DRUGS, CRIME,
AND THEIR RELATIONSHIPS

THEORY, RESEARCH, PRACTICE, AND POLICY

Glenn D. Walters, PhD

Department of Criminal Justice
Kutztown University
Kutztown, PA

JONES & BARTLETT
LEARNING

World Headquarters
Jones & Bartlett Learning
5 Wall Street
Burlington, MA 01803
978-443-5000
info@jblearning.com
www.jblearning.com

Jones & Bartlett Learning books and products are available through most bookstores and online booksellers. To contact Jones & Bartlett Learning directly, call 800-832-0034, fax 978-443-8000, or visit our website, www.jblearning.com.

Substantial discounts on bulk quantities of Jones & Bartlett Learning publications are available to corporations, professional associations, and other qualified organizations. For details and specific discount information, contact the special sales department at Jones & Bartlett Learning via the above contact information or send an email to specialsales@jblearning.com.

Production Credits

Publisher: Cathleen Sether	Composition: diacriTech
Acquisitions Editor: Sean Connelly	Cover Design: Karen Leduc
Editorial Assistant: Caitlin Murphy	Rights & Photo Research Assistant: Ashley Dos Santos
Editorial Assistant: Audrey Schwinn	Cover Image: prison door: © iStockphoto/Thinkstock; woman with drugs:
Production Manager: Tracey McCrea	© Artem Furman/ShutterStock, Inc.
Marketing Manager: Lindsay White	Printing and Binding: Courier Companies
Manufacturing and Inventory Control Supervisor: Amy Bacus	Cover Printing: Courier Companies

To order this product, use ISBN: 978-1-284-02117-2

Library of Congress Cataloging-in-Publication Data
Walters, Glenn D.
  Drugs, crime, and their relationships : theory, research, practice, and policy / Glenn Walters.
    pages cm
  Includes bibliographical references and index.
  ISBN 978-1-4496-8846-2 (pbk.)
1. Drug abuse and crime—United States. 2. Drug abuse—United States—Prevention. 3. Crime prevention—United States. I. Title.
  HV5825.W381265 2014
  364.2—dc23
                                                                              2012034917

6048
Printed in the United States of America
17 16 15 14 13   10 9 8 7 6 5 4 3 2 1

BRIEF CONTENTS

CONTENTS

3 Crime: Definitions, Classification, and Theory — 73

4 Drug–Crime Relationships — 109

III Practice 257

9 Drugs and the Criminal Justice System 259

10 Assessing the Drug-Involved Offender 293

Surveys administered to high school students, studies carried out on jail and prison inmates, and interviews conducted with substance abusers undergoing treatment all point to the same conclusion: that is, drugs and crime are strongly correlated. Why they are correlated is harder to decipher. Comprehending the nature and implications of this relationship could go a long way toward managing the ubiquitous problem of drugs and crime in society. A cursory review of the literature reveals that the drug–crime connection is complex and multifaceted; so complex, in fact, that it is a misnomer to refer to the relationship in the singular as there are multiple drug–crime connections. In an attempt to understand these connections, this book explores several different drug–crime nexuses, from the simple unidirectional model (drugs cause crime or crime causes drugs), to the more intricate bidirectional model (drugs and crime are reciprocally related), to several third-variable models (moderation, mediation, epiphenomenal).

The purpose of this book is to provide an overview and analysis of the many facets of drug–crime relationships. To accomplish this, the book is divided into four parts. The first part contains the first four chapters of the book and provides an introduction and overview of theories on drugs, crime, and their relationships. The next four chapters are covered in the second part of the book, which explores the relevant research on the biological, psychological, sociological, and static/situational correlates of drug–crime relationships. The three chapters that comprise the third part of this book explore the practical implications of drug–crime connections for the criminal justice system, offender assessment, and treatment programming. The fourth part of this book encompasses the final four chapters and examines the policy implications of the drug–crime relationship as they pertain to prevention, harm reduction, and society's response to drugs and drug-related crime.

Given the overlap that exists between drugs and crime, it is not surprising that it is often difficult to separate the two. The opening chapters of this book nevertheless attempt to do just this by discussing drugs and crime separately to set the stage for later discussions on drug–crime relationships. Chapter 2, for instance, focuses exclusively on drugs and Chapter 3 concentrates solely on crime. As the book proceeds, however, the boundaries between drugs and crime begin to blur. In Part II (Research), the drug, crime, and drug–crime correlates of each biological, psychological, sociological, and status/situational variable are reviewed in sequential subsections, whereas in Part III (Practice) drugs and crime are discussed in the same subsection. By the time we get to Part IV (Policy), the overlap is nearly complete. Here, drugs and crime are no longer discussed separately but simultaneously. All of this is designed to provide the reader with a complete understanding of drugs, crime, and their relationships.

ACKNOWLEDGMENTS

We would like to thank the following individuals for reviewing this text:

Robert M. Beuler, Hilbert College

Stacey Burroughs, Harrisburg Area Community College

Dana C. De Witt, Mount Marty College

Beverly Edwards, Arkansas State University

Christopher R. Freed, University of South Alabama

N. Gelman, Oakland Community College

Mary S. Jackson, East Carolina University

Shepherd M. Jenks, Jr., Central New Mexico Community College

Gloria J. Lawrence, Wayne State College, Nebraska

Al Martinez, Hartnell College

Jennifer Myers, Fairmont State University

James F. Quinn, University of North Texas

Cheryn Rowell, Stanly Community College

Cher A. Shannon, Gateway Community College

Elvira M. White-Lewis, Texas A&M—Commerce

Beth A. Wiersma, University of Nebraska at Kearney

PART I

THEORY

Courtesy of Professor Albert Bandura.

Courtesy of the National Library of Medicine.

Courtesy of the National Library of Australia.

CHAPTER 1

AN INTRODUCTION TO DRUGS AND CRIME

© John Birdsall/age fotostock

It is generally assumed that drugs and crime are linked. This assumption must be tested before it can be accepted, and if accepted it will serve as a stepping-stone to future discussions in this book. The first objective of this chapter, then, is to test this assumption in a review of research on the drug–crime relationship. Other objectives for this chapter include:

- Providing a brief history of drugs and crime in America.
- Exploring the role of politics in drugs and crime.
- Acknowledging the limitations of science in understanding drugs and crime.
- Gaining a sense of direction for the rest of the book.

Is There a Relationship Between Drugs and Crime?

Before discussing the nature of the drug–crime relationship it needs to be established that a relationship does, in fact, exist between these two variables. Three primary methodologies can be used to shed light on this issue:

- General surveys of drug use and delinquency in students and young adults
- Studies on drug use in offender populations
- Studies on crime in drug using populations

General Surveys of Drug Use and Delinquency in Students and Young Adults

Kandel, Simcha-Fagan, and Davies administered surveys to 1,004 high school students in grades 10–11 inquiring about the students' use of drugs and involvement in delinquency. The researchers then readministered the surveys to the same group of individuals 8 years later when the students were young adults. Examining participant responses during adolescence, it was clear that adolescent boys and girls reporting the highest levels of drug use also reported the highest levels of delinquency. Viewing participant responses from high school to early adulthood, it was apparent that drug use persisted more than delinquency and that those participants who had not entered conventional adult social roles (military, marriage, occupation) after 8 years were significantly more likely to be using drugs than those who had assumed conventional adult social roles by young adulthood.[1]

Huizinga, Loeber, Thornberry, and Cothern interviewed more than 4,000 inner-city youths from three urban areas: Denver, Colorado; Rochester, New York; and Pittsburgh, Pennsylvania. Participants were 7 to 15 years of age when first interviewed and the results showed evidence of a robust correlation between drug use and delinquency. In addition, sex appeared to moderate this relationship. A **moderator variable** alters the relationship between an independent variable and dependent variable, in this case drug use and delinquency. Huizinga et al. determined that drug-using boys engaged in delinquency more often than delinquent boys engaged in drug use, whereas delinquent girls engaged in drug use more often than drug-using girls engaged in delinquency (see **Figure 1-1**).[2] Hence, in boys, drug use was a better indicator of delinquency than delinquency was of drug use, whereas in girls, delinquency was a better indicator of drug use than drug use was of delinquency.

The 2007 **Youth Risk Behavior Surveillance (YRBS)** is a nationally representative sample of 14,000 students enrolled in public and private high schools throughout the United States and District of Columbia.[3] When self-reported drug use and crime were compared, more than

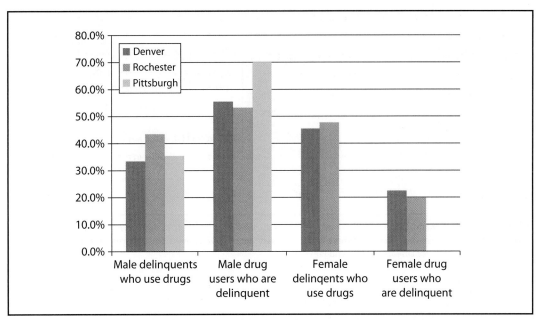

Figure 1-1
Drug use in delinquents and delinquency in drug users for male and female participants in three samples. (For the Pittsburgh study, all participants were male.)

Data from: Huizinga, D., Loeber, R., Thornberry, T. P., & Cothern, L. (2000). Co-occurrence of delinquency and other problem behaviors. *Juvenile Justice Bulletin* (NCJ 182211). Washington, DC: Office of Juvenile Justice and Delinquency Prevention.

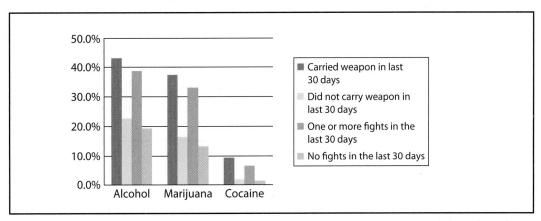

Figure 1-2
Criminality in adolescents from the Youth Risk Behavior Surveillance (YRBS) sample who had five or more drinks, used marijuana, or used cocaine in the last 30 days.

Data from: Eaton, D. K., Kann, L., Kinchen, S., Shanklin, S., Ross, J., Hawkins, J., et al. (2008, June 6). *Morbidity and Mortality Weekly Report* (Vol. 57): Youth risk behavior surveillance—United States, 2007. Atlanta, GA: Department of Health and Human Services Centers for Disease Control and Prevention.

twice as many students who acknowledged consuming five or more drinks, using marijuana, or using cocaine in the last 30 days also acknowledged carrying a weapon or getting into a fight than students who took fewer than five drinks, did not use marijuana, or did not use cocaine (see **Figure 1-2**). By the same token, more than twice as many students who reported carrying a weapon or getting into a fight in the last 30 days also acknowledged taking five or more drinks, using marijuana, or using cocaine in the last 30 days (see **Figure 1-3**).

Another national youth survey, the **National Longitudinal Study of Adolescent Health (Add Health)**, has also shed light on the drug–crime relationship. The Add Health study was conducted in four waves on an original sample of 26,666 American youth. Wave 1 data were collected in 1994–1995 when participants were in grades 7–12 and between the ages of 12 and 18. Wave 2 data were collected in 1996 when participants were between the ages of 13 and 20. Data for Wave 3 were gathered between 2001 and 2002 when participants

Figure 1-3
Drug use in adolescents for the Youth Risk Behavior Surveillance (YRBS) sample who carried a weapon or participated in a fight in the last 30 days.

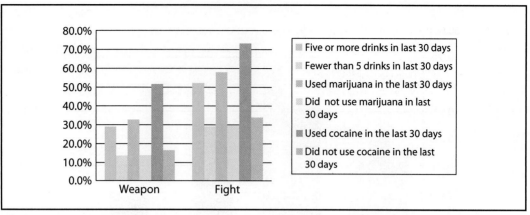

Data from: Eaton, D. K., Kann, L., Kinchen, S., Shanklin, S., Ross, J., Hawkins, J., et al. (2008, June 6). *Morbidity and Mortality Weekly Report* (Vol. 57): Youth risk behavior surveillance—United States, 2007. Atlanta, GA: Department of Health and Human Services Centers for Disease Control and Prevention.

Figure 1-4
Changes in the relationship between drunkenness and criminality and between marijuana use and criminality over the four waves of the National Longitudinal Study of Adolescent Health (Add Health) sample.

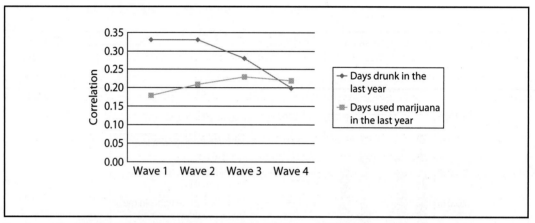

Data from: Udry, J. R. (2003). *The National Longitudinal Study of Adolescent Health (Add Health)*. Chapel Hill, NC: Carolina Population Center, University of North Carolina.

were between the ages of 18 and 26. The final wave of data was assembled in 2007–2008 when participants were between the ages of 24 and 32.[4] Correlating the number of times a participant was drunk in the last 12 months or used marijuana in the last 30 days with a composite measure of crime (one point for participation in each of the following six criminal acts over the past 12 months: property damage, serious fight, stealing item worth > $50, burglary, selling drugs, using or threatening to use a weapon) revealed a significant relationship across all four waves of the Add Health sample. However, the correlation between alcohol and crime dropped rather sharply between Waves 2 and 3 and then again between Waves 3 and 4, whereas the correlation between marijuana and crime rose steadily during the first three waves before leveling off at Wave 4 (see **Figure 1-4**). One possible explanation for these results is that as alcohol became legal (age 21) for a greater portion of the sample its association with crime weakened but remained significant nonetheless (during Waves 1 and 2 alcohol was illegal for the entire sample, in Wave 3 alcohol was legal for over half the sample, and in Wave 4 alcohol was legal for the entire sample).

All four studies reviewed in this section indicate that a strong relationship exists between drugs and crime in surveys of general population respondents. One of the limitations of this line of research, however, is that it measures drug use and crime exclusively from self-report. It is possible, then, that certain response styles account for these results. For instance, individuals who are defensive about their drug use would also likely be defensive about their involvement in crime and consequently deny both behaviors, whereas individuals who want to view themselves as rebels might tend to endorse both drug and crime items, whether or not they actually engaged in these behaviors. Because of this, the drug–crime relationship observed in survey research needs to be verified with nonself-report measures.

Studies on Drug Use in Criminal Populations

One way to reduce reliance on self-report data is to study incarcerated offenders. The fact that the crime portion of the drugs–crime relationship is assessed, not by self-report, but by a participant's presence in jail or prison suggests that studies on prison and jail inmates hold promise of further clarifying the drug–crime relationship. Adopting this approach, Karberg and James discovered that 68% of the more than 610,000 jail inmates they surveyed satisfied criteria for substance (alcohol or drug) abuse or dependence (see **Table 1-1**).[5] When a similar methodology was adopted with state and federal prison inmates it was noted that 53.4% of the state inmates and 45.5% of the federal inmates satisfied criteria for drug abuse or dependence (see **Figure 1-5**).[6] These percentages fall short of the 68% of jail inmates with diagnoses of substance abuse and dependence, but it should be noted that in the jail study alcohol and drugs were combined whereas in the prison study only drug misuse was examined. In two of the three samples (jail, state) female offenders reported a slightly higher rate of drug involvement than male offenders and in all three samples marijuana was the most frequently used illegal substance (see **Figure 1-6**).[7–8] Finally, as shown in **Table 1-2**, more extensive drug use in state and federal prisoners was associated with a more extensive criminal history.[9]

Evidence of heightened self-reported alcohol and drug abuse in jail and prison inmates aside, there is still a need to verify the drug–crime relationship independent of self-reported drug use. Such an opportunity is provided by the **Arrestee Drug Abuse Monitoring (ADAM II)** federal data collection program. The protocol for ADAM II requires that all males arrested in 10 U.S. cities be tested for 10 different drugs within 24 hours of arrest.

Table 1-1 Prevalence of Substance Dependence or Abuse Among Jail Inmates, 2002

Diagnosis	Estimated number of inmates[a]	Percent of jail inmates		
		Alcohol	**Drugs**	**Alcohol or drugs**
Any dependence or abuse	415,242	46.6%	53.5%	68.0%
Dependence and abuse	269,632	22.2	34.4	44.2
Dependence only	6,084	0.6	1.4	1.0
Abuse only	139,530	23.8	17.7	22.9
No dependence or abuse[b]	195,054	53.4	46.5	32.0

Note: See *References* for sources on measuring dependence or abuse based on the *Diagnostic and Statistical Manual of Mental Disorders*, fourth edition (DSM-IV).
[a]Excludes 20,945 inmates for whom data were unknown.
[b]Includes inmates who did not use alcohol or drugs.

Reproduced from Karberg, J. C., & James, D. J. (2005). Substance dependence, abuse, and treatment of jail inmates, 2002. *Bureau of Justice Statistics Special Report* (NCJ 209588). Washington, DC: U.S. Department of Justice.

Figure 1-5
Illegal drug use by state and federal inmates, 2004.

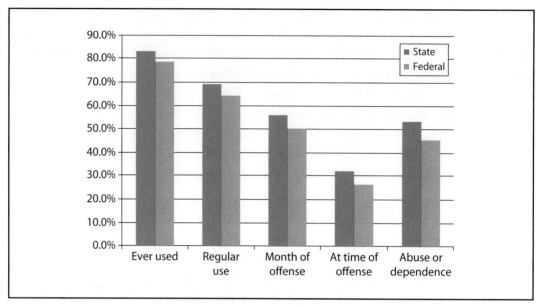

Data From: Mumola, C. J., & Karberg, J. C. (2006). Drug use and dependence, state and federal prisoners, 2004. *Bureau of Justice Statistics Special Report* (NCJ 213530). Washington, DC: U.S. Department of Justice.

Table 1-2 Criminal History of State and Federal Prisoners, by Drug Dependence or Abuse, 2004

| | Percent of prisoners — | | | |
| | State | | Federal | |
Characteristic	Dependence or abuse	Other inmates	Dependence or abuse	Other inmates
Criminal justice status at arrest				
None	51.9%	62.8%	70.1%	75.4%
Any status	48.1	37.2	29.9	24.6
On parole	20.9	15.9	12.1	12.6
On probation	26.7	21.0	17.2	11.7
Criminal history				
None	15.6%	32.1%	25.2%	42.8%
Priors	84.4	67.9	74.8	57.2
Violent recidivists	46.8	40.6	28.1	23.5
Drug recidivists only	4.0	2.8	10.2	6.8
Other recidivists*	33.6	24.5	36.5	26.9
Number of prior probation/ incarceration sentences				
0	16.9%	34.0%	27.1%	44.2%
1	14.1	17.4	14.4	16.8
2	15.8	16.4	16.1	14.6
3-5	28.5	21.7	25.9	16.5
6-10	16.5	7.9	11.4	5.9
11 or more	8.2	2.7	5.2	2.0

*Includes recidivists with unknown prior offense types.

Reproduced from Mumola, C. J., & Karberg, J. C. (2006). Drug use and dependence, state and federal prisoners, 2004. *Bureau of Justice Statistics Special Report* (NCJ 213530). Washington, DC: U.S. Department of Justice.

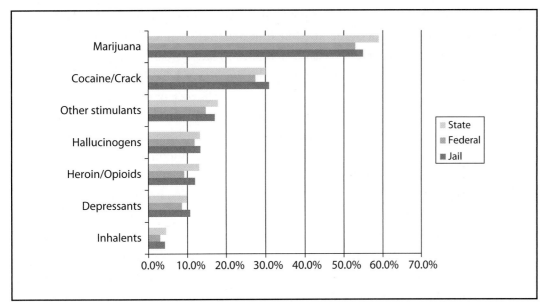

Figure 1-6
Proportion of state, federal, and jail inmates reporting regular use of drugs, by drug type.

Data From: Karberg, J. C., & James, D. J. (2005). Substance dependence, abuse, and treatment of jail inmates, 2002. *Bureau of Justice Statistics Special Report* (NCJ 209588). Washington, DC: U.S. Department of Justice; and Mumola, C. J., & Karberg, J. C. (2006). Drug use and dependence, state and federal prisoners, 2004. *Bureau of Justice Statistics Special Report* (NCJ 213530). Washington, DC: U.S. Department of Justice.

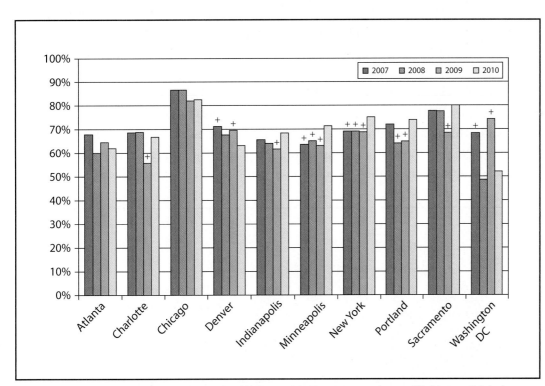

Figure 1-7
Percentage of new arrestees testing positive for any drug in the 10 sites participating in the ADAM II data collection program, 2007–2010.
+ = difference between identified year and 2010 is significant (p < .10).

Reproduced from Office of National Drug Control Policy. (2011). ADAM II: 2010 annual report. Washington, DC: Author.

Figure 1-7 compares the proportion of arrestees testing positive for any one of 10 drugs across the 10 sites between 2007 and 2010. The results indicate a strong and consistent relationship between arrest and a positive drug test, with most sites identifying drug use in 60 to 80% of arrestees. Marijuana (46.8%), cocaine (22.4%), and heroin (14.4%) were the three most commonly identified substances across the 10 sites, although wide variations were sometimes found between sites. Methamphetamine, for instance, was detected in no more than 4% of specimens in eight of the sites but appeared more frequently in testing conducted in two west-coast cities: Sacramento, California (33.2%) and Portland, Oregon (19.8%).[10]

Another way to test the drug–crime relationship without relying on self-report is to calculate the proportion of offenders who were under the influence of drugs at the time of the offense based on reports from crime victims. One of the questions asked on the **National Crime Victimization Survey (NCVS)** is whether the perpetrator appeared to be under the influence of alcohol or other drugs at the time of the offense. Victim reports over several different years of the NCVS show that approximately half the victims who were able to form an opinion about an offender's sobriety believed the perpetrator to have been under the influence of alcohol or drugs at the time of the offense. The results for victims of violent crime in the 2007 NCVS are presented in Figure 1-8.[11]

Research conducted on substance use and misuse in criminal populations supports the results of survey research showing a robust relationship between drugs and crime. These studies do more than just confirm the results of general surveys on child, adolescent, and adult samples; they actually extend the survey findings by demonstrating that the drug–crime relationship is equally prominent whether self-report or nonself report measures are used as proxies for drug use and crime. As a general rule, it would appear that approximately two out of three offenders suffers from a significant substance abuse problem, although the actual proportion of substance abuse in offender populations may vary across important demographic (gender), background (criminal history), and location (site) parameters.

Crime in Substance Abusing Populations

Studies from the 1980s conducted on habitual heroin users in three east-coast U.S. cities (New York, Miami, and Baltimore) revealed a strong relationship between drug use and crime. Over 95% of the 201 heroin users from New York City contacted by Johnson et al. reported obtaining some of their recent income from illegal activities.[12] Likewise, 99.7%

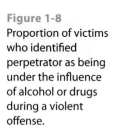

Figure 1-8
Proportion of victims who identified perpetrator as being under the influence of alcohol or drugs during a violent offense.

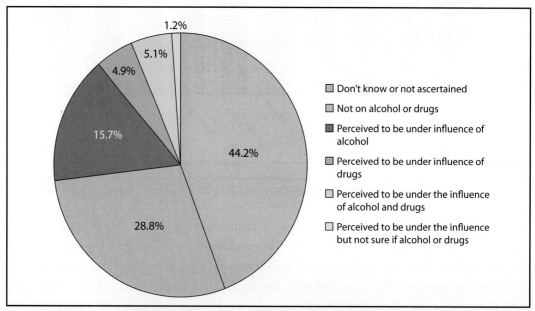

Data From: Bureau of Justice Statistics. (2010). *Criminal victimization in the United States, 2007* (NCJ 227669). Washington, DC: Author.

of the male heroin users and 98.9% of the female heroin users from Miami surveyed by James Inciardi acknowledged participating in at least one crime within the past year. These 574 male and female heroin users recalled committing 215,105 crimes during the previous year, an average of 375 offenses per person, or more than one offense a day. Whereas the majority of crimes were for property offenses and drug sales, violence did occur:[13]

- 82,000 drug sales
- 25,000 minor larceny offenses (shoplifting)
- 45,000 other crimes of larceny and fraud
- 6,700 burglaries
- 6,000 robberies and assaults

In a study conducted on opiate users in Baltimore and New York, Nurco et al. determined that 95% of the male heroin users they interviewed reported involvement in criminal activity during an average 12-year "at-risk" period. The results of this study also showed that criminal activity was highest during periods of heaviest use.[14]

Criminal justice involvement was also prevalent in the backgrounds of juveniles enrolled in an adolescent drug treatment program located near Baltimore, Maryland. The majority of program participants acknowledged past involvement in crime (83%), with over half (56.7%) reporting that they had been on probation in the last 90 days and 14.4% reporting that they had been in a juvenile detention or confinement facility in the last 90 days. Nearly one out of every two participants had committed a prior violent or serious offense (see **Figure 1-9**) and one in five (20.1) had begun their criminal careers before the age of 10. In addition, over half the sample felt pressure from the criminal justice system to enter drug treatment (55.7%).[15] It should be noted that there is research evidence suggesting that substance abusing offenders may respond as well to compulsory interventions as they do to noncompulsory interventions.[16]

High rates of criminality have been observed in drugs users outside the United States as well. Mats Fridell and colleagues followed a large group of drug users recruited from a detoxification and short-term rehabilitation center in Sweden and found that the majority of participants were criminally active during the follow-up period. Although a diagnosis of Antisocial

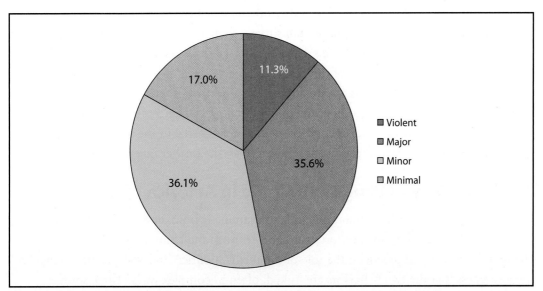

Figure 1-9
Most serious past crime committed by participants in a juvenile drug treatment facility.

Data From: Battjes, R. J., Gordon, M. S., O'Grady, K. E., Kinlock, T. W., Katz, E. C., & Sears, E. A. (2004). Evaluation of a group-based substance abuse treatment program for adolescents. *Journal of Substance Abuse Treatment, 27*, 123–134.

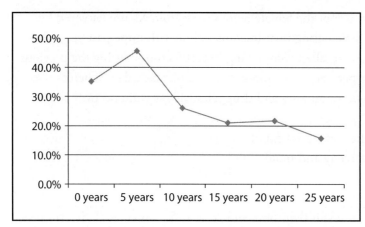

Data From: Fridell, M., Hesse, M., Jæger, M. M., & Kühlhorn, E. (2008). Antisocial personality disorder as a predictor of criminal behavior in a longitudinal study of a cohort of abusers of several classes of drugs: Relation to types of substances and types of crime. *Addictive Behaviors, 33,* 799–811.

Personality Disorder (ASPD) was associated with higher rates of subsequent criminality (97%), even participants without an ASPD diagnosis had high rates of criminality (90%). The crime rate in this sample peaked after 5 years but was still significant, at 15%, 20 years later (see **Figure 1-10**). In this study, the primary drug of abuse had an effect on the types of crimes committed. For instance, stimulant abuse was associated with an increased rate of subsequent violent and nonviolent criminality, whereas opiate abuse was associated with an increased rate of subsequent theft, fraud, and drug offenses. Marijuana abuse, on the other hand, was associated with lower rates of subsequent violent and nonviolent criminality.[17]

In a recent **meta-analysis** of 30 studies on the drugs-crime nexus, Trevor Bennett, Katy Holloway, and David Farrington calculated the odds of offending at 2.8 to 3.8 times higher in drug users than in nondrug users. They further noted that the relationship between illegal drug use and crime varied as a function of the drug used. Crack cocaine use, for instance, displayed the strongest relationship with crime (mean odds ratio = 6.09), followed by heroin (mean odds ratio = 3.08) and powder cocaine (mean odds ratio = 2.56). Recreational drug use also correlated with crime but at a lower level. Users of amphetamine were 1.93 times more likely to offend than nonusers of amphetamine and users of marijuana were 1.46 times more likely to offend than nonusers of marijuana.[18]

The results of research on criminality in adults and juveniles who abuse drugs mirror the results found in general surveys of drug and criminal involvement and studies on drug use in criminal populations. General population surveys show that individuals who report high levels of drug use also report high levels of delinquency and crime, research conducted in jails and prisons indicate that two out of three offenders have a serious problem with alcohol and/or drugs, and studies carried out on adults who abuse drugs reveal that the vast majority of these individuals have engaged in crime in the recent past. Hence, the question of whether there is a relationship between drugs and crime can be answered in the affirmative. The nature and complexity of this relationship, however, awaits further investigation and analysis.

A Brief History of Drugs and Crime in America

One way to gain perspective on a problem is to examine it from an historical point of view. By taking an historical perspective on drugs and crime in the United States we can see the changing attitudes and practices; the role of the media, politics, and science; and the growing awareness that the two behaviors are linked, often in complex ways. Three sources, particularly the Shmoop "Drugs in America" timeline, were used to construct a chronology of events in American history bearing on the country's ongoing problems, concerns, and preoccupations with drugs, crime, and their relationship.[19–21]

1492

- On his first day in the New World, Columbus meets friendly natives who offer him a gift of tobacco. Columbus is unsure of what to do with the gift, but many of his men enjoy smoking the dried leaves and the practice soon catches on in Europe.

1604

- Alarmed by his subjects' growing preoccupation with the smoking habit, England's King James I publishes *A Counterblaste to Tobacco*, in which he outlines the dangers of tobacco smoking. Later that same year he tries to impose a 4000% increase in the tobacco tax but this has little impact on tobacco consumption in England.

1607

- The first permanent English colony in North America is established at Jamestown, Virginia. Within a year nearly two-thirds of the 144 colonists perish because of the harsh conditions.

1612

- Jamestown colonists begin to plant tobacco, which then becomes a valuable cash crop and saves the fledgling colony from financial ruin.

1619

- The first African slaves arrive in North America. Many are put to work in the tobacco fields.
- Virginia colonists create the first local government. That same year, a law goes into effect prohibiting colonists from selling tobacco for less than 3¢ per pound.

1661

- The Massachusetts General Court contends that excess production of rum is threatening the orderly running of the colony and jeopardizing the health of the citizenry.

1669

- England and much of Europe import large amounts of tobacco, coffee, tea, and rum from the Americas.

1770

- Because water purification has not yet been invented and there is a strong belief that alcohol invigorates people and is capable of curing a variety of ailments, the 1.7 million colonists are consuming 7.5 million gallons of rum a year. This represents an average of 4.4 gallons of alcohol for every man, woman, and child in the 13 colonies.

1773

- American colonists, angered by British taxation of colonial trade, stage the Boston Tea Party whereby tea from an English merchant ship is dumped into Boston Harbor. Rejection of the English habit of tea drinking will eventually make coffee a more popular beverage than tea in the United States.

1790

- The Walnut Street Jail is opened in Philadelphia. It is the first jail in North America to assign inmates to separate cells and provide them with individualized work details.

1829

- Eastern Penitentiary, outside of Philadelphia, opens. Based on the Pennsylvania model, it is designed to give inmates the opportunity to reflect on their crimes and find penitence. As such, inmates eat, sleep, and work in solitude and a strict code of silence is enforced. Severe punishments are administered to those who violate the code of silence.

1841

- John Augustus, a Boston shoemaker and philanthropist, vouches for a defendant of good character with an alcohol problem. He convinces the judge that the defendant would be more effectively managed in the community than in jail. The judge releases the defendant to Augustus' care, giving birth to probation.

1865

- During the American Civil War morphine is widely administered to relieve the suffering of wounded soldiers on both sides. Morphine and opium addiction is so prevalent among Civil War veterans that opiate addiction becomes known as "the army disease."

1876

- Zebulon Brockway is made superintendant of the Elmira (New York) adult reformatory where he experiments with good time, educational programming, and parole.

1884

- The American medical community embraces cocaine as a miracle cure for a wide variety of ailments, including morphine and alcohol addiction.

1886

- American John Pemberton invents Coca-Cola by chemically combining two stimulant drugs: cocaine from the South American coca leaf and caffeine from the African kola nut. It is initially marketed as a medicine.

1895

- Coca-Cola stops marketing itself as a medicine and starts marketing itself as a soft drink; sales increase dramatically.

1898

- The German drug company, Bayer, markets heroin, a derivative of morphine, as a cough suppressant. It is sold in drug stores as an over-the-counter medicine and can even be ordered through the Sears and Roebuck catalogue.

1899

- The first juvenile court is established in Cook County (Chicago) Illinois.

1906

- Congress passes the Pure Food and Drug Act. This act requires truth in labeling for both food and drugs and seeks to ban adulterated food products and poisonous substances that were being passed off as medicines at the time.

1911

- An article in the *New York Times* warns that cocaine is being used to corrupt young girls and force them into prostitution. Cocaine figures prominently in the Harrison Act, which will be passed just 3 years later.

1914

- The Harrison Act is passed by Congress, making it illegal to prescribe opiates and cocaine to addicts. Although physicians are still permitted to prescribe these controlled substances to patients, they are prohibited from prescribing them to addicts. A number of physicians are jailed for prescribing opiates and cocaine to addicts, thereby leading the medical profession to conclude that prescribing opiates and cocaine to addicts is inadvisable. Some of the impetus for the Harrison Act grew out of concern for public health, but much of it was fueled by prejudice and racism (cocaine was associated with African-Americans and prostitution, whereas opiates were associated with Chinese immigrants who were viewed as strange and dangerous).
- Henry Ford condemns cigarettes as gateway drugs.

1919

- The Eighteenth Amendment is ratified, making the manufacture, sale, and transportation of "intoxicating liquors" illegal. Alcohol prohibition in the United States is commonly referred to as the "noble experiment." The crime rate rises dramatically as bootleggers and gangsters vie for control of the lucrative illegal alcohol trade.

1930

- The Federal Bureau of Narcotics (FBN) is established as an agency in the Department of the Treasury. Harry J. Anslinger is appointed the first commissioner of the FBN, where he will remain until his retirement in 1962.

1933

- Congress ratifies the Twenty-First Amendment, repealing Prohibition; the "noble experiment" is over.

1935

- The federal government opens the U.S. Narcotic Farm in Lexington, Kentucky for the treatment of drug-using federal prisoners and nonprisoner volunteers.

1936

- The movie *Reefer Madness* is released under the title *Tell Your Children*. It provides a highly unrealistic picture of the consequences of marijuana use, to include manslaughter, suicide, attempted rape, and psychosis. In separate campaigns, Harry Anslinger and Randolph Hearst, the newspaper magnate, attempt to tie marijuana use to violent crime. Congress will pass the Marijuana Tax Act 1 year later, the first step in criminalizing marijuana use in the United States.

1944

- A committee appointed by New York mayor Fiorello LaGuardia concludes that the claims about the dangers of marijuana have been greatly exaggerated. This angers Harry Anslinger who has been actively campaigning against marijuana and who characterizes the committee's report as unscientific.

1950

- The American Medical Association publishes the first U.S. study showing a correlation between smoking and lung cancer. The first international study showing a link between tobacco smoking and lung cancer was actually conducted in Nazi Germany in 1939.

1954

- Major tobacco companies band together to promote a public campaign challenging the emerging scientific evidence that smoking is dangerous to one's health.
- The American Medical Association reverses its previous views on alcoholism and declares that alcohol abuse and dependence are diseases.

1965

- Illegal drug use grows. Marijuana and the hallucinogen, LSD, are particularly popular with adolescents and young adults. In fact, both drugs become symbols of youthful rebellion and are considered threats to the American way of life by many older Americans.

- The war in Vietnam gives rise to a new generation of drug users. Although alcohol and marijuana were the drugs of choice for men and women serving in Vietnam, heroin was readily available and used with some degree of frequency. Research indicates that very few of these heroin-using servicemen continued using heroin upon their return to the United States, primarily because the environmental cues that supported drug craving in Vietnam were no longer in effect once the servicemen returned home.

1966

- Warning labels are placed on cigarette packs. The weak language used in the message (i.e., "Cigarette smoking may be hazardous to your health") was the result of heavy lobbying by the tobacco industry.

1970

- Congress passes the Comprehensive Drug Abuse Prevention and Control Act. Whereas the act reduces the penalty for marijuana possession, it grants law enforcement broader powers in conducting drug-related searches and seizures.

1971

- President Richard Nixon declares a war on drugs, referring to it as "public enemy number one" and coining the term "**War on Drugs**."

1973

- The Drug Enforcement Agency (DEA) is created; its mission, to enforce the controlled substance laws and regulations of the United States.

1980

- A Presidential Commission on drugs concludes that illegal drug trafficking is a threat to national security; more money is pumped into drug enforcement.

1986

- President Ronald Reagan signs the Anti-Drug Act of 1986, which creates mandatory sentences for drug crimes, leading to an unprecedented increase in the federal prison population.

- The 2-hour CBS News Special, "48 Hours on Crack Street" is watched by 15 million Americans. This stimulates media interest in crack cocaine and leads to exaggerated claims of an alleged crack epidemic.

1988

- American politicians react to the alleged crack epidemic by passing harsh new drug laws, whereby possession of crack cocaine is punished by a significantly longer prison sentence than possession of powder cocaine; this is viewed as racially biased by many, in that blacks are significantly more likely to be involved in the sale of crack cocaine than whites.

1989

- The first drug court is established in Miami, Florida.

1995

- All Federal Bureau of Prisons facilities are locked down for a 2-week period after riots break out over racial inequities in the crack law.

2006

- Violence escalates in Mexico as rival drug gangs vie for power; some of the violence overflows into the United States, giving rise to calls for more stringent laws and measures, greater restrictions on entry into the United States, and an increase in the number of Mexican inmates housed in U.S. prisons.

2008

- The worst economic crisis since the Great Depression hits the United States, stretching correctional resources to dangerous levels and encouraging states and local governments to start investigating alternatives to prison.

Drugs, Crime, and Politics

After reviewing the history of drugs and crime in the United States, it should be clear that politics plays a leading role in the drug–crime relationship. From the Harrison Act of 1914 to the Anti-Drug Act of 1986 and from Harry Anslinger's efforts to criminalize marijuana to the more recent hysteria surrounding the "crack epidemic," politics, along with the media, have helped shape our views on drugs and crime. Nowhere is this more evident than in America's "War on Drugs." It would appear that the "War on Drugs" has more to do with politics and power acquisition than with public health and law enforcement. Dan Baum views the "War on Drugs" as a classic "smoke and mirrors" tactic that distracts voters from more pressing issues while garnering significant power for those who espouse it.[22] Consequently, the "War on Drugs," like the "noble experiment" of American Prohibition that preceded it, has been an abject failure, though this has not discouraged politicians from using it for political gain. Fear of crime has also been deployed as a weapon in the "War on Drugs" and as a tool in law and order politics.[23]

One thing that Democrats and Republicans can agree upon is that it is good to be reelected. They further understand that they are unlikely to be elected or reelected if they appear soft on crime or weak on drugs, and this is exactly how they will be portrayed by their opponents if they show any leniency on either issue. Conversely, the legal drugs are supported by political lobbies designed to keep the drug legal and accessible to as many people as possible. In 2011, the tobacco and alcoholic beverage industries spent $17 million and $18.9 million, respectively, to promote their interests in Washington and various state capitols.[24] These numbers, although large, are dwarfed by the $149 million dollars spent on lobbying efforts by pharmaceutical manufacturing companies.[25] Between the fear of being seen as soft on crime or weak on drugs and the desire to receive the financial backing of lobbyists pushing legal substances, the status quo is maintained: legal drugs, regardless of their degree of harm, remain legal, and illegal drugs, irrespective of the harm they may or may not create, remain illegal.

When it comes to negotiating the intricate and convoluted path between politics and drug prohibition, no administration has been more adroit or successful than the Clinton administration. In fact, the Clinton administration may have held the most enlightened views on drugs of any American administration in recent memory. Nevertheless, there were limitations to what the Clinton administration could tolerate politically and it would deliberately steer clear of controversial issues such as the possible legalization or decriminalization of drug use. When Joycelyn Elders, Clinton's first Surgeon General, suggested that the issues of drug decriminalization and legalization should be studied she drew immediate fire from conservatives in Congress. Her openness to discussing drug decriminalization and legalization coupled with several statements she made about masturbation at an international AIDS conference sealed her fate and she was asked to resign a week after the conference. This suggests that politics play a potentially important role in defining the relationship between drugs and crime, a relationship that cannot be understood without first understanding the politics involved. The politics of crime as it pertains to DNA testing is highlighted in News Spot 1-1.

NEWS SPOT 1-1

Title: Other View: Walker's Proposal to Collect DNA at Arrest Deserves Careful Study
Source: *The Chippewa (Chippewa Falls, WI) Herald*
Reporter: Oshkosh Northwestern
Date: April 15, 2012

A politician can never go wrong by being tough on crime. Every voter wants safe communities and justice for crime victims. But is there such a thing as being too tough on crime?

We ask the question because Gov. Scott Walker proposed last week to expand the collection of DNA samples to include suspects arrested in some felony and sex crimes as an enhanced crime-fighting tool. Currently, DNA only can be collected when police obtain a warrant or upon conviction of a felony or certain misdemeanor sex crimes.

Twenty-two other states have laws requiring collection of DNA samples from suspects arrested in felony, sex or burglary investigations. Walker argued Wisconsin needs similar crime-fighting tools.

DNA science has unquestionably revolutionized crime investigation. DNA evidence has led to convictions in hard-to-prosecute cases and exonerations in other cases where suspects were wrongly convicted. However, the governor's proposal gives us pause for several reasons.

First and foremost is the question the proposal raises regarding civil liberties and the right to privacy. There is nothing more personal than an individual's DNA. Obtaining and cataloging DNA from suspects who are never charged or convicted unfairly brands them a suspect for life. The proposal carries a certain "big brother" connotation that has chilling implications. Not surprisingly the Wisconsin chapter of the American Civil Liberties Union has weighed in against the proposal.

A lesser concern, but one that must be considered, is the practicality and cost of the proposal. Although Walker did not specify which alleged crimes would trigger a DNA sample from a suspect, the proposal could add tens of thousands of DNA samples to the state's database. The question becomes one of cost and logistics. It most certainly would mean expansion of the state crime lab resources to handle the workload. But the governor did not address whether local law enforcement agencies would be reimbursed for the additional costs associated with a significant increase in the number of samples collected....

Questions to Ponder
1. **How far should law enforcement be allowed to go in collecting information on citizens who commit felonies and misdemeanors?**
2. **What might motivate a politician to push for such legislation?**
3. **Do you see any potential problems if such a law were passed?**

Drugs, Crime, and Science

Science is often conceptualized as a means of arriving at some indisputable truth. Although science is one way of accumulating knowledge, it has its limitations. In fact, science is filled with traps, roadblocks, and detours that can mislead rather than inform if one is not careful. Richard Hammersley maintains that by adopting an attitude of **pragmatic realism** we can avoid common traps in the misapplication of scientific methods.[26] These traps can also be avoided by gaining a broader understanding of the knowledge acquisition process.

Pragmatic Realism

By pragmatic realism, Hammersley means that there is no guarantee of us ever knowing the truth about something because our perception of reality is so heavily influenced by our experiences, prejudices, and personal limitations.[27] We should consequently remain skeptical of the methods we use to form our conclusions, being careful not to cross the line into cynicism. Maintaining an attitude of healthy skepticism or pragmatic realism can be helpful in avoiding the conceptual traps and pitfalls set by such knowledge-inhibiting influences as **grand theories**, **reductionism**, and **naïve empiricism**.

Grand theories assume that complex behavior can be explained with a few constructs. The goal of theory building is to simplify but when such simplification leads us to conclude that drug use or crime are caused by one or two factors we are falling into the grand theory trap.[28] Many theories of substance abuse conceptualize drug use as a stable trait impervious to temporary states and situational events such as the user's mind set or the circumstances under which the drug is taken. Many theories of crime are also guilty of grand theorizing as represented by the popularity of single-variable theories in the field of criminology. As important as low self-control,[29] antisocial peers,[30] and secondary deviance[31] are to crime, viewing any one of these factors as a complete explanation for crime is a prime example of the knowledge-inhibiting effects of grand theories.

Reductionism is another common trap confronting those who would follow a rigid path to knowledge acquisition.[32] Because reductionism involves breaking complex phenomena down into their constituent parts, it is grounded in the assumption that the constituent parts fully account for the behavior in question. This is another way of saying that molar constructs are best understood by breaking them down into their molecular subcomponents. The substance abuse field is replete with examples of biological reductionism, whereby the causes of drug use are reduced to the level of the gene or neuron. Sociologic criminology, on the other hand, suffers from the opposite problem, focusing on molar constructs like social structure to the detriment of the decision-making apparatus of the individual actor. A certain degree of reductionism is required in any science; where we run into problems is when we start assuming that reductionism is the only avenue to truth. A systems-within-systems view of science, in which the molar and molecular levels are balanced, would appear to hold greater potential for advancing our understanding of the drug–crime relationship than an exclusive focus on either molar or molecular constructs.

Some researchers seem to be of the opinion that all major scientific questions can be answered with a few well-designed and definitive studies. Fortunately, this is a minority opinion, but when expressed reflects what Hammersley refers to as naïve empiricism.[33] The fact of the matter is that there never will be a definitive study because each study is limited by the sample it selects, the methodology it adopts, the assumptions it makes, and the statistics it uses. This is why virtually every research study published in a peer-reviewed journal has a limitations section. A sample is, by definition, a subcomponent of the population to which we wish to generalize our results. To ensure generalization, the sample we select must adequately cover the groups that comprise the population of interest. Stratified random sampling, where we randomly select participants in proportion to their representation in the overall population, does the best job of creating a sample with good **external validity**, yet it still does not guarantee full **generalizability**. Moreover, the indicators we select to represent the constructs we are investigating are imperfect and subject to criticism. The lesson to be learned from all this is that there is no such thing as a flawless study. We can partially compensate for these limitations, nonetheless, by taking note of the knowledge accumulation process.

Knowledge Accumulation

The best way to compensate for the limitations of individual studies is to examine the results of multiple studies on a single topic. This has traditionally been accomplished with

Figure 1-11
Correlation coefficients and Cohen's *d* values associated with small, medium, and large effect sizes.

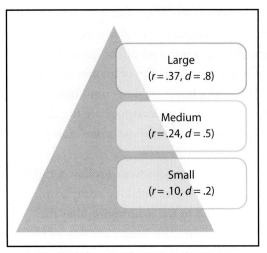

Data From: Cohen, J. (1988). *Statistical power analysis for the behavioral sciences* (2nd ed.). Hillsdale, NJ: Lawrence Erlbaum.

a literature review in which the results of different studies are examined, critiqued, and compared. Literature reviews, however, have been characterized as overly subjective, unsystematic, and potentially biased.[34] Many scientists are consequently abandoning the qualitative or narrative literature review for the more objective and quantitative meta-analytic review. A meta-analysis involves pooling the results of multiple studies on the same topic to determine the degree of relationship between two variables or the effect of one variable on another variable. A measure known as the **effect size** is the foundation upon which meta-analyses are based. The effect size is calculated for each study or sample (sometimes there are multiple samples from the same study and these are usually treated separately) and then pooled.

The two most popular effect size measures are Pearson's *r* and Cohen's *d*. Pearson's *r* assesses the correlation or covariation between two variables. It can range from −1.00 (perfect inverse relationship) to +1.00 (perfect direct relationship), with .00 representing a total absence of relationship. Cohen's *d* is computed as the difference between two means divided by the means' pooled standard deviation. The magnitude of effect can be classified as small, medium, and large based on guidelines provided by Cohen for *d* and *r* (see **Figure 1-11**).[35] The effect size results for the different studies in a meta-analysis are pooled and a mean effect size and confidence interval (range of values that contains the true effect size 95% or 99% of the time) calculated. Meta-analysis is a prime example of knowledge accumulation and so the results of meta-analytic studies will be reported whenever they are available to shed light on major aspects of the drug–crime connection.

The Complexity of Drug–Crime Relationships

In this chapter I demonstrate how drugs and crime are linked, how both individually and collectively they have been instrumental at various points in American history, how drug and crime policy can be politically motivated, and how science, despite its limitations, may still be our best means of understanding the drug–crime relationship. We are now in a position to examine these issues in greater detail, particularly as they relate to theory, research, practice, and policy. By understanding that a relationship exists between drugs and crime, we can begin delving into this relationship for the purpose of determining how it can best be managed clinically, practically, and bureaucratically. It is unrealistic to think that there is any one drug–crime relationship, however, and I underscore this point by replacing the term drug–crime relationship with drug–crime relationships from here on in.

It is vital that the reader understand that drug–crime relationships are formidably complex. Before we can understand this complexity, though, we must first appreciate the contextual nature of these relationships. Substance-using offenders treated in substance abuse programs display reduced levels of both drug use and crime, yet many successful treatment programs for substance-using offenders, such as Moral Reconation Therapy and Thinking for a Change, spend little if any time discussing drugs or drug abuse.[36] Heroin shortages are often accompanied by lower levels of heroin use and decreased levels of drug-related crime, yet shortages can encourage users to switch to other, sometime more dangerous, substances.[37] During Prohibition thousands of Americans died and hundreds of thousands suffered permanent physical disabilities after drinking ethanol substitutes like wood alcohol.[38] In modern-day Russia, addicts who cannot afford heroin inject substitute drugs like Fentanyl, Coaxil, and Desmorphine, better known as "Krokodil" because its poisonous ingredients quickly turn the skin a scaly green (see News Spot 1-2).

NEWS SPOT 1-2

Title: DEA Closely Watching Krokodil, a Morphine Derivative That is Deadly
Source: *Detroit Examiner*
Author: Michael Velardo
Date: June 29, 2011

Call it a designer drug on steroids, krokodil is a morphine derivative that is destroying people, and it may be on its way to America.

The Drug Enforcement Administration, (DEA), have their eyes on this reptilian drug madness overseas, and doesn't believe it has hit the U.S. yet DEA spokesman Rusty Payne told FoxNews.com.

Krokodil, or "despmorphine" has been making it's rounds in Russia where about 65 million doses have been confiscated in the first few months of this year according to Russia's Federal Drug Control Service as told to Time.

"To produce the potentially deadly drug, which has a comparable effect to heroin but is much cheaper to make, users mix codeine with gasoline, paint thinner, iodine, hydrochloric acid and red phosphorous.Codeine, a controlled substance in the United States used to treat mild to moderate pain, is widely available over the counter in Russia," reported FoxNews.com.

The drug is at epidemic proportions in Russia where an estimated 1 million people where (sic) injecting this concoction in 2010.

Krokodil, a take on the word crocodile, is so named because the skin at the sites of the injection turn green, and scaly from ruptured blood vessels, and then die.

Reports indicate that the drug first appeared in Siberia in 2002.

"Dr. Lewis Nelson, a medical toxicologist at Bellevue Hospital Center in New York, said he doubts krokodil will reach the United States due to the availability of other cheap, powerful drugs such as black tar heroin and Oxycontin," reported FoxNews.com.

Let's hope Dr. Lewis, and the DEA are right. If this snake of a drug reaches our kids, many of them already experimenting with research chemicals, prescription, and other drugs, krokodil will make those substances look like licking Blow Pop suckers in comparison.

Questions to Ponder
1. **What would possess someone to inject a substance into his or her body that causes the skin to turn green and rot away?**
2. **Relate this situation to Prohibition in American where some people died and went blind from drinking wood alcohol.**
3. **What can law enforcement do to keep Krokodil out of the hands of U.S. citizens?**

The complexity of drug–crime relationships becomes more apparent when we examine drug–crime relationships at the individual level. Turning our attention to individuals we find that in some cases drug use precedes crime, in other cases crime precedes drug use, and in still other cases the two behaviors surface around the same time. Thus, although the correlation between drugs and crime is strong and consistent at the group level, there are many variations at the individual level. Drugs also differ in their **criminogenic** (crime-causing) potential. A drug like heroin or alcohol is more criminogenic than marijuana; but that does not mean marijuana cannot be criminogenic in certain individual cases or under specific environmental conditions. The first step in understanding and potentially altering drug–crime relationships is appreciating the complexity of these behaviors and the relationships that form between them. This chapter takes the first step by providing the reader with an appreciation for the complexity of drugs, crime, and various drug–crime relationships.

Summary and Conclusions

- There is sufficient empirical evidence to support the conclusion that a robust relationship exists between drugs and crime. This support comes from three primary sources: general surveys of high school students and young adults, studies on drug use in criminal populations, and studies on crime in drug using populations.
- The history of drugs and crime begins with Christopher Columbus and continues to the present day. The role of politics, the influence of the media, and the subjugation of science to personal interests is clearly evident in this history.
- Politics clearly influence how society approaches drugs, crime, and their relationships. If significant change is to occur in American drug policy then the politics will have to change as well.
- Science may be our best means of understanding drug–crime relationships but it has its drawbacks. Understanding these drawbacks and working toward knowledge accumulation is one way of compensating for the weaknesses of the scientific method while taking advantage of its strengths.
- There is no single drug–crime relationship but rather multiple drug–crime relationships and the primary objective is to make sense of these relationships.

Key Terms

Arrestee Drug Abuse Monitoring (ADAM II)   Data monitoring federal program in which arrestees in 10 U.S. cities are tested for 10 different drugs within 24 hour of arrest.

Confidence Interval   Range of values or scores that contain the true population value or score at a specific level of confidence: i.e., 95% of the time in the case of a 95% confidence interval and 99% of the time in the case of a 99% confidence interval.

Criminogenic   Capable of causing crime.

Effect Size   Measure of the relationship between two variables or the effect of one variable on another.

External Validity   (see Generalizability).

Generalizability   Extent to which results obtained in a particular sample apply to the population of interest.

Grand Theories   Models that presume complex behavior can be explained with a small number of variables.

Meta-Analysis   Statistical technique that combines the results of multiple studies.

Moderator Variable   Measured variable that affects the direction or size of the relationship between two other variables.

Naïve Empiricism   Belief that a scientific study can answer all relevant questions.

National Crime Victimization Survey (NCVS)   Stratified multistage cluster sample of American household interviewed to assess the frequency, characteristics, and consequences of victimization.

National Longitudinal Study of Adolescent Health (Add Health)   Nationally representative sample of 26,666 American youth collected in four waves.

Pragmatic Realism   Perspective that is mindful of the limitations of science.

Reductionism   Tendency of a theory to break complex, global phenomena down into simpler and smaller constituent parts.

"War on Drugs"   Policy of drug prohibition followed in the United States in which supply-side strategies like interdiction and incarceration of drug users are emphasized over demand-side strategies like treatment and harm reduction.

Youth Risk Behavior Surveillance (YRBS)   Nationally representative sample of 14,000 students enrolled in public and private high schools in 50 U.S. states and District of Columbia.

Critical Thinking

1. Which studies do you find most compelling as evidence of a drug–crime connection—general surveys of drug use and delinquency, drug use in criminal populations, or crime in drug-using populations?
2. Can you find anything in the history of crime and drug use in the United States that might explain America's current preoccupation with drugs?
3. How can researchers and scientists avoid falling into the reductionism, grand theorizing, and naïve empiricism traps?

Notes

1. Kandel, D., Simcha-Fagan, O., & Davies, M. (1986). Risk factors for delinquency and illicit drug use from adolescence to young adulthood. *Journal of Drug Issues, 16,* 67–90.
2. Huizinga, D., Loeber, R., Thornberry, T. P., & Cothern, L. (2000). Co-occurrence of delinquency and other problem behaviors. *Juvenile Justice Bulletin* (NCJ 182211). Washington, DC: Office of Juvenile Justice and Delinquency Prevention.
3. Eaton, D. K., Kann, L., Kinchen, S., Shanklin, S., Ross, J., Hawkins, J., et al. (2008, June 6). Youth risk behavior surveillance—United States, 2007. *Morbidity and Mortality Weekly Report* (Vol. 57). Atlanta, GA: Centers for Disease Control and Prevention, U.S. Department of Health and Human Services.
4. Udry, J. R. (2003). *The National Longitudinal Study of Adolescent Health (Add Health).* Chapel Hill, NC: Carolina Population Center, University of North Carolina.
5. Karberg, J. C., & James, D. J. (2005). Substance dependence, abuse, and treatment of jail inmates, 2002. *Bureau of Justice Statistics Special Report* (NCJ 209588). Washington, DC: U.S. Department of Justice.
6. Mumola, C. J., & Karberg, J. C. (2006). Drug use and dependence, state and federal prisoners, 2004. *Bureau of Justice Statistics Special Report* (NCJ 213530). Washington, DC: U.S. Department of Justice.
7. Karberg & James (2005).
8. Mumola & Karberg (2006).
9. Mumola & Karberg (2006).
10. Office of National Drug Control Policy. (2011). *ADAM II: 2010 annual report.* Washington, DC: Author.
11. Bureau of Justice Statistics. (2010). *Criminal victimization in the United States, 2007* (NCJ 227669). Washington, DC: Author.
12. Johnson, B. D., Goldstein, P., Preble, E., Schmeidler, J., Lipton, D. S., Spunt, B., et al. (1985). *Taking care of business: The economics of crime by heroin abusers.* Lexington, MA: Lexington Books.
13. Inciardi, J. A. (1986). *The war on drugs: Heroin, cocaine, and public policy.* Palo Alto, CA: Mayfield.
14. Nurco, D. N., Hanlon, T. E., Kinlock, T. W., & Slaght, E. (1989). *Final report: Drug offender typology development.* (National Institute of Justice Grant No. 86-IJ-CX-0030). Submitted to the National Institute of Justice, June 2, 1989.
15. Battjes, R. J., Gordon, M. S., O'Grady, K. E., Kinlock, T. W., Katz, E. C., & Sears, E. A. (2004). Evaluation of a group-based substance abuse treatment program for adolescents. *Journal of Substance Abuse Treatment, 27,* 123–134.
16. Farabee, D., Prendergast, M., & Anglin, M. D. (1998). The effectiveness of coerced treatment for drug-abusing offenders. *Federal Probation, 62*(1), 3–10.
17. Fridell, M., Hesse, M., Jæger, M. M., & Kühlhorn, E. (2008). Antisocial personality disorder as a predictor of criminal behavior in a longitudinal study of a cohort of abusers of several classes of drugs: relation to types of substances and types of crime. *Addictive Behaviors, 33,* 799–811.
18. Bennett, T. H., Holloway, K., & Farrington, D. P. (2008). The statistical association between drug misuse and crime: A meta-analysis. *Aggression and Violent Behavior, 13,* 107–118.
19. Musto, D. F. (2008). *Drugs in America: A documentary history.* New York: NYU Press.
20. Oliver, W. M., & Hilgenberg, J. F. (2010). *A history of crime and criminal justice in America* (2nd ed.). Durham, NC: Carolina Academic Press.
21. Shmoop Editorial Team. (2008). *History of drugs in America.* Retrieved January 22, 2012, from http://www.shmoop.com/drugs-america/timeline.html.
22. Baum, D. (1996). *Smoke and mirrors: The war on drugs and the politics of failure.* New York: Little Brown.
23. Ditton, J., & Farrall, S. (2000). *The fear of crime.* Aldershot, England: Dartmouth.
24. OpenSecrets.org. *Influence and Lobbying: Interest Groups.* Retrieved January 18, 2012, from http://www.opensecrets.org/influence/index.php.
25. OpenSecrets.org. *Influence and Lobbying: Interest Groups.* Retrieved January 18, 2012, from http://www.opensecrets.org/influence/index.php.

26. Hammersley, R. (2008). *Drugs and crime*. Cambridge, England: Polity Press.

27. Hammersley (2008).

28. Hammersley (2008).

29. Gottfredson, M. R., & Hirschi, T. (1990). *A general theory of crime*. Stanford, CA; Stanford University Press.

30. Sutherland, E. H., & Cressey, D. R. (1978). *Criminology* (10th ed.). Philadelphia: Lippincott.

31. Bernburg, J. G., & Krohn, M. D. (2003). Labeling, life chances, and adult crime: The direct and indirect effects of official intervention in adolescence on crime in early adulthood. *Criminology, 41*, 1287–1318.

32. Hammersley (2008).

33. Hammersley (2008).

34. Lipsey, M. W., & Wilson, D. B. (2001). *Practical meta-analysis* (Applied Social. Research Methods Series, Vol. 49). Thousand Oaks, CA: Sage.

35. Cohen, J. (1988). *Statistical power analysis for the behavioral sciences* (2nd ed.). Hillsdale, NJ: Lawrence Erlbaum.

36. Inciardi, J. A., Martin, S. S., & Butzin, C. A. (2004). Five-year outcomes of therapeutic community treatment of drug-involved offenders after release from prison. *Crime and Delinquency, 50*, 88–107.

37. Moffatt, S., Weatherburn, D., & Donnelly, N. (2005). What caused the drop in property crime? *Crime and Justice Bulletin* (No. 86). Sydney: New South Wales Bureau of Crime Statistics and Research.

38. Behr, E. (1997). *Prohibition: Thirteen years that changed America*. New York: Arcade Publishing.

DRUGS: DEFINITIONS, CLASSIFICATION, AND THEORY

Drug use and abuse are a major problem in modern-day America. A recent news report indicated that in 2009 drug-related deaths exceeded deaths from traffic accidents for the first time in recorded United States history (see News Spot 2-1). **Figure 2-1** depicts how rapidly drug-related deaths have climbed in the last 11 years.[1] In an effort to understand the role of drugs in modern American society, the current chapter is organized around three primary objectives:

- Define what is meant by the terms drug and drug effect
- Explore several possible classification systems for drugs of abuse
- Review and evaluate major theories of drug use and abuse

NEWS SPOT 2-1

Title: Drug Deaths Now Outnumber Traffic Fatalities in U.S., Data Show
Source: Copyright © 2011. *Los Angeles Times*. Reprinted with Permission.
Author: Lisa Girion, Scott Glover, and Doug Smith
Date: September 17, 2011

Propelled by an increase in prescription narcotic overdoses, drug deaths now outnumber traffic fatalities in the United States, a *Times* analysis of government data has found.

Drugs exceeded motor vehicle accidents as a cause of death in 2009, killing at least 37,485 people nationwide, according to preliminary data from the U.S. Centers for Disease Control and Prevention.

Although most major causes of preventable death are declining, drugs are an exception. The death toll has doubled in the last decade, now claiming a life every 14 minutes. By contrast, traffic accidents have been dropping for decades because of huge investments in auto safety.

Public health experts have used the comparison to draw attention to the nation's growing prescription drug problem, which they characterize as an epidemic. This is the first time that drugs have accounted for more fatalities than traffic accidents since the government started tracking drug-induced deaths in 1979.

Fueling the surge in deaths are prescription pain and anxiety drugs that are potent, highly addictive and especially dangerous when combined with one another or with other drugs or alcohol. Among the most commonly abused are OxyContin, Vicodin, Xanax, and Soma. One relative newcomer to the scene is Fentanyl, a painkiller that comes in the form of patches and lollipops and is 100 times more powerful than morphine.

Such drugs now cause more deaths than heroin and cocaine combined.

Questions to Ponder

1. **Why do drug deaths continue to rise when most forms of preventable death are declining?**
2. **What, if anything, can be done to reverse this trend?**
3. **Why are prescription drugs causing more deaths than illegal drugs?**

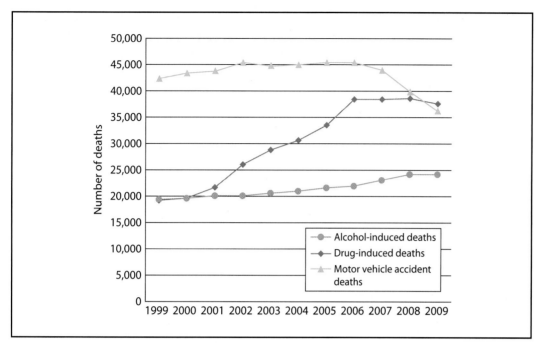

Figure 2-1
Annual rates of drug-induced, alcohol-induced, and motor vehicle accident deaths, 1999–2009.

Data From: National Vital Statistics Report, Centers for Disease Control.

Definitions

The term **drug** can have different meanings and connotations depending on whom you ask. Therefore I begin this chapter with a brief discussion of what I mean by the term drug. When I use the term drug I am referring to a chemical substance other than food that alters the structure or function of the body. A particular category of drug is of interest here; namely, a psychoactive substance capable of generating a subjective state of pleasure, relief, or change that the user finds reinforcing. Through the integrated action of biologic, psychologic, sociologic, and situational processes, a portion of users are motivated to continue using the substance in an effort to reexperience this subjective reinforcing state of pleasure, relief, or change. The chemical substance contributes only partially to this "**drug effect**," however. Nonchemical factors are at least as important as the pharmacologic action of the drug in promoting the subjective reinforcing effect of pleasure, relief, or change. Norman Zinberg's views on drug, set, and setting are particularly helpful in defining the effect of these nonpharmacologic factors on the overall drug experience.[2]

Drug

The chemical ingredients in a drug interact with receptors in the central and peripheral nervous systems to bring about a change in physiology. These changes are not interpreted uniformly across people, in part because of individual differences in physiology and in part because of individual differences in the psychology, sociology, and context of drug use. Hence, the chemical ingredients in a drug are only partially responsible for the effect of the drug on the individual. Zinberg reminds us that craving, withdrawal, and overdose are influenced as much by psychologic, sociologic, and situational factors as they are by the pharmacologic action of the drug.[3] Furthermore, although higher doses of a drug are normally associated with larger effects, drug-response curves tend to be curvilinear and complex. In a meta-analysis of 34 prospective studies, Di Castelnuovo and colleagues

Figure 2-2
Unintentional drug overdose deaths for opioid analgesics, cocaine, and heroin in the United States, 1999–2008.

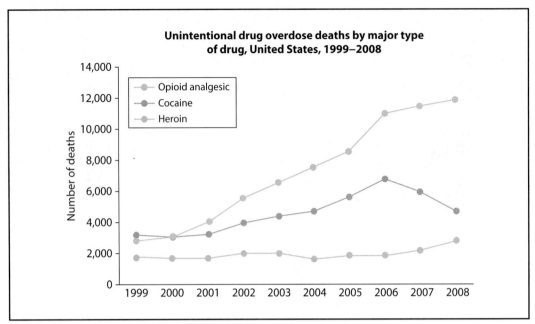

Unintentional drug overdose deaths by major type of drug, United States, 1999–2008

Reproduced from NIDA, 2011, Topics in Brief: Prescription Drug Abuse.

(2006) observed a j-shaped drug-response curve for alcohol whereby men who consumed two to four alcoholic drinks per day and women who consumed one or two alcoholic drinks per day had below average rates of mortality and men and women who drank more than this experienced progressively higher rates of mortality.[4]

Whether a substance is legal or illegal is largely a matter of convention and has little to do with its status as a drug. Some legal drugs can be quite deadly, partly because they are legal and therefore more available to people. Alcohol is responsible for more deaths than all of the illegal drugs combined and tobacco is responsible for more deaths than alcohol and illegal drugs combined. Juergen Rehm, director of Switzerland's Addiction Research Institute, examined the death rates for tobacco, alcohol, and illegal drugs and determined that tobacco was responsible for 4.9 million deaths, alcohol for 1.8 million deaths, and illegal drugs for 223,000 deaths in 2000. Even overdose deaths are more often the result of legal drugs than illegal ones.[5] **Figure 2-2** depicts the changing pattern of overdose deaths in the past 10 years. During the most recent year of the survey (2008), overdose deaths for opioid-based prescription medications like hydrocodone (Vicodin) and oxycodone (OxyContin) exceeded overdose deaths for cocaine and heroin combined.[6]

Set

Psychological **set** can be defined as a person's state of mind at the time a drug is consumed. Zinberg notes that a person's mindset or mood can have a powerful impact on the overall drug experience.[7] An individual who takes a drug in a positive frame of mind is more likely to have a pleasant experience than an individual who takes a drug when angry, depressed, or paranoid. In fact, in many cases, the drug will amplify these negative emotions. Psychological set can influence any drug experience but certain drugs are more susceptible to psychological set than others. People's experiences with marijuana and the hallucinogen LSD seem to be particularly sensitive to a person's psychological set.[8–9] Andrew Weil, in fact, refers to most drugs of abuse as active placebos, suggesting that although they affect the neurophysiology of the brain, the drug experience itself is more a function of psychological processes than it is of biological ones, particularly at low to moderate doses.[10]

A **placebo** is an inert substance made to look like an active drug. A placebo effect is a person's response to the placebo. One of the ways researchers test the efficacy of a drug is by comparing it to a placebo (sugar pill) made to look like the active drug. Findings from such research indicate that a good portion of the effect of most psychoactive substances on mood and behavior is due to a placebo effect. Three-quarters to 80% of the therapeutic effect of antidepressant medication on mood, for instance, is the result of a placebo effect.[11–12] There is also evidence that the placebo effect is mediated by the release of an endogenous opiate in the user's brain known as endorphin.[13] Hence, the placebo effect may act very much like a drug, interacting with various neurotransmitter systems, to produce a response that is indistinguishable from the drug's pharmacological effect.

The **balanced placebo design** (see **Table 2-1**) was used in a classic study by Alan Marlatt and colleagues to demonstrate the effect of alcohol and expectancies on drinking behavior.[14] Half the group was administered the drug (vodka and tonic) and half were administered a placebo (tonic only); half of the participants in each group were then told that they were drinking vodka and tonic and the other half were informed that they were drinking tonic only. In both alcoholics and social drinkers, the expectancy of receiving alcohol had a much greater impact on the amount of beverage consumed than whether the drink contained alcohol (see **Figure 2-3**).

Table 2-1 The Four Cells of the Balanced Placebo Design

	Given Drug	**Given Placebo**
Told Drug	Drug Effect + Placebo Effect	Placebo Effect
Told Placebo	Drug Effect	Baseline

Similar results have been obtained when alcohol expectancies for aggression, mood, and sexual arousal have been studied and when the balanced placebo design has been extended to nicotine and marijuana use.[15–17]

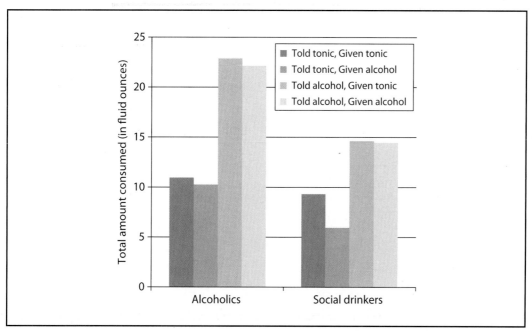

Figure 2-3
Effect of alcohol content and expectancies on amount of beverage consumed.

Data From: Marlatt, G. A., Demming, B., & Reid, J. B. (1973). Loss of control drinking in alcoholics: An experimental analogue. *Journal of Abnormal Psychology*, 81, 233–241.

Setting

The **setting** for drug consumption is the physical environment where the drug is taken as well as the psychological meaning the user invests in that environment. Research indicates that this can also have a significant impact on the overall drug experience. Drug use by soldiers in Vietnam is a prime example of a setting effect. A fair number of combat veterans used heroin in Vietnam, but the vast majority discontinued the habit once they returned home, largely as a consequence of the change in setting.[18] Once back in the United States, the environmental cues that supported drug use in Vietnam were no longer present and so most of these individuals did not experience the level of craving and **withdrawal** symptomatology that frequently lead to relapse in former heroin users.

With repeated consumption in the same setting, environmental cues for drugs form an opponent process. Hence, some cues generate a druglike effect and other cues generate a compensatory or drug-opposite effect.[19] The problem is that the drug-opposite effect grows more rapidly than the druglike effect (see **Figure 2-4**). This opponent process helps explain several phenomena, including tolerance, withdrawal, and craving. Because the drug-opposite effect grows more rapidly than the druglike effect, regular users will experience craving and withdrawal as soon as they enter the room or building where they normally use drugs. Once they start using, they will require progressively higher doses of the drug (tolerance) to counteract the rising drug opposite effect. By the same token, a person who accommodates to a specific dose of medication in one environment (hospital) can overdose on the same dose of medication in an environment where they have not yet formed a drug-opposite effect (home).

Environmental factors can either increase or decrease the behavioral problems associated with drug use. Establishments that encourage people to drink heavily or that tolerate drunken behavior experience higher levels of drunken and violent behavior than bars and pubs that do not encourage heavy drinking or do not tolerate drunken behavior.[20] Environmental enrichment, on the other hand, successfully reversed cocaine addiction in laboratory mice in a recent study by Marcello Solinas and colleagues (see **Figure 2-5**).[21] How well these findings generalize to humans is uncertain at this time, yet they suggest that environmental stimulation and enrichment could play an important role in recovery and relapse prevention.

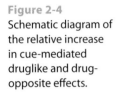

Figure 2-4
Schematic diagram of the relative increase in cue-mediated druglike and drug-opposite effects.

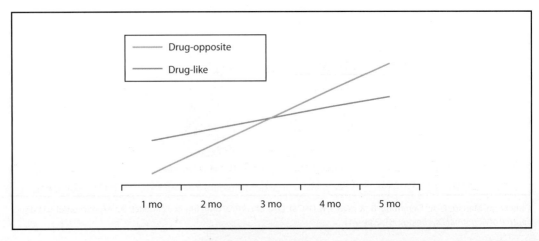

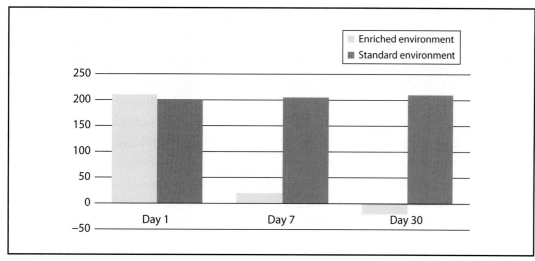

Figure 2-5
Cocaine preference
scores (in seconds)
for cocaine-
addicted mice
exposed to standard
and enriched
environments after
1, 7, and 30 days.

Data From: Solinas, M., Chauvet, C., Thiriet, N., El Rawas, R., & Jaber, M. (2008). Reversal of cocaine addiction by environmental enrichment. *PNAS*, 105, 17145–17150.

Classification

The fourth edition of the *Diagnostic and Statistical Manual of Mental Disorders* (DSM-IV) divides substance use disorders into two main categories:

- Substance Dependence
- Substance Abuse

Substance Dependence

The DSM-IV defines substance dependence as a maladaptive pattern of substance use characterized by at least three of the following seven symptoms in the same 12-month period:[22]

- Tolerance
- Withdrawal
- Using in larger amounts or over longer periods than intended
- Persistent desire or unsuccessful attempts to cut down or stop
- Time spent obtaining or using the substance
- Social, occupational, or recreational activities sacrificed
- Continued use despite physical or psychological problems

Tolerance

Tolerance refers to the fact that with continued use of a drug the user requires increasingly higher doses to achieve the desired effect. With the possible exception of caffeine, most drugs of abuse produce tolerance. Tolerance is held to be a function of three mechanisms: metabolic tolerance, pharmacodynamic tolerance, and behavioral conditioning.[23] Metabolic tolerance refers to the fact that the liver produces enzymes following repeated exposure to a substance designed to metabolize or break down the substance. Pharmacodynamic tolerance means that neurons respond to the continued presence of the drug in the brain by reducing the number or sensitivity of receptors for the neurotransmitters involved in the drug response. Behavioral conditioning involves the creation of an opponent-process that gives rise to cue-elicited druglike and drug-opposite effects.

Withdrawal Symptoms

When an individual who has been using a drug regularly abruptly stops using that drug he or she may experience withdrawal symptoms. Withdrawal symptoms tend to be the flip side of the drug effect in the sense that they are the compensatory component of the opponent-process. As such, withdrawal symptoms vary from one drug to the next. Withdrawal symptoms for alcohol range from mild (hangover) to severe (delirium tremens) and involve sweating, headache, insomnia, and hand tremors at the mild level and fever, convulsions, and visual hallucinations at the severe level. Withdrawal from opiates is uncomfortable but rarely fatal and includes nausea, shakes, sweats, and bodily aches and pains. Typical withdrawal symptoms for cocaine include low mood, insomnia, lack of energy, and other signs of depression. LSD, by contrast, does not appear to give rise to withdrawal symptoms.

Using in Larger Amounts or over Longer Periods than Intended

Someone who is dependent on a drug will often consume a larger amount of the drug or spend more time using the drug than originally intended. One example might be an individual who stops by the local bar to have a drink and ends up consuming a dozen beers and several shots of whiskey. Another example would be an individual who stops by a party where cocaine is being used with the intent of spending a few minutes with friends but who remains at the party for 14 hours, leaving only after all the cocaine is gone.

Persistent Desire or Unsuccessful Attempts to Cut Down or Stop

As the negative consequences of habitual drug use begin to mount the individual may feel the need to stop or cut down on his or her usage. Most such attempts are unsuccessful in that people who are dependent on drugs have learned to use drugs to cope with the problems of everyday living and so when they experience negative affect they often turn to drugs as a means of coping with these uncomfortable feelings. The individual may be capable of stopping or cutting down for short periods of time but the duration of these periods of abstinence or controlled drug usage is normally brief.

Time Spent Obtaining or Using the Drug

Those who are dependent on a drug often spend an inordinate amount of time obtaining, using, and thinking about drugs. This is sometimes referred to as "chasing the high." For instance, someone who is dependent on prescription medication may go to multiple doctors or spend hours forging drug prescriptions to get access to their drug of choice, whereas someone who is dependent on marijuana may drive many miles to pick up their weekly stash. Some cocaine and heroin users will spend days at a time in crack houses where cocaine is being used or shooting galleries where heroin is being used. A chain smoker will spend much of his or her day with a cigarette in his or her mouth, engaging in various smoking rituals.

Social, Occupational, or Recreational Activities Sacrificed

As a person's dependence on drugs grows he or she will abandon or greatly reduce his or her involvement with family, friends, and acquaintances. The person may frequently call in "sick" to work, quit, or even purposely get fired so that he or she can spend more time with drugs. Recreational activities (sports, hobbies) the individual may have engaged in for years no longer seem important unless they can be incorporated into the drug lifestyle.

Continued Use Despite Physical or Psychological Problems

There are a number of physical and psychological problems that can arise from habitual drug use. The individual will tend to ignore these problems or at least deny that there is a connection between these problems and their drug use. Examples include the individual who continues snorting cocaine despite the physical (nose bleeds) and psychological (paranoia) problems this creates and the individual who continues drinking even though he or she has developed an ulcer and gastritis that are aggravated by alcohol.

In the *Addiction Concept*, Walters defines addiction as a behavioral pattern composed of four symptom clusters: progression, preoccupation, perceived loss of control, and persistence in the face of negative long-term consequences.[24] Progression means that the individual's involvement with the drug grows over time. Preoccupation refers to the fact that drugs begin to structure the individual's time and dominate his or her daily schedule. Perceived loss of control means that addicted individuals view themselves as having little control over the drug or their behavior while on the drug. Finally, the behavior persists despite a growing number of negative long-term consequences. Each of the seven criteria for drug dependence is subsumed by one of the four clusters in the addiction concept and so the concept may be of some help to readers looking for a way to remember the seven criteria.

- Progression
  - Tolerance
  - Withdrawal
- Preoccupation
  - Inordinate amount of time spent obtaining and using drugs
- Perceived Loss of Control
  - Using larger amounts or for longer periods than intended
  - Unsuccessful attempts to stop or cut down on usage
- Persistence in the Face of Negative Long-Term Consequences
  - Restrictions in social/occupational/recreational activities
  - Physical and psychological problems stemming from drug use

Substance Abuse

Substance abuse, as defined in the DSM-IV, consists of a maladaptive pattern of recurrent substance use leading to impaired functioning or psychological distress. A clinician will first attempt to diagnose substance dependence. If the criteria for substance dependence are not met then the next step is to see if the criteria for substance abuse can be satisfied. There are four criteria for substance abuse. If a person satisfies at least one of the criteria in a 12-month period a diagnosis of substance abuse can be made.[25]

Failure to Fulfill Major Role Obligations at Work, at School, or in the Home

A pattern of substance abuse is indicated when use of the drug significantly interferes with the individual's behavior or performance at work or school or causes significant family problems.

Use of the Substance in Situations that Are Physically Hazardous

If the individual drives impaired, operates machinery while high on drugs, or regularly gets into physical fights while intoxicated he or she would satisfy the criterion for using the substance in situations that are physically hazardous.

Substance-Related Legal Problems

Examples of substance-related legal problems that qualify one for a diagnosis of substance abuse include an arrest for domestic violence in which alcohol or drugs played a role, an arrest or conviction for driving under the influence of alcohol or drugs, or a court date for possessing illegal drugs in an individual with a history of personal drug use.

Continued Use Despite Recurrent Drug-Related Social or Interpersonal Problems

Continuing to use drugs even though such use interferes with interpersonal relationships at school or work or causes relationship problems with family or friends also qualifies one for a diagnosis of substance abuse.

There are three facts about drug misuse that are important to kept in mind:

1. The misuse of alcohol, perhaps because alcohol is legal and therefore more available, is more common than the misuse of illegal drugs.
2. Substance abuse is a more common pattern than substance dependence.
3. Men display higher rates of alcohol and drug misuse than women.

Simultaneous documentation of these three facts can be found in a large-scale study by Compton and colleagues, the results of which are presented in **Figure 2-6**.[26]

Expert Ratings of Harm

Another way to classify drugs is by the harm they create for both the user and society. David Nutt, Leslie King, and Lawrence Phillips recently asked a panel of experts to rate major drugs of abuse on 16 harm criteria broken down into three general categories (physical harm, psychological harm, and social harm).[27] Nine of the criteria were specific to users (e.g., drug-related physical damage, dependence, loss of relationships) and seven of the criteria were specific to others (e.g., injury, economic loss, crime). Using a scale of 100 and a sophisticated weighting scheme these researchers came to the following conclusions: (1) alcohol created the most harm to others and the most harm overall; (2) crack cocaine, heroin, and methamphetamine created the most harm to self; and (3) heroin and crack cocaine created the most crime. The level of harm to self and to others, with crime separated out from harm to others, for the 10 drugs evaluated in the Nutt et al. study are delineated in **Figure 2-7**.[28]

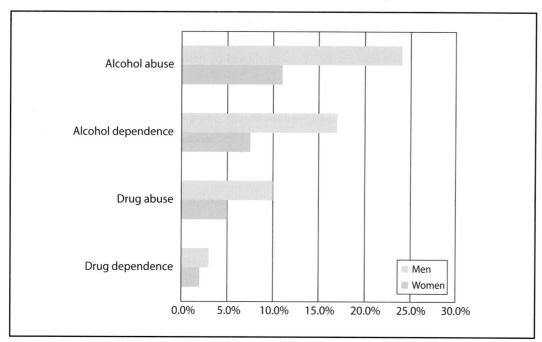

Figure 2-6
Proportion of men and women with alcohol and drug abuse and dependency diagnoses.

Data From: Compton, W. M., Thomas, Y. F., Stinson, F. S., & Grant, B. F. (2007). Prevalence, correlates, disability, and comorbidity of DSM-IV drug abuse and dependence in the United States. *Archives of General Psychiatry*, 64, 566–576.

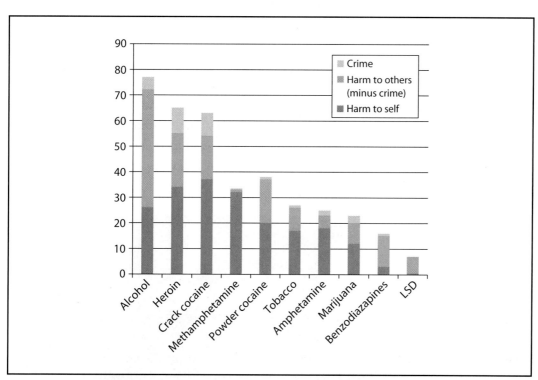

Figure 2-7
Expert ratings of the harm created to self and others for major drugs of abuse.

Data From: Nutt, D. J., King, L. A., & Phillips, L. D. (2010). Drug harms in the UK: A multicriteria decision analysis. *Lancet*, 376, 1558–1565.

Taxometrics and Latent Structure

The **taxometric** method was developed by Paul Meehl in an effort to determine whether the underlying organization (**latent structure**) of a construct was categorical or dimensional.[29] Using procedures developed by Meehl and an interpretative strategy created by John Ruscio and colleagues, it is possible to assess whether individual differences on a construct, such as drug dependence, reflect a difference in kind (categorical) or a difference in degree (dimensional).[30] Large-scale studies conducted on alcohol and nicotine seem to suggest that both alcohol and nicotine dependence may be underpinned by categorical latent structure.[31–32] Hence, it may be more appropriate to divide drugs into categories (alcohol vs. marijuana vs. cocaine) and subcategories (Type 1 and Type 2 alcoholism[33]) than to view them as points along multiple dimensions. Of course, it is also possible that some aspects of substance abuse and dependence are categorical and other aspects are dimensional.

Drugs of Abuse

Although there are too few taxometric studies to conclude that categories exist between individual drugs of abuse and fairly strong evidence that most drug users do not have a drug of choice but rather select a substance based on availability,[34] it may still be useful to discuss major drugs of abuse, allowing for the possibility of significant overlap between some of the categories. Seven major categories of commonly abused substances are discussed in this section, with each section being divided further into subsections (brief description, routes of administration, prevalence, short-term effects, and long-term effects). Unless otherwise noted, the primary source for information on prevalence rates was *Monitoring the Future* (*MTF*)[35] and the primary source for data in the remaining subsections was the National Institute of Drug Abuse (NIDA) drug abuse Web site.[36]

Alcohol

Brief Description

Ethyl alcohol or ethanol is produced from fermented yeast, sugars, and starches and is found in beer, wine, and liquor. It is absorbed into the bloodstream from the stomach and small intestine and travels to the brain. The rate of absorption varies as a function of the beverage's concentration of alcohol, volume and rate of consumption, the user's weight, and whether there is

Alcohol is the most frequently used drug in all age groups.

© Digital Vision/Thinkstock

food present in the stomach. Alcohol is considered a central nervous system (CNS) depressant, although at low doses it can act like a stimulant, and it achieves its effect, in part, by activating inhibitory neurotransmitters like Gamma-aminobutyric acid (GABA) and stimulating the parasympathetic branch (relaxation response) of the Autonomic Nervous System (ANS).

Routes of Administration

The most common route of administration for alcohol is oral. Although alcohol enemas are sometimes used by those looking for a more intense high, this is a potentially dangerous way of administering alcohol because it bypasses the normal filters in the digestive tract that protect the individual when alcohol is taken orally. Alcohol enemas, in fact, can lead to a sudden and potentially lethal rise in the blood alcohol concentration (BAC) level.

Prevalence

MTF data for 2010 indicate that 13.8% of 8th graders, 28.9% of 10th graders, 41.2% of 12th graders, 65.0% of college students, and 68.4% of young adults (ages 19-28) reported that they used alcohol at least once in the last month. In addition, 5.0% of 8th graders, 14.7% of 10th graders, 26.8% of 12th graders, 43.6% of college students and 39.4% of young adults reported getting drunk at least once in the last 30 days. Annual alcohol use was at least twice as common as yearly illicit drug use in the *MTF* between 1991 and 2011 (see **Figure 2-8**).[37]

Short-Term Effects

After being absorbed into the bloodstream, alcohol is broken down into acetaldehyde by the liver enzyme alcohol dehydrogenase. Fortunately, this highly toxic and carcinogenic substance is broken down further into acetate by another liver enzyme, aldehyde

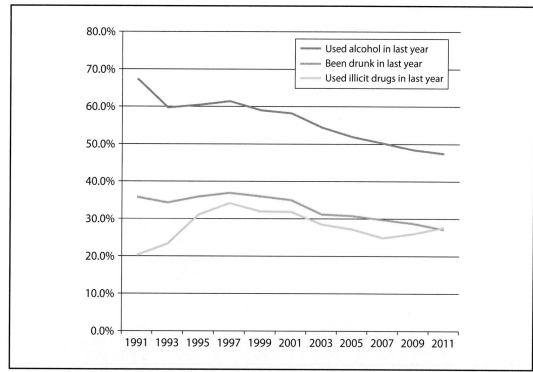

Figure 2-8
Percentage of students in grades 8, 10, and 12 who used alcohol, have been drunk, and used illicit drugs in the last year, 1991–2011.

Data From: Johnston, L. D., O'Malley, P. M., Bachman, J. G., & Schulenberg, J. E. (2011). *Monitoring the future: 1975–2010, Vols. 1 and 2.* Ann Arbor, MI: Institute for Social Research, University of Michigan.

dehydrogenase.[38] The manner in which alcohol is metabolized in the system is diagrammed in **Figure 2-9**. Given alcohol's status as a toxin and fact that acetaldehyde is even more toxic than alcohol, some of the short- and long-term effects of alcohol are the result of these poisons interacting with various bodily tissues and organs. The initial short-term effects of alcohol are facial flushing, reduced inhibitions, increased rate of speech, and a general sense of well-being. With continued consumption, the effect changes to one of sedation, slurred speech, and a gradual loss of coordination. At higher doses, the short-term effects of alcohol can include increased aggressive behavior, impaired memory in the form of blackouts, and stupor or coma.

Long-Term Effects

Heavy drinking over time can lead to a number of negative health consequences, including cancer, ulcers, gastritis, pancreatitis, and cirrhosis of the liver. Because the liver produces the enzymes that detoxify alcohol, serious liver disease can lead to a state of reverse tolerance whereby the individual requires less alcohol to get the same effect. Problems with both short- and long-term memory are observed with some degree of regularity in people who drink heavily for prolonged periods of time.[39] **Korsakoff syndrome** is believed to be the result of neurological damage caused by both vitamin deficiencies in the diets of many chronic alcoholics and the long-term effects of alcohol on various parts of the brain.[40] Social, occupational, and legal problems are additional negative long-term consequences of chronic heavy drinking.

Nicotine

Brief Description

Nicotine is what makes tobacco so addictive. Tobacco is produced in many countries but the world's top tobacco producers are China (39.6%), India (8.3%), Brazil (7.0%), and the United States (4.6%).[41] When tobacco is smoked, inhaled, or chewed it is absorbed into the bloodstream where it then travels to the brain and interacts with the central and autonomic nervous systems. Smoking provides the most direct route to the brain where it stimulates

Figure 2-9
How the body metabolizes alcohol.

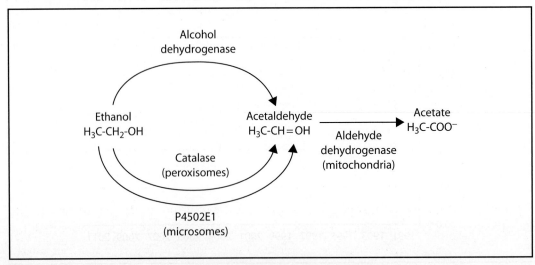

Reproduced from Alchohol Alert, No. 72, "Alcohol Metabolism: An Update," NIAAA, April 2007.

© Saharrr/ShutterStock, Inc.

Cigarettes are responsible for more deaths each year than alcohol and illegal drugs combined.

certain neurotransmitters—dopamine (DA), norepinephrine (NE), and serotonin (5HT), in particular.

Routes of Administration

The most popular route of administration for nicotine is to smoke it in cigarettes, cigars, or pipe tobacco. Nicotine is also consumed through chewing and inhalation (snuff).

Prevalence

The 2010 *MTF* revealed that 7.1% of 8th-grade students, 13.6% of 10th-grade students, 19.2% of 12th-grade students, 16.4% of college students, and 22.4% of young adults (ages 19–28) reported smoking one or more cigarettes in the last 30 days.

Short-Term Effects

Nicotine activates the sympathetic branch of the ANS. The sympathetic branch of the ANS controls the "fight or flight" response and acts on a number of different organ systems. As a stimulator of sympathetic response, nicotine interacts with the cardiovascular system to increase heart rate and blood pressure, relaxing the airways of the lungs to change breathing patterns, and shutting down the digestive system to reduce gastric motility. At high doses, nicotine is toxic. One drop of purified nicotine can actually kill a person. The lethality of nicotine is so well known, in fact, that it has been used in pesticides for centuries.

Long-Term Effects

There is growing evidence that people develop tolerance to nicotine and go through withdrawal when they stop using the drug. Typical withdrawal symptoms include irritability, insomnia, increased appetite, and strong cravings for tobacco. The most alarming long-term consequence of habitual nicotine consumption is the risk of fatal disease. Lung disease (bronchitis, emphysema), cancer (lung, mouth, throat), and heart disease are the primary culprits. Tobacco smoking causes more deaths per year than all other drugs (including alcohol) combined. On average, habitual smokers have a life expectancy that is 14 years shorter than nonsmokers. People who do not smoke can also experience cigarette-related health problems. Secondhand smoke is responsible for the deaths of 50,000 people each year.[42]

Cocaine and Amphetamine

Brief Description

Like nicotine, cocaine and amphetamine are stimulant drugs. As such, both activate dopaminergic (DA), noradrenergic (NE), and serotonergic (5HT) receptors in the brain. Cocaine is extracted from the leaf of the coca plant that grows abundantly in the Andes Mountains of South America. Amphetamines are produced synthetically in large company laboratories or in small makeshift labs. Some of the materials used to make amphetamine are highly combustible and so it is not uncommon to hear of an illegal methamphetamine lab exploding.

Routes of Administration

Cocaine can be snorted, injected, or smoked (freebasing). Amphetamine can be taken orally, snorted, injected, or smoked. The most intense effects are achieved by smoking or injecting these drugs.

Prevalence

According to the results of the 2010 *MTF*, 0.6% of 8th-grade students, 0.9% of 10th-grade students, 1.3% of 12th-grade students, 1.0% of college students, and 1.4% of young adults (ages 19–28) acknowledged consuming cocaine at least once in the past month.

Snorting remains the most popular route of cocaine administration.

© George Doyle/Stockbyte/Thinkstock

Amphetamines use was more frequent, with 1.8% of 8th graders, 3.3% of 10th graders, 3.3% of 12th graders, 4.1% of college students, and 2.9% of young adults reporting amphetamine use in the past month.

Short-Term Effects

Like nicotine, cocaine and amphetamine stimulate the sympathetic branch of the ANS. Consequently, the short-term effects of cocaine and amphetamine are much like those of nicotine except that they are more pronounced. Because amphetamines have a longer half-life than cocaine, the effects of amphetamines persist longer than the effects of cocaine. Individuals using cocaine and amphetamine experience a rush of energy, an exaggerated sense of control and intense feelings of euphoria and well-being. These drugs are also associated with decreased appetite (amphetamines have traditionally been used as diet pills) and reduced need for sleep (amphetamines are sometimes used by truck drivers and college students who wish to remain awake for a prolonged period of time). Acute overdoses are not uncommon and when they occur they are normally accompanied by irregular heartbeat that could lead to a heart attack, vascular constriction that could lead to a stroke, or convulsions that could lead to death.

Long-Term Effects

Prolonged use of cocaine and amphetamine can lead to periods of psychosis marked by auditory and visual hallucinations, delusions of grandeur and persecution, and extreme paranoia. Repeated use of cocaine, particularly crack cocaine, has been found to be associated with crime and violence. Ninety-seven percent of a sample of habitual crack cocaine users reported being involved in violence in the last 6 months and 68% reported being in a physical fight in the last 6 months. Crimes committed by the majority of participants in the sample included robbery, theft, and drug trafficking.[43] When cocaine and alcohol are used together a substance known as **cocaethylene** is formed; this substance intensifies the euphoric effects of cocaine but also increases the user's risk of cardiac arrest and sudden death.[44]

Sedatives and Tranquilizers

Brief Description

Like alcohol, sedatives (barbiturates, e.g., Seconal) and tranquilizers (benzodiazepines, e.g., Xanex) are central nervous system depressants, and like alcohol, they activate the parasympathetic branch of the ANS and the inhibitory neurotransmitter GABA. Barbiturates and benzodiazepines are used in medicine to treat insomnia and anxiety. Benzodiazepines have largely replaced barbiturates in general medical practice because they are less likely to lead to overdose. Nonetheless, both barbiturates and benzodiazepines are used for their antianxiety properties and have high abuse potential.

Routes of Administration

Barbiturates and tranquilizers are normally taken orally but can also be injected intramuscularly.

Barbiturates and benzodiazepines can produce cross-tolerance to alcohol.

© kubais/ShutterStock, Inc.

Prevalence

In 2010, the *MTF* sedative question was not posed to 8th and 10th graders, but 2.2% of 12th graders, 0.6% of college students, and 1.1% of young adults (ages 19–28) reported using sedatives in the last 30 days. The tranquilizer question was asked of all five groups, the results of which indicated that 1.2% of 8th-grade students, 2.2% of 10th-grade students, 2.5% of 12th-grade students, 1.3% of college students, and 2.2% of young adults reported using tranquilizers (benzodiazepines) in the last 30 days.

Short-Term Effects

At low doses, sedatives and tranquilizers produce decreased heart rate, reduced blood pressure, slowed respiration, and a general sense of calm. At moderate doses, they often produce feelings of euphoria, lack of coordination, and disinhibition of sexual impulses. At high doses, sedatives and tranquilizers can produce slurred speech, dizziness, stupor, and even coma. At moderate to high doses, sedatives and tranquilizers can impair judgment and reduce coordination, thereby creating a safety hazard if the individual is attempting to drive or operate machinery. Paradoxical reactions have been observed with both sedatives and tranquilizers. One such paradoxical reaction is a rage reaction whereby the individual experiences increased levels of anger, anxiety, hostility and, in some cases, violence.[45]

Long-Term Effects

Sedatives and tranquilizers produce both tolerance and withdrawal. Similar levels of tolerance have been reported for the three major CNS depressants (alcohol, sedatives, tranquilizers) and cross-tolerance appears to form between the drugs such that a preexisting tolerance to alcohol will automatically increase tolerance to barbiturates and vice versa.[46] Withdrawal symptoms are similar for sedatives and tranquilizers (anxiety, agitation, insomnia, tension, perceptual abberations) but they tend to be more severe with sedatives. Barbiturates also have a high overdose potential and have been implicated in a number of suicides, including Marilyn Monroe's. This does not mean that tranquilizers in the benzodiazepine class are harmless when it comes to withdrawal and overdose. A withdrawal syndrome has been described for benzodiazepines in which symptoms can last for up to a year.[47]

Heroin

Brief Description

Heroin comes from the milky sap of the egg-shaped seed pod in the opium poppy, which is then refined into a brown or white powder or black, sticky substance. Before it is distributed to users, heroin is mixed and cut with sugar, baby powder, starch, quinine, or even strychnine to reduce the purity. Because purity levels vary widely and users do not normally test their supply before using, overdose is common. Heroin achieves its effect by interacting with endogenous opiate (endorphin, enkephalin) receptors in the brain.

Routes of Administration

Heroin can be smoked, snorted, or injected. Mainlining (injecting the drug directly into a vein) is considered the optimal route of administration, although if the purity level is high enough, snorting and smoking heroin can produce as quick and as intense a response as injecting the drug.

Prevalence

Heroin is one of the least often used drugs in the *MTF*. The 2010 survey revealed that 0.4% of 8th graders, 0.4% of 10th graders, 0.4% of 12th graders, 0.1% of college students, and 0.2% of young adults (ages 19–28) used heroin at least once in the last month. Only 0.3%

© JordiDelgado/ShutterStock, Inc.

Those heroin users who share needles with other users are at increased risk for a number of health problems, to include hepatitis and AIDS.

of 8th graders, 0.2% of 10th graders, 0.4% of 12th graders, 0.0% of college students, and 0.1% of young adults indicated that they had injected heroin in the last 30 days. Prescription opiates (OxyContin, Vicodin, Percocet) were several times more popular than heroin with respondents. Although the question was not posed to 8th or 10th graders, 3.6% of 12th graders, 2.3% of college students, and 3.4% of young adults in the 2010 *MTF* reported using prescription opiates at least once in the last 30 days.

Short-Term Effects

Almost immediately after heroin is injected into the bloodstream the individual feels an intense sense of euphoria and well-being commonly referred to as a "rush." The positive mood usually only lasts 30–60 minutes and some users will spend years trying to recapture their initial high (a process sometimes referred to as "chasing the dragon"). In some novice users, heroin can induce nausea or vomiting, although this only lasts a few minutes and is quickly replaced by euphoria as heroin starts interacting with endorphin and enkephalin receptor sites. Additional short-term effects of heroin intoxication include increased sensitivity to sights and sounds, blocking of pain signals, clouded consciousness, and alternating periods of wakefulness and drowsiness (or "nodding"). Heroin also slows the heart rate and depresses respiration, the latter of which contributes to many of the overdose deaths observed with heroin.

Long-Term Effects

Heroin produces rapid tolerance and frequent dependence. This leads many users into a chronic, relapsing pattern of use that can last for years, if not decades. Yih-Ing Hser, Valarie Hoffman, Christine Grella, and Douglas Anglin followed a large group of male heroin users admitted to a mandatory drug treatment program in 1962–1964 for a period of 33 years. The results of three follow-up interviews conducted 11 years apart, revealed a growing mortality rate (with the most common cause of death being accidental overdose) and a slightly decreasing but still significant number of active users after 33 years (see **Figure 2-10**).[48] Given the uncertain purity of these drugs and a rapidly growing tolerance, accidental overdose is one of the primary negative long-term consequences of heroin use. Other negative long-term consequences include weight loss, abscesses, collapsed veins, infections of the heart lining, hepatitis, and AIDS. Withdrawal symptoms (pain, diarrhea, motor tremors) peak 24–48 hours after last usage and can last up to 1 week, and although uncomfortable, are usually not fatal. Heroin users will often engage in property and drug crime in order to get money to pay for their growing drug habit.

Hallucinogens

Brief Description

Hallucinogens are manufactured in makeshift laboratories and achieve their effect by interacting with norepinephrine (NE) and serotonin (5HT) receptors in the occipital region of the brain (posterior part of the brain). Lysergic acid diethylamide (LSD), peyote (mescaline), ecstasy (MDMA), and phencyclidine (PCP) are several of the more popular hallucinogen drugs.

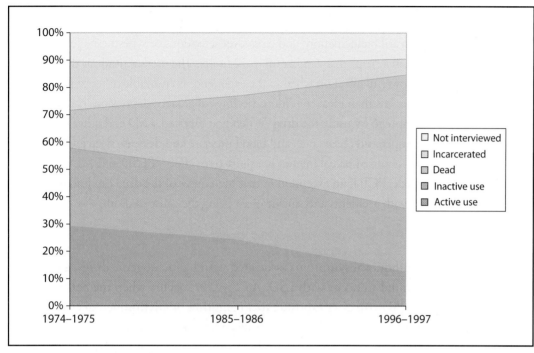

Figure 2-10
Changes in the status of narcotics addicts over 33 years; results from the three follow-up interviews.

Data From: Hser, Y.-I., Hoffman, V., Grella, C. E., & Anglin, M. D. (2001). A 33-year follow-up of narcotics addicts. *Archives of General Psychiatry, 58,* 503–508.

Routes of Administration

Most hallucinogens are administered orally, although PCP can also be sniffed, injected, or smoked.

Prevalence

Hallucinogens were used in the last 30 days by 1.0% of the 8th-grade students, 1.6% of the 10th-grade students, 1.9% of the 12th-grade students, 1.4% of college students, and 1.0% of young adults (ages 19–28) in the 2010 *MTF* sample.

© Line Tscherning Damgaard/iStockphoto

MDMA or Ecstacy is an hallucinogen with stimulant properties.

Short-Term Effects

LSD produces colorful visual hallucinations and cross-over sensations or synesthesias (e.g., hearing colors or seeing sounds), in a "trip" that can last up to 12 hours. The user's attitude at the time they ingest LSD can have a powerful effect on whether the experience is enjoyable or terrifying. Those who consume LSD under less than ideal conditions (feelings of anxiety, depression, paranoia) are likely to be made even more so by using the drug. When first ingested, LSD and other hallucinogens increase body temperature, heart rate, and blood pressure and decrease sleep and appetite. Heightened sexuality or increased sexual interest is a short-term effect of LSD and MDMA. Most hallucinogens are not toxic. PCP is an exception in that high doses of the drug can lead to convulsions, coma, and death, with accidents and suicide often being the cause of death.

Long-Term Effects

There are no known withdrawal symptoms associated with hallucinogenic drugs, although flashbacks have been found to occur with LSD. A **flashback** occurs when the person relives part or all of a former LSD trip after exposure to an emotion or environmental cue associated with the prior drug experience. These flashbacks do not occur in all users and tend to weaken over time. Psychosis and permanent distortions in visual perception known as Hallucinogen Persisting Perception Disorder (HPPD) have been reported in a small number of cases, although these findings require more extensive study before they can be attributed to effects of hallucinogenic drugs.[49] One of the more serious long-term outcomes of hallucinogens, in this case PCP, is an increase in the number of accidents people experience while intoxicated on the drug.[50]

Marijuana

Brief Description

Marijuana or cannabis comes from the dried leaves and flowers of the hemp plant. The active ingredients in marijuana are 9-tetrahydrocannabinol (THC) and cannabidol.

Marijuana is now the number one cash crop in the United States.

© sara22/ShutterStock, Inc.

A recent news story indicates that THC and cannabinol affect different parts of the brain and may be responsible for the contradictory effects sometimes observed in those who consume marijuana (see News Spot 2-2). Marijuana creates its effect by interacting with cannabinoid receptors in various parts of the brain.

NEWS SPOT 2-2

Title: Paranoid or Placid? Scans Show Pot's Effect on Brain
Source: *HealthDay*
Author: Alan Mozes
Date: January 6, 2012

Smoking marijuana can mean different things to different people—for some, anxiety and paranoia can set in, while others mellow out.

Now, a unique brain scan study suggests two ingredients in pot may work independently to achieve these effects.

British scientists who watched the effects of the two marijuana ingredients—9-tetrahydrocannabinol (THC) and cannabidiol (CBD)—on the brains of 15 young men say the research shows how the drug can either ease or agitate the mind.

"People have polarized views about marijuana," said study lead author Dr. Sagnik Bhattacharyya, a researcher in the department of psychosis studies at the Institute of Psychiatry, King's College London. "Some consider it to be essentially harmless but potentially useful as a treatment in a number of medical conditions, and others link it to potentially severe public health consequences in terms of mental health. This study explains why the truth is somewhere in between."…

In the new study, the researchers used functional MRI brain imaging on 15 healthy men, roughly 27 years old on average and described as "occasional cannabis users."…

The team found that THC and CBD appeared to affect the brain in different and opposite ways.

Ingesting THC brought about irregular activity in two regions of the brain (the striatum and the lateral prefrontal cortex) that are key to the way people perceive their surroundings. THC seemed to boost the brain's responses to otherwise insignificant stimuli, while reducing response to what would typically be seen as significant or salient.

In other words, under the influence of THC, healthy individuals might give far more importance to details in their environment than they would have without the chemical in their brain.

THC also prompted a significant uptick in paranoid and delusional thinking, the authors said, and the more that "normal" brain responses were set off kilter, the more severe the paranoid or even psychotic reaction.

The effect of the other main pot ingredient, CBD, was nearly the opposite, however.

Ingesting the CBD capsule appeared to prompt brain activity linked to *appropriate* responses to significant stimuli in the environment, the team reported.

Questions to Ponder

1. **What role might marijuana play in the development of psychiatric disorders?**
2. **What role might marijuana play in the treatment of psychiatric disorders?**
3. **In your opinion, is marijuana more or less dangerous than alcohol?**

Routes of Administration

Marijuana is normally smoked in hand-rolled cigarettes known as joints or blunts, through a long tube known as a bong, or in a pipe. It can also be taken orally by mixing it in with food (brownies, cookies) or by brewing it in tea, but oral administration of marijuana normally requires a dose several times larger than the dose used to achieve a comparable effect by smoking.

Prevalence

The 2010 *MTF* indicates that marijuana is the most frequently used illegal substance in American youth. According to the survey, 8.0% of 8th-grade students, 16.7% of 10th-grade students, 21.4% of 12th-grade students, 17.4% of college students, and 16.1% of young adults (ages 19–28) reported using marijuana in the last 30 days.

Short-Term Effects

The short-term effects of marijuana consumption include a pervasive sense of well-being, memory impairment, increased heart rate, distorted perception (particularly of time), and difficulty thinking and solving problems. At low doses most people feel happy but at higher doses some people report increased levels of anxiety or paranoia. This could be a dose-response relationship or it could be the result of the differing effects of THC and cannabidiol. It has been estimated that users have a 4.8-fold increase in the risk of heart attack in the first hour after smoking marijuana.[51] This could be the result of a change in heart rate, a change in heart rhythm, or an increase in palpitations, all of which have been observed with marijuana use. The risk of heart attack from smoking marijuana may be greater in aging populations or in those with a history of cardiac problems.

Long-Term Effects

It is uncertain whether tolerance develops in all users of marijuana but there is some indication that heavy users may need to increase their dosage to achieve the desired effect. Mild withdrawal symptoms have been reported whereby chronic marijuana users experience increased irritability, anxiety, sleeplessness, and craving after cessation. Marijuana smoke contains more carcinogens than tobacco smoke and is an irritant to the lungs, although a direct causal link between marijuana smoking and cancer has not yet been established and an increased rate of lung cancer and pulmonary problems could be due to the fact that most marijuana users also smoke tobacco. In one study of participants with no history of tobacco smoking, those who smoked marijuana had more health problems and more days missed from work than those who did not smoke marijuana.[52] A correlation has also been observed between marijuana use and later mental health problems, particularly in individuals who start using marijuana in childhood or early adolescence, although there is no evidence at this point that the relationship is causal.[53]

Theory

A theory is a set of principles designed to explain, predict, and manage a phenomenon. In this chapter the phenomenon of interest is drugs. There are many different findings and observations related to drugs, crime, and the drug–crime nexus. A theory simplifies these complex relationships by boiling them down into a small number of principles designed to describe, explain, predict, and manage the phenomenon of interest. If you notice that most homeless people use drugs you may come up with the theory that homelessness causes drug use. This theory simplifies the drug–homelessness situation because all you need to know is that a person is homeless and you can predict that he or she will have a drug problem. Further testing may reveal that your theory is in need of modification but even with modifications your theory will be more practical than trying to understand the drug–homelessness relationship on a case-by-case basis.

By simplifying complex relationships a theory can be of substantial value to researchers, clinicians, and policy-makers. Whoever first said "there is nothing more practical than a good theory"—whether it was Kurt Lewin, Albert Einstein, or some obscure scholar—was clearly correct. There really is nothing more practical than a good theory. By the same token, there is nothing more misleading than a bad theory. Accordingly, we need to find ways to differentiate between good and bad theories. Theories are not judged, however, by an absolute standard of validity but by their usefulness to researchers, clinicians, and policy-makers. There are several criteria that have been applied to theories as a means of evaluating their usefulness. I have selected four criteria that I believe are particularly helpful in evaluating the theories of drug abuse, crime, and the drug–crime nexus for this text: comprehensiveness, parsimony, precision, and **fruitfulness**.

Comprehensiveness

A useful theory is one that sufficiently covers the area of interest. If the area covered by a theory is too narrow then the theory's practical utility is compromised. Rarely will a theory cover all major aspects of a phenomenon but the degree to which it does is a measure of its comprehensiveness.

Parsimony

Theories provide general principles. Some theories, however, can get bogged down in excessive detail or sidetracked by a large number of assumptions. These theories are less useful than theories which keep their assumptions and principles to a minimum. In a manner of speaking, **comprehensiveness** and **parsimony** are at cross-purposes. The most useful theories, then, are those that cover the widest area of a phenomenon with the fewest number of assumptions and principles.

Precision

Theories must be clear, understandable, and precise to be useful. Otherwise, researchers, clinicians, and policy-makers will not be in a position to use them. Theories that do not clearly define their concepts in precise behavioral terms will confuse rather than clarify the types of relationships theories are designed to explain. Having reliable (consistent) and valid (relevant and meaningful) measures of key constructs within a theory can be a major boost to the theory's **precision**.

Fruitfulness

To be useful, a theory should be fruitful. A fruitful theory is one that encourages new ideas and applications. One way a theory is fruitful is by stimulating research. However, a theory must be falsifiable to stimulate meaningful research. What I mean by this is that a theory should be capable of producing specific predictions that can be tested and proven false. More fruitful theories stimulate scholarly debate, clinical practice, and policy changes, whereas less fruitful theories have little impact on a field.

In evaluating six theories of drug use and abuse I will periodically return to these four criteria of a useful theory as a means of demonstrating the relative utility of these six theories.

Disease Model

The **disease model** of addiction is probably the most prominent model of addiction among lay people and treatment providers, although it is much less popular with scientists and researchers. There are actually several different disease models, most of which can be classified into one of two categories: medical disease models, with an emphasis on genetics and physiology, and spiritual disease models, with an emphasis on overcoming basic character defects. The spiritual disease model is the foundation of such self-help programs as Alcoholics Anonymous (AA), Narcotics Anonymous (NA), Marijuana Anonymous (MA), and other 12-step programs.

Fundamental Assumptions, Principles, and Concepts

According to the disease model of addiction, the abuse of alcohol and other drugs is a progressive disease process that is fatal if not addressed. The belief is that the individual is not responsible for the development of his or her disease (whether it be genetics or character flaws) but is responsible for overcoming the disease. The model is supported by four primary principles.[54] First, the disease of addiction is characterized by loss of control. The disease model predicts that people who suffer from the disease of addiction will eventually lose control over their drug use. Consequently, abstinence is the only acceptable goal for change, the disease model's second principle. Third, in order not to fall back into a pattern of denial the individual must label him or herself an alcoholic or addict. Fourth, because the disease is incurable, the individual is never fully recovered but rather is "in recovery" for the rest of his or her life. The means of change in the disease model is to find a sponsor (more experienced fellowship member who serves as an advisor or guide) and follow the 12 steps (see **Table 2-2**).

Table 2-2 The Twelve Steps of Alcoholics Anonymous (with all references to God highlighted in red)

1. We admitted we were powerless over alcohol—that our lives had become unmanageable.
2. Came to believe that a Power greater than ourselves could restore us to sanity.
3. Made a decision to turn our will and our lives over to the care of **God** *as we understood Him*.
4. Made a searching and fearless moral inventory of ourselves.
5. Admitted to **God**, to ourselves, and to another human being the exact nature of our wrongs.
6. We're entirely ready to have **God** remove all these defects of character.
7. Humbly asked **Him** to remove our shortcomings.
8. Made a list of all persons we had harmed, and became willing to make amends to them all.
9. Made direct amends to such people wherever possible, except when to do so would injure them or others.
10. Continued to take personal inventory and when we were wrong promptly admitted it.
11. Sought through prayer and meditation to improve our conscious contact with **God** *as we understood Him*, praying only for knowledge of **His** will for us and the power to carry that out.
12. Having had a spiritual awakening as the result of these steps, we tried to carry this message to alcoholics, and to practice these principles in all our affairs.

The Twelve Steps are reprinted with permission of Alcoholics Anonymous World Services, Inc. Permission to reprint the Twelve Steps does not mean that A.A. has reviewed or approved the contents of this publication, nor that A.A. agrees with the views expressed herein, programs and activities which are patterned after A.A., but which address other problems, or in any other non-A.A. context, does not imply otherwise.

Research Support

There is very little research support for the disease model, primarily because there has been very little research conducted on the model. A recent book by Gene Heyman, however, finds evidence that operant conditioning principles and choice are vital to understanding drug abuse and dependence.[55] The official position of the disease model is that willpower or choice cannot be trusted and that lasting change can only be found by surrendering to a higher power.[56]

Strengths of the Disease Model

Prior to the advent of AA and the disease model of addiction, those with drug and alcohol problems were viewed as drunks and derelicts. The disease model helped reduce the stigma associated with addiction by shifting the blame from the individual to the "disease." This may have helped instill hope in some individuals previously racked by guilt or incapacitated by fatalism, who then sought help for their problem. Many of those who have abused drugs for any length of time have burned their bridges with family and friends. Twelve-step programs provide them with a built-in system of social support, which research suggests is one of the most important factors in promoting long-term change in those who are recovering from a drug or alcohol problem.[57] The disease model is strong on parsimony in that it is simple and consists of only a few principles.

Weaknesses of the Disease Model

Because of its simplicity, the disease model cannot account for much of the complexity of substance abuse and almost completely ignores environmental factors in its approach to substance use and abuse. Moreover, it has stimulated very little research, in part because of fuzzy conceptualizations and weak operationalization (behavioral referents) of terms. Third, its quasi-religious tenor (see Table 2-2) makes it unacceptable to a large portion of the substance abusing community. Fourth, the model has been accused of circular reasoning by arguing that people use drugs because they have a disease and then drawing on their drug use as evidence that they have the disease.[58] There have been a number of studies conducted on topics such as loss of control and expectancies in response to a placebo and evidence of controlled drinking that run counter to fundamental assumptions and principles of the disease model.[59–60]

Unified Biosocial Model

Robert Cloninger originally developed the **unified biosocial model** to explain chronic cognitive and somatic anxiety but in a 1987 paper he applied the unified model to alcoholism.[61] In his theory, Cloninger postulates the existence of three genetically independent but interacting dimensions of personality, which he labels novelty seeking (NS), harm avoidance (HA), and reward dependence (RD). These three dimensions can be measured using Cloninger's **Tridimensional Personality Questionnaire** (TPQ).[62]

Fundamental Assumptions, Principles, and Concepts

Novelty seeking (NS), as defined by Cloninger, is the tendency to approach novel, interesting, and appetitive stimuli. Individuals high in NS are said to be impulsive, fickle, excitable, and quick tempered. Individuals with low NS are thought to be reflective, rigid, orderly, and even tempered. In that NS is thought to be part of the behavioral activation system (BAS) of the brain it is mediated by dopaminergic (DA) neurons and receptor sites.[63]

The second major construct in the unified biosocial model of alcoholism, **Harm Avoidance** (HA), is defined by Cloninger as the tendency to avoid aversive and other negative conditioned stimuli (i.e., punishment). Individuals high in HA tend to be cautious, tense, fearful, and worrisome. Individuals low in HA are said to be carefree, outgoing, uninhibited, and relaxed. Given its relationship to the behavioral inhibition system (BIS) of the brain, HA is believed to be mediated by serotonergic (5HT) neurons and receptor sites.[64]

Cloninger defines **Reward Dependence** (RD) as the tendency to resist extinction of previously rewarded behaviors. Individuals high in RD are often rated as ambitious, sentimental, and persistent, whereas individuals low in RD are rated as detached, tough minded, and irresolute. Cloninger proposes that RD is part of the behavioral maintenance system (BMS) and as such, is mediated by noradrenergic (NE) neurons and receptor sites.[65]

The unified biosocial theory of alcoholism postulates the existence of Type 1 and Type 2 alcoholism, with Type 1 being low in NS, high in HA, and high in RD and Type 2 being high in NS, low in HA, and low in RD. Whereas Type 1 alcoholism (milieu-limited) has moderate heritability, a relatively late age of onset, minimal criminal involvement, and responds nicely to treatment, Type 2 alcoholism (male-limited) has strong heritability (father to son), onset during the late teens or early twenties, extensive criminal involvement, and is viewed by Cloninger as less amenable to treatment.[66]

Research Support

The unified biosocial model of alcoholism has generated a moderate degree of research interest, although the results of this research have been mixed. Whereas NS is largely capable of differentiating between groups of Type 1 and Type 2 alcoholics classified according to age of onset and other characteristics that normally separate the two types (e.g., gender, criminality), there is much less support for the utility of HA and RD as type differentiators.[67-68] High HA, however, may be a useful marker of the intensity of substance use.[69] Questions concerning the factor structure of the TPI have been raised because the three factors proposed by Cloninger rarely surface in research conducted by independent researchers.[70-71]

Strengths of the Unified Biosocial Model

The model is reasonably precise in that the three dimensions (NS, HA, RD) are operationally defined by scores on the TPQ. As previously mentioned, however, research on the TPQ has produced mixed results, particularly with respect to the inventory's factor structure. There is strong support for the utility of the NS scale, nevertheless, and so researchers and clinicians should probably rely more on this scale in differentiating between Type 1 and Type 2 alcoholics than on the HA or RD scales. With respect to the Type 1–Type 2 breakdown, there is preliminary support from a large-scale taxometric study for categories of alcoholism consistent with Cloninger's Type 1–Type 2 dichotomy.[72] The unified biosocial model has been moderately fruitful, particularly in terms of generating interest in the Type 1–Type 2 dichotomy.

Weaknesses of the Unified Biosocial Model

One weakness of Cloninger's theory is that it is rather narrow in scope; hence, it suffers from weak comprehensiveness. In addition, empirical research has consistently only supported the NS dimension. More work is required to determine whether HA and RD have a role in the theory or need to be replaced by other constructs. Cloninger's (1987) initial application of the unified biosocial model to alcoholism has been criticized for using small samples and indirect measures of family functioning.[73] The Type 1–Type 2 dichotomy is nonetheless popular with researchers and clinicians, though it could also benefit some from revision. There is growing evidence, for instance, that the Type 2 pattern, which Cloninger held to be male limited, may also apply to females.[74-75]

Cross-Cultural Theory

Robert Freed Bales proposed a cross-national theory of alcohol abuse and dependence that focused on several categories of cultural influence. In contrast to the molecular (individual-level) leanings of the disease and unified biosocial models, **cross-cultural theory** adopts a molar perspective on alcohol and drug abuse.

Fundamental Assumptions, Principles, and Concepts

According to Bales, cultures differ in the degree to which they arouse inner tension and adjustment problems in their members, provide viable tension-reducing and recreation-enhancing alternatives to alcohol and drugs, and approve of alcohol and drugs as ways of reducing tension and promoting self-interest. The core of Bales' theory is the cultural attitude of which there are four: abstinence or total prohibition, ritualistic, convivial, and utilitarian. Strong prohibitions against alcohol and drug use, as are found in the Mormon and Muslim cultures, can lead to a polarization of attitudes and a pattern in which most people do not drink or use drugs, but those who do experience significant levels of guilt and severe psychological problems. The interaction of the tension-arousing features of a culture, coupled with its attitude toward alcohol and drugs as a means of managing this tension, and the presence of nondrug tension-reducing alternatives in a culture will determine the population's level of both substance use and abuse.[76]

Research Support

There has been very little research on cross-cultural theory. Although evidence for a cultural interpretation of drinking and drug use behavior exists, very little of it directly tests Bales' model.[77] Of the few studies that have been conducted on the theory, most have produced mixed or negative results. For instance, Bales predicted that countries holding ritualistic attitudes toward alcohol use would experience lower levels of alcoholism than countries professing a utilitarian attitude. Using data compiled by de Lint[78], Walters discovered that a country with a social-ritualistic attitude toward alcohol use (Italy) had an alcohol abuse rate several times that of a country promoting a utilitarian view of alcohol use (Ireland).[79] In addition, whereas Bales attributed the low rate of alcoholism in Jewish groups to their ritualistic approach to alcohol, a more recent study found that religious attitudes may play an even greater role in controlling problem drinking in this particular culture.[80]

Strengths of Cross-Cultural Theory

Parsimony is the principal strength of Bales' cross-cultural theory to the extent that postulates and core constructs have been kept to a minimum. A further strength of the cross-cultural interpretation of alcohol and drug abuse is that it provides a perspective that has traditionally been neglected by researchers and practitioners in the substance abuse field, namely, **emergentism** instead of reductionism. Unlike the molecular approach adopted by most theories of alcohol and drug abuse, cross-cultural theory examines alcohol and drug abuse from a molar perspective. Hence, even thought the theory is parsimonious it is also moderately comprehensive.

Weaknesses of Cross-Cultural Theory

There has been little direct research on cross-cultural theory, making it one of the least fruitful theories covered in this chapter. Lack of precision is a second major weakness of Bales' cross-cultural theory of alcohol and drug abuse. This lack of precision is probably the result of fuzzy operationalization of key terms and weak specification of certain relationships. For example, the criteria used to define ritualistic, convivial, and utilitarian attitudes toward alcohol and drug use could be more clearly articulated.

Self-Medication Hypothesis

The **self-medication hypothesis** has been advanced by members of both the psychoanalytic (Leon Wurmser, Edward Khantzian) and behavioral (John Conger, David Duncan) communities. Psychoanalysts and behaviorists make strange bedfellows, although this is not the first time the two models have been combined.[81] According to proponents of the self-medication hypothesis, people abuse drugs in order to self-medicate against anxiety, depression, and other serious psychological issues and concerns. In contrast to the disease model, which holds that drug abuse causes psychological problems, proponents of the self-medication hypothesis contend that psychological problems cause drug abuse (see **Figure 2-11**). Drugs temporarily disable the threatening internal signals associated with past traumas and self-doubt (psychoanalytic version) or reduce tension and thereby become highly reinforcing (behavioral version).

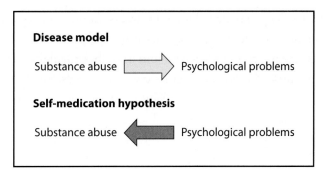

Disease model

Substance abuse ⟹ Psychological problems

Self-medication hypothesis

Substance abuse ⟸ Psychological problems

Figure 2-11
Relationship between substance abuse and psychological problems in the Disease and Self-Medication models.

Fundamental Assumptions, Principles, and Concepts

Four core concepts define the self-medication hypothesis. **Tension reduction** is the principal construct contributed by behaviorists to the self-medication hypothesis. Drugs, particularly alcohol, are consumed because of their ability to reduce tension and anxiety and some people learn to use alcohol and drugs as a means of escape from negative affect.[82] The psychoanalytic version of the self-medication hypothesis is based on three constructs: addictive search, adventitious entrance, and drug specificity. **Addictive search** refers to the psychological hunger or craving that drives a person to search for something to relieve the inner turmoil.[83] **Adventitious entrance** is random introduction of an addictive activity into the person's life. If an individual uses drugs and they serve to relieve the inner turmoil that is driving the person's addictive search then he or she will be motivated to continue using the substance to momentarily relieve the inner turmoil.[84] Finally, some psychoanalytic versions of the self-medication hypothesis propose the existence of **drug specificity** whereby a relationship forms between specific categories of drug and specific psychological issues and concerns. For instance, alcohol is believed to be particularly effective in neutralizing guilt and anxiety, whereas narcotics are most helpful in controlling rage, stimulants in reducing depression, and hallucinogens in relieving boredom.[85]

Research Support

Studies conducted on tension reduction and alcohol use indicate that alcohol does, in fact, reduce tension in a fair number of cases, although there is also evidence that it can increase tension in certain situations and in some individuals.[86] The absence of a universal tension-reducing response to alcohol and other depressant drugs has led some researchers to propose that the active mechanism behind drinking and using drugs to reduce tension is actually an outcome expectancy for reduced physical tension from drinking and drug use.[87] The aspect of the psychoanalytic version of the self-medication hypothesis that has received the most empirical attention is drug specificity. Research has fairly convincingly demonstrated, however, that a specific relationship does not exist between different drugs and different underlying emotional issues.[88–89]

Strengths of the Self-Medication Hypothesis

As a theory, the self-medication hypothesis is parsimonious. In addition, it has stimulated a fair amount of research. Unfortunately, the research has only been partially supportive of the hypothesis. In fact, one of the core principles of the self-medication hypothesis, i.e., drug specificity, has virtually no research support. On the other hand, the self-medication hypothesis highlights the importance of psychological factors in the initiation and maintenance of drug use behavior and as such, provides more avenues of intervention than either the unified biosocial or cross-cultural models. Furthermore, the self-medication hypothesis emphasizes the role of availability and access as necessary preconditions for the development of drug use patterns and problems.

Weaknesses of the Self-Medication Hypothesis

The self-medication hypothesis is rather narrow in scope in that it focuses on negative reasons (anxiety, depression, rage) for drug use, whereas research indicates that people often start using drugs for positive reasons (pleasure, excitement, having fun with friends) rather than negative reasons.[90] Precision also appears to be a weakness of the self-medication hypothesis in that several of the key terms (tension-reduction, adventitious search, drug specificity) are rather poorly defined. Although the self-medication hypothesis has been moderately fruitful in terms of encouraging research, the research has not always been supportive of key principles. For instance, drug specificity has failed to find support when either diagnostic or personality assessment measures have been used to assess psychological differences between drug users.[91-92] In addition, the "drug of choice" concept, so essential to the drug specificity principle of the self-medication hypothesis, does not appear to characterize the behavior of most drug users.[93]

Gateway Theory

The **gateway theory** of drug abuse was developed by Denise Kandel who proposed that drug problems follow a sequential pattern of gates that often lead to more serious future drug involvement, from substances that are licit for adults (alcohol and tobacco), to marijuana, to other illegal drugs, and finally to prescription medications. Gateway theory is less extreme and more flexible than its predecessor, stepping stone theory, which held that alcohol, tobacco, and marijuana lead inexorably to the use of harder drugs.

Fundamental Assumptions, Principles, and Concepts

Gateway theory asserts that drug use normally begins with drugs that are licit for adults (alcohol, tobacco). Kandel and colleagues made a refinement in the theory when it was determined that although both alcohol and tobacco formed the first stage for female youth, only alcohol served as the initial stage for male youth (see **Figures 2-12** and **2-13**). The second stage of gateway theory centers on marijuana. Unlike the discredited stepping stone theory, gateway theory does not hold to the rigid view that marijuana use invariably leads to the use of other illegal drugs, but it does maintain that those who use other illegal drugs have passed through the marijuana gate. The third stage of gateway theory is occupied by drugs like cocaine and heroin, whereas the final stage involves the use of prescriptions medications. Age of onset and frequency of use are said to predict movement to a higher stage and a direct pharmacological or behavioral link between earlier and later stages is proposed by advocates of gateway theory.[94-95]

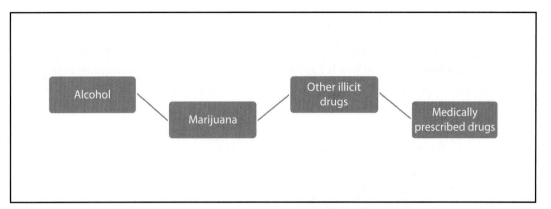

Figure 2-12
Gateways for male substance use and abuse.

Data From: Kandel, D. B., Yamoguchi, K., & Chen, K. (1992). Stages of progression in drug involvement from adolescence to adulthood: Further evidence from gateway theory. *Journal of Studies on Alcohol,* 53, 447–457.

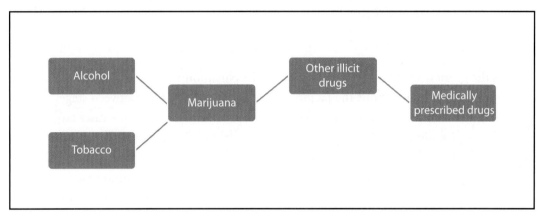

Figure 2-13
Gateways for female substance use and abuse.

Data From: Kandel, D. B., Yamoguchi, K., & Chen, K. (1992). Stages of progression in drug involvement from adolescence to adulthood: Further evidence from gateway theory. *Journal of Studies on Alcohol,* 53, 447–457.

Research Support

There is no doubt that most people who use hard drugs often used marijuana first.[96] This is a far cry, however, from proving that using marijuana directly causes a significant portion of people to pursue the use of hard drugs. There are four recent studies that bring the central tenets of gateway theory into serious question. First, a study by a group of researchers from the Rand Corporation revealed a correlation between earlier marijuana use and later hard drug use but the results were as easily explained by a common factor model in which both marijuana and hard drug use were the result of a third variable, drug use propensity, than by the more complex formulations proposed by gateway theory.[97] Second, Ralph Tarter and colleagues conducted a 12-year longitudinal study of 214 boys originally interviewed when they were 10 to 12 years of age. Although the progression proposed by gateway theory was observed, so was a progression from marijuana to alcohol and tobacco use. Moreover, there were no differences in the seriousness of future drug use behavior between the two progressions.[98] Third, in a secondary analysis of data from two national surveys, Golub and Johnson determined that hard drug-using criminals were less, rather than more, likely to start off using alcohol and tobacco exclusively than those who did not become hard drug-using criminals.[99] Fourth, whereas Choo, Roh, and Robinson uncovered support for the progression proposed by gateway theory, the risk factors associated with transition from one stage to the next were inconsistent with predictions from gateway theory.[100]

Strengths of Gateway Theory

The principal strength of gateway theory is its fruitfulness. Not only has it stimulated a great deal of academic research but it has also had an impact on drug prevention policy. The zero tolerance policies adopted in the United States are very much in line with gateway theory and the theory is often used to justify these policies. In addition, gateway theory is more comprehensive than most of the other theories described in this chapter. By entertaining both genetic/biological factors and developmental/environmental influences and using longitudinal designs, the theory's level of methodological sophistication clearly surpasses that of many of its competitors. The notion that different sets of risk factors are important in moving between different stages of the model is intriguing and potentially important for prevention, although research has tended not to support the specific risk factor constellations proposed by gateway theory.[101]

Weaknesses of Gateway Theory

Perhaps the greatest weakest of gateway theory is its parsimony. The theory makes rather complicated assumptions about the factors responsible for transitions between stages when research suggests that much simpler explanations often suffice and in some cases are superior to the explanations offered by gateway theory.[102–103] Hence, whereas individuals who use alcohol and tobacco often also use marijuana and individuals who use marijuana sometimes progress to harder drugs, correlation does not constitute causation. Common factor explanations, like drug use propensity and exposure to new drug connections, need to be entertained before it can be concluded that there is a direct causal link between using certain categories of drug at an earlier age and using other categories of drug at a later age.

Social Learning Theory

Social learning theory is based on the work of Albert Bandura and Alan Marlatt, and postulates that individuals learn the attitudes and behaviors associated with drug use and abuse from other people. In addition to using basic learning principles such as reinforcement and conditioning to explain drug use behavior, social learning theory proposes that the organism plays an active role in the learning process. This is sometimes referred to as the S-O-R theory of learning, with S representing the stimulus, O the internal processes (thoughts, needs, motives) operating within the organism, and R the response (see **Figure 2-14**).

Fundamental Assumptions, Principles, and Concepts

Albert Bandura is responsible for many of the core concepts and principles in social learning theory and Alan Marlatt was instrumental in applying many of these concepts and principles to alcohol and drug abuse.[104–105] Besides the fundamental behavioral tenets of conditioning, reinforcement, and punishment, there are four cognitive-behavioral constructs central to the social learning theory of drug and alcohol abuse: modeling, outcome expectancies, efficacy expectancies, and causal attributions. Modeling means learning through observation. By observing drug use in parents, peers, and media figures, children and adolescents learn the techniques of drug use as well as the motives, expectancies, and

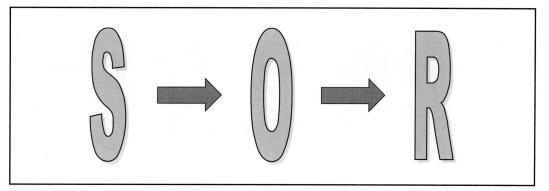

Figure 2-14
The S (stimulus), O (organism), R (response) model upon which social learning theory is based.

rationalizations that support drug use behavior. **Outcome expectancies** for drugs are the beliefs one has about the likely consequences of drug use. These expectancies are initially learned through observation but are subsequently shaped by direct experience. **Efficacy expectancies** constitute people's appraisal of their ability to successfully perform a specific behavior. **Attributions**, on the other hand, are a person's appraisal of the probable cause of an event. Research indicates that attributing a drinking lapse to internal, stable, and global factors has a much better chance of leading to full-blown relapse than when the lapse is attributed to external, unstable, and specific factors.[106]

Research Support

Social learning theory is probably the most heavily researched theory of drug and alcohol abuse in existence. Furthermore, most of the studies on the social learning theory of drug and alcohol abuse at least partially support the underlying tenets of the approach. Outcome expectancies, for instance, are acquired through social learning channels and can play a major role in predicting and managing drug use problems. Research indicates that alcohol expectancies are socially shared beliefs between parents and their children and although positive outcome expectancies for alcohol (tension reduction, increased sociability, sexual enhancement) predict level of drinking, negative outcome expectancies (low self-control, feeling sick, lack of coordination) predict abstention.[107–108] Both general outcome expectancies for alcohol and specific outcome expectancies for aggression appear to mediate the relationship between drinking behavior and subsequent aggression.[109–110]

Strengths of Social Learning Theory

The social learning theory of drug and alcohol abuse has been extremely fruitful and is supported by an impressive array of research evidence. Moreover, it covers a larger number of topics relating to substance abuse than most theories of addiction and can be considered moderately comprehensive. The theory has strong applicability across gender, culture, and content areas because moral views tend to be relatively consistent across these domains.[111] In addition, social learning theory has given rise to two of the most successful forms of intervention for substance abuse: cognitive-behavioral therapy and relapse prevention.

Table 2-3 Summary of an Evaluation of Six Theories of Drug Abuse

Theory	Comprehensiveness	Parsimony	Precision	Fruitfulness
Disease Model	L	H	L	L
Unified Biosocial	L	M	M	M
Cross-Cultural	M	H	L	L
Self-Medication	L	H	L	M
Gateway Theory	M	L	M	H
Social Learning	M	M	L	H

Weaknesses of Social Learning Theory

The principal weakness of the social learning theory of drug and alcohol abuse is low precision. It receives low marks for precision, not because of poor operationalization of terms but because of low coherence or internal consistency. The social learning theory of drug and alcohol abuse is not a particularly elegant or well-integrated theory; it is more like a series of minitheories strung together. In addition, it fails to provide a strong developmental framework for the majority of its constructs. Weak internal consistency and inattention to developmental issues serve to limit the theory's usefulness for researchers, clinicians, and policy-makers.

Each of the six theories reviewed in this chapter has both strengths and weaknesses. Most of the reviewed theories received one high rating and at least one low rating (see **Table 2-3**). This illustrates that none of these theories provides a sufficiently complete explanation of drug use and abuse to be maximally useful on its own but that each is capable of contributing to our understanding of drug use and abuse. The solution would appear to be either a synthesis of ideas from several different theories or flexible application of the theories so that one theory can be used to explain one aspect of drug use and abuse (for example, gateway theory and development) and other theories are used to explain other aspects of drug use or abuse (for example, self-medication and motivation or social learning theory and behavioral acquisition).

Summary and Conclusions

- Drug use is defined as a substance other than food that alters the structure or function of the body. A drug effect involves an interaction of drug (chemical substance), set (user's current mindset), and setting (environment in which drug use takes place).
- Drugs can be classified according to their effect on personal and social adjustment (diagnostic criteria for drug abuse and dependence), by the amount of harm they cause the user and others, and by their chemical structure and subjective effects (alcohol, nicotine, stimulants, depressants, heroin, hallucinogens, and marijuana).
- Six theories of drug use and abuse were reviewed in this chapter (disease model, unified biosocial model, cross-cultural theory, self-medication hypothesis, gateway theory, social learning theory) and each was found to have both strengths and weaknesses. For the purposes of understanding drug use and abuse better, a synthesis or flexible interchange of theories may be helpful.

Key Terms

Addictive Search   Searching for something to relieve one's inner turmoil.

Adventitious Entrance   Random pairing of drug use with relief from inner turmoil.

Attributions   A person's appraisal of the probable causes of an event.

Balanced Placebo Design   Research design composed of four groups of participants, one in which participants receive an active drug and are told they are being given an active drug, one in which participants receive an active drug and are told they are being given a placebo, one in which participants receive a placebo and are told they are being given an active drug, and one in which participants receive a placebo and are told they are being given a placebo.

Cocaethylene   Substance created when alcohol and cocaine are taken simultaneously and that increases the chances of heart attack and sudden death in users.

Comprehensiveness   Scope or the degree to which a theory covers the range of information within the field of inquiry it is designed to explain.

Cross-Cultural Theory   Theory of drug use and abuse that breaks cultural attitudes toward alcohol into abstinent, ritualistic, convivial, and utilitarian.

Disease Model   Theory of drug use and abuse that holds that people with drug and alcohol problems suffer from either a medical (genetic) or spiritual disease process.

Drug   Substance other than food that alters the structure or function of the body.

Drug Effect   Impact of the drug on an individual user, as represented by drug, set, and setting.

Drug Specificity   Belief that people use specific drugs to neutralize specific psychological issues and concerns.

Efficacy Expectancies   Belief about one's ability to successfully perform a behavior.

Emergentism   Philosophical argument that the whole is greater than the sum of the individual parts and information is lost when we try to break processes down into their smallest component parts.

Flashback   Long-term effect of some hallucinogenic drugs, LSD in particular, whereby the individual experiences portions of a prior drug event when not using the drug.

Fruitfulness   Ability of a theory to stimulate research, clinical, and policy-making interest, as well as make accurate predictions and generate useful information.

Gateway Theory   Theory in which alcohol and tobacco use are believed to lead to marijuana use and marijuana use is believe to lead to the use of hard drugs.

Harm Avoidance   Tendency to avoid aversive and other negative conditioned stimuli.

Korsakoff Syndrome   Long-term effect of chronic alcohol use in which affected individuals experience severe memory gaps, often filling in the gaps with erroneous information (confabulation).

Latent Structure   Underlying organization of a construct as to how it handles individual differences between cases; either by grouping them into categories or placing them along a dimension.

Novelty Seeking   Tendency to approach novel, exciting, and appetitive stimuli.

Outcome Expectancies   Belief about the likely outcome should one engage in a specific behavior.

Parsimony   Simplicity or the ability of a theory to account for a phenomenon with the fewest number of assumptions and principles.

Placebo   Inert substance made to look like an active drug, sometime referred to as a sugar pill; used to evaluate and rule out expectancy effects for various drugs.

Precision   Ability of a theory to provide clear behavioral definitions of key concepts and offer internally consistent assumptions and principles.

Reward Dependence   Tendency to resist extinction of previously rewarded behaviors.

Self-Medication Hypothesis   Theory that maintains people use drugs to relieve inner turmoil and reduce stress.

Set   Psychological mindset of the drug user at the time the drug is consumed.

Setting   Environment conditions under which a drug is taken.

Social Learning Theory   Theory based on the S-O-R principle that factors within the organism (modeling, outcome expectancies, efficacy expectancies, attributions) mediate the learning of drug use behaviors.

Taxometrics   A statistical procedure used to determine whether a construct has an underlying categorical or dimensional latent structure.

Tension Reduction   Proposition that alcohol and other drugs are reinforcing because they reduce tension.

Tolerance   The need for greater amounts of a drug to achieve the desired effect.

Tridimensional Personality Questionnaire   Personality inventory designed to measure the three components of the unified biosocial model (novelty seeking, harm avoidance, and reward dependence).

Unified Biosocial Model   Theory that alcohol use problems can be effectively classified and understood using three personality dimensions (novelty seeking, harm avoidance, reward dependence).

Withdrawal   Symptoms experienced when a person stops using a drug that he or she is physically dependent on.

Critical Thinking

1. How do drug, set, and setting help define and explain drug abuse?
2. The DSM-5 workgroup is proposing elimination of the drug abuse-dependence differentiation. What are the pros and cons of such a proposal?

3. How would you evaluate a theory that is popular with policy-makers (gateway theory), with one that is popular with practitioners, judges, and probation officers (disease model) and one that is popular with scientists (unified biosocial model)?

Notes

1. Centers for Disease Control and Prevention (2012). *National Vital Statistics Reports* (Vol. 61). Atlanta, GA: Author.

2. Zinberg, N. E. (1986). *Drug, set, and setting: The basis for controlled intoxicant use.* New Haven, CT: Yale University Press.

3. Zinberg (1986).

4. Di Castelnuovo, A., Costanza, S., Bagnardi, V., Donati, M. B., Iacoveillo, L., & de Gaetano, G. (2006). Alcohol dosing and total mortality in men and women: An updated meta-analysis of 34 prospective studies. *Archives of Internal Medicine, 166,* 2437–2445.

5. Rehm, J., Greenfield, T. K., & Rogers, J. D. (2001). Average volume of alcohol consumption, patterns of drinking, and all-cause mortality: Results from the US National Alcohol Survey. *American Journal of Epidemiology, 153,* 64–71.

6. National Institute on Drug Abuse (NIDA). (2012). *Topics in brief: Prescription drug abuse.* Washington, DC: Author. Retrieved from http://www.drugabuse.gov/publications/topics-in-brief/prescription-drug-abuse

7. Zinberg (1986).

8. Becker, H. S. (1967). History, culture, and subjective experience: An exploration of the social bases of drug-induced experiences. *Journal of Health and Social Behavior, 8,* 163–176.

9. Weil, A. (1972). *The natural mind: A new way of looking at drugs and the higher consciousness.* Boston: Houghton-Mifflin.

10. Weil (1972).

11. Kirsch, I., Moore, T. J., Scoboria, A., & Nicholls, S. S. (2002). The emperor's new drugs: An analysis of antidepressant medication data submitted to the U.S. Food and Drug Administration. *Prevention and Treatment, 5*(23).

12. Kirsch, I., & Sapirstein, G. (1998). Listening to Prozac but hearing placebo: A meta-analysis of antidepressant medication. *Prevention and Treatment, 1* (Article 0002a).

13. Levine, J. D., Gordon, N. C., & Fields, H. L. (1979). The role of endorphins in placebo analgesia. In J. J. Bonica, J. C. Liebeskind, & D. Albe-Fessard (Eds.), *Advances in pain research and therapy* (Vol. 3, pp. 547–551). New York: Raven.

14. Marlatt, G. A., Demming, B., & Reid, J. B. (1973). Loss of control drinking in alcoholics: An experimental analogue. *Journal of Abnormal Psychology, 81,* 233–241.

15. Hull, J. G., & Bond, C. F. (1986). The social and behavioral consequences of alcohol consumption and expectancy: A meta-analysis. *Psychological Bulletin, 99,* 347–360.

16. Juliano, L. M., & Brandon, T. H. (2002). Effects of nicotine dose, instructional set, and outcome expectancies on the subjective effects of smoking in the presence of a stressor. *Journal of Abnormal Psychology, 111,* 88–97.

17. Metrik, J. (2010). Balanced-placebo design successfully adapted for use with marijuana. *Brown University Digest of Addiction Theory and Application, 29,* p. 8.

18. Zinberg (1986).

19. Siegel, S. (2005). Drug tolerance, drug addiction, and drug anticipation. *Current Directions in Psychological Science, 14,* 296–300.

20. Forsyth, A. J. M., Cloonan, M. & Barr, J. (2005). On-line Report. *Factors Associated with Alcohol-related Problems within Licensed Premises.* Glasgow: Greater Glasgow NHS Board. Retrieved March 1, 2012, from http://www.nhsggc.org.uk/content/assetList.asp?aType=15&aSType=184&page=s775_2.

21. Solinas, M., Chauvet, C., Thiriet, N., El Rawas, R., & Jaber, M. (2008). Reversal of cocaine addiction by environmental enrichment. *PNAS, 105*, 17145–17150.

22. American Psychiatric Association. (2000). *Diagnostic and statistical manual of mental disorders* (4th ed., text rev.). Washington, DC: Author.

23. Julien, R. (2001). *A primer of drug action* (9th ed.). New York: W. H. Freeman & Co.

24. Walters, G. D. (1999). *The addiction concept: Working hypothesis or self-fulfilling prophesy?* Boston: Allyn & Bacon.

25. American Psychiatric Association (2000).

26. Compton, W. M., Thomas, Y. F., Stinson, F. S., & Grant, B. F. (2007). Prevalence, correlates, disability, and comorbidity of DSM-IV drug abuse and dependence in the United States. *Archives of General Psychiatry, 64*, 566–576.

27. Nutt, D. J., King, L. A., & Phillips, L. D. (2010). Drug harms in the UK: A multicriteria decision analysis. *Lancet, 376*, 1558–1565.

28. Nutt et al. (2010).

29. Meehl, P. E. (1995). Bootstraps taxometrics: Solving the classification problem in psychopathology. *American Psychologist, 50*, 266–275.

30. Ruscio, J., Haslam, N., & Ruscio, A. M. (2006). *Introduction to the taxometric method: A practical guide.* Mahwah, NJ: Erlbaum.

31. Green, B. A., Ahmed, A. O., Marcus, D. K., & Walters, G. D. (2011). The latent structure of alcohol use pathology in an epidemiological sample. *Journal of Psychiatric Research, 45*, 225–233.

32. Goedeker, K. C., & Tiffany, S. T. (2008). On the nature of nicotine addiction: A taxometric analysis. *Journal of Abnormal Psychology, 117*, 896–909.

33. Cloninger, C. R. (1987). Neurogenetic adaptive mechanisms in alcoholism. *Science, 236*, 410–416.

34. Kendler, K. S., Jacobson, K. C., Prescott, C. A., & Neale, M. C. (2003). Specificity of genetic and environmental risk factors for use and abuse/dependence of cannabis, cocaine, hallucinogens, sedatives, stimulants, and opiates in male twins. *American Journal of Psychiatry, 160*, 687–695.

35. Johnston, L. D., O'Malley, P. M., Bachman, J. G., & Schulenberg, J. E. (2011). *Monitoring the future: 1975-2010* (Vols. 1-2). Ann Arbor, MI: Institute for Social Research, University of Michigan.

36. NIDA. (2012). *Drug abuse website.* Retrieved February 12, 2012, from http://www.drugabuse.gov/drugs-abuse.

37. Johnston, L. D., O'Malley, P. M., Bachman, J. G., & Schulenberg, J. E. (2012). *Monitoring the future: National results on adolescent drug use. Overview of key findings, 2011.* Ann Arbor, MI: Institute for Social Research, University of Michigan.

38. National Institute of Alcohol Abuse and Alcoholism (NIAAA). (2007). *Alcohol alert* (no. 72). Washington, DC: U.S. Department of Health and Human Services.

39. NIAAA (2007).

40. Kopelman, M. D., Thomson, A. D., Guerrini, I., & Marshall, E. J. (2009). The Korsakoff syndrome: Clinical aspects, psychology and treatment. *Alcohol and Alcoholism, 44*, 148–154.

41. U.S. Census Bureau. (2005). *Foreign trade statistics.* Washington, DC: Author.

42. Centers for Disease Control and Prevention. (2010). Vital signs: Nonsmokers' exposure to secondhand smoke—United States, 1999–2008. *Morbidity and Mortality Weekly Report, 59*(35), 1141.

43. de Carvalho, H. B., & Seibel, S. D. (2009). Crack cocaine and its relationship with violence and HIV. *Clinics, 64*, 857–866.

44. Harris, D. S., Everhart, E. T., Mendelson, J., & Jones, R. T. (2003). The pharmacology of cocaethylene in humans following cocaine and ethanol administration. *Drug and Alcohol Dependence, 72*, 169–182.

45. Paton, C. (2002). Benzodiazepines and disinhibition: A review. *The Psychiatrist, 26*, 460–462.

46. Liang, J., Spigelman, I., & Olsen, R. W. (2009). Tolerance to sedative/hypnotic actions of GABAergic drugs correlates with tolerance to potentiation of extrasynaptic tonic currents of alcohol-dependent rats. *Journal of Neurophysiology, 102*, 224–233.

47. Ashton, C. H. (1991). Protracted withdrawal syndromes from benzodiazepines. *Journal of Substance Abuse Treatment, 8,* 19–28.

48. Hser, Y.-I., Hoffman, V., Grella, C. E., & Anglin, M. D. (2001). A 33-year follow-up of narcotics addicts. *Archives of General Psychiatry, 58,* 503–508.

49. Abraham, H. D., & Aldridge, A. M. (1993). Adverse consequences of lysergic acid diethylamide. *Addiction, 88,* 1327–1334.

50. Sharp, J. G., & Graeven, D. B. (1981). The social, behavioral, and health effects of phencyclidine (PCP) use. *Journal of Youth and Adolescence, 10,* 487–499.

51. Mittleman, M. A., Lewis, R. A., Maclure, M., Sherwood, J. B., & Muller, J. E. (1993). Triggering myocardial infarction by marijuana. *Circulation, 103,* 2805–2809.

52. Polen, M. R., Sidney, S., Tekawa, I. S., Sadler, M., & Friedman, G. D. (1993). Health care use by frequent marijuana smokers who do not smoke tobacco. *Western Journal of Medicine, 158,* 596–601.

53. National Survey on Drug Use and Health. (2005). *The NSDUH report: Age at first us of marijuana and past year serious mental illness.* Washington, DC: U.S. Department of Health and Human Services.

54. Gorski, T. T. (1996, October 4). *Disease model of addiction.* Paper presented at the tenth annual Dual Disorder Conference, Las Vegas, NV.

55. Heyman, G. (2009). *Addiction: A disorder of choice.* Cambridge, MA: Harvard University Press.

56. Gorski (1996).

57. Booth, B. M., Russell, D. W., Soucek, S., & Laughlin, P. R. (1992). Social support and outcome of alcohol treatment: An exploratory analysis. *American Journal of Drug and Alcohol Abuse, 18,* 87–101.

58. Heather, N., & Robertson, I. (1985). *Problem drinking: The new approach.* Harmondsworth, England: Penguin.

59. Marlatt et al. (1973).

60. Walters, G. D. (2000). Behavioral self-control training for problem drinkers: A meta-analysis of randomized control studies. *Behavior Therapy, 31,* 135–149.

61. Cloninger (1987).

62. Cloninger, C. R., Przybeck, T. R., & Svrakic, D. M. (1991). The Tridimensional Personality Questionnaire: U.S. normative data. *Psychological Reports, 69,* 1047–1057.

63. Cloninger (1987).

64. Cloninger (1987).

65. Cloninger (1987).

66. Cloninger (1987).

67. Howard, M. O., Kivlahan, D., & Walker, R. D. (1997). Cloninger's tridimensional theory of personality and psychopathology: Applications to substance use disorders. *Journal of Studies on Alcohol, 58,* 48–66.

68. Lim, S.-W., Oh, K.-S., Shin, Y.-C., Kang, S.-G., Kim, L., et al. (2008). Clinical and temperamental differences between early- and late-onset alcoholism in Korean men. *Comprehensive Psychiatry, 49,* 94–97.

69. Howard et al. (1997).

70. Stewart, M. E., Ebmeier, K. P., & Deary, I. J. (2004). The structure of Cloninger's Tridimensional Personality Questionnaire in a British sample. *Personality and Individual Differences, 36,* 1403–1418.

71. Howard et al. (1997).

72. Green et al. (2011).

73. Hesselbrock, V. M., & Hesselbrock, M. N. (2006). Are there empirically supported and clinically useful subtypes of alcohol dependence? *Addiction, 101,* 99–103.

74. Green et al. (2011)

75. Hesselbrock & Hesselbrock (2006).

76. Bales, R. F. (1946). Cultural differences in rates of alcoholism. *Quarterly Journal of Studies on Alcohol, 6,* 480–499.

77. Amodeo, M., & Jones, L. K. (1997). Viewing alcohol and other drug use cross-culturally: A cultural framework for clinical practice. *Families in Society: The Journal of Contemporary Human Services, 78,* 240–254.

78. de Lint, J. (1976). The etiology of alcoholism with specific reference to sociocultural factors. In M. W. Everett, J. O. Waddell, & D. B. Heath (Eds.), *Cross-cultural approaches to the study of alcohol: An introductory perspective* (pp. 323–339). Paris: Mouton.

79. Walters, G. D. (1994). *Escaping the journey to nowhere: The psychology of alcohol and other drug abuse.* Washington, DC: Taylor & Francis.

80. Luczak, S. E., Shea, S. H., Carr, L. G., Li, T. K., & Wall, T. L. (2002). Binge drinking in Jewish and non-Jewish white college students. *Alcoholism: Clinical and Experimental Research, 26,* 1773–1778.

81. Wachtel, P. L. (1997). *Psychoanalysis, behavior therapy, and the relational world.* Washington, DC: American Psychological Association.

82. Duncan, D. F. (1974). Reinforcement of drug abuse: Implications for prevention. *Clinical Toxicology Bulletin, 4,* 69–75.

83. Wurmser, L. (1984). The role of superego conflicts in substance abuse and their treatment. *International Journal of Psychoanalytic Psychotherapy, 10,* 227–258.

84. Wurmser (1984).

85. Khantzian, E. J. (1980). An ego-self theory of substance dependence. In D. J. Lettieri, M. Sayers, & H. W. Pearsons (Eds.), *Theories of addiction* (NIDA Research Monograph No. 30, DHHS Publication No. ADM 80-967). Washington, DC: U.S. Government Printing Office.

86. Sayette, M. A. (1999). Does drinking reduce stress? *Alcohol Research and Health, 23,* 250–255.

87. Kushner, M. G., Sher, K. J., Wood, M., & Wood, P. K. (1994). Anxiety and drinking behavior: Moderating effects of tension-reduction expectancies. *Alcoholism: Clinical and Experimental Research, 18,* 852–860.

88. Aharonovich, E., Nguyen, H. T., & Nunes, E. V. (2001). Anger and depressive states among treatment-seeking drug abusers: Testing the psychopharmacological specificity hypothesis. *American Journal of Addiction, 10,* 327–334.

89. Weiss, R. D., Griffin, M. L., & Mirin, S. M. (1992). Drug abuse as self-medication for depression: An empirical study. *American Journal of Drug & Alcohol Abuse, 18,* 121–129.

90. Johnston, L. D. (1998). Reasons for use, abstention, and quitting illicit drug use by American adolescents. *Monitoring the Future: Occasional Paper 44.* Ann Arbor, MI: Institute for Social Research, University of Michigan.

91. Aharonovich et al. (2001).

92. Weiss et al. (1992).

93. Kendler et al. (2003).

94. Kandel, D. (1975). Stages in adolescent involvement in drug use. *Science, 190,* 912–914.

95. Kandel, D. B., Yamoguchi, K., & Chen, K. (1992). Stages of progression in drug involvement from adolescence to adulthood: Further evidence from gateway theory. *Journal of Studies on Alcohol, 53,* 447–457.

96. Golub, A., & Johnson, B. D. (2001). Variations in youthful risks of progression from alcohol and tobacco to marijuana and to hard drugs across generations. *American Journal of Public Health, 91,* 225–232.

97. Morral, A. R., McCaffrey, D. F., & Paddock, S. M. (2002). Reassessing the marijuana gateway effect. *Addiction, 97,* 1493–1504.

98. Tarter, R. E., Vanyukov, M., Kirisci, L., Reynolds, M., & Clark, D. B. (2006). Predictors of marijuana use in adolescents before and after licit drug use: Examination of the gateway hypothesis. *American Journal of Psychiatry, 163,* 2134–2140.

99. Golub, A., & Johnson, B. D. (2002). The misuse of "Gateway Theory" in U.S. policy on drug abuse control: A secondary analysis of the muddled deduction. *International Journal of Drug Policy, 13,* 5–19.

100. Choo, T., Roh, S., & Robinson, M. (2008). Assessing the "gateway hypothesis" among middle and high school students in Tennessee. *Journal of Drug Issues, 38,* 467–492.

101. Choo et al. (2008).

102. Lynskey, M. T., Fergusson, D. M., & Horwood, L. J. (1998). The origins of the correlations between tobacco, alcohol and cannabis use during adolescence. *Journal of Child Psychology and Psychiatry, 39,* 995–1007.

103. Morral et al. (2002).

104. Bandura, A. (1986). *Social foundations of thought and action: A social cognitive theory.* Englewood Cliffs, NJ: Prentice Hall.

105. Marlatt, G. A. (1985). Relapse prevention: Theoretical rationale and overview of the model. In G. A. Marlatt & J. R. Gordon (Eds.), *Relapse prevention* (pp. 250–280). New York: Guilford.

106. Marlatt, G. A., & Gordon, J. R. (Eds.), *Relapse prevention.* New York: Guilford.

107. Donovan, J. E., Molina, B. S. G., & Kelly, T. M. (2009). Alcohol outcome expectancies as socially shared and socialized beliefs. *Psychology of Addictive Behaviors, 23,* 248–259.

108. Leigh, B. C., & Stacy, A. W. (2004). Alcohol expectancies and drinking in different age groups. *Addiction, 99,* 215–227.

109. Barnwell, S. S., Borders, A., & Earleywine, M. (2006). Alcohol-aggression expectancies and dispositional aggression moderate the relationship between alcohol consumption and alcohol-related violence. *Aggressive Behavior, 32,* 517–527.

110. McMurran, M. (2007). The relationship between alcohol-aggression proneness, general alcohol expectancies, hazardous drinking, and alcohol-related violence in adult male prisoners. *Psychology, Crime & Law, 13,* 275–284.

111. Santrock, J. W. (2008). *Life-span development* (12th ed.). New York: McGraw-Hill.

CRIME: DEFINITIONS, CLASSIFICATION, AND THEORY

As the crime rate in the United States has dropped (see **Figure 3-1**),[1] so too have people's fears and concerns about crime. Crime nonetheless continues to play a major role in American life and can often be found near the top of the list of concerns expressed by U.S. citizens on various regional and national surveys. Nearly half the Americans participating in a recent Pew Research Center survey, in fact, indicated that crime should be a top priority of the Obama administration and Congress in 2012 (see **Table 3-1**).[2] In an effort to understand crime and its impact on modern-day American society, the current chapter is structured around three primary objectives:

- Define what is meant by the terms crime and criminality.
- Explore several possible classification systems for crime.
- Review and evaluate major theories of criminality.

Figure 3-1
Total per capita crime rate in the United States, 1960–2010.

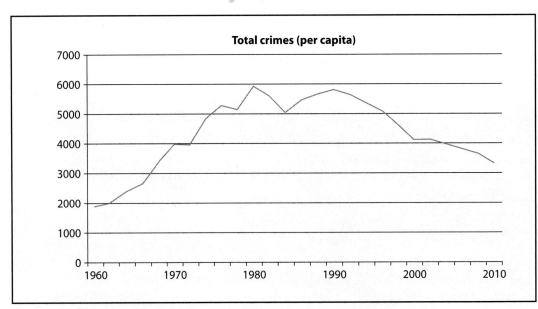

Data From: Federal Bureau of Investigation. (2011). *Uniform crime reports, 2010.* Washington, DC: Author.

Table 3-1 U.S. Citizen views on the Top Policy Priorities for the President and Congress in 2007 and 2012

Policy Priority	January 2007	January 2012	Change
Economy	68%	86%	+18
Jobs	57%	82%	+25
Terrorism	80%	69%	−11
Budget Deficit	53%	69%	+16
Education	69%	65%	−4
Energy	57%	52%	−5
Crime	62%	48%	−14
Environment	57%	43%	−14
Illegal Immigration	55%	39%	−16
Global Warming	38%	25%	−13

Data From: Pew Research Center. (2012, January 23). *Public priorities: Deficit rising, terrorism slipping.* Washington, DC: Author.

Definitions

Crime

Crime can be defined as an act performed in violation of a law forbidding it (e.g., robbery) or not performed in violation of a law requiring it (e.g., paying taxes). This is a technical definition that is probably not very useful to most readers. In real life, a great deal more subjectivity goes into defining a behavior as criminal. Police officers, prosecutors, judges, corrections officials, and probation and parole officers continually make judgments about whether an activity is of sufficient severity to warrant their time and effort. In a study conducted in a suburban Chicago school, it was determined that teachers were more apt to label an act a crime when it was committed by a black student than when it was committed by a white student.[3] **Definitions** may be just as subjective if the decision maker is a police officer or federal prosecutor. Furthermore, many laws derive from **mala prohibita** (actions made illegal by legislation) rather than from **mala in se** (natural law) and so a subjective element is clearly part of the definition used to classify these behaviors as crimes. Transforming and assembling these individual crimes into a set of crime statistics, as we will soon see, is an equally subjective process.

Official arrest or conviction data are commonly used to compile crime statistics. The Federal Bureau of Investigation's (FBI) Uniform Crime Reports (UCR), from which **Figure 3-1** was constructed, is a particularly popular source of crime statistics. The problem is, about half of all crime goes unreported, and because the rate of unreported crime varies by offense, jurisdiction, and victim–perpetrator relationship, we cannot simply assume that the actual rate is twice that of the measured rate. This has led to the development of several alternative measures (see **Table 3-2**). Self-report surveys, for instance, are sometimes administered to high school students as a way of estimating the crime rate. This has the advantage of providing a more complete picture of crime than official records, although it has several drawbacks, chief of which are its tendency to focus on minor or relatively trivial offenses and its reliance on respondents (offenders themselves) who may be less than forthcoming. Victim surveys are a second alternative to official crime data. The advantage of a procedure like the National Crime Victimization Survey is that it provides a more complete picture of crime than official data and is based on a national stratified sample of respondents. Expense and widespread reliance on victim memory are two disadvantages of victim surveys.[4] Some combination of official records, self-report data, and victimization surveys may consequently be required for optimally accurate results.

Table 3-2 Advantages and Disadvantages of Official, Self-Report, and Victimization Survey Measures of Crime

Measure	Advantages	Disadvantages
Official	Convenience Availability	Most crime goes unreported Only certain crime categories covered
Self-Report	More inclusive than official data Correlates well with official data	Weighted toward minor and trivial crimes Nonresponse and defensiveness
Victimization Survey	More inclusive than official data Stratified sampling	Relatively expensive Heavily reliant on victim memory

A number of contextual factors potentially moderate definitions of crime, including culture, offender age, war, and politics. In some cultures, murder is justified if it can be demonstrated that a family member has dishonored the family by becoming the victim of rape, engaging in premarital sex, practicing homosexuality, or refusing to abide by an arranged marriage. It is estimated that as many of 5,000 of these honor killings take place each year and that many of the cultures in which they occur either openly or tacitly accept the practice.[5] Offender age is another important contextual factor. If a robbery is committed by a 17-year-old, unless he or she is tried as an adult, then a crime has not been committed; although the act would clearly be defined as a crime if it was committed by an 18-year-old. In time of war, killing goes from being a crime to an objective. Finally, as indicated in News Spot 3-1, members of Congress do not have to follow the same laws and restrictions the rest of the U.S. population does. Crime should therefore not be considered a purely objective concept but rather a socially constructed and highly contextualized process that is open to both interpretation and negotiation.

NEWS SPOT 3-1

Title: Congress, Legislate Thyself
Source: *San Francisco Chronicle*
Author: Editorial
Date: November 28, 2011

It's an issue of basic fairness. It is illegal for corporate executives and others to trade stocks based on insider information. It ought to be illegal for members of Congress to buy and sell based on inside information as well, but it is not illegal because Congress has exempted itself from insider-trading laws.

In 2006, when Rep. Louise Slaughter, D-N.Y., introduced the Stop Trading on Congressional Knowledge—or STOCK—Act to prohibit members of Congress and their staff from trading stocks based on nonpublic information, her bill attracted only 14 cosponsors.

"60 Minutes" changed all that. This month, the CBS news magazine aired a segment about politicians who had access to insider briefings and made fortuitous purchases in the market. As Steve Kroft reported, in 2008 after federal officials briefed congressional leaders about the pending financial meltdown, the then-ranking Republican on the House Financial Services Committee, Rep. Spencer Bachus, R-Ala., bought options that bet the market would fall. In a week, Bachus turned a profit of more than $5,000.

Bachus later told National Public Radio that with Wall Street in turmoil and Lehman Brothers failing earlier that week, any savvy investor could have made the same call. That sounds reasonable. It also is reasonable for taxpayers to flinch when they learn that the now chairman of the Financial Services Committee was betting on the market to drop.

Peter Schweizer, a fellow at Stanford's Hoover Institution, believes that some in Congress see the public trust as a "venture opportunity" that allows them to leverage information not available to the general public.

Slaughter's STOCK Act would not stop members or staffers from dabbling in the markets. The legislation, however, would make Capitol Hill insiders subject to prosecution if they buy or sell securities based on nonpublic information. It also would cut into K Street's latest boutique business practice—"political intelligence"—that allows lobbyists to gather inside financial information which they can give to hedge-fund clients.

Before the "60 Minutes" story, the STOCK Act had nine cosponsors.... Since the story aired, the list of STOCK Act cosponsors has snowballed from 9 to 61 a week ago; the roster hit 99 last week. On December 6, the House Financial Services Committee will hold a hearing on the bill.

Republished with the permission of the *San Francisco Chronicle*, permission conveyed through Copyright Clearance Center, Inc.

Questions to Ponder
  1. **What is insider trading?**
  2. **Should Congress be exempt from certain laws?**
  3. **What should be the penalty for someone who uses an elected position for financial gain?**

Using the subjective definitions of crime described in this section presents several problems for those interested in studying drug–crime relationships. First, if the criterion for crime is committing one or more crimes then nearly everyone satisfies this criterion because practically everyone has violated a law, no matter how small or trivial, at some point in time. This makes comparisons meaningless because virtually everyone would be classified as a criminal. Second, the drug–crime relationship might vary as a function of the contextual variables previously described. Although I previously acknowledged the possibility that multiple drug–crime relationships exist, wide variations in these relationships based on contextual factors make crime per se a poor choice as a criterion measure. Finally, the same individuals tend to be labeled "criminals" and "drug addicts," in part, because they lack social status, influence, and power, a situation that could artificially inflate the correlation between drugs and crime.[6] What is required, then, is a construct that reveals a pattern of behavior rather than an isolated and potentially uncharacteristic act. The construct I have come up with is criminality.

Criminality

Just as the term drug effect does a better job of capturing the drug experience than the term drug, so too does the term **criminality** do a better job of capturing a pattern of antisocial behavior than the term crime. Accordingly, criminality should be more useful than crime to those interested in studying drug–crime relationships. I define criminality as a person's propensity to commit crime as manifest by six elements: age, criminal history, age of onset, antisocial cognition, antisocial peer associations, and antisocial personality processes (see **Figure 3-2**). Four of the elements—criminal history, antisocial cognition, antisocial peer associations, and antisocial personality process—have been referred to as the "big four" predictors of criminality and recidivism.[7] The other two elements—age and age of onset—are frequently considered among the best predictors of the frequency (age) and chronicity (age of onset) of offending behavior.[8-9] Taken as a whole, these six variables do a much better job of defining a pattern or lifestyle of crime or criminality than any single act, no matter how violent or remarkable.

Figure 3-2
Elements of
Criminality.

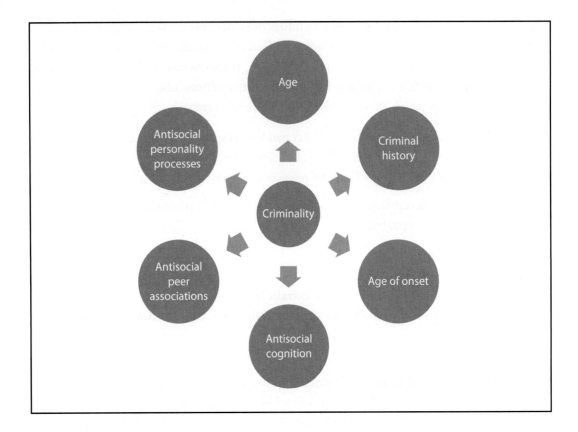

It should be noted that although criminality is defined as the propensity to commit crime, this propensity is not a stable trait. As the individual ages the propensity weakens. The age–crime relationship is one of the "brute facts" of crime, at least according to Hirschi and Gottfredson.[10] As such, this relationship is held to be invariant across time, culture, and types of offenses. Although this view has been challenged, it is still widely held.[11] Irrespective of how invariant the age–crime relationship is, the importance of age in defining criminality highlights the fact that propensity changes, not only in response to age but also in response to some of its other elements (e.g., antisocial cognition, antisocial peers, antisocial personality processes). Changes in these three elements correspond to a person's odds of committing another crime. Because it is a function of both static (age, criminal history, age of onset) and dynamic (antisocial cognition, antisocial peer associations, antisocial personality processes) risk factors, propensity is both stable and changeable.

Classification

Taxometric Research

The results of a handful of taxometric studies on substance misuse indicate that the latent structure of alcohol and nicotine abuse/dependence appears to be categorical. There have been many more taxometric studies performed on the crime-related constructs of psychopathy, antisocial personality, and criminal lifestyle and the consensus is that, with a few exceptions,[12–13] the latent structure of these constructs is dimensional.[14–27] If the latent structure of a construct is dimensional, as it appears to be with criminality, then individual differences in criminality are quantitative (differences of degree) rather than qualitative (differences in kind) in nature. Accordingly, classification is less a matter of assigning people to their proper category (criminal, noncriminal) than it is placing them along a continuum (degree of criminality) and assessment procedures designed to evaluate the construct should be set up to identify the individual's position on this continuum.

Models of Crime Classification

There are several different ways to classify crime and criminality. Four of the more popular ways to classify crime are described next:

- crime vs. delinquency
- violent vs. nonviolent
- person vs. property
- felony vs. misdemeanor

Crime vs. Delinquency

Crime is an illegal act committed by an adult; an adult being defined as someone 18 years of age or older. **Delinquency** is an illegal act committed by a minor or someone under the age of 18. The difference between crime and delinquency is somewhat arbitrary, however, in that the age at which one is considered an adult is not the same in every jurisdiction or for every purpose. For example, the age of majority (legal adulthood) is 19 in Alabama and 21 in Mississippi. In most states, someone under the age of 18 can be prosecuted as an adult and thereby convicted of a crime if the court is willing to certify the individual as an adult. Status offenses, like truancy, running away from home, and underage drinking, are restricted to juveniles in that they would not be considered offenses if committed by an adult. Again, the problem is that the age at which one is considered an adult varies by offense. A 19-year-old would not generally be considered a status offender for skipping school or running away from home but would be considered a status offender for drinking alcohol.

The justification for distinguishing between crime and delinquency is that adults and juveniles who violate the law should be treated differently. Hence, the adult correctional system is concerned first and foremost with punishing and incapacitating adult criminals and only secondarily with rehabilitation. Rehabilitation, however, is the primary purpose of the juvenile correctional system and the very reason for its existence. Because juvenile offenders are viewed as less culpable or responsible for their actions than adult offenders and more deserving of rehabilitation than of punishment, it is thought that they should be treated differently from adult criminals. In fact, legislation keeping status offenders out of detention can be found in most state charters.[28] The practice of distinguishing between juvenile and adult offending, although admirable, does not alter the fact that it is based on an arbitrary division given the high degree of overlap that exists between adult and juvenile crime.

Violent vs. Nonviolent

Violent crimes are normally defined as the use of force or the threatened use of force against another person. Taking into account the interpersonal nature of violence, a violent offense often entails a violation of someone else's personal space. Nonviolent crimes, on the other hand, are free of force or the threat of force and do not constitute a violation of personal space. This again, is an arbitrary distinction. Furthermore, the criteria for violence can vary widely from one jurisdiction or country to the next. This makes it difficult to compare violent crime rates across nations and indicates that definitions of violent and nonviolent crime are anything but universal.[29]

In the United States, violent crime is normally classified into five categories: murder, forcible rape, robbery, aggravated assault, and simple assault. Homicide, attempted murder, assault, sexual offenses, robbery, and abductions are categories of violent crime in Canada. In England, all violence against the person, sexual offenses, and robbery are classified as violent crimes. Australia classifies homicide, manslaughter, attempted murder, assault, assaultive and non-assaultive sexual offenses, abduction, robbery, and extortion as violent crime, whereas New Zealand classifies homicide, robbery, abduction, kidnapping, assault, intimidation, threats, and group assembly as violent crimes.[30] Divergent definitions of violent crime make it nearly impossible to conduct meaningful cross-national research on violent crime.

Person vs. Property

Person crimes like murder, rape, assault, and robbery involve the use of force or the threatened use of force against one or more other people. Property crimes like theft, larceny, burglary, and arson involve taking or destroying property. These two categories overlap extensively with the violent vs. nonviolent classification and with each other. Robbery involves taking property but is classified as a **person crime** because it usually implies the threat of violence. As was the case with crime vs. delinquency and violent vs. nonviolent crime, differences between person and **property crime** are more apparent than real. The small differences that exist between person and property crime when they are compared over time (person crime peaked more before declining in the mid-1990s: see **Figures 3-3** and **3-4**), across age (person crime peaks a few years later than property crime: see **Figure 3-5**), and between gender (the male-to-female ratio is higher for person than property crimes: see **Figure 3-6**) are not sufficient to justify treating them as distinct entities.[31]

Figure 3-3
Violent crime in the United States, 1986–2004.

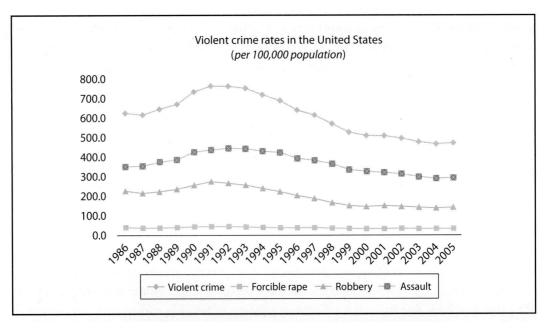

Data From: Federal Bureau of Investigation. (2011). *Uniform crime reports, 2010*. Washington, DC: Author.

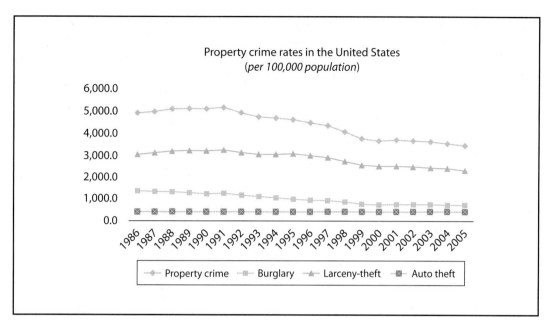

Data From: Federal Bureau of Investigation. (2011). *Uniform crime reports, 2010*. Washington, DC: Author.

Figure 3-4
Property crime in the United States, 1986–2005.

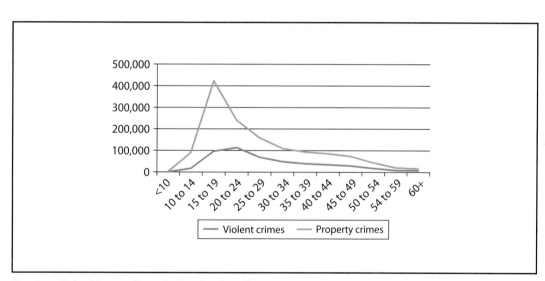

Data From: Federal Bureau of Investigation. (2011). *Uniform crime reports, 2010*. Washington, DC: Author.

Figure 3-5
Age-violent crime and age-property crime relationships.

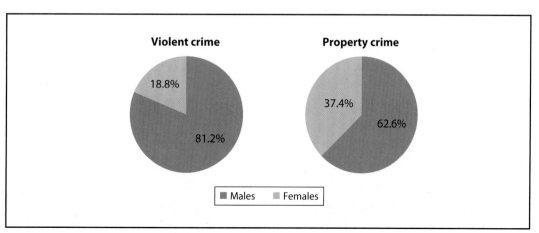

Data From: Federal Bureau of Investigation. (2011). *Uniform crime reports, 2010*. Washington, DC: Author.

Figure 3-6
Male and female involvement in person and property crimes.

Felony vs. Misdemeanor

A **felony** is classified as a more serious or severe offense punishable by a prison term of 1 year or longer. A misdemeanor, on the other hand, is classified as a less serious or severe offense punishable by a jail or prison term of less than 1 year. This distinction is not generally considered particularly useful by most legal scholars and has actually been dropped by some jurisdictions. In California, for instance, there is now a category of crime known as a **wobbler** in which the same crime can be classified as either a **misdemeanor** or felony, depending on the circumstances.[32] Furthermore, research indicates that many high-risk offenders commit both felonies and misdemeanors and that some low-risk offenders commit only felonies.[33]

One reason why the violent-nonviolent, person-property, and felony-misdemeanor differentiations are not particularly helpful or meaningful is that offenders do not generally confine themselves to any one category of crime. Instead, they commit crimes from different categories, violent as well as nonviolent, person as well as property, and felonies as well as misdemeanors. This pattern of offending, commonly referred to as criminal versatility, has even been observed in offender groups traditionally considered more specialized (e.g., sex offenders).[34] This, along with the dimensional nature of crime-related constructs, indicates that dividing crimes into categories is an arbitrary exercise of questionable utility. Perhaps criminality lends itself better to classification.

Models of Criminality Classification

There are several potential criminality classification systems, three of which are discussed here:

- Conduct disorder
- Antisocial personality disorder
- Proactive and reactive dimensions of criminality

Conduct Disorder

The fourth edition of the *Diagnostic and Statistical Manual of Mental Disorders* (DSM-IV) classifies **conduct disorder** as a repeated pattern of behavior in which the rights of others and/or major social norms are violated. It is normally only diagnosed in children and adolescents. A **diagnosis** of conduct disorder requires the presence of at least 3 of the following 15 symptoms in the last 12 months, with at least one of the symptoms occurring in the last 6 months:[35]

- Bullying, threatening, or intimidating others
- Initiating physical fights
- Using a weapon against someone
- Physical cruelty toward people
- Physical cruelty toward animals
- Stealing through intimidation (robbery)
- Forcing someone into sexual activity
- Setting fires with the intention of causing property damage
- Deliberately destroying property
- Breaking into a house, building, or car
- Lying to obtain goods or to avoid obligations

- Stealing items of nontrivial value
- Staying out at night in violation of parental prohibitions prior to age 13
- Running away from home overnight on at least two separate occasions
- Truant from school on multiple occasions starting before age 13

Epidemiology

Using data collected on male and female 5- to 15-year-old participants from the British Child Mental Health Survey, Barbara Maughan and colleagues determined that nearly three times as many boys as girls could be diagnosed with conduct disorder (2.1% vs. 0.8%). They also discovered that the prevalence of conduct disorder increased with age.[36] The gender and age trends for participants in this sample are reproduced in **Figure 3-7**.

Comorbidity

There is a great deal of overlap or **comorbidity** between conduct disorder and the other two DSM-IV childhood externalization disorders: oppositional defiant disorder (ODD) and attention deficit/hyperactivity disorder (ADHD). In the Maughan et al. study, for instance, conduct disorder and ODD achieved 62% overlap in boys and 56% overlap in girls. The overlap between conduct disorder and ADHD was almost 30% and twice that of the overlap between conduct disorder and childhood internalizing disorders like depression and anxiety.[37] A developmental sequence has been observed in which conduct disorder symptoms proceed from mild to moderate to severe, with ODD sometimes, but not always, forming the mild phase of the disorder.[38]

Prognosis

The course and predicted long-term outcome of conduct disorder is mixed but there is evidence that a good portion of children with conduct disorder grow up to become anti-social and criminal adults. Early onset Conduct Disorder (age 10 years or younger) and

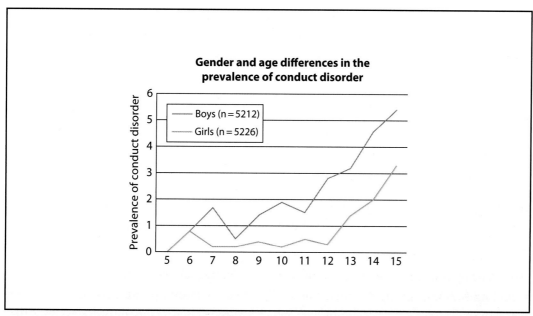

Figure 3-7
Sex and age differences in the prevalence (percentage with a diagnosis) of conduct disorder.

Data From: Maughan, B., Rowe, R., Messer, J., Goodman, R., & Meltzer, H. (2004). Conduct disorder and oppositional defiant disorder in a national sample: Developmental epidemiology. *Journal of Child Psychology and Psychiatry, 45*, 609–621.

greater diversity in delinquent and antisocial behavior increase the probability of adult anti-social personality disorder.[39] In addition, conduct disorder has been found to correlate with more rapidly progressing substance abuse problems and poorer response to treatment.[40] Conduct disorder and ADHD alone or in combination predict future adult criminality and violent recidivism.[41] The combination of conduct disorder and ADHD is particularly prognostic of future criminal violence, at least in men.[42] Conduct disorder and other externalization behaviors also predict higher levels of mortality in early to middle adulthood.[43]

Diagnosis

Although there have been no taxometric studies done specifically on conduct disorder, taxometric investigations of childhood aggression and adolescent psychopathy indicate that these behaviors possess a dimensional latent structure.[44–45] Conduct disorder can therefore be conceptualized as a dimension, measured with a scale composed of all 15 conduct disorder symptoms, and classified using the juvenile's position on the continuum rather than as a category, measured with a dichotomous scale, and classified using class membership based on an arbitrary cutoff score of 3.

Antisocial Personality Disorder

DSM-IV defines **Antisocial Personality Disorder** as a chronic pattern of behavior in which the rights of others are disregarded and the rules of society are violated by an individual who is at least 18 years of age. In addition to satisfying three or more of seven criteria for adult antisocial behavior, the individual must also satisfy 3 of the 15 conduct disorder criteria, with onset prior to age 15 years. The seven adult antisocial behavior criteria for Antisocial Personality Disorder are:[46]

- Engaging in behavior that could lead to arrest
- Lying, conning, and deceitfulness
- Impulsivity and failure to follow a life plan
- Irritability and aggressiveness as represented by physical fights and assaults
- Recklessness and disregard for the safety of self and others
- Irresponsibility as represented by failure to meet obligations at work or home
- Lack of remorse or guilt for harm caused to others

Epidemiology

Antisocial Personality Disorder is several times more common in males than it is in females. Results from the National Co-Morbidity Study and National Institute of Mental Health Epidemiologic Catchment Area Study indicate that the lifetime prevalence of Antisocial Personality Disorder is significantly higher in men (5%) than in women (1.8%).[47–48] The gender gap in prevalence for Antisocial Personality Disorder narrows considerably when incarcerated samples are examined, although male inmates still tend to outnumber female inmates when it comes to receiving a diagnosis of Antisocial Personality Disorder (40% vs. 30%).[49]

Comorbidity

Antisocial personality disorder is comorbid with a number of Axis I and Axis II diagnoses, including ADHD, anxiety disorders, mood disorders, somatoform disorders, and borderline personality disorder.[50] The diagnosis with which antisocial personality disorder overlaps the most, however, is substance use disorder.[51] The abuse of alcohol and other drugs is particularly prevalent in individuals with early onset conduct disorder and a current diagnosis of antisocial personality disorder.[52]

Prognosis

Individuals diagnosed with antisocial personality disorder are at increased risk for criminal behavior. Recidivism rates are substantially elevated in individuals diagnosed with antisocial personality disorder, particularly when they also satisfy the diagnostic criteria for psychopathy.[53] Requiring a diagnosis of conduct disorder before age 15 as a precondition for a diagnosis of antisocial personality disorder does a better job of identifying individuals at risk for future behavioral problems than does a simple requirement of satisfying three of the seven adult criteria for antisocial personality disorder. Glenn Walters and Raymond Knight, for instance, determined that inmates satisfying the conduct disorder criteria and adult criteria for antisocial personality disorder displayed a significantly greater level of criminal thinking and experienced significantly more adjustment problems in prison than inmates who satisfied only the adult criteria for antisocial personality disorder.[54]

Diagnosis

Like conduct disorder, antisocial personality disorder is probably dimensional even though it is treated as categorical in DSM-IV. When the DSM-IV categorical model for antisocial personality disorder was compared to a dimensional model (total number of criteria satisfied), the dimensional model achieved significantly more accurate results (see **Figure 3-8**).[55] The dimensionality of personality disorders like antisocial personality disorder has not escaped the notice of clinicians and researchers involved in revising the Diagnostic and Statistical Manual and plans for DSM-5 include a dimensional approach for the personality disorder diagnoses (see News Spot 3-2).

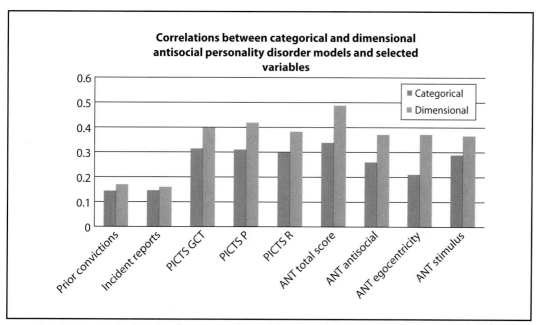

Figure 3-8
Correlations between categorical and dimensional antisocial personality disorder models and selected variables.

Note: PICTS = Psychological Inventory of Criminal Thinking Styles; GCT = General Criminal Thinking score; P = Proactive score; R = Reactive score; ANT = Antisocial Features scale of the Personality Assessment Inventory; Antisocial = Antisocial Behaviors subscale; Egocentricity = Egocentricity subscale; Stimulus = Stimulus Seeking subscale.

Data From: Walters, G. D., & Knight, R. A. (2010). Antisocial personality disorder with and without antecedent childhood conduct disorder: Does it make a difference? *Journal of Personality Disorders, 24,* 165–178.

Title: Michigan State University-Led Research Team Proposes New Way to Classify Personality Disorders
Source: *Michigan State University News*
Author: Andy Henion
Date: October 12, 2010

Research led by a Michigan State University psychologist is playing a key role in the effort to change the way mental health clinicians classify personality disorders.

The study by Christopher Hopwood and colleagues calls for a more scientific and practical method of categorizing personality disorders—a proposal that ultimately could improve treatment, Hopwood said.

"We're proposing a different way of thinking about personality and personality disorders," said Hopwood, MSU assistant professor of psychology and an experienced clinician. "There's widespread agreement among personality disorder researchers that the current way to conceptualize personality disorders is not working."

The study is being cited by the team of experts that currently is developing criteria for the manual used to diagnose personality disorders—the fifth edition of the Diagnostic and Statistical Manual of Mental Disorders, or DSM-5, slated to come out in 2013.

The study is being considered for inclusion in the DSM-5. The DSM, published by the American Psychiatric Association, is considered the bible of the U.S. mental health industry and is used by insurance companies as the basis for treatment approval and payment. The study also will appear in an upcoming issue of the *Journal of Personality Disorders*.

The current method of classifying personality disorders, as spelled out in the fourth edition of the DSM, or DSM-IV, breaks personality disorders into 10 categories, Hopwood said. That system is flawed, he said, because it does not take into account severity of personality disorders in an efficient manner and often leads to overlapping diagnoses.

"It's just not true that there are 10 types of personalities disorders, and that they're all categorical—that you either have this personality disorder or you don't," Hopwood said. "Scientifically, it's just not true."

Hopwood and colleagues propose a new three-stage strategy for diagnosing personality disorders:

Stage One: Consider a patient's normal personality traits, such as introversion/extroversion…

Stage Two: Create a numerical score to represent severity of the disorder….

Stage Three: Condense the list of 10 personality disorder categories to five dimensional ratings.

Questions to Ponder
   1. What are the advantages of a categorical system of diagnosis?
   2. What are the advantages of a dimensional system of diagnosis?
   3. Can a diagnosis be both categorical and dimensional?

Proactive and Reactive Dimensions of Criminality

Taxometric analysis is helpful in determining whether the latent structure of a construct is categorical or dimensional but it cannot determine the number of categories or dimensions in a construct. Once the taxometric approach indicates that the latent structure of a construct is categorical or dimensional, the next step is to use another statistical technique to identify the number of categories or dimensions in the construct. Using the dimensionally oriented statistical procedure of factor analysis and indicators from three crime-related constructs (psychopathy, antisocial personality, and criminal lifestyle), Walters identified two dimensions that he subsequently labeled **proactive** and **reactive criminality**.[56] Several of the characteristics that differentiate between proactive and reactive criminality are listed in **Table 3-3**.

Proactive and reactive criminality can be considered overlapping dimensions. In fact, these two dimensions have been found to correlate anywhere from .50 and .75.[57–59] Despite the overlap, the two dimensions form countervailing (equal force in opposite directions) relationships with important outside criteria. Using the Proactive (P) and Reactive (R) criminal thinking scores from the Psychological Inventory of Criminal Thinking Styles (PICTS) as proxies for proactive and reactive criminality, respectively, Walters and colleagues demonstrated that where proactive criminal thinking correlated with a history of instrumental crimes (robbery and burglary), reactive criminal thinking correlated with a history of impulsive crimes (assault).[60] In another study, proactive criminal thinking correlated with positive outcome expectancies for crime (beliefs about what can be accomplished through crime) but not hostile attribution biases (misinterpreting innocuous interpersonal situations as threatening), whereas reactive criminal thinking correlated with hostile attribution biases but not positive outcome expectancies for crime.[61] Hence, crime patterns and cognitive processes tend to differ between these two overlapping dimensions.

The proactive-reactive dimensional model has three advantages as a classification system for criminality. First, there is a developmental precedent for a proactive-reactive model of adult criminality in Dodge's proactive and reactive model of childhood aggression.[62] The two models propose similar levels of overlap and countervailing correlations (proactive aggression with positive outcome expectancies for aggression and reactive aggression with hostile attribution biases), although longitudinal research is required to determine whether proactive and reactive childhood aggression lead to

Table 3-3 Comparing the Characteristics of Proactive and Reactive Criminality

Proactive	Reactive
Instrumental	Hostile
Cold-blooded	Hot-blooded
Calculated	Spontaneous
Goal-directed	Impulsive
Future-oriented	Present-oriented
Offensive	Defensive

proactive and reactive adult criminality. Second, the proactive-reactive dimensional model has important implications for clinical practice. It not only suggests the need for an integrated program of assessment but also calls for the development of interventions for **proactive criminality** to complement the skill-based programs currently available for reactive criminality.[63] Finally, proactive and reactive criminality appear to have differing levels of relevance to drug abuse, with preliminary research showing that reactive criminality may be more closely associated with drug abuse than proactive criminality.[64]

Theory

Theories of crime—and substance abuse, for that matter—can be organized into three general categories: propensity, developmental, and interactive. **Propensity theories** assume that one or more time-stable characteristics are responsible for drug abuse or crime. **Developmental theories** postulate that life experiences or developmental trajectories are at the root of drug abuse or crime. **Interactive theories** explain drug abuse or crime by postulating an interaction of time-stable characteristics and developmental/life experiences. The six theories of crime to be reviewed in this chapter are the psychopathy model, self-control theory, the **developmental taxonomy**, age-graded theory, the **biosocial model**, and social learning theory. The manner in which these six theories and the six theories of drug abuse fit into the three general categories of propensity, developmental, and interactive is illustrated in **Figure 3-9**.

Psychopathy Model

Robert Hare is the individual most responsible for popularizing the concept of psychopathy. In his attempt to operationalize Hervey Cleckley's 16 traits of the psychopathic personality, Hare created a commonly used measure of psychopathy known as the **Psychopathy Checklist**.[65–66]

Fundamental Assumptions, Principles, and Concepts

In a 1988 paper, Hare and several colleagues postulated that psychopathy is caused by a left-hemisphere linguistic processing deficit that interferes with the person's ability to learn from punishment. This linguistic processing deficit is conceptualized by Hare and colleagues to be a time-stable trait with roots in genetics and early neurological problems.[67]

Figure 3-9
Propensity, developmental, interactive theories of drug abuse and crime.

Category	Drug abuse	Crime
Propensity	Disease model	Psychopathy model
	Self-medication hypothesis	Self-control theory
Developmental	Cross-cultural theory	Developmental taxonomy
	Gateway theory	Age-graded theory
Interactive	Unified biosocial model	Biosocial model
	Social learning theory	Social learning theory

Accordingly, Hare is pessimistic about the possibility of effecting change in the psychopathic individual and estimates the prevalence of psychopathy at around 1% in the general population and at 15% to 25% in prison populations, which is why much of the research on psychopathy has been conducted in prison.[68] The 20-item Psychopathy Checklist-Revised (PCL-R) may be Hare's greatest contribution to the field in that it provides a reliable means by which psychopathy can be assessed and studied. Each item on the PCL-R is scored using a three-point scale (0 = not present, 1 = may be present, 2 = present) and a total score that ranges from 0 to 40.[69] The four primary factors or facets of psychopathy, as measured by the PCL-R, along with the items that comprise each facet, are listed in **Table 3-4**.

Table 3-4 Content of the Four PCL-R Facets

Facet 1: Interpersonal
- Glib and superficially charming
- Egocentric
- Lying/conning
- Manipulative

Facet 2: Affective
- Shallow emotional life
- Lack of guilt or remorse
- Callous and lack of empathy
- Failure to accept responsibility for own actions

Facet 3: Impulsive Lifestyle
- Easily bored
- Impulsive
- Irresponsible
- Parasitic lifestyle
- Lack of realistic long-term goals

Facet 4: Antisocial Behavior
- Early behavior problems
- Poor behavioral control
- Juvenile delinquency
- Revocation of conditional release
- Criminal versatility

Data From: Hare, R. D. (2003). *The Hare Psychopathy Checklist—Revised manual.* (2nd ed.). Toronto, Canada: Multi-Health Systems.

Research Support

A number of cortical and subcortical areas have been implicated as putative neuroanatomical markers of psychopathy, from the prefrontal cortex to the amygdala.[70–71] Hare's supposition that psychopathy is caused by a left hemisphere processing deficit has not received much in the way of empirical support, yet there is evidence that a right hemisphere processing deficit may be involved in psychopathy.[72] In fact, there have been so many conflicting findings in research on the neuroanatomy of psychopathy that some researchers have speculated on the possibility of multiple forms or types of psychopathy, each with its own unique neuroanatomical signature.[73] Although this is an interesting and potentially fruitful line of research it comes precariously close to falling into the same biological reductionistic trap that has ensnared much of the biological research on substance abuse.

The PCL-R has traditionally done an outstanding job of predicting general and violent recidivism.[74] More recent studies, however, suggest that the PCL-R owes the bulk of its predictive efficacy to a single component; namely, the antisocial facet. Incremental validity analyses are conducted to determine whether a variable continues to predict a criterion after other relevant variables have been controlled. Using an incremental validity design, Walters and colleagues determined that when the antisocial facet was entered into the regression equation behind the first three facets (thereby effectively controlling for the first three facets) it continued to predict general and violent recidivism but that when the other three facets were entered into the equation behind the antisocial facet (thereby controlling for the antisocial facet) they failed to predict general and violent recidivism.[75] In addition, there is research questioning the feasibility of extending the PCL-R to juvenile and female offenders.[76–77]

Strengths of the Psychopathy Model

Hare's model is one of the more precise theories of crime in existence given the strength of its methodology. By operationally defining psychopathy using criteria from a reliable and well-validated measure (PCL-R) Hare has advanced the study of psychopathy and made it more accessible to researchers and clinicians alike. Moreover, the **psychopathy model** has been researched extensively and is generally considered a highly fruitful approach. It only receives moderate ratings on fruitfulness, however, because a good portion of the research runs counter to some of Hare's fundamental ideas and hypotheses on psychopathy. Another major strength of the psychopathy model is that it emphasizes the proactive features of criminality, a topic overlooked by most criminological theories.

Weaknesses of the Psychopathy Model

There is minimal support for Hare's argument that a left-hemisphere deficit in verbal linguistic processing is responsible for psychopathy.[78] In addition, Hare's view that psychopaths do not change over time, either spontaneously or through treatment, is inconsistent with the results of Randall Salekin's comprehensive review of the research in this area.[79] The parsimony of Hare's theory can also be called into question based on the fact that some of the complicated genetic-biological explanations he offers may be better accounted for by environmental factors. For instance, Hare's notion that the central nervous systems of psychopaths are underaroused by threats of punishment because of genetics may simply reflect the fact that psychopaths have been desensitized to violence by virtue of their involvement in a violent lifestyle. Finally, controversy continues to rage over whether Facet 4 (antisocial) is a core feature of psychopathy.[80] If Facet 4 accounts for much of the PCL-R's predictive efficacy but is not a core feature of the psychopathy construct then we must question the comprehensiveness of the psychopathy model and the relevance of the PCL-R to crime and criminal justice.

Self-Control Theory

Another propensity theory of crime is offered by Michael Gottfredson and Travis Hirschi in their 1990 book, *A General Theory of Crime*. In their general theory of crime, Gottfredson and Hirschi contend that all crime is a function of low self-control.

Fundamental Assumptions, Principles, and Concepts

According to Gottfredson and Hirschi, **low self-control** has its origins in inadequate parental control and socialization whereby weak parental monitoring, supervision, and discipline lead to low self-control on the part of the child. Gottfredson and Hirschi maintain that self-control is a trait composed of six interrelated personality dimensions (diligence, prudence, sensitivity, high-level cognitive functioning, delay of gratification, and anger control). They further contend that the trait normally stabilizes by the time a child is 8 to 10 years of age. Crime, say Gottfredson and Hirschi, is a function of three primary factors: low self-control, choice, and opportunity. Desistance from crime occurs because opportunities for crime

Table 3-5 Five Core Postulates of Self-Control Theory

Postulate	Definition
Stability	Low self-control is stable relative to one's age-mates after age 8–10 years
Resiliency	Low self-control is resilient or impervious to intervention after age 8–10 years
Exclusivity	Low self-control is caused exclusively by weak parental control and supervision
Universality	Low self-control is the universal cause of crime and explains even white-collar crime
Versatility	Low self-control leads to criminal versatility whereby the individual commits a range of different crimes

decrease as a person ages, a consequence of physical changes (reduced strength and stamina) occurring with age, improvements in absolute self-control (although relative self-control, defined as one's level of self-control in comparison to age-mates, is held to be stable), and a rapidly shrinking pool of available criminal associates.[81] The five core postulates in **self-control theory** are listed and described in **Table 3-5**.

Research Support

In a meta-analysis of 21 studies on the self-control construct, Pratt and Cullen recorded mean effect sizes (r) of moderate strength (.26–.28).[82] Research on the five core **postulates**, however, has produced mixed results. Self-control is reasonably stable in most people after ages 8–10 but a significant minority of individuals demonstrate substantial shifts in absolute and relative self-control after this age.[83–84] There is less support for the **resiliency postulate** in the sense that evidence-based interventions are capable of effecting significant change in self-control.[85] The **exclusivity postulate** has received minimal support in the research literature, with studies showing that factors other than parenting, including genetics, prenatal injury, and neighborhood context, play an important role in the development of low self-control.[86–87] Low self-control applies to a wide variety of different crimes, although questions about its applicability to white-collar crime have been raised, thus providing mixed support for the **universality postulate**.[88] The **versatility postulate**, on the other hand, has received consistent empirical support and is generally considered the strongest of Gottfredson and Hirschi's five postulates.[89]

Strengths of Self-Control Theory

Self-control theory is more comprehensive than Hare's psychopathy model but nowhere near as complete an explanation of offending as one would expect of a general theory of crime. Hence, the theory possesses only moderate comprehensiveness. Parsimony and fruitfulness, on the other hand, are exceptionally strong. With only a few major constructs and a handful of principles, self-control theory is extremely parsimonious. The theory is quite fruitful as well, in that it has probably generated more research in the last 2 decades than any other theory in the field of criminology. Research conducted on self-control theory indicates that low self-control predicts future criminality and recidivism as well as if not better than other important criminological constructs, such as labeling and antisocial associates.[90] Several of the theory's core postulates have also received consistent support (**stability** and versatility in particular). In addition, self-control theory emphasizes the second major dimension of criminality—reactive criminality.

Weaknesses of Self-Control Theory

With its exclusive focus on reactive criminality, self-control theory cannot be considered a general theory of crime. Therefore, while it is moderately comprehensive, it is less comprehensive than several other theories described in this chapter. In addition, the theory suffers from low precision in that low self-control is never adequately defined or distinguished from criminality. Akers and Sellers, in fact, contend that self-control theory is an exercise in tautology to the extent that the predictor (low self-control) may simply be another term for the criterion (criminality).[91] A self-report measure has been devised to assess low self-control (Grasmick et al.[92]) and has been used extensively in research on low self-control, but Gottfredson and Hirschi contend that low self-control is best measured behaviorally.[93] Unfortunately, there is no generally agreed upon behavioral measure of low self-control at this time. Support for the notion that self-control mediates the relationship between poor parenting and delinquency is limited, at best.[94]

Developmental Taxonomy

Terrie Moffitt has constructed a developmental theory of crime in which early antisocial patterns form distinct developmental trajectories useful in understanding and predicting future criminality. A key feature of Moffitt's theory is that developmental factors are instrumental in defining the three trajectory groups in her theory.

Fundamental Assumptions, Principles, and Concepts

In her developmental taxonomic theory of crime, Moffitt postulates that delinquency conforms to three developmental patterns which she refers to as **life-course-persistent** (LCP), **adolescence-limited** (AL), and nondelinquent (ND). The LCP trajectory has a prevalence rate of 3–16% and is characterized by childhood or preadolescent onset, early environmental deprivation, verbal and executive functioning deficits, poor social adjustment, and termination in middle adulthood. The AL pattern is more prevalent (45–55%) than the LCP pattern and marked by midadolescent onset, minimal environmental deprivation, average to above average verbal and executive function skills, good social adjustment, and termination in late adolescence or early adulthood. In contrast to the deep pathology of the LCP pattern, the AL pattern is viewed by Moffitt as a normative reaction to the social pressures and responsibilities of impending adulthood. The ND pattern has a prevalence rate of 29–52% and is characterized by normal development and minimal contact with the criminal justice system.[95] A schematic representation of the three trajectories is provided in **Figure 3-10**.

Research Support

The three trajectories in Moffitt's theory were rationally derived. In other words, after examining delinquency data Moffitt arrived at the conclusion that there were three distinct groups of delinquents: those who started early and ended late (LCP), those that started late and ended early (AL), and those who did not start at all (ND). Growth mixture modeling and latent class growth analysis are two statistical procedures that can be used to group longitudinal data into trajectories. Studies using these procedures to evaluate longitudinal

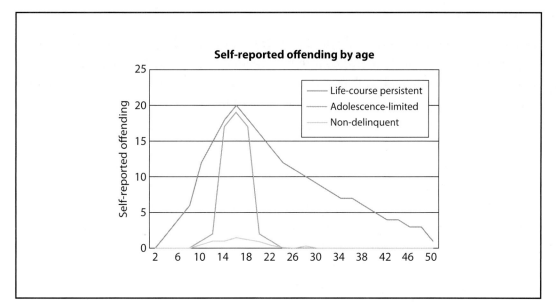

Figure 3-10
Schematic representation of the delinquency patterns present in the three trajectories proposed by Moffitt.

delinquency data support the presence of multiple trajectories but often identify more than three.[96] Even so, these studies support Moffitt's belief that delinquency can be divided into multiple trajectories. In addition, there is evidence that delinquents classified as LCP display more neuropsychological and early environmental problems, greater genetic liability for delinquency, an earlier age of onset and later age of desistence, and poorer adult outcomes than delinquents classified as AL.[97–101] Moffitt maintains that AL offenders learn the attitudes and techniques of crime by observing the actions of LCP offenders through a process known as **social mimicry**. Research has supported this aspect of her theory as well.[102]

Strengths of the Developmental Taxonomy

Moffitt's theory is highly fruitful in that it has stimulated a great deal of research in both the psychology and criminology fields. In addition, much of this research has tended to support the major assumptions and principles found in Moffitt's theory. The theory is also moderately comprehensive and parsimonious. Viewing crime as a developmental process is particularly attractive to policy-makers in that it suggests possible avenues for prevention and intervention. Moffitt's position that a small group of LCP offenders account for the lion's share of serious adult crime is consistent with prior research showing that less than 10% of the adult and juvenile criminal populations account for over half the crime.[103–104]

Weaknesses of the Developmental Taxonomy

The greatest weakness in Moffitt's theory is its lack of precision. Some of the major concepts could be more precisely defined (e.g., social mimicry) and the boundaries between the three trajectories could be more clearly articulated. This may be why studies often identify more than three different trajectories and why there is a lack of consensus as to how many trajectories exist for delinquency. Even more problematic is the fact that several recent taxometric studies have failed to identify a taxonic boundary between the different trajectories in Moffitt's model, which suggests that LCP and AL delinquency may be different points along the same continuum rather than distinct categories of behavior.[105–106]

Age-Graded Theory

Like Moffitt, Robert Sampson and John Laub view crime as both continuous and changeable. Unlike Moffitt, who confined continuity to one trajectory (LCP) and change to another (AL), Sampson and Laub conceptualize change and continuity as complementary components of a single trajectory in their **age-graded theory** of crime.

Fundamental Assumptions, Principles, and Concepts

Sampson and Laub's age-graded theory of crime emphasizes informal and indirect patterns of social control over formal and direct patterns of social control. Whereas the police, courts, and criminal justice system exercise formal social control and parental discipline provides direct control over a child's behavior, a person's social network of family, friends, coworkers, and classmates serves as sources of informal social control. Sampson and Laub theorize that people accumulate **social capital** through informal social control networks and that those with low social capital are more likely to follow a trajectory of crime than those with high social capital. Though Sampson and Laub do not deny the existence of individual differences in criminal propensity or the importance of early experiences in shaping future behavior, they focus their attention on proximal events (marriage, occupation) rather than distal ones. Sampson and Laub maintain that incarceration, labeling, and other negative consequences of delinquent and criminal behavior lead to a "knifing off" of opportunities for corrective prosocial experiences like marriage, military service, and an occupation. They refer to this process as **cumulative disadvantage** and consider it a primary reason why individuals remain in a trajectory of crime long after it has stopped being fun.[107]

Research Support

Research indicates that informal social bonds predict desistance from crime independent of a person's level of self-control.[108–109] Moreover, marriage has been found to promote desistance by reducing, and in some cases eliminating, time spent with antisocial peers.[110] There is also evidence that alcohol and illegal drugs encourage future criminality by loosening the social bonds, like marriage and employment, that facilitate desistance from crime.[111–112] All three sets of findings are consistent with Sampson and Laub's age-graded theory. Contrasting the age-graded theory with social relations theory and Gottfredson and Hirschi's general theory of crime in a large sample of high school students, Brent Benda discovered that the age-graded theory provided the best explanation for self-reported offending in both male and female participants.[113] Examining minority status, delinquency, and detention decisions, McGuire uncovered qualified support for Sampson and Laub's cumulative disadvantage hypothesis.[114]

Strengths of the Age-Graded Model

The age-graded model incorporates Hirschi's original views on informal social control and social bonding into a modern theory of crime and desistance.[115] This is important because interest in the informal aspects of social control seemed to fade after Gottfredson and Hirschi's general theory of crime came onto the scene and formal social control apparently began to replace informal social control in the hearts of many control theorists. Owing to the fact that the age-graded model incorporates concepts from a number of different models, such as informal social control theory, differential association theory, labeling theory, and strain theory, it is more comprehensive than most theories of crime. Even though the age-graded model borrows extensively from other theories, it still possesses moderate internal consistency and precision. The model's ability to accommodate a single trajectory makes it consistent with a growing body of evidence showing that crime-related constructs are dimensional rather than categorical in nature. Finally, unlike most theories of crime, which focus primarily on offending, Sampson and Laub's age-graded model emphasizes desistance.

Weaknesses of the Age-Graded Model

Given the number of constructs that have been integrated into the age-graded theory it makes sense that parsimony would be the theory's greatest weakness. The theory is fruitful but not nearly as fruitful or as popular as Gottfredson and Hirschi's low self-control model or Moffitt's developmental taxonomy. In addition, much of the foundational research for Sampson and Laub's theory comes from a reanalysis of the classic Glueck and Glueck study.[116] Because the Gluecks collected their data in the late 1920s it is uncertain just how relevant these data are to current patterns of delinquency and crime. Moreover, Glueck and Glueck oversampled serious offenders and relied on official crime reports rather than self-report data, raising further questions about the appropriateness of these data for testing some of Sampson and Laub's hypotheses. Despite the severity and chronicity of offending displayed by participants in the Glueck's sample, it is interesting that most eventually desisted from crime (see **Figure 3-11**).[117] Finally, some studies testing the age-graded theory have failed to find a relationship between criminality and attachment to school, spouse, or job, contrary to Sampson and Laub's views on informal social control and desistance.[118]

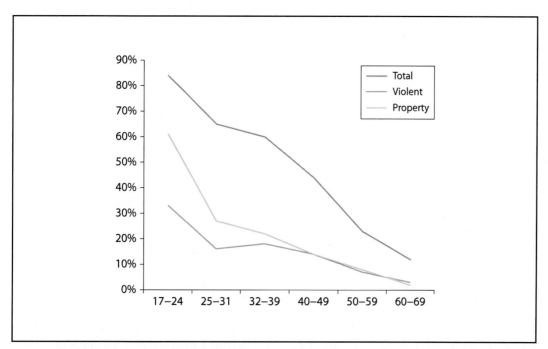

Figure 3-11
Proportion of participants with official arrests at different ages, from Glueck and Glueck (1968).

Data From: Sampson, R. J., & Laub, J. H. (2005). A life-course view of the development of crime. *Annals of the American Academy of Political and Social Science, 602,* 12–45.

Figure 3-12
Conceptual model for the low self-control phenotype, with the putative genotypes in the right column and the proposed endophenotypes in the middle column.

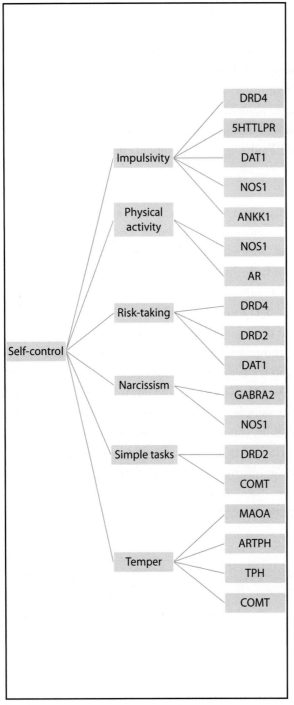

Adapted from: DeLisi, M., Wright, J. P., Beaver, K., & Vaughn, M. G. (2011). Teaching biosocial criminology I: Understanding endophenotypes using Gottfredson and Hirachi's self-control construct. *Journal of Criminal Justice Education, 22*, 360–376.

Biosocial Theory of Crime

Kevin Beaver, Matt DeLisi, Michael Vaughn, and John Paul Wright have proposed a biosocial theory of crime in which genetics are hypothesized to interact with social environment to increase liability or risk for future criminal behavior. Sarnoff Mednick and Adrian Raine introduced earlier versions of this same basic approach.

Core Assumptions, Principles, and Concepts

Beaver, DeLisi, Vaughn, and Wright reinterpret popular criminological constructs like low self-control and delinquent peer associations as biosocial concepts. For instance, they reinterpret low self-control as a genetically based predisposition to weak executive functioning and delinquent peer associations as a genetically based preference for certain friendship patterns. They have also examined a number of gene–environment interactions and correlations in an effort to more effectively predict and understand criminal behavior. In creating their theory, they have focused a significant amount of attention on three biological constructs: genotype, phenotype, and endophenotype. The **genotype** is the genetic code or composite for a particular behavior. The **phenotype** is the behavioral expression of the genetic composite, and the **endophenotype** connects the genetic liability to the behavioral expression of that liability.[119] Putative genotypes for the six components or endophenotypes of low self-control are listed in **Figure 3-12**.[120]

Research Support

Using behavioral genetic methods, Beaver and colleagues discovered that 52–64% of the variance in low self-control and 58–74% of the variance in delinquent peers were

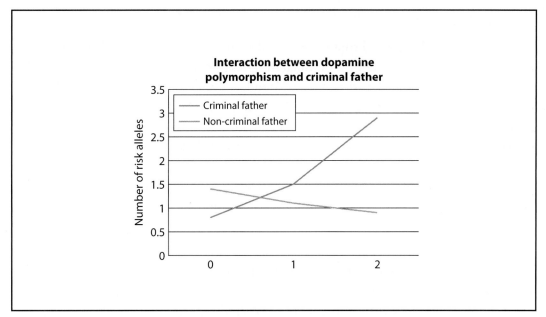

Data From: DeLisi, M., Beaver, K. M., Vaughn, M. G., & Wright, J. P. (2009). All in the family: Gene x environment interaction between DRD2 and criminal father is associated with five antisocial phenotypes. *Criminal Justice and Behavior, 36,* 1187–1197.

accounted for by genetic factors.[121–122] This team of researchers has also investigated the effect of different gene–environment interactions on criminal behavior. For instance, DeLisi et al. observed that a **polymorphism** (variant of a gene) for a dopamine receptor gene and a criminal father interacted to increase liability for serious delinquency in a group of adolescent African American girls. The results of this study revealed no relationship between the polymorphism and delinquency in girls with noncriminal fathers but indicated a rising level of delinquency involvement in girls with criminal fathers as the number of risk **alleles** increased from 0 to 2 (see **Figure 3-13**).[123] In a second study, Beaver et al. determined that growing up in a disadvantaged neighborhood only correlated with crime in individuals with one of two dopamine polymorphisms.[124] In a study particularly relevant to drug–crime relationships, Vaughn et al. identified a relationship between polymorphisms in two dopamine genes and polysubstance abuse that was mediated by neuropsychological problems, deviant peers, maternal disengagement, and low self-control.[125]

Strengths of the Biosocial Theory of Crime

Criminologists have traditionally been dismissive of biological explanations of criminal behavior. Accordingly, biology has often been overlooked as a possible explanation for crime. Biosocial theory attempts to remedy this situation by reframing popular criminological constructs in biosocial terms and showing how gene-environment interactions may be more helpful than biology or sociology alone in explaining criminal behavior. By integrating biological and environmental explanations of crime, biosocial theory is one of the more comprehensive theories of crime available. Although this is a relatively new theory, the leading proponents of this approach (Beaver, DeLisi, Vaughn, and Wright) are prolific researchers who have already developed a fairly substantial base of knowledge in just a few years.

Figure 3-13
Serious delinquency as a function of number of risk alleles for a dopamine polymorphism and having a criminal father.

Weaknesses of the Biosocial Theory of Crime

Because it is relatively new and runs counter to the current zeitgeist of sociological criminology, biosocial theory has not yet captured the attention of most researchers in the fields of criminology and criminal justice. As such, it suffers from low fruitfulness and will probably require research from scholars outside the small circle of advocates before gaining wide acceptance in the field. In addition, other than an obvious focus on genetic and biological processes in crime causation, biosocial theory seems to lack a set of core beliefs about biology, environment, and crime, and its precision suffers as a result. The theory runs the risk of biological reductionism, particularly if the supporting research continues to rely on twin studies, a method that tends to produce elevated heritability estimates.[126]

Social Learning Theory

Ronald Akers revised Edwin Sutherland's influential **differential association** theory of delinquency by integrating it with B. F. Skinner's operant conditioning model and Albert Bandura's social cognitive theory. The result has been the creation of a **social learning theory** of crime.

Fundamental Assumptions, Principles, and Concepts

Akers proposed that people learn both criminal and noncriminal forms of behavior through four processes: differential association, definitions, differential reinforcement, and imitation. Differential association is the process by which one's actions are influenced by those with whom one interacts or associates. Akers and Sutherland both contend that close and frequent association with deviant behavioral patterns, norms, and values greatly increase a person's odds of future criminal involvement. Definitions are people's attitudes toward crime (in general as well as toward specific crimes) based on a moral code and the meaning the individual attaches to the behavior. The acceptance of antisocial attitudes and the rejection of prosocial attitudes is a foundation for criminal behavior. Rewards are the reinforcements people receive for their behavior. Individuals who differentially receive more reinforcement from crime than from conventional behavior will tend to engage in crime. Finally, **imitation** is learning through observation. People who interact regularly with criminals will tend to model the behavior of these criminals, particularly if they perceive that the criminals are rewarded for their antisocial behavior.[127]

Research Support

Pratt and colleagues[128] recently conducted a meta-analysis of Akers' version of social learning theory and determined that the differential association and definitions components achieved results comparable to those obtained in an earlier meta-analysis on self-control theory[129] and superior to those obtained in a previous meta-analysis of deterrence or rational choice theory.[130] Mean effect sizes (r) for the other two components, **differential reinforcement** and imitation/modeling, although significant, were half the size of the mean effects attained by differential association and definitions (see **Figure 3-14**). Furthermore, the differential association effect for peers was twice that of the differential association effect

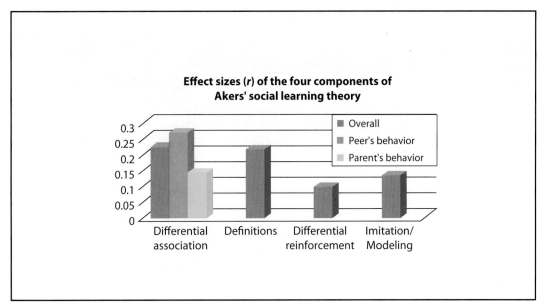

Figure 3-14
Results of a meta-analysis on Akers' social learning theory.

Data From: Pratt, T. C., Cullen, F. T., Sellers, C. S., Winfree, T., Madensen, T. D.,...Gau, J. M. (2010). The empirical status of social learning theory: A meta-analysis. *Justice Quarterly, 27*, 765–802.

for parents. However, research shows that when friends' direct reports of criminality are studied instead of a respondent's perception of their friends' criminality, the differential association effect drops significantly.[131] Hence, the single most important component of social learning theory may be criminological attitudes and beliefs (definitions).

Strengths of Social Learning Theory

Akers' social learning theory of crime pulls from a number of different theories in both criminology and psychology and as a consequence is at least moderately comprehensive. In addition, it has stimulated a significant amount of research but not as much as its individual components (i.e., differential association, operant conditioning, observational learning). Social learning theory has direct application to the criminal justice system in terms of both classification (assignments based on security level in order to keep less sophisticated inmates from being adversely affected by association with more sophisticated inmates) and supervision (standard parole/probation condition of forbidding association with known felons). Finally, social learning theory has received a great deal of support in the psychological literature and provides excellent guidance for evidence-based intervention in the form of cognitive-behavior therapy.

Weaknesses of Social Learning Theory

Although Akers's social learning theory explains many types of crimes, there are some crimes it appears to have difficulty explaining, such as crimes committed alone. The theory also fails to incorporate opportunity and as such, fails to explain why juvenile offenders differentially associate with drug-using peers rather than with their own parents.[132] In addition, some of the constructs in Akers's social learning theory, as is also the case with Sutherland's original differential association theory, are difficult, if not impossible, to

Table 3-6 Summary of an Evaluation of Six Theories of Crime

Theory	Comprehensiveness	Parsimony	Precision	Fruitfulness
Psychopathy	L	L	H	M
Low Self-Control	M	H	L	H
Dev. Taxonomy	M	M	L	H
Age-Graded	H	L	M	M
Biosocial	H	M	L	L
Social Learning	M	M	L	M

operationalize. What exactly did Sutherland mean by definitions favorable or unfavorable to the law and how does Akers' theory address cognition? The results of the Pratt et al. meta-analysis seem to suggest that cognition may be the single most important feature of social learning theory, but Akers's model does not do a particularly good job of clarifying the role of cognition in crime.

The six theories of crime reviewed in this chapter have both strengths and weaknesses. Five of the six theories received at least one high rating and all six received at least one low rating (see **Table 3-6**). Hence, the conclusion reached with theories of drug abuse applies equally to theories of crime: no single theory provides a sufficiently satisfactory explanation of crime to be maximally useful as a stand-alone procedure or theory. This is particularly true of criminological theory where single-variable models have dominated the field. The solution, as before, is to either provide a synthesis of ideas from different theories, as the biosocial theory is attempting to do, or adopt theoretical eclecticism and apply different theories in different situations, depending on which seems most appropriate for the purpose at hand.

Summary and Conclusions

- Crime is defined as an act performed in violation of a law forbidding it or not performed in violation of a law requiring it. Because nearly everyone has violated a law at one time or another, this concept may not be particularly helpful in furthering our understanding of drug–crime relationships. Accordingly, a related term, criminality, defined as a person's propensity to commit crime, serves as the point of reference whenever the term crime is used.

- Crime-related constructs like psychopathy, antisocial personality, and criminal lifestyle appear to have a dimensional latent structure. As such, criminality should be organized into dimensions rather than into categories. A model by which crime is conceived as overlapping dimensions of proactive and reactive criminality was therefore introduced.

- Six theories of crime were reviewed in this chapter (psychopathy, self-control theory, developmental taxonomy, age-graded theory, biosocial model, and social learning theory) and each was found to have strengths and weaknesses. For the purposes of understanding crime, a synthesis of the different models or a flexible use of different models in different situations is required.

Key Terms

Adolescence-limited Developmental trajectory marked by a relatively brief period of delinquency between midadolescence and late adolescence or early adulthood.

Age-Graded Theory Theory that emphasizes proximal developmental events (marriage, occupation) as the principal cause of desistance from crime.

Allele One member of a pair or series of genes.

Antisocial Personality Disorder Adult personality disorder characterized by chronic violation of and disregard for the rights of others and conventions of society.

Biosocial Model Theory in which an interaction between genetic and social influences is held to be the cause of crime.

Comorbidity Presence of two or more coexisting disorders.

Conduct Disorder Childhood disorder in which the rights of others and/or major social norms are violated.

Crime Act performed in violation of a law forbidding it or not performed in violation of a law requiring it.

Criminality The propensity to commit crime as manifested by age, criminal history, age of onset, antisocial cognition, antisocial peer associations, and antisocial personality processes.

Cumulative Disadvantage Involvement in delinquent and criminal behavior leading to a knifing off of opportunities for corrective prosocial experience (e.g., marriage, job).

Definitions Attitudes either favorable or unfavorable to violations of the law.

Delinquency Illegal act committed by a minor or someone under the age of 18 years.

Developmental Taxonomy Theory that postulates the presence of three primary developmental trajectories for crime: life-course-persistent, adolescence-limited, and nondelinquent.

Developmental Theories Group of theories that presume that criminality is a function of life experiences or developmental trajectories.

Diagnosis Clinical classification of a disorder.

Differential Association Process by which one's actions are influenced by those with whom one interacts.

Differential Reinforcement Degree to which one receives rewards for crime versus rewards for conventional behavior.

Endophenotype Connection between the genetic liability for a behavior (genotype) and the behavioral expression of that liability (phenotype).

Epidemiology Study of the distribution and pattern of disorders.

Exclusivity Postulate Assumption that low self-control is caused exclusively by weak parental control and supervision.

Felony More serious crime punishable by a year or more in prison.

Genotype Genetic code, composite, or liability for a particular behavior.

Imitation   Learning through observation; also known as modeling.

Interactive Theories   Group of theories that presume that criminality is a function of an interaction between time-stable characteristics and developmental/life experiences.

Life-Course-Persistent   Developmental trajectory characterized by early onset of delinquency, chronic offending during adolescence and early adulthood, and desistance in middle adulthood.

Low Self-Control   Disposition to engage in antisocial behavior marked by poor behavioral controls and stimulation-seeking tendencies.

Mala in se   Natural law.

Mala Prohibita   Act made illegal by legislation.

Misdemeanor   Less serious crime punishable by less than a year in jail or prison.

Person Crime   Offense involving the use of force or threatened use of force against another person.

Phenotype   Behavioral expression of a genetic composite or genotype.

Polymorphism   Variant of a gene.

Postulate   Theoretical principle or hypothesis.

Proactive Criminality   Planned, organized, and cold-blooded patterns of criminal conduct.

Prognosis   Prediction of the probable course and long-term outcome of a disorder.

Propensity Theories   Set of theories that presume that criminality is a function of one or more time-stable characteristics.

Property Crime   Offense involving taking or destroying property.

Psychopathy Checklist   20-item rating scale designed to measure psychopathic personality disorder.

Psychopathy Model   Theory in which psychopathic personality processes are held to be the principal cause of crime.

Reactive Criminality   Impulsive, spontaneous, and hot-blooded patterns of criminal conduct.

Resiliency Postulate   Assumption that low self-control is impervious to intervention after ages 8–10 years.

Self-Control Theory   Theory in which poor parental supervision and control are held to result in low self-control and eventual delinquency and crime.

Social Capital   Investment in the conventional social order.

Social Learning Theory   Theory of human behavior in which reinforcement, modeling, and cognitive (attitudinal) factors play a major role.

Social Mimicry   Learning crime by observing the antisocial actions of more experienced delinquents.

Stability Postulate   Assumption that low self-control does not change after ages 8–10 years.

Universality Postulate   Assumption that all crime is explained by low self-control.

Versatility Postulate   Assumption that low self-control is characterized by involvement in a variety of different offenses.

Wobbler   Crime that can be classified as either a misdemeanor or felony depending on the circumstances.

Critical Thinking

1. Why is it important to distinguish between crime and criminality?
2. What is the rationale for not diagnosing anyone under the age of 18 with Antisocial Personality Disorder? Do you think this same reasoning should apply to a diagnosis of psychopathy or psychopathic personality disorder?
3. Which do you think provides a better explanation of crime—propensity theories or developmental theories—and why?

Notes

1. Federal Bureau of Investigation. (2011). *Uniform crime reports, 2010*. Washington, DC: Author.
2. Pew Research Center. (2012, January 23). *Public priorities: Deficit rising, terrorism slipping*. Washington, DC: Author.
3. Manley, T. (2006). *From Columbine, Colorado to Chicago, Illinois: The criminalization of success and failure by placing white youth at promise and youth of color at risk*. Paper presented at the International Symposium at De Montfort University, Leicester, England.
4. Coleman, C., & Moynihan, J. (1996). *Understanding crime data: Haunted by the dark figure*. Philadelphia, PA: Open University Press.
5. United Nations Population Fund. (2000). *Ending violence against women and girls*. Retrieved August 22, 2012, from http://www.unfpa.org/swp/2000/english/ch03.html.
6. Hammersley, R. (2008). *Drugs and crime*. Cambridge, England: Polity Press.
7. Andrews, D. A., & Bonta, J. (2006). *The psychology of criminal conduct* (4th ed.). Newark, NJ: LexisNexis.
8. Warr, M. (1998). Life-course transitions and desistance from crime. *Criminology, 36*, 183–216.
9. DeLisi, M. (2006). Zeroing in on early arrest onset: Results from a population of extreme career criminals. *Journal of Criminal Justice, 34*, 17–26.
10. Hirschi, T., & Gottfredson, M. (1983). Age and the explanation of crime. *American Journal of Sociology, 89*, 522–584.
11. Steffensmeier, D., Allan, E., Harer, M., & Streifel, C. (1989). Age and the distribution of crime. *American Journal of Sociology, 94*, 803–831.
12. Harris, G. T., Rice, M. E., & Quinsey, V. L. (1994). Psychopathy as a taxon: Evidence that psychopaths are a discrete class. *Journal of Consulting and Clinical Psychology, 62*, 387–397.
13. Harris, G. T., Rice, M. E., Hilton, N. Z., Lalumière, J. L., & Quinsey, V. L. (2007). Coercive and precocious sexuality as a fundamental aspect of psychopathy. *Journal of Personality Disorders, 21*, 1–27.
14. Edens, J. F., Marcus, D. K., Lilienfeld, S. O., & Poythress, N. G. (2006). Psychopathic, not psychopath: Taxometric evidence for the dimensional structure of psychopathy. *Journal of Abnormal Psychology, 115*, 131–144.
15. Edens, J. F., Marcus, D. K., & Vaughn, M. G. (2011). Exploring the taxometric status of psychopathy among youthful offenders: Is there a juvenile psychopath taxon? *Law and Human Behavior, 35*, 13–24.
16. Guay, J.-P., Ruscio, J., Knight, R. A., & Hare, R. D. (2007). A taxometric analysis of the latent structure of psychopathy: Evidence for dimensionality. *Journal of Abnormal Psychology, 116*, 701–716.

17. Marcus, D. K., John, S. L., & Edens, J. F. (2004). A taxometric analysis of psychopathic personality. *Journal of Abnormal Psychology, 113*, 626–635.

18. Marcus, D. K., Lilienfeld, S. O., Edens, J. F., & Poythress, N. G. (2006). Is antisocial personality disorder continuous or categorical? A taxometric analysis. *Psychological Medicine, 36*, 1571–1581.

19. Marcus, D. K., Ruscio, J., Lilienfeld, S. O., & Hughes, K. T. (2008). Converging evidence for the latent structure of antisocial personality disorder: Consistency of taxometric and latent class analysis. *Criminal Justice and Behavior, 35*, 284–293.

20. Walters, G. D. (2007). The latent structure of the criminal lifestyle: A taxometric analysis of the Lifestyle Criminality Screening Form and Psychological Inventory of Criminal Thinking Styles. *Criminal Justice and Behavior, 34*, 1623–1637.

21. Walters, G. D., Brinkley, C. A., Magaletta, P. R., & Diamond, P. M. (2008). Taxometric analysis of the Levenson Self-Report Psychopathy scale. *Journal of Personality Assessment, 90*, 491–498.

22. Walters, G. D., Diamond, P. M., Magaletta, P. R., Geyer, M. D., & Duncan, S. A. (2007). Taxometric analysis of the antisocial features scale of the Personality Assessment Inventory in federal prison inmates. *Assessment, 14*, 351–360.

23. Walters, G. D., Duncan, S. A., & Mitchell-Perez, K. (2007). The latent structure of psychopathy: A taxometric investigation of the Psychopathy Checklist-Revised in a heterogeneous sample of male prison inmates. *Assessment, 14*, 270–278.

24. Walters, G. D., Gray, N. S., Jackson, R. L., Sewell, K. W., Rogers, R., Taylor J., et al. (2007). A taxometric analysis of the Psychopathy Checklist: Screening Version (PCL:SV): Further evidence of dimensionality. *Psychological Assessment, 19*, 330–339.

25. Walters, G. D., Marcus, D. K., Edens, J. F., Knight, R. A., & Sanford, G. M. (2011). In search of the psychopathic sexuality taxon: Indicator size does matter. *Behavioral Sciences and the Law, 29*, 23–39.

26. Walters, G. D., & McCoy, K. (2007). Taxometric analysis of the Psychological Inventory of Criminal Thinking Styles in incarcerated offenders and college students. *Criminal Justice and Behavior, 34*, 781–793.

27. Walters, G. D., & Ruscio, J. (2009). To sum or not to sum: Taxometric analysis with ordered categorical assessment items. *Psychological Assessment, 21*, 99–111.

28. Steinberg, L., Haskins, R., & Steinberg, L. (2008). *Keeping adolescents out of prison*. Policy Brief. Princeton, NJ: The Future of Children, Retrieved August 22, 2012, from http://www.princeton.edu/futureofchildren/publications/docs/18_02_PolicyBrief.pdf.

29. Segessenmann, T. (2002, June). *Section 2—International comparisons of recorded violent crime rates for 2000*. Wellington, New Zealand: Research & Evaluation Unit, Ministry of Justice.

30. Segessenmann (2002).

31. Federal Bureau of Investigation. (2011).

32. California Penal Code 17 PC—Classification of offenses, Section 872.

33. DeLisi (2006).

34. Harris, D. A., Knight, R. A., Smallbone, S., & Dennison, S. (2011). Postrelease specialization and versatility in sexual offenders referred for civil commitment. *Sexual Abuse: A Journal of Research and Treatment, 23*, 243–259.

35. American Psychiatric Association. (2000). *Diagnostic and statistical manual of mental disorders* (4th ed., text rev.). Washington, DC: Author.

36. Maughan, B., Rowe, R., Messer, J., Goodman, R., & Meltzer, H. (2004). Conduct disorder and oppositional defiant disorder in a national sample: Developmental epidemiology. *Journal of Child Psychology and Psychiatry, 45*, 609–621.

37. Maughan et al. (2004).

38. Burke, J. D., Loeber, R., & Birmaher, B. (2002). Oppositional defiant disorder and conduct disorder: A review of the past 10 years, Part II. *Journal of the American Academy of Child and Adolescent Psychiatry, 41*, 1275–1293.

39. Myers, M. G., Stewart, D. G., & Brown, S. A. (1998). Progression from conduct disorder to antisocial personality disorder following treatment for adolescent substance abuse. *American Journal of Psychiatry, 155*, 479–485.

40. Connor, D. F., Ford, J. D., Albert, D. B., & Doerfler, L. A. (2007). Conduct disorder subtype and comorbidity. *Annals of Clinical Psychiatry, 19*, 161–168.

41. Soderstrom, H., Sjodin, A.-K., & Carlstedt, A. (2004). Adult psychopathic personality with childhood-onset hyperactivity and conduct disorder: A central problem constellation in forensic psychiatry. *Psychiatry Research, 121*, 271–280.

42. Babinski, L. M., Hartsough, C. S., & Lambert, N. M. (1999). Childhood conduct problems, hyperactivity-impulsivity, and inattention as predictors of adult criminal activity. *Journal of Child Psychology and Psychiatry and Allied Disciplines, 40*, 347–355.

43. Jokela, M., Ferrie, J., & Kivimäki, M. (2009). Childhood problem behaviors and death by midlife: The British National Child Development Study. *Journal of the American Academy of Child and Adolescent Psychiatry, 48*, 19–24.

44. Edens et al. (2011).

45. Walters, G. D., Ronen, T., & Rosenbaum, M. (2010). The latent structure of childhood aggression: A taxometric analysis of self-reported and teacher-rated aggression in Israeli schoolchildren. *Psychological Assessment, 22*, 628–637.

46. APA (2000).

47. Kessler, R. C., McGonagle, K. A., Zhao, S., Nelson, C. B., Hughes, M., Eshleman, S., et al. (1994). Lifetime and 12-month prevalence of DSM-III-R psychiatric disorders in the United States. Results from the National Comorbidity Survey. *Archives of General Psychiatry, 51*, 8–19.

48. Robins, L. N., & Price, R. K. (1991). Adult disorders predicted by childhood conduct problems: Results from the NIMH Epidemiologic Catchment Area project. *Psychiatry, 54*, 116–132.

49. Lewis, C. F. (2010). Childhood antecedents of adult violent offending in a group of female felons. *Behavioral Sciences and the Law, 28*, 224–234.

50. Compson, W. M., Conway, K. P., Stinson, F. S., Colliver, J. D., & Grant, B. F. (2005). Prevalence, correlates, and comorbidity of DSM-IV antisocial personality syndromes and alcohol and specific drug use disorders in the United States: Results from the national epidemiologic survey on alcohol and related conditions. *Journal of Clinical Psychiatry, 66*, 677–685.

51. Black, D. W., Gunter, T., Loveless, P., Allen, J., & Sieleni, B. (2010). Antisocial personality disorder in incarcerated offenders: Psychiatric comorbidity and quality of life. *Annals of Clinical Psychiatry, 22*, 113–120.

52. Mueser, K. T., Crocker, A. G., Frisman, L. B., Drake, R. E., Covell, N. H., & Essock, S. M. (2006). Conduct disorder and antisocial personality disorder in persons with severe psychiatric and substance use disorders. *Schizophrenia Bulletin, 32*, 626–636.

53. Kosson, D., Lorenz, A. R., & Newman, J. P. (2005). Effects of comorbid psychopathy on criminal offending and emotion processing in male offenders with antisocial personality disorder. *Journal of Abnormal Psychology, 115*, 798–806.

54. Walters, G. D., & Knight, R. A. (2010). Antisocial personality disorder with and without antecedent childhood conduct disorder: Does it make a difference? *Journal of Personality Disorders, 24*, 165–178.

55. Walters & Knight (2010).

56. Walters, G. D. (2008). Self-report measures of psychopathy, antisocial personality, and criminal lifestyle: Testing and validating a two-dimensional model. *Criminal Justice and Behavior, 35*, 1459–1483.

57. Walters (2008).

58. Walters, G. D. (2009). Latent structure of a two-dimensional model of antisocial personality disorder: Construct validation and taxometric analysis. *Journal of Personality Disorders, 23*, 647–660.

59. Walters, G. D. (2011). Taking the next step: Combining incrementally valid indicators to improve recidivism prediction. *Assessment, 18*, 227–233.

60. Walters, G. D., Frederick, A. A., & Schlauch, C. (2007). Postdicting arrests for proactive and reactive aggression with the PICTS proactive and reactive scales. *Journal of Interpersonal Violence, 22*, 1415–1430.

61. Walters, G. D. (2007). Measuring proactive and reactive criminal thinking with the PICTS: Correlations with outcome expectancies and hostile attribution biases. *Journal of Interpersonal Violence, 22*, 371–385.

62. Dodge, K. A., & Coie, J. D. (1987). Social-information processing factors in reactive and proactive aggression in children's peer groups. *Journal of Personality and Social Psychology, 53*, 1146–1158.

63. Walters, G. D. (2009). Anger management training in incarcerated male offenders: Differential impact on proactive and reactive criminal thinking. *International Journal of Forensic Mental Health, 8*, 214–217.

64. Walters, G. D. (2012). Substance abuse and criminal thinking: Testing the countervailing, mediation, and specificity hypotheses. *Law and Human Behavior, 36*, 506–512.

65. Cleckley, H. (1976). *The mask of sanity* (5th ed.). St. Louis, MO: Mosby. (Original work published 1941)

66. Hare, R. D. (2003). *The Hare Psychopathy Checklist-Revised manual.* (2nd ed.). Toronto, Canada: Multi-Health Systems.

67. Hare, R. D., Williamson, S. E., & Harpur, T. J. (1988). Psychopathy and language. In T. E. Moffitt & S. A. Mednick (Eds.), *Biological contributions to crime causation* (pp. 68–92). Dordrecht, Netherlands: Nijhoff Martinus.

68. Hare, R. D. (1998). The Hare PCL-R: Some issues concerning its use and misuse. *Legal and Criminological Psychology, 3*, 99–119.

69. Hare (2003).

70. Raine, A. (2002). Annotation: The role of prefrontal deficits, low autonomic arousal, and early health factors in the development of antisocial and aggressive behavior in children. *Journal of Child Psychology and Psychiatry, 43*, 417–434.

71. Blair, R. J. (2006). Subcortical brain systems in psychopathy: The amygdala and associated structures. In C. J. Patrick (Ed.), *Handbook of psychopathy* (pp. 296–312). New York: Guilford.

72. Kiehl, K. A., Smith, A. M., Medrek, A., Forster, B. B., Hare, R. D., & Liddle, P. F. (2004). Temporal lobe abnormalities in semantic processing by criminal psychopaths as revealed by functional magnetic resonance imaging. *Psychiatry Research, 130*, 27–42.

73. Raine, A., & Yang, Y. (2006). The neuroanatomical bases of psychopathy: A review of brain imaging findings. In C. J. Patrick (Ed.), *Handbook of psychopathy* (pp. 278–295). New York: Guilford.

74. Hemphill, J. F., Hare, R. D., & Wong, S. (1998). Psychopathy and recidivism: A review. *Legal and Criminological Psychology, 3*, 141–172.

75. Walters, G. D., Knight, R. A., Grann, M., & Dahle, K.-P. (2008). Incremental validity of the Psychopathy Checklist facet scores: Predicting release outcome in six samples. *Journal of Abnormal Psychology, 117*, 396–405.

76. Skeem, J. L., & Cauffman, E. (2003). Views of the downward extension: Comparing the youth version of the Psychopathy Checklist with the Youth Psychology Trait Inventory. *Behavioral Sciences and the Law, 21*, 737–770.

77. Vitale, J. E., Smith, S. S., Brinkley, C. A., & Newman, J. P. (2002). The reliability and validity of the Psychopathy Checklist-Revised in a sample of female offenders. *Criminal Justice and Behavior, 29*, 202–231.

78. Raine & Yang (2006).

79. Salekin, R. T. (2002). Psychopathy and therapeutic pessimism. Clinical lore or clinical reality? *Clinical Psychology Review, 22*, 79–112.

80. Skeem, J. L., & Cooke, D. J. (2010). Is criminal behavior a central component of psychopathy? Conceptual directions for resolving the debate. *Psychological Assessment, 22*, 433–445.

81. Gottfredson, M. R., & Hirschi, T. (1990). *A general theory of crime.* Stanford, CA; Stanford University Press.

82. Pratt, T. C., & Cullen, F. T. (2000). The empirical status of Gottfredson and Hirschi's general theory of crime: A meta-analysis. *Criminology, 38*, 931–964.

83. Hay, C., & Forrest, W. (2006). The development of self-control: Examining self-control theory's stability thesis. *Criminology, 44*, 739–774.

84. Turner, M. G., & Piquero, A. R. (2002). The stability of self-control. *Journal of Criminal Justice, 30*, 457–471.

85. Andrews, D. A., & Bonta, J. (2003). *The psychology of criminal conduct* (3rd ed.). Cincinnati, OH: Anderson.

86. Beaver, K. M., Wright, J. P., DeLisi, M., & Vaughn, M. G. (2008). Genetic influence on the stability of low self-control: Results from a longitudinal sample of twins. *Journal of Criminal Justice, 36*, 478–485.

87. Pratt, T. C., Turner, M. G., & Piquero, A. R. (2004). Parental socialization and community context: A longitudinal analysis of the structural sources of low self-control. *Journal of Research in Crime and Delinquency, 41*, 219–243.

88. Benson, M. L., & Moore, E. (1992). Are white-collar and common offenders the same? An empirical and theoretical critique of a recently proposed general theory of crime. *Journal of Research in Crime and Delinquency, 29*, 251–272.

89. Chapple, C. L., & Hope, T. L. (2003). An analysis of the self-control and criminal versatility of gang and dating violence offenders. *Violence and Victims, 18*, 671–690.

90. Pratt & Cullen (2000).

91. Akers, R. L., & Sellers, C. S. (2004). *Criminological theories: Introduction, evaluation, and application* (4th ed.). Los Angeles, CA: Roxbury Publishing Company.

92. Grasmick, H. G., Tittle, C. R., Bursick, R. J., & Arneklev, B. J. (1993). Testing the core implications of Gottfreson and Hirschi's general theory of crime. *Journal of Research in Crime and Delinquency, 30*, 5–29.

93. Gottfredson & Hirschi (1990).

94. Perrone, D., Sullivan, C. J., Pratt, T. C., & Margaryan, S. (2004). Parental efficacy, self-control, and delinquency: A test of a general theory of crime on a nationally representative sample of youth. *International Journal of Offender Therapy and Comparative Criminology, 48*, 298–312.

95. Moffitt, T. E. (1993). Adolescence-limited and life-course-persistent antisocial behavior: A developmental taxonomy. *Psychological Review, 100*, 674–701.

96. Van Dulmen, M., Goncy, E., Vest, A., & Flannery, D. (2009). Group-based trajectory modeling of externalizing behavior problems from childhood through adulthood: Exploring discrepancies in the empirical findings. In J. Savage (Ed.). *The development of persistent criminality* (pp. 288–314). New York: Oxford University Press.

97. Barnes, J. C., Beaver, K. M., & Boutwell, B. B. (2011). Examining the genetic underpinnings to Moffitt's developmental taxonomy: A behavioral genetic analysis. *Criminology, 49*, 923–954.

98. Mazerolle, P., & Maahs, J. (2002). *Developmental theory and battery incidents: Examining the relationship between discrete offender groups and intimate partner violence* (Final report). Washington, DC: Office of Justice Programs.

99. Moffitt, T. E., & Caspi, A. (2001). Childhood predictors differentiate life-course persistent and adolescence-limited pathways among males and females. *Development and Psychopathology, 13*, 355–375.

100. Piquero, A. R., Brame, R., & Lynam, D. (2004). Studying criminal career length through early adulthood among serious offenders. *Crime and Delinquency, 50*, 412–435.

101. Piquero, A. R., Daigle, L. E., Gibson, C., Piquero, N. L., & Tibbetts, S. G. (2007). Are life-course-persistent offenders at risk for adverse health outcomes? *Journal of Research in Crime and Delinquency, 44*, 185–207.

102. Juvonen, J., & Ho, A. Y. (2008). Social motives underlying antisocial behavior across middle school grades. *Journal of Youth and Adolescence, 37*, 749–756.

103. Vaughn, M. G., & DeLisi, M. (2008). Were Wolfgang's chronic offenders psychopaths? On the convergent validity between psychopathy and career criminality. *Journal of Criminal Justice, 36*, 33–42.

104. Wolfgang, M. E., Figlio, R., & Sellin, T. (1972). *Delinquency in a birth cohort*. Chicago, IL: University of Chicago Press.

105. Walters, G. D. (2011). The latent structure of life-course-persistent antisocial behavior: Is Moffitt's developmental taxonomy a true taxonomy? *Journal of Consulting and Clinical Psychology, 79*, 96–105.

106. Walters, G. D., & Ruscio, J. (in press). Trajectories of youthful antisocial behavior: Categories or continua? *Journal of Abnormal Child Psychology.*

107. Sampson, R. J., & Laub, J. H. (1993). *Crime in the making*. Cambridge, MA: Harvard University Press.

108. Doherty, E. E. (2006). Self-control, social bonds, and desistance: A test of life-course interdependence. *Criminology, 44*, 807–833.

109. Eggleston, D. E. (2006). Self-control, social bonds and desistance: A test of life-course interdependence. *Criminology, 44*, 807–833.

110. Sampson, R. J., Laub, J. H., & Wimer, C. (2006). Does marriage reduce crime? A counterfactual approach to within-individual causal effects. *Criminology, 44,* 465–508.

111. Laub, J. H., & Sampson, R. J. (2003). *Shared beginnings, divergent lives: Delinquent boys to age 70.* Cambridge, MA: Harvard University Press.

112. Schroeder, R. D., Giordano, P. C., & Cernkovich, S. A. (2007). Drug use and desistance processes. *Criminology, 45,* 191–222.

113. Benda, B. (2002). A test of three competing theoretical models of delinquency using structured equation modeling. *Journal of Social Science Research, 29,* 55–91.

114. McGuire, D. (2002). Cumulative disadvantage as an explanation for observed disproportionality within the juvenile justice system: An empirical test. *Juvenile and Family Court Journal, 53,* 1–17.

115. Hirschi, T. (1969). *Causes of delinquency.* Berkeley: University of California Press.

116. Glueck, S., & Glueck, E. (1968). *Delinquents and nondelinquents in perspective.* Cambridge, MA: Harvard University Press.

117. Sampson, R. J., & Laub, J. H. (2005). A life-course view of the development of crime. *Annals of the American Academy of Political and Social Science, 602,* 12–45.

118. Giordano, P. C., Cernkovich, S. A., & Rudolph, J. L. (2002). Gender, crime, and desistance: Toward a theory of cognitive transformation. *American Journal of Sociology, 107,* 990–1064.

119. Beaver, K. M., & Wright, J. P. (2005). Biosocial development and delinquent involvement. *Youth Violence and Juvenile Justice, 3,* 168–192.

120. DeLisi, M., Wright, J. P., Beaver, K., & Vaughn, M. G. (2011). Teaching biosocial criminology I: Understanding endophenotypes using Gottfredson and Hirachi's self-control construct. *Journal of Criminal Justice Education, 22,* 360–376.

121. Beaver et al. (2008).

122. Beaver, K. M., Gibson, C. L., Turner, M. G., DeLisi, M., Vaughn, M. G., & Holand, A. (2010). Stability of delinquent peer associations: A biosocial test of Warr's sticky-friends hypothesis. *Crime and Delinquency, 57,* 907–927.

123. Beaver, K. M., Gibson, C. L., DeLisi, M., Vaughn, M. G., & Wright, P. J. (2011). The interaction between neighborhood disadvantage and genetic factors in the prediction of antisocial outcomes. *Youth Violence and Juvenile Justice, 10,* 25–40.

124. DeLisi, M., Beaver, K. M., Vaughn, M. G., & Wright, J. P. (2009). All in the family: Gene x environment interaction between DRD2 and criminal father is associated with five antisocial phenotypes. *Criminal Justice and Behavior, 36,* 1187–1197.

125. Vaughn, M. G., Beaver, K. M., DeLisi, M., Perron, B. E., & Schelbe, L. (2009). Gene-environment interplay and the importance of self-control in predicting polydrug use and substance related problems. *Addictive Behaviors, 34,* 112–116.

126. Walters, G. D. (1992). A meta-analysis of the gene-crime relationship. *Criminology, 30,* 595–613.

127. Akers, R. L. (2001). Social learning theory. In R. Paternoster & R. Bachman (Eds.), *Explaining criminals and crime: Essays in contemporary criminological theory* (pp. 192–210). Los Angeles, CA: Roxbury.

128. Pratt, T. C., Cullen, F. T., Sellers, C. S., Winfree, T., Madensen, T. D., Daigle, L. E., et al. (2010). The empirical status of social learning theory: A meta-analysis. *Justice Quarterly, 27,* 765–802.

129. Pratt & Cullen (2000).

130. Pratt, T. C., Cullen, F. T., Blevins, K. R., Daigle, L. E., & Madensen, T. D. (2006). The empirical status of deterrence theory: A meta-analysis. In F. T. Cullen, J. P. Wright, & K. R. Blevins (Vol. Eds.), *Taking stock: The status of criminological theory—Advances in criminological theory* (Vol. 15, pp. 367–396). New Brunswick, NJ: Transaction.

131. Haynie, D. L., & Osgood, D. W. (2005). Reconsidering peers and delinquency: How do peers matter? *Social Forces, 84,* 1109–1130.

132. Cloward, R., & Ohlin, L. (1960). *Delinquency and opportunity: A theory of delinquent gangs.* Glencoe, IL: Free Press.

DRUG–CRIME RELATIONSHIPS

Up to this point, the focus has either been on drugs *or* crime. In this chapter the focus shifts to drugs *and* crime. From the research reviewed thus far, there can be little doubt that drugs and crime are related.[1] The present chapter asks a different question: how are drugs and crime related? There appear to be three major possibilities: (1) drug–crime relationships are noncausal and the result of each variable's common association with some third variable; (2) drug–crime relationships are unidirectional to the extent that drug use causes crime or crime causes drug use; (3) drug–crime relationships are bidirectional in the sense that drug abuse and crime are both a cause and effect of each other. This chapter is consequently organized around the following four objectives:

- Evaluate third-variable explanations of drug–crime relationships
- Explore the two primary unidirectional explanations of drug–crime relationships (drug use as a cause of crime and crime as a cause of drug use)
- Examine major bidirectional explanations of drug–crime relationships
- Appreciate the complexity of drug–crime relationships

Third-Variable Explanations of Drug–Crime Relationships

Third-variable or **epiphenomenal** (a phenomenon that accompanies and is caused by another phenomenon) explanations of drug–crime relationships assume that any connection observed between drugs and crime is illusory, spurious, and noncausal. In other words, drugs and crime are connected, not because one causes the other or both are part of a reciprocal causal network, but because both correlate with the same third variable. Hence, drugs and crime are not causally connected but rather spuriously connected by virtue of their common or mutual association with a third variable (see **Figure 4-1**). Several different **third-variable explanations** have been offered in an attempt to account for drug–crime relationships. Six of these explanations are examined in this section: parallel developmental processes, age, general deviance, low self-control, societal labeling, and response styles.

Parallel Developmental Processes

In a survey of inner-city youth, Fagan, Weis, and Cheng ascertained that serious substance abuse was more prevalent and frequent in youth who engaged in serious acts of delinquency but that serious substance abuse was generally high regardless of the youth's level of delinquency. On the basis of these results, Fagan et al. concluded that substance abuse and delinquency, rather than being causally connected, were artificially linked by a third variable. The third variable in this case was a developmental process in which substance abuse and crime are embedded in parallel, yet independent, social networks.[2] Ford uncovered partial support for the argument that **parallel developmental processes** between crime and drug abuse account for drug–crime connections.[3]

Figure 4-1
Schematic diagram of the epiphenomenal view of drug–crime relationships.

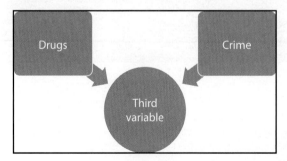

Age

Age is another third variable potentially capable of supporting an epiphenomenal explanation of the drug–crime relationship based on the fact that the age–drug and age–crime curves are similar. It is an established fact that young people use more drugs and commit more crime than older adults. Research confirms that drug use and crime both peak during the adolescent years and then drop off dramatically from there.[4] Plotting curves with data from the second wave of the Adolescent Health sample, it can be seen that whereas both crime (shoplifting, burglary) and drug use (heavy drinking, marijuana use) peaked during adolescence, crime tended to peak about 4 years earlier than drug use (see **Figure 4-2**).[5] In addition, Corwyn and Benda discovered that although age partially moderated the overlap between drug use and crime in a large sample of adolescents, it did not fully account for the overlap.[6] Therefore, similarities in the age–crime and age–drug curves may explain a portion of the overlap between drugs and crime, but this still leaves the majority of overlap unexplained.

General Deviance

General deviance is yet another candidate for the third variable in an epiphenomenal model of drug–crime relationships. Nearly 40 years ago, Richard and Shirley Jessor proposed a general deviance syndrome in which drugs, crime, and several other deviant behaviors were viewed to be components of a latent construct they called general deviance (see **Figure 4-3**).[7] General deviance theory has received its share of support in studies on adolescent criminality and alcohol use.[8–10] Marc LeBlanc and Stéphane Girard conducted a series of factor analyses on two separate cohorts of Canadian respondents and found consistent support for a large first factor (general deviance) on which all six deviant behaviors (vandalism, school and family rebellion, minor theft, serious theft, aggression, drug use) loaded.[11] General deviance may not account for every instance of drug–crime overlap, but it would appear to be a viable explanation under some circumstances.

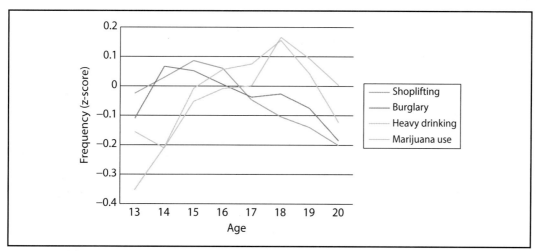

Figure 4-2
Age relationships for two crimes (shoplifting and burglary) and two drug use behaviors (heavy drinking and marijuana use).

Data From: Created from data from Wave 2 of the Add Health sample; Udry, J. R. (2003). *The National Longitudinal Study of Adolescent Health (Add Health)*. Chapel Hill, NC: Carolina Population Center, University of North Carolina.

Figure 4-3
Elements of the
General Deviance
Syndrome.

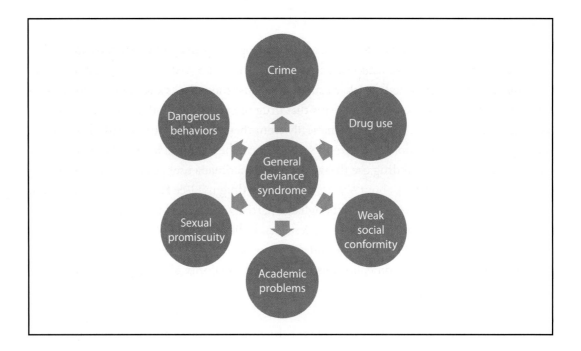

Low Self-Control

In presenting their general theory of crime, Gottfredson and Hirschi advance a propensity theory of crime and a third-variable explanation for the drug–crime relationship. Gottfredson and Hirschi contend that the drug–crime connection is **spurious** rather than causal, the result of a third variable. The third variable in this case is low self-control.[12] Studying drug abuse and crime in 317 adolescent male offenders, Bradley Connor, Judith Stein, and Douglas Longshore determined that only a multidimensional model, in which the six core elements of the self-control construct served as separate dimensions, effectively predicted drug abuse and crime. As shown in **Table 4-1**, only two of the dimensions (impulsivity, volatile temper) effectively predicted drug abuse and only three of the dimensions (physical activity, risk taking, volatile temper) effectively predicted crime.[13] Therefore, although low self-control, like age and general deviance, may explain a portion of the overlap between drugs and crime it is not a complete explanation for drug–crime relationships.

Table 4-1 Components of Self-Control as Predictors of Drug Use and Crime in a Sample of 317 Juvenile Male Offenders.

Component	Drug Use	Property Crime	Violent Crime
Impulsiveness	**.18**	.13	.07
Physical Activity	-.05	.13	.12
Risk Taking	.08	**.25**	**.19**
Self-Centeredness	.05	.10	.08
Simple Tasks	.06	.04	.09
Volatile Temper	.13	**.21**	**.18**

Note: red = $p < .05$, bolded red = $p < .01$
Data From: Connor, B., T., Stein, J. A., & Longshore, D. (2009). Examining self-control as a multidimensional predictor of crime and drug use in adolescents with criminal histories. *Journal of Behavioral Health Services and Research, 36*, 137–149.

Societal Labeling

Often, the same individual is labeled a drug addict and a criminal. Lack of social and political power makes such individuals open targets for negative societal labeling.[14] The fact that the same individuals tend to be labeled drug addicts and criminals could inflate the correlation between drugs and crime and serve as the third variable in an epiphenomenal theory of drug–crime relationships. The deleterious effects of **labeling** could further inflate the overlap between drugs and crime by establishing a self-fulfilling prophesy capable of leading drug users to consume more drugs and criminals to commit more crime and cut off potential avenues of correction and change.[15]

Response Style

Many of the studies that have been cited as evidence for the existence of a drug–crime connection have measured the incidence and/or frequency of drug use and crime with self-report measures. Given the fact that self-report measures can be influenced by the **response style** or test-taking set of the person completing the survey or taking the test it is possible that a portion of the variance in drug–crime relationships is a consequence of certain response styles.[16] An overly defensive individual will tend to deny past drug use as well as past criminality; an acquiescent individual will tend to acknowledge both past drug use and past criminality. The result in both cases would be an elevated correlation between drugs and crime, complements of the epiphenomenal effect of the individual's test-taking response style.

Of the six theories of drug abuse (Disease Model, Unified Biosocial, Cross-Cultural, Self-Medication, Gateway Theory, Social Learning) and of the six theories of crime (Psychopathy, Low Self-Control, Developmental Taxonomy, Age-Graded, Biosocial Theory, Social Learning), four seem to propose an epiphenomenal explanation for drug–crime relationships. Of the drug abuse theories, the unified biosocial model and self-medication hypothesis provide the best examples of third-variable theories of drug–crime overlap. Whereas Cloninger would appear to hold novelty seeking responsible for the drug–crime connection in his unified biosocial model, self-medication theorists apparently treat psychological problems as the third variable in their epiphenomenal explanation of the overlap between drugs and crime. Of the crime theories, Gottfredson and Hirschi's general theory of crime and Moffitt's developmental taxonomy offer the best examples of epiphenomenal accounts of the drug–crime nexus. As previously mentioned, Gottfredson and Hirschi contend that **low self-control** is primarily responsible for the drug–crime connection, whereas Moffitt seems to view early developmental problems and concerns as the third variable in an epiphenomenal model linking delinquency to drug abuse.

Unidirectional Explanations of Drug–Crime Relationships

Third-variable explanations of drug–crime relationships assume that the drug–crime connection is spurious and fully accounted for by one or more third variables. As such, they are not required to show evidence of a directional relationship between drugs and crime. The same cannot be said of **unidirectional** (one direction) and **bidirectional** (two directions) explanations of drug–crime connections. Because they assume that drugs and crime form a causal nexus (either drugs cause crime, crime causes drugs, or drugs and crime cause each other) they are obligated to demonstrate a **temporal order** or directional relationship over time. Hence, if drug use causes crime then drug use should precede crime and if crime causes drug use then crime should precede drug use. It therefore follows that whereas third-variable explanations can use **cross-sectional designs** (data collected at a single point in time) to statistically demonstrate that drugs and crime are connected solely by their common association with a third variable, unidirectional and bidirectional explanations must make use of longitudinal designs, whereby data are collected at several different points in time.

Theorists who favor third-variable explanations of drug–crime relationships are often critical of longitudinal designs, calling them expensive and unnecessary.[17] Longitudinal studies are a must, however, for theorists advancing unidirectional or bidirectional explanations of drug–crime relationships. Without them, a **causal relationship** cannot be established. There are three conditions that must be satisfied before one can make a causal statement. First, the variables, in this case, drug use and crime, must be correlated. Second, temporal order must be established such that the putative causal variable appears before the putative effect variable. Third, viable alternate explanations should be tested and ruled out. The third condition (i.e., ruling out viable alternate explanations) is an ongoing process but the second condition (i.e., temporal ordering) requires a longitudinal design. In this section we examine two simple unidirectional models of drug–crime association (drug use causes crime and crime causes drug use); this is followed by a section on the more intricate bidirectional or **reciprocal effects** model.

The structure for this section comes from the pioneering work of Paul Goldstein, who developed a tripartite system to explain drug-related crime. In Goldstein's model, three mechanisms are held to be responsible for drug–crime relationships: a **psychopharmacological** mechanism, an economic-compulsive mechanism, and a **systemic** mechanism. Psychopharmacological mechanisms encompass the direct effects of a drug on the emotions, thinking, and behavior of the individual. Economic-compulsive mechanisms, on the other hand, play an indirect causal role by encouraging individuals to rob and steal in order to get money to pay for their drugs. Systemic mechanisms involve a combination of direct and indirect causal effects created by means of a drug user's contact with the illicit supply system.[18] Trevor Bennett and Katy Holloway investigated Goldstein's model and extended it to situations in which crime might be considered a cause of drug use.[19]

Drug Use Causes Crime

Newcomb and McGee determined that early alcohol use predicted later delinquency in both male and female offenders but that early delinquency had no bearing on later alcohol use.[20] Judith Brook and colleagues likewise found that illegal drug use in early adolescence effectively predicted delinquency in later adolescence and adulthood.[21] These results are somewhat anomalous, however, in that most studies indicate that minor delinquency precedes a person's initial use of drugs. These same studies also denote that drug use, once initiated, can have a powerful facilitative effect on more serious forms of criminality.[22–24] This would seem to suggest that in some cases, given the right circumstances, drug use and abuse can cause crime. This relationship is highlighted in News Spot 4-1, after which the three ways Goldstein believed drug use and abuse cause crime are discussed.[25]

Title: Chief: Drugs Drive City's Rising Crime Rate
Source: *The Galax (VA) Gazette*
Author: April Wright
Date: February 22, 2012

Drugs continue to be the motivating factor in the increase of property and violent crimes in the city, Galax Police Chief Rick Clark told Galax City Council on Feb. 13.

During 2011, the Galax Police Department recorded 1,375 crimes, compared to 1,242 in 2010 a 10.7% increase.

"Many are using burglary to feed their drug habit," said Clark.

The police department recorded 18,951 calls for service last year, an 18.7% increase from 15,965 in 2010.

Over the past couple of years, the city has experienced an increase in robbery, aggravated assault, simple assault, shoplifting, larceny, forgery, credit card fraud, embezzlement, vandalism, and drug offenses.

In 2010, 775 arrests were made, compared to 712 arrests in 2011.

The department recorded 70 drug arrests last year. The Twin County Drug Task Force investigated 119 drug offenses committed by 80 offenders.

Of these drug offenses, 61 offenders were prosecuted in Grayson and Carroll circuit courts; and 19 were prosecuted in federal court.

Galax police officers were involved in the investigation of 189 drug offenses and arrests of 150 individuals in 2010.

Questions to Ponder
1. **How does a 10.7% increase in crime compare to national trends?**
2. **Do you agree with the police chief that drugs are fueling this rise in crime?**
3. **If drugs are fueling a crime rise in this city, what can be done to rectify the situation?**

Psychopharmacological Mechanism: Stimulating Violence

One way drug use can cause crime is by adversely affecting a person's mood, judgment, or capacity for self-control. There is a well-documented link between alcohol consumption and violence but it is uncertain how well this link extends to illegal drugs.[26] Early research found illegal drug use to be either unrelated or negatively related to violence.[27–28] Using data from the **ADAM II** project, Carole Barnes and Bruce Taylor discovered that heavy drinking correlated significantly with arrests for domestic violence, but that there was no relationship between illegal drug use and domestic violence. In fact, the greatest proportion of domestic violence arrests occurred in arrestees who reported heavy alcohol use but did not test positive for illegal drugs.[29] The results of several other studies, nevertheless, suggest that illegal drug use may play a role in violence. Valdez, Kaplan, and Cepeda, for instance, determined that drug use interacted with various individual and situational factors to increase violence in Mexican-American gang members.[30] Likewise, Fernández-Montalvo and colleagues ascertained that 40% of a group of 252 substance abuse patients reported problems with violence.[31] However, because the data for these two studies were collected cross-sectionally, it was not possible to test temporal ordering. In fact, whereas there is clear evidence of a relationship between drugs and violence, the only causal connection that has been documented is the one between alcohol and violent behavior.[32]

Economic-Compulsive Mechanism: Drugs and Property Crime

Given the high cost of some illegal drugs, it makes sense that some users might commit economically oriented crime in order to pay for their drugs. Longitudinal studies conducted on heroin addicts living in Baltimore,[33] Harlem,[34] California,[35] and Great Britain[36] showed that economically oriented crime was most common during periods of heavy drug usage. Twenty percent of the heroin and cocaine users interviewed at the Manhattan site of the **Drug Use Forecasting** (DUF) study indicated that they supported their drug habit exclusively with illegal money, whereas 55% reported no illegal income at all. The rest of the participants in this study supported themselves with a combination of legal and illegal money. It would seem likely, then, that although heroin and cocaine users frequently commit crimes to support their habits, their income is based as much on legal sources of income as it is on illegal sources of income (see **Figure 4-4**).[37]

Figure 4-4
Sources of monthly income for DUF participants in Manhattan, New York.

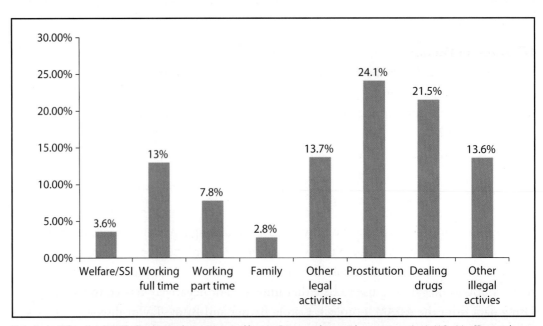

Data From: Riley, K. J. (1997). *Crack, powder cocaine, and heroin: Drug purchase and use patterns in six U.S. cities* [Research Report]. Washington, DC: National Institute of Justice.

Systemic Mechanism: Exposure to the Illicit Supply System

The regular use of drugs can bring a user into contact with the illicit drug supply system. Philip Bean and Christine Wilkinson interviewed a small group of heroin, cocaine, and intravenous amphetamine users in the greater Nottingham (England) area and discovered that nearly all had a history of criminal involvement. Over 90% of the sample reported at least one prior felony conviction and over 60% acknowledged participating in crime in the last 6 months. Whereas Bean and Wilkinson found little evidence that drug use directly caused crime or that crime directly caused drug use, they did garner support for the hypothesis that contact with the illicit drug supply system led to increased criminal involvement, not only with respect to drug transactions but also with respect to other crimes (theft, stolen property) committed within the context of a drug transaction. Participants who were receiving treatment (scripts for methadone maintenance) were just as likely to be involved in the **illicit supply system** as participants not receiving treatment (see **Figure 4-5**).[38]

Contact with the illicit supply system not only increases opportunities for crime but also encourages a subtle and gradual erosion of a person's respect for the law. Daily interactions with habitual lawbreakers, from whom the drug user purchases illegal substances, can lead to the formation of antisocial attitudes and criminal thinking in users. **Differential association** theory posits that associating with criminal offenders is one of the primary means by which criminal attitudes and beliefs are transmitted to nonoffenders. In a series of classic studies conducted in the 1970s, Don Andrews and colleagues discovered that community volunteers who participated in group discussions with young offenders became more accepting of rule violations and more criminal in their attitudes as a consequence of their exposure to the attitudes and beliefs of the criminal offenders with whom they met weekly.[39] If previously unaffiliated community residents are affected by associating with offenders, then individuals who rely on criminals to supply them with drugs are most assuredly affected as well.

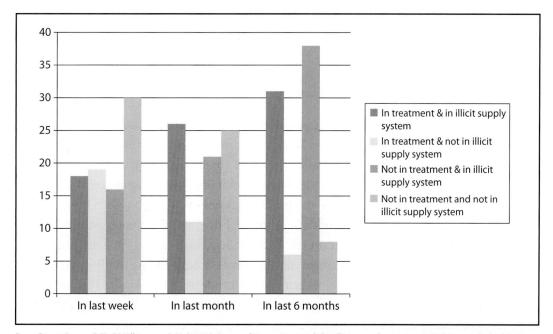

Figure 4-5
Number of drug users involved and not involved in the illicit supply system in last week, last month, and last 6 months, by treatment status.

Data From: Bean , P. T., & Wilkinson, C. K. (1988). Drug taking, crime and the illicit supply system. *British Journal of Addiction, 83*, 533–539.

Crime Causes Drug Use

Just as drug use can cause crime, so too can crime cause drug use. In terms of the temporal order between initial crime and initial drug use, research is fairly consistent in showing that crime normally precedes drug use rather than the other way around.[40–44] Using a Markov chain model to analyze the crime- and drug-related activities of 431 high-rate offenders in Philadelphia, Leon Pettiway and colleagues found that crime-related activities were significantly more apt to lead to drug use than drug-related activities were to culminate in crime.[45] Using a matched sample that controlled for individual differences in the propensity for deviance, Elaine Doherty, Kerry Green, and Margaret Ensminger determined that serious adolescent delinquency often preceded the onset of marijuana and cocaine use. These results are consistent with a crime causing drug use explanation of the drugs–crime connection but are inconsistent with popular third-variable explanations that posit general deviance or low self-control as the sole cause of this relationship.[46] Three of the more likely scenarios in which crime may cause drug use, based again on Goldstein's tripartite system, are described next.

Psychopharmacological Mechanism: Chemical Courage

Many offenders are apprehensive about breaking into a house or robbing someone. Drugs can facilitate the criminal act by reducing the actor's fear or anxiety. Walters describes cutoff as a psychological process whereby the individual uses a word or phrase, like "fuck it," to eliminate deterrents to crime.[47] Drugs can also serve as a cutoff. Alcohol has been known to increase "false courage" and lead to violent confrontations, heroin is capable of calming one's "nerves" before a robbery, and cocaine can sharpen attention and promote a sense of invulnerability prior to breaking into a home or building. Burglars have been known to use alcohol and other drugs as a crime lubricant prior to committing a property crime.[48] Drugs do not normally make someone a more efficient criminal—in fact, the exact opposite is probably more often the case—yet when used as a cutoff they provide the individual with a false sense of confidence, which in the end probably increases their chances of both committing the crime and getting caught.

Economic/Compulsive Mechanism: Chemical Celebration

Following a successful criminal venture, many criminals celebrate. The celebration often includes alcohol and drugs, among other things. This is another mechanism by which crime causes drug use.[49] Likewise, a bonanza of illegal funds obtained through one's involvement in a financially successful crime can also lead to a substantial rise in drug usage. Many heroin addicts maintain themselves on low-moderate doses of opiates but then dramatically augment their usage, as well as their odds of overdose, once money becomes available, as would be the case following a significant rise in their illegal income. Uggen and Thompson note that drug users increase and decrease the amount of drugs they use in direct proportion to the rising and falling fortunes of their criminal endeavors.[50] A windfall of money achieved by way of a successful criminal venture is not unlike winning the lottery for some drug-using offenders (see News Spot 4-2).

Title: Why Winning the Lotto Should Carry a Health Warning
Source: *Irish Independent (Ireland)*
Author: None Indicated
Date: July 28, 2009

Could winning the lottery be bad for you? If you find it hard to resist temptation, the answer, it seems, is a definite "yes." In a survey of jackpot scoopers, researchers have found overnight wealth can lead to long-term health problems—largely as a consequence of reckless overpartying as the new minted millionaires embrace a champagne and cigars lifestyle.

So common is the phenomenon of Lottery winners cavorting their way to an early grave, economists have even coined a term for it: "positive income shock."

In simple English this means that, with an unlimited fortune suddenly at their disposal, people have a tendency to kick back and live the good life—no matter that the good life may actually exact a costly toll on their health….

Consider the case of infamous "Lotto Lout" Michael Carroll. Former bin-man Carroll won the equivalent of €12m in 2002 and immediately embarked on a two-year binge—a life of wanton overindulgence that quickly turned self-destructive.

Writing in his autobiography, Carroll describes scenes of all-night partying that would have made an attendee at a Roman orgy blush.

"Almost every night and most afternoons we had the wildest parties," he recalled. "It was full of my mates, women, drink and drugs. We would act like Roman generals. We had sword fights with real swords and drank ourselves into a stupor. The girls would be bed-hopping round the house. We would treat them like servants and they loved it. They served us cocaine on silver platters."

The wheels finally came off in 2004 when he was sent to prison having failed to comply with a drug treatment order. He was jailed a second time after going on the rampage with a baseball bat at a music festival. Clearly Carroll was an unstable personality—which raises the question of whether he would have ended up behind bars regardless of his financial status?

We'll never know. One thing's for sure, however: wealth didn't solve his problems, but merely exacerbated them.

Questions to Ponder

1. **How does gaining newfound wealth through crime compare to winning the lotto?**

(continued)

2. **Why do some people act so irresponsibly after they acquire a lot of money quickly?**
3. **Do you think Michael Carroll would have ended up in jail even if he hadn't won the lotto?**

Systemic Mechanism: Inhibition of the Maturing Out Process

In 1962, Charles Winick published the results of his classic analysis of records from the U.S. Public Health Service Hospital in Lexington, Kentucky. Based on his findings, he concluded that even with a higher than normal rate of death among drug addicts, most of these individuals became abstinent between the ages of 23 and 37. He attributed this to a "maturing out" process, whereby the negative aspects of the drug lifestyle gradually begin to outweigh the positive aspects and the individual starts integrating into conventional society by way of marriage and the job market (see **Figure 4-6**).[51] Douglas Anglin and colleagues discovered that the **maturing out** of drug use was inhibited by continued involvement in crime and drug dealing.[52] By the same token, continued drug usage has been shown to retard and inhibit the natural maturing out of crime that occurs, even in most habitual offenders, during the fourth decade of life.[53] Both effects have been observed in more recent investigations on the maturing out of drug and maturing out of crime processes.[54–55]

Figure 4-6
The maturing out process as reflected in changes in the frequency of drug use in heavy drug users over time.

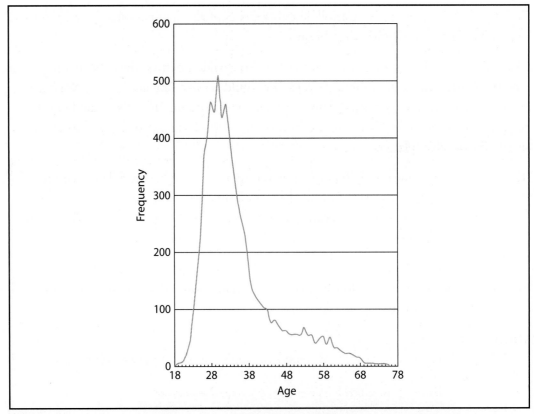

From *U.S. Bulletin on Narcotics*. Maturing out of narcotic addiction. by Winick, C. 14, 1-7. © 1962 United Nations. Reprinted with permission of the United Nations.

The two most common drug–crime connections observed in the Bennett and Holloway study were the drug causing crime psychopharmacological and drug causing crime **economic-compulsive** mechanisms, but all six mechanisms were reported by at least some of the drug users participating in this study (see **Figure 4-7**). Unidirectional explanations of drug–crime relationships would appear to be time limited in that they often become bidirectional when examined over a long enough period of time.[56–57] In fact, only 2 of the 12 theories mentioned earlier hold consistently to a unidirectional explanation of the drug–crime nexus. The Disease model of addiction appears committed to a unidirectional explanation of drug–crime relationships implicating drug use as the cause of crime in the sense that the disease of addiction is considered the primary problem and all other behaviors, including crime, are a consequence of this primary disease. Of the six crime theories, Hare's psychopathy model would appear to come closest to a crime as the cause of drug use explanation of the drug–crime connection, at least for individuals diagnosed with psychopathic personality disorder.

Bidirectional Explanations of Drug–Crime Relationships

Richard Hammersley and Valerie Morrison conducted a series of structured interviews with 28 active heroin users to determine whether drugs and crime were reciprocally related. The results indicated that heroin use and crime not only interacted with one another, but appeared to form reciprocal relationships that varied in direction and intensity with the introduction of additional drugs of abuse.[58] In a further test of the reciprocal hypothesis, Brook, Whiteman, and Finch examined drug–crime relationships in a three-wave longitudinal panel study. Intercorrelations between early childhood aggression, early and later adolescent delinquency, and early and later adolescent drug use revealed that early childhood aggression (Wave 1: ages 5–10) predicted adolescent drug use and delinquency, and that early adolescent drug use (Wave 2: ages 13–18) correlated with early adolescent delinquency and predicted later drug use and delinquency (Wave 3: ages 15–20).[59] David and Judith Brook, along with several colleagues, discovered that **externalization** or conduct disorder

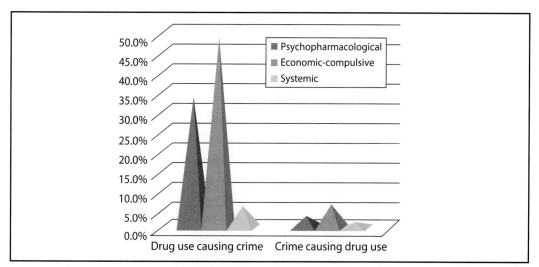

Figure 4-7
Drug–crime relationships reported by 41 English prisoners.

Data From: Bennett, T., & Holloway, K. (2009). The causal connection between drug misuse and crime. *British Journal of Criminology, 49*, 513–531.

problems often preceded illicit drug use but illicit drug use did a better job than early externalization problems of predicting future violent behavior.[60]

A team of researchers under the direction of Alex Mason investigated bidirectional interpretations of drug–crime relationships. Two of their studies have produced outcomes that are particularly relevant to the current discussion. Based on the results of a 2002 study, Mason and Windle concluded that a bidirectional relationship exists for drug use and crime in boys but not in girls. They also observed a small but consistent effect of delinquency on subsequent drug use and a larger but less consistent effect of drug use on subsequent delinquency.[61] In a 2007 study, Mason, Hitchings, McMahon, and Spoth observed both direct and indirect effects of delinquency on alcohol use and later problem drinking. The indirect effect was mediated by peer drug use. Hence, individuals who engaged in delinquency often associated with peers who committed crimes and used drugs. It was the differential association of these individuals with antisocial and drug using peers, coupled with past delinquency, that increased their odds of having a future drinking problem.[62]

Recruiting participants from the Los Angeles juvenile probation department, Elizabeth D'Amico and colleagues conducted a four-wave longitudinal panel study on the relationship between substance use and crime. Controlling for age, gender, ethnicity, and time spent in a controlled environment, these authors observed significant cross-lag correlations between substance use (at an earlier wave) and crime (at a later wave) and between crime (at an earlier wave) and substance use (at a later wave) across all three crime categories examined (i.e., violent, property, and drug). The results revealed a stable reciprocal relationship between substance use and crime across the four waves of the study, although it should be kept in mind that the entire study took only 12 months to complete. D'Amico et al. discuss how the bidirectional relationship between drug use and crime forms a cycle of mutual reinforcement. To break free of this cycle the individual, with support from family members and people in the community, must stop using drugs and committing crime. This is easier said than done because of the insidious nature of drug–crime relationships.[63]

Thornberry's Interactional Theory

Terence Thornberry developed an **interactional theory** of crime that may have something to contribute to our understanding of bidirectional or reciprocal relationships between drugs and crime. In his interactional theory of crime, Thornberry maintains that attachment to parents, belief in conventional values, commitment to school, commitment to family, commitment to conventional activities, delinquent values, delinquent peer associations, and delinquent behavior form a system of interacting reciprocal and bidirectional effects.[64] This model could easily accommodate the drug–crime relationship in that drug use has been found to interact with some of these same variables, especially delinquent peer associations, delinquent values, weak commitment to school, and weak family ties. A particularly useful feature of Thornberry's theory is the proposition that these reciprocal relationships change over time and have a tendency to gain strength as the individual moves from early adolescence, to middle adolescence, to late adolescence (see **Figures 4-8** to **4-10**).

Several empirical tests have been conducted on Thornberry's interactional theory. Using data from the first three waves of the Rochester Youth Development Study, Thornberry and colleagues discovered several complex bidirectional relationships between delinquency and social bonding. Whereas a weak family or school bond correlated with subsequent delinquency, delinquency weakened the bonds further. This supports the interactional prediction that bonding and delinquency are reciprocally related.[65] Krohn, Lizotte, Thornberry, Smith, and McDowall applied interactional theory to drug use in a five-wave longitudinal study of high-risk youth. Results indicated that peer drug use and beliefs about drugs were both reciprocally related to drug consumption. In this study, drug consumption had a slightly stronger effect on peer drug use than peer drug use had on drug consumption and drug consumption had a significantly stronger effect on beliefs about drugs than beliefs about drugs had on drug consumption. In addition, the impact of peer drug use on beliefs about

Association with delinquent peers ↔ Delinquent behavior

Attachment to parents ↔ Commitment to school

Attachment to parents ↔ Delinquent behavior

Commitment to school ↔ Delinquent behavior

Commitment to school ↔ Delinquent peer associations

Data From: Thornberry, T. P. (1987). Toward an interactional theory of delinquency. *Criminology, 25*, 863–891.

Figure 4-8 Strong (orange) and weak (black) reciprocal relationships proposed by Thornberry during early adolescence.

Delinquent peer associations ↔ Delinquent behavior

Delinquent peer associations ↔ Delinquent values

Delinquent values ↔ Delinquent behavior

Belief in conventional values ↔ Commitment to school

Commitment to school ↔ Delinquent behavior

Commitment to school ↔ Delinquent peer associations

Data From: Thornberry, T. P. (1987). Toward an interactional theory of delinquency. *Criminology, 25*, 863–891.

Figure 4-9 Strong (orange) and weak (black) reciprocal relationships proposed by Thornberry during middle adolescence.

Delinquent peer associations ↔ Delinquent behavior

Delinquent peer associations ↔ Delinquent values

Delinquent values ↔ Delinquent behavior

Belief in conventional values ↔ Commitment to conventional activity

Belief in conventional values ↔ Commitment to family

Commitment to conventional activity ↔ Delinquent behavior

Data From: Thornberry, T. P. (1987). Toward an interactional theory of delinquency. *Criminology, 25*, 863–891.

Figure 4-10 Strong (orange) and weak (black) reciprocal relationships proposed by Thornberry during late adolescence.

drugs was stronger during later waves of this longitudinal study than during earlier waves.[66] The interactional model appears capable of explaining drug use and crime separately but research is required to determine how well it explains drug–crime relationships.

Walters' Overlapping Lifestyles Model

Glenn Walters proposes a bidirectional theory of drug–crime relationships in which drug abuse and crime are conceptualized as overlapping lifestyles. In this model, a **lifestyle** is defined as a routinized pattern of cognitive-behavioral interactions. The drug and criminal lifestyles are viewed as partially overlapping in the sense that they share some of the same behavioral and cognitive traits and features in common. The partially overlapping behavioral styles of the drug and criminal lifestyles are depicted in **Figure 4-11**. Overlapping features of the two behavioral systems, highlighted in orange, include irresponsibility and social rule breaking. The cognitive factors that overlap between the drug and criminal lifestyles, also in orange, are identified in **Figure 4-12**. It should be noted that even when separate terms are used to describe different facets of behavior and cognition, the similarities

Figure 4-11
Overlap in behavioral styles between the criminal and drug lifestyles.

Criminal Lifestyle	Drug Lifestyle
Irresponsibility	Irresponsibility/Pseudoresponsibility
Self-Indulgence	Stress–Coping Imbalance
Interpersonal Intrusiveness	Interpersonal Triviality
Social Rule Breaking	Social Rule Breaking/Bending

Figure 4-12
Overlap in cognitive features between the criminal and drug lifestyles.

Criminal Lifestyle	Drug Lifestyle
Thinking Styles Proactive and Reactive	Thinking Styles Reactive
Attributions Hostile Attribution Biases	Attributions Self-Labeling
Outcome Expectancies Positive for crime	Outcome Expectancies Positive for drugs
Efficacy Expectancies Strong crime, weak prosocial	Efficacy Expectancies Strong drugs, weak sobriety
Goals Short-term to Intermediate-term	Goals Short-term
Values Physical and mental hedonism	Values Physical hedonism

between the two lifestyles tend to be greater than the differences. For example, stress–coping imbalance (drug lifestyle) is simply an advanced form of self-indulgence (criminal lifestyle) and the mechanisms underlying positive outcome expectancies for drugs are similar to the mechanisms underlying positive outcome expectancies for crime. Just as Thornberry proposes that reciprocal relationships strengthen with time, Walters theorizes that the overlap between lifestyles grows with increased involvement in either lifestyle (see **Figure 4-13**).[67]

Walters recently tested a core feature of the drug lifestyle–criminal lifestyle overlap by postulating that the reactive (impulsive) dimension of criminal thinking, but not the proactive (planned) dimension, would correlate with prior substance abuse. Analyses revealed that, as predicted, only reactive criminal thinking correlated with a history of substance abuse as well as the total number of different drugs abused in the past (see **Figure 4-14**). Furthermore, when the alternate dimension was statistically controlled using a partial correlation (i.e., proactive criminal thinking controlled when reactive criminal thinking and past drug use were correlated and reactive criminal thinking controlled when proactive criminal thinking and past drug use were correlated), the reactive criminal thinking correlations remained significant and the proactive criminal thinking correlations became negative but remained nonsignificant. Using these same data, Walters demonstrated that reactive criminal thinking partially mediated the relationship between a prior history of substance abuse and subsequent criminal recidivism.[68] As is discussed in the next section of this chapter, partial mediation is a cardinal feature of bidirectional theories designed to explain drug–crime relationships.

Of the 12 previously reviewed theories of drug abuse or crime, 4 theories are consistent with a bidirectional explanation of drug–crime relationships. By emphasizing propensity, development, and their interaction, Sampson and Laub seem to be promoting a reciprocal or bidirectional explanation of the drug–crime connection. The biosocial theory of crime would also appear to be taking a bidirectional approach to drug–crime relationships by examining the interaction of biological and sociological factors. Finally, both the social learning theory of substance abuse and the social learning theory of crime are compatible with a bidirectional interpretation of drug–crime relationships. The emphasis that both

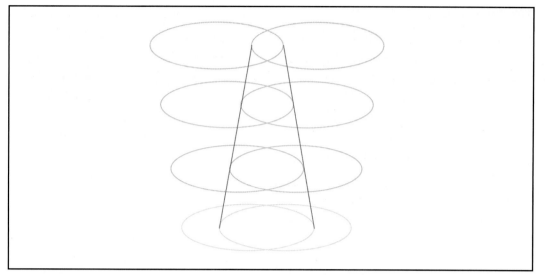

Figure 4-13
Expanding overlap
between the drug
(left) and criminal
(right) lifestyles as a
person proceeds from
an early (top) to a later
(bottom) phase of
lifestyle development.

Data From: Walters, G. D. (1998). *Changing lives of crime and drugs: Intervening with substance-abusing offenders.* Chichester, England: Wiley.

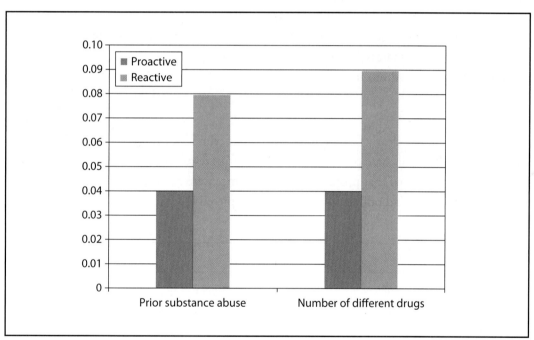

Figure 4-14
Correlations between
proactive and reactive
criminal thinking
and presence of prior
substance abuse and
number of different
drugs used.

Data From: Walters, G. D. (2012b). Substance abuse and criminal thinking: Testing the countervailing, mediation, and specificity hypotheses. *Law and Human Behavior, 36,* 506–512.

social learning models place on mediation and reciprocity clearly place them in the bidirectional camp of theories designed to explain the connection between drugs and crime.

Understanding the Complexity of Drug–Crime Relationships

There is little doubt that the connection between drugs and crime is complex. Not only are there multiple drug–crime relationships but these relationships often vary as a function of the context, situation, and presence of additional variables. In this final section, I address five contexts that should be taken into account when interpreting drug–crime relationships in all their complexity.

The Drug Context

Not all drugs are equally **criminogenic**. In the previously mentioned meta-analysis by Holloway, Bennett, and Farrington, heroin and crack cocaine were found to be highly criminogenic, powder cocaine and amphetamines were classified as moderately criminogenic, and marijuana was evaluated as mildly criminogenic.[69] The criminogenic status of alcohol, particularly as a psychopharmacological agent of violence, is also well documented.[70] These results are reasonably consistent with the harm ratings Nutt and colleagues compiled on these same drugs.[71] The criminogenic status of marijuana, however, remains a point of contention between politicians and scientists. Whereas government officials and policy-makers tend to rate marijuana as moderately criminogenic, scientists place marijuana near the bottom of the criminogenic continuum. A recent longitudinal study by Willy Pedersen and Torbjørn Skardhamer revealed that marijuana use in adolescence and early adulthood was associated with later criminality, although nearly all of the criminality was for simple use or distribution of marijuana.[72] There is no evidence, then, to support a psychopharmacological or economic-compulsive interpretation of the marijuana–crime nexus and scant evidence that marijuana and crime are connected systemically (mostly by way of gateway theory). In short, drugs like heroin, alcohol, and crack cocaine tend to group near the top of the criminogenic continuum, whereas drugs like marijuana, LSD, and ecstasy tend to fall near the bottom of this same continuum.[73]

The Crime Context

Some crimes are more clearly tied to drugs than other crimes. In interviews conducted with inmates confined in jail, state prison, and federal prison, researchers from the Bureau of Justice Statistics determined that property and drug crimes were more closely associated with drug use than violent and public order crimes. As depicted in **Figure 4-15**, property offenders

Figure 4-15
Percentage of jail, state prison, and federal prison inmates who report committing their current offense in order to get money for drugs, by current offense.

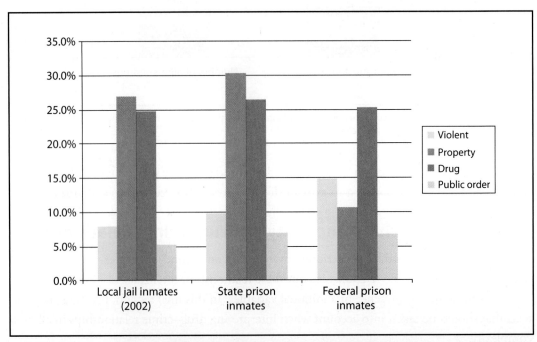

Data From: Karberg, J. C., & James, D. J. (2005). *Substance dependence, abuse, and treatment of jail inmates, 2002. Bureau of Justice Statistics Special Report* (NCJ 209588). Washington, DC: U.S. Department of Justice.

in jail and state prison were more likely to acknowledge committing their offense in order to get money for drugs than any of the other three categories of crime. The results are somewhat more ambiguous with respect to federal prisoners, where individuals serving time for drug offenses and violent crimes were more likely than property offenders to report committing their crimes for money to buy drugs.[74–75] Violent crime, by contrast, is more likely to occur when one is using alcohol.[76] Whereas any crime can be drug connected, the crimes least likely to overlap with drug or alcohol abuse are the public order offenses referenced in the Bureau of Justice Statistics studies, weapons violations and fraud being two of the more common crimes included in this category. In addition, white-collar crime is probably only weakly tied to drug use and this may explain why federal offenders classified as property offenders, many of whom were serving time for white-collar crimes, had such low levels of drug use.

The Drug–Crime Context

Some drug–crime connections are more common than others. Two of the more frequently encountered connections are the alcohol–violent crime relationship and the heroin–property crime relationship. As shown in **Figure 4-16**, both relationships were clearly represented in the 41 prisoners interviewed by Bennett and Holloway about their past involvement with drugs and crime. Heroin was the drug most often associated with robbery and property crime (around 30% each) and alcohol was the drug most heavily represented in assaults (42%). Other noteworthy findings from this study were as follows:[77]

- Crack cocaine was several times more likely to be associated with robbery, property crime, and assault than powder cocaine.
- Amphetamine and marijuana, although not extensively criminogenic, were present most often in drug offenses and property crimes.
- LSD did not appear to play a significant role in any of the 10 categories of crime considered.

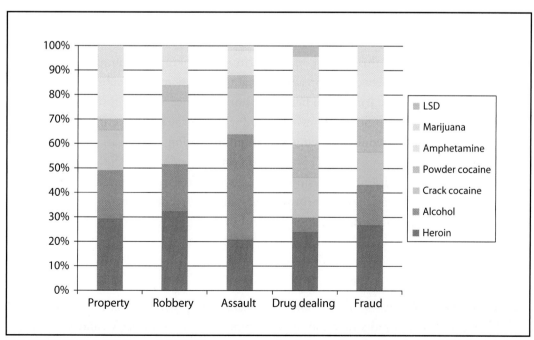

Figure 4-16
Proportion of offenders reporting the presence of a connection between a specific crime and a specific drug in their past.

Data From: Bennett, T., & Holloway, K. (2009). The causal connection between drug misuse and crime. *British Journal of Criminology, 49,* 513–531.

Although these results are based on a small sample, they suggest that there is some correspondence between specific drugs and specific crimes.

The Variable Context

Variables other than drugs and crime can also play an important role in drug–crime relationships. They do so by strengthening, weakening, moderating, and mediating the relationship between drugs and crime. Third-variable theories, for instance, assume that one or more third variables fully explain the drug–crime connection and that controlling these variables in a multiple regression analysis or partial correlation will eliminate the commonly observed relationship between drugs and crime. When propensity for deviance was controlled in a study by Doherty et al., however, a substantial drug–crime correlation persisted, thereby disputing the third-variable explanation in this particular research context.[78] In some contexts, a third variable may weaken the relationship between drugs and crime but not eliminate it, and in other contexts, a third variable may strengthen the relationship between drugs and crime. The former is suggested by the countervailing correlations between drug use and intelligence and between crime and intelligence and the latter by the increase in drug–crime correlations in women exposed to childhood sexual victimization.

Variables can moderate and mediate drug–crime relationships. A moderating effect occurs when a third variable alters the strength or direction of the relationship between two variables (see **Figure 4-17**).[79] Moderation is represented statistically by a significant interaction between the predictor and moderator variables where the relationship between the predictor and outcome varies at different levels of the moderator variable. Loxley and Adams discerned that gender moderated the temporal ordering of drug use and crime, such that boys more often started committing crime before using drugs whereas girls more often started using drugs before committing crime.[80] A mediating effect occurs when a third variable accounts for a portion or the totality of relationship between two temporally ordered variables.[81] Mediation is represented statistically by a significant correlation between the mediating variable and predictor and outcome variables in a design where the **predictor variable** comes before and the **outcome variable** comes after the **mediator variable**. In a study reviewed earlier in this chapter, reactive criminal thinking was found to partially mediate the relationship between prior substance abuse (predictor) and subsequent recidivism (outcome).[82] Had the correlation between prior substance abuse and subsequent recidivism become nonsignificant following introduction of the reactive criminal thinking intervening variable, this would have constituted full mediation. Third-variable theorists do not generally rely on **longitudinal research designs** but would view full mediation as evidence that a causal relationship does not exist between drugs and crime. Unidirectional theorists rely heavily on **moderator variable** effects and bidirectional theorists place moderation and mediation effects on equal footing within the context of reciprocal variable relationships.

The Developmental Context

The developmental context of drug–crime relationships simply means that these relationships change over time or as a function of development. Both Thornberry's and Walters'

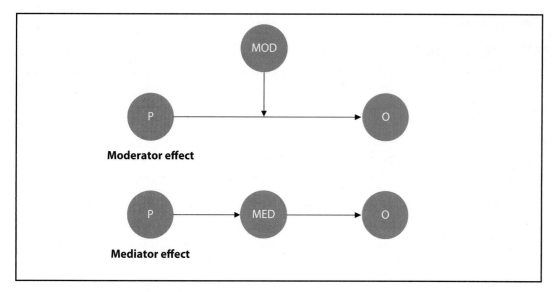

Figure 4-17
A moderator variable (MOD) affects the strength or direction of the relationship between a predictor variable (P) and outcome variable (O). A mediator variable (MED) accounts for a portion or the full relationship between a predictor variable (P) and outcome variable (O).

bidirectional theories of drug–crime relationships emphasize a change in variable relationship strength as the adolescent ages (Thornberry) or the drug and criminal lifestyles evolve (Walters). Furthermore, the longer a researcher follows a group of individuals the greater the opportunity and likelihood of observing bidirectional or reciprocal effects. In studies where either drug use precedes delinquency or delinquency precedes drug use, bidirectional relationships are nearly always eventually observed.[83–84] Rather than directly causing crime, habitual drug use may simply intensify a person's tendency toward deviance which, in turn, leads to crime.[85] Consequently, drug–crime relationships may conform to a unidirectional model in the short term but in the long term they nearly always show evidence of bidirectionality.

Summary and Conclusions

- Third-variable explanations of drug–crime relationships hold that the well-established correlation between drugs and crime is spurious and the result of their common association with some third variable. Six putative "third variables" were examined in this chapter: parallel developmental processes, age, general deviance, low self-control, societal labeling, and response style.
- Unidirectional explanations of drug–crime relationships assert that drug use causes crime or that crime causes drug use. Three mechanisms believed to underlie unidirectional explanations of drug–crime relationships—psychopharmacological, economic-compulsive, and systemic—were also reviewed.
- Bidirectional explanations of drug–crime relationships maintain that drug use and crime are reciprocally related in the sense that drug use causes crime as much as crime causes drug use. Two theoretical models—Thornberry's interactional theory and Walters' overlapping lifestyles model—were also introduced and reviewed.
- Drug–crime relationships are formidably complex and should be understood within various contexts, five of which were discussed in this chapter: the drug context, the crime context, the drug–crime context, the variable context, and the developmental context.

Key Terms

ADAM II   Arrestee Drug Abuse Monitoring Program; program in which arrestees in 10 cities are tested for 10 different illegal drugs, including marijuana, cocaine, heroin, and methamphetamine.

Bidirectional   Causal relationship that goes in both directions; from drug use to crime and from crime to drug use.

Causal Relationship   A predictive relationship that meets the following three conditions: (1) correlation, (2) direction, and (3) ruling out of viable alternative explanations.

Criminogenic   Capable of causing crime.

Cross-Sectional Research Design   Research design in which participants are sampled from a cross-section of the population, and where all measures are taken at the same time.

Differential Association   Theory that asserts that crime is learned in close association with those who violate the law.

Drug Use Forecasting   Program in which arrestees in various cities are interviewed about their drug histories and involvement in treatment and are tested for drugs; forerunner of ADAM II.

Economic-Compulsive   Mechanism by which drugs cause crime by encouraging economically oriented crime to pay for drugs.

Epiphenomenal   A phenomenon that accompanies and is caused by another phenomenon.

Externalization Disorders   Group of childhood disorders characterized by problems in outward behavior; includes conduct disorder, hyperactivity/attention deficit disorder, and oppositional defiant disorder.

General Deviance   Tendency or propensity to engage in a variety of deviant activities, including crime/delinquency, substance use, sexual promiscuity, and various other forms of risk-taking behavior.

Illicit Supply System   Network of relationships whereby drugs are bought and sold.

Interactional Theory   Theory that holds that a series of social factors—e.g., commitment to school, association with delinquent or drug-using peers, belief in conventional values—form reciprocal relationships with delinquent and drug-using behavior.

Labeling Theory   Theory that holds that applying labels to behavior reinforces and perpetuates the labeled behavior.

Lifestyle Theory   Theory that holds that drug use and crime can be conceptualized as lifestyles composed of specific cognitive and behavioral features and that the drug–crime connection is a function of overlap between the drug and criminal lifestyles.

Longitudinal Research Design   Research design in which the same group of individuals is followed for a specified period of time during which they are evaluated or tested at prespecified intervals (commonly referred to as waves).

Low Self-Control   Tendency or propensity to engage in reckless behavior as characterized by impulsiveness, physical activity, risk-taking, self-centeredness, preference for simple tasks, and volatile temper.

Maturing Out   Process by which drug users significantly reduce or essentially stop using drugs as a result of age and the accumulated effects of a drug lifestyle; concept has also been applied to criminal behavior.

Mediator Variable   Third variable that partially or fully accounts for the relationship between a predictor variable and outcome variable, with the third (mediating) variable coming after the predictor variable but before the outcome variable.

Moderator Variable   Third variable that alters the strength or direction of a relationship between two other variables.

Outcome Variable   Dependent or criterion variable in an experiment that is predicted by the independent variable; in a causal analysis it is the putative effect.

Parallel Developmental Processes   Epiphenomenal explanation for the drug–crime connection in which substance abuse and crime are said to be embedded in parallel, yet independent, social networks.

Predictor Variable   Independent or manipulated variable that is used to predict the dependent variable; in a causal analysis it is the putative cause.

Psychopharmacological   Mechanism by which drugs cause crime by directly affecting the user's moods, thoughts, or actions.

Reciprocal Effects   Variables in a causal relationship that are both a cause and effect of one another.

Response Style   Test-taking behavior derived from a respondent's attitudes or tendencies rather than from the content of the items being answered.

Spurious   False or noncausal.

Systemic   Mechanism by which drugs cause crime by bringing individual into contact with the illicit supply system.

Temporal Order   The requirement that a predictor variable come before an outcome variable in establishing a causal relationship.

Third Variable   Variable other than the two variables that are the current focus of attention.

Third Variable Explanations   The relationship between two variables is spurious, illusory, or noncausal and a consequence of the variables' correlation with a common or third variable.

Unidirectional   Causal relationship that goes in one direction; from drug use to crime or from crime to drug use.

Critical Thinking

1. How does a third-variable or epiphenomenal explanation of the drug–crime connection account for drug–crime correlations?

2. When would you use Goldstein's tripartite model of drug–crime relationships to explain drug–crime relationships?

3. Why is it that unidirectional relationships often give way to bidirectional relationships when the period of observation is expanded?

Notes

1. Bennett, T. H., Holloway, K., & Farrington, D. P. (2008). The statistical association between drug misuse and crime: A meta-analysis. *Aggression and Violent Behavior, 13*, 107–118.

2. Fagan, J., Weis, J. G., & Cheng, Y. (1990). Delinquency and substance use among inner-city students. *Journal of Drug Issues, 20*, 351–402.

3. Ford, J. A. (2005). Substance use, the social bond, and delinquency. *Sociological Inquiry, 75*, 109–128.

4. Telesca, D., Erosheva, E. A., Kreager, D. A., & Matsueda, R. L. (2011). Modeling criminal careers as departures from a unimodal population age-crime curve: The case of marijuana use. Working paper no. 113, Center for Statistics and the Social Science, University of Washington. http://www.csss.washington.edu/Papers/wp113.pdf.

5. Udry, J. R. (2003). *The National Longitudinal Study of Adolescent Health (Add Health)*. Chapel Hill, NC: Carolina Population Center, University of North Carolina.

6. Corwyn, R. F., & Benda, B. B. (2002). The relationship between use of alcohol, other drugs, and crime among adolescents: An argument for a delinquency syndrome. *Alcoholism Treatment Quarterly, 20*(2), 35–49.

7. Jessor, R., & Jessor, S. L. (1977). *Problem behavior and psychological development: A longitudinal study of youth*. New York: Academic Press.

8. Baer, J. S. (2002). Student factors: Understanding individual variation in college drinking. *Journal of Studies on Alcohol,* (Suppl. 14), 40–53.

9. Clapper, R. L., Martin, C. S., & Clifford, P. R. (1994). Personality, social environment, and past behavior as predictors of late adolescent alcohol use. *Journal of Substance Abuse, 6*, 305–313.

10. Norwood, W. D., Jouriles, E. N., McDonald, R., & Swank, P. R. (2004). *Domestic violence and deviant behavior* (NCJ 199713). Washington, DC: National Institute of Justice.

11. LeBlanc, M., & Girard, S. (1997). The generality of deviance: Replication over two decades with a Canadian sample of adjudicated adolescents. *Canadian Journal of Criminology, 39*, 171–183.

12. Gottfredson, M. R., & Hirschi, T. (1990). *A general theory of crime*. Stanford, CA; Stanford University Press.

13. Connor, B, T., Stein, J. A., & Longshore, D. (2009). Examining self-control as a multidimensional predictor of crime and drug use in adolescents with criminal histories. *Journal of Behavioral Health Services and Research, 36*, 137–149.

14. Hammersley, R. (2008). *Drugs and crime*. Cambridge, England: Polity Press.

15. Bernburg, J. G., & Krohn, M. D. (2003). Labeling, life chances, and adult crime: The direct and indirect effects of official intervention in adolescence on crime in early adulthood. *Criminology, 41*, 1287–1318.

16. Baumgartner, H., & Steenkamp, J.-B. E. M. (2001). Response styles in marketing research: A cross-national investigation. *Journal of Marketing Research, 38*, 143–156.

17. Gottfredson, M., & Hirschi, T. (1987). The methodological adequacy of longitudinal research on crime. *Criminology, 25*, 581–614.

18. Goldstein, P. (1985). The drugs/violence nexus: A tripartite conceptual framework. *Journal of Drug Issues, 15*, 493–506.

19. Bennett, T., & Holloway, K. (2009). The causal connection between drug misuse and crime. *British Journal of Criminology, 49*, 513–531.

20. Newcomb, M. D., & McGee, L. (1989). Adolescent alcohol use and other delinquent behaviors: A one year longitudinal analysis controlling for sensation seeking. *Criminal Justice and Behavior, 16*, 345–369.

21. Brook, J. S., Whiteman, M., Finch, S. J., & Cohen, P. (1996). Young adult drug use and delinquency: Childhood antecedents and adolescent mediators. *Journal of the American Academy of Child and Adolescent Psychiatry, 35*, 1584–1592.

22. Allen, C. (2005). The links between heroin, crack cocaine, and crime: Where does street crime fit in? *British Journal of Criminology, 45*, 355–372.

23. Huizinga, D., Loeber, R., & Thornberry, T. P. (1993). Longitudinal study of delinquency, drug use, sexual activity, and pregnancy among children and youth in three cities. *Public Health Reports, 108*, 90–96.

24. Makkai, T., & Payne, J. (2003). Key findings from the Drug Use Careers of Offenders (DUCO) study. *Trends and Issues in Crime and Criminal Justice* (No. 267). Canberra, Australia: Australian Institute of Criminology.

25. Goldstein (1985).

26. Collins, J. J. (Ed.). (1981). *Drinking and crime*. New York: Guilford Press.

27. Fagan et al. (1990).

28. Valdez, A., Kaplan, C. D., Curtis, R. L., & Yin, Z. (1995). Illegal drug use, alcohol and aggressive crime among Mexican American and white male arrestees in San Antonio. *Journal of Psychoactive Drugs, 27*, 135–143.

29. Barnes, C., & Taylor, B. G. (2000). *Prevalence of intimate partner violence in a sample of arrestees in Sacramento, California, 1999* [computer file]. Washington, DC: National Institute of Justice.

30. Valdez, A., Kaplan, C. D., & Cepeda, A. (2006). The drugs-violence nexus among Mexican-American gang members. *Journal of Psychoactive Drugs, 38*, 109–121.

31. Fernández-Motalvo, J., López-Gana, J., & Arteaga, A. (2012). Violent behaviors in drug addiction: Differential profiles of drug-addicted patients with and without violence problems. *Journal of Interpersonal Violence, 27*, 142–157.

32. Kuhns, J. B., & Clodfelter, T. A. (2009). Illicit drug-related psychopharmacological violence: The current understanding within a causal context. *Aggression and Violent Behavior, 14*, 69–78.

33. Ball, J. C., Shaffer, J. W., & Nurco, D. N. (1983). The day-to-day criminality of heroin addicts in Baltimore: A study in the continuity of offense rates. *Drug and Alcohol Dependence, 12*, 119–142.

34. Johnson, B. A., Goldstein, P., Preble, E., Schmeidler, J., Lipton, D. S., Spunt, B., et al. (1985). *Taking care of business: The economics of crime by heroin abusers*. Lexington, MA: Lexington Books.

35. Anglin, M. D., & Speckart, G. (1988). Narcotics use and crime: A multisample, multimethod analysis. *Criminology, 26*, 197–233.

36. Jarvis, G., & Parker, H. (1989). Young heroin users and crime: How do the "new users" finance their habits? *British Journal of Criminology, 29*, 175–185.

37. Riley, K. J. (1997). *Crack, powder cocaine, and heroin: Drug purchase and use patterns in six U.S. cities* [Research Report]. Washington, DC: National Institute of Justice.

38. Bean, P. T., & Wilkinson, C. K. (1988). Drug taking, crime and the illicit supply system. *British Journal of Addiction, 83*, 533–539.

39. Andrews, D. A. (1980). Some experimental investigations of the principles of differential association through deliberate manipulations of the structures of service systems. *American Sociological Review, 45*, 448–462.

40. Allen (2005).

41. Deitch, D., Koutsenok, I., & Ruiz, A. (2000). Relationship between crime and drugs: What we have learned in recent decades. *Journal of Psychoactive Drugs, 32*, 391–397.

42. Huizinga et al. (1993).

43. Makkai & Payne (2003).

44. Menard, S., Mihalic, S., & Huizinga, D. (2001). Drugs and crime revisited. *Justice Quarterly, 18*, 269–299.

45. Pettiway, L. E., Dolinsky, S., & Grigoryan, A. (1994). The drug and criminal activity patterns of urban offenders: A Markov chain analysis. *Journal of Quantitative Criminology, 10*, 99–107.

46. Doherty, E. E., Green, K. M., & Ensminger, M. E. (2008). Investigating the long-term influence of adolescent delinquency on drug use initiation. *Drug and Alcohol Dependence, 93*, 72–84.

47. Walters, G. D. (2012a). *Crime in a psychological context: From career criminals to criminal careers.* Thousand Oaks, CA: Sage.

48. Cromwell, P., Olson, J., & Avary, D. (1991). *Breaking and entering: An ethnographic analysis of burglary.* Newbury Park, CA: Sage.

49. Menard et al. (2001).

50. Uggen, C., & Thompson, M. (2003). The socioeconomic determinants of ill-gotten gains: within-person changes in drug use and illegal earnings. *American Journal of Sociology, 109*, 146–185.

51. Winick, C. (1962). Maturing out of narcotic addiction. *U.S. Bulletin on Narcotics, 14*, 1–7.

52. Anglin, M. G., Brecht, M.-L., Woodward, J. A., & Bonett, D. G. (1986). An empirical study of maturing out: Conditional factors. *International Journal of the Addictions, 21*, 233–246.

53. Beck, A. J., & Shipley, B. E. (1989). Recidivism of prisoners released in 1983. *Bureau of Justice Statistics Special Report* [NCJ 116261]. Washington, DC: National Institute of Justice.

54. Prins, E. H. (2008). "Maturing out" and the dynamics of the biographical trajectories of hard drug addicts. *Qualitative Social Research, 9*(1), Art. 30.

55. Welte, J. W., Barnes, G. M., Hoffman, J. H., Wieczorek, W. F., & Zhang, L. (2005). Substance involvement and the trajectory of criminal offending in young males. *American Journal of Drug and Alcohol Abuse, 31*, 267–284.

56. Huizinga et al. (1993).

57. Makkai & Payne (2003).

58. Hammersley, R., & Morrison, V. (1987). Effects of polydrug use on the criminal activities of heroin-users. *British Journal of Addiction, 82*, 899–906.

59. Brook, J. S., Whiteman, M. M., & Finch, S. (1992). Childhood aggression, adolescent delinquency, and drug use: A longitudinal study. *Journal of Genetic Psychology, 153*, 369–383.

60. Brook, D. W., Brook, J. S., Rubenstone, E., Zhang, C., & Saar, N. S. (2011). Developmental associations between externalizing behavior, peer delinquency, drug use, perceived neighborhood crime, and violent behavior in urban communities. *Aggressive Behavior, 37*, 349–361.

61. Mason, W. A., & Windle, M. (2002). Reciprocal relations between adolescent substance use and delinquency: A longitudinal latent variable analysis. *Journal of Abnormal Psychology, 111*, 63–76.

62. Windle, W. A., Hitchings, J. E., McMahon, R. J., & Spoth, R. L. (2007). A test of three alternative hypotheses regarding the effects of early delinquency on adolescent psychosocial functioning and substance involvement. *Journal of Abnormal Child Psychology, 35*, 831–843.

63. D'Amico, E. J., Edelen, M. O., Miles, J. N. V., & Morral, A. R. (2008). The longitudinal association between substance use and delinquency among high-risk youth. *Drug and Alcohol Dependence, 93*, 85–92.

64. Thornberry, T. P. (1987). Toward an interactional theory of delinquency. *Criminology, 25*, 863–891.

65. Thornberry, T. P., Lizotte, A. J., Krohn, M. D., Farnsworth, M., & Jang, S. J. (1991). Testing interactional theory: An examination of reciprocal causal relationships among family, school, and delinquency. *Journal of Criminal Law and Criminology, 82*, 3–35.

66. Krohn, M. D., Lizotte, A. J., Thornberry, T. P., Smith, C., & McDowall, D. (1996). Reciprocal causal relationships among drug use, peers, and beliefs: A five-wave panel model. *Journal of Drug Issues, 26*, 405–428.

67. Walters, G. D. (1998). *Changing lives of crime and drugs: Intervening with substance-abusing offenders.* Chichester, England: Wiley.

68. Walters, G. D. (2012b). Substance abuse and criminal thinking: Testing the countervailing, mediation, and specificity hypotheses. *Law and Human Behavior, 36*, 506–512.

69. Bennett, Holloway, & Farrington (2008).

70. Kuhns & Clodfelter (2009).

71. Nutt, D. J., King, L. A., & Phillips, L. D. (2010). Drug harms in the UK: A multicriteria decision analysis. *Lancet, 376*, 1558–1565.

72. Pedersen, W., & Skardhamar, T. (2009). Cannabis and crime: Findings from a longitudinal study. *Addiction, 105*, 109–118.

73. Nutt et al. (2010).

74. Karberg, J. C., & James, D. J. (2005). Substance dependence, abuse, and treatment of jail inmates, 2002. *Bureau of Justice Statistics Special Report* (NCJ 209588). Washington, DC: U.S. Department of Justice.

75. Mumola, C. J., & Karberg, J. C. (2006). Drug use and dependence, state and federal prisoners, 2004. *Bureau of Justice Statistics Special Report* (NCJ 213530). Washington, DC: U.S. Department of Justice.

76. Kuhns & Clodfelter (2009).

77. Bennett & Holloway (2009).

78. Doherty et al. (2008).

79. Baron, R. M., & Kenney, D. A. (1986). The moderator-mediator variable distinction in social psychological research: Conceptual, strategic, and statistical considerations. *Journal of Personality and Social Psychology, 51*, 1173–1182.

80. Loxley, W., & Adams, K. (2009). *Women, drug use and crime: Findings from the Drug Use Monitoring in Australia program.* Canberra, Australia: Australian Institute of Criminology.

81. Baron & Kenney (1986).

82. Walters (2012b).

83. Brook et al. (1996)

84. Huizinga et al. (1993)

85. Inciardi, J. A. (1992). *The War on Drugs II: The continuing epic of heroin, cocaine,crack, crime, AIDS, and public policy.* Mountainview, CA: Mayfield Publishing Company.

RESEARCH

© iStockphoto/Thinkstock

© iStockphoto/Thinkstock

© iStockphoto/Thinkstock

Whereas Part I of this book dealt with definitions and theories of drug abuse and crime, Part II deals with research relevant to drugs, crime, and their relationships. The research on drugs, crime, and the drug–crime connection is broken down into four chapters: one on the biological foundations of research on drugs, crime, and their relationships; one on the psychological foundations of research on drugs, crime, and their relationships; one on the sociological foundations of research on drugs, crime, and their relationships; and one on the static/situational foundations of research on drugs, crime, and their relationships. Whenever possible, the relevance of these research findings to the theories described in Chapters 2, 3, and 4 of this text is noted and discussed because not only is it important for the reader to be informed about theory, research, practice, and policy on drug–crime relationships, but it is also imperative that he or she appreciate the interrelationships between the four domains.

CHAPTER 5

BIOLOGICAL FOUNDATIONS OF DRUG–CRIME RELATIONSHIPS

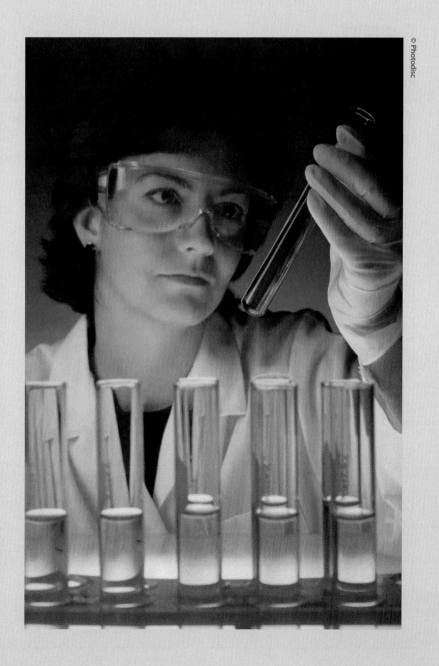

© Photodisc

This chapter is divided into four sections. Each section represents one of the four primary objectives of this chapter:

- Understand the genetic foundations of drug use, crime, and their relationships.
- Comprehend the role of neurophysiology in drug use, crime, and the drug–crime nexus.
- Identify major brain systems relevant to drug use, crime, and the drug–crime nexus.
- Appreciate the role of the autonomic nervous system in organizing a person's reaction to drugs, crime, and drugs and crime in combination.

Each section of this chapter is divided into four subsections: an introductory subsection, a subsection on the relevance of biological factors to drug use and abuse, a subsection on the relevance of biological factors to crime, and a subsection on the relevance of biological factors to drug–crime relationships.

Genetics

The human genome is made up of 20,000 to 25,000 genes, all of which are located on 23 pairs of chromosomes.[1] A **chromosome** is a microscopic threadlike process composed of two linear strands of **deoxyribonucleic acid** (DNA) twisted in the shape of a double helix. A **gene** is a basic unit of heredity located on a chromosome. Like chromosomes, genes come in pairs, also known as **alleles**, and there is a specific place on the chromosome where each specific gene is located (**locus**). Human cells contain 46 chromosomes grouped into 23 pairs: 44 autosomes and two sex chromosomes (see **Figure 5-1**). The two sex

Figure 5-1
The normal **karotype** consists of 23 pairs of chromosomes.

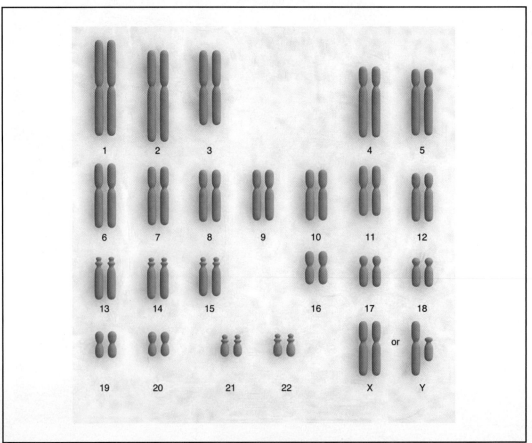

chromosomes (X and Y), when combined, form offspring that are either male (XY) or female (XX). The only cells that do not have paired chromosomes are the gametes (ova, sperm). Gametes contain 23 unpaired chromosomes, which when joined with 23 unpaired chromosomes from an opposite-sex partner (23 chromosomes from the mother and 23 chromosomes from the father), yield a new organism with 23 pairs of chromosomes.

DNA is like a spiral staircase. The steps of the staircase are composed of two ring-shaped carbon-nitrogen molecules known as nucleotide bases, each of which are connected by a hydrogen bond (see **Figure 5-2**). Four nucleotide bases make up a chain of DNA: adenine (A), thymine (T), guanine (G), and cytosine (C). DNA serves two basic functions: **translation** and **transmission**.

The first function, translation, refers to the fact that DNA codes for the production of proteins responsible for the structure and function of cells. These cells, in turn, contribute to the formation of various physical characteristics (e.g., height, eye color), psychomotor

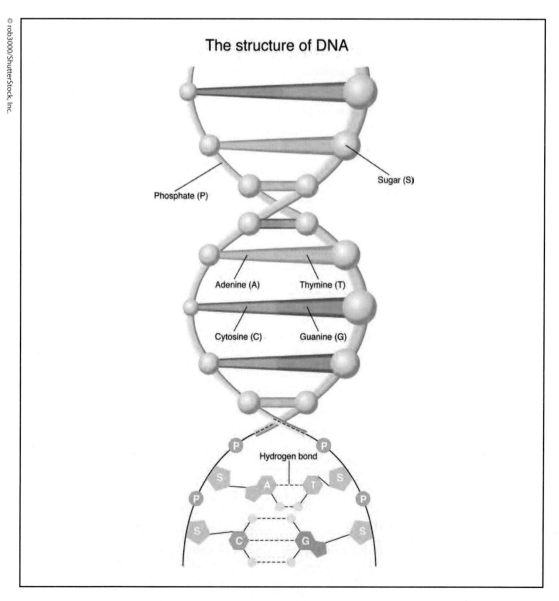

Figure 5-2
The structure of Deoxyribonucleic Acid (DNA).

abilities (e.g., eye–hand coordination, intelligence), and behavioral tendencies (e.g., temperament, excitement-seeking). The second function of DNA, transmission, is to replicate and transmit genetic material to the next generation. Once in every billion replications a mutation may occur, which then gives rise to genetic variability.[2]

Over 100 years ago Gregor Mendel, after years of research on pea plants, discovered the basic principles of genetic transmission. The two basic principles of genetic transmission identified by Mendel were **dominant transmission** and **recessive transmission**. Dominant transmission occurs when a single (dominant) allele determines a behavior. Examples of dominant traits include freckles, hazel or green eyes, and the neuropsychological condition known as Huntington's disease. Recessive transmission means that both alleles must be present for the characteristic or trait to appear. A bent thumb, blue or gray eyes, and the metabolic disease phenylketonuria (PKU) are all examples of recessive traits. Humans are more complex than pea plants and so most human characteristics and traits are passed down in ways other than simple dominant and recessive transmission. One way human parents pass their genes down to their offspring is through **polygenetic additive transmission**. Here, multiple genes from different loci and in various combinations contribute to a behavior. There are no necessary or sufficient genes in additive transmission. **Emergenesis** is a nonadditive form of multiple gene transmission. Here, a specific necessary and sufficient combination of genes from different loci is required for behavioral expression of a trait.[3]

An important distinction to make when studying the role of genes in drug use and crime is differentiating between genotypes and phenotypes. A **genotype** consists of the actual alleles present in a particular genome. A **phenotype** is the behavioral expression of this genotype in the form of an observed characteristic (hair color) or behavior (impulsivity). The same genotype can lead to somewhat different phenotypes depending on how it interacts with other genes and with the environment. **Gene–environment interaction** means that a gene is expressed in one environment but not in another. Hence, a genetic predisposition to irritable temperament may be expressed only in children whose mothers are anxious about childrearing.[4] Likewise, the effect of environmental factors may depend on the presence of certain genotypes, such as in a recent study by Craig Olsson and colleagues where insecure attachment led to increased use of tobacco and marijuana in adolescents with an abnormal allele for the **neurotransmitter dopamine**. However, insecure attachment did not lead to tobacco and marijuana use in adolescents without the abnormal allele.[5] Gene–environment interaction plays an important role in the biosocial theory of crime.[6-7]

In some situations, genes and environment may correlate without interacting. Three major forms of **gene–environment correlation** have been identified: passive, active, and reactive. Passive gene–environment correlation occurs because parents not only pass their genes on to their offspring but also provide an environment for their child that is influenced to some extent by the parents' own genetic background. Hence, alcoholic parents who engage in a pattern of problem drinking in the home not only provide their children with a genetic predisposition to problem drinking but also an environmental role model for alcohol misuse. Active gene–environment correlation means that children seek out environments consistent with their genetic makeup. This can be viewed as a form of niche seeking. An impulsive adolescent who is rejected by conventional peers may seek solace and support from similarly impulsive and rejected peers. Reactive or evocative gene–environment correlation means that the child's genetic predispositions evoke a response from the environment that then reinforces or advances the inherited trait. An example of reactive gene–environment correlation might be a child with a hyperactive or rebellious temperament who elicits physical punishment and abuse from frustrated parents.[8]

Behavioral geneticists employ three primary methodologies in an attempt to gauge the **heritability** of various behavioral traits: **family studies**, **twin studies**, and **adoption studies**. The logic behind family studies is that increased prevalence of a behavior in the family tree can be construed as a possible genetic effect in that **first-degree relatives** (siblings, offspring) share 50% of their genes in common, **second-degree relatives** (grandparents, aunt/uncle, half-siblings) share 25% of their genes in common, third-degree relatives (first cousins) share 12.5% of their genes in common, and unrelated individuals share 0% of their genes in common. Twin studies operate under the assumption that greater **concordance** (presence of the same trait in both members of a pair of twins) between **monozygotic** (MZ) twins (who share 100% of their genes in common) than between **dizygotic** (DZ) twins (who share only 50% of their genes in common) could signal a genetic effect. Adoption studies compare concordance rates between adopted children and their biological parents (who contributed to the child's genetic makeup but did not raise the child) with concordance rates for these same adopted children and their adoptive parents (who raised the child but did not contribute to the child's genetic makeup). A genetic effect is indicated when concordance between the child and a biological parent is greater than concordance between the child and an adoptive parent.

Each behavioral genetic method has its limitations. The family study method, the most problematic of the three, frequently confounds genetics with environment. This is because family members not only share many of the same genes in common but also frequently grow up in the same home environment. The twin method, although stronger than the family method, rests on the **equal environments assumption**. The equal environments assumption holds that the environments of MZ twins are no more similar than the environments of DZ twins. Research on twinning and mutual identity, however, suggests that because MZ or identical twins look exactly alike and are very difficult to tell apart, they are often treated more similarly by the people with whom they come into contact and experience a greater sense of mutual identity than DZ or fraternal twins.[9]

Of the three behavioral genetic methods, scientists prefer the adoption method, although even here there are problems. Most children who serve as participants in adoption studies were not adopted at birth and even those who were adopted at birth spent 9 months in the womb environment of the biological mother. If the mother used drugs during pregnancy or failed to practice good prenatal care then this could have a significant detrimental effect on the child's early development. In addition, many adoption agencies in the Scandinavian countries, where much of the adoption research has been conducted, attempt to match the adoptive and biological homes on such potentially important environmental factors as socioeconomic status and urban versus rural setting. Finally, there is the problem of assortative mating, defined as the human tendency to select partners who are similar in certain genetically based traits, such as intelligence and impulsivity. Whereas **assortative mating** inflates heritability estimates in family and adoption studies by giving the child a "double dose" of certain genetically related traits, it deflates heritability estimates in twin studies. This is because there is no room for increased genetic similarity in MZ twins who are already 100% alike genetically, but there is room for an assortative mating-influenced increase in genetic similarity for DZ twins.[10]

Heritability is the degree to which a trait or behavior is genetic. It is normally calculated as a percentage of the total variance in liability for a trait or behavior. Hence, 50% heritability means that half the variance in a particular trait is due to genetic factors. In twin studies, heritability can be expressed as the correlation between MZ twins on a trait or behavior or the concordance for MZ twins minus the concordance for DZ twins times two. Because the equal environments assumption is often violated in twin research, twin-based heritability estimates are often inflated. A more conservative and probably more accurate estimate of heritability can be obtained from adoption studies, where the concordance rate between the adoptee and adoptive parent is subtracted from concordance rate between the adoptee and biological parent and the remainder multiplied by two. In addition to heritability, behavioral geneticists also calculate the variance attributable to living in the same environment (**shared environment**) and individualized experiences (**nonshared environment**). The three estimates—heritability, shared environment, and nonshared environment—when combined, should add up to 100%.[11]

Genetic Studies on Alcohol

There was a great deal of fanfare in 1990 when researchers at the University of Texas Health Sciences Center in San Antonio reported that they had discovered a gene for alcoholism.[12] The gene, a mutant allele of the D_2 dopamine receptor (DRD2) located on chromosome 11, was three and one-half times more prevalent in the autopsied brains of 35 individuals with histories of alcoholism than in the autopsied brains of 35 individuals without histories of alcoholism. A number of methodological problems have hindered attempts to make sense of these results, however, and although there were several successful replications of these findings,[13–14] most studies failed to verify the alleged role of the DRD2 gene as a biological marker for alcoholism.[15–20] Despite the fact most scientists now dismiss the notion of an alcoholism gene, many people have not heard that the single gene theory has been discredited, because whereas the initial press releases were widely disseminated, the retractions have received much less attention (see News Spot 5-1).

NEWS SPOT 5-1

Title: Genetic Studies Yield Opposite Results
Source: *The Washington Post*
Author: David Brown
Date: October 2, 1991

The murky realm of science in which genes are searched for possible effects on complex human behaviors presented itself for inspection this week with two mutually contradictory studies about the risks for alcoholism laid out back-to-back in the same scientific journal.

One study found a strong relationship between alcoholism and possible defects in a particular gene active in the brain. The other found no relationship whatsoever.

The papers represent the sort of conflict that may become increasingly common in an era when it is easy to find genes or genetic markers in large groups of people without knowing at the outset what the genes actually do.

At issue is the chemical dopamine, a substance known to play a role in several neurological illnesses, such as Parkinson's disease, and felt to play a part in the brain's complex circuitry that governs feelings of reward and pleasure. Like all "neurotransmitters," dopamine exerts its effects by stimulating proteins called receptors on the outer surfaces of nerve cells.

A research team at the University of Texas and the University of California surprised the neuroscience world in April 1990, when it reported that more than 69 percent of severe alcoholics carried a DNA marker, called A1- DRD2, that lies very close to the gene for the dopamine receptor on chromosome 11. Only 20 percent of nonalcoholics in that study had A1- DRD2…

In the first of the studies published today in the *Journal of the American Medical Association*, researchers at the City of Hope Medical Center in Duarte, Calif., not only confirm the original findings, but also greatly expand the list of neurological and psychiatric illnesses that A1- DRD2 appears to mark.

"We think it is associated with a spectrum of impulsive, compulsive, or addictive behaviors," said David Comings, a geneticist who headed the study…

In the second study in *JAMA*, researchers at Yale University and the West Haven (Conn.) Veterans Affairs Hospital found that 43 percent of alcoholics and 35 percent of "normal" people carried the A1- DRD2 gene marker—a difference that was not statistically significant. Both the study group and the control group included white participants only.

"I and my collaborators feel quite strongly that there is now no causal relationship (between A1- DRD2 and alcoholism) that has been proved," said Joel Gelernter, a psychiatrist at Yale who headed that study.

Questions to Ponder

1. **What is the media's responsibility when it comes to reporting scientific findings?**
2. **Why did these two studies arrive at such different conclusions?**
3. **Do you believe that a gene for alcoholism will ever be found?**

The alcoholism gene fiasco notwithstanding, the evidence is fairly consistent in showing that genes contribute significantly to the tendency to misuse alcohol. Using data from the Australian twin registry, Andrew Heath and colleagues compared concordance rates for diagnoses of alcohol dependence in 1,328 MZ and 765 DZ twins. The results revealed greater concordance for MZ male and female twins than for DZ male and female twins, with heritability estimates of 50% (38.9% MZ vs. 13.9% DZ) and 23% (20.9% MZ vs. 9.2% DZ) respectively.[21] In a major adoption study on alcoholism, Sigvardsson, Bohman, and Cloninger uncovered evidence of a genetic effect for alcohol dependence in male (24.1% Bio vs. 12.8% Adopt, 23% heritability) but not in female (0.9% Bio vs. 1.3% Adopt) members of the Stockholm adoption cohort.[22] Even though most of the genetic research on substance abuse has focused on alcohol, there is evidence that the use and abuse of other drugs, including tobacco and marijuana, may also be genetically linked.[23] These findings tend to support the predictions of medical disease models of alcoholism and drug abuse, which hold that substance misuse is caused in large part by genetic factors.

Whereas several of the more enthusiastic supporters of genetic models of alcoholism estimate the heritability of alcohol use problems to be somewhere in the neighborhood of 40 to 60%,[24] the actual figure is probably closer to 25%. In a meta-analysis of 50 family, twin, and adoption studies on problem drinking and alcohol dependence, Glenn Walters calculated 27% heritability for alcohol abuse and alcoholism, an 8% effect for shared environment, and a 65% effect for nonshared environment. He also discovered that heritability was stronger for males than for females and higher for more severe definitions of alcohol abuse (alcoholism and alcohol dependence) than for less severe definitions of alcohol use and abuse (problem drinking). Based on these results, he estimated the upper limit of heritability for alcohol use problems (i.e., males with more severe diagnoses) at 30 to 36%.[25] In a subsequent analysis of 41 twin and adoption studies, most of which were included in the original 2002 meta-analysis, Walters obtained a heritability estimate of 23%.[26]

Genetic Studies on Crime

Karl Christiansen examined criminality in an unselected sample of 73 MZ and 146 DZ Danish twin pairs. The results indicated significantly greater concordance between MZ twins than between DZ twins on several different measures of criminality (33% MZ vs. 11% DZ, 44% heritability). Christiansen determined that the MZ/DZ discrepancy was highest when a narrow or more restrictive definition of criminality was employed (i.e., more serious crimes or more serious patterns of criminality).[27] Using a cross-fostering analysis of data collected on 14,427 Danish adoptees, Sarnoff Mednick, William Gabrielli, and Barry Hutchings recorded conviction rates of 13.5%, 14.7%, 20.0%, and 24.5% for adoptees with no criminal parents, a criminal adoptive parent but no criminal biological parent, a criminal biological parent but no criminal adoptive parent, and a criminal biological parent and a criminal adoptive parent, respectively. In this study the genetic effect was significant (20.0% vs. 13.5%) but the environmental effect was not (14.7% vs. 13.5%), although the strongest effect was observed when both genetic and environmental components were positive for crime (24.5%).[28]

Walters performed a meta-analysis of genetic studies on crime a decade before he performed his meta-analysis on genetic studies on alcohol abuse. The results of this meta-analysis revealed 14% heritability for crime, a figure about half that obtained in the later alcohol abuse meta-analysis.[29] However, the shared environment effect for crime was three times higher than the shared environment effect for alcohol abuse obtained in the Walters meta-analysis of alcohol abuse studies (see **Figure 5-3**). This suggests that although genetics play a more salient role in alcohol abuse than in crime, shared family experiences play a more important role in crime than in alcohol abuse. In addition, whereas heritability for alcohol use problems is higher for males than for females, the situation is reversed with crime in that females experience higher heritability for crime than males (see **Figure 5-4**).

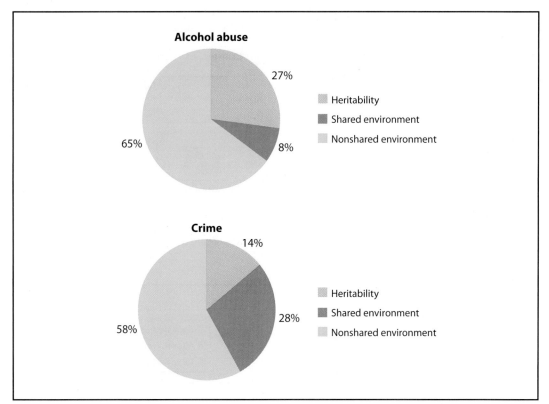

Figure 5-3
Heritability, shared environment, and nonshared environment for alcohol abuse and crime.

Data From: Walters, G. D. (1992). A meta-analysis of the gene-crime relationship. *Criminology*, 30, 595–613 & Walters, G. D. (2002). The heritability of alcohol abuse and dependence: A meta-analysis of behavior genetic research. *American Journal of Drug and Alcohol Abuse*, 28, 557–584.

The two meta-analyses by Walters used a case-to-case statistical model to analyze genetic data on alcohol abuse and crime. In a case-to-case approach the presence or absence of the identified behavior (crime, alcohol abuse) is crossed with a dichotomous measure of genetic liability (i.e., MZ vs. DZ or Bio vs. Adopt). This procedure can be criticized for potentially lowering the ceiling of the measured genetic effect when applied to low base-rate behaviors like crime and drug abuse. To test this possibility, Walters compared twin and adoption studies for alcohol abuse and crime with 19 twin and adoption studies on schizophrenia, another low base-rate behavior believed to have a strong genetic component. Using the case-to-case approach with twin and adoption studies on schizophrenia, alcohol abuse, and crime, Walters observed 70% heritability in schizophrenia, 23% heritability in alcohol abuse, and 17% heritability in crime (see **Figure 5-5**).[30] These results suggest that the moderate and modest heritability found for alcohol abuse and crime, respectively, were not simply a function of the methodology used in the original Walters meta-analyses. Furthermore, whereas alcohol abuse and crime are both influenced by genetic factors, environmental factors are even more important in the development of these behaviors.

Genetic Studies on Alcohol and Crime

There have been at least two studies in which **cross-concordance** for alcohol and criminal behavior has been compared across MZ and DZ twins. Matthew McGue, Roy Pickens, and Dace Svikis determined that cross-concordance for alcohol in the **proband** twin (member

Figure 5-4
Effect sizes (*r*) for twin and adoption studies on alcohol abuse and crime broken down by gender.

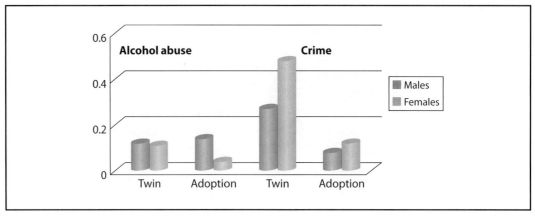

Data From: Walters, G. D. (1992). A meta-analysis of the gene-crime relationship. *Criminology*, 30, 595–613 & Walters, G. D. (2002). The heritability of alcohol abuse and dependence: A meta-analysis of behavior genetic research. *American Journal of Drug and Alcohol Abuse*, 28, 557–584.

Figure 5-5
Effect sizes (*r*) obtained with twin and adoption studies on schizophrenia, alcohol abuse, and crime.

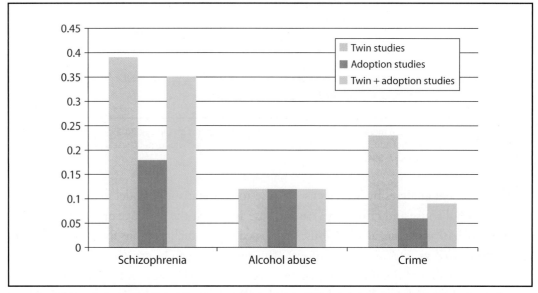

Data From: Walters, G. D. (2006). Pattern inheritance and the genetics of lifestyle behavior. In G. D. Walters, *Lifestyle Theory: Past, Present, and Future* (pp. 87–102). New York: Nova Science.

of a twin pair that is the focus of investigation) and conduct disorder in the **cotwin** (member of a twin pair that is not the focus of investigation) was twice as high in male MZ twins as in male DZ twins, although female MZ and DZ twins failed to differ in their cross-concordance for alcohol and crime.[31] In an earlier study, Gurling, Oppenheim, and Murray discovered that the cross-concordance for alcoholism and criminal convictions was actually higher in DZ than in MZ twins.[32] The Gurling et al. study is limited, however, by the fact that it included only 14 MZ and 14 DZ twin pairs.

Several adoption studies have also explored cross-concordance for alcohol and crime. In an early study, Donald Goodwin, Fini Schulsinger, and Leif Hermansen observed greater concordance between adoptees and their adoptive parents than between adoptees and their biological parents, a finding that runs counter to the genetic hypothesis.[33] In several Swedish adoption studies, however, there was greater cross-concordance between adoptees and their biological parents than between adoptees and their adoptive parents in male but not female adoptees.[34–35] In a sample of male and female Iowan adoptees, Remi Cadoret and colleagues witnessed three-times greater concordance between alcohol abuse in a biological parent and antisocial personality disorder in the adoptee (44.4%) than between alcohol abuse in an adoptive parent and antisocial personality disorder in the adoptee (14.3%). They also observed slightly better concordance between antisocial behavior in a biological parent and alcohol abuse in the adoptee than between antisocial behavior in an adoptive parent and alcohol abuse in the adoptee (33.3% vs. 20.0%).[36]

In a meta-analysis of cross-concordance studies on alcohol abuse and crime, Walters obtained a mean effect size of .065 for males and a mean effect size of -.000 for females.[37] Although the male figure is small, it needs to be evaluated in light of the fact that the average genetic variance of the involved patterns (alcohol abuse and crime) is also small (~.11). Comparing the proportion of cross-concordance to total concordance for alcohol abuse and crime (.065/.11 = .59) reveals that cross-concordance accounts for approximately 59% of the total genetic effect for male alcohol abuse and crime. This finding is consistent with the results of a behavioral genetic study by Wendy Slutske and colleagues in which 70% of the association between alcohol abuse and conduct disorder was attributed to a common inherited risk factor.[38] It could therefore be argued that at least in males, a greater portion of the genetic variance in crime and alcohol abuse can be traced back to a general deviance or low self-control factor than to genetic effects specific to either individual pattern.

Neurophysiology

The central nervous system is composed of the brain and the spinal cord. A drug is taken into the body through ingestion, inhalation, smoking, injection, or enema, and is eventually carried to the brain through the blood stream. To enter the brain, however, the drug must pass through the blood–brain barrier. The blood–brain barrier is a series of densely packed capillaries that do not allow substances to easily diffuse through their walls. Because most drugs are lipid (fat) soluble, they pass easily through the capillary wall into the brain. Drugs like cocaine, that are not lipid soluble, have to be transported through the capillary wall by special carrier proteins. Once in the brain, the drug interacts with the fundamental element of the central nervous system, the **neuron**, to create certain physical and psychological changes.[39]

A neuron can be defined as an electronically excitable cell capable of both processing and transmitting information. The neuron gathers information from neighboring brain cells and then passes this information on to cells further along in the chain by means of an electrochemical process. The function of a neuron can perhaps best be understood by examining its structure. The neuron can be divided into four parts: cell body, **dendrites**, **axon**, and **terminal buttons**. Two of the most important structures in the cell body are the **nucleus** and **mitochondria**. The nucleus is where the chromosomes are located and the mitochondria help convert food into energy the cell needs to meet its high daily energy requirements. Dendrites are treelike structures that receive signals from other cells, sending the signals down a long,

Figure 5-6
Components of
a neuron.

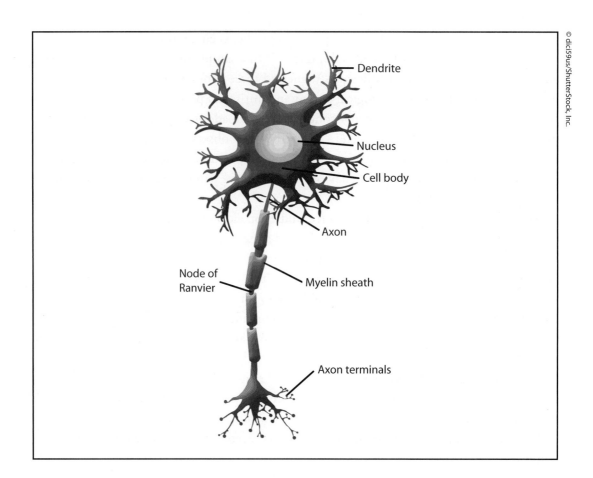

slender projection known as the axon. The signal eventually reaches the terminal buttons where it stimulates the release of whatever neurotransmitter is stored there (see **Figure 5-6**).[40]

As multiple inputs are summed, the cell membrane becomes increasingly more permeable to sodium, a positively charged ion. When the negative resting potential of the cell changes to become less negative the ion channels open and sodium rushes into the cell, depolarizing the cell (i.e., changing its potential from negative to positive). This is known as an **action potential** (see **Figure 5-7**). The action potential then propagates down the length of the axon. Because the speed of propagation is a function of the diameter of the axon and axons in the human brain are microscopic, there is a need for additional mechanisms to speed up the transfer of information. One such mechanism is **myelin**, a white lipoprotein covering that wraps itself tightly around the axon. Transmembrane current flow only occurs in the unmyelinated sections (**nodes of Ranvier**) of the axon (see **Figure 5-8**). The action potential consequently jumps from node to node, skipping over the myelinated sections. This process, which substantially increases the speed of propagation, is called **saltatory conduction**.[41]

Eventually, the action potential reaches the terminal button. This is where the neurotransmitter substance is located. During an action potential the **vesicles** where the neurotransmitter molecules are stored migrate toward the presynaptic membrane. When the vesicle comes into contact with the presynaptic membrane it bursts, spilling its contents into

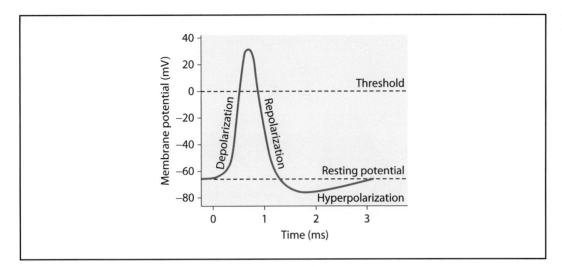

Figure 5-7
The action potential.

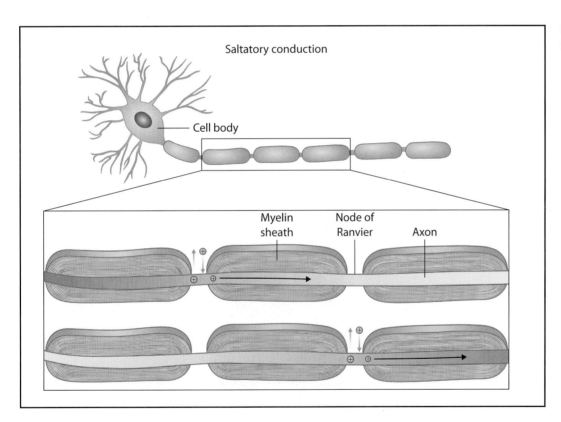

Figure 5-8
Saltarory conduction.

the synaptic cleft, a process known as **exocytosis** (see **Figure 5-9**). The neurotransmitter molecules then diffuse across the synaptic cleft, eventually attaching themselves to postsynaptic receptor sites where they cause a momentary change in the permeability of the postsynaptic membrane by opening ion channels and allowing a free exchange of ions. A reuptake mechanism in the presynaptic membrane then reabsorbs the transmitter molecules, breaks them down, and recycles them through a process known as **endocytosis** (see **Figure 5-10**).[42]

Figure 5-9
Release of
neurotransmitter into
synapse.

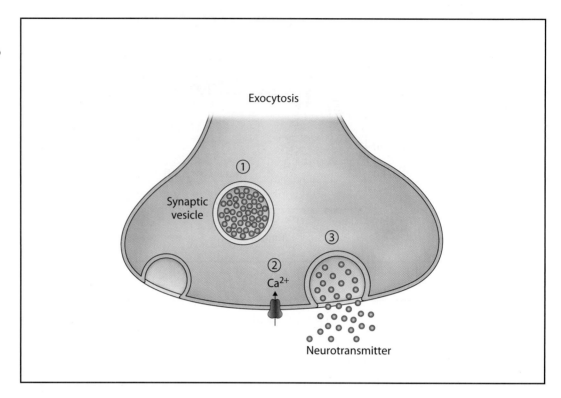

Figure 5-10
Recycling of vessicles
by means of
endocytosis.

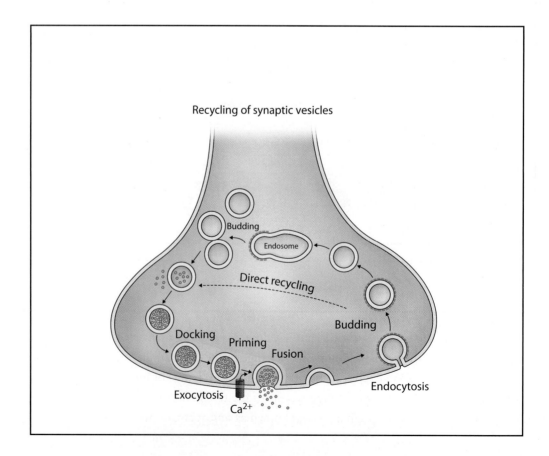

Table 5-1 Major Neurotransmitters

Neurotransmitter	effect	precursor	Functions
Dopamine (DA)	Excitatory	L-Dopa	Schizophrenia Parkinson's Disease Reward System
Gamma-Aminobutyric Acid (GABA)	Inhibitory	Glutamic Acid	Anxiety reduction Muscle relaxation
Norepinephrine (NE)	Excitatory/Inhibitory	Dopamine	Alertness/wakefulness Sympathetic arousal
Serotonin (5-HT)	Inhibitory/Excitatory	Tryptophan	Regulation of mood Control of sleep/arousal Regulation of pain

It is important to understand that neurons communicate with one another by means of an electrochemical process:

- Electrical—**depolarization** and the movement of the action potential down the axon by means of changes in membrane permeability or saltatory conduction.
- Chemical—neurotransmitter molecules cross the synaptic cleft and occupy the postsynaptic receptor site to either increase (excitatory effect) or decrease (inhibitory effect) the receiving neuron's chances of depolarizing (firing).

Neurotransmitter substances important in the development of drug use and criminal behavior include dopamine (DA), **gamma-aminobutyric acid** (GABA), **norephinephrine** (NE), and **serotonin** (5-HT). Although a neurotransmitter can have only one of two effects on the receiving neuron, excitatory or inhibitory, many neurotransmitters have both excitatory and inhibitory properties, depending on where in the central nervous system the effect takes place. Basic information on these four neurotransmitters can be found in **Table 5-1**.[43]

Neurophysiology and Drugs

The human brain has evolved to the point where repetition of life-sustaining activities is associated with pleasure or reward in the form of activation of the dopamine-rich **mesolimbic system**, which runs from the ventral tegmental area of the midbrain to major limbic structures like the amygdala, hippocampus, and nucleus accumbens.[44] The compulsive aspect of drug use can be traced back, in part, to the effect drugs have on the action of dopamine in the mesolimbic system. There are three competing theories designed to explain the causal effect of the mesolimbic dopamine system on reward. One theory holds that dopamine triggers a hedonistic or "liking" response in the organism. A second theory holds that dopamine helps the individual predict or "learn" to anticipate future reward. A third theory maintains that dopamine creates a "wanting" response in the organism by focusing the organism's attention on reward-related stimuli. Although there is evidence to support each of these three theories, a recent review of the literature by Kent Berridge (2007) indicates that the "wanting" hypothesis has received more support than the "liking" and "learning" explanations.[45]

Twenty-five years ago, Di Chiara and Imperato determined that drugs of abuse stimulate 2 to 10 times as much dopamine release as natural rewards and nonpharmacological reinforcers.[46] Since that time, interest in the effects of various drugs of abuse on the dopamine-rich reward pathways of the mesolimbic system has grown. In a systematic review of the neurochemical correlates of five drugs of abuse (stimulants, nicotine, alcohol, marijuana, and opiates) strong evidence was found that stimulants, nicotine, and alcohol are used because of their dopamine-enhancing properties. Marijuana and opiates also appear to be used in part because of their dopamine-enhancing effects, but in the case of marijuana there is too little research to understand the full extent of the effect and in the case of opiates there are dopamine-independent mechanisms operating as well (e.g., endorphins).[47] There are several ways drugs enhance the action of dopamine (see **Figure 5-11**). Most drugs of abuse stimulate the direct release of dopamine. In addition, drugs like cocaine and amphetamine block the

Figure 5-11
Different ways the action of dopamine can be potentiated.

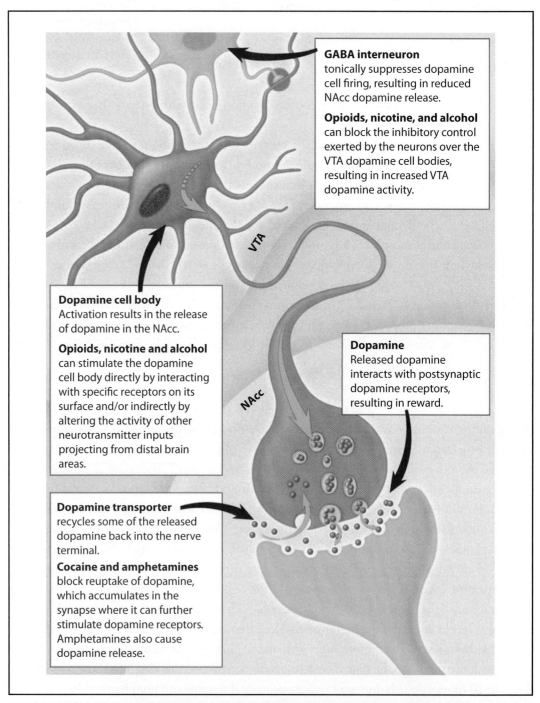

GABA interneuron
tonically suppresses dopamine cell firing, resulting in reduced NAcc dopamine release.

Opioids, nicotine, and alcohol
can block the inhibitory control exerted by the neurons over the VTA dopamine cell bodies, resulting in increased VTA dopamine activity.

Dopamine cell body
Activation results in the release of dopamine in the NAcc.

Opioids, nicotine and alcohol
can stimulate the dopamine cell body directly by interacting with specific receptors on its surface and/or indirectly by altering the activity of other neurotransmitter inputs projecting from distal brain areas.

Dopamine
Released dopamine interacts with postsynaptic dopamine receptors, resulting in reward.

Dopamine transporter
recycles some of the released dopamine back into the nerve terminal.

Cocaine and amphetamines
block reuptake of dopamine, which accumulates in the synapse where it can further stimulate dopamine receptors. Amphetamines also cause dopamine release.

VTA

NAcc

reuptake of dopamine into the presynaptic terminal so that the neurotransmitter can remain in the **synapse** longer and thereby exert a more sustained effect on the postsynaptic receptor sites. Finally, drugs like alcohol, nicotine, and opiates enhance dopaminergic activity by interacting with a neurotransmitter (GABA) that sometimes inhibits dopamine. By inhibiting the inhibitor the action of dopamine is disinhibited or potentiated.[48]

The brain responds to the rise in dopamine, secondary to habitual drug use, by producing less dopamine and reducing the number and/or sensitivity of dopamine receptors. Dopamine depletion with habitual drug use has been well documented in animals[49] but has also been observed in humans. With continued use of drugs, dopamine's natural effect on the reward pathways of the brain is attenuated to such an extent that the user has trouble experiencing pleasure without the drug. Even with the drug, the experience is no longer as intense as it was during initial usage, thus giving rise to the phenomenon of chasing in which subsequent usage is, in part, a futile attempt to recapture the initial drug experience. At this point, the habitual drug user consumes drugs just to feel "normal" and feeling normal often means increasing the dosage (tolerance).[50] Remaining abstinent from the drug for a sufficient period of time, which in some cases means not using the drug for 24 months or longer, can bring dopamine levels back to normal (see **Figure 5-12**).[51]

Neurophysiology and Crime

Neurotransmitters, particularly dopamine, may be as instrumental in motivating crime as they are in motivating drug use. Several genes responsible for the production of dopamine have been found to be associated with aggression and conduct disorder in children.[52] Risk taking, as measured by the Novelty Seeking Scale of the Tridimensional Personality Questionnaire,[53] was found to correlate with dopamine receptor availability in a small group of neurologically and psychiatrically healthy adults. Novelty seekers and risk takers may have fewer dopamine autoreceptors than normal, making it difficult for them to terminate an ongoing reinforcing activity.[54] Joshua Buckholtz, David Zald and other researchers at Vanderbilt University have identified a number of dopamine-related deficits in offenders, particularly those individuals classified as psychopathic, that encourage them to pursue rewards irrespective of the cost.[55] The

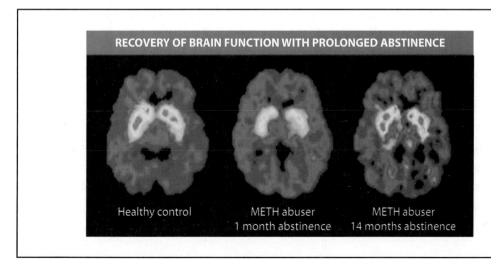

Figure 5-12
Distribution of dopamine transporters (lighter areas) in the striatum of a normal individual and methamphetamine abuser after 1 and 14 months of abstinence.

Zickle, P. (2002, April). Methamphetamine abuse linked to impaired cognitive and motor skills despite recovery of dopamine transporters. *NIDA Notes*, Vol. 17, No. 1.

pursuit of reward irrespective of the cost is a long-recognized feature of criminality and this study suggests that such a tendency can perhaps be traced to dysregulation in the mesolimbic dopamine system. The Buckholtz study, as the reader might guess, has attracted its share of popular media attention (see News Spot 5-2).

News spot 5-2

Title: Impulsive-Antisocial Personality Traits Linked to a Hypersensitive Brain Reward System
Source: *NIH News*
Author: NIDA Press Team
Date: March 15, 2010

Normal individuals who scored high on a measure of impulsive/antisocial traits display a hypersensitive brain reward system, according to a brain imaging study by researchers at Vanderbilt University. The findings provide the first evidence of differences in the brain's reward system that may underlie vulnerability to what's typically referred to as psychopathy.

The study in the current issue of the journal Nature Neuroscience was funded by the National Institute on Drug Abuse (NIDA), a component of the National Institutes of Health.

Psychopathy is a personality disorder characterized by a combination of superficial charm, manipulative and antisocial behavior, sensation-seeking and impulsivity, blunted empathy and punishment sensitivity, and shallow emotional experiences. Psychopathy is a particularly robust predictor of criminal behavior and recidivism.

Since psychopathic individuals are at increased risk for developing substance use problems, the Vanderbilt team decided to investigate possible links between the brain's reward system (activated by abused substances and natural reward), and a behavioral trait (impulsive/antisociality) characteristic of psychopathy. Researchers used two different technologies to measure the brain's reward response. …

The results in both cases show that individuals who scored high on a personality assessment that teases out traits like egocentricity, manipulating others, and risk taking had a hypersensitive dopamine response system. The picture that emerges from these high resolution PET and fMRI scans suggests that alterations in the function of the brain's reward system may contribute to a latent psychopathic trait. …

Questions to ponder
1. **When you hear the term psychopath, what comes to mind?**
2. **If psychopaths are "hardwired" for risk-taking, does this excuse them from criminal responsibility for crimes committed out of a sense of excitement or frustration?**
3. **What might some of the components of the latent psychopathic trait described in this article be?**

Whereas dopamine may explain a certain portion of crime, its interaction with other neurotransmitters may explain even more crime. Serotonin, for example, often modulates the reward-seeking features of dopamine. One possibility, then, is that antisocial behavior is partly a function of inadequate modulation of dopamine by serotonin in that a 2002 meta-analysis showed reduced levels of the serotonin metabolite, 5-hydroxyindoleacetic acid (5-HIAA), in antisocial individuals.[56] Henrik Soderstrom and colleagues examined the dopamine-serotonin relationship in 28 violent and sexual offenders between the ages of 18 and 45 and detected an abnormally high homovanillic acid (HVA, a metabolite of dopamine) to 5-HIAA ratio, indicating impaired serotonergic modulation of dopamine. These authors discovered a particularly high HVA to 5-HIAA ratio for such Factor 2 Psychopathy Checklist traits as impulsivity, irresponsibility, and need for stimulation as well as for a history of childhood conduct disorder and hyperactivity. Based on these results, Soderstrom et al. speculate that dopamine modulating drugs, alone or in combination with serotonin reuptake inhibitors like Prozac, may be of some value in treating psychopathy.[57]

Neurophysiology, Drugs, and Crime

There has been virtually no research exploring the possibility of a neurophysiogical connection between drugs and crime, but it is interesting that both drug use and crime seem to stimulate the release of dopamine. If the preliminary research of Zald et al. is correct and individuals high in novelty seeking and risk taking suffer from decreased dopamine receptor availability,[58] this may provide a partial explanation for the connection between drugs and crime and help account for the fact that over two-thirds of offenders seriously abuse alcohol or illegal drugs.[59-60] An individual born with a smaller than average number of dopamine receptors will seek out excitement in its various forms to attain the level of reward most other people achieve naturally. Owing to the fact that natural reward experiences will normally be insufficient to achieve the desired effect in someone with fewer than normal dopamine receptors, he or she may use drugs or engage in crime as a way of achieving an optimal level of dopamine stimulation and reward in that both behaviors appear to provide greater release of dopamine than natural rewards.[61-62] Because of an abnormally low number of dopamine autoreceptors and/or ineffective modulation of dopamine by the serotonin system, once the individual starts engaging in drug use and crime, the system tends to become flooded with dopamine, thereby making it difficult for the individual to stop the rewarding behavior in which he or she is currently engaged.[63] In combination with various biological, psychological, sociological, and situational factors, this could provide a partial (third variable) explanation for the drug–crime nexus.

Brain systems

Jeffrey Gray has postulated the existence of two interacting brain systems: a **behavioral activation system** (BAS) and a **behavioral inhibition system** (BIS). The BAS is an approach-oriented, positive-incentive system grounded in the dopamine-rich fibers of the mesolimbic system.[64-65] It is goal directed, reward sensitive, and thrill seeking. In Cloninger's unified biosocial theory of addiction, the BAS is represented by the novelty seeking personality dimension.[66] The BIS is an avoidance-oriented, negative-incentive system grounded in the serotonin-rich fibers of the prefrontal cortex-limbic system. It is nongoal directed, threat sensitive, and responsive to punishment. The BIS projects from the prefrontal cortex to the limbic system (see **Figure 5-13**). The BAS and BIS have opposing effects: the BAS activates the limbic system, the BIS inhibits it. According to Gray, it is the balance of these two systems that determines various behavioral patterns, from drug use to crime.[67] In Cloninger's unified biosocial theory, the BIS is represented by the harm avoidance personality dimension.[68]

Brain Systems and Drugs

Zisserson and Palfai ascertained that heavy drinkers demonstrated appetitive responses (BAS) in response to the sight and smell of their favorite alcoholic beverage.[69] In comparing male heroin addicts to controls, Jeddi Abdalehzade and colleagues discerned that although heroin addicts scored significantly higher on a BAS scale (particularly the Fun-Seeking subscale), there were no differences between the two groups on the BIS scale.[70] Knyazev examined drug use in a large sample of college and university students and found that behavioral activation was the best personality predictor of drug use. Peer and parental support decreased the strength of association between behavioral activation and drug use in females but not in males.[71] The results of these studies suggest that whereas drug use is associated with a strong BAS response, there is no apparent relationship between drug use and BIS response.

Brain Systems and Crime

Don Fowles hypothesized that psychopathy was a function of a weak BIS.[72] Research conducted on this proposition, however, reveals that weak BIS is a less consistent correlate of psychopathy than strong BAS.[73] Baskin-Sommers and colleagues nonetheless tested Fowles' hypothesis and determined that psychopathic offenders were significantly less sensitive to BIS-related cues than controls.[74] Hence, whereas drug use is consistently associated with a strong BAS response, serious offending, as represented by the construct of psychopathy, is

Figure 5-13
Brain structures that are part of the Behavioral Activation and Behavioral Inhibition Systems.

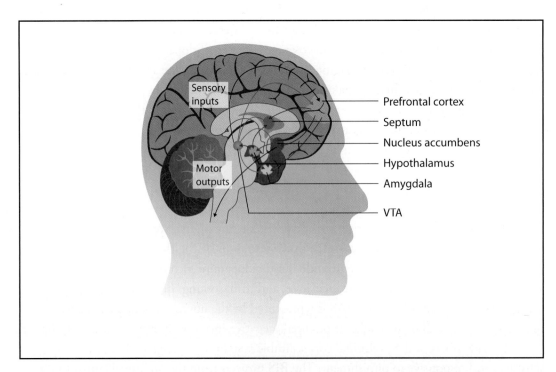

associated with a strong BAS response and a weak BIS response. Offenders, it would seem, are not only attracted to reward but also have trouble inhibiting their behavior in response to punishment or the threat of punishment.

Brain Systems, Drugs, and Crime

Jeanette Taylor, Mark Reeves, Lisa James, and Leonardo Bobadillo performed a cluster analysis of various BIS and BAS scales and identified five clusters, two of which were associated with elevated levels of drug use and antisocial behavior. One of the two clusters suggested the presence of a "disinhibited" pattern characterized by strong BAS tendencies, weak BIS tendencies, heavy illegal drug use, and antisocial personality disorder. The other cluster suggested a "high affectivity" pattern characterized by strong BIS tendencies, heavy illegal drug use, and a mixture of antisocial, narcissistic, and borderline personality traits.[75] These results suggest the presence of multiple drug use and crime patterns based on the relative strength of BAS and BIS activation and are partially consistent with the self-medication hypothesis, which holds that people abuse drugs to deal with underlying personality and emotional problems.

Investigating BAS and BIS mediation of disinhibition in conduct disorder and binge drinking, Natalie Castellanos-Ryan, Katya Rubia, and Patricia Conrod tested two different causal models: one from impulsivity at age 14 to conduct disorder at age 16 and one from sensation seeking at age 14 to binge drinking at age 16. The study was conducted on a group of 76 adolescents followed for a period of 2 years. The outcome indicated that the relationship between impulsivity and conduct disorder was mediated by weak BIS functioning whereas the relationship between sensation seeking and binge drinking was mediated by strong BAS functioning. The authors interpret these findings as evidence of dual cognitive/motivational pathways to drug use and crime that are mediated differentially by the BIS and BAS, respectively.[76]

Autonomic Nervous System

The **autonomic nervous system** (ANS) is part of the peripheral nervous system. Its principal function is to control involuntary physiological responses like circulation, digestion, and respiration. To accomplish this task the ANS is divided into two parts: a **sympathetic** branch and a **parasympathetic** branch. The sympathetic branch of the ANS flows from cell bodies in the thoracic and lumbar regions of the spinal cord (hence, the term thoracolumbar outflow) to create a "fight or flight" response. In other words, sympathetic activation occurs when the organism perceives a threat, which then encourages the organism to either confront the threat or run from it. As part of the sympathetic response, the heart rate will increase, the blood vessels will constrict, the pupils will dilate, the bronchi in the lungs will relax, and digestive activity will decrease (see **Figure 5-14a**). These responses are all designed to prepare the organism to fight or flee from threat.[77]

The parasympathetic branch of the ANS is activated by cell bodies in the cranial nerves and sacral or lower section of the spinal cord (hence, the term craniosacral outflow). Its primary function is to create a resting or relaxation response to help balance the "fight or flight" response of the sympathetic branch. Too much time spent in sympathetic activation can lead to physical and psychological exhaustion and dysfunction. The parasympathetic response accordingly allows the organism to rest and replenish itself. When the parasympathetic division is active, heart rate is decreased, blood vessels are dilated, the pupils constrict, the bronchi in the lungs constrict, and the digestive system tends to speed up (see Figure 5-14b). Parasympathetic activation is designed to increase the organism's level of stored energy so that it is in a better position to meet the demands and responsibilities of everyday living.[78]

The ANS and Drugs

Stimulant drugs like cocaine, amphetamine, and nicotine activate the sympathetic branch of the ANS, whereas depressant drugs like alcohol, sedatives, and tranquilizers activate the parasympathetic branch. Other drugs, such as the opiates, produce a mixed autonomic response: activating portions of the parasympathetic division (decreased heart rate, reduced breathing) as well as portions of the sympathetic division (reduced gastric motility leading to constriction of the intestinal muscles and constipation). Habitual drug use can disrupt the delicate balance between the sympathetic and parasympathetic branches of the ANS and lead to several long-term problems, including cardiovascular neuropathy, orthostatic hypotension, and erectile dysfunction.[79]

The ANS and Crime

There is minimal research on the relationship between ANS activation and crime. However, the buildup to crime could be viewed as a form of sympathetic arousal and successful completion of a crime could well lead to a state of parasympathetic rest and relaxation. Adrian Raine, Peter Venables, and Sarnoff Mednick are one of the few research teams to actively investigate the relationship between sympathetic activation and crime. They discovered that children with low resting heart rates (indicative of reduced sympathetic activity) at age 3 were more likely to engage in physical violence at age 11 than 3-year-old children with normal or high resting heart rates tested at age 11. They speculate that sympathetic underarousal may place an individual at risk for future violence and criminal behavior by virtue of crime's ability to act like a stimulant drug and elevate the individual's normally weak level of sympathetic arousal.[80] Deficits in sympathetic arousal are consistent with Hare's psychopathy model of crime.[81]

ANS, Drugs, and Crime

There is mounting evidence that drug abuse may be categorical.[82-83] Whether we draw the line between brain systems (BAS vs. BIS)[84] or personality–neurotransmitter patterns (harm avoidance-serotonin vs. novelty seeking-dopamine),[85] there is evidence that criminality may interact differentially with various drug-use types. For instance, Cloninger proposes that **Type 1 alcoholism** has a later age of onset, moderate heritability, and no connection to crime, whereas **Type 2 alcoholism** has an earlier age of onset, strong inheritance, and a significant connection to crime.[86] Should it turn out that Type 2 alcoholics also have strong novelty seeking and weak harm avoidance and that both alcohol and crime are an attempt to overcome a low baseline level of sympathetic arousal, this would support a third variable

Sympathetic system

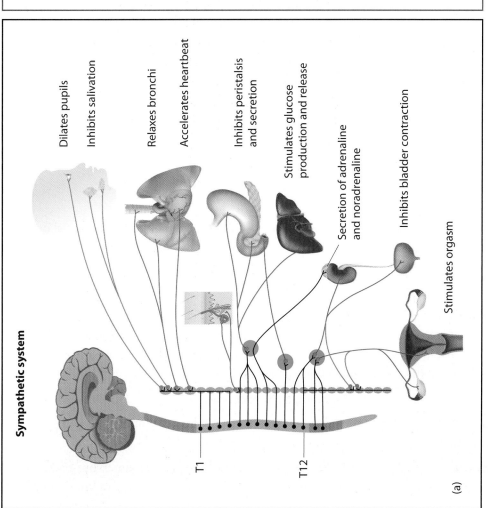

Dilates pupils

Inhibits salivation

Relaxes bronchi

Accelerates heartbeat

Inhibits peristalsis and secretion

Stimulates glucose production and release

Secretion of adrenaline and noradrenaline

Inhibits bladder contraction

Stimulates orgasm

T1

T12

(a)

Parasympathetic system

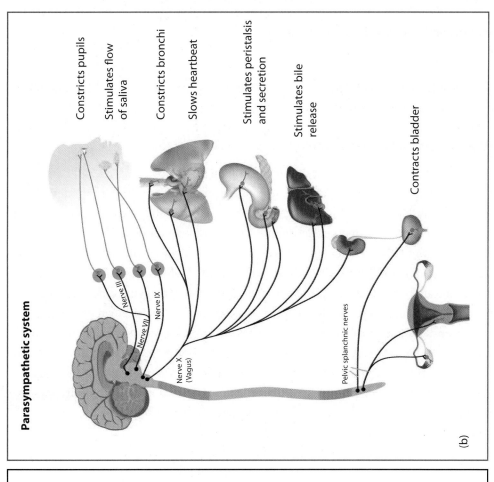

Constricts pupils

Stimulates flow of saliva

Constricts bronchi

Slows heartbeat

Stimulates peristalsis and secretion

Stimulates bile release

Contracts bladder

Nerve III

Nerve VII

Nerve IX

Nerve X (Vagus)

Pelvic splanchnic nerves

(b)

Figure 5-14

The sympathetic (a) and parasympathetic (b) branches of the Autonomic Nervous System (ANS).

interpretation of the drug–crime nexus, similar to the low dopamine sensitivity/availability hypothesis described earlier in this chapter.

summary and Conclusions

- Genetic factors appear to play a significant role in both alcohol abuse and crime. Heritability for these behaviors tends to range from modest (crime) to moderate (alcohol abuse) and is significantly lower than the heritability of a disorder with well-documented genetic roots (i.e., schizophrenia). Cross-concordance between alcohol abuse and crime in several behavioral genetic studies suggests that the inherited liability for these disorders is primarily due to a third variable with which alcohol abuse and crime are both correlated, one possible candidate being general deviance.
- Neurophysiological studies indicate that drug use and crime stimulate the dopamine-rich reward circuits of the brain that run from the ventral tegmental area of the mid-brain to various structures in the limbic system. This provides additional support for a third variable explanation of biologically based drug–crime relationships. There is also preliminary evidence to suggest that it is the ratio of dopamine (novelty seeking) to serotonin (harm avoidance) that is important in determining drug use and criminal behavior.
- The behavioral activation system (BAS) and behavioral inhibition system (BIS) may also be important in drug use and crime. Several subtypes have been identified and two disinhibition subtypes in one study (strong BAS/weak BIS and strong BIS) may be particularly useful in making sense of drug–crime relationships.
- Stimulant drugs activate the sympathetic ("fight or flight") branch of the autonomic nervous system (ANS), whereas depressant drugs activate the parasympathetic ("relaxation and restoration") branch. Low sympathetic arousal may encourage some individuals to use drugs and/or commit crime in order to achieve an optimal level of sympathetic arousal.

Key terms

Action Potential   Momentary depolarization of a cell in which the electrical potential on the surface of a neuron changes rapidly from negative to positive and then back again to negative.

Additive Transmission   Multiple genes from different loci and in various combinations contribute to a behavior.

Adoption Studies   Behavioral genetic method in which concordance between adoptees and their biological parents is compared to concordance between adoptees and their adoptive parents; a genetic effect is suggested when adoptee–biological parent concordance is greater than adoptee–adoptive parent concordance.

Allele   One of a pair of genes found on a chromosome.

Assortative Mating   Human tendency to select mates who are similar in certain genetically related traits.

Autonomic Nervous System (ANS)   A component of the peripheral nervous system designed to control involuntary responses like circulation, digestion, and respiration.

Axon Long, slender projection of a neuron that directs electrical impulses from the cell body to the terminal buttons.

Behavioral Activation System Approach-oriented, positive-incentive system grounded in the mesolimbic system.

Behavioral Inhibition System Avoidance-oriented, negative-incentive system grounded in the prefrontal cortex-limbic system.

Chromosome Microscopic thread-like process composed of two linear strands of DNA that holds the genes; a normal human has 23 pairs of chromosomes.

Concordance Agreement between pairs of twins or between an adoptee and his/her biological or adoptive parents.

Cotwin Member of a twin pair that is not the principal focus of investigation.

Cross-Concordance Agreement between twins or between an adoptee and his/her biological or adoptive parents across different behaviors (e.g., crime and alcohol abuse).

Dendrites Treelike structures on a neuron that receive signals from other neurons.

Deoxyribonucleic acid (DNA) Nucleic acid that carries the information for heredity.

Depolarization Change in a cell's membrane potential, making it less negative or more positive; commonly referred to as a "firing" neuron.

Dizygotic (DZ) Two-egg twin pair; also referred to as fraternal twins.

Dominant Transmission Only one of two copies (alleles) of a gene are required for the trait or behavior to surface.

Dopamine Excitatory neurotransmitter substance.

Emergenesis Nonadditive form of multiple gene transmission in which a specific combination of genes from different loci is required for behavioral expression of a trait.

Equal Environments Assumption Assumption that the environments of monozygotic twins are no more similar than are the environments of dizygotic twins.

Endocytosis Recycling of neurotransmitter substance in the presynaptic button.

Exocytosis Release of a neurotransmitter substance into the synaptic cleft.

Family Studies Behavioral genetic method in which family relationships are studied in an effort to determine the genetic inheritance of various behavioral traits.

First-Degree Relatives Share 50% of their genes in common: parents, children, and siblings.

Gamma-Aminobutyric Acid (GABA) Inhibitory neurotransmitter substance.

Gene Basic unit of heredity; located on chromosomes.

Gene–Environment Correlation Gene and environment correlate but do not interact through one of three mechanisms: passive, active, and reactive.

Gene–Environment Interaction Gene and environment interact such that a gene is expressed in one environment but not another environment.

Genotype Actual alleles present in a particular genome.

Heritability Degree to which a trait or behavior is inherited; expressed as a percentage out of 100.

Karotype   The number, form, and size of chromosomes that characterize a species.

Locus   Position on a chromosome where a gene is located.

Mesolimbic System   Reward system of the brain that runs from the ventral tegmental area of the mesencephelon to various limbic structures, to include the amygdala, hippocampus, and nucleus accumbens.

Mitochondria   Membrane-enclosed organelle found in the cell body of a neuron and responsible for converting food into energy.

Monozygotic (MZ)   Single-egg twin pair; also referred to as identical twins.

Myelin   White insulating material that surrounds the axon of a neuron and significantly speeds up the transmission of a signal down the axon.

Neuron   Electronically excitable cell capable of both processing and transmitting information.

Neurotransmitter   Substance capable of increasing or decreasing the propensity of a neuron to depolarize or fire.

Node of Ranvier   Small unmyelinated sections of an axon.

Nonshared Environment   Degree to which a trait or behavior is the result of unique, unshared experiences; expressed as a percentage out of 100.

Norepinephrine   Neurotransmitter substance capable of both exciting and inhibiting other neurons.

Nucleus   Membrane-enclosed organelle located in the cell body of a neuron.

Parasympathetic   Division of the autonomic nervous system designed to create a relaxation or resting response.

Phenotype   Behavioral expression of a genotype in the form of an observable characteristic or behavior.

Polygenetic   Involving multiple genes.

Proband   Member of a twin pair that is the focus of investigation.

Recessive Transmission   Both copies (alleles) of a gene are required for the trait or behavior to surface.

Saltatory Conduction   Rapid transmission of an action potential down the axon by skipping over the myelinated sections.

Second-Degree Relatives   Share 25% of their genes in common: half-sibling, grandparents, aunts/uncles.

Serotonin   Neurotransmitter substance capable of both exciting and inhibiting other neurons.

Shared Environment   Degree to which a trait or behavior is the result of common, often family, experiences; expressed as a percentage out of 100.

Sympathetic   Division of the autonomic nervous system designed to manage threat by creating a "fight or flight" response in the organism.

Synapse   Gap between two neurons, across which neurotransmitter substances travel.

Terminal Buttons   End point of a neuron where the neurotransmitter is manufactured, stored, and released.

Translation One of two functions of DNA in which DNA codes for the production of proteins responsible for the structure and function of cells.

Transmission One of two functions of DNA in which DNA is passed on to the next generation.

Twin Studies Behavioral genetic method in which monozygotic and dizygotic twins are compared; a genetic effect is indicated when there is greater concordance between monozygotic twins than between dizygotic twins.

Type 1 Alcoholism Pattern of alcoholism characterized by moderate heritability, later age of onset, and minimal criminal involvement.

Type 2 Alcoholism Pattern of alcoholism characterized by strong heritability, early age of onset, and extensive criminal involvement.

Vesicles Tiny organelles filled with neurotransmitter substance found in the terminal buttons of neurons.

Critical thinking

1. How do behavioral scientists study genetics?
2. Why is dopamine the neurotransmitter of choice for most researchers studying the neurophysiology of drugs?
3. What roles do the Behavioral Activity System (BAS) and Behavioral Inhibition System (BIS) play in drug abuse and crime?
4. Drugs clearly affect the Autonomic Nervous System (ANS), but does crime interact with the ANS as well?

Notes

1. International Human Genome Sequencing Consortium. (2004). Finishing the euchromatic sequence of the human genome. *Nature, 431*, 931–945.
2. Pierce, B. A. (2000). *Genetics: A conceptual approach.* New York: Freeman.
3. Lykken, D. T. (2006). The mechanism of emergenesis. *Genes, Brain and Behavior, 5*, 306–310.
4. Ivorra, J. L., Sanjuan, J., Jover, M., Carot, J. M., Frutos, R., & Molto, M. D. (2010). Gene–environment interaction of child temperament. *Journal of Developmental and Behavioral Pediatrics, 31*, 545–554.
5. Olsson, C. A., Moyzis, R. K., Williamson, E., Ellis, J. E., Parkinson-Bates, M., Patton, G. C., et al. (in press). Gene-environment interaction in problematic substance use: Interaction between DRD4 and insecure attachments. *Addiction Biology.*
6. Beaver, K., & Belsky, J. (2012). Gene–environment interaction and the intergenerational transmission of parenting: Testing the differential-susceptibility hypothesis. *Psychiatric Quarterly, 83*, 29–40.
7. Beaver, K. M., Gibson, C. L., DeLisi, M., Vaughn, M. G., & Wright, J. P. (2012). The interaction between neighborhood disadvantage and genetic factors in the prediction of antisocial outcomes. *Youth Violence and Juvenile Justice, 10*, 25–40.
8. Jaffee, S. R., & Price, T. S. (2007). Gene–environment correlations: A review of the evidence and implications for prevention of mental illness. *Molecular Psychiatry, 12*, 432–442.
9. Walters, G. D., & White, T. W. (1989). Heredity and crime: Bad genes or bad research? *Criminology, 27*, 455–485.
10. Walters & White (1989).
11. Plomin, R., DeFries, J. C., McClearn, G. E., & McGuffin, P. (2008). *Behavioral genetics* (5th ed.). New York: Freeman.

12. Blum, K., Nobel, E. P., Sheridan, P. J., Montgomery, A., Ritchie, T., Jagadeeswaran, P., et al. (1990). Allelic association of human Dopamine D2 Receptor Gene in alcoholism. *Journal of the American Medical Association, 263*, 2055–2060.

13. Blum, K., Nobel, E. P., Sheridan, P. J., Finley, O., Montgomery, A., Ritchie, T., et al. (1991). Association of the A1 allele of the D_2 dopamine receptor gene with severe alcoholism. *Alcohol, 8*, 409–416.

14. Comings, D. E., Comings, B. G., Muhleman, D., Dietz, G., Shahbahrami, B., Tast, D., et al. (1991). The dopamine D_2 receptor locus as a modifying gene in neuropsychiatric disorders. *Journal of the American Medical Association, 256*, 1793–1800.

15. Bolos, A. M., Dean, M., Lucas-Derse, S., Ramsburg, M., Brown, G. L., & Goldman, D. (1990). Population and pedigree studies reveal a lack of association between the Dopamine D2 Receptor Gene and alcoholism. *Journal of the American Medical Association, 264*, 3156–3160.

16. Gelernter, J., O'Malley, S., Risch, K., Kranzler, H. R., Krystal, J., Merikangas, K., et al. (1991). No association between an allele at the D_2 dopamine receptor gene (DRD2) and alcoholism. *Journal of the American Medical Association, 256*, 1801–1807.

17. Schwab, S., Soyka, M., Niederecker, M., Ackenheil, M., Scherer, J., & Wildenauer, D. B. (1991). Allelic association of human D_2-receptor DNA polymorphism ruled out in 45 alcoholics. *American Journal of Human Genetics, 49*, 203.

18. Arinami, T., Itokawa, M., Komiyama, T., Mitshushio, H., Mori, H., Mifune, H., et al. (1993). Association between severity of alcoholism and the A1 allele of the dopamine D_2 receptor gene TaqI A RFLP in Japanese. *Biological Psychiatry, 33*, 108–114.

19. Geijer, T., Neiman, J., Rydberg, U., Gyllander, A., Jönsson, E., Sedvall, G., et al. (1994). Dopamine D_2-receptor gene polymorphisms in Scandinavian chronic alcoholics. *European Archives of Psychiatry and Clinical Neuroscience, 244*, 26–32.

20. Sander, T., Harms, H., Podschus, J., Finck, U., Nickel, B., Rolfs, A., et al. (1995). Dopamine D_1, D_2, and D_3 receptor genes in alcohol dependence. *Psychiatric Genetics, 5*, 171–176.

21. Heath, A. C., Bucholz, K. K., Madden, A. F., Dinwiddie, S. H., Slutske, W. S., Bierut, L. J., et al. (1997). Genetic and environmental contributions to alcohol dependence risk in a national twin sample: Consistency of findings in women and men. *Psychological Medicine, 27*, 1381–1396.

22. Sigvardsson, S., Bohman, M., & Cloninger, C. R. (1996). Replication of the Stockholm Adoption Study of Alcoholism: Confirmatory cross-fostering analysis. *Archives of General Psychiatry, 53*, 681–687.

23. Fowler, T., Lifford, K., Shelton, K., Rice, F., Thapar, A., Neale, M. C., et al. (2007). Exploring the relationship between genetic and environmental influences on initiation and progression of substance use. *Addiction, 102*, 413–422.

24. McGue, M. (1999). The biological genetics of alcoholism. *Current Directions in Psychological Science, 8*, 109–115.

25. Walters, G. D. (2002). The heritability of alcohol abuse and dependence: A meta-analysis of behavior genetic research. *American Journal of Drug and Alcohol Abuse, 28*, 557–584.

26. Walters, G. D. (2006). Pattern inheritance and the genetics of lifestyle behavior. In G. D. Walters, *Lifestyle Theory: Past, Present, and Future* (pp. 87–102). New York: Nova Science.

27. Christiansen, K. O. (1970). Crime in a Danish twin population. *Acta Geneticae Medicae Gemellologiae: Twin Research, 19*, 323–326.

28. Mednick, S. A., Gabrielli, W. F., & Hutchings, B. (1984). Genetic influence in criminal convictions: Evidence from an adoption cohort. *Science, 224*, 891–894.

29. Walters, G. D. (1992). A meta-analysis of the gene-crime relationship. *Criminology, 30*, 595–613.

30. Walters (2006).

31. McGue, M., Pickens, R. W., & Svikis, D. S. (1992). Sex and age effects on the inheritance of alcohol problems. *Journal of Abnormal Psychology, 101*, 3–17.

32. Gurling, H. M. D., Oppenheim, B. E., & Murray, R. M. (1984). Depression, criminality, and psychopathology associated with alcoholism: Evidence from a twin study. *Acta Geneticae Medicae Gemellologiae: Twin Reseach, 33*, 333–339.

33. Goodwin, D. W., Schulsinger, F., & Hermansen, L. (1973). Alcoholism problems in adoptees raised apart from alcoholic biological parents. *Archives of General Psychiatry, 28*, 238–243.

34. Bohman, M. (1978). Some genetic aspects of alcoholism and criminality: A population of adoptees. *Archives of General Psychiatry, 35*, 269–276.

35. Cloninger, C. R., Bohman, M., & Sigvardsson, S. (1981). Inheritance of alcohol abuse: Cross-fostering analysis of adopted men. *Archives of General Psychiatry, 38*, 861–868.

36. Cadoret, R. J., O'Gorman, T., Troughton, E., & Heywood, E. (1985). Alcoholism and antisocial personality: Interrelationships, genetic and environmental factors. *Archives of General Psychiatry, 42*, 161–167.

37. Walters (2006).

38. wSlutske, W. S., Heath, A. C., Dinwiddie, S. H., Madden, P. A. F., Bucholtz, K. K., Dunne, M. P., et al. (1998). Common genetic risk factors for conduct disorder and alcohol dependence. *Journal of Abnormal Psychology, 107*, 363–374.

39. Carlson, N. R. (2009). *Physiology of behavior* (10th ed.). Boston: Allyn & Bacon.

40. Carlson (2009).

41. Carlson (2009).

42. Carlson (2009).

43. Cooper, J. R, Bloom, F. E., & Roth, R. H. (2003). *The biochemical basis of neuropharmacology* (8th ed.). New York: Oxford University Press.

44. Nesse, R. M. (1990). Evolutionary explanations of emotions. *Human Nature, 1*, 261–289.

45. Berridge, K. C. (2007). The debate over dopamine's role in rewards: The case for incentive salience. *Psychopharmacology, 191*, 391–431.

46. Di Chiara, G., & Imperato, A. (1988). Drugs abused by humans preferentially increase synaptic dopamine concentrations in the mesolimbic system of freely moving rats. *Proceedings of the National Academy of Sciences, 85*, 5274–5278.

47. Pierce, R. C., & Kumaresan, V. (2006). The mesolimbic dopamine system: The final common pathway for the reinforcing effect of drugs of abuse? *Neuroscience and Biobehavioral Reviews, 30*, 215–238.

48. Wise, R. A., & Bozarth, M. A. (1987). A psychomotor stimulant theory of addiction. *Psychological Review, 94*, 469–492.

49. Atianjoh, F. E., Ladenheim, B., Krasnova, N., & Cadet, J. L. (2008). Amphetamine causes dopamine depletion and cell death in the mouse olfactory bulb. *European Journal of Pharmacology, 589*, 94–97.

50. O'Sullivan, S., Evans, A. H., & Lees, A. J. (2009). Dopamine dysregulation syndrome: An overview of its epidemiology, mechanisms and management. *CNS Drugs, 23*, 157–170.

51. Zickle, P. (2002, April). Methamphetamine abuse linked to impaired cognitive and motor skills despite recovery of dopamine transporters. *NIDA Notes, 17*(1).

52. Grigorenko, E. L., Urban, A. E., & Mencl, E. (2010). Behavior, brain, and genome in genomic disorders: Finding the correspondences. *Journal of Developmental and Behavioral Pediatrics, 31*, 602–609.

53. Cloninger, C. R., Przybeck, T. R., & Svrakic, D. M. (1991). The Tridimensional Personality Questionnaire: U.S. normative data. *Psychological Reports, 69*, 1047–1057.

54. Zald, D. H., Cowan, R. L., Riccardi, P., Baldwin, R. M., Ansari, M. S., Li, R., et al. (2009). Midbrain dopamine receptor availability is inversely associated with novelty-seeking traits in humans. *Journal of Neuroscience, 28*, 14372–14378.

55. Buckholtz, J. W., Treadway, M. T., Cowan, R. L., Woodward, N. D., Benning, S. D., Li, R., et al. (2010). Mesolimbic dopamine reward system hypersensitivity in individuals with psychopathic traits. *Nature and Neuroscience, 13*, 419–421.

56. Moore, T. M., Scarpa, A., & Raine, A. (2002). A meta-analysis of serotonin metabolite 5-HIAA and antisocial behavior. *Aggressive Behavior, 28*, 299–316.

57. Soderstrom, H., Blennow, K., Sjodin, A.-K., & Forsman, A. (2003). New evidence for an association between the CSF HVA:5-HIAA ratio and psychopathic traits. *Journal of Neurology, Neurosurgery, and Psychiatry, 74*, 918–921.

58. Zald et al. (2009).

59. Karberg, J. C., & James, D. J. (2005). Substance dependence, abuse, and treatment of jail inmates, 2002. *Bureau of Justice Statistics Special Report* (NCJ 209588). Washington, DC: U.S. Department of Justice.

60. Mumola, C. J., & Karberg, J. C. (2006). Drug use and dependence, state and federal prisoners, 2004. *Bureau of Justice Statistics Special Report* (NCJ 213530). Washington, DC: U.S. Department of Justice.

61. Buchholtz et al. (2010).

62. Di Chiara & Imperato (1988).

63. Zald et al. (2009).

64. Gray, J. A. (1981). A critique of Eysenck's theory of personality. In H. J. Eysenck (Ed.), *A model for personality* (pp. 246–276). Berlin: Springer-Verlag.

65. Gray, J. A. (1990). Brain systems that mediate both emotion and cognition. *Cognition and Emotion, 4,* 269–288.

66. Cloninger, C. R. (1987). Neurogenetic adaptive mechanisms in alcoholism. *Science, 236,* 410–416.

67. Gray (1990).

68. Cloninger (1987).

69. Zisserson, R. N., & Palfai, T. P. (2007). Behavioral Activation System (BAS) sensitivity and reactivity to alcohol cues among hazardous drinkers. *Addictive Behaviors, 32,* 2178–2186.

70. Abdalehzade, J. A., Hashemi, N. T., Moradi, A. R., & Farzad, V. (2010). The role of brain behavioral systems in predicting of drug abuse. *Journal of (Iranian) Clinical Psychology, 2*(2, 6), 37–45.

71. Knyazev, G. G. (2010). Reward seeking as a predictor of drug use in youth: Effect of gender and social environment. *Open Addiction Journal, 3,* 1–8.

72. Fowles, D. (1980). The three arousal model: Implications of Gray's two-factor learning theory for heart rate, electrodermal activity, and psychopathy. *Psychophysiology, 17,* 87–104.

73. Blackburn, R. (2006). Other theoretical models of psychopathy. In C. J. Patrick (Ed.), *Handbook of psychopathy* (pp. 35–57). New York: Guilford.

74. Baskin-Sommers, A., Wallace, J., MacCoon, D., Curtin, J., & Newman, J. (2010). Clarifying the factors that undermine behavioral inhibition system functioning in psychopathy. *Personality Disorders: Theory, Research, and Treatment, 1,* 203–217.

75. Taylor, J., Reeves, M., James, L., & Bobadilla, L. (2006). Disinhibitory trait profile and its relation to Cluster B personality disorder features and substance use problems. *European Journal of Personality, 20,* 271–284.

76. Castellanos-Ryan, N., Rubia, K., & Conrod, P. J. (2011). Response inhibition and reward response bias mediate the predictive relationships between impulsivity and sensation seeking and common and unique variance in conduct disorder and substance misuse. *Alcoholism: Clinical and Experimental Research, 35,* 140–155.

77. Carlson (2009).

78. Carlson (2009).

79. Robertson, D., Biaggioni, I., Burnstock, G., Low, P. A., & Paton, J. F. R. (Eds.). (2012). *Primer on the autonomic nervous system* (3rd ed.). Waltham, MA: Academic Press.

80. Raine, A., Venables, P. H., & Mednick, S. A. (1997). Low resting heart rate at age 3 predisposes to aggression at age 11 years: Evidence from the Mauritius Child Health Project. *Journal of the American Academy of Child and Adolescent Psychiatry, 36,* 1457–1464.

81. Hare, R. D., Williamson, S. E., & Harpur, T. J. (1988). Psychopathy and language. In T. E. Moffitt & S. A. Mednick (Eds.), *Biological contributions to crime causation* (pp. 68–92). Dordrecht, Netherlands: Nijhoff Martinus.

82. Green, B. A., Ahmed, A. O., Marcus, D. K., & Walters, G. D. (2011). The latent structure of alcohol use pathology in an epidemiological sample. *Journal of Psychiatric Research, 45,* 225–233.

83. Walters, G. D. (2008). The latent structure of alcohol use disorders: A taxometric analysis of structured interview data obtained from male federal prison inmates. *Alcohol and Alcoholism, 43,* 326–333.

84. Gray (1990).

85. Howard, M. O., Kivlahan, D., & Walker, R. D. (1997). Cloninger's tridimensional theory of personality and psychopathology: Applications to substance use disorders. *Journal of Studies on Alcohol, 58,* 48–66.

86. Cloninger (1987).

PSYCHOLOGICAL FOUNDATIONS OF DRUG–CRIME RELATIONSHIPS

© kali9/iStockphoto

Psychology can be broadly defined as the study of behavior. Because of its size and scope, however, the field of psychology is often divided into subfields. Three of these subfields were used to structure the current chapter: developmental psychology, personality psychology, and social psychology. Developmental psychology is the study of human development and change, from birth to death. Four developmental issues relevant to drugs, crime, and their interrelationships are covered in this chapter: intelligence, temperament, moral reasoning, and age of onset. Personality psychology is the study of individual differences in behavior, in this case, drug use, crime, and the drug–crime nexus. Current research on the Five Factor Model (FFM) of personality receives the major portion of attention in this section. Social psychology is the study of behavior as it relates to social processes present in an individual's environment. Four different cognitive processes central to social-cognitive psychology are examined in this section: thinking styles, attributions, outcome expectancies, and efficacy expectancies.

The three principal objectives of this chapter are:

- Appraise the role of early development and change in initiating and maintaining drug use, crime, and the drug–crime connection.
- Determine whether individual differences in personality, as outlined in the FFM, are helpful in explaining important aspects of drug use, crime, and the drug–crime overlap.
- Decipher the process by which four quasi-time-stable cognitive factors mediate a person's interactions with the social-psychological environment, thereby increasing the person's propensity for drug use or crime and providing a context for drug–crime relationships.

Early Developmental Problems

Intelligence

Intelligence was defined by David Wechsler, creator of the Wechsler intelligence scales, as the "aggregate or global capacity of the individual to act purposively, to think rationally, and to deal effectively with his environment."[1] Intelligence tests are designed to measure intelligence with a score known as the **intelligence quotient** (IQ). Most IQ tests have a mean of 100 and standard deviation of 15 and in a stratified random sample of sufficient size will yield a distribution of scores that approximate the normal bell-shaped curve (see **Figure 6-1**). Accordingly, 68% of the population will score within one standard deviation of the mean (85–115) and 95% of the population will score within two standard deviations of the mean (70–130). Whereas the reliability and validity of intelligence tests have improved since Alfred Binet first introduced the IQ test back in 1905, a score on an IQ test should not be interpreted independent of other information. This is because an IQ test measures what an individual has learned rather than his or her innate ability. Hence, IQ tests are subject to bias and are influenced by a range of contextual factors.[2] These limitations notwithstanding, we move into a review of the research on the relationship between intelligence, drug use, and crime.

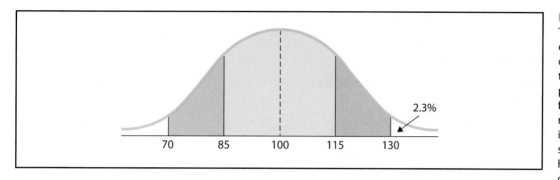

Figure 6-1
The bell-shaped curve of the IQ score distribution. Note that 2.3% of the population should fall into the mentally retarded range of intelligence and 2.3% should fall into the highly superior range of intelligence.

Intelligence and Drug Use

According to the **Savanna-IQ interaction hypothesis**, general intelligence is associated with the tendency to acquire, espouse, and embrace evolutionarily novel **values**.[3] To the extent that alcohol, tobacco, and illicit drug use are evolutionarily novel, the Savanna-IQ interaction hypothesis predicts that more intelligent individuals should use greater amounts of alcohol, tobacco, and illicit drugs than less intelligent individuals. Satoshi Kanazawa and Josephine Hellberg tested this hypothesis in two large, nationally representative longitudinal samples, one from the United States and one from the United Kingdom, in which IQ was tested during childhood and substance use behaviors were measured in adulthood. The results partially supported Kanazwa's Savanna-IQ interaction hypothesis. More intelligent children in both countries grew up to consume more alcohol. In addition, more intelligent children in the United States grew up to consume more tobacco and more intelligent children in the United Kingdom grew up to consume more illegal drugs (see **Figure 6-2**). The authors speculate that **openness to experience** or sensation seeking may mediate the relationship between childhood intelligence and adult substance use (see News Spot 6-1).[4]

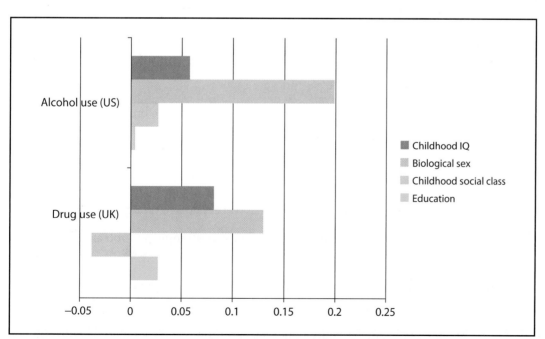

Figure 6-2
Effect size estimates (standardized beta coefficients from a regression equation) obtained by childhood IQ, biological sex, childhood social class, and education as predictors of adult alcohol use in the United States and illicit drug use in the United Kingdom.

Adapted From: S. Kanazawa. Why intelligent people drink more alcohol. *The Scientific Fundamentalist*, published on 10–10–10.

Title: Crime Might Pay, a Little
Source: *The Weatherford (TX) Democrat*
Author: Phil Riddle
Date: October 3, 2008

I've always suspected the old saying about crime not paying is pretty accurate.

I'll admit, the political antics in an election season make me wonder, but, on average, I have to believe crime is a bad career choice.

No benefits.

No guaranteed salary.

The ever-present possibility the police will roust you from a sound sleep and take you downtown for a Nick Nolte-esque mug shot and a single phone call.

Plus, you spend so much of your work day around other criminals discussing your next victim. Sort of like being in Congress.

But the one aspect of taking up a life of crime is requirements for employment are so low.

There is no drug test, no background check and, perhaps most importantly, no intelligence test.

A prime example of the need for at least minimum standards for any crooks' union is a semi-successful robbery of an armored car in Kuala Lumpur recently.

It seems a group of ambitious, but apparently mentally deficient robbers hijacked a van with about $1.3 million inside.

But, upon making the switch from the easily spotted armored vehicle to a compact car, the thieves had to leave half of their booty, since it wouldn't fit in the getaway vehicle.

There had to be a financial trade-out involved. The tiny car wouldn't carry all the robbers and all the cash, but it got incredible gas mileage.

The Associated Press reports the robbers swiped the compact car before holding up guards in the security van at a shopping center. Witnesses say one thief drove the van, while another followed in the too-small car.

This is where my theory bears out.

Had the robbers had the benefit of an IQ test, maybe they'd have thought this out better.

"If you leave Kuala Lumpur at 6:30 p.m. driving south at 40 mph, and rob an armored vehicle, what kind of car should you steal to make your getaway?" …

Police say the abandoned van was recovered with nine bags containing 2.7 million ringgit, about $786,000 in real money.

"The bags are quite big," District Police Chief Shakaruddin Che Mood said. "I consider them quite stupid. Their planning was very shortsighted."

Phil Riddle, originally published on October 3, 2008 in the Weatherford Democrat.

Questions to Ponder
  1. **What do you make of these robbers' dumb behavior?**
  2. **Kanasawa considers crime evolutionary familiar and drug use evolutionary novel. Could this explain why IQ correlates positively with drug use and negatively with crime?**
  3. **Can you think of any evolutionary novel crimes?**

Intelligence and Crime

James Q. Wilson and Richard Herrnstein, in their book, *Crime and Human Nature*, draw several links—some direct, others indirect—between intelligence and crime. Their overall conclusion, however, is that intelligence and crime are inversely related.[5] In an early meta-analysis on intelligence and crime, Hirschi and Hindelang calculated a significant inverse correlation between intelligence and crime ($r = -.20$) that persisted after race and social class were controlled. Although the effect was significant for both officially measured and self-reported offending, it was stronger for officially measured crime.[6] The magnitude of difference was on the order of 8–10 IQ points, which places the average IQ of the delinquent and criminal population at the bottom of the average range of intelligence (90–92). In an attempt to form a better understanding of the IQ–delinquency relationship, McGloin, Pratt, and Maahs tested several indirect relationships between the two variables and found that school performance, deviant peers, and self-control all mediated the IQ–delinquency relationship.[7] Lower IQ in offender populations is consistent with the Savanna-IQ interaction hypothesis to the extent that murder, theft, and robbery represent evolutionary familiar activities designed to improve one's competitive advantage in the ancestral environment and general intelligence is designed to solve problems that diverge significantly from ancestral tasks.[8]

Intelligence, Drug Use, and Crime

Whereas the Savanna-IQ interaction hypothesis suggests that drug use and crime form countervailing (opposing) relationships with intelligence, there is at least one study in which drug use and crime both correlated negatively with IQ. Fergusson, Horwood, and Ridder determined that IQ measured at ages 8–9 correlated negatively with alcohol dependence, nicotine dependence, illicit drug dependence, and crime in adolescence and early adulthood. The nicotine dependence and crime predictive effects remained significant but the correlations between intelligence and alcohol and drug dependence became positive when early conduct problems were controlled.[9] Therefore, when early conduct problems are controlled, the Savanna-IQ hypothesis is supported. Even the robust negative correlation between tobacco dependence and IQ is not necessarily incompatible with the Savanna-IQ interaction hypothesis given that the hypothesis focuses more on drug use than drug dependence; similar to what has been observed with social class,[10] even though higher intelligence (like higher social class) is associated with tobacco use, lower intelligence (like lower social class) may be associated with tobacco dependence and tobacco-related problems.

Temperament

Temperament is the innate disposition to respond to the environment in a particular way. As such, it is the forerunner of **personality** and the original or constitutional individual difference variable. Alexander Thomas and Stella Chess (1977) grouped children into three general temperament categories: easy child, difficult child, and slow-to-warm-up child.[11] It is more common, however, to conceptualize temperament as a series of dimensions rather than as a set of categories, a practice supported by taxometric research showing that the latent structure of childhood temperament is dimensional rather than categorical in nature.[12] Several of the more popular temperament dimensions are **activity level**, **positive emotionality**, **negative emotionality**, **novelty seeking**, **self-regulation** (effortful control), and **sociability**/inhibition. Descriptions for each of these temperament dimensions are provided in **Table 6-1**.

Temperament and Substance Use

Longitudinal research indicates that high activity level, negative emotionality, and weak effortful control measured in childhood and early adolescence predict drug use in late adolescence and early adulthood.[13–14] Other studies indicate that the temperament–drug use relationship may be mediated by various psychological and sociological variables. Hanneke Creemers and colleagues, for instance, determined that early temperament had both a direct and indirect effect on subsequent drug use. In this study, shyness and weak effortful control at ages 10–12 predicted regular use of marijuana at ages 15–18, an effect that was partially mediated by substance-using peers at ages 12–15.[15] It should be noted that temperament, particularly novelty seeking, plays a central role in Cloninger's unified biosocial theory of alcohol abuse.[16]

Temperament and Crime

Diane Smart and members of the Australian Temperament Project conducted a large-scale study of temperament as a correlate of antisocial behavior and discovered that the most persistent offending youth in their sample were rated by their parents as high in activity level, high in negative reactivity, low in positive emotionality, and low in effortful control (see **Figure 6-3**).[17] Dustin Pardini also explored the relationship between temperament and crime and ascertained

Table 6-1 Descriptions of Common Temperament Dimensions

Temperament Dimension	Description
Activity Level	Degree and rate of motor output and behavioral response displayed across various situations
Positive Emotionality	Intensity and frequency of positive affect in the form of happiness, joy, and contentment
Negative Emotionality	Intensity and frequency of negative affect in the form of anger, anxiety, and depression
Novelty Seeking	Tendency to seek out new experiences and unfamiliar stimuli and avoid routine
Self-Regulation (effortful control)	Ability to control one's actions and anticipate the likely consequences of one's behavior
Sociability	Tendency to approach interpersonal stimuli and situations (sociability) rather than avoiding interpersonal stimuli and situations (shyness or inhibition)

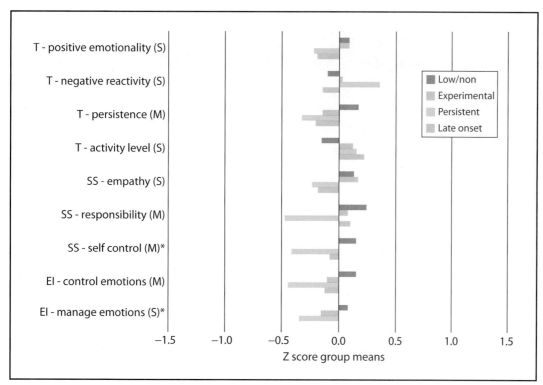

Figure 6-3
Relationship between parent-rated temperament and degree of antisocial involvement (low, experimental, persistent, and late onset). S = small effect; M = medium effect

Smart, D., Richardson, N., Sanson, A., Dussuyer, I., & Marshall, B. (2005). *Patterns and precursors of adolescent antisocial behavior: Outcomes and connections*. Melbourne, Australia: Australian Institute of Family Studies.

that low negative emotionality in the form of **fearlessness** increased a juvenile's risk for severe violent delinquency as mediated by low punishment concern and an attitude of callousness.[18] It should be noted, however, that this was a cross-sectional rather than longitudinal study and so no causal conclusions can be drawn from the results.

Temperament, Drug Use, and Crime

Disorders of childhood and adolescence are often classified as **externalizing** (attention deficit disorder, conduct disorder, oppositional defiant disorder) and internalizing (anxiety, depression). Youth who abuse drugs often satisfy the criteria for both internalizing and externalizing disorders,[19] whereas delinquent youth are almost always diagnosed with externalizing disorders.[20] In comparing children with internalizing and externalizing disorders, Nancy Eisenberg and colleagues concluded that negative emotionality was a general risk factor for both internalizing and externalizing disorders of childhood, whereas weak effortful control (**disinhibition**) was primarily a risk factor for externalizing disorders alone.[21] Mary Rothbart and colleagues have identified three higher order temperament dimensions: positive emotionality, negative emotionality, and effortful control.[22–23] Replacing positive emotionality with a higher order temperament dimension of fearlessness (low negative emotionality other than anger)[24] and expanding effortful control to encompass disinhibition or reactive criminality leaves us with a modified three-dimensional model of temperament that may be of some help in explaining drug–crime relationships.

Of the three higher order temperament dimensions proposed in this modified model (i.e., negative emotionality, disinhibition, fearlessness), negative emotionality would seem to relate best to **internalizing disorders**. Because the aggressive or angry features of negative emotionality may relate equally well to internalizing and externalizing disorders,[25] I have restricted the modified model to the nonaggressive features of negative emotionality.

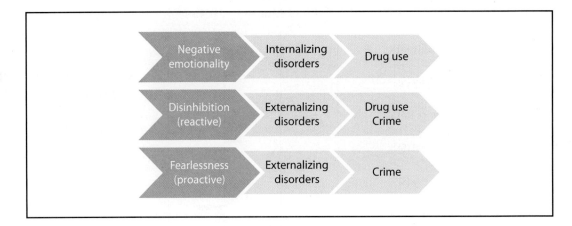

Disinhibition (reactive dimension) and fearlessness (proactive dimension), on the other hand, appear to relate best to externalizing disorders. I would contend that drug use, which overlaps with both internalizing and externalizing disorders, is most closely tied to the negative emotionality and disinhibition (reactive) temperament dimensions, whereas crime, which overlaps nearly exclusively with externalizing disorders, is more closely tied to the disinhibition (reactive) and fearlessness (proactive) temperament dimensions (see **Figure 6-4**).

Moral Reasoning

Lawrence Kohlberg developed a three-level, six-stage model of moral reasoning based on Jean Piaget's early work on moral development. The three levels in Kohlberg's theory are preconventional moral reasoning, conventional moral reasoning, and postconventional moral reasoning. Kohlberg believed that internalization of a coherent moral code was the key factor in distinguishing between the three levels. Thus, preconventional, conventional, and post-conventional reasoning are associated with no, moderate, and full internalization of a moral code, respectively. The levels and stages of Kohlberg's theory are listed in **Table 6-2**.[26]

Table 6-2 Levels and Stages of Kohlberg's Theory of Moral Development

Level 1	**Preconventional Reasoning (no internalization)**	
Stage 1	Heteronomous Morality	Obey out of a fear of punishment
Stage 2	Instrumental Morality	Pursue own interests, seek rewards
Level 2	**Conventional Reasoning (intermediate internalization)**	
Stage 3	Mutual Interpersonal Expectations	Emphasize trust, caring, and loyalty
Stage 4	Social Systems Morality	Emphasize social order, justice, and duty
Level 3	**Postconventional Reasoning (full internalization)**	
Stage 5	Social Contract	Laws are needed to protect basic human rights
Stage 6	Universal ethical principles	Moral standard based on universal human rights

Moral Reasoning and Drug Use

Abide, Richards, and Ramsay tested two hypotheses in two groups of college students. The first hypothesis predicted that students who believed drug use was morally wrong would report using fewer drugs than students who viewed drug use as a personal choice. The second hypothesis held that individuals functioning at higher levels of moral reasoning would demonstrate greater consistency between their moral beliefs about drugs and their actual use of drugs. Analyses supported both hypotheses. Hence, students capable of higher levels of moral reasoning showed greater consistency between their attitudes and behaviors, irrespective of whether or not they reported using drugs.[27]

Moral Reasoning and Crime

It has been observed that male and female delinquents and adult criminals tend to score significantly lower on measures of moral reasoning than nondelinquents and noncriminals. Thus, whereas the average nondelinquent or noncriminal tends to function at Stage 3 of Kohlberg's model, most offenders function no higher than Stage 2.[28–29] Aleixo and Norris observed lower levels of moral reasoning (mostly at the preconventional level) in a group of offenders but failed to discern a relationship between moral reasoning and self-reported offending.[30] This would seem to suggest that offenders display lower levels of moral reasoning, using Kohlberg's scheme, than nonoffenders, but that moral reasoning is not useful in identifying the level or extent of criminal offending, at least where self-reported offending is concerned.

Moral Reasoning, Drug Use, and Crime

Kuther and Higgins-D'Alessandro explored the relationship between moral reasoning in high school students and self-reported involvement in both drug use and antisocial behavior. Results indicated that when drug use or antisocial behavior was viewed as a moral behavior, higher levels of moral reasoning were associated with lower levels of involvement in these activities. In students who viewed drug use and antisocial behavior as a personal choice, however, there was no relationship between moral reasoning and self-reported involvement in drug use and antisocial behavior.[31] These findings indicate that before moral reasoning can influence behavior and serve as a foundation for intervention, the individual must construe the behavior as a moral decision rather than as a personal choice. The problem of moral reasoning not always matching up with moral behavior has, in fact, been a major criticism of Kohlberg's theory.[32]

Age of Onset

Age of onset, defined as the age at which drug use or delinquency/crime begins, is another potentially important developmental factor in understanding drug–crime relationships. It is thought to be important because it helps define the severity of the problem. The earlier the age of onset, the more severe the problem, regardless of whether we are talking about drug use or crime.

Age of Onset and Drug Use

Studying a large nationally representative sample of the U.S. population, Bridget Grant and Deborah Dawson noted that early onset drug use was a powerful predictor of subsequent drug problems. In fact, lifetime drug abuse and dependence were reduced by 4% and 5%, respectively, for each year of delay in drug use onset.[33] In the 2005 National Survey on Drug Use and Health, serious mental health problems were associated with an earlier onset of marijuana use, with the prevalence of serious mental illness (SMI) in individuals who started using marijuana before age 12 being twice that of individuals who started using marijuana at age 18 or later (see **Figure 6-5**).[34] Recently, Griffin, Bang, and Botvin discovered that an earlier onset of drug use correlated with higher levels of adult drug use and more drug-related social and occupational problems.[35] Early onset alcohol use (< age 15 years) is also associated with an increased probability of future diagnoses of alcohol abuse and dependence.[36]

Age of Onset and Crime

It has long been recognized that the age of onset of antisocial behavior is one of the better predictors of the frequency, duration, and seriousness of future offending. Age of onset of antisocial behavior, in fact, is the cornerstone of Moffitt's developmental taxonomy of criminality, with the life-course-persistent pattern demonstrating a significantly earlier age of onset than the adolescence-limited pattern.[37] In a review of the literature on age of onset and delinquency, David Farrington and colleagues concluded that age of onset may be the single best predictor of the severity and course of antisocial behavior.[38] In fact, age of onset has been incorporated into the *Diagnostic and Statistical Manual of Mental Disorders*, Fourth Edition (DSM-IV) criteria for antisocial personality disorder, such that an individual must meet the criteria for conduct disorder prior to age 15 before receiving a diagnosis of antisocial personality disorder.[39] Research supports the utility of the age of onset criterion for antisocial personality disorder.[40]

Figure 6-5
Age of onset of marijuana use and prevalence of past year serious mental illness.

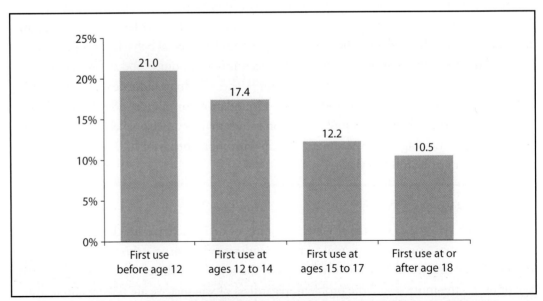

Substance Abuse and Mental Health Services Administration. (2006). *National Survey on Drug Use and Health, 2005.* Washington, DC: United States Department of Health and Human Services.

Age of Onset, Drug Use, and Crime

As with many of the research topics covered in this section there appears to be significant overlap between drug use and crime with respect to age of onset. Zhang, Wieczorek, and Welte, for instance, found that early onset substance use predicted later delinquency, a relationship that was mediated by continued alcohol and drug use, association with delinquent peers, and ongoing deviant behavior.[41] Conversely, Gordon, Kinlock, and Battjes determined that early onset delinquency predicted higher levels of subsequent drug use.[42] The order of drug–crime onset may also have a bearing on the types of crimes an individual commits. David Farabee and colleagues discovered that those individuals who used drugs before their initial arrest were more likely to engage in victimless crimes and commit a wider range of offenses (criminal versatility), whereas those individuals who were arrested before they started using drugs were more likely to engage in violent or predatory crime.[43–44]

It would appear that both early onset drug use and early onset delinquency promote future drug and crime problems and may be partially responsible for the overlap between drugs and crime that occurs in adolescence and adulthood. The exact mechanism behind the effect of age of onset on future drug use and crime, however, is poorly understood. Three possibilities nonetheless suggest themselves. First, early involvement with drugs or crime could interfere with the individual's early personal and social development, which might then interfere with the individual's later personal and social adjustment. Second, factors that correlate with early onset (e.g., association with antisocial or drug using peers, neurological deficits) may account for the early onset–future problem relationship. Matt McGue and colleagues, for instance, discovered that the connection between early onset alcohol use and later alcohol dependence was largely a consequence of preexisting differences in disinhibitory behavior and psychopathology.[45] A third possibility is that early onset of drug use/crime is a marker for disinhibition (reactive dimension) yet also has an independent causal effect on later drug/crime problems.

Personality

Personality can be defined as a relatively enduring pattern of behavior that is unique to the individual and predictable across situations. There are four core elements in this definition. First, personality has an internal (person-oriented) rather than external (situation-oriented) locus. Second, personality is more concerned with individual differences (uniqueness) than with shared attributes or experiences. Third, personality is reasonably consistent (predictable) across situations. Fourth, personality is reasonably stable (relatively enduring) over time.

Before proceeding, it is important for the reader to understand the difference between the personality variables described in this section and constructs like the addictive and criminal personalities.[46–47] The addictive personality and criminal personality are popular constructions of dubious value to scientists (see News Spot 6-2). The personalities of those involved with drugs and crime are too diverse to be classified under a single or unitary personality construct. As the reader will soon learn, there are similarities in the personalities of those who abuse drugs and commit crime; yet, there is no single set of personality traits or characteristics that applies to all drug users or all criminals.

Title: Predicting Who Gets Hooked and Who Doesn't
Source: *Miami (FL) Herald*
Author: Ena Naunton
Date: December 29, 1985

The psychiatrist's voice developed that slight edge that occurs when a polite person's patience is about to be exhausted.

"Let's forget this business of 'addictive personality,'" said Dr. David Fishbain. "Quit talking about it, because no such thing exists, scientifically."

It has, however, become a grab-bag label in South Florida, where the nature of addiction is not just a topic for researchers and doctors who treat the addicted. Parents look at their children, wives at husbands, husbands at wives, employers at employees—all wondering if there is some common denominator to predict who will and who won't be caught up in the omnipresent drug scene.

But prediction is still an imprecise activity at best, and most professionals are in the business of handling drug addiction after the fact rather than being able to step in before it gets started.

Dr. Stephen Kahn, a psychiatrist and clinical director of the Recovery Center at Highland Park General Hospital in Miami, said researchers' attempts to use psychological tests on large groups of high school students to predict who would grow up as addicts failed completely.

"I think the notion of an addictive personality is certainly much overdone," said Dr. Irl Extein, medical director at Fair Oaks Hospital in Delray Beach, a center for the 1-800-COCAINE drug hotline. "That concept has been replaced by a more useful notion that alcohol and drug addiction are diseases."

One problem with the "addictive personality" theory, Extein said, is that people who are addicted get hung up on the notion that they need to understand why they are addicted instead of how to break their habit.

"Some people engage in psychotherapy for years, continuing to drink and use drugs while figuring out 'Why do I use them?' That can be a dead-end road," Extein said....

Questions to Ponder
1. **Why is the concept of an addictive personality so popular?**
2. **Do you consider the notion that drug and alcohol abuse are diseases a better explanation for addiction?**
3. **How else might you explain the tendency of people to get involved in a variety of negative behaviors without resorting to the concept of an addictive personality?**

Personality overlaps extensively with temperament. As the reader may recall from discussions taking place in the previous section, temperament is a constitutionally based (innate) construct, although it is also influenced by the child's early environment. Ongoing temperament–environment interactions eventually give rise to personality development. Where temperament ends and personality begins is not always easy to discern and the two appear to blend into one another. Personality becomes increasingly more important as the person makes the transition from adolescence to adulthood.

Biologically based theories of childhood temperament and early personality development frequently posit the existence of three dimensions: approach, avoidance, and aggression/dyscontrol.[48] The approach dimension is characterized by behavioral activation, extraversion, and positive affect. The avoidance dimension is characterized by behavioral inhibition, anxiety, and negative affect. The aggression-dyscontrol dimension is characterized by behavioral maintenance, impulsivity, and nonspecific arousal. These three dimensions parallel the three temperament dimensions identified by Rothbart and discussed in an earlier section of this chapter: positive emotionality, negative emotionality, and effortful control.[49]

As the reader may recall, I made some alterations to Rothbart's three dimensions, restricting negative affect to fear, anxiety, and depression; substituting fearlessness (low negative emotionality except for anger, which is high) for positive emotionality; and expanding effortful control to incorporate aspects of impulsivity and sensation seeking to form the higher order temperament dimension of disinhibition. I did this in an attempt to make the dimensions more relevant to research on drug use and crime. The three temperament dimensions of negative emotionality, fearlessness, and disinhibition may serve as the biological precursors of personality factors important in the development of drug abuse and crime. It is these personality factors that now attract our attention.

Personality and Factor Analysis

Factor analysis is a statistical procedure in which a correlational matrix formed by crossing various items or variables with each other is analyzed for the purpose of determining the number of underlying factors or latent dimensions. A simplified example is provided in **Figure 6-6**. In this example there are two factors, one made up of Variables 1, 2, and 3 (correlations in red) and the other made up of Variables 4, 5, and 6 (correlations in green). Once identified, these factors need to be correlated with external criteria to see whether or not they produce useful or meaningful results.

One of the first factor-based theories of personality was Eysenck's three-factor model: introversion vs. extraversion, neuroticism vs. emotional stability, and psychoticism vs. superego.[50] Other factor analytic theories of personality soon followed. These included Cloninger's Tridimensional model (behavioral activation, behavioral inhibition, behavioral maintenance),[51] Atkinson's Motivational model (approach motivation, avoidance motivation),[52] and Tellegen's Temperament model (positive affect, negative affect, constraint).[53]

Figure 6-6
Correlation matrix upon which factor analysis is based.

	V1	V2	V3	V4	V5	V6	V7
V1		.45	.51	.01	.12	.08	.10
V2			.47	.04	.00	.10	−.05
V3				.06	.01	.09	−.02
V4					.54	.49	.05
V5						.63	.11
V6							.04
V7							

The Five-Factor Model

In an attempt to synthesize these different models, Robert McCrae and Paul Costa created the **five-factor model** (FFM). The acronym OCEAN can be helpful as a mnemonic device in remembering the five components of the FFM:

- *Openness to Experience* and its six facets: fantasy, aesthetics, feelings, actions, ideas, and values.
- *Conscientiousness* and its six facets: competence, orderliness, dutifulness, achievement striving, self-discipline, and deliberation.
- *Extraversion* and its six facets: warmth, gregariousness, assertiveness, activity, excitement seeking, and positive feelings.
- *Agreeableness* and its six facets: trust, straightforwardness, altruism, compliance, modesty, and tendermindedness.
- *Neuroticism* and its six facets: anxiety, angry hostility, depression, self-consciousness, impulsiveness, and vulnerability.[54]

Given the fact that personality appears to evolve from temperament and knowing that temperament is heavily influenced by genetic factors, it should come as no surprise that personality is at least moderately heritable. Thomas Bouchard and Matthew McGue computed heritability estimates for the five factors of the FFM from the results of several twin studies and came up with the following results: Openness (57% heritable), **Conscientiousness** (49% heritable), **Extraversion** (54% heritable), **Agreeableness** (42% heritable), and **Neuroticism** (48% heritable).[55] Although these figures may be somewhat inflated owing to the fact that they were derived exclusively from twin data and twin studies tend to overestimate heritability, they do suggest a moderately strong heritable component for each of the five factors.

There have been several different self-report and structured interview procedures developed to assess the FFM. The most popular measure is a self-report personality inventory, now in its third edition, known as the NEO-Personality Inventory-3 (NEO-PI-3). The NEO-PI-3 is a 240-item inventory that takes 35–45 minutes to complete. This measure of the FFM generates scores for the 5 domains (factors) and 30 facets (6 per domain). Reliability and validity data are strong and the inventory has been used extensively in cross-cultural research on personality.[56] Much of the FFM research reported in the next section was based on data provided by the NEO-PI-3 or one of its predecessors (NEO-PI, NEO-PI-R).

The FFM and Drug Use

John Malouff, Einar Thorsteinsson, and Nicola Schutte performed a meta-analysis of nine studies ($N = 4,720$) examining the relationship between the FFM and tobacco smoking. The results of this meta-analysis revealed that smoking was associated with significantly higher scores on the Neuroticism (N) scale and significantly lower scores on the Agreeableness (A) and Conscientiousness (C) scales.[57] Previous research had shown that Extraversion (E) was also elevated in smokers,[58] but in the Malouff et al. meta-analysis E correlated with smoking only in earlier studies and in studies conducted outside of North America. In more recent studies conducted in North America, E was not significantly higher in smokers than in nonsmokers.[59] In one of the studies reviewed in the Malouff et al. meta analysis, Michael Hooten and colleagues determined that high N, low A, and low C predicted poorer outcomes for smoking cessation programs. These authors note that although smoking cessation programs often attempt to reduce negative affect and stress-related smoking (N), most make no effort to increase A or C, but if they did, perhaps they would be more effective.[60]

Malouff, Thorsteinsson, Rooke, and Schutte also conducted a meta-analysis of studies on the FFM and alcohol involvement. This meta-analysis encompassed 20 studies and 7,886 participants. As in their previous meta-analysis on smoking, alcohol involvement correlated positively with N and negatively with A and C. Heavy drinkers in this meta-analysis scored particularly low on a superordinate factor called self-control, which is similar to the disinhibition (reactive) factor described previously in the section on temperament. Mixed-gender samples achieved weaker effect sizes, indicating that gender may obscure or moderate the relationship between the FFM and alcohol involvement. Treatment samples, on the other hand, had stronger effect sizes, perhaps because those with more serious problems are more often referred for treatment.[61] **Figure 6-7** depicts the similarity in effect sizes for the five factors in the FFM across the two Malouff et al. meta-analyses.

Several more recent studies not included in the Malouff meta-analyses have recorded results similar to those obtained by Malouff and his colleagues. Terracciano et al., for instance, ascertained that compared to individuals who never smoked cigarettes, current cigarette smokers were significantly higher on N and significantly lower on C; compared to individuals who never consumed cocaine or heroin, current cocaine and heroin users scored significantly higher on N, particularly the Vulnerability facet, and significantly lower on C, particularly the competence, achievement-striving, and deliberation facets; compared to individuals who never used marijuana, current marijuana users scored significantly higher on Openness to Experience (O) and significantly lower on A and C.[62] Administering a

Figure 6-7
Mean effect sizes obtained in meta-analyses of the relationship between the Five Factor Model and alcohol and smoking.

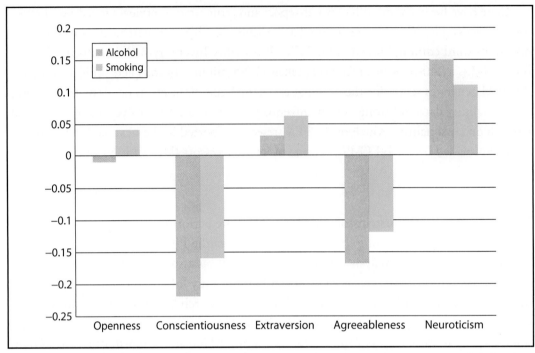

Data From: Malouff, J. M., Thorsteinsson, E. B., & Schutte, N. S. (2006). The five-factor model of personality and smoking: A meta-analysis. *Journal of Drug Education, 36,* 47–58 & Malouff, J. M., Thorsteinsson, E. B., Rooke, S. E., & Schutte, N. S. (2007). Alcohol involvement and the five-factor model of personality: A meta-analysis. *Journal of Drug Education, 37,* 277–294.

personality questionnaire to a group of college students, Raynor and Levine discovered that students high in C were less likely to smoke cigarettes, consume alcohol, and binge drink and more likely to follow harm reduction principles than students low in C, and that students high in Extraversion (E) were more likely to smoke cigarettes, consume alcohol, and binge drink and less likely to follow harm reduction principles than students low in E.[63]

The FFM and Crime

Thomas Widiger and Donald Lynam predicted that the personality features of psychopathy (i.e., Factor 1 of the PCL-R) would correlate with low A and N and high E, whereas the behavioral features of psychopathy (i.e., Factor 2 of the PCL-R) would correlate with low A and C and high N.[64] Subsequent research has tended to support this hypothesis. Miller, Lynam, Widiger, and Leukefeld constructed a Psychopathy Resemblance Index (PRI) by comparing an individual's NEO-PI-R profile to the NEO-PI-R profile of a prototypic psychopath and found that it correlated significantly with both criminal and drug use behavior (see **Figure 6-8**).[65] Ross, Lutz, and Bailley compared the FFM for individuals scoring high in either primary (similar to Factor 1 of the PCL-R) or secondary (similar to Factor 2 of the PCL-R) psychopathy. The results indicated that primary psychopathy was associated with low scores on A, and secondary psychopathy was associated with low scores on A and C and high scores on N.[66]

Whereas much of the FFM research on drug use has focused on individual differences between drug users and nonusers, much of the FFM research on crime has focused on individual differences within various groups of offenders. Christen Clower and Robert Bothwell examined the relationship between the FFM and recidivism and discovered that low O and C were associated with increased rates of recidivism. The combination of low O and C was particularly toxic in terms of a person's odds of remaining crime free in the community.[67]

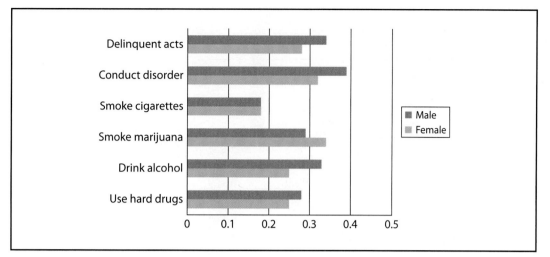

Figure 6-8
Correlations between the Psychopathy Resemblance Index (PRI) and measures of criminality and drug use, across gender.

Data From: Miller, J. D., Lynam, D. R., Widiger, T. A., & Luekefeld, C. (2001). Personality disorder as extreme variants of common personality dimensions: Can the five-factor model adequately represent psychopathy? *Journal of Personality, 69,* 253–276.

Comparing the NEO scores of a group of child molesters to the NEO normative sample, Madsen, Parsons, and Grubin discovered that child molesters scored significantly higher on N and significantly lower on C. In addition, child molesters with personality disorders had higher N and lower A than child molesters without personality disorders.[68] Further evidence that the FFM may be helpful in differentiating between offenders is provided by Trninić, Barančić, and Nazor, who discovered that self-reported aggressiveness in incarcerated offenders was associated with high N and low C and A.[69]

The FFM, Drug Use, and Crime

Mark Ruiz, Aaron Pincus, and John Schinka recently carried out a major meta-analysis of studies covering the relationships between the FFM and substance use and antisocial personality disorders. Gathering data from 63 samples, totaling 15,331 participants, Ruiz et al. scrutinized 22 substance use disorder (SUD) samples, 35 antisocial personality disorder (APD) samples, and 6 combined (SUD/APD) samples. The results indicated that SUD was associated with moderately high N scores and moderately low A and C scores, APD was associated with moderately low A and C scores, and SUD/APD was associated with moderately high N scores and moderately low A and C scores (see **Figure 6-9**). Significant group differences were observed on N (SUD and SUD/APD > APD) and A (SUD > APD and SUD/APD).[70]

Analysis of 11 studies from the Ruiz et al. meta-analysis for which facet-level data were available revealed several interesting relationships. First, APD and SUD did not differ on the N facets of hostility and impulsiveness but APD displayed significantly lower scores on the remaining four N facets (see **Figure 6-10**). Second, APD recorded significantly higher scores than SUD on five of the six E facets (warmth, assertiveness, activity, excitement seeking, and positive emotions). Third, APD recorded significantly lower scores than SUD on five of the six A facets (straightforwardness, altruism, compliance, modesty, tendermindedness). Fourth, APD and SUD differed on only two of the C facets (competence, dutifulness), both of which were lower in APD.[71]

Of the six theories of drug abuse (disease model, unified biosocial model, cross-cultural theory, self-medication hypothesis, gateway theory, social learning theory) and six theories

Figure 6-9
Mean effect sizes (r) on the four domains for the substance using (SUD), antisocial personality (APD), and co-occurring (SUD/APD) groups.

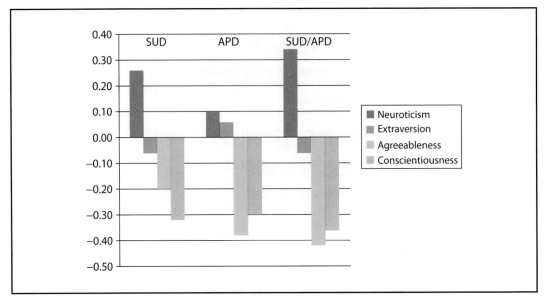

Data From: Ruiz, M. A., Pincus, A. L., & Schinka, J. A. (2008). Externalizing pathology and the five-factor model: A meta-analysis of personality traits associated with antisocial personality disorder, substance use disorder, and their co-occurrence. *Journal of Personality Disorders, 22,* 365–388.

Figure 6-10
Mean effect sizes (r) on the six facets of the neuroticism domain for the substance using (SUD), antisocial personality (APD), and co-occurring (SUD/APD) groups.

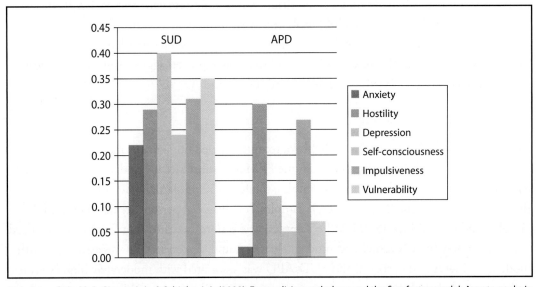

Data From: Ruiz, M. A., Pincus, A. L., & Schinka, J. A. (2008). Externalizing pathology and the five-factor model: A meta-analysis of personality traits associated with antisocial personality disorder, substance use disorder, and their co-occurrence. *Journal of Personality Disorders, 22,* 365–388.

of crime (psychopathy model, self-control theory, developmental taxonomy, age-graded theory, biosocial model, social learning theory), the personality approach is most consistent with Cloninger's unified biosocial model and Hare's psychopathy approach, respectively. As far as characterizing the drug–crime nexus goes, research on the FFM denotes the presence of overlapping conditions, with drug abuse being associated with temperament-personality features indicative of negative emotionality and disinhibition (reactive dimension) and crime being associated with temperament-personality features indicative of fearlessness (proactive dimension) and disinhibition (reactive dimension). In situations where drugs and crime coexist, there may be an additive effect. Based on the Ruiz et al. meta-analysis, samples of substance-abusing offenders appeared to get the worst of both worlds: i.e., high levels of N from the drug association and low levels of A and C from the crime association.[72]

Cognition

Cognition consists of mental processes designed to assist people in interpreting, comprehending, and acting on their environment. In addition, these mental processes allow people to reflect on their environment and their role in it. As such, cognition is vital to self-regulation and self-control. Thanks to the pioneering work of Albert Bandura in his cognitive-social learning theory, we now understand the critical role cognitive variables play in mediating stimulus–response relationships.[73] The cognitive variables discussed in this section (thinking styles, attributions, efficacy expectancies, and outcome expectancies), in fact, have their greatest impact on the drug–crime connection as mediators of important drug- and crime-based relationships. Social learning theory holds to an S → O → R model of behavior in which the organism (thoughts, feelings, and impulses) intervenes between the stimulus and response of traditional learning theory. As we make our way through the next four subsections on the cognitive foundations of drug–crime relationships, it is essential that the reader keep in mind that these variables exert their most powerful influence as mediators of other variables.

Thinking Styles

Thinking styles are the attitudes and beliefs an individual holds toward certain activities. Much of the research on drug use and crime has centered around **criminal thinking** styles and the instruments that have been constructed to assess criminal thinking styles tend to focus on either criminal thought content (what a criminal thinks) or criminal thought process (how a criminal thinks). An instrument developed by Walters to assess the eight thinking styles in his criminal lifestyle model, known as the Psychological Inventory of Criminal Thinking Styles (PICTS), is first and foremost, a measure of criminal thought process.[74] Recently, a hierarchic structure has been proposed for the thinking styles in Walters' cognitive model. At the top of the hierarchy is general criminal thinking, this then branches off into the two overlapping dimensions of proactive and reactive criminal thinking, and these two dimensions then branch off into more specific thinking styles (see **Figure 6-11**).[75] **Table 6-3** provides brief descriptions of each of the criminal thinking styles in Walters' model.

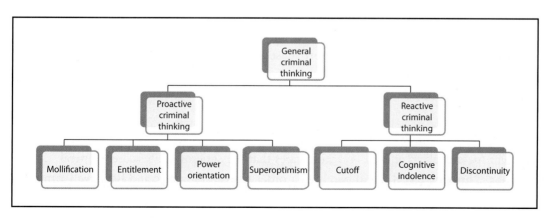

Figure 6-11
Hierarchical organization of criminal thinking.

Table 6-3 Descriptions for the Eight Criminal Thinking Styles

Thinking Style	Factor	Description
Mollification	Proactive	Making excuses, rationalizing behavior, blaming external circumstances, and generally failing to take responsibility for own criminal actions and their consequences.
Cutoff	Reactive	Rapid elimination of deterrents to crime though a single phrase, such as "fuck it," a musical theme, or the use of alcohol and/or drugs.
Entitlement	Proactive	Sense of ownership, privilege, or prerogative. Sometimes expressed as the misidentification of wants as needs.
Power Orientation	Proactive	Desire for power and control over others and a sense of personal weakness or ineffectiveness when not in control of a situation.
Sentimentality	None[1]	Self-centered attempt to gain favor or eliminate guilt by engaging in good deeds designed to eliminate the harm done by one's criminal actions.
Superoptimism	Proactive	Belief that one can continue to engage in criminal behavior and not suffer the same negative consequences that so many others have experienced.
Cognitive Indolence	Reactive	Shortcut or lazy thinking; failure to critically evaluate one's thoughts and plans, thereby culminating in impulsive decision making.
Discontinuity	Reactive	Tendency to be easily sidetracked by events going on around one; general failure to maintain a commitment or consistent goal-directed pattern of behavior.

[1] Sentimentality loads on neither one of the two higher order factors (proactive or reactive) nor on the superordinate factor (general criminal thinking).

Criminal Thinking and Drugs

A measure of drug-related thinking, modeled after the PICTS and called the Psychological Inventory of Drug-Based Thinking Styles (PIDTS), is available for use and has been shown to predict drug use behavior in nonoffenders.[76–77] However, in light of the fact that low agreeableness (A) and conscientiousness (C) are prominent features of FFM profiles in both drug using and criminal populations and many drug users are in regular contact with the illicit supply system or regularly violate the law in order to participate in drug use (e.g., drinking and driving), it may make more sense to use the PICTS in evaluating drug users whether or not they have an official arrest record, given the much greater body of research available on the PICTS.

Criminal Thinking and Crime

A recent meta-analysis of the PICTS indicates that the superordinate score, General Criminal Thinking (GCT), and two higher order scores, (Proactive and Reactive Criminal

Thinking) effectively predict recidivism, with a slight advantage going to the GCT score. In addition, the GCT score was capable of predicting recidivism after controlling for the top two static risk factors for recidivism (i.e., age and criminal history).[78] Criminal thinking has also demonstrated an ability to mediate relationships between important criminal justice constructs. In separate studies, the PICTS was found capable of mediating the relationship between a history of mental illness and violence in prison,[79] the relationship between race and recidivism,[80] and the relationship between past crime and future crime.[81] Its mediating role in the past crime–future crime relationship is particularly noteworthy because it suggests that early antisocial behavior and delinquency shape criminal thinking, which, in turn, shapes future adult criminal behavior.

Criminal Thinking, Drug Use, and Crime

Walters recently determined that reactive but not proactive criminal thinking correlated with a prior history of drug use in a large sample of incarcerated offenders. In addition, reactive criminal thinking mediated the relationship between a history of prior drug abuse and subsequent recidivism.[82] These findings lend further credence to the tripartite model of temperament-personality previously mentioned in this chapter, whereby negative emotionality is more closely aligned with drug use, fearlessness or proactive criminality is principally linked to crime, and disinhibition or reactive criminality seems to encompass both drug use and crime. Reactive criminal thinking and general criminal thinking have also been found to interfere with treatment engagement and progress in offenders enrolled in drug programming.[83–84] Consequently, it would seem important for programs to address criminal thinking in general, and reactive criminal thinking in particular, prior to the onset of treatment or at least during the early stages of an intervention as a means of preparing participants for change.

Attributions

Attributions derive from research in social psychology and refer to beliefs people have about the causes of their own and others' behavior. There are four dimensions along which attributions are commonly evaluated: internal versus external, stable versus unstable, controllable versus uncontrollable, and global versus specific. An internal attribution ascribes behavior to the person (dispositional), whereas an external attribution ascribes behavior to the environment (situational). A stable attribution makes reference to a durable causal agent, whereas an unstable attribution makes reference to a fluid causal agent. A controllable attribution suggests that the behavior is under the person's control, whereas an uncontrollable attribution suggests that the behavior cannot be controlled. Global attributions involve all aspects of a person or situation, whereas specific attributions are restricted to a single attribute. The definitions I have provided should not be interpreted to mean that attributions are dichotomous (internal or external). Like crime itself, attributions are dimensionally organized and so a person's causal attributions can fall at various points along each of the four attribution dimensions. In addition, a person can change his or her position on a dimension over time.

Attributions and Drug Use

The **Abstinence Violation Effect** (AVE) occurs when an individual violates strict prohibitions against drug use, as set forth by groups like Alcoholics Anonymous and Narcotics Anonymous. This then leads to a sense of failure and a significantly greater chance that the slip or lapse will turn into a full-blown relapse. Alan Marlatt and Judith Gordon proposed that relapse has a greater likelihood of occurring when the actor attributes the lapse or slip to factors that are internal (something is wrong with me), stable (the thing that is wrong with me cannot be changed), and global (the thing that is wrong with me is part of everything I do) than when the lapse or slip is attributed to factors that are external (a situation caused the problem), unstable (the situation can be changed), and specific (there is something specific about the situation that I can change).[85] Research on the AVE has been mixed, with retrospective accounts of users attempting to explain the reasons for their relapse supporting an AVE–relapse relationship but ongoing real-time analyses showing that the AVE frequently does not lead to relapse.[86]

Attributions and Crime

Although there is no AVE for crime, there is evidence that attributions may be important not only in initiating criminal behavior but in maintaining it as well. Investigating blame attributions, McKay, Chapman, and Long discovered that child molesters attributed their prior sexual offending and current sexual arousal to internal, stable, and uncontrollable factors; violent offenders did much the same thing in accounting for their past violent crimes. Rapists and property offenders, by comparison, attributed their past crimes to external, stable, and uncontrollable factors.[87] All four groups held stable and uncontrollable attributions for past criminality, which means that their attributions were more likely to maintain criminal behavior than ameliorate it.

Attributions can be applied to other people's behavior as well. An attribution for another person's behavior with relevance to crime is the **hostile attribution bias**. This occurs when a person assumes that an unintentional behavior (e.g., someone accidently bumping into you) was an intentional hostile act. In a meta-analysis of studies on hostile attribution bias, Bram Orobio de Castro and colleagues detected a robust relationship between hostile attribution biases and aggression in children and noted that the effect was strongest for more severe forms of aggression, such as violent delinquency.[88] A link has also been observed between hostile attribution biases and aggression in adults.[89] It should be noted that hostile attribution biases are more likely to be found on the reactive dimension of criminality than on the proactive dimension.

Attributions, Drugs, and Crime

Wagdy Loza and Paul Clements studied the blame attributions of 179 Canadian penitentiary inmates classified into four groups: rapist/alcohol abusers, rapist/nonalcohol abusers, nonrapist/alcohol abusers, and nonrapist/nonalcohol abusers. The results indicated that alcohol abusers blamed alcohol significantly more often than nonalcohol abusers and that rapists blamed victims significantly more often than nonrapists. Inmates attributing the most blame to victims were the rapist/nonalcohol abusers.[90] Without alcohol to blame, they may have directed their externalization efforts to the victim. Externalization of blame was also evident in a large sample of Australian offenders, whereby females attributed their current offense to drugs or alcohol (39%) significantly more often than males (24%). In addition, property offenders were significantly more likely to attribute their most recent offense to drugs or alcohol than nonproperty offenders.[91] Attributing criminal involvement to drugs does not mean that the drugs necessarily caused the crime, but it does suggest that cognitive factors such as attribution biases play a vital role in drug–crime relationships regardless of which (drugs or crime) is held to be the cause of the other.

Outcome Expectancies

Expectancy theory holds that people are motivated to select or choose behaviors for which they anticipate a positive outcome (reinforcement) and to avoid behaviors for which they anticipate a negative outcome (punishment). These behavioral expectations are referred to by proponents of expectancy theory as outcome expectancies. These outcome expectancies are often learned through observation (parents, peers, media) and are shaped further by personal experience.[92] Hence, positive outcome expectancies are potentially important mediators of drug use and criminal outcomes.

Outcome Expectancies for Drugs

Outcome expectancies for alcohol are well-known mediators of key alcohol-related connections. The disinhibition (reactive criminality) dimension that plays such a vital role in drug use–crime relationships is made up of several subdimensions, to include sensation seeking and impulsivity. Róbert Urbán, Gyöngyi Kökönyei, and Zsolt Demetrovics, in fact, determined that alcohol expectancies mediated the relationship between sensation seeking and alcohol use,[93] whereas Matthew Gullo and colleagues ascertained that alcohol expectancies mediated the relationship between impulsivity and hazardous drinking.[94] The well-established connection between the behavioral activation system (BAS) and drinking behavior may also be mediated by outcome expectancies for alcohol.[95] Outcome expectancies for tobacco,[96] cannabis,[97] and stimulants[98] have also been found to correlate with and potentially mediate drug use behavior.

Individuals participating in an **expectancy challenge** are provided with a **placebo** they are told is an active drug (usually alcohol). Individuals frequently respond to the suggestion by acting as if they are under the influence of the alleged chemical substance. Later they are informed that they had actually consumed a placebo and the effect of expectancies on drug use behavior and subjective experience is discussed. This procedure has been found to reduce alcohol and drug consumption, particularly problematic alcohol and drug consumption in student and treatment samples.[99] Despite the obvious relevance of positive outcome expectancies for alcohol treatment, Jones, Corbin, and Fromme found evidence inconsistent with the position that reducing positive outcome expectancies for alcohol reduced future alcohol consumption, although they did note that increasing negative outcome expectancies for alcohol did, in fact, reduce subsequent alcohol consumption.[100]

Outcome Expectancies for Crime

Although the majority of studies on outcome expectancies have dealt with alcohol and drugs, several attempts have been made to extend the outcome expectancies concept to crime. Walters, for instance, has developed a measure of outcome expectancies for crime that is divided into a negative outcome expectancies for crime scale (death, jail or prison, loss of family, loss of job) and three positive outcome expectancies for crime scales: social (acceptance, love, respect, and security), control (control, excitement, freedom, and power), and identity (approval, prestige, purpose, and status). Using this measure, Walters has determined that:

- positive outcome expectancies for crime correlate with proactive but not reactive criminal thinking[101]
- black inmates hold stronger positive outcome expectancies for crime than white inmates[102]
- positive outcome expectancies for crime tend to fall and negative outcome expectancies for crime tend to rise following a course of cognitive-behavioral therapy[103]

Outcome Expectancies for Drugs and Crime

A common **outcome expectancy** for alcohol is that it stimulates aggression. Mary McMurran has studied alcohol-related expectancies for violence in adolescent and young adult offenders and recorded a connection between alcohol expectancies for violence and actual aggressive behavior.[104] In a recent study on this issue, McMurran and McCulloch determined that recalling expectancies of alcohol-related aggression led to a significant but short-lived (2-week) increase in alcohol-related aggression following the intervention.[105] This suggests that outcome expectancies exert their impact by mediating important relationships between other variables. In fact, a research group headed by Sven Barnow determined that alcohol expectancies and peer delinquency/drug use mediated the relationship between aggressive/impulsive delinquent problems and subsequent alcohol consumption (see **Figure 6-12**).[106] Hence, it would seem that alcohol expectancies mediate relationships both when alcohol is the predictor and when alcohol is the outcome. As such, they serve as vital linchpins in a bidirectional model of drug–crime relationships.

Efficacy Expectancies

Efficacy expectancies or self-efficacy refers to a person's belief in his or her ability to successfully perform a particular behavior and in so doing, achieve specific **goals**. In a manner of speaking, self-efficacy is one's confidence in being able to successfully complete or

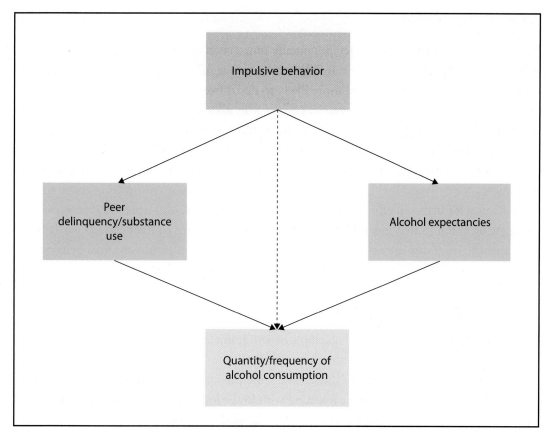

Figure 6-12
Mediating effect of alcohol expectancies and peer delinquency/substance use on the impulsive behavior–alcohol consumption relationship.

Barnow, S., Schultz, G., Lucht, M., Ulrich, I., Preuss, U.-W., & Freyberger, H.-J. (2004). Alcohol expectancies and peer delinquency/substance use mediate the relationship between impulsivity and drinking behavior in adolescence? *Alcohol and Alcoholism, 39*, 213–219. By permission of Oxford University Press.

master specific tasks. The key to self-efficacy is that it is focused on specific actions and behaviors.[107] Hence, a person can have high self-efficacy for committing crime but low self-efficacy for successfully completing drug treatment.

Efficacy Expectancies for Drugs

Research indicates that higher levels of coping self-efficacy are associated with lower levels of problem drinking,[108] marijuana use,[109] and heroin use.[110] In a review of research on how people recover in Alcoholics Anonymous (AA), Kelly, Magill, and Stout discovered that change depended less on specific AA practices and the program's emphasis on spirituality than on the intermediating effects of coping skills development and increased self-efficacy.[111] In a study previously reviewed, Gullo et al. determined that positive outcome expectancies for alcohol and low refusal self-efficacy mediated the impulsivity–alcohol misuse relationship.[112] Impulsivity mediated the relationship between AA attendance and drinking outcome and self-efficacy appeared to mediate the relationship between impulsivity and drinking outcome in a study by Daniel Blonigen and colleagues.[113] This last study illustrates the complex relationships that exist between impulsivity or disinhibition and self-efficacy and how both may be playing mediating roles in important drug-relevant relationships.

Efficacy Expectancies for Crime

There are two ways that self-efficacy potentially impacts on crime. First, individuals with high levels of self-efficacy for crime are likely to continue offending, whereas individuals with low self-efficacy for crime are more likely to desist from offending. When the wife of the Nicolas Cage character in the movie, *Lord of War*, asks him why he continues to deal illegal arms after making more money than he would ever need, he responds, "because I'm good at it." This reflects high self-efficacy for crime and one reason why some offenders remain in crime long after their financial needs have been met. Second, individuals with low self-efficacy for conventional behavior are more likely to continue committing crime than individuals with high-self efficacy for conventional behavior. With respect to this second point, Walters found that low self-efficacy to avoid future police contact (arrest) partially mediated the relationship between a history of delinquency and future criminal behavior.[114]

Efficacy Expectancies for Drugs and Crime

Research on the role of self-efficacy in drug–crime relationships is sparse, contradictory, and largely inconclusive. Two-thirds of a sample of 188 homeless veterans enrolled in substance abuse programming reported that they were involved in at least one crime in the past year and 41% reported multiple crimes during the same time period. In this study, higher levels of self-efficacy and resilience were associated with lower levels of self-reported criminality.[115] The results of a study by Schaub and colleagues, however, revealed that self-efficacy did not predict treatment retention in substance-abusing offenders participating in an 18-month five-country European longitudinal panel study.[116] One possible explanation for these results is that the treatment protocol was not evidence based or efficacious, although more research is required to determine whether this is a reasonable explanation for these results and ascertain whether self-efficacy plays a meaningful role in drug–crime relationships.

Psychological Inertia

The four cognitive factors described in this section relate most directly to social learning theories of drug use and crime and the bidirectional models of Thornberry and Walters. As such, they exert both mediating and reciprocal effects on drug use and crime. They mediate important relationships between other variables and create reciprocal or bidirectional associations with drug use, crime, and the drug–crime connection. Just as criminal thinking and self-efficacy are shaped by early delinquent experiences, subsequent adult criminality is shaped by criminal thinking and self-efficacy. By virtue of their mediating effect, cognitive variables are both a cause and effect of important drug- and crime-based relationships. These quasi-time-stable cognitive variables and the bidirectional relationships to which they give rise maintain behavioral patterns like drug use and crime through what Walters refers to as **psychological inertia**. Psychological inertia is the process by which quasi-time-stable cognitive variables interact to create a state of relative behavioral continuity. This is one reason why people continue engaging in a behavior long after it has stopped being overtly reinforcing.[117] Crossing the three temperament-personality dimensions with the four quasi-time-stable cognitive variables provides a picture of the factors that support psychological inertia (see **Table 6-4**).

Table 6-4 Foundations of Psychological Inertia Broken Down by the Three Temperament-Personality Dimensions of Negative Emotionality, Disinhibition, and Fearlessness

Cognitive Variable	Negative Emotionality	Disinhibition (Reactive)	Fearlessness (Proactive)
Thinking Styles		Reactive Criminal Thinking	Proactive Criminal Thinking
Attributions	Abstinence Violation Effect	Hostile Attribution Biases	
Outcome Expectancies	Positive Outcome Expectancies for Alcohol & Drugs		Positive Outcome Expectancies for Crime
Efficacy Expectancies	Low Self-Efficacy for Coping with Stress	Low Self-Efficacy for Conventional Behavior	High Self-Efficacy for Crime

Summary and Conclusions

- Higher levels of intelligence appear to be associated with increased use of drugs and decreased involvement in crime. Certain temperaments (negative emotionality) appear to be more closely tied to drug use, other temperaments (fearlessness or proactive) are more closely tied to crime, and still other temperaments (disinhibition or reactive) are more closely tied to both drug use and crime. Moral development has not been sufficiently studied to know what value it holds in explaining the drug–crime nexus, but an early age of onset of either drug use or crime clearly predicts more severe patterns of future drug use and crime.

- The FFM of personality has been used to study a number of behaviors and appears to have relevance to research on drug use and crime. A review of the literature and the results of several major meta-analyses indicate the presence of high neuroticism (N) and low agreeableness (A) and conscientiousness (C) in drug users and low A and C in criminals. Drug-using offenders, on the other hand, appear to demonstrate the highest levels of N and the lowest levels of A and C.

- The four quasi-time-stable cognitive variables of criminal thinking, attributions, outcome expectancies, and efficacy expectancies play an important mediating role in relationships involving drugs, crime, and the drug–crime overlap. These variables help create a web of bidirectional influences that stabilize drug and crime patterns and give rise to a state of psychological inertia.

Key Terms

Abstinence Violation Effect (AVE) Violation of strict prohibition against drug use leads to a sense of failure and increases the individual's chances of relapse.

Activity Level Temperament dimension characterized by the degree and rate of motor output and behavioral response displayed across various situations.

Age of Onset Age at which an individual starts using drugs or committing crime.

Agreeableness (A) One of the "big five" factors in the Five Factor Model; characterized by altruism, compliance, and tendermindedness.

Attributions   People's beliefs about the causes of their own or another's behavior.

Conscientiousness (C)   One of the "big five" factors in the Five Factor Model; characterized by thoughtfulness, self-control, and achievement striving.

Criminal Thinking   Set of attitudes or beliefs that help maintain criminal behavior as well as drug use.

Disinhibition   Higher order temperament dimension marked by weak personal control, impulsiveness, and sensation-seeking tendencies.

Efficacy Expectancies   Person's belief in his or her ability to successfully perform a specific behavior and achieve certain goals.

Expectancy Challenge   Intervention in which participants are administered a placebo they are told is an active drug; after responding to the placebo participants are informed that they have consumed a placebo.

Externalizing Disorder   Broad category of childhood disorders involving outward behavior and including attention deficit/hyperactivity disorder, conduct disorder, and oppositional defiant disorder.

Extraversion (E)   One of the "big five" factors in the Five Factor Model; characterized by sociability, talkativeness, and excitement seeking.

Factor Analysis   Statistical procedure in which a correlational matrix composed of several items or variables is created and analyzed to determine the number of underlying factors or latent dimensions.

Fearlessness   Higher order temperament dimension marked by low fear, anxiety, and depression; moderate to high anger; callousness in interpersonal relationships; and a tendency to engage in instrumental aggression.

Five Factor Model (FFM)   Theory of personality that encompasses five main factors: openness to experience, conscientiousness, extraversion, agreeableness, and neuroticism.

Goals   Objectives people pursue in life; they can be short term, intermediate term, or long term.

Hostile Attribution Bias   Automatically attributing an intentional hostile motive to an ambiguous situation or event.

Intelligence   Aggregate ability to solve problems and deal effectively with the environment.

Intelligence Quotient (IQ)   Score from a test designed to measure intelligence; normally has a mean of 100 and standard deviation of 15.

Internalizing Disorder   Broad category of childhood disorders involving internal thoughts and feelings like anxiety and depression.

Negative Emotionality   Temperament dimension characterized by intensity and frequency of negative affect in the form of anger, anxiety, and depression; also a higher order temperament dimension marked by anxiety, fear, and depression.

Neuroticism (N)   One of the "big five" factors in the Five Factor Model; characterized by emotional instability, hostility, and impulsiveness.

Novelty Seeking   Temperament dimension characterized by the tendency to seek out new experiences and unfamiliar stimuli and avoid routine.

Openness to Experience (O)   One of the "big five" factors in the Five Factor Model; characterized by aestheticism, imagination, and insight.

Outcome Expectancy   Person's belief about what will happen should he or she engage in a specific behavior.

Personality   Relatively enduring patterns of behavior that are unique to the individual and consistent across situations.

Placebo   Inert substance made to look like an active drug.

Positive Emotionality   Temperament dimension characterized by intensity and frequency of positive affect in the form of happiness, joy, and contentment.

Psychological Inertia   Process by which quasi-time-stable cognitive variables interact to create a state of relative behavioral continuity.

Savanna-IQ Interaction Hypothesis   Theory that holds general intelligence to be associated with the tendency to acquire, espouse, and embrace evolutionarily novel values and practices.

Self-Regulation   Temperament dimension characterized by the ability to control one's actions and anticipate the likely consequences of one's behavior; also known as effortful control.

Sociability   Temperament dimension characterized by the tendency to approach interpersonal stimuli and situations rather than avoid interpersonal stimuli and situations.

Temperament   Innate disposition to respond to environmental stimuli in a particular way.

Values   Relative significance or priority people assign to specific behaviors.

Critical Thinking

1. How does early development, particularly an early age of onset of drug use or delinquency, influence a person's future propensity for drug abuse and crime.
2. Is there such a thing as an addictive or criminal personality? If not, is there still a role that personality can play in the development of a drug or crime problem?
3. How might criminal thinking and positive outcome expectancies for alcohol interact to increase a person's propensity to both abuse drugs and commit crime?

Notes

1. Matarazzo, J. D. (1972). *Wechsler's Measurement and appraisal of adult intelligence* (5th ed.). Baltimore, MD: Williams & Wilkins (p. 79).
2. Kaufman, A. S., & Lichtenberger, E. O. (2006). *Assessing adolescent and adult intelligence* (3rd ed.). Hoboken, NJ: Wiley.
3. Kanazawa, S. (2008). Temperature and evolutionary novelty as forces behind the evolution of general intelligence. *Intelligence, 36*, 99–108.
4. Kanazawa, S., & Hellberg, J. E. E. U. (2010). Intelligence and substance use. *Review of General Psychology, 14*, 382–396.

5. Wilson, J. Q., & Herrnstein, R. (1985). *Crime and human nature*. New York: Simon and Schuster.

6. Hirschi, T., & Hindelang, M. (1977). Intelligence and delinquency: A revisionist review. *American Sociological Review. 32*, 571–587.

7. McGloin, J. M., Pratt, T. C., & Maahs, J. (2004). Rethinking the IQ-delinquency relationship: A longitudinal analysis of multiple theoretical models. *Justice Quarterly, 21*, 603–635.

8. Kanazawa & Hellberg (2010).

9. Fergusson, D. M., Horwood, L. J., & Ridder, E. M. (2005). Show me the child at seven. II: Childhood intelligence and later outcomes in adolescence and young adulthood. *Journal of Child Psychology and Psychiatry, 46*, 850–858.

10. Room, R. (2004, February 25–27). *Thinking about how social inequalities relate to alcohol and drug use and problems*. Presented at the First International Summer School on Inequalities and Addictions, National Centre for Education and Training in Addictions, Adelaide, South Australia.

11. Thomas, A., & Chess, S. (1977). *Temperament and development*. New York: Brunner/Mazel.

12. Walters, G. D. (2011). Childhood temperament: Dimensions or types? *Personality and Individual Differences, 50*, 1168–1173.

13. Ivanov, I., Schulz, K. P., London, E. D., & Newcorn, J. H. (2008). Inhibitory control deficits in childhood and risk for substance use disorders: A review. *American Journal of Drug and Alcohol Abuse, 34*, 239–258.

14. Windle, M., & Windle, R. C. (2006). Adolescent temperament and lifetime psychiatric and substance abuse disorders assessed in young adulthood. *Personality and Individual Differences, 41*, 15–25.

15. Creemers, H. E., Dijkstra, J. K., Vollebergh, W. A. M., Ormel, J., Verhulst, F. C., & Huizink, A. C. (2010). Predicting life-time and regular cannabis use during adolescence: The roles of temperament and peer substance use. The TRAILS study. *Addiction, 105*, 699–708.

16. Cloninger, C. R. (1987). Neurogenetic adaptive mechanisms in alcoholism. *Science, 236*, 410–416.

17. Smart, D., Richardson, N., Sanson, A., Dussuyer, I., & Marshall, B. (2005). *Patterns and precursors of adolescent antisocial behavior: Outcomes and connections*. Melbourne, Australia: Australian Institute of Family Studies.

18. Pardini, D. A. (2006). The callousness pathway to severe violent delinquency. *Aggressive Behavior, 32*, 590–598.

19. Clark, D. B., Bukstein, O. G., Smith, M. G., Kaczynski, N. A., Mezzick, A. C., & Donovan, J. E. (1995). Identifying anxiety disorders in adolescents hospitalized for alcohol abuse or dependence. *Psychiatric Services, 46*, 618–620.

20. Hudziak, J. J., Copeland, W., Stanger, C., & Wadsworth, M. (2004). Screening for DSM-IV externalizing disorders with the Child Behavior Checklist: A receiver-operating characteristic analysis. *Journal of Child Psychology and Psychiatry and Allied Disciplines, 45*, 1299–1307.

21. Eisenberg, N., Guthrie, I. K., Fabes, R. A., Shepard, S., Losoya, S., Murphy, B. C., et al. (2000). Prediction of elementary school children's externalizing problem behaviors from attentional and behavioral regulation and negative emotionality. *Child Development, 71*, 1367–1382.

22. Gartstein, M., & Rothbart, M. (2003). Studying infant temperament via the revised infant behavior questionnaire. *Infant Behavior & Development, 26*, 64–86.

23. Rothbart, M. (2007). Temperament, development, and personality. *Current Directions in Psychological Science, 16*, 207–212.

24. Lykken, D. T. (1995). *The antisocial personalities*. Hillsdale, NJ: Lawrence Erlbaum.

25. Evans, D. E., & Rothbart, M. K. (2007). Development of a model for adult temperament. *Journal of Research in Personality, 41*, 868–888.

26. Kohlberg, L. (1981). *Essays on moral development: Vol. 1. The philosophy of moral development*. San Francisco: Harper and Row.

27. Abide, M. M., Richards, H. C., & Ramsay, S. G. (2001). Moral reasoning and consistency of belief and behavior: Decisions about substance abuse. *Journal of Drug Education, 31*, 367–384.

28. Bartek, S. E., Krebs, D. L., & Taylor, M. C. (1993). Coping, defending, and the relations between moral judgment and moral behavior in prostitutes and other female juvenile delinquents. *Journal of Abnormal Psychology, 102*, 65–73.

29. Hayes, S. C., & Walker, W. I. (1986). Intellectual and moral development in offenders: A review. *Australian and New Zealand Journal of Criminology, 19*, 53–64.

30. Aleixo, P. A., & Norris, C. E. (2000). Personality and moral reasoning in young offenders. *Personality and Individual Differences, 28*, 609–623.

31. Kuther, T. L., & Higgins-D'Alessandro, A. (2000). Bridging the gap between moral reasoning and adolescent engagement in risky behavior. *Journal of Adolescence, 23*, 409–422.

32. Krebs, D. L., & Denton, K. (2006). Explanatory limitations of cognitive-developmental approaches to morality. *Psychological Review, 113*, 672–675.

33. Grant, B. F., & Dawson, D. A. (1998). Age at onset of drug use and its association with DSM–IV drug abuse and dependence: Results from the National Longitudinal Alcohol Epidemiologic Survey. *Journal of Substance Abuse, 10*, 163–173.

34. Substance Abuse and Mental Health Services Administration. (2006). *National Survey on Drug Use and Health, 2005.* Washington, DC: U.S. Department of Health and Human Services.

35. Griffin, K. W., Bang, H., & Botvin, G. J. (2010). Age of alcohol and marijuana use onset predicts weekly substance use and related psychosocial problems during young adulthood. *Journal of Substance Use, 15*, 174–183.

36. Grant, B. F., & Dawson, D. A. (1997). Age of onset of alcohol use and its association with DSM–IV alcohol abuse and dependence: Results from the National Longitudinal Alcohol Epidemiological Survey. *Journal of Substance Abuse, 9*, 103–110.

37. Moffitt, T. E. (1993). Adolescence-limited and life-course-persistent antisocial behavior: A developmental taxonomy. *Psychological Review, 100*, 674–701.

38. Farrington, D. P., Loeber, R., Elliott, D. S., Hawkins, J. D., Kandel, D. B., Klein, M. W., et al. (1990). Advancing knowledge about the onset of delinquency and crime. In B. Lahey & A. Kazdin (Eds.), *Advances in clinical child psychology* (Vol. 13, pp. 283–342). New York: Plenum.

39. American Psychiatric Association. (2000). *Diagnostic and statistical manual of mental disorders* (4th ed., text rev.). Washington, DC: Author.

40. Walters, G. D., & Knight, R. A. (2010). Antisocial personality disorder with and without antecedent childhood conduct disorder: Does it make a difference? *Journal of Personality Disorders, 24*, 165–178.

41. Zhang, L., Wieczorek, W. F., & Welte, J. W. (1997). The impact of age of onset of substance use on delinquency. *Journal of Research in Crime and Delinquency, 34*, 253–268.

42. Gordon, M. S., Kinlock, T. W., & Battjes, R. J. (2004). Correlates of early substance use and crime among adolescents entering outpatient substance abuse treatment. *American Journal of Drug and Alcohol Abuse, 30*, 39–59.

43. Farabee, D., Joshi, V., & Anglin, M. D. (2001). Addiction careers and criminal specialization. *Crime and Delinquency, 47*, 196–220.

44. Hegamin, A., Farabee, D., Lu, A. T.-H., & Longshore, D. (2007). Substance abuse and criminal specialization in an arrestee sample. In K. Knight & D. Farabee (Eds.), *Treating addicted offenders: A continuum of effective practices* (pp. 1.1–1.11). Kingston, NJ: Civic Research Institute.

45. McGue, M., Iacono, W. G., Legrand, L. N., Malone, S., & Elkins, I. (2001). Origins and consequences of age at first drink. I. Associations with substance-use disorders, disinhibitory behavior and psychopathology, and p3 amplitude. *Alcoholism: Clinical and Experimental Research, 25*, 1156–1165.

46. Nakken, C. (1996). *The addictive personality: Understanding the addictive process and compulsive behavior* (2nd ed.). Center City, MN: Hazelden.

47. Yochelson, S., & Samenow, S. (1976). *The criminal personality: Vol. I. A profile for change.* New York: Aronson.

48. Revelle, W. (1995). Personality processes. *Annual Review of Psychology, 46*, 295–328.

49. Rothbart (2007).

50. Eysenck, H. J. (1967). *The biological basis of personality.* Springfield, IL: Thomas.

51. Cloninger (1987).

52. Atkinson, J. W. (1957). Motivational determinants of risk-taking behavior. *Psychological Review, 64*, 359–372.

53. Tellegen, A. (1985). Structure of mood and personality and their relevance to assessing anxiety, with an emphasis on self-report. In A. H. Tuma & J. D. Maser (Eds.), *Anxiety and the anxiety disorders* (pp. 681–706). Hillsdale, NJ: Lawrence Erlbaum.

54. McCrae, R. R., & Costa, P. T., Jr. (1997). Personality trait structure as a human universal. *American Psychologist, 52*, 509–516.

55. Bouchard, T. J., & McGue, M. (2003). Genetic and environmental influences on human psychological differences. *Journal of Neurobiology, 54*, 4–45.

56. McCrae, R. R., Costa, P. T., Jr., & Martin, T. A. (2005). The NEO-PI-3: A more readable revised NEO Personality Inventory. *Journal of Personality Assessment, 84*, 261–270.

57. Malouff, J. M., Thorsteinsson, E. B., & Schutte, N. S. (2006). The five-factor model of personality and smoking: A meta-analysis. *Journal of Drug Education, 36*, 47–58.

58. Gilbert, D. G. (1995). *Smoking: Individual differences, psychopathology, and emotion*. Washington, DC: Taylor & Francis.

59. Malouff et al. (2006).

60. Hooten, W. M., Wolter, T. D., Ames, S. C., Hurt, R. D., Vickers, K. S., Hurt, R. D., et al. (2005). Personality correlates related to tobacco abstinence following treatment. *International Journal of Psychiatry in Medicine, 35*, 59–74.

61. Malouff, J. M., Thorsteinsson, E. B., Rooke, S. E., & Schutte, N. S. (2007). Alcohol involvement and the five-factor model of personality: A meta-analysis. *Journal of Drug Education, 37*, 277–294.

62. Terracciano, A., Löckenhoff, C. E., Crum, R. M., Bienvenu, J., & Costa, P. T., Jr. (2008). Five-factor model personality profiles of drug users. *BMC Psychiatry, 8*, 22.

63. Raynor, D. A., & Levine, H. (2009). Associations between the five-factor model of personality and health behaviors among college students. *Journal of American College Health, 58*, 73–82.

64. Widiger, T. A., & Lynam, D. R. (1998). Psychopathy from the perspective of the five-factor model of personality. In T. Millon, E. Simonsen, M. Birket-Smith, & R. D. Davis (Eds.), *Psychopathy: Antisocial, criminal, and violent behaviors* (pp. 171–187). New York: Guilford Press.

65. Miller, J. D., Lynam, D. R., Widiger, T. A., & Leukefeld, C. (2001). Personality disorder as extreme variants of common personality dimensions: Can the five-factor model adequately represent psychopathy? *Journal of Personality, 69*, 253–276.

66. Ross, S. R., Lutz, C. J., & Bailley, S. E. (2004). Psychopathy and the five factor model in a noninstitutionalized sample: A domain and facet analysis. *Journal of Psychopathology and Behavioral Assessment, 26*, 213–223.

67. Clower, C. E., & Bothwell, R. K. (2001). An exploratory study of the relationship between the big five and inmate recidivism. *Journal of Research in Personality, 35*, 231–237.

68. Madsen, L., Parsons, S., & Grubin, D. (2006). The relationship between the five-factor model and DSM personality disorder in a sample of child molesters. *Personality and Individual Differences, 40*, 227–236.

69. Trninić, V., Barančić, M., & Nazor, M. (2008). The five-factor model of personality and aggressiveness in prisoners and athletes. *Kinesiology, 40*, 170–181.

70. Ruiz, M. A., Pincus, A. L., & Schinka, J. A. (2008). Externalizing pathology and the five-factor model: A meta-analysis of personality traits associated with antisocial personality disorder, substance use disorder, and their co-occurrence. *Journal of Personality Disorders, 22*, 365–388.

71. Ruiz et al. (2008).

72. Ruiz et al. (2008).

73. Bandura, A. (1986). *Social foundations of thought and action: A social cognitive theory*. Englewood Cliffs, NJ: Prentice Hall.

74. Walters, G. D. (1995). The Psychological Inventory of Criminal Thinking Styles: Part I. Reliability and preliminary validity. *Criminal Justice and Behavior, 22*, 307–325.

75. Walters, G. D. (2012). *Crime in a psychological context: From career criminals to criminal careers*. Thousand Oaks, CA: Sage.

76. Walters, G. D., & Willoughby, F. W. (2000). The Psychological Inventory of Drug-Based Thinking Styles (PIDTS): Preliminary data. *Alcoholism Treatment Quarterly, 18*, 51–66.

77. Morris, C., & Moore, E. (2009). An evaluation of group work as an intervention to reduce the impact of substance misuse for offender patients in a high security hospital. *Journal of Forensic Psychiatry and Psychology, 20*, 559–576.

78. Walters, G. D. (2012). Criminal thinking and recidivism: Meta-analytic evidence on the predictive and incremental validity of the Psychological Inventory of Criminal Thinking Styles (PICTS). *Aggression and Violent Behavior, 17*, 272–278.

79. Walters, G. D. (2011). Criminal thinking as a mediator of the mental illness-prison violence relationship: A path analytic study and causal mediation analysis. *Psychological Services, 8*, 189–199.

80. Walters, G. D. (in press). Relationships among race, education, criminal thinking and recidivism: Moderator and mediator effects. *Assessment.*

81. Walters, G. D. (in press). Cognitive mediation of crime continuity: A causal mediation analysis of the past crime-future crime relationship. *Crime and Delinquency.*

82. Walters, G. D. (2012). Substance abuse and criminal thinking: Testing the countervailing, mediation, and specificity hypotheses. *Law and Human Behavior, 36*, 506–512.

83. Best, D., Day, E., Campbell, A., Flynn, P. M., & Simpson, D. D. (2009). Relationship between drug treatment engagement and criminal thinking style among drug-using offenders. *European Addiction Research, 15*, 71–77.

84. Walters, G. D., & Geyer, M. D. (2005). Construct validity of the psychological inventory of criminal thinking styles in relationship to the PAI, disciplinary adjustment, and program completion. *Journal of Personality Assessment, 84*, 252–260.

85. Marlatt, G. A., & Gordon, J. R. (Eds.). (1985). *Relapse prevention: Maintenance strategies in the treatment of addictive behaviors.* New York: Guilford.

86. Brandon, T. H., Vidrine, J. I., & Litvin, E. B. (2007). Relapse and relapse prevention. *Annual Review of Clinical Psychology, 3*, 257–284.

87. McKay, M. M., Chapman, J. W., & Long, N. R. (1996). Causal attributions for criminal offending and sexual arousal: Comparison of child sex offenders with other offenders. *British Journal of Clinical Psychology, 35*, 63–75.

88. de Castro, B. O., Veerman, J. W., Koops, W., Bosch, J. D., & Monshouwer, H. J. (2002). Hostile attribution of intent and aggressive behavior: A meta-analysis. *Child Development, 73*, 916–934.

89. Epps, J. B., & Kendall, P. C. (1995). Hostile attributional bias in adults. *Cognitive Therapy and Research, 19*, 159–178.

90. Loza, W., & Clements, P. (1991). Incarcerated alcoholics' and rapists' attributions of blame for criminal acts. *Canadian Journal of Behavioural Science, 23*, 76–83.

91. Loxley, W., & Adams, K. (2009). *Women, drug use, and crime: Findings from the Drug Use Monitoring in Australia program.* Canberra, Australia: Australian Institute of Criminology.

92. Bandura (1986).

93. Urbán, R., Kökönyei, G., & Demetrovics, Z. (2008). Alcohol outcome expectancies and drinking motives mediate the association between sensation seeking and alcohol use among adolescents. *Addictive Behaviors, 33*, 1344–1352.

94. Gullo, M. J., Dawe, S., Kambouropoulos, N., Staiger, P. K., & Jackson, C. J. (2010). Alcohol expectancies and drinking refusal self-efficacy mediate the association of impulsivity with alcohol misuse. *Alcoholism: Clinical & Experimental Research, 34*, 1386–1399.

95. Wardell, J. D., Read, J. P., Colder, C. R., & Merrill, J. E. (2012). Positive outcome expectancies mediate the influence of the behavioral activation system on alcohol use: A prospective path analysis. *Addictive Behaviors, 37*, 435–443.

96. Cohen, L. M., McCarthy, D. M., Brown, S. A., & Myers, M. G. (2002). Negative affect combines with smoking outcome expectancies to predict smoking behavior over time. *Psychology of Addictive Behaviors, 16*, 91–97.

97. Alfonso, J., & Dunn, M. E. (2007). Differences in the marijuana expectancies of adolescents in relation to marijuana use. *Substance Use and Misuse, 42*, 1009–1025.

98. Labbe, A. K., & Maisto, S. A. (2010). Development of the stimulant medication outcome expectancies questionnaire for college students. *Addictive Behaviors, 35*, 726–729.

99. Darkes, J., & Goldman, M. S. (1993). Expectancy challenge and drinking reduction: Experimental evidence for a mediational process. *Journal of Consulting and Clinical Psychology, 61*, 344–353.

100. Jones, B. T., Corbin, W., & Fromme, K. (2001). A review of expectancy theory and alcohol consumption. *Addiction, 96*, 57–62.

101. Walters, G. D. (2007). Measuring proactive and reactive criminal thinking with the PICTS: Correlations with outcome expectancies and hostile attribution biases. *Journal of Interpersonal Violence, 22*, 371–385.

102. Walters, G. D. (2011). Black–white differences in positive outcome expectancies for crime: A study of male federal prison inmates. *Journal of Criminal Justice, 39*, 192–197.

103. Walters, G. D. (2004). Changes in positive and negative crime expectancies in inmates exposed to a brief psychoeducational intervention: Further data. *Personality and Individual Differences, 37*, 505–512.

104. McMurran, M. (2007). The relationships between alcohol-aggression proneness, general alcohol expectancies, hazardous drinking, and alcohol-related violence in adult male prisoners. *Psychology, Crime & Law, 13*, 275–284.

105. McMurran, M., & McCulloch, A. (2009). Alcohol-aggression outcome expectancies and their responsiveness to event recall. *Addiction Research and Theory, 17*, 54–63.

106. Barnow, S., Schultz, G., Lucht, M., Ulrich, I., Preuss, U.-W., & Freyberger, H.-J. (2004). Alcohol expectancies and peer delinquency/substance use mediate the relationship between impulsivity and drinking behavior in adolescence? *Alcohol and Alcoholism, 39*, 213–219.

107. Bandura (1986).

108. Long, C. G., Hollin, C. R., & Williams, M. J. (1998). Self–efficacy, outcome expectations, and fantasies as predictors of alcoholics' posttreatment drinking. *Substance Use and Misuse, 33*, 2383–2402.

109. Stephens, R. S., Wertz, J. S., & Roffman, R. A. (1995). Self-efficacy and marijuana cessation: A construct validity analysis. *Journal of Consulting and Clinical Psychology, 63*, 1022–1031.

110. Senbanjo, R., Wolff, K., Marshall, E. J., & Strong, J. (2009). Persistence of heroin use despite methadone treatment: Poor coping self-efficacy predicts continued heroin use. *Drug and Alcohol Review, 28*, 608–615.

111. Kelly, J. F., Magill, M., & Stout, R. L. (2009). How do people recover from alcohol dependence? A systematic review of the research on mechanisms of behavior change in Alcoholics Anonymous. *Addiction Research and Theory, 17*, 236–259.

112. Gullo et al. (2010).

113. Blonigen, D. M., Timko, C., Finney, J. W., Moos, B. S., & Moos, R. H. (2011). Alcoholics Anonymous attendance, decreased in impulsivity and drinking and psychosocial outcomes over 16 years: Moderated-mediation from a developmental perspective. *Addiction, 106*, 2167–2177.

114. Walters, G. D. (in press). Cognitive mediation of crime continuity: A causal mediation analysis of the past crime-future crime relationship. *Crime and Delinquency*.

115. Benda, B., Rodell, D., & Rodell, L. (2003). Crime among homeless military veterans who abuse substances. *Psychiatric Rehabilitation Journal, 26*, 332–345.

116. Schaub, M., Stevens, A., Haug, S., Berto, D., Hunt, N., Kerschl, V., et al. (2011). Predictors of retention in the "voluntary" and "quasi-compulsory" treatment of substance dependence in Europe. *European Addiction Research, 17*, 97–105.

117. Walters, G. D. (2012). *Crime in a psychological context: From career criminals to criminal careers*. Thousand Oaks, CA: Sage.

CHAPTER 7

SOCIOLOGICAL FOUNDATIONS OF DRUG–CRIME RELATIONSHIPS

© Jack Hollingsworth/Photodisc/Thinkstock

203

In contrast to psychological factors, which emphasize the role of the individual, sociological factors emphasize the role of the environment. Allowing for the fact that the person x situation interaction is probably more important than isolated individual or environmental factors in explaining drug use, crime, and drug–crime relationships, best practice still requires that we understand the individual and environmental factors responsible for drug use and crime before trying to decipher and disentangle the complexities of their interaction. The focus of the current chapter is on two broad environmental factors of major concern to sociologists, social workers, and social psychologists interested in the study of drug use, crime, and the drug–crime connection. First, there are the adverse social conditions created by social inequities, unemployment, and physical and sexual abuse. Second, there is the process of socialization whereby the individual acquires both deviant and conventional definitions of behavior through association with parents, peers, and the media.

Both adverse social conditions and socialization effects are vital to the development of drug use, crime, and drug–crime relationships. As such, they figure prominently in the two principal objectives of this chapter:

- Determine the extent to which social inequities, unemployment, and physical and sexual abuse explain drug use, crime, and various features of the drug–crime nexus.
- Ascertain how socialization to deviant definitions of behavior and failed socialization to conventional definitions of behavior contribute to drug use, crime, and drug–crime relationships by way of parents, **peers**, and the **media**.

Adverse Social Conditions

This section examines the relevance of three **adverse social conditions** (social inequities, employment status, physical and sexual abuse) to drug use, crime, and drug–crime relationships.

Social Inequities

Social inequities arise because the wealth and economic capital of most societies is not evenly distributed across the population. Hence, there are the haves and the have-nots. It is the have-nots that I am speaking about when I raise the issue of social inequities. Social inequities in the form of lower social class or **socioeconomic status** (SES), poverty, and lack of education are capable of explaining drug use, crime, and the drug–crime connection, according to many sociologists.

Social Inequities and Drug Use

The relationship between the molar construct of social inequity and drug use is formidably complex and conflicting results have often surfaced in research on social inequities and drug use. This is because the relationship tends to vary as a function of the social inequity measure employed (social class, poverty, education), the level of drug involvement studied (use, abuse, dependence), and various sample characteristics (gender, race, nationality). In a review of the literature on social class and drug use, Robin Room concluded that there is no clear relationship between the two variables.[1] Some studies, in fact, suggest that more affluent people tend to drink more, smoke more, and use more illegal drugs than less affluent people (see **Figure 7-1**).[2] More serious forms of substance abuse, problem drinking, single-episode harm (overdose, accidents, violence), and drug-related health problems, however, tend to be concentrated in the lower social classes where poverty runs rampant and people have fewer years of education (see **Figure 7-2**).[3–4]

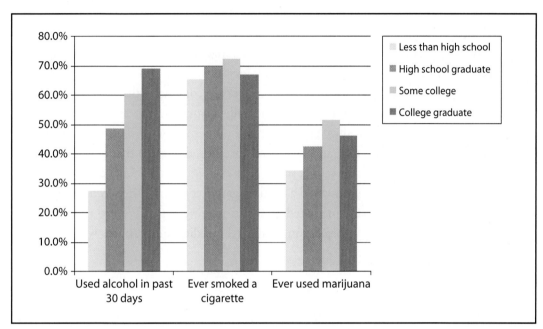

Figure 7-1
Percentage of individuals age 18 and older who reported using alcohol in the last 30 days, ever smoked cigarettes, and ever used marijuana by educational level, 2010.

Data From: Center for Behavioral Health Statistics and Quality. (2012). *Results from the 2010 National Survey on Drug Use and Health*. Rockville, MD: Substance Abuse and Mental Health Services Administration.

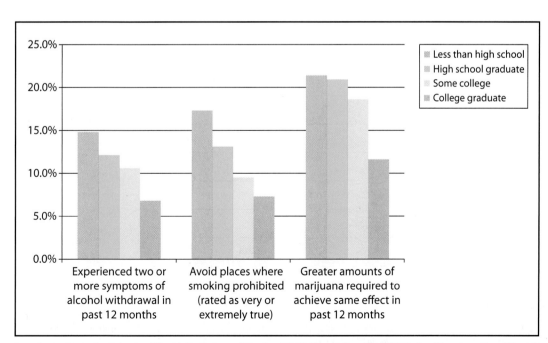

Figure 7-2
Percentage of individuals age 18 and older who reported two or more withdrawal symptoms to alcohol in the last 12 months, avoided places where smoking was prohibited, or needed to use more marijuana to get the same effect in the last 12 months by educational level, 2010.

Data From: Center for Behavioral Health Statistics and Quality. (2012). *Results from the 2010 National Survey on Drug Use and Health*. Rockville, MD: Substance Abuse and Mental Health Services Administration.

Social Inequities and Crime

Charles Tittle, Wayne Villemez, and Douglas Smith performed a meta-analysis of studies addressing the social class–crime relationship and uncovered a small negative or inverse correlation. In a negative correlation, the variables go in opposite directions: i.e., as one variable increases the other variable decreases. Hence, as crime goes up, social class goes down. The results of this meta-analysis also indicated that the social class–crime relationship was strongest for official crime data, primarily from **ecological studies** where social class and crime are compared across areas (e.g., neighborhoods within a city). Furthermore, earlier and less methodologically sound studies witnessed a substantially stronger negative correlation between social class and crime than later and more methodologically sound studies (see **Figure 7-3**).[5]

Based on the results of their meta-analysis, Tittle et al.[6] concluded that the highly touted relationship between social class and crime was actually a "myth." More recent studies on the social class–crime relationship have confirmed the results of the Tittle et al. meta-analysis. Dunaway, Cullen, Burton, and Evans, for instance, discerned that regardless of how they measured social class and crime, social class exerted minimal impact on crime.[7] Jonas Ring and Robert Svensson observed a small negative correlation between social class and delinquency that was partially mediated by school achievement.[8] What this means is that the social class–delinquency correlation weakened but did not disappear when school achievement was controlled.

Social Inequalities, Drug Use, and Crime

Using data from the 24 metropolitan areas included in the 1992 Drug Use Forecasting (DUF) survey, Avelardo Valdez, Charles Kaplan, and Russell Curtis determined that male arrestees booked for a violent crime were more likely to report a history of alcohol abuse and

Figure 7-3
Correlations between social class broken down by data source (self-report, official) and date of publication.

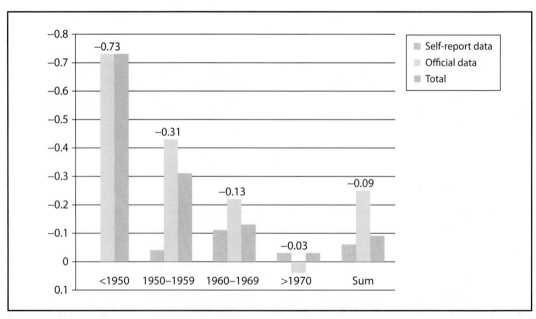

Data From: Tittle, C., Villemez, W. J., & Smith, D. (1978). The myth of social class and criminality: An empirical assessment of the evidence. *American Sociological Review, 43*, 643–656.

Note: The correlation coefficients listed in the graph are for the total (purple) bar.

less likely to test positive for illegal drugs.[9] This is consistent with previous research showing that alcohol tends to promote violence in some individuals, whereas illegal drug use is more often associated with nonviolent economically oriented crime designed to acquire money to pay for drugs.[10–11] Valdez et al. also found evidence that community-level concentrations of poverty and individual-level measures of social attachment mediated the different substance use–crime relationships observed in their study. Thus, whereas alcohol and illegal drugs formed countervailing (opposite) associations with violent crime, social inequality appeared to mediate both relationships.[12] One way to interpret these results is that living in an impoverished urban environment amplifies existing alcohol–violent crime and illegal drug–nonviolent crime relationships, perhaps by increasing stress or decreasing coping resources.

Occupational Status

As with social class, poverty, education, and other measures of social inequity, the occupational status of people who abuse drugs and commit crime is often less stable than the occupational status of people who do not abuse drugs or commit crime. Many sociologists believe that when a person loses his or her job the chances are good that he or she will turn to drugs or crime to cope with the frustration or to make ends meet. People are more resilient than sociologists often give them credit for, however. Galatzer-Levy, Bonanno, and Mancini discovered that people were often upset just before and just after losing a job but within a year most had bounced back and were dealing well with the adversity.[13] **Resilience** aside, some people do succumb to substance abuse or engage in crime as a reaction to losing a job or being unemployed. This research is reviewed next.

Occupational Status and Drug Use

After conducting a comprehensive review of research on **unemployment** and substance use, Dieter Henkel arrived at the following conclusions:

- Unemployment is associated with increased alcohol, tobacco, and illicit drug use and abuse.
- Problematic drug use decreases a person's chances of finding a job and increases his or her chances of being fired from an existing job.
- Unemployment is a risk factor for substance abuse.
- Unemployment increases a person's odds of relapse following a course of substance abuse treatment.
- As the economy worsens and the unemployment rate goes up, alcohol and tobacco use tend to decline, whereas adolescent drug use seems to increase.[14]

From the results of this review it would seem likely that a qualified relationship exists between unemployment and drug use and abuse.

Occupational Status and Crime

Van Der Geest, Bijleveld, and Blokland followed a group of high-risk men for a period of 14 years, beginning when the men were 18 years old and ending around the time the men turned 32, and determined that employment had a dampening effect on crime in several different crime trajectories. The effect appeared to be strongest in individuals with good initial social and educational/occupational skills, adolescence-limited offenders, as Moffitt would call them, and weakest in individuals following trajectories with a chronic course, such as the life-course-persistent pattern. Overall, however, being employed full time or temporarily had both a selection and direct effect on future criminality. In other words, better adjusted individuals desisted from crime and were considered more employable (selection effect) and having a job reduced both the incentive and opportunities for crime (direct effect). In fact, when men in this study went from continuous unemployment to regular employment, offending dropped by 46%.[15]

NEWS SPOT 7-1

Title: Can Cops Control Crime?
Source: *Associated Press*
Author: Matt Apuzzo
Date: August 23, 2004

When Connecticut's largest city was mired in the economic slump of the early 1990s, drug dealers and gang leaders charged tolls to cross their turf.

Every year, Bridgeport flirted with setting its own state record for homicides.

And when economic relief came in the late 1990s, it was no surprise that violent crime rates fell in turn, riding the national wave of big-city crime reduction.

It seemed obvious: Lead the state in unemployment, lead the state in homicides. Stop the recession, stop the violence.

But recent years have turned that thinking on its head. The collapse of the stock market in 2000 brought tough economic times to Bridgeport. The region lost more than 8,000 manufacturing jobs and city unemployment more than doubled.

Violent crime, meanwhile, fell 32 percent over that span.

It wasn't an aberration. From San Jose, Calif., to Chattanooga, Tenn., cities across the country dramatically reduced violent crime despite a recession, spikes in unemployment, and dips in the stock market.

It's a trend that's forcing police and criminologists to question the premise that crime is a product of the economy and only so much can be done to prevent it.

"They're absolutely wrong," Bridgeport Police Chief Wilbur Chapman said. "I couldn't be more diametrically opposed to the idea that the economy drives crime."

Bridgeport saw 15 homicides last year, down from 60 a decade ago and down from 32 during the height of the late 1990s economic boom. Chapman, a product of the New York City Police Department, attributes the decline not to an increase in officers (he's down 57) but to the statistics-driven policing model credited with polishing the Big Apple.

"The results have been nothing short of phenomenal," Mayor John Fabrizi said…

Questions to Ponder

1. **What role do you think the economy plays in both drug use and crime?**
2. **Do law-abiding citizens actually start committing crime after they lose their jobs?**
3. **How do you reconcile the fact that during the worst recession since the Great Depression (2008–2011), the crime rate actually went down (see Figures 7-4 and 7-5)[16]**

Occupational Status, Drug Use, and Crime

Analyzing data on Norwegian men who had lost their jobs because of the economic downturn in Europe during the early 1980s, Mari Rege and colleagues detected a slight upswing in the use of substances and a small rise in nonacquisition crime following a major plant closing (see **Figure 7-6**). This suggests that instead of committing crime to pay the bills, these individuals were dealing with the stress of losing their jobs by drinking, using drugs, and engaging in nonproperty crimes, fueled perhaps by alcohol.[17] Further research is required to determine whether increased alcohol usage mediated the weak relationship between unemployment and nonacquisition crime or whether unemployment acted as a third variable in creating the semblance of a drug–crime (epiphenomenal) relationship.

Physical and Sexual Abuse

Findings from the Fourth National Incidence Study of Child Abuse and Neglect (NIS-4) revealed that more than 1.25 million children in the United States experienced some form of maltreatment during a 1-year period between 2005 and 2006. Hence, one child in 58

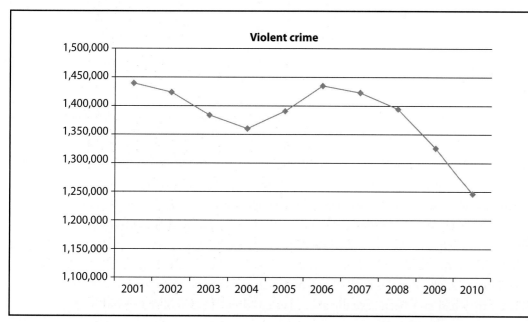

Figure 7-4
Total number of violent crimes in the United States, 2001–2010.

Data From: Federal Bureau of Investigation. (2011). *Uniform crime reports, 2010.* Washington, DC: Author.

Figure 7-5
Total number of property crimes in the United States, 2001–2010

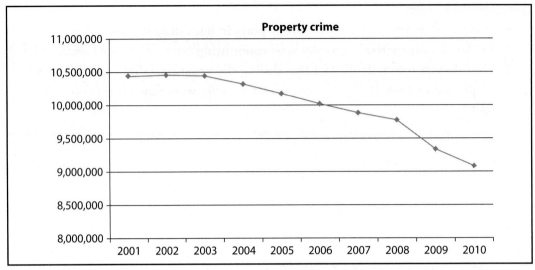

Data From: Federal Bureau of Investigation. (2011). *Uniform crime reports, 2010.* Washington, DC: Author.

Figure 7-6
Effects of plant closings on crime in Norway.

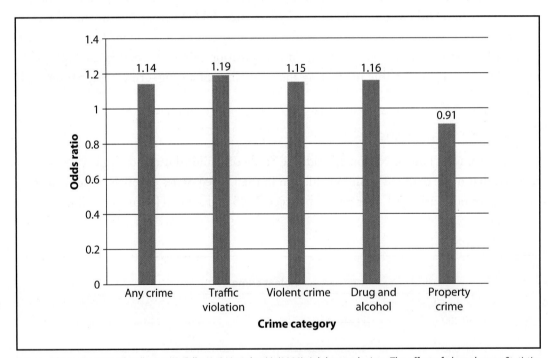

Adapted from: Rege, M., Skardhamar, T., Telle, K., & Votruba, M. (2009). Job loss and crime: The effect of plant closure. *Statistics Norway* (Discussion Papers No. 593). Accessed on March 15, 2012 from http://www.ssb.no/publikasjoner/pdf/dp593.pdf.

suffered neglect, physical abuse, or sexual abuse during that time frame. Whereas over 60% of the sample had experienced neglect, a total of 771,700 cases, there were also 323,000 cases of physical abuse, 148,500 cases of emotional abuse, and 135,300 cases of sexual abuse. Boys were slightly more likely than girls to suffer physical abuse but girls were four times more likely to suffer sexual abuse.[18] These proportions are similar to the rates obtained through the retrospective accounts of adults. Asked if they had ever been physically abused as children, 22.2% of males and 19.5% of females answered in the affirmative, and when asked if they had ever been sexually abused as children, 14.2% of males and 32.3% of females answered in the affirmative.[19]

Physical/Sexual Abuse and Drugs

Butt, Chou, and Brown reviewed studies on the relationship between **childhood physical abuse** (CPA)/**childhood sexual abuse** (CSA) and illicit drug use. The results of their review revealed:[20]

- qualified support for a relationship between CPA/CSA and illicit drug use.
- a relationship between CSA (but not CPA) and drug use when analyses were restricted to better designed studies.
- that most studies in this area are cross-sectional and retrospective, thus indicating the need for more longitudinal and prospective research.

Results from two early longitudinal studies suggested that CPA/CSA failed to predict illicit drug usage and substance abuse problems in females.[21–22] Two more recent longitudinal investigations, however, identified a relationship between CPA/CSA and subsequent illicit drug use and substance abuse problems in both males and females.[23–24] The results were not only **statistically significant** but **clinically significant** as well. In the Huang et al. study, for instance, individuals exposed to CPA/CSA were 37% more likely to use illicit drugs than individuals not exposed to CPA/CSA.[25]

Anderson, Teicher, Polcari, and Renshaw compared **fMRI** scans obtained from 8 young adults with a history of child sexual abuse and brain scans obtained from 16 matched controls. The results indicated possible damage or dysfunction in the cerebellar vermis region of the brains of adults with a history of CSA. Because the cerebellar vermis is highly susceptible to stress and is involved in dopamine transport and communication, it is believed that drugs may be favored by these individuals because of their ability to stimulate dopamine receptors in the dopamine-depleted regions of the cerebellar vermis.[26]

Physical/Sexual Abuse and Crime

Cathy Spatz Widom refers to the relationship between physical/sexual abuse and crime as the "**cycle of violence**" and makes reference to its role in the intergenerational transmission of violence. Widom examined the abuse and criminal histories of 1,500 individuals and observed a moderate relationship between the two variables. This investigation was superior to many of the studies previously conducted on CPA/CSA in that it was prospective rather than retrospective in nature and included a control group for comparative purposes (see **Figure 7-7**).[27]

Using data from the Survey of Inmates in State and Federal Correctional Facilities, Richard Felson and Kelsea Lane discovered that offenders tend to model behaviors to which they have been exposed; a finding consistent with the basic tenets of social learning theory. For instance, male offenders who were sexually abused as children were significantly more likely to commit sexual crimes against children. Offenders who were physically abused as children, on the other hand, were significantly more likely to commit a violent crime than a nonviolent offense.[28]

Physical/Sexual Abuse, Drugs, and Crime

In a study of Australian detainees, Lubica Forsythe and Kerryn Adams found that gender moderated the relationship between childhood sexual abuse, drug use, and crime in the sense that the relationship was much stronger in female offenders than it was in male offenders.[29] Victimization would appear to play a particularly powerful role in female

Figure 7-7
Relationship between different forms of abuse and juvenile, adult, and sexual arrests.

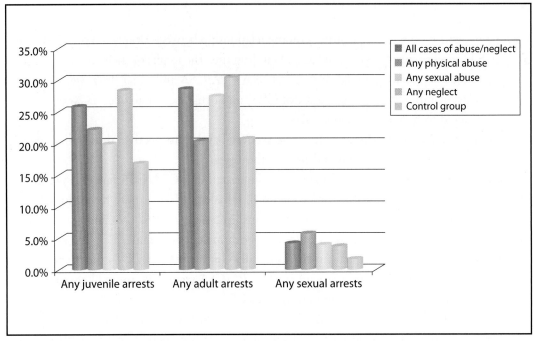

Data From: Widom, C. S. (1995). *Victims of childhood sexual abuse—Later criminal consequences.* National Institute of Justice: Research in Brief. Washington, DC: Department of Justice.

Figure 7-8
Prior sexual abuse in male and female offenders.

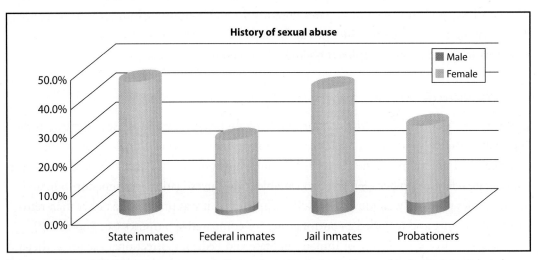

Data From: Harlow, C. W. (1999). *Prior abuse reported by inmates and probationers.* Bureau of Justice Statistics: Selected Findings. Washington, DC: Department of Justice.

offending, as indicated by the preponderance of female to male offenders with a history of physical or sexual abuse (see **Figure 7-8**). The ratio of female-to-male inmates who have been physically or sexually abused are:[30]

- 3:1 in state inmates
- 5:1 in federal inmates
- 4:1 in jail inmates
- 4:1 in probationers

The gendered relationship that appears to exist between childhood physical/sexual abuse, drug use, and crime intimates that the CPA/CSA–drug/crime relationship is moderated by gender and that the effects of physical and sexual abuse are more closely tied to drug use and criminality in women than in men. In addition, running away from home has been found to mediate the relationship between early physical and psychological abuse and later delinquency.[31] The latter result implies that running away from an abusive home environment may encourage delinquency development by decreasing **parental control** and supervision and/or by bringing the child into contact with delinquent and drug-using peers.

Socialization

Socialization is the process by which a culture or subculture transmits its values, norms, customs, and ideologies to members. Drug use and crime may be the result of failed socialization to conventional definitions of behavior or of successful socialization to deviant definitions of behavior. The agents of socialization that contribute the most to future drug use and crime are parents, peers, and the media.

Parental Support and Control

Although all members of a person's immediate family are potential agents of socialization, the greatest influence is exerted by those who occupy the parental or caregiver role. The caregiver role is normally assumed by one or both biological parents but if the role is assumed by a surrogate parent, such as an aunt, grandparent, or older sibling, this individual is not only a caregiver but also a source of support and control in the eyes of the child. This means that a surrogate parent can have as strong a socializing influence over a child from a nontraditional home as biological parents have on a child from a traditional home.

Parental socialization effects can either be **direct** or **indirect**. Parents socialize their children indirectly by forging an emotional bond with the child, thereby making the child feel loved and accepted. This is known as the support dimension of parental socialization. Parents also socialize their children directly by monitoring the child's behavior, establishing rules, implementing discipline, and placing demands on the child. This is known as the control dimension of parental socialization.

Travis Hirschi was one of the first criminologists to recognize the importance of informal social control and the support dimension in socializing children to conventional definitions of behavior.[32] Robert Sampson and John Laub subsequently incorporated family-based informal social control and emotional bonds into a larger network of socializing influences as part of their age-graded theory of informal social control.[33] These theories hold that people with strong attachments to their parents tend not to use drugs or commit crime because they do not want to disappoint or embarrass their parents.

In a review of the research literature on early predictors of male delinquency, Rolf Loeber and Thomas Dishion identified parental family management style, in the form of supervision and discipline, as the single most powerful predictor of male delinquency (see **Figure 7-9**).[34] Gottfredson and Hirschi's general theory of crime is based on the premise that weak parental supervision and discipline lead to low self-control in children and low self-control in children leads to drug use and delinquency.[35] According to the theory, people exposed to strong and consistent models of parental control tend not to use drugs or commit crime because they have developed internal controls and self-discipline.

Figure 7-9
Meta-analysis of
studies on various
historical and social-
environmental factors
as predictors of
male delinquency,
using mean relative
improvement over
chance (RIOC) as the
effect size measure.

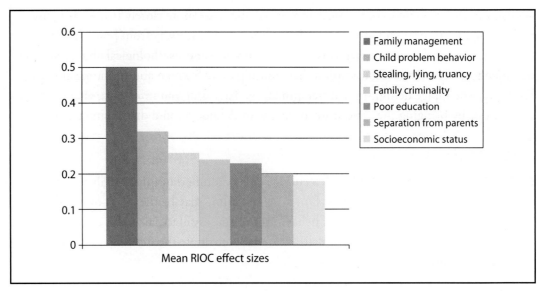

Data From: Loeber, R., & Dishion, T. (1983). Early predictors of male delinquency: A review. *Psychological Bulletin, 94*, 68–99.

Although support and control can be viewed as competing explanations for parental socialization, they could also be considered complementary. Diana Baumrind has created a model of parenting styles (**authoritarian**, **authoritative**, **indulgent**, **neglectful**) that incorporates both support and control (see **Table 7-1**), with the parenting style most likely to promote low levels of drug use and crime (i.e., authoritative) being a combination of high support and high control.[36] In reviewing research on the impact of **parental support** and control on drug use, crime, and drug–crime relationships the reader would be well advised to focus less on how the dimensions differ than on how they complement one another. Parental support, it is argued, permits parents more opportunities to exercise control, whereas parental control establishes the optimal conditions for support.

Parental Support/Control and Drug Use

Research investigating the relationship between parental support/control and offspring alcohol and drug use denotes that support and control are equally important in the development of drug use and drug use problems. In an early longitudinal study on this issue, Stice, Barrera, and Chassin ascertained that extremes in either support or control

Table 7-1 Four Parenting Styles Formed by Crossing Support and Control

	High Support	**Low Support**
High Control	Authoritative	Authoritarian
Low Control	Indulgent	Neglectful

Data From: Baumrind, D. (1991). The influence of parenting style on adolescent competence and substance use. *Journal of Early Adolescence, 11*, 56–95.

(very high or very low) were associated with an increased rate of alcohol, but not illicit drug, use in adolescent offspring.[37] A moderate degree of each or balance between the two would seem to be the best alternative and is clearly consistent with Baumrind's notion of authoritative parenting.[38] Colleen Pilgrim and several others working at the University of Michigan's Institute for Social Research uncovered a negative cross-sectional correlation between parental involvement and offspring drug use that they believed was mediated by school success and time spent with peers. In this study, children who enjoyed higher levels of parental involvement and support achieved greater school success and spent less time with friends, both of which then decreased their chances of regular substance use.[39]

Marie Choquet and associates observed that French adolescents whose parents exerted an appropriate level of control used fewer substances than adolescents whose parents exercised too little control or were inconsistent in their control efforts. The effect was stronger for tobacco and marijuana than for alcohol and for girls than for boys. Although parental control had a stronger effect than parental support on offspring drug use in this study, parental support was moderately effective in reducing substance use in females.[40] Analyzing adolescent data gathered from various schools in the southwestern region of the United States, Monica Parsai, Stephen Kulis, and Flavio Marsiglia determined that the 13- to 15-year-old adolescent participants they surveyed seemed to benefit from having unambiguous rules about the use of substances and understanding that their behavior had clear consequences. In this study, parental control correlated better with offspring attitudes toward drug use than with actual drug use behavior, implying that drug use attitudes may mediate the relationship between parental support/control and offspring drug use behavior.[41]

A **longitudinal panel study** of African American youth conducted by Michael Cleveland and colleagues revealed that parental monitoring, warmth, and communication predicted lower levels of alcohol, tobacco, and marijuana use 5 years later, an effect that was mediated by participants' thoughts about substances or drug use attitudes. Neighborhood status moderated the effect of parental support and control on drug use in the sense that the **protective effect** of parental monitoring, warmth, and communication was strongest in families living in high-risk neighborhoods where drug use and crime were prevalent.[42]

Parental Support/Control and Crime

Machteld Hoeve and colleagues recently completed a meta-analysis of 161 published and unpublished studies on the relationship between parenting and delinquency. Moderate effect sizes were recorded for the general support and control dimensions, with affection and monitoring displaying the strongest individual effects (see **Figure 7-10**). Authoritative parenting, featuring inductive discipline, was negatively correlated with delinquency, whereas authoritarian parenting and coercive discipline correlated positively with delinquency. It was also noted that lack of warmth and support from the father was more strongly associated with delinquency than lack of warmth and support from the mother, particularly in male children.[43] The results of this meta-analysis indicate that parental support and control contribute equally to the development of future delinquency.

Given the role weak parental discipline appears to play in delinquency development, one means of intervention might be to enhance the child management skills of the parents of high-risk youths. The results of a meta-analysis covering 63 peer-reviewed treatment studies revealed that parenting training is effective in reducing disruptive behavior in children. Overall, the effect was strongest when:[44]

- younger children from disadvantaged homes with more severe externalizing symptoms were targeted
- treatment was implemented using an individual rather than group format
- parents but not children received treatment

Figure 7-10
Average effect sizes
(*r*) achieved in the
Hoeve et al. (2009)
meta-analysis.

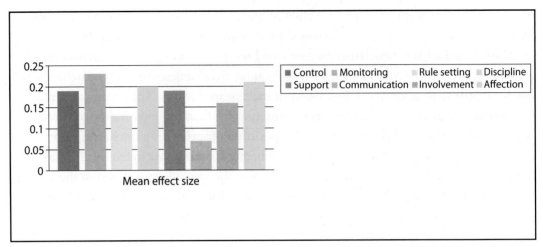

Data From: Hoeve, M., Dubas, S., Eichelsheim, V. I., van der Laan, P. H., Smeenk, W., & Gerris, J. R. M. (2009). The relationship between parenting and delinquency: A meta-analysis. *Journal of Abnormal Child Psychology, 37*, 749–775.

These findings indicate that the control dimension of parental socialization can be improved with training. More attention needs to be directed, however, at finding ways to reinforce the support dimension based on previously reviewed research showing that the support dimension may be just as important as the control dimension in delinquency development.

It should be noted that the behavior of children may have as much influence on their parents as the behavior of parents has on their children. This points once again to the power of reciprocal relationships. In a short-term longitudinal study, Muñoz, Pakalniskiene, and Frick discovered that the parents of children with callous-unemotional traits reduced their monitoring behavior over time and became less consistent in implementing the monitoring behaviors they did employ.[45] Additional research is required to further document this putative bidirectional relationship and determine which factors, other than callous-unemotional traits, moderate and potentially mediate the child behavior–parental control relationship.

Parental Support/Control, Drug Use, and Crime

Studying a representative sample of 699 U.S. adolescents and their parents and controlling for age, race, sex, family structure, and family history of alcohol problems, Grace Barnes and Michael Farrell ascertained that parental support and control had a significant impact on adolescent substance use and deviance (mild delinquency). The effects of maternal support and parental monitoring on offspring substance use and deviance are depicted in **Figures 7-11** and **7-12**, respectively. In both cases, higher levels of maternal support and higher levels of parental monitoring were associated with lower levels of substance use and delinquency. This study also revealed that peer associations were important predictors of drinking behavior and delinquency and that these associations tended to interact with parenting factors.[46]

Jeffrey Cookston compared the effects of **family structure** (single-mother, single-father, intact family) and parental supervision (low to high) on adolescent alcohol use, illicit drug use, and delinquency and determined that intact families offered their offspring more supervision than single-parent families and that higher levels of supervision were associated with fewer behavioral problems. Accordingly, adolescents from intact families had the fewest number of behavioral problems, adolescents from single-father homes had the most behavioral problems,

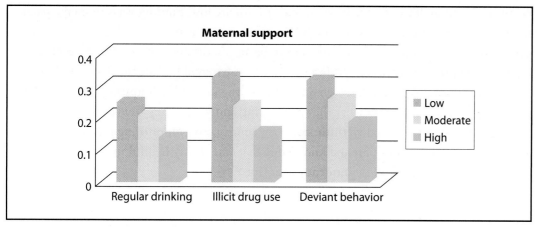

Figure 7-11
Impact of maternal support on drinking, illicit drug use, and deviant (delinquent) behavior in adolescent offspring.

Data From: Barnes, G. M., & Farrell, M. P. (1992). Parental support and control as predictors of adolescent drinking, delinquency, and related problem behaviors. *Journal of Marriage and the Family, 54,* 763–776.

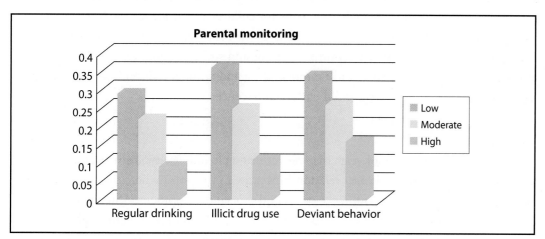

Figure 7-12
Impact of parental monitoring on drinking, illicit drug use, and deviant (delinquent) behavior in adolescent offspring.

Data From: Barnes, G. M., & Farrell, M. P. (1992). Parental support and control as predictors of adolescent drinking, delinquency, and related problem behaviors. *Journal of Marriage and the Family, 54,* 763–776.

and adolescents from single-mother homes had an intermediate number of behavioral problems. Interestingly, girls seemed to be more adversely affected by living in a low-supervision home than boys and boys seemed to benefit more from living in a high-supervision home than girls.[47]

Kenneth Griffin, Gilbert Botvin, Lawrence Scheier, Tracy Diaz, and Nicole Miller explored the relationship between family structure/parental supervision and sixth graders' use of alcohol and cigarettes and involvement in delinquency and violence; they discerned that boys and girls from single-parent families were more likely to engage in problem behaviors than boys and girls from two-parent homes. In addition, greater parental monitoring was associated with lower levels of delinquency in both boys and girls, lower levels of alcohol use in boys, and lower levels of cigarette smoking in girls. They also noted that eating family dinners together, a good indicator of both family cohesion and parental control, served as a protective factor in the sense that youths from single-parent homes who ate dinner with their families experienced lower levels of delinquency and aggression than youths from single-parent homes who did not eat dinner with their families.[48]

The research reviewed in this section indicates that parental support and control are equally important in managing the behavior of children and that drug and delinquency problems are more likely to occur when one or both are low. Finding ways to merge parental support and control by way of a higher level construct, as represented in one study by eating family dinners together, would seem to be an important topic for future research. One such construct may be something referred to as parental knowledge. Fletcher, Steinberg, and Williams-Wheeler discovered that both drug use and delinquency were lower in children whose parents knew what they were doing and where they were over the course of a day. In their study, parental warmth, concern, control, and monitoring merged to form a higher order construct of parental knowledge that was clearly helpful in reducing future occurrences of drug use and delinquency behavior.[49]

Peers

Parents are not the only socialization agents capable of influencing a child's propensity to experiment with and use drugs or experiment with and commit crime. Peers and the media may also function as socializing agents for children and adolescents. In fact, peer relationships open the door to companionship as the individual enters adolescence, offering opportunities for enhanced community status and social acceptance.[50] It is therefore not surprising that peers play a leading role in drug and crime initiation, maintenance, and escalation, particularly once the child enters adolescence.

Peers and Drug Use

It is during the middle school years that cigarette and alcohol use typically begin.[51] This is also the period during which peer relationships grow to the point where they begin to supplant parents as the primary influence on a child's social development.[52] Stephen Bahr, John Hoffmann, and Xiaoyan Yang surveyed a sample of 4,230 junior and senior high school students for the purpose of testing the ability of peer and family factors to predict adolescent alcohol use, binge drinking, tobacco consumption, marijuana use, and involvement with other illicit drugs. The results of their analyses indicated that peer drug use exerted a moderately strong direct effect on adolescent drug use and partially mediated the effect of tolerant parental attitudes and sibling drug use on adolescent drug use. The family also had a direct effect on adolescent drug use in this study.[53]

Kimberly Henry examined the mediating effect of peers on drug use in a large sample of middle school students. The results indicated that the relationship between weak family attachment and drug use was mediated by poor school attachment and involvement with drug-using peers, whereas poor school attachment correlated with drug use by way of drug-using friends. This study supports the hypothesis that disengagement from prosocial agents of socialization leads to increased involvement with antisocial agents of socialization and eventual drug use and abuse.[54] The relationship between parental support and control and peer associations requires further study because it may hold the key to understanding socialization influences and drug use.

Peers and Delinquency

In a review of the literature on peers and delinquency, Gifford-Smith, Dodge, Dishion, and McCord concluded that peers were critical in initiating, accelerating, and maintaining delinquent behavior. They further surmised that the peer effect was due to direct exposure to delinquent peer role models and attitudes rather than selection bias because the effect persisted even after prior levels of delinquency were controlled.[55] The direct effect of deviant peers is particularly prominent in situations where the juvenile's exposure to prosocial peers is limited.[56] Although there was clear evidence of a direct **peer socialization** effect in the Gifford-Smith et al. review, **peer selection**, whereby juveniles make friends with those who think and act as they do, may also be operating in a number of situations. In all probability, peer socialization and peer selection effects are equally responsible for the strong correlations observed between self- and peer delinquency during adolescence.

There is evidence that **impulsivity**, parental attachment, and community factors moderate the relationship between peer delinquency and an adolescent's personal involvement in antisocial behavior. Vitulano, Fite, and Rathert, for instance, noted that peer and self-delinquency correlated in youth with low impulsivity but not in youth with high impulsivity. Apparently, impulsivity was sufficient in and of itself to promote delinquency but in individuals with good self-control or low impulsivity, associating with delinquent peers significantly enhanced their chances of engaging in delinquent behavior.[57] Examining the effects of parental monitoring and attachment on the peer–self delinquency relationship, Vitaro, Brendgen, and Tremblay determined that peer and self-delinquency correlated only in situations where parental attachment was weak. Parental monitoring, on the other hand, did not appear to moderate the peer–self-delinquency relationship.[58] Finally, Mennis and Harris observed **spatial contagion** in several thousand male juvenile offenders processed through the Philadelphia family court. Repeat offending in this sample was crime and neighborhood specific in the sense that youths reoffended by committing crimes that were typical of other delinquents in their neighborhood. Hence, juveniles from neighborhoods with a high rate of peer drug offending were more often rearrested for a drug crime, whereas juveniles from neighborhoods with a high rate of peer property offending were more often rearrested for a property crime.[59]

Peers, Drug Use, and Delinquency

Battin-Pearson, Thornberry, Hawkins, and Krohn compared three groups of juveniles: gang members, individuals who reported that two or more of their three closest friends had been arrested or had engaged in behavior that could have gotten them arrested, and individuals who reported that fewer than two of their three closest friends had been arrested or had engaged in behavior that could have gotten them arrested. The authors assumed that gang members would have the strongest delinquent peer ties, followed by individuals with two or more delinquent friends, and that individuals with fewer than two delinquent friends would have the weakest delinquent peer ties. Consistent with their predictions, gang members engaged in the most self-reported delinquency, official offending, and drug use, and individuals with fewer than two delinquent friends displayed the lowest levels of self-reported delinquency, official offending, and drug use (see **Figures 7-13**, **7-14**, and **7-15**).[60]

Lening Zhang, William Wieczorek, and John Welte tested a model in which early onset alcohol and drug use was predicted to have an indirect effect on subsequent delinquency via four mediating variables: continued alcohol use, continued drug use, association with delinquent peers, and involvement in deviant behavior (see **Figure 7-16**). Applying their model

Figure 7-13
Self-reported individual offense rates at age 15.

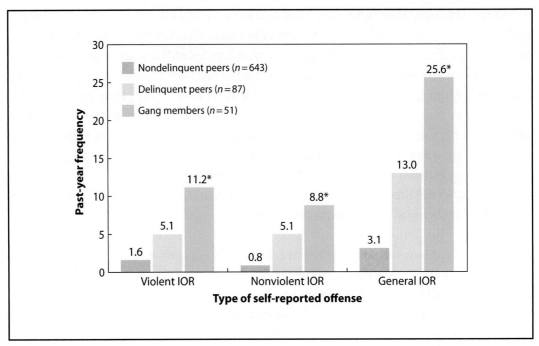

Battin-Pearson, S., Thornberry, T. P., Hawkins, J. D., & Krohn, M. D. (1998). *Gang membership, delinquent peers, and delinquent behavior*. Washington, DC: U.S. Department of Justice.

Figure 7-14
Court-recorded individual offense rates at age 15.

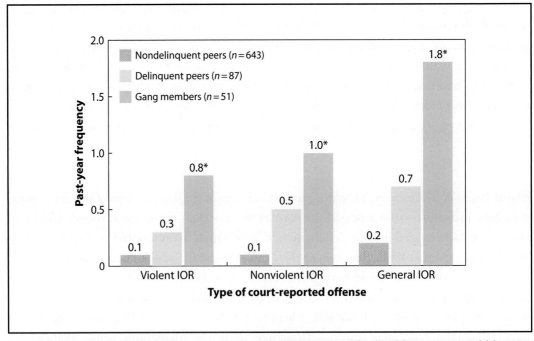

Battin-Pearson, S., Thornberry, T. P., Hawkins, J. D., & Krohn, M. D. (1998). *Gang membership, delinquent peers, and delinquent behavior*. Washington, DC: U.S. Department of Justice.

to data from the Buffalo Longitudinal Survey of Young Men, Zhang et al. determined that delinquent peers and involvement in deviant behavior had a robust mediating effect on the relationship between age of onset of drug use and later delinquency. Although continued substance use also played a mediating role, the role was attenuated and applied only to general and index delinquency.[61]

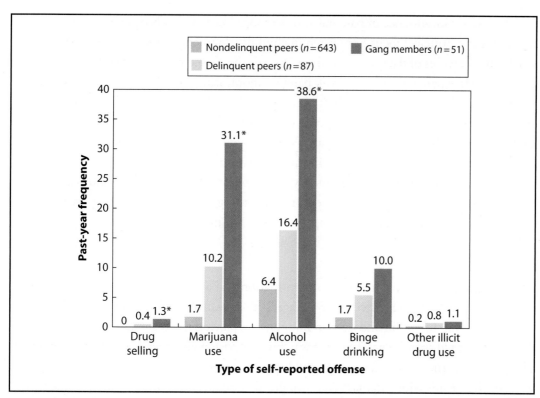

Battin-Pearson, S., Thornberry, T. P., Hawkins, J. D., & Krohn, M. D. (1998). *Gang membership, delinquent peers, and delinquent behavior*. Washington, DC: U.S. Department of Justice.

Figure 7-15
Self-reported rates of drug selling and substance use at age 15.

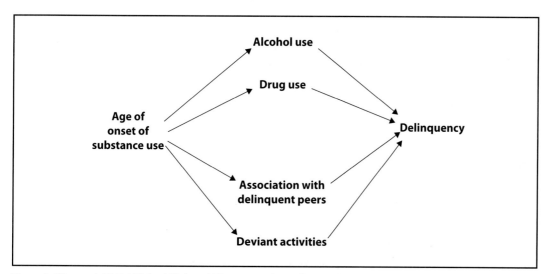

Zhang, L., Wieczorek, W. F., & Welte, J. W. (1997). The impact of age of onset of substance use on delinquency. *Journal of Research in Crime and Delinquency, 34*, 253–265. Reprinted by Permission of SAGE Publications.

Figure 7-16
Mediating relationships proposed to link early age of onset of substance use and delinquency.

Parents appear to have the strongest effect on children during the preschool and primary school years, but peers exert an increasingly powerful influence over a child's behavior as he or she enters adolescence. Analyzing data provided by 14- to 19-year-old adolescent participants in the National Youth Survey (NYS), Daniel Mears and Samuel Field determined that peers had a stronger impact on drug-related offending (getting drunk, using marijuana, selling drugs) in older adolescents than in younger adolescents. For nondrug forms of delinquency, such as fighting, burglary, and theft, the results were inconclusive.[62]

The relative importance of parental and peer socialization to subsequent drug use and crime is a principal focus of research in child development and juvenile delinquency. Analyzing six waves of data obtained from 506 youths, Grace Barnes and colleagues discerned that low parental support, weak parental monitoring, and delinquent peer associations predicted future levels of both drug use and crime. These results also implied that parental monitoring and parental support may have served as protective factors in terms of buffering the individual from the negative effects of antisocial peers.[63] Even though difficult temperament did not come into play in the Barnes study, it did play a role in a study by Ronald Simons and colleagues. Specifically, the results of the Simons study showed that early difficult temperament moderated the effect of parenting on future delinquency by reducing parental involvement and increasing opportunities for interaction with deviant peers.[64]

Media

The media has become a vital source of information and a major vehicle for entertainment in modern-day American society. The average 2- to 5-year-old child spends nearly 25 hours a week watching television and over an hour a week playing video games. The average 6- to 11-year-old child spends over 22 hours watching television and over 2 hours a week playing video games.[65] The average school-age child spends almost as much time in front of the TV as he or she spends with parents.[66] Accordingly, the media plays an important socializing role for youth and may have a part to play in the development of a drug or delinquency problem.

Media and Drug Use

Gunasekera, Chapman, and Campbell analyzed depictions of drug use in 200 popular films released between 1983 and 2003 and discovered that cannabis (8%) and other noninjecting illicit drug (7%) use was less common than alcohol intoxication (32%) and tobacco use (68%). Of particular concern, however, was the fact that there was a tendency to portray drug use in a positive light with few if any negative consequences.[67] How, we might ask, does this affect young viewers? A team of researchers under the direction of Kate Hunt attempted to answer this very question by comparing film depictions of tobacco use with adolescent cigarette use. In a survey of 1,999 15- and 16-year-old students from 13 Scottish schools, Hunt et al. determined that students reporting high exposure to film smoking were significantly more likely to have consumed one or more cigarettes in the last year than students reporting low exposure to film smoking. In addition, students whose parents had established rules about their film-viewing habits were less likely to have smoked in the last year than students whose parents had no such rules.[68]

Media and Violent Crime

The relationship between media violence and crime is more complex and controversial and less straightforward than the peer–delinquency relationship. Based on a review of five meta-analyses and one quasi-systematic review, Browne and Hamilton-Giachritsis concluded that violent images from television programs, feature films, and computer games can lead to a moderate short-term increase in aggressive or fearful behavior on the part of younger children, particularly boys. The short-term effect of media violence on older children and the long-term effect on all children is currently unknown.[69]

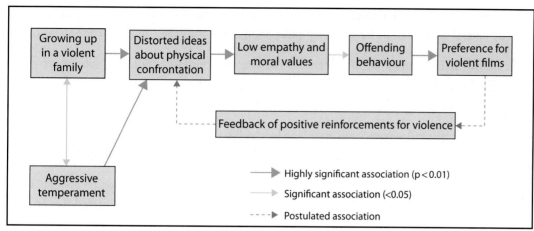

Figure 7-17
Model of aggression proposed by Browne & Pennell (2000) and the proposed role of violent film viewing on violence.

Reprinted from Browne, K. D., & Hamilton-Giachritsis, C. (2005). The influence of violent media on children and adolescents: A public-health approach. Reprinted from *The Lancet, 365*, 702–710, with permissions from Elsevier.

The link between media violence and later criminality is weak at best.[70] Nevertheless, in combination with other factors, such as an angry temperament[71] or a violent home environment,[72] media violence could very well play a significant role in some forms of criminal and domestic violence. A model proposed by Browne and Pennell shows how media violence potentially interacts with other variables to increase a child's propensity for violent criminality (see **Figure 7-17**).[73] Given the growing popularity of video games, some scientists and policy-makers have shifted their concern from television and movies to graphically violent computer and video games (see News Spot 7-2).

NEWS SPOT 7-2

Title: Killer Games in the Crosshairs—Legislators Wrestle with First Amendment, Violent Video Games
Source: *The Toledo (OH) Blade*
Author: Karen MacPherson
Date: June 28, 2003

Rep. Joe Baca (D, Ca.) is no fan of "Grand Theft Auto: Vice City," the best-selling video game in America last year.

Mr. Baca doesn't begrudge the millions of adults who want to play the game, which features graphic violence and sex, including prostitution and the murders of police officers.

Mr. Baca does object to the fact—documented by the Federal Trade Commission—that "Vice City" and other similar violent video games are readily available to children and young teens.

In an effort to limit children's exposure to violent video games, Mr. Baca has introduced legislation that would make it a federal crime for retailers to rent or sell video games with graphic violent and sexual content to kids ages 17 or younger.

"We as parents have to take responsibility for our children," Mr. Baca said. "But stores also have a responsibility. When kids can walk into their neighborhood stores and buy games with graphic violent and sexual content, parents are cut out of the decision-making process. If local, state or federal governments have to help put parents back into the equation, then so be it."

Officials of the Interactive Digital Software Association, the industry group representing video game manufacturers, stress that they, too, believe that violent video games aren't meant to be played by children.

But they argue that video games are protected by the First Amendment and that it is parents—not the government—who should determine whether children are permitted to play such games.

That's why the industry says it created its rating system for video games, which ensures that games with graphic violence and sexual content are clearly labeled for mature audiences, IDSA officials said.

Under the system, games are rated "EC" (early childhood), "E" (everyone), "T" (teen), "M" (mature) or "AO" (adults only.). "Grand Theft Auto: Vice City" is rated "M."

In fact, FTC studies have found that parents are involved in the purchase or rental of video games more than 82 percent of the time, IDSA officials add...

IDSA officials contend that "the most objective and methodologically sound studies have found no causation between game playing and violent activity." Among those studies is a 2001 report by the U.S. Surgeon General that stated that "the impact of video games on violent behavior remains to be determined."

Reprinted with permission from The Blade, Toledo, Ohio.

Questions to Ponder
1. **Do you personally know of anyone who was adversely affected by exposure to violent video games?**
2. **What measures other than government regulation could and/or should be taken to keep violent video games out of the hands of children and young teens?**
3. **Scientists tell us that the link between playing violent video games and engaging in violent behavior has not yet been established. What do you think?**

Media, Drug Use, and Crime

There has been very little research on the overlap between the media, drug use, and crime, although there is one study that has taken a look at the media's tendency to downplay the role of alcohol and drugs in violent crime and serious accidents. Comparing television, news, and magazine stories linking alcohol and drugs to homicide, automobile accidents, and other accidents with the actual rate of alcohol and drug involvement in these events, Slater, Long, and Ford discovered that the media underreported the contributions of alcohol and drugs to these problem behaviors by 53 to 2,114% (see **Figure 7-18**).[74] In a follow-up to this study, Slater, Hayes, Goodall, and Ewoldsen determined that mentioning alcohol in a crime news story increased reader support for alcohol-control laws.[75] Hence, if the media

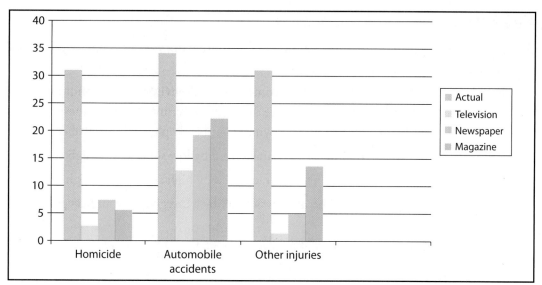

Figure 7-18
Proportion of homicides, automobile accidents, and fatal accidents that are alcohol related compared to the percentages portrayed in the media.

Data From: Slater, M. D., Long, M., & Ford, V. L. (2006). Alcohol, illegal drugs, violent crime, and traffic-related and other unintended injuries in U.S. local and national news. *Journal of Studies on Alcohol, 67*, 904–910.

were more accurate in its reporting of the link between certain drugs (including alcohol) and accidents or violence, people's attitudes might well change in a positive direction.

Summary and Conclusions

- Adverse social conditions like social inequity, occupational status, and childhood physical and sexual abuse appear to relate to one degree or another to drug use and crime. Childhood physical and sexual abuse may be the adverse social condition with the most to offer a general theory of drug–crime relationships.
- Socialization is particularly important in understanding drug use, crime, and the drug–crime connection. Parents are often the primary agents of socialization in younger children. Once the child enters school, however, peers begin to take a more active role in socializing children and by the time the child reaches adolescence peers are often their primary source of both reinforcement and socialization. The media is a third agent of socialization capable of influencing a child's future propensity for drug use and crime.
- Physical/sexual abuse and socialization may interact with cognitive mediator variables, such as outcome expectancies, goals, and values, and in so doing, influence a person's chances of future drug and criminal involvement (see **Figure 7-19**). The application of this model to actual data and future research studies may well hold value in explaining drug use, crime, and the drug–crime connection.

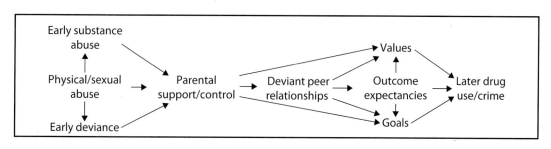

Figure 7-19
Social and cognitive factors important in the development of drug–crime relationships.

Key Terms

Acquisition Crime   A criminal act committed to acquire money; most property crimes are included in this definition.

Adverse Social Conditions   Negative or detrimental social-environmental conditions capable of increasing one's chances of future drug use and crime; several of these conditions include social class, poverty, unemployment, and early physical/sexual abuse.

Authoritarian Parenting   Parenting style characterized by low support and high control.

Authoritative Parenting   Parenting style characterized by high support and high control.

Childhood Physical Abuse   A deliberate physical act by a caregiver that inflicts pain or injury on a child.

Childhood Sexual Abuse   A form of child abuse in which an adult or older adolescent uses a child for sexual stimulation or pleasure.

Clinical Significance   A statistically significant correlation or group difference that is sufficiently large to be practically meaningful and noteworthy.

Cycle of Violence   The intergenerational transmission of violence; tendency for individuals who are physically abused to abuse others and continue the cycle.

Direct Parenting Effect   Parental discipline or monitoring of a child's behavior.

Ecological Studies   Investigations in which geographic areas (cities, neighborhoods) serve as subjects.

Family Structure   Organization or structure of the family unit: one-parent, two-parent, adoptive parent.

fMRI   Functional Magnetic Resonance Imaging, a technique for measuring brain activity by monitoring changes in blood flow within the brain.

Impulsivity   Tendency of an individual to act with minimal consideration of the possible consequences.

Indirect Parenting Effect   Formation of an affective bond between the child and caregiver.

Indulgent Parenting   Parenting style characterized by high support and low control.

Longitudinal Panel Study   Research design whereby the same group of individuals is followed over time.

Media   Mass communication technologies designed to reach a large audience.

Negligent Parenting   Parenting style characterized by low support and low control.

Nonacquisition Crime   A crime committed for reasons other than financial gain; a nonproperty crime.

Parental Control   Parental management of child behavior by monitoring, setting limits, and disciplining the child.

Parental Support   Parental management of child behavior through development of a positive and accepting relationship.

Peers   Friendship networks.

Peer Selection   Person selects the peers with whom he or she associates.

Peer Socialization   Person's attitudes, beliefs, and behaviors are shaped by the peers with whom he or she associates.

Protective Effect   Variable that buffers an individual against the negative effects of stress or other risk factors.

Resilience   Person's ability to deal effectively with adversity and cope with harsh social conditions.

Social Inequities   Below average social status (social class, poverty, education).

Socialization   The process by which a culture or subculture transmits its values, norms, customs, and ideology to members.

Socioeconomic Status   Person's relative position or standing in a hierarchy of social structure; normally determined by occupation, income, education, and place of residence.

Spatial Contagion   Individuals from the same small geographical region (city or neighborhood) engaging in similar forms of criminal conduct.

Statistical Significance   Observed correlation or group difference is unlikely to be the result of (statistical) chance.

Unemployment   Losing one's job or not having a job.

Critical Thinking

1. What are gendered pathways to crime and how might these pathways be traced back to differential rates of physical and sexual abuse in boys and girls?
2. In what manner do parents and peers influence the drug use and delinquent behavior of children and adolescents and is there an interaction between the two whereby weak parenting increases the influence of peers and strong parenting reduces the influence of peers?
3. Does the media have a responsibility to provide accurate and nonsensationalistic information on drugs and crime?

Notes

1. Room, R. (2004, February 25–27). *Thinking about how social inequalities relate to alcohol and drug use and problems.* Presented at the 1st International Summer School on Inequalities and Addictions, National Centre for Education and Training in Addictions, Adelaide, South Australia. Retrieved from http://www.robinroom.net/inequal.htm.
2. Center for Behavioral Health Statistics and Quality. (2012). *Results from the 2010 National Survey on Drug Use and Health.* Rockville, MD: Substance Abuse and Mental Health Services Administration.
3. Center for Behavioral Health Statistics and Quality (2012).
4. Room (2004).
5. Tittle, C., Villemez, W. J., & Smith, D. (1978). The myth of social class and criminality: An empirical assessment of the evidence. *American Sociological Review, 43,* 643–656.
6. Tittle et al. (1978)

7. Dunaway, R. G., Cullen, F. T., Burton, V. S., & Evans, T. D. (2000). The myth of social class and crime revisited: An examination of class and adult criminality. *Criminology, 38*, 589–632.

8. Ring, J., & Svensson, R. (2007). Social class and criminality among young people: A study considering the effects of school achievement as a mediating factor on the basis of Swedish register and self-report data. *Journal of Scandinavian Studies in Criminology and Crime Prevention, 8*, 210–233.

9. Valdez, A., Kaplan, C. D., & Curtis, R. L. (2007). Aggressive crime, alcohol and drug use, and concentrated poverty in 24 U.S. urban areas. *American Journal of Drug and Alcohol Abuse, 33*, 595–603.

10. Collins, J. J. (Ed.) (1981). *Drinking and crime*. New York: Guilford Press.

11. Jarvis, G., & Parker, H. (1989). Young heroin users and crime: How do the "new users" finance their habits? *British Journal of Criminology, 29*, 175–185.

12. Valdez et al. (2007).

13. Galatzer-Levy, I. R., Bonanno, G. A., & Mancini, A. D. (2010). From Marianthal to latent growth mixture modeling: A return to the exploration of individual differences in response to unemployment. *Journal of Neuroscience, Psychology, and Economics, 3*, 116–125.

14. Henkel, D. (2011). Unemployment and substance use: A review of the literature (1990–2010). *Current Drug Abuse Reviews, 4*, 4–27.

15. Van Der Geest, V. R., Bijleveld, C. C. J. H., & Blokland, A. J. (2010). The effect of employment on longitudinal trajectories of offending: A follow-up of high-risk youth from 18 to 32 years of age. *Criminology, 49*, 1195–1234.

16. Federal Bureau of Investigation. (2011). *Crime in the United States, 2010*. Washington, DC: Author.

17. Rege, M., Skardhamar, T., Telle, K., & Votruba, M. (2009). The effect of plant closure on crime. *Statistics Norway* (Discussion Papers No. 593). Retrieved March 15, 2012, from http://www.ssb.no/publikasjoner/pdf/dp593.pdf.

18. Sedlak, A. J., Mettenburg, J., Basena, M., Petta, I., McPherson, K., Greene, A., & Li, S. (2010). *Fourth National Incidence Study of Child Abuse and Neglect (NIS–4): Report to Congress*. Washington, DC: U.S. Department of Health and Human Services, Administration for Children and Families.

19. Briere, J., & Elliott, D. M. (2003). Prevalence and psychological sequelae of self-reported childhood physical and sexual abuse in a general population sample of men and women. *Child Abuse and Neglect, 27*, 1205–1222.

20. Butt, S., Chou, S., & Browne, K. (2011). A rapid systematic review on the association between childhood physical and sexual abuse and illicit drug use among males. *Child Abuse Review, 20*, 6–38.

21. Silverman, A. B., Reinherz, H. Z., & Giaconia, R. M. (1996). The long-term sequelae of child and adolescent abuse: A longitudinal community study. *Child Abuse and Neglect, 20*, 709–723.

22. Widom, C. S., Weilder, B. L., & Cottier, L. B. (1999). Childhood victimization and drug abuse: A comparison of prospective and retrospective findings. *Journal of Consulting and Clinical Psychology, 67*, 867–880.

23. Huang, S., Trapido, E., Fleming, L., Arheart, K., Crandall, L., French, M., et al. (2011). The long-term effects of childhood maltreatment experiences on subsequent illicit drug use and drug-related problems in young adulthood. *Addictive Behaviors, 36*, 95–102.

24. Thompson, M. P., Kingree, J. B., & Desai, S. (2004). Gender differences in long-term health consequences of physical abuse of children: Data from a nationally representative survey. *American Journal of Public Health, 94*, 599–604.

25. Huang et al. (2011).

26. Anderson, C. M., Teicher, M. H., Polcari, A., & Renshaw, P. F. (2002). Abnormal T2 relaxation time in the cerebellar vermis of adults sexually abused in childhood: Potential role of the vermis in stress-enhanced risk for drug abuse. *Psychoneuroendocrinology, 27*, 231–244.

27. Widom, C. S. (1995). Victims of childhood sexual abuse—Later criminal consequences. *National Institute of Justice: Research in Brief*. Washington, DC: U.S. Department of Justice.

28. Felson, R. B., & Lane, K. J. (2009). Social learning, sexual and physical abuse, and adult crime. *Aggressive Behavior, 35*, 489–501.

29. Forsythe, L., & Adams, K. (2009). Mental health, abuse, drug use and crime: Does gender matter? *Trends and Issues in Crime and Criminal Justice* (No. 384). Canberra, Australia: Australian Institute of Criminology.

30. Harlow, C. W. (1999). Prior abuse reported by inmates and probationers. *Bureau of Justice Statistics: Selected Findings*. Washington, DC: U.S. Department of Justice.

31. Kim, M. J., Tajima, E. A., Herrenkohl, T. I., & Huang, B. (2009). Early child maltreatment, runaway youths, and risk of delinquency and victimization in adolescence: A meditational model. *Social Work Research, 33*, 19–28.

32. Hirschi, T. (1969). *Causes of delinquency*. Berkeley: University of California Press.

33. Sampson, R. J., & Laub, J. H. (1993). *Crime in the making*. Cambridge, MA: Harvard University Press.

34. Loeber, R., & Dishion, T. (1983). Early predictors of male delinquency: A review. *Psychological Bulletin, 94*, 68–99.

35. Hirschi, T., & Gottfredson, M. (1983). Age and the explanation of crime. *American Journal of Sociology, 89*, 522–584.

36. Baumrind, D. (1991). The influence of parenting style on adolescent competence and substance use. *Journal of Early Adolescence, 11*, 56–95.

37. Stice, E. M., Barrera, M., Jr., & Chassin, L. (1993). Relation of parental social support and control to adolescents' externalizing symptomatology and substance use. *Journal of Abnormal Child Psychology, 21*, 609–629.

38. Baumrind (1991).

39. Pilgrim, C. C., Schulenberg, J. E., O'Malley, P. M., Bachman, J. G., & Johnston, L. D. (2006). Mediators and moderators of parental involvement on substance use: A national study of adolescents *Prevention Science, 7*, 75–89.

40. Choquet, M., Hassler, C., Morin, D., Falissard, B., & Chau, N. (2008). Perceived parenting styles and tobacco, alcohol and cannabis use among French adolescents: Gender and family structure differentials. *Alcohol and Alcoholism, 43*, 73–80.

41. Parsai, M., Kulis, S., & Marsiglia, F. F. (2010). Parental monitoring, religious involvement and drug use among Latino and non-Latino youth in the southwestern United States. *British Journal of Social Work, 40*, 100–114.

42. Cleveland, M. J., Gibbons, F. X., Gerrard, M., Pomery, E. A., & Brody, G. H. (2005). The impact of parenting on risk cognitions and risk behavior: A study of mediation and moderation in a panel of African American adolescents. *Child Development, 76*, 900–916.

43. Hoeve, M., Dubas, S., Eichelsheim, V. I., van der Laan, P. H., Smeenk, W., & Gerris, J. R. M. (2009). The relationship between parenting and delinquency: A meta-analysis. *Journal of Abnormal Child Psychology, 37*, 749–775.

44. Lundahl, B. W., Nimer, J., & Parsons, B. (2996). Preventing child abuse: A meta-analysis of parent training programs. *Research on Social Work Practice, 16*, 251–262.

45. Muñoz, L. C., Pakalniskiene, V., & Frick, P. J. (2011). Parental monitoring and youth behavior problems: Moderation by callous-unemotional traits over time. *European Child Adolescent Psychiatry, 20*, 261–269.

46. Barnes, G. M., & Farrell, M. P. (1992). Parental support and control as predictors of adolescent drinking, delinquency, and related problem behaviors. *Journal of Marriage and the Family, 54*, 763–776.

47. Cookston, J. T. (1999). Parental supervision and family structure: Effects on adolescent problem behaviors. *Journal of Divorce & Remarriage, 32*, 107–122.

48. Griffin, K. W., Botvin, G. J., Scheier, L. M., Diaz, T., & Miller, N. L. (2000). Parenting practices as predictors of substance use, delinquency, and aggression among urban minority youth: Moderating effects of family structure and gender. *Psychology of Addictive Behaviors, 14*, 174–184.

49. Fletcher, A. C., Steinberg, L., & Williams-Wheeler, M. (2004). Parental influences on adolescent problem behavior: Revisiting Stattin and Kerr. *Child Development, 75*, 781–796.

50. Collins, W. A., & Steinberg, L. (2006). Adolescent development in interpersonal context. In N. Eisenberg (Ed.), *Handbook of child psychology: Vol. 3. Social, emotional, and personality development* (6th ed., pp. 1003–1067). Hoboken, NJ: Wiley.

51. Johnston, L. D., O'Malley, P. M., Bachman, J. G., & Schulenberg, J. E. (2005). *Monitoring the Future: National survey results on drug use, 1975–2004. Vol. I: Secondary school students* (NIH Publication No. 05-5727). Washington, DC: National Institutes of Health.

52. Rubin, K. H., Bukowski, W., & Parker, J. (2006). Peer interactions, relationships, and groups. In N. Eisenberg (Ed.), *Handbook of child psychology: Vol. 3. Social, emotional, and personality development* (6th ed., pp. 571–645). Hoboken, NJ: Wiley.

53. Bahr, S. J., Hoffmann, J. P., & Yang, X. (2005). Parental and peer influence on the risk of adolescent drug use. *Journal of Primary Prevention, 26*, 529–551.

54. Henry, K. L. (2008). Low prosocial attachment, involvement with drug-using peers, and adolescent drug use: A longitudinal examination of mediational mechanisms. *Psychology of Addictive Behaviors, 22*, 302–308.

55. Gifford-Smith, M., Dodge, K. A., Dishion, T. J., & McCord, J. (2005). Peer influence in children and adolescents: Crossing the bridges from developmental to intervention science. *Journal of Abnormal Child Psychology, 33*, 255–265.

56. Dishion, T. J., McCord, J., & Poulin, F. (1999). When interventions harm. *American Psychologist, 54*, 755–764.

57. Vitulano, M., Fite, P. J., & Rathert, J. (2010). Delinquent peer influence on childhood delinquency: The moderating effect of impulsivity. *Journal of Psychopathology and Behavioral Assessment, 32*, 315–322.

58. Vitaro, F., Brendgen, M., & Tremblay, R. E. (2000). Influence of deviant friends on delinquency: Searching for moderator variables. *Journal of Abnormal Child Psychology, 28*, 313–325.

59. Mennis, J., & Harris, P. (2011). Contagion and repeat offending among urban juvenile delinquents. *Journal of Adolescence, 34*, 951–963.

60. Battin-Pearson, S., Thornberry, T. P., Hawkins, J. D., & Krohn, M. D. (1998). *Gang membership, delinquent peers, and delinquent behavior*. Washington, DC: U.S. Department of Justice.

61. Zhang, L., Wieczorek, W. F., & Welte, J. W. (1997). The impact of age of onset of substance use on delinquency. *Journal of Research in Crime and Delinquency, 34*, 253–265.

62. Mears, D. P., & Field, S. H. (2002). A closer look at the age, peers, and delinquency relationship. *Western Criminology Review, 4*, 20–29.

63. Barnes, G. M., Hoffman, J. H., Welte, J. W., Farrell, M. P., & Dintcheff, B. A. (2006). Effects of parental monitoring and peer deviance on substance use and delinquency. *Journal of Marriage and Family, 68*, 1084–1104.

64. Simons, R. L., Chao, W., Conger, R. D., & Elder, G. H. (2001). Quality of parenting as mediator of the effect of childhood deviance on adolescent friendship choices and delinquency: A growth curve analysis. *Journal of Marriage and Family, 63*, 63–79.

65. McDonough, P. (2009). *TV viewing among kids at an eight-year high*. Retrieved August 31, 2012 from http://blog.nielsen.com/nielsenwire/media_entertainment/tv-viewing-among-kids-at-an-eight-year-high/

66. Vandewater, E. A., Bickham, D. S., & Lee, J. H. (2006). Time well spent? Relating television use to children's free-time activities. *Pediatrics, 117*, 181–191.

67. Gunasekera, H., Chapman, S., & Campbell, S. (2005). Sex and drugs in popular movies: An analysis of the top 200 films. *Journal of the Royal Society of Medicine, 98*, 464–470.

68. Hunt, K., Henderson, M., Wight, D., & Sargent, J. D. (2011). Exposure to smoking in films and own smoking among Scottish adolescents: A cross-sectional study. *Thorax, 66*, 866–874.

69. Browne, K. D., & Hamilton-Giachritsis, C. (2005). The influence of violent media on children and adolescents: A public-health approach. *Lancet, 365*, 702–710.

70. Savage, J. (2004). Does viewing violent media really cause criminal violence? A methodological review. *Aggression and Violent Behavior, 10*, 99–128.

71. Engelhardt, C. R., Bartholow, B. D., & Saults, J. S. (2011). Violent and nonviolent video games differentially affect physical aggression for individuals high vs. low in dispositional anger. *Aggressive Behavior, 37*, 539–546.

72. Orue, I., Bushman, B. J., Calvete, E., Thomaes, S., de Castro, B. O., & Hutteman, R. (2011). Monkey see, monkey do, monkey hurt: Longitudinal effects of exposure to violence on children's aggressive behavior. *Social Psychological and Personality Science, 2*, 432–437.

73. Browne, K. D., & Pennell, A. E. (2000). The influence of film and video on young people and violence. In G. Boswell (Ed.), *Violent children and adolescents: Asking the question why* (pp. 151–168). Philadelphia: Whurr.

74. Slater, M. D., Long, M., & Ford, V. L. (2006). Alcohol, illegal drugs, violent crime, and traffic-related and other unintended injuries in U.S. local and national news. *Journal of Studies on Alcohol, 67*, 904–910.

75. Slater, M. D., Hayes, A. F., Goodall, C. E., & Ewoldsen, D. R. (2012). Increasing support for alcohol-control enforcement through news coverage of alcohol's role in injuries and crime. *Journal of Studies on Alcohol and Drugs, 73*, 311–315.

CHAPTER 8

STATIC AND SITUATIONAL FOUNDATIONS OF DRUG–CRIME RELATIONSHIPS

© iStockphoto/ericsphotography

Biological, psychological, and sociological factors encompass much of the basic research on drug use, crime, and the drug–crime connection. Another area of basic research is static and **situational** correlates of drug use and crime. Static and situational factors constitute the two ends of a popular tripartite model of risk assessment in which risk is classified as static, stable dynamic, and acute dynamic.[1–2] A **static risk** factor, being historical in nature, does not change. A **dynamic risk** factor, by comparison, is subject to change. The change can either be slow and gradual (stable dynamic) or rapid and sudden (acute dynamic). **Stable dynamic risk** factors include antisocial personality processes, antisocial cognition, and antisocial peers. The present chapter, however, focuses on the upper and lower ends of the tripartite model, i.e., static risk and acute dynamic risk.

The principal objectives of this chapter are to:

- Understand how static risk factors can serve as effective predictors of drug use, crime, and the drug–crime overlap.
- Appreciate the utility of situational or acute dynamic risk factors in preventing drug use, crime, and drug–related crime.

Static Risk

Four static risk factors are examined in this chapter: age, gender, race, and behavioral history.

Age

Age is considered a static risk factor because despite the fact it changes over time, the change is stable relative to others. Consequently, as long as we are alive, I will always be 21 years younger than my father and 24 years older than my son. Age acquires its well-deserved reputation as a key static risk factor by virtue of its association with nervous system maturity, drug/crime opportunities, changes in strength and stamina, and alterations in sensory stimulation from drugs. The frontal lobes of the human brain are not fully developed until early adulthood and their development brings with them advancements in impulse control;[3] moreover, drug and crime opportunities, strength, stamina, and sensory stimulation from drugs tend to diminish with age.[4]

Age and Drug Use

Older adolescents and young adults tend to use more drugs than younger adolescents and older adults. Results from the 2010 **National Survey of Drug Use and Health (NSDUH)** clearly support the conclusion that illicit drug use is more heavily concentrated in late adolescence and early adulthood (see **Figure 8-1**). Alcohol follows a similar, albeit less dramatic, pattern that peaks a few years later than the illicit drug pattern (see **Figure 8-2**).[5]

Age and Crime

Hirschi and Gottfredson refer to the **age–crime** relationship as one of the few brute facts of criminology. The relationship, often identified as a j-shaped curve, is invariant across time, place, crime category (person vs. property), data source (official vs. self-report), gender, and race. Hirschi and Gottfredson used the age–crime relationship to argue against the career criminal and life-course paradigms and to argue for cross-sectional research designs.[6]

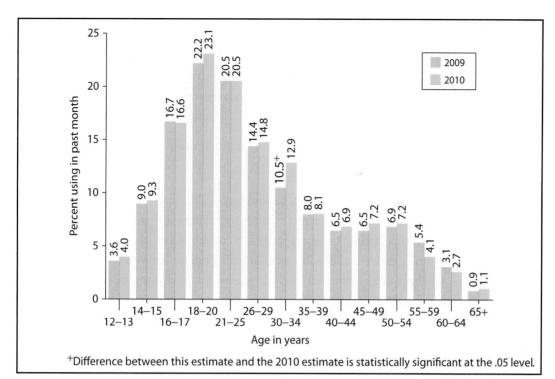

Figure 8-1
Illicit drug use in past month broken down by age.

⁺Difference between this estimate and the 2010 estimate is statistically significant at the .05 level.

Substance Abuse and Mental Health Services Administration. (2011). *Results from the 2010 National Survey on Drug Use and Health: Summary of National Findings, NSDUH Series H-41, HHS Publication No. (SMA) 11-4658*. Rockville, MD: Substance Abuse and Mental Health Services Administration.

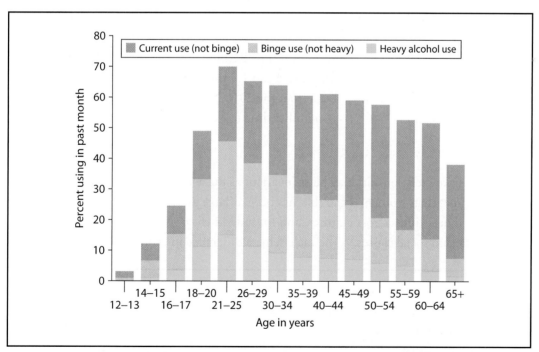

Figure 8-2
Current, binge, and heavy alcohol use broken down by age.

Substance Abuse and Mental Health Services Administration. (2011). *Results from the 2010 National Survey on Drug Use and Health: Summary of National Findings, NSDUH Series H-41, HHS Publication No. (SMA) 11-4658*. Rockville, MD: Substance Abuse and Mental Health Services Administration.

Although Hirschi and Gottfredson's conclusions concerning the invariance of the drug–crime relationship have been challenged,[7] this does not alter the fact that age is one of the most robust and consistent predictors of crime.

Age, Drug Use, and Crime

Mumola and Karberg examined drug use in state and federal inmates by age and obtained figures (see **Figure 8-3**) that were similar to those reported in the 2010 NSDUH for the U.S. general population.[8] Forging consistent inverse relationships (negative correlations) with drug use, crime, and the drug–crime nexus, age is an important static risk factor and potent predictor of both drug use and crime.

Gender

Sex is a biological characteristic expressed in certain physical differences between males and females. **Gender**, on the other hand, is a social role based on this innate, biological characteristic. Gender acquires its status as a key static risk factor by virtue of sex-related differences in physiology and gender-based differences in socialization. Testosterone, the male sex hormone, is associated with increased levels of aggression, and women's smaller physical stature means that alcohol and drugs will affect them differently than men.[9] In addition, boys are socialized to be more aggressive than girls. Hence, it is more socially acceptable for boys to engage in crime and drug-use behaviors than girls.[10]

Gender and Drug Use

Drug use, abuse, and dependence have always been more prevalent in males than in females, although there is evidence that the gender gap in drug use has narrowed in recent years. Shelly Greenfield and her colleagues determined that the 5:1 ratio of male to female drug use/ abuse from the 1980s was closer to 3:1 in 2010.[11] Results from the National Epidemiologic Survey on Alcohol and Related Conditions (NESARC) indicate that 2.3 times more men than women satisfy the criteria for drug abuse and 1.9 times more men than women satisfy the criteria for drug dependence.[12] Data from the 2010 NSDUH also show clear evidence of a gender gap in alcohol (**Figure 8-4**) and other drug (**Figure 8-5**) abuse and dependence.[13]

Gender and Crime

The gender–crime relationship may be as invariant as the age–crime relationship. Men commit more crimes than women, a gap that has been as large as 9:1 in the past. This has been demonstrated over time, across cultures, and for individuals of varying races, educational backgrounds, and social classes.[14] The male-female difference in crime has been observed in

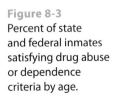

Figure 8-3
Percent of state and federal inmates satisfying drug abuse or dependence criteria by age.

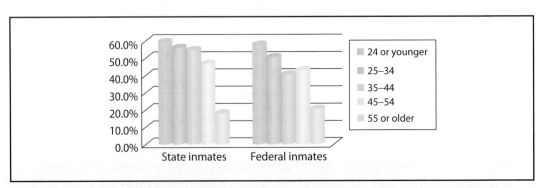

Data From: Mumola, C. J., & Karberg, J. C. (2006). *Drug use and dependence, state and federal prisoners, 2004.* Bureau of Justice Statistics Special Report (NCJ 213530).

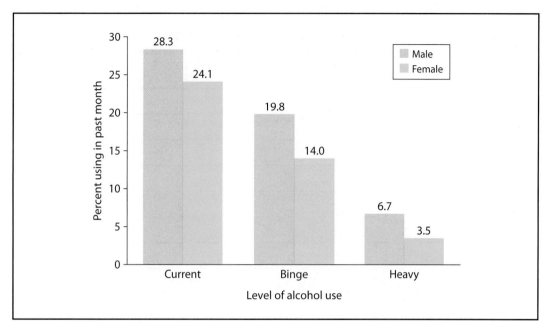

Figure 8-4
Current, binge, and heavy alcohol use broken down by gender.

Substance Abuse and Mental Health Services Administration. (2011). *Results from the 2010 National Survey on Drug Use and Health: Summary of National Findings, NSDUH Series H-41, HHS Publication No. (SMA) 11-4658.* Rockville, MD: Substance Abuse and Mental Health Services Administration.

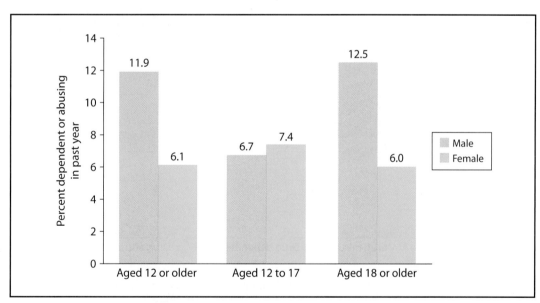

Figure 8-5
Substance abuse or dependence broken down by age and gender.

Substance Abuse and Mental Health Services Administration. (2011). *Results from the 2010 National Survey on Drug Use and Health: Summary of National Findings, NSDUH Series H-41, HHS Publication No. (SMA) 11-4658.* Rockville, MD: Substance Abuse and Mental Health Services Administration.

all major offense categories (except prostitution) but is greater for more serious crimes than for less serious crimes. Like the gender gap in drug use, the gender gap in crime has showed signs of narrowing in recent years (see **Figure 8-6**).[15–16]

Gender, Drug Use, and Crime

Males clearly use more drugs and commit more crimes than females but female offenders often display slightly higher rates of substance misuse than male offenders (see **Figures 8-7** and **8-8**).[17–18] Female offenders are also more likely than male offenders to have mental health

Figure 8-6
Violent crime by
gender, 1973–2003.

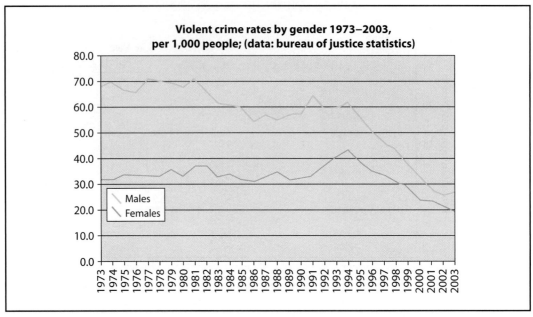

From: Bureau of Justice Statistics.

Figure 8-7
Percentage of male
and female jail
inmates reporting any
drug misuse, drug
dependence, and
drug abuse.

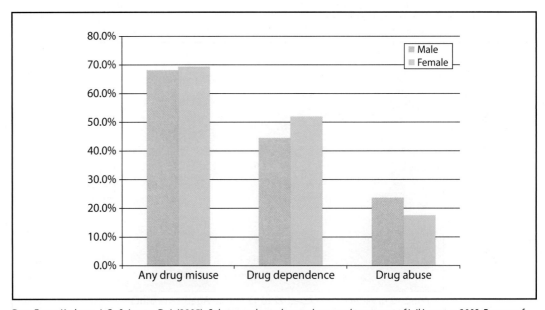

Data From: Karberg, J. C., & James, D. J. (2005). *Substance dependence, abuse, and treatment of jail inmates, 2002.* Bureau of Justice Statistics Special Report (NCJ 209588). Washington, DC: U.S. Department of Justice.

problems, relationship issues, and sexual or physical abuse histories.[19] This indicates the presence of gendered pathways for drug use, crime, and drug–crime overlap that need to be taken into account by criminal justice researchers, practitioners, and policy-makers trying to make sense of male-female differences in offending.

Race

Race, like gender, is a socially constructed variable with foundations in certain genetic and physical characteristics, which in this case involve skin color, facial form, and eye shape. In many ways, classifying people by race is a highly arbitrary process that combines genetic and cultural information to form a single variable. Nonetheless, race has been shown to correlate

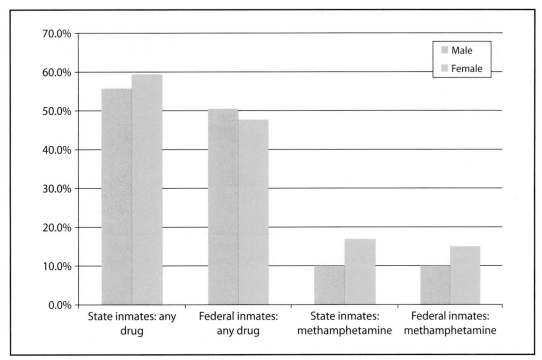

Figure 8-8
Percentage of male and female state and federal inmates reporting any drug or methamphetamine use within 1 month of arrest.

Data From: Mumola, C. J., & Karberg, J. C. (2006). *Drug use and dependence, state and federal prisoners, 2004*. Bureau of Justice Statistics Special Report (NCJ 213530).

with both drug use and crime. It acquires its status as a key static risk factor by virtue of its correlation with social inequality (poverty, social class) and various cultural and subcultural factors that are instrumental in either promoting or discouraging drug use and crime.[20]

Race and Drug Use

Racial differences in drug use and abuse are relatively minor, although there are a few consistent findings. First, Asians tend to have lower alcohol and drug use/abuse rates than whites, blacks, and Hispanics. In the 2010 National Survey of Drug Use and Health (NSDUH), Asians reported the lowest rates of alcohol/drug use and abuse among the six racial groups examined. Second, Native Americans exhibited comparatively high rates of alcohol and drug use and abuse. Native Americans and Alaska Natives had among the highest rates of illicit drug use and substance abuse/dependence diagnoses of the six groups included in the 2010 NSDUH. Third, mixed race individuals tend to engage in more problematic alcohol and drug use than whites and blacks but less than Native Americans. This is also supported by results from the 2010 NSDUH. Fourth, there are normally few meaningful differences in drug use and abuse between black and white Americans. According to the 2010 NSDUH, African Americans and Caucasian Americans were equivalent in substance abuse diagnoses but there were twice as many Caucasian Americans as African Americans who reported prior episodes of binge drinking (see **Figure 8-9**).[21]

Race and Crime

The odds of going to prison are much greater for African Americans, and to a lesser extent, Hispanics, than for whites (see **Figure 8-10**).[22] There are at least two ways to interpret these findings. First, it could reflect racial bias in the American criminal justice system. Second, it could

Figure 8-9
Binge drinking, illicit drug use, and substance abuse/dependence in individuals 12 years of age and older, by race.

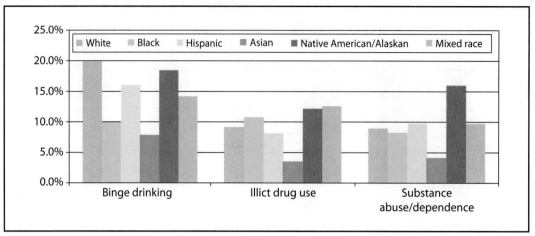

Substance Abuse and Mental Health Services Administration. (2011). *Results from the 2010 National Survey on Drug Use and Health: Summary of National Findings, NSDUH Series H-41, HHS Publication No. (SMA) 11-4658.* Rockville, MD: Substance Abuse and Mental Health Services Administration.

Figure 8-10
Lifetime chances of going to state or federal prison, by race.

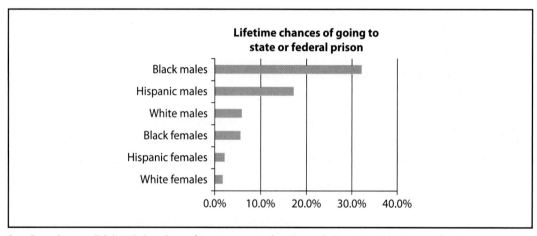

Data From: Bonczar, T. P. (2003). *Prevalence of imprisonment in the U.S. population, 1974–2001.* Bureau of Justice Statistics Special Report (NCJ 197976). Washington, DC: U.S. Department of Justice.

reflect genuine differences in criminal offending. The bulk of empirical evidence suggests that it is differential involvement in crime, not criminal justice system bias, that accounts for the large difference in incarceration rates observed between racial groups. In an early study on this issue, Alfred Blumstein determined that 80% of the black-white gap in imprisonment was the result of greater involvement of blacks in serious offending.[23] A decade later, Steve Crutchfield and colleagues demonstrated that 90% of the black-white gap in imprisonment was a consequence of differences in offending between blacks and whites.[24] This issue was recently investigated by Jon Sorensen, Robert Hope, and Don Stemen, who, based on their analyses of national arrest and prison admission data, concluded that racial disparities in state prison admissions are better explained by racial discrepancies in arrest rates than by bias in the criminal justice system.[25]

Race, Drug Use, and Crime

A majority of offenders have a history of regular drug usage, if not a significant drug problem. White offenders, it would seem, display higher rates of substance misuse than black and Hispanic offenders (see **Figure 8-11**).[26] It may be that drugs play a more instrumental

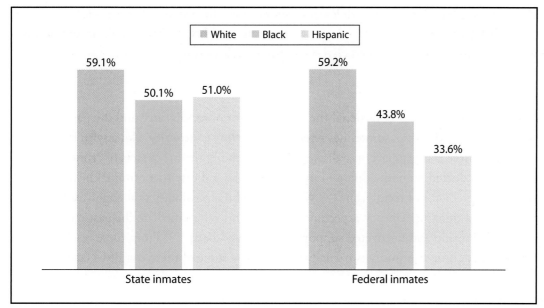

Figure 8-11
Proportion of state and federal inmates satisfying criteria for substance abuse/dependence.

Data From: Mumola, C. J., & Karberg, J. C. (2006). *Drug use and dependence, state and federal prisoners, 2004.* Bureau of Justice Statistics Special Report (NCJ 213530).

role in the crimes committed by white offenders than in the crimes committed by black and Hispanic offenders. This moderation of the drug–crime relationship by racial status may be the result of certain intervening cognitive variables. Research indicates that black offenders tend to hold more positive outcome expectancies for crime (a correlate of proactive criminal thinking) than white offenders.[27] In addition, self-esteem and offending are positively correlated in blacks but negatively (inversely) correlated in whites.[28] It is conceivable, then, that racial moderation of the drug–crime relationship (i.e., stronger correlation in whites than blacks) is mediated by proactive issues like positive outcome expectancies and self-esteem.

Behavioral History

A prior history of substance abuse or criminality, referred to generically as behavioral history, is another static risk factor capable of predicting future substance abuse and criminality. Behavioral history acquires its status as a key static risk factor by way of the old psychological adage that the "best predictor of future behavior is past behavior," whether the behavior in question is drug use or crime.

Substance History and Drug Use

Much of the research in this section comes from researchers affiliated with the gateway theory of drug involvement. In testing a multiple risk factor theory of drug use vulnerability, Michael Newcomb and Maria Felix-Ortiz ascertained that:

- Frequency, severity, and chronicity of prior substance abuse were robust predictors of future drug and alcohol usage.
- **Polysubstance abuse** was particularly predictive of future drug and alcohol problems.[29]

Lewinsohn, Rohde, and Brown studied the prognostic value of prior cigarette smoking for the purpose of predicting subsequent drug use in a longitudinal study and discovered that smoking cigarettes during adolescence significantly increased a person's odds of using marijuana, hard drugs, and multiple drugs in young adulthood. Daily smoking and an earlier age of onset of smoking predicted the highest levels of subsequent drug use.[30]

Criminal History and Crime

Criminal history is often considered the best predictor of recidivism[31] and the past crime–future crime relationship, sometimes referred to as **crime continuity**, along with the age-crime curve and gender-crime discrepancy, are among the brute facts of crime. Meta-analyses conducted on both adult and juvenile samples indicate that criminal history is the single best predictor of recidivism.[32–33] Walters tested the possibility that cognitive factors like criminal thinking, efficacy expectancies, goals, and values mediate the past crime–future crime relationship and uncovered support for this hypothesis.[34–35] From these results, we can surmise that crime continuity is partially mediated by some of these cognitive factors.

Behavioral History, Drug Use, and Crime

There also appears to be cross-domain predictability between drugs and crime in the sense that early drug use is capable of predicting subsequent criminality and early criminality is capable of predicting subsequent drug use. Gresnigt, Breteler, Schippers, and van den Hurk, in a study of male inmates released from various Dutch prisons, noted that the total score on the Addiction Severity Index (ASI) successfully predicted recidivism in this group 2 years later.[36] Conversely, Helen Wilson and Cathy Spatz Widom identified several different drug use trajectories in a cohort of 374 men and 332 women. The chronic, persistent drug pattern was associated with a history of prior criminal arrest.[37] Hence, prior crime is capable of predicting both future crime and future drug use, whereas prior drug use is capable of predicting both future drug use and future crime.

Meta-analyses indicate that each of the four static risk factors reviewed in this section (age, gender, race, and criminal history), along with substance abuse, are among the best predictors of institutional adjustment and recidivism in criminal populations. Results from two of the largest meta-analyses, both conducted by a group of researchers under the direction of Paul Gendreau, are summarized in **Table 8-1**.[38–39] Although there are no meta-analytic studies on static risk factors and drug use, early drug use and behavioral problems are principal risk factors for future drug use.[40] Two of the four factors (age, criminal history) are frequently considered in sanction and release decision making but it would be unethical and unconstitutional to include the other two factors (gender, race) in these decisions.

Table 8-1 Effect Sizes from Institutional Adjustment and Recidivism

Predictor	Institutional Adjustment	Recidivism
Age	-.11 ($k = 28$)	-.11 ($k = 56$)
Gender		.06 ($k = 17$)
Race	.05 ($k = 21$)	.17 ($k = 21$)
Criminal History	.12 ($k = 82$)	.17 ($k = 164$)
Substance Abuse	.05 ($k = 104$)	.10 ($k = 60$)

Note: All figures are correlations (r); k = number of effect sizes included in the analysis.
Data From: Gendreau, P., Little, T., & Goggin, C. (1996). A meta-analysis of the predictors of adult offender recidivism: What works! Criminology, 34, 575–608 & Gendreau, P., Goggin, C., & Law, M. A. (1997). Predicting prison misconducts. Criminal Justice and Behavior, 24, 414–431.

Stable Dynamic Risk Factors

Dynamic risk factors are changeable. When the term stable is placed in front of dynamic it means that the risk factor changes slowly and gradually rather than quickly and suddenly. Whereas static risk factors are most useful in predicting behavior, stable dynamic risk factors are most useful in establishing goals for treatment and intervention. Antisocial history, antisocial cognition, antisocial personality processes, and antisocial peer associations are commonly referred to as the "**Big Four**" risk factors. Three of the "Big Four" are stable dynamic risk factors, whereas antisocial history is the sole static risk factor in the "Big Four." The "Big Four" plus family/marital status, lack of educational/occupational achievement, lack of prosocial leisure activities, and substance abuse make up the "**Central Eight**" risk factors. Several of these factors are normally classified as stable dynamic risk factors, but can also serve as **acute dynamic risk** factors (see **Table 8-2**).[41]

Acute Dynamic Risk Factors

Like stable dynamic risk factors, acute dynamic risk factors are changeable; unlike stable dynamic risk factors, acute dynamic risk factors change quickly and suddenly rather than slowly and gradually. Another unique aspect of acute dynamic risk factors is that they are more **situational** and less **dispositional** than stable dynamic risk factors. This is another way of saying that they are highly sensitive to momentary changes in a person's environment, mood, or current situation. Two general classes of acute dynamic risk factor are examined in this section: **access** and **stress**.

Access

Before a drug can be used it must be available in one's environment and before a crime can be committed a **criminal opportunity** must be present. Both **drug availability** and criminal opportunity come under the heading of access-related acute dynamic risk factors.

Drug Availability

Increased availability is an important facilitator of drug use and abuse. Increased availability of opiate-based prescription drugs, for instance, resulted in a 65% increase in the number of hospitalizations and a 47% increase in the number of overdoses in a study conducted between 1999 and 2006.[42] In 1980, Reginald Smart introduced a model of substance use that continues to be applicable today. According to Smart's **availability-proneness model**, substance use is a function of a drug's availability in the physical, social, and economic

Table 8-2 Big Four and Central Eight Risk Factors as Stable and Acute Dynamic Risk Factors

• BIG FOUR RISK FACTORS	• REMAINING CENTRAL EIGHT RISK FACTORS
▥ Antisocial History	▥ Family/Marital
▥ Antisocial Cognition	▥ Lack of Achievement in Education/ Occupation
▥ Antisocial Peers	▥ Lack of Prosocial Leisure Activities
▥ Antisocial Personality Pattern	▥ Substance Abuse

Blue = stable dynamic risk factors; Purple = stable and acute dynamic risk factors environment as well as the person's proneness to drug use. High availability means that lower than normal levels of proneness are required for drug use and abuse, whereas high proneness means that lower than normal levels of availability are required for drug use and abuse.[43]

Just as an increase in the availability of drugs can lead to an increase in the use of drugs, so too, can a decrease in the availability of drugs lead to a decrease in the use of drugs. A sudden and dramatic reduction in the supply of heroin in Australia in 2001, for instance, was followed by a rapid increase in the price of heroin, a marked decrease in heroin consumption, and a significant reduction in the types of **acquisitive** (property) **crimes** normally committed by addicts in need of cash to pay for heroin. Unfortunately, there was also a countervailing rise in cocaine usage and an associated spike in violent criminality.[44] Community policing initiatives, such as community–police partnerships and "weed-and-seed" programs, designed to limit access to drugs by reducing supply, demand, or both, have been found to be successful in reducing drug use and drug-related crime.[45]

Even the availability of legal drugs like alcohol can be manipulated in an effort to reduce drug use and its associated problems. Ways in which the availability of alcohol can be reduced include raising the legal drinking age, imposing restrictions on when and where alcohol can be sold or served, and boosting the price of alcohol through taxation. Alex Wagenaar and colleagues recently conducted a meta-analysis of 1,003 effect sizes from 112 different studies and discovered that raising the cost of alcohol through taxation and price increases resulted in moderate reductions in both alcohol consumption and problem drinking.[46] There are certain additional advantages to controlling alcohol usage through taxation. According to Phillip Cook, "[taxation strategies] help curtail alcohol abuse and its consequences without a direct restriction on freedom of choice. They can be set high or low or anywhere in between, providing the possibility of a calibrated response to the costs of alcohol related problems" (p. 11).[47]

Criminal Opportunity

Criminal opportunity plays a major role in several criminological theories, including Gottfredson and Hirschi's general theory of crime,[48] Simon's gender theory of crime,[49] and Cloward and Ohlin's **differential opportunity theory**.[50] No criminological theory has focused more on opportunity, however, than Cohen and Felson's routine activities theory. **Routine activities theory** holds that crime is most likely to occur when three conditions are met, the last two of which center around opportunity and situational concerns:[51]

- Presence of a motivated offender
- Appearance of a suitable target or victim
- Absence of capable guardians against crime

A meta-analysis by Travis Pratt and Francis Cullen on macrolevel theories of crime uncovered moderate support for basic principles and fundamental constructs of routine activities theory.[52]

Economic conditions or technological advancements can augment or dampen opportunities for crime. Major armed conflicts, like World Wars I and II, have been shown to be followed by several years of increased violent criminality in the populations of countries that participated in the conflicts.[53] The sharp rise in shoplifting incidents occurring in England between 1950 and 1960 corresponded to a thirteenfold increase in the number of self-service groceries.[54] A huge rise in the market value of gold and silver in the 1970s led to a shift in items targeted in burglaries, such that jewelry was preferred over TV sets and cash.[55] In the first two instances, opportunity facilitated crime, by increasing access to firearms or groceries; in the third instance, one item, gold and silver jewelry, was specifically targeted because it commanded a high price.

In recent years there has been an explosion of crime on the Internet, from identity theft, to fraud, to extortion, to child pornography. Consequently, the Internet has become an arena in which new opportunities for crime and antisocial behavior play out. By the same token, the Internet has also provided new opportunities for innovative policing techniques and government policies (cyberpolicing) designed to catch Internet thieves and predators and limit their negative and ever-expanding influence on society (see News Spot 8-1).

NEWS SPOT 8-1

Title: Our Brave New Cyber World—It's a Jungle Out There, Let's Hope the President's New Cyber Czar Can Tame the Proliferating Threats to Our Security
Source: *Pittsburgh Post-Gazette*
Author: Jeffrey Hunker
Date: June 7, 2009

President Obama's creation of a cyber security "czar" with a broad mandate to protect the nation's computer networks marks a step long overdue, and is a good start. But the announcement, and his cyber security policy review, leave unanswered how we're really going to address the problems of cyber crime and cyber war. These problems are spinning dangerously out of control.

Cyber criminals now operate in a sophisticated virtual underworld, a sort of computerized version of Prohibition.

At the recent World Economic Forum in Davos, cyber crime against business was estimated to cost the global economy $1 trillion per year. Individuals suffer, too: Identity theft on the Internet is rampant. Cyber extortion ("pay us or we'll shut down your organization's Web site") has become a global protection racket. Any information that's otherwise difficult to get—ranging from e-mail addresses of potential Viagra buyers to national security secrets—has value on the virtual black markets run by cyber-crime organizations.

The national security threat from espionage and cyber war is growing. In March, researchers uncovered a vast electronic spying operation that had infiltrated computers (including the Dalai Lama's) across 103 countries. The U.S. government admitted that both Russian and Chinese hackers have broken into secret computer systems in the Pentagon. In what looked to be the first cases of real cyber war, Russia is widely believed to have disabled vital computer systems during disputes with the former Soviet republics of Estonia and Georgia.

What's most troubling is that most attacks now are launched from virtual networks of thousands of infected computers— including possibly yours. Cyber security is no longer somebody else's problem. Now it's everybody's concern.

Questions to Ponder

1. **How can you protect yourself from cybercriminals and Internet predators?**
2. **Do you think greater regulation of the Internet might cut down on cybercrime?**
3. **What do you think should be done with cybercriminals?**

There are several ways to reduce opportunities for crime through situational crime control and prevention. One strategy is to increase the perceived effort of crime through the use of **target hardening** principles (steering column locks, self-defense training) or **access control** (password protection, watchdogs). A second strategy is to increase the perceived risk to the offender by increasing **formal surveillance** (burglar alarms, private security patrols) and **natural surveillance** (nighttime lighting, neighborhood watch). A third strategy is to decrease the anticipated reward of criminal behavior through **target removal** (detachable car stereo, women's shelter) or **property identification** (vehicle identification numbers, cattle branding).[56]

Drug and Crime Access

Drug availability and criminal opportunity provide the individual with access to various drug and criminal options. As with behavioral history, there may be important cross-domain relationships, such that increased access to drugs leads to increased criminality and increased access to crime leads to increased drug usage. Brad Myrstol documented a rapid acceleration in drug use approximately 90 days before arrest in a small group (~20%) of males followed as part of the 2002–2003 ADAM protocol in Anchorage, Alaska. This pattern occurred for all five drugs included in the ADAM protocol (marijuana, methamphetamine, crack cocaine, powder cocaine, heroin).[57] This would seem to suggest that increased access to drugs may open up new or reintroduce old opportunities for crime.

The converse may also be true; i.e., that decreased access to drugs can lead to reductions in future criminality. According to Nora Volkow, director of the National Institute on Drug Abuse (NIDA), "studies have consistently shown that comprehensive drug treatment works. It not only reduces drug use but also curtails criminal behavior and recidivism."[58] Research conducted at the Justice Policy Institute in Washington, DC lends support to Volkow's assertion, as indicated by the results depicted in **Figure 8-12**.[59]

In 1985, a strict alcohol policy went into effect in Russia whereby state alcohol production was reduced, the number of outlets selling alcohol was decreased, the price of alcohol was increased, alcohol was banned in public places, the age at which alcohol could be purchased was raised, and penalties for selling homemade alcohol were enhanced. Between 1984, the year before the policy went into effect, and 1987:

- Alcohol sales dropped by 61%
- Alcohol consumption fell by 29%
- Alcohol-related deaths were reduced by 51%
- Total violent deaths were reduced by 33%

The campaign was discontinued in late 1988 because of its unpopularity, at which point the alcohol-related and violent death rates returned to their precampaign levels.[60]

Figure 8-12
Effect of treatment on
criminal involvement.

U.S. Department of Health and Human Services, Substance Abuse and Mental Health Services Association, Center for Substance Abuse Treatment. (1997). *The National Treatment Improvement Evaluation Study (NTIES) highlights.* Rockville, MD: U.S. Department of Health and Human Services.

There is a dearth of research on the ability of criminal opportunities to promote drug use or whether reducing criminal opportunities through treatment is capable of reducing drug use. It would make sense that a cross-domain relationship between criminal opportunities and drug use similar to the well-documented cross-domain relationship between drug availability and crime exists. Before this can be viewed as anything more than an interesting hypothesis, however, hard research data are required.

Stress

Stress is a second major situational variable capable of increasing a person's odds of drug use and crime. In his **general strain theory** of crime, Robert Agnew established stress or strain as the primary motive for crime and anger as the primary concomitant emotion.[61] His model may also be applicable to drug use. Agnew mentions three sources of stress, all of which would appear to be relevant to drug use and crime:

- Failure to achieve positively valued goals (see **Table 8-3**)
- Loss of positive stimuli (see **Table 8-4**)
- Introduction of negative stimuli (see **Table 8-5**)

Table 8-3 Stress Created by Failure to Achieve Positively Valued Goals on Drug Use and Crime

• Goals of Drug Use
   ▪ Positive Affect
   ▪ Social Acceptance
   ▪ Sexual Enhancement
   ▪ Cognitive Improvement
• Goals of Crime
   ▪ Money
   ▪ Power
   ▪ Status
   ▪ Respect
	• Failure to achieved these positively valued goals culminates in:

Table 8-4 Stress Created by Loss of Positive Stimuli on Drug Use and Crime

• Positive Stimuli for Drugs
  ▪ Positive Affect
  ▪ Social Acceptance
  ▪ Personal Empowerment
  ▪ Cognitive Ability
• Positive Stimuli for Crime
  ▪ Money
  ▪ Power
  ▪ Status
  ▪ Respect
	• Loss of these positive stimuli culminates in:
	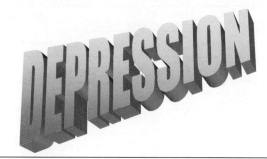

Table 8-5 Stress Created by Introduction of Negative Stimuli on Drug Use and Crime

• Negative Stimuli for Drugs
  ▪ Negative Affect
  ▪ Social Rejection
  ▪ Sexual Inhibition
  ▪ Cognitive Impairment
• Negative Stimuli for Crime
  ▪ Economic hardship
  ▪ Being taken advantage of
  ▪ Boredom
  ▪ Being put down
	• Introduction of these negative stimuli culminates in:

Stress and Drugs

The link between stress and drug use/abuse has been extensively researched. In a recent literature review, Logrip, Zorilla, and Koob noted that the rate of substance abuse and dependence was elevated in individuals diagnosed with posttraumatic stress disorder,[62] and in a recent meta-analysis, DiMaggio, Galea, and Li determined that 7–14% of the general population of nations subjected to a terrorist attack reported increased alcohol consumption within 2 years of the attack.[63] Other studies have shown that a poor home situation significantly increased both alcohol and drug use in homeless intravenous drug users,[64] and the desire to escape from uncomfortable emotions and physical discomfort correlated significantly with the frequency of drug usage in homosexual and bisexual men with histories of methamphetamine abuse.[65] Behavioral coping strategies, on the other hand, have been found to be highly efficacious in managing the high-risk situations that elicit the negative emotions that give rise to relapse.[66]

Stress and Crime

Richard Felson and Henry Steadman discovered that person and choice factors, like the desire for retaliation, played a key role in serious assaults and homicides but that specific behaviors on the part of the victim and various bystanders also influenced how a violent scenario played out. Victim and bystander behavior may increase the likelihood of a more serious crime taking place, in part, by their ability to raise the perpetrator's stress level. Victims in the Felson and Steadman study, for instance, were more likely to be killed when they were intoxicated, physically aggressive, or in possession of a weapon than when they were sober, nonaggressive, and unarmed.[67] Further analysis of these data revealed that third parties also played a significant role in a potentially violent scenario, either as antagonists (aggravating effect) or mediators (mitigating effect).[68] What are the moral and legal responsibilities of bystanders who witness a crime in progress? This is a topic addressed in News Spot 8-2.

NEWS SPOT 8-2

Title: Can Bystanders Be Charged in Richmond, California, Gang Rape? Experts Disagree
Source: *San Francisco Examiner*
Author: Ed Walsh
Date: November 2, 2009

Police say that as many as 24 bystanders stood and watched, some taking cell phone video and photos, as a 15-year-old girl was gang raped. The attack took place on Saturday, October 24, outside of a homecoming dance in Richmond, California. The City of Richmond (pop. 102,000) is in the San Francisco Bay Area, about 20 minutes north of Oakland, and has a high crime rate.

The question many are asking is whether the bystanders can be charged.

"No," criminal defense attorney Richard Herman told CNN. He noted the California law that states that witnesses are only obligated to report sexual assaults when they are committed against a person under 15 years old.

But Civil Rights Attorney Avery Friedman said charges could be filed if there is evidence that the bystanders were goading or encouraging people to commit a crime. The lawyer added that there "may be an aiding and abetting opportunity" for prosecutors.

Both attorneys agreed that the school district is liable in civil court for inadequate security at the school.

"There are going to be multi-million dollar lawsuits filed against this school district for failing to supervise this event," Herman said. "They had nobody walking around, no monitors and it is alleged that when the police finally arrived after two-and-a-half hours of torture, she was still being tortured."

Questions to Ponder
1. **What might possess a person not to act when they witness such an horrific crime?**
2. **Are there any policy changes you can think of that might encourage people to report violent crime more often?**
3. **Do you believe the school should be held liable for what happened to this girl? Are there any other parties you think should be held liable along with or instead of the school system?**

Stress can also be aroused by changes in the immediate environment, such as the **ambient temperature** to which a person is exposed. In separate studies, Craig and Dona Anderson and John Cotton unearthed modest positive correlations between ambient temperature and violent crime. The aggregate results for the three cities covered by these two studies are provided in **Figure 8-13**.[69–70] In a subsequent study, Craig Anderson discovered that hot days (maximum temperature ≥ 90 degrees), warmer months of the year (April through September), and years with more hot days than normal correlated with a higher rate of violent crime, even after controlling for differences in nonviolent crime. Anderson estimated that a year with 10 more hot days than average would produce a 7% increase in violent criminality. These results were independent of seasonal and time cycle effects, thereby ruling out the alternative hypothesis that it was not ambient temperature but the opportunity for interpersonal interaction and conflict that occurs when the weather is warmer that was responsible for the increased violence.[71]

Stress, Drugs, and Crime

In a 1990 editorial in the *British Journal of Addiction*, Trevor Bennett speculated that situational factors could hold a great deal of importance in explaining the drug–crime overlap by increasing access and augmenting stress within the context of an ongoing interaction between the criminal event and the drinking/drug-using environment. One possibility mentioned by Bennett is that drugs and crime are related via conditional factors present in situations where alcohol and drugs are consumed. In other words, the bar setting may reinforce the effect of alcohol on behavior (i.e., getting drunk and violent in a bar is expected, if not acceptable). Another possibility mentioned by Bennett would be that whereas the bar setting does not cause criminal behavior directly, it does provide increased opportunities for criminal behavior by bringing certain individuals into contact with one another (i.e., criminals may congregate in a bar to plan a crime or because of low self-control get into a confrontation that could eventually leads to serious violence).[72]

Figure 8-13

A:N (aggressive to nonaggressive crime) ratio as a function of ambient temperature, aggregated data from three cities: Des Moines, Iowa, Houston, Texas, and Indianapolis, Indiana.

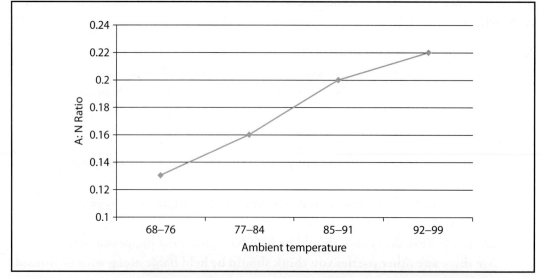

Data From: Anderson, C. A., & Anderson, D. C. (1984). Ambient temperature and violent crime: Tests of the linear and curvilinear hypotheses. *Journal of Personality and Social Psychology, 46*, 91–97 & Cotton, J. L. (1986). Ambient temperature and violent crime. *Journal of Applied Social Psychology, 16*, 786–801.

David Matza discussed situational factors in his **social drift theory** of delinquency, which may be as relevant to drug abuse as it is to crime. According to Matza, many juveniles (and some adults) drift in and out of delinquency and crime in response to various situational factors. Matza grouped these situational factors into two categories: preparation and desperation.[73] To the extent that preparation consists of opportunity and peer influence and desperation focuses on stress and intoxication they would seem to correspond with the two general groupings of acute dynamic risk factors covered in this section—access and stress, respectively. The lack of attention given to intoxication in this chapter should in no way be interpreted as evidence that it is unimportant. Richard Felson and Jeremy Staff, in fact, found that alcohol intoxication exerted its strongest effect on homicide and sexual/physical assault but was also involved in burglary and robbery. A dose-effect relationship (more violence being associated with higher levels of intoxication) was also noted, although homicide and physical assaults occurred even in moderately intoxicated offenders.[74]

Whereas static risk factors are primarily useful as predictors and stable dynamic factors are primarily useful in planning interventions, acute dynamic risk factors are most helpful in identifying effective forms of prevention. In other words, the best way to deal with access and stress is to prevent them from occurring in the first place.

A Word about Choice

Situational factors, as represented by increased availability of drugs, increased opportunities for crime, and the presence of drug- and crime-promoting stress, highlight the importance of choice and decision making in explaining aspects of the drug–crime nexus. This contrasts sharply with the positivistic or deterministic leanings of much of the research being conducted on drugs and crime. The classical or decision-making approach to drug use and crime was addressed in the second half of this chapter, as part of a discussion on acute dynamic or situational risk factors. The criminal justice system, the topic of discussion in the next chapter, is more closely aligned with classicism and the notion of an offender's ability to choose.

Summary and Conclusions

- Static risk factors like age, gender, race, and behavioral history are all effective predictors of drug use, crime, and drug-related crime. They may also interact with one another and with various biological, psychological, and sociological variables to moderate drug–crime relationships.
- Stable dynamic risk factors can serve an important role in establishing goals for intervention.
- Acute dynamic risk or situational factors are the least studied of the three risk categories but no less important. Two general classes of acute dynamic risk factors were examined in this chapter: access and stress. The primary function of acute dynamic risk factors is to identify effective preventive measures. Situational factors also highlight the salience of choice and decision making in drug use, crime, and drug–crime relationships.

Key Terms

Access   Degree to which drugs are available and criminal opportunities are present in the current situation.

Access Control   Situational crime control strategy in which control is exerted over who can access a particular resource.

Acquisitive Crimes   Offenses committed out of a desire to acquire goods or money; also known as property crimes.

Acute Dynamic Risk   Alterable risk factors marked by rapid and sudden change.

Age-Crime Curve   Well-documented relationship between age and crime in which crime peaks during midadolescence and then falls off sharply in late adolescence or early adulthood.

Ambient Temperature   The overall temperature in a person's immediate environment.

Availability-Proneness Model   Theory of drug use that holds that drug use/abuse is a function of the availability of drugs in one's environment and one's proneness or propensity to use drugs.

Big Four   The four risk factors that are generally considered to be the best predictors of future crime and recidivism; the list includes antisocial history, antisocial cognition, antisocial personality processes, and antisocial companions.

Central Eight   The eight risk factors that are generally considered the top predictors of future crime and recidivism; includes the Big Four and four additional factors: family/marital status, lack of educational/occupational achievement, lack of prosocial leisure activities, and substance abuse.

Crime Continuity   Based on the fact that crime is concentrated in people with a prior history of criminality and so those who have committed crime in the past are the ones most likely to commit crime in the future.

Criminal Opportunity   Circumstances favorable to the commission of a criminal act.

Differential Opportunity Theory   Theory of criminology in which people are said to have differential degrees of opportunity for legitimate and illegitimate activity that then influences their probability of committing a crime.

Dispositional   Pertaining to stable and internal characteristics of the individual; opposite of situational.

Drug Availability   Circumstances favorable to the use of a particular drug.

Dynamic Risk   Cognitive, developmental, or changeable variables like antisocial peers or intoxication that are capable of predicting future behavior and are useful in identifying goals for intervention and assessing change.

Formal Surveillance   Situational crime control strategy that produces a deterrent effect through the use of specialized security devices and personnel.

Gender   Social-cultural construction of a person's biological sex.

General Strain Theory   Theory of criminology that holds to the belief that a subjective state of strain encourages future crime through three conditions capable of creating stress: (1) failure to achieve positively valued goals, (2) loss of positive stimuli, and (3) introduction of negative stimuli.

National Survey of Drug Use and Health (NSDUH)   National- and state-level data centered on the use of tobacco, alcohol, and illicit drugs, as well as mental health, in the United States.

Natural Surveillance   Situational crime control strategy that produces a deterrent effect by increasing the perception that a potential offender can be seen.

Polysubstance Abuse   Pattern of abuse involving multiple substances.

Property Identification   Situational crime control strategy that deters crime by marking items.

Race   Socially constructed classification variable that uses certain genetically based characteristics, such as skin color, facial form, and eye shape, to classify individuals into broad categories.

Routine Activities Theory   Theory of criminology in which crime opportunities are said to involve the convergence in time and place of three elements: (1) a motivated offender, (2) a suitable target or victim, and (3) the absence of capable guardians against crime.

Sex   Biological properties that give rise to primary and secondary physical characteristics used to classify an individual as male or female (compare with gender).

Situational   Relating to one's current environmental situation; opposite of dispositional.

Social Drift Theory   Theory of criminology in which juveniles drift into and out of delinquency in response to various situational factors.

Stable Dynamic Risk   Alterable risk factors marked by slow and gradual change.

Static Risk   Historical or unchangeable variables like age and drug/criminal history that are helpful in predicting future behavior.

Stress   A mentally or emotionally unpleasant state created by changes in the internal or external environment; if not properly managed, stress can lead to drug use, crime, and a variety of adverse mental and physical conditions.

Target Hardening   Situational crime control strategy in which physical barriers are erected to prevent or limit crime.

Target Removal   Situational crime control strategy in which an offender's opportunities for crime are reduced or eliminated by removing a potential target or victim from the environment.

Critical Thinking

1. Why are age and criminal history the two best predictors of recidivism? What are the best predictors of drug relapse?
2. What person and situational factors can transform a conflict situation into a homicide or serious assault?
3. How can adolescent alcohol abuse and alcohol-related problems be reduced by restricting adolescents' access to alcohol?

Notes

1. Hanson, R. K., Harris, A. J. R., Scott, T. L., & Helmus, L. (2007). *Assessing the risk of sexual offenders on community supervision: The dynamic supervision project.* Ottawa: Public Safety Canada.
2. Heilbrun, K. (2009). *Evaluation for risk of violence in adults.* New York: Oxford University Press.
3. Spencer-Smith, M., & Anderson, V. (2009). Healthy and abnormal development of the prefrontal cortex. *Developmental Neurorehabilitation, 12,* 279–297.
4. Vaughn, M. G., Shook, J. J., & McMillen, J. C. (2008). Aging out of foster care and legal involvement: Toward a typology of risk. *Social Service Review, 82,* 419–446.
5. Substance Abuse and Mental Health Services Administration. (2011). *Results from the 2010 National Survey on Drug Use and Health: Summary of National Findings.* NSDUH Series H-41, HHS Publication No. (SMA) 11-4658. Rockville, MD: Substance Abuse and Mental Health Services Administration.
6. Hirschi, T., & Gottfredson, M. (1983). Age and the explanation of crime. *American Journal of Sociology, 89,* 522–584.
7. Steffensmeier, D., Allan, E., Harer, M., & Streifel, C. (1989). Age and the distribution of crime. *American Journal of Sociology, 94,* 803–831.
8. Mumola, C. J., & Karberg, J. C. (2006). Drug use and dependence, state and federal prisoners, 2004. *Bureau of Justice Statistics Special Report* (NCJ 213530). Washington, DC: U.S. Department of Justice.
9. Sánchez-Martín, J. R., Azurmendi, A., Pascual-Sagastizabal, E., Cardas, J., Braza, F., Braza, P., et al. (2011). Androgen levels and anger and impulsivity measures as predictors of physical, verbal and indirect aggression in boys and girls. *Psychoneuroendocrinology, 36,* 750–760.
10. Côté, S. M. (2007). Sex differences in physical and indirect aggression: A developmental perspective. *European Journal on Criminal Policy & Research, 13,* 183–200.
11. Greenfield, S. F., Back, S. E., Lawson, K., & Brady, K. T. (2010). Substance abuse in women. *Psychiatric Clinics of North America, 33,* 339–355.
12. Compton, W. M., Thomas, Y. E., Stinson, F. S., & Grant, B. F. (2007). Prevalence, correlates, disabilities, and comorbidities of DSM-IV drug abuse and dependence in the United States. *Archives of General Psychiatry, 64,* 566–576.
13. Substance Abuse and Mental Health Services Administration (2011).
14. Steffensmeier, D., & Allan, E. (1996). Gender and crime: Toward a gendered theory of female offending. *Annual Review of Sociology, 22,* 459–487.
15. Heimer, K. (2000). Changes in the gender gap in crime and women's economic marginalization. In G. La Free (Ed.), *The nature of crime: Continuity and change; Criminal Justice 2000* (Vol. 1, pp. 427–483). Washington, DC: National Institute of Justice.
16. Lauritsen, J. L., Heimer, K., & Lynch, J. P. (2010). Trends in the gender gap in violent offending: New evidence from the National Crime Victimization Survey. *Criminology, 47,* 361–399.
17. Karberg, J. C., & James, D. J. (2005). Substance dependence, abuse, and treatment of jail inmates, 2002. *Bureau of Justice Statistics Special Report* (NCJ 209588). Washington, DC: U.S. Department of Justice.
18. Mumola & Karberg (2006).
19. Palmer, E. J., Jinks, M., & Hatcher, R. M. (2010). Substance use, mental health, and relationships: A comparison of male and female offenders serving community sentences. *International Journal of Law and Psychiatry, 33,* 89–93.
20. Ore, T. (2008). *The social construction of difference and inequality: Race, class, gender and sexuality* (4th ed.). New York: McGraw-Hill.
21. Substance Abuse and Mental Health Services Administration (2011).
22. Bonczar, T. P. (2003). Prevalence of imprisonment in the U.S. population, 1974–2001. *Bureau of Justice Statistics Special Report* (NCJ 197976). Washington, DC: U.S. Department of Justice.
23. Blumstein, A. (1982). On the racial disproportionality of United States prison populations. *Journal of Law and Criminology, 73,* 1259–1281.
24. Crutchfield, R. D., Bridges, G. S., & Pritchford, S. R. (1994). Analytical and aggregation biases in analyses of imprisonment: Reconciling discrepancies in studies of racial disparity. *Journal of Research in Crime and Delinquency, 31,* 166–182.

25. Sorensen, J., Hope, R., & Stemen, D. (2003). Racial disproportionality in state prison admissions: Can regional variation be explained by differential arrest rates? *Journal of Criminal Justice, 31*, 73–84.

26. Mumola & Karberg (2006).

27. Walters, G. D. (2011). Black-white differences in positive outcome expectancies for crime: A study of male federal prison inmates. *Journal of Criminal Justice, 39*, 192–197.

28. Hubbard, D. J. (2006). Should we be targeting self-esteem in treatment for offenders: Do gender and race matter in whether self-esteem matters? *Journal of Offender Rehabilitation, 44*, 39–57.

29. Newcomb, M. D., & Felix-Ortiz, M. (1992). Multiple protective and risk factors for drug use and abuse: Cross-sectional and prospective findings. *Journal of Personality and Social Psychology, 63*, 280–296.

30. Lewinsohn, P. M., Rohde, P., & Brown, R. A. (1999). Level of current and past adolescent cigarette smoking as predictors of future substance abuse disorders in adulthood. *Addiction 94*, 913–921.

31. Farrington, D. P. (1987). Predicting individual crime rates. In *Crime and Justice. Vol. 9: Prediction and Classification: Criminal Justice Decision-Making* (pp. 53–101). Chicago: University of Chicago Press.

32. Cottle, C. C., Lee, R. J., & Heilbrun, K. (2001). The prediction of criminal recidivism in juveniles: A meta-analysis. *Criminal Justice and Behavior, 28*, 367–394.

33. Gendreau, P., Little, T., & Goggin, C. (1996). A meta-analysis of the predictors of adult offender recidivism: What works! *Criminology, 34*, 575–608.

34. Walters, G. D. (in press). Cognitive mediation of crime continuity: A causal mediation analysis of the past crime-future crime relationship. *Crime and Delinquency*.

35. Walters, G. D. (in press). Short-term goals and physically hedonistic values as mediators of the past crime-future crime relationship. *Legal and Criminological Psychology*.

36. Gresnigt, J., Breteler, M., Schippers, G., & van den Hurk, A. (2000). Predicting violent crime among drug-using inmates: The Addiction Severity Index as a prediction instrument. *Legal and Criminological Psychology, 5*, 83–95.

37. Wilson, H. W., & Widom, C. S. (2010). Predictors of drug-use patterns in maltreated children and matched controls followed up into middle adulthood. *Journal of Studies on Alcohol and Drugs, 71*, 801–809.

38. Gendreau, P., Goggin, C., & Law, M. A. (1997). Predicting prison misconducts. *Criminal Justice and Behavior, 24*, 414–431.

39. Gendreau et al. (1996).

40. Hawkins, J. D., Catalano, R. E., & Miller, J. Y. (1992). Risk and protective factors for alcohol and other drug problems in adolescence and early adulthood: Implications for substance abuse prevention. *Psychological Bulletin, 112*, 64–105.

41. Andrews, D. A., Bonta, J., & Wormith, J. S. (2006). The recent past and near future of risk and/or need assessment. *Crime and Delinquency, 52*, 7–27.

42. Coben, J. H., Davis, S. M., Furbee, P. M., Sikora, R. D., Tillotson, R. D., & Bossare, R. M. (2010). Hospitalizations for poisoning by prescription opioids, sedatives, and tranquilizers, *American Journal of Preventive Medicine, 38*, 517–524.

43. Smart, R. G. (1980). An availability-proneness theory of illicit drug abuse. *NIDA Research Monograph, 30*, 46–49.

44. Degenhardt, L., Conroy, E., Gilmour, S., & Collins, L. (2005). The effect of a reduction in heroin supply in Australia upon drug distribution and acquisitive crime. *British Journal of Criminology, 45*, 2–24.

45. Office of Justice Programs. (2000). *Promising strategies to reduce substance abuse*. Washington, DC: U.S. Department of Justice.

46. Wagenaar, A. C., Salois, M. J., & Komro, K. A. (2009). Effects of beverage alcohol price and tax levels on drinking: A meta-analysis of 1003 estimates from 112 studies. *Addiction, 104*, 179–190.

47. Cook, P. J. (2008, Spring). Paying the tab: The costs and benefits of alcohol control (book review). *Prevention Review*, pp. 10–11.

48. Gottfredson, M. R., & Hirschi, T. (1990). *A general theory of crime*. Stanford, CA; Stanford University Press.

49. Simon, R. (1975). *The contemporary woman and crime*. Washington, DC: National Institute of Mental Health.

50. Cloward, R., & Ohlin, L. (1960). *Delinquency and opportunity.* New York: Free Press.

51. Cohen, L. E., & Felson, M. (1979). Social change and crime rate trends: A routine activity approach. *American Sociological Review, 44,* 588–608.

52. Pratt, T. C., & Cullen, F. T. (2005). Assessing macro-level predictors and theories of crime: A meta-analysis. *Crime and Justice, 32,* 373–450.

53. Archer, D., & Gartner, R. (1984). *Violence and crime in cross-national perspective.* New Haven, CT: Yale University Press.

54. Walsh, D. P. (1978). *Shoplifting: Controlling a major crime.* London: Macmillan.

55. Conklin, J. E. (2009). *Criminology* (10th ed.). Boston: Allyn & Bacon.

56. Clarke, R.V., & Homel, R. (1997). A revised classification of situational crime prevention techniques. In: S.P. Lab (Ed.), *Crime prevention at a crossroads* (pp. 21–35). Cincinnati, OH: Anderson Publishing.

57. Myrstol, B. A. (2009, Summer). Drug use trajectories of Anchorage male arrestees: 2002–2003. *Alaska Justice Forum, 26*(2), 1, 7–12.

58. Volkow, N. D. (2006, August 19). Treat the addict, cut the crime rate [editorial]. *Washington Post,* A17.

59. Justice Policy Institute. (2008, January). *Substance abuse treatment and public safety.* Washington, DC: Author.

60. Nemtsov, A. V. (1998). Alcohol-related harm and alcohol consumption in Moscow before, during, and after a major alcohol campaign. *Addiction, 93,* 1501–1510.

61. Agnew, R. (1992). Foundations for a general strain theory of crime and delinquency. *Criminology, 30,* 47–87.

62. Logrip, M. L., Zorrilla, E. P., & Koob, G. F. (2012). Stress modulation of drug self-administration: Implications for addiction comorbidity with post-traumatic stress disorder. *Neuropharmacology, 62,* 552–564.

63. DiMaggio, C., Galea, S., & Li, G. (2009). Substance use and misuse in the aftermath of terrorism: A Bayesian meta-analysis. *Addiction, 104,* 894–904.

64. Stein, J. A., Leslie, M. B., & Nyamathi, A. (2002). Relative contributions of parent substance use and childhood maltreatment to chronic homelessness, depression, and substance abuse problems among homeless women: Mediating roles of self-esteem and abuse in adulthood. *Child Abuse and Neglect, 26,* 1011–1027.

65. Halkitis, P. N., Parsons, J. T., & Wilton, L. (2003). An exploratory study of contextual and situational factors related to methamphetamine use among gay and bisexual men in New York City. *Journal of Drug Issues, 33,* 413–432.

66. Schmitz, J. M., Oswald, L. M., Damin, P., & Mattis, P. (1995). Situational analysis of coping in substance-abusing patients. *Journal of Substance Abuse, 7,* 189–204.

67. Felson, R. B., & Steadman, H. J. (1983). Situational factors in disputes leading to criminal violence. *Criminology, 21,* 59–74.

68. Felson, R. B., Ribner, S. A., & Siegel, M. S. (1984). Age and the effect of third parties during criminal violence. *Sociology and Social Research, 68,* 452–462.

69. Anderson, C. A., & Anderson, D. C. (1984). Ambient temperature and violent crime: Tests of the linear and curvilinear hypotheses. *Journal of Personality and Social Psychology, 46,* 91–97.

70. Cotton, J. L. (1986). Ambient temperature and violent crime. *Journal of Applied Social Psychology, 16,* 786–801.

71. Anderson, C. A. (1987). Temperament and aggression: Effects on quarterly, yearly, and city rates of violent and nonviolent crime. *Journal of Personality and Social Psychology, 52,* 1161–1173.

72. Bennett, T. (1990). Editorial: Links between drug misuse and crime. *British Journal of Addiction, 85,* 833–835.

73. Matza, D. (1964). *Delinquency and drift.* New York: Wiley.

74. Felson, R. B., & Staff, J. (2010). The effects of alcohol intoxication on violent versus other offending. *Criminal Justice and Behavior, 37,* 1343–1360.

PRACTICE

Whereas Part II (Research) of this book (with the notable exception of the second half of Chapter 8) relied heavily on deterministic models of drug use and crime, Part III (Practice) is grounded in choice and free will. Hence, in moving from Part II to Part III we are moving from the deterministic positivism of Cesare Lombroso to the **classical** criminology of Cesare Beccaria.

DRUGS AND THE CRIMINAL JUSTICE SYSTEM

Cesare Lombroso proposed that criminals were evolutionary throwbacks or **atavisms** to an earlier stage of human development. These "born criminals," as Lombroso called them, could be identified by their large protruding ears, sloping foreheads, and jutting jaws. Although this theory is no longer taken seriously, Lombroso is often credited with being the father of **positivism** and the originator of the scientific study of crime. Cesare Beccaria was a reformer who believed that crime could be deterred with a program of punishment that was swift, certain, and severe. In addition, he believed that people possessed free will and that they were responsive to the anticipated consequences of their behavior. With its emphasis on choice, free will, and deterrence, Beccaria's theory is the foundation of modern criminal justice systems.

The criminal justice system is composed of three principal components: law enforcement, the courts, and corrections. Each component gives rise to a different objective for this chapter:

- Understand the manner in which law enforcement detects, gathers intelligence on, and apprehends drug-involved offenders.
- Appreciate how the court system processes and adjudicates drug-involved offenders.
- Discover the means by which the correctional system classifies, manages, and attempts to reintegrate drug-involved offenders.

Drugs and Law Enforcement

When it comes to dealing with drug-involved offenders, the police serve three vital functions, each of which are supported by a number of subfunctions. The three primary functions are:

- Surveillance
- Intelligence
- Apprehension

Surveillance

Patrolling

Increased police presence can have a short-term deterrent effect on street-level drug dealing and public drug use, but it should not be considered a long-term solution to either drug dealing or use. This is because dealers and users will move to another area or temporarily stop selling or using drugs but then start up again once the police leave. There is also concern on the part of some policy-makers and community leaders that police patrols target poor and minority neighborhoods, although this is where much of the overt drug dealing occurs.[1] Eliminating or reducing police patrols can be even more damaging to the community than targeting poorer neighborhoods, in that situational factors, left alone, can actually magnify the problem. In an Australian study, for instance, Ross Homel and colleagues determined that lack of police **surveillance** in terms of oversight and **patrolling** resulted in increased levels of bar-related violence.[2]

Police patrols provide only a short-term solution to the problem of drug dealing.

Video Surveillance

Video surveillance has helped reduce theft and shoplifting in stores and plays an indispensible role in store security. It can also be used to reduce drug dealing, but the strategy one adopts is vital to the success of these operations. Charest, Tremblay, Boivin, and D'Elia compared two different strategies of video surveillance in a study conducted in Montreal, Canada. The first strategy used video surveillance as a proactive and integral element of a problem-solving initiative targeting an area where drugs were dealt openly. The second and more common strategy was essentially a passive/reactive approach in which cameras were dispersed along a street with an active bar scene and a large number of clubs. The results indicated that video surveillance, when administered in a proactive fashion (identifying problems and looking for solutions to the problems using an integrated law enforcement approach), was significantly more effective in reducing both drug dealing and violent crime than the passive-reactive approach (see **Figure 9-1**).[3]

Undercover Operations

Darin Logue, a former undercover officer, has discussed the pros and cons of undercover drug operations. The pros include:

- Undercover work can be personally rewarding.
- Undercover work can be effective in identifying the higher echelons of drug organizations.
- Undercover work can supplement other law enforcement efforts when conducted as part of a team approach.

Figure 9-1
Percentage reduction in offending, averaged across two different sites, after surveillance cameras installed using proactive and reactive strategies.

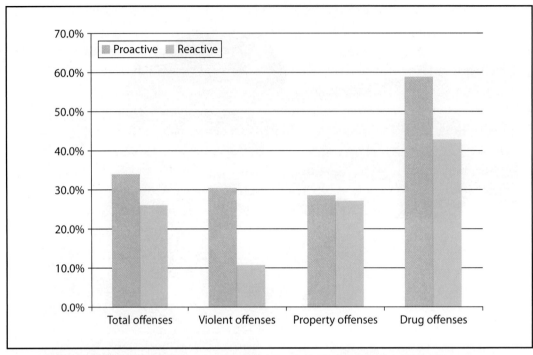

Data From: Charest, M., Tremblay, P., Boivin, R., & D'Elia, M. (2010). Police video surveillance in public places: Learning technologies. *Canadian Journal of Criminology and Criminal Justice, 52*, 449–470.

There are also cons to undercover work, according to Logue:[4]

- Undercover work can be dangerous.
- Undercover work can be stressful and difficult for one's personal and family life.
- Undercover work can be expensive because it requires a great deal of training, funds, and a high degree of professionalism.
- **Undercover operations** often take a long time to develop because drug dealers generally do not trust anyone they do not already know.

Confidential Informants

Confidential informants (CIs) are individuals who provide "inside information" to law enforcement. The Drug Enforcement Administration divides CIs into two categories: Class I or criminal informants and Class II or citizen informants. The majority of CIs who work with the police on drug cases come from Class I.[5] Law enforcement agencies typically prefer CIs over undercover operatives, particularly when investigating drug rings. There are several reasons for this. First, unlike undercover agents, CIs do not need to abide by the law. Some CIs are so heavily ensconced in the criminal lifestyle, in fact, that it causes problems for their law enforcement handlers. In several cases, handlers have actually ended up in jail themselves for negligent oversight of their CIs. Second, most CIs already have an "in" with the drug organization that law enforcement is trying to infiltrate. As such, information is more immediately forthcoming with CIs. Third, using CIs is cheaper than running a full undercover operation. In 1989, the federal government paid $63 million to CIs from public funds and seized assets and local authorities paid another $60 million, yet this is still cheaper than the cost of funding dozens of undercover operations.[6]

Given the inherent dangers of the drug trade and fact that CIs may be risking their lives, many law enforcement officials feel justified in providing CIs with more than just remuneration. Some receive leniency in criminal court and others receive protection from retaliation. There are nonetheless concerns about corruption and misuse of funds because CIs have been known to **entrap** defendants in order to make a case and several well-known professional CIs have earned over $100,000 a year in cash and drugs. Moreover, because they are typically involved in regular drug use, the reliability of their testimony is open to question.[7]

There are several reasons why people become CIs, but the most common reason, according to the results of a study by J. Mitchell Miller, is legal duress in which an individual who has been arrested for a crime hopes that by cooperating with the authorities he or she will receive leniency from the court. Then, there are the mercenary informants, who turn state's evidence for money and drugs, the vengeful informants, who are attempting to get even with someone by tying them to an illegal activity, and the police buffs, who want to be accepted as cops. The most valuable CIs, according to Miller, are those in the legal duress and mercenary categories.[8]

Wiretaps and Recording Devices

Wiretapping phones plays less of a role than undercover agents or CIs in law enforcement drug operations. In 2010, there were only 3,194 criminal wiretaps authorized, the majority of which were for mobile phones in drug cases. The average wiretap lasted 45 days and information gathered from these taps led to 4,711 **arrests** and 800 convictions.[9] Undercover agents and CIs wear recording devices to tape conversations. These tapes are then used to prosecute drug cases. Agents do not ordinarily wear a wire, however, when making what is known as a controlled buy. A **controlled buy** is where the officer buys a quantity of drug from a dealer. First, however, the officer is searched to make sure he or she has no contraband on his/her person. Next, the officer is given prerecorded funds and transported to a location where drug dealing is known to occur. Upon arriving at the location, the officer purchases drugs from the dealer (without enticing or entrapping the dealer) and is searched again. Then the drugs he or she has bought are field tested to make sure they are actually an illegal substance. It should be pointed out that the officer making the controlled buy is under constant surveillance by other law enforcement officers from the time he or she leaves the station until the time the drugs are field tested.[10]

Drug-Detecting Canines

A dog's sense of smell is 1,000 times stronger than a human's. Law enforcement accordingly uses canines to detect illegal drugs, among other things. Some lawyers maintain that drug-detecting canines violate the Fourth Amendment right against unreasonable search and seizure, but in a 6-2 decision, the U.S. Supreme Court ruled that police do not need to have reasonable suspicion that a crime has been committed to use drug-detecting canines because the detection is specific to contraband:

> We have held that any interest in possessing contraband cannot be deemed "legitimate," and thus, governmental conduct that *only* reveals the possession of contraband "compromises no

A well-trained drug-sniffing canine can detect drug residuals several hours after a drug has been removed from a car or locker, giving rise to concerns about false positive results.

legitimate privacy interest"…In *United States v. Place* (1983), we treated a canine sniff by a well-trained narcotics-detection dog as "*sui generis*" because it "discloses only the presence or absence of narcotics, a contraband item (see also *Indianapolis v. Edmond* (2000)…This conclusion is entirely consistent with our recent decision that the use of a thermal-imaging device to detect the growth of marijuana in a home constituted an unlawful search (*Kyllo v. United States*, 2001). Critical to that decision was the fact that the device was capable of detecting lawful activity—in that case, intimate details in a home, such as "at what hour each night the lady of the house takes her daily sauna and bath."[11]

Another concern with drug-detecting canines is a high false positive rate (i.e., the dog senses drugs that cannot be found). Those who advocate for the use of drug-detecting canines contend that a dog's sense of smell is so sensitive that it can detect drug residuals hours or even days after a drug has been removed from an area. Detractors argue that drug-detecting canines produce too many false positives to be effective. Most experts agree, however, that well-trained dogs and handlers make significantly fewer errors than poorly trained dogs and handlers (see News Spot 9-1). In many jurisdictions a positive signal from a drug-detecting canine is considered probable cause for officers to search an automobile, locker, residence, or person.

Sobriety checkpoints are effective in reducing alcohol-related crashed but perhaps not as effective as saturation patrols.

NEWS SPOT 9-1

Title: Tribune Analysis: Drug-Sniffing Dogs In Traffic Stops Often Wrong
Source: *Chicago Tribune*
Authors: Dan Hinkel and Joe Mahr
Date: January 6, 2011

Drug-sniffing dogs can give police probable cause to root through cars by the roadside, but state data show the dogs have been wrong more often than they have been right about whether vehicles contain drugs or paraphernalia.

The dogs are trained to dig or sit when they smell drugs, which triggers automobile searches. But a Tribune analysis of three years of data for suburban departments found that only 44 percent of those alerts by the dogs led to the discovery of drugs or paraphernalia.

For Hispanic drivers, the success rate was just 27 percent.

Dog-handling officers and trainers argue the canine teams' accuracy shouldn't be measured in the number of alerts that turn up drugs. They said the scent of drugs or paraphernalia can linger in a car after drugs are used or sold, and the dogs' noses are so sensitive they can pick up residue from drugs that can no longer be found in a car.

But even advocates for the use of drug-sniffing dogs agree with experts who say many dog-and-officer teams are poorly trained and prone to false alerts that lead to unjustified searches. Leading a dog around a car too many times or spending too long examining a vehicle, for example, can cause a dog to give a signal for drugs where there are none, experts said.

"If you don't train, you can't be confident in your dog," said Alex Rothacker, a trainer who works with dozens of local drug-sniffing dogs. "A lot of dogs don't train. A lot of dogs aren't good."

The dog teams are not held to any statutory standard of performance in Illinois or most other states, experts and dog handlers said, though private groups offer certification for the canines.

Civil rights advocates and Latino activists say the findings support complaints that police unfairly target Hispanic drivers for invasive and embarrassing roadside vehicle searches.

"We know that there is a level of racial profiling going on, and this is just another indicator of that," said Virginia Martinez, a Chicago-based staff attorney for the Mexican American Legal Defense and Educational Fund.

Questions to Ponder

1. **How accurate do drug-detecting dogs need to be to justify their use at roadside stops?**
2. **To what would you attribute the majority of "false positive" responses given by drug-detecting dogs: poor training, the sensitivity of a dog to scent even when the drug has been removed, or some other factor?**
3. **Do you believe that racial profiling could be a problem with respect to drug-detecting dogs, and if so, how?**

Sobriety Checkpoints

According to the **National Highway Traffic Safety Administration**, alcohol-impaired driving was responsible for 31% of all traffic deaths in 2010: this translates into one fatality every 51 minutes.[12] When police suspect a driver of being under the influence of alcohol or other drugs the typical procedure is to ask the person to submit to a **breathalyzer** test. The relative risk of an accident rises significantly once an individual produces a **blood-alcohol concentration (BAC)** of .08 or higher (see **Figure 9-2**).[13] If an individual passes the breathalyzer test but still exhibits signs of intoxication, the officer can escort the suspected impaired driver to a setting where blood/urine/hair specimen tests for drugs can be administered. In some jurisdictions, officers carry equipment that can be used to field test for illegal drugs. Based on the results of a meta-analysis of 23 different studies, researchers at the Centers for Disease Control (CDC) concluded that **sobriety checkpoints** reduced fatal crashes by 20%.[14] An FBI study, on the other hand, noted that **saturation patrols**, where police actively search for drivers showing behavioral signs of impairment, may be even more effective than sobriety checkpoints.[15]

Intelligence

Gathering intelligence on drug activities and organizations is a second major function of law enforcement. The intelligence function involves the use of surveillance, technology, undercover operations, informants, and coordination between enforcement and nonenforcement agencies to prevent, reduce, and manage drug-related crime. Jerry Ratcliffe has written extensively on intelligence as applied to drug networks. In his writings, Ratcliffe describes three levels of criminal intelligence helpful in combating drug dealing at the local, state, national, and international levels: tactical, operational, and strategic.[16]

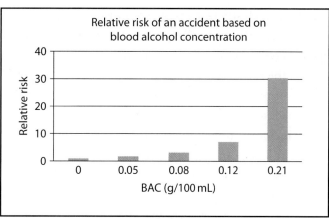

Figure 9-2
Relative risk of being involved in an auto accident as a function of blood alcohol concentration (BAC) level.

Data From: Kloeden, C. N., McLean, A. J., Moore, V. M., & Ponte, G. (1997). *Traveling speed and the risk of crash involvement: Vol 1. Findings.* Canberra, Australia: NHMRC Road Accident Research Unit, University of Adelaide.

Tactical Intelligence

Tactical intelligence assumes a microlevel focus and is designed to support frontline law enforcement officers taking case-specific action against local criminals. This is the most common form of intelligence used by law enforcement agencies working with narcotics and drug enforcement. Because it is an approach with which most law enforcement officers are familiar it is easy to explain to local law enforcement and can be extremely helpful in targeting and managing the most recidivistic and problematic individual offenders. An exclusive tactical approach, without input and support from operational and strategic sources of intelligence, however, provides only a short-term solution to the drug problem.[17]

Operational Intelligence

Operational intelligence provides area commanders and regional managers with information vital in reducing drug distribution across a broader geographical area than can be achieved with tactical intelligence. This mesolevel approach to drug enforcement consequently focuses on an entire city or state rather than restricting itself to the local community. The operational approach can be useful in targeting criminal organizations functioning at the state and regional levels and can be particularly helpful in prioritizing operations. Operational intelligence can also be helpful to area commanders, regional managers, and administrative policy-makers who must decide how to allocate limited resources to programs designed to discourage drug use and disrupt drug distribution networks in a city or state.[18]

Strategic Intelligence

Strategic intelligence takes a macrolevel approach to the drug problem by focusing on longstanding criminal patterns and taking note of how the criminal environment functions. Each of the three levels of intelligence gathering is successively more future oriented and proactive, with strategic intelligence being the most future-oriented and proactive approach of the three. Effective collaboration between law enforcement and nonlaw enforcement agencies (community planners, medical and mental health agencies, courts, corrections) is vital to the success of strategic intelligence initiatives. Strategic intelligence provides valuable information to top-level policy-makers interested in developing solutions to crime in the broadest sense, keeping in mind that drug trafficking organizations operate on multiple levels, including the international level.[19]

Stuart Kirby, Amanda Quinn, and Scott Keay compared 100 individuals caught dealing Class A drugs in Great Britain using an intelligence-led proactive approach with a group of 100 individuals caught dealing Class A drugs using a traditional reactive approach. Offenders arrested through the intelligence-led approach were older, more often unemployed, lived closer to their drug market, and had a higher incidence of prior offending than offenders arrested through the traditional reactive approach. Kirby and colleagues concluded that the intelligence-led approach was more effective than the reactive approach in identifying prolific and problematic drug dealers.[20] The proactive approach provides information that may be useful in making **selective incapacitation** (policy of targeting the most prolific dealers for incarceration) and rehabilitation (targeting the highest risk offenders for intervention) decisions.

Apprehension

Two procedures commonly used to apprehend drug-involved offenders, are arrest and booking.

Arresting the Drug-Involved Offender

The FBI's 2011 Uniform Crime Reports (UCR) indicate that 1,638,846 arrests were made for drugs in 2010. This translates into one arrest for drug charges every 19 seconds. Nearly half of all arrests for drugs in 2010 (45.8%) were for simple possession of marijuana (see **Figure 9-3**). The rate of drug arrests is up only slightly from the 1,633,582 arrests made in 2009, but this needs to be interpreted in light of the significant drop in violent and property crime that has occurred over the last decade. Consequently, whereas the number of drug arrests has stabilized at historically high levels, arrests for other offenses have significantly declined. Between 2001 and 2010, for instance, drug arrests went up 8.3% compared to a 30% reduction in arrests for property crime and a 35% reduction in arrests for violent crime.[21]

Regardless of whether the offense involves a legal substance like alcohol (driving while intoxicated or DWI) or an illegal substance like marijuana or heroin (drug possession, drug distribution), the standard procedure is to arrest the individual and bring him or her to the police station. However, in a growing number of states a small amount of marijuana is classified as a misdemeanor and handled with a summons, citation, or fine. There are also states where marijuana has been legalized for medical treatment of nausea, vomiting, poor appetite, weight loss, neurogenic pain, debilitating muscle spasms, and glaucoma.[22] States where marijuana has been decriminalized for personal use, legalized for medical treatment, or both are identified in **Figure 9-4**.

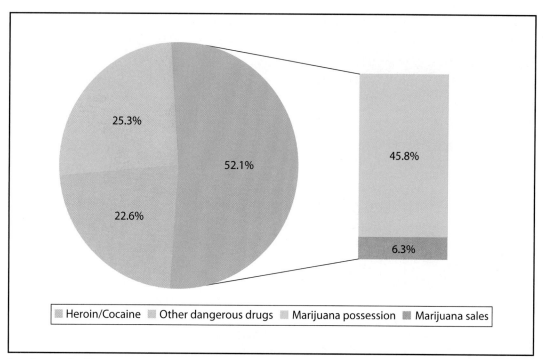

Figure 9-3
Breakdown of arrests for drugs, 2010.

Legend: Heroin/Cocaine | Other dangerous drugs | Marijuana possession | Marijuana sales

Data From: Federal Bureau of Investigation. (2011). *Uniform crime reports, 2010.* Washington, DC: Author.

An individual who is visibly intoxicated or high on drugs presents several potential problems to an officer attempting to make an arrest. The most common problems include:[23]

- emotional lability and mental confusion
- elevated risk of violence and combativeness
- increased probability of suicide
- withdrawal symptoms that may occur in habitual offenders, which in the case of a drug like alcohol or barbiturates, could be fatal

For one or more of these reasons, a newly arrested offender may require immediate medical or mental health attention or perhaps medically supervised detoxification.

Booking the Drug-Involved Offender

Once the escorting officer arrives at the station with the arrestee the next step is for the officer to book and process the arrestee. **Booking** means fingerprinting and photographing the arrestee, taking and inventorying any money or property the arrestee may have in his or her possession, and then either placing the individual in a jail cell or releasing the individual to a family member or on his or her own recognizance. Before being placed in a jail cell the individual is showered and deloused, given jail clothing, and allowed to make one phone call (although some jurisdictions allow two phone calls). Whether the arrestee is released or placed in a jail cell, he or she is normally scheduled for a preliminary hearing in front of a judge or magistrate, where the judge or magistrate sets bail (in the event the individual is currently jailed) and asks for a preliminary plea.

In some jurisdictions, instead of arresting and booking the drug-involved offender, the police take the individual directly to drug treatment. This is commonly referred to as drug **diversion**. Drug diversion can occur at any point in the law enforcement sequence,

Figure 9-4
Legal status of
marijuana in the
50 U.S. states.

State with legal medical cannabis.
State with decriminalized cannabis possession laws.*
State with both medical and decriminalization laws.
State with legalized cannabis.

either before or after charges have been brought against the individual, and is designed
to reduce the negative labeling that frequently occurs with official processing through the
criminal justice system.[24] When drug diversion is initiated by law enforcement personnel
it is normally precharge and referred to as police drug diversion. An innovative program in
Seattle, Washington known as Law Enforcement Assisted Diversion (LEAD) is an example
of a precharge police drug diversion program (see News Spot 9-2).

NEWS SPOT 9-2

Title: Seattle Program Aims to Break the Habit of Incarceration
Source: *Seattle (WA) Times*
Author: Sara Jean Green
Date: October 13, 2011

Seven men were arrested for street-level drug crimes last month during a two-day buy-bust
operation by Seattle police in Belltown.

Two of them caught a huge break.

Instead of being locked up, they were offered the first spots in a new program borne out of
collective fatigue with the criminal-justice system's approach to managing the low-level drug
dealers, addicts and prostitutes who revolve through King County's jails and courthouses.

The two men are now being given the chance to break the cycle of arrest and incarceration
by signing on to a program aimed at changing their lives and, in a small way, the community. The idea is to help the drug-addicted kick their habits and give people who survive by
selling drugs a chance at legitimate employment and a future.

No one knows if it'll work, but the creation of Law Enforcement Assisted Diversion (LEAD) has made partners out of professional adversaries and brought shared hope to those dealing with the ramifications of the country's war on drugs.

Funded by private foundations, the $950,000-a-year, four-year pilot program offers hand-picked participants individualized alternatives to arrest, from inpatient drug treatment and educational opportunities to housing assistance and microloans for would-be business owners.

Belltown, Seattle's drug-plagued neighborhood just north of downtown, is the program's launchpad, to be followed later this year by Skyway, just south of Seattle in unincorporated King County....

"Most of these people will have been to jail many times. These are frequent fliers through the system, but no one has ever offered them help," King County Prosecutor Dan Satterberg said of the population LEAD hopes to reach.

Clearly, jail or prison stints did nothing to curb their involvement in the drug trade, he said, "because they're right back in an alley putting a needle in their arm."

An unscientific survey by West Precinct police officers found that 54 individuals most frequently contacted by police in Belltown had been collectively arrested 2,704 times—and the majority now live in shelters, assisted-living facilities or jail-alternative housing in the neighborhood. The count, which does not include out-of-state convictions, includes 266 felony arrests for crimes such as murder, rape, robbery and assault.

But the LEAD program won't be offered to everyone and is an option only for low-level offenders. Police officers on the street—who best know the neighborhood's dealers, users, and prostitutes—will be the ones to decide who gets a shot at immediate access to treatment and other services, such as rental assistance, job training, and mental-health programs.

"If this is going to work, we need the men and women who patrol the streets to believe in this option and use their best judgment to decide who should receive this chance," Satterberg said.

Sgt. Sean Whitcomb, a spokesman for the Seattle Police Department, said officers know that "locking people up for low-level drug offenses" is expensive and rarely results in rehabilitation.

"Officers are frustrated arresting the same people over and over again. We know it's not working," Whitcomb said.

Questions to Ponder

1. Do you think that police diversion of low-level dealers and drug users is a good idea? Why or why not?
2. List some of the agencies that need to be involved in a program of this magnitude?
3. How can the policy-makers who developed this program help ensure that the police officers who run the program support it and give it a chance of succeeding?

Drugs and the Court System

The court system, as indicated by **Figure 9-5**, can be quite complex.[25] Nevertheless, the role of the courts in the lives of drug-involved offenders can be boiled down to two functions, the second of which can be broken down further into two subfunctions. The first function of the courts with respect to drug-involved offenders is pretrial services. The second function is adjudication, which can be broken down further into disposition and sentencing.

Pretrial Services

The **pretrial services** officer gathers information that will be helpful to the judge or magistrate in making initial decisions about a case, such as setting bail. The pretrial services officer conducts an interview and gathers information about the defendant's criminal history, escape history, family and social history, residency status, mental health and substance abuse history, educational background, and employment status. The pretrial officer will also gather information on the charges but avoids asking questions pertaining to guilt or innocence. He or she will then submit a report to the judge or magistrate in charge of the case, who will then decide whether the defendant can be released from pretrial confinement. If so, it must be determined whether the individual can be released on a recognizance bond, cash-only bond, or property bond. If released on bond there will be certain conditions the individual must satisfy (e.g., avoid any drug use), which if violated could result in bond being revoked and the individual being returned to jail.[26]

John Clark and Alan Henry note that nearly 70% of all pretrial service agencies drug test their supervisees, whereas 50% conduct random breathalyzer tests for alcohol.[27] The success of these programs has been brought into serious question, however. Pretrial drug testing programs in Arizona, Florida, Maryland, and Wisconsin failed to increase compliance or reduce criminality in drug-using offenders on bail.[28–30] Pretrial release nevertheless plays a potentially important role in managing drug-involved offenders, if for no other reason than its ability to reduce jail overcrowding without appreciably jeopardizing public safety.[31]

Drug Diversion

Diversion of lower risk, first- or second-time, nonviolent offenders can occur at any point during the pretrial or adjudication stage of the criminal justice process. Judicial officers who divert drug users from the criminal justice system into a drug program are cognizant of research showing that drug treatment reduces both drug use and crime.[32] In addition, an intervention program conducted in the community is significantly more effective than a program administered in jail or prison.[33] Taken together, these findings indicate that a program of community-based intervention has the best chance of effectively reducing drug use and crime in drug-involved offenders. In a review of 20 nonrandomized studies, Evelyn Harvey and her colleagues concluded that drug diversion holds promise of reducing both drug use and crime.[34]

What is the sequence of events in the criminal justice system?

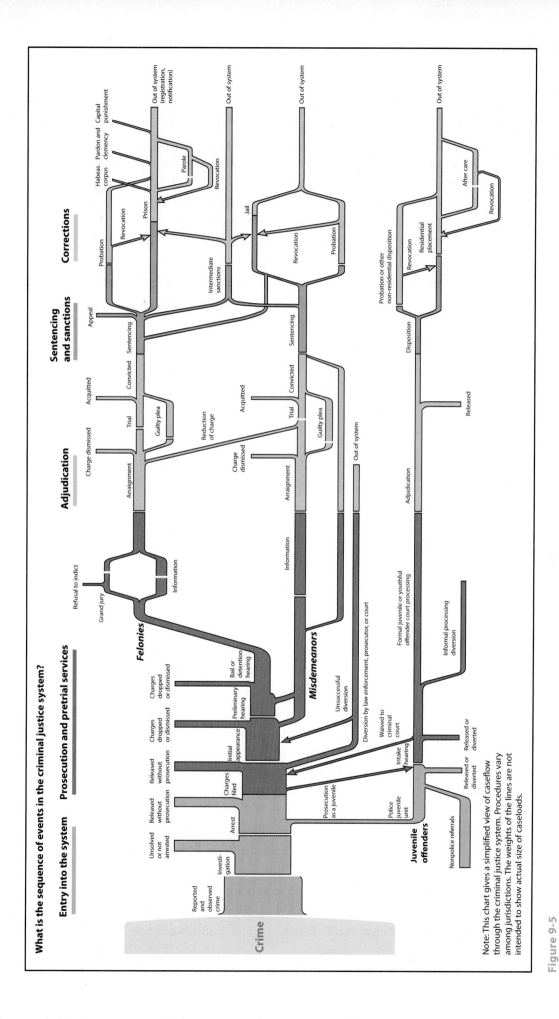

Note: This chart gives a simplified view of caseflow through the criminal justice system. Procedures vary among jurisdictions. The weights of the lines are not intended to show actual size of caseloads.

Figure 9-5

The criminal justice system.

Prepared by the Bureau of Justice Statistics in 1997 and adapted from The challenge of crime in a free society. President's Commission on Law Enforcement and Administration of Justice, 1967.

Treatment Alternatives to Street Crime (TASC)

TASC is an outpatient drug treatment program for drug-involved offenders initiated in the early 1970s that is frequently used for drug diversion. Douglas Anglin, Douglas Longshore, and Susan Turner have argued that TASC provides the following advantages over traditional drug programs:

- coordination of criminal justice and treatment services
- legal sanctions to encourage participants to enter and remain in treatment
- matching offenders to treatment based on offender needs
- mandatory drug testing to evaluate compliance with program objectives

In this same paper, Anglin et al. conducted one of the more comprehensive evaluations of TASC. Using two experimental and three quasi-experimental comparisons of pretrial diversion and posttrial samples, they uncovered evidence that TASC worked, although the outcomes were:[35]

- mostly modest in magnitude
- restricted to high risk offenders
- strongest for drug use and drug-related crimes
- mixed and difficult to interpret with respect to technical violations and nondrug-related crimes

Adjudication

Drug-using offenders who progress to the adjudication stage of the criminal justice sequence can either be processed through the regular courts or transferred to a specialized court like a drug court or DWI court. The court is then responsible for providing a disposition and imposing sentence.

Providing a Disposition

Drug Courts

The first **drug court** was established in Miami, Florida in 1989 as a means of coping with the rising crack problem and the growing number of drug cases being processed through the regular courts. Since that time, the number of drug courts has increased dramatically. By December 31, 2010 there were 2,633 drug courts operating throughout the United States, with at least one drug court in every U.S. state and territory.[36] In the late 1980s and early 1990s the burgeoning drug offending population was clogging up the regular court system and threatening many Americans' right to a fair and speedy trial. Drug courts significantly reduced the burden by diverting drug-using first-time/nonviolent offenders and noncriminal drug users from the regular court system into a special court designed specifically for them.

A Bureau of Justice Assistance (BJA) pamphlet identifies 10 key components of drug courts that distinguish them from regular courts. These include:

1. **Integration** of alcohol/drug treatment and criminal justice processing
2. **Nonadversarial** approach in which the prosecution and defense work together to protect public safety, promote client change, and preserve due process
3. **Early identification** of problems and prompt placement in programming
4. **Continuum** of treatment and rehabilitation services, to include drug and alcohol programming and other relevant services (e.g., mental health counseling, education, occupational training, housing assistance)

5. **Monitoring** through regular drug and alcohol testing
6. **Coordinated strategy** in which compliance is rewarded and noncompliance is met with increased supervision/sanctions
7. **Ongoing judicial interaction** whereby client meets with the judge on a regular basis
8. **Program evaluation** conducted at regular intervals to ensure that program goals are being met
9. **Education and training** of drug court staff to maintain program integrity
10. **Partnerships** forged with community agencies to improve coordination with private and public entities and maintain positive relationships with community leaders[37]

Meta-analyses indicate that those who participate in drug courts commit 8–26% (adults) and 3–5% (juveniles) fewer subsequent crimes than comparison subjects who do not participate in drug courts (see **Figure 9-6**).[38–43] In a recent study comparing 23 drug courts and 6 comparison sites, Shelli Rossman and colleagues observed significantly lower levels of self-reported criminal involvement and illegal drug use 6 and 18 months after program initiation (see **Figures 9-7** and **9-8**). At 18 months, official recidivism (40% vs. 53%) and saliva tests positive for illegal drugs (29% vs. 46%) were also significantly lower in drug court participants. Moreover, drug court participants reported less of a need for employment, educational, and financial assistance than comparison offenders.[44]

A principal strength of drug courts is that they are cost-effective alternatives to processing a drug user through the regular court system. Drug courts produce an average direct benefit to the criminal justice system of $2.21 for every dollar spent. The savings are even greater ($3.36 for every dollar spent) when higher risk offenders are targeted.[45] In fact, high-risk individuals are twice as likely to benefit from participating in a drug court as low-risk individuals (see **Figure 9-9**). What is more, drug courts allow an individual to remain in the community where there are more effective programs, community ties can be maintained, and reintegration is not required. The principal criticism of drug courts is that they lend themselves to net-widening, in that unlike drug diversion, individuals who go through drug court are being processed through the criminal justice system.[46] It has also been argued that drug courts load up on good prognosis clients, a process known as creaming, thus increasing their chances of observing a positive outcome even if the program is ineffective.[47] However, if higher risk individuals are targeted—higher risk being defined by both drug use and criminality—then net-widening and creaming are less of a problem and the procedure is made more effective.

DWI Courts

DWI courts are based on the drug court model and are designed for repeat DWI offenders with serious alcohol problems. A 2-year follow-up of DWI graduates in Michigan revealed that graduates were significantly less likely to be arrested for any offense (4.5% vs. 13.7%) or for another DWI (2.2% vs. 10.3%) than control subjects.[48] In Wisconsin, three-time DWI offenders processed through a DWI court were significantly less likely to be charged with a DWI or other criminal offense than controls in a 2-year follow-up.[49] In a review of three DWI courts in Georgia, significantly lower recidivism rates were noted in DWI court participants compared to control subjects followed over a period of 4 years.[50] In a

Figure 9-6
Results for six meta-analyses of drug court programs.

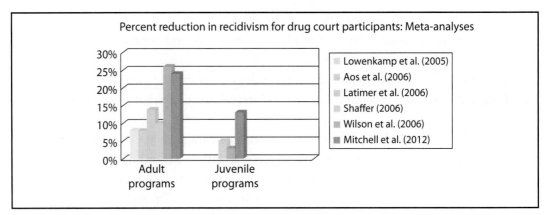

Data from the six sources are indicated in the figure's legend.

Figure 9-7
Percentage of drug court and comparison group participants who reported using drugs in prior 6 months.

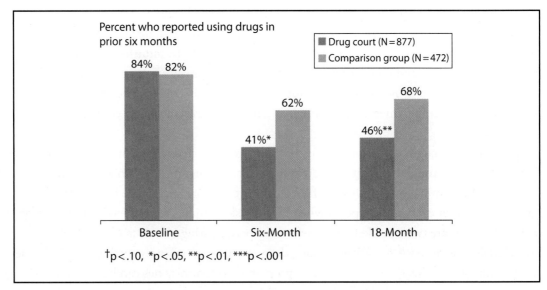

Rossman, S. B., Roman, J. K., Zweig, J. M., Rempel, M., & Lindquist, C. H. (2011). *The multi-site adult drug court evaluation: Executive summary.* Washington, DC: Urban Institute. Reprinted with permission of the Urban Institute.

Figure 9-8
Percentage who reported committing a crime in the prior 6 months.

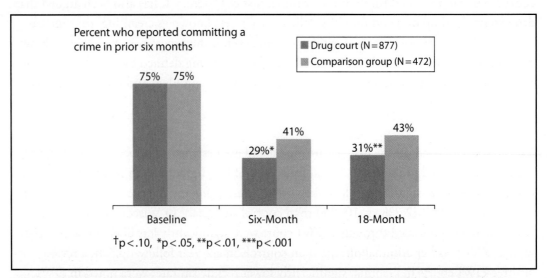

Rossman, S. B., Roman, J. K., Zweig, J. M., Rempel, M., & Lindquist, C. H. (2011). *The multi-site adult drug court evaluation: Executive summary.* Washington, DC: Urban Institute. Reprinted with permission of the Urban Institute.

meta-analysis performed by Ojmarrh Mitchell and others, it was determined that DWI court participants and graduates achieved reductions in recidivism (24%) that were comparable to reductions achieved in drug court, although a lack of experimental studies prompted Mitchell et al. to recommend further experimental research on DWI courts.[51]

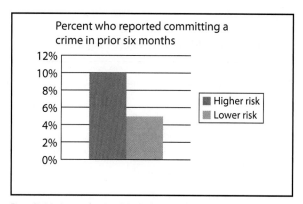

Figure 9-9
Percentage of reduction in recidivism in drug court participants by risk level.

Data From: Lowenkamp, C. T., Holsinger, A. M., & Latessa, E. J. (2005). Are drug courts effective? A meta-analytic review. *Journal of Community Corrections,* Fall, 5–28.

Regular Courts

Most individuals charged with drug offenses are adjudicated through the regular court system. History indicates that drug offenders did not ordinarily receive prison terms but this all changed with the "War on Drugs." The most common disposition for drug offenders, in fact, is prison. In 1998, during the height of the "War on Drugs," nearly 315,000 individuals were sentenced in state court on drug charges; of these, 42% were sentenced to prison, 26% were sentenced to a short jail sentence, and 32% received **probation** and/or treatment.[52] The issue of sentencing is taken up next.

Imposing a Sentence

Marc Mauer and Ryan King provide an overview of changes in sentencing practice for drug offenses in response to the "War on Drugs." In the mid- to late-1980s state legislatures began allotting harsher sentences for drug law offenses. The states were actually taking their lead from the federal government and the **Sentencing Reform Act of 1984**. Changes in federal sentencing guidelines created **mandatory minimum** prison sentences for drug offenders. The states were encouraged to follow suit and many did. With the advent of mandatory minimums, federal judges had very little discretion in sentencing defendants in federal court. Relatively small departures from the guidelines were permitted but they had to be justified in writing. This led to an increase in the number of drug users and small time dealers serving rather substantial sentences in federal prison.[53]

The state and federal prison populations experienced unprecedented growth between 1980 and 2009 (see **Figure 9-10**). There was a sixfold increase in the federal Bureau of Prisons (BOP) inmate population between 1984, the year I started working for the BOP, and 2011, the year I retired from government service. There are currently over 210,000 inmates housed in BOP facilities. One of the reasons given for the rapid growth of the BOP has been the large number of drug offenders sentenced to prison. The proportion of defendants sentenced to federal prison rather than to federal probation has clearly risen in the last 27 years, but this does not fully account for the sixfold increase in the BOP inmate population between 1984 and 2011. A substantial increase in the mean sentence of federal prisoners and discontinuation of federal **parole**, additional ramifications of the 1984 Sentencing Reform Act, have also contributed to rapid growth in the federal prison population, making the BOP the largest prison system in the United States.[54]

Figure 9-10
Number of sentenced
prisoners under
state and federal
jurisdiction per
100,000 from 1980 to
2009.

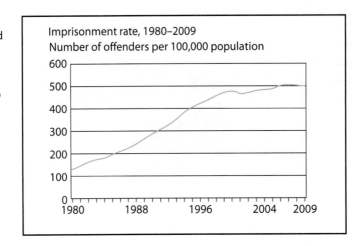

Imprisonment rate, 1980–2009
Number of offenders per 100,000 population

Bureau of Justice
Statistics, Key Facts at
a Glance, http://bjs.
ojp.usdoj.gov/content/
glance/incrt.cfm.

The federal system now gives judges greater discretion in sentencing individuals convicted in federal court. State judges have always had significant leeway in sentencing drug and nondrug offenders. Accordingly, a modest proportion of federal drug offenders and about a third of state drug offenders are sentenced to something other than incarceration. The nonincarceration alternatives most commonly used by state and federal judges include:[55]

Drug court is much
less adversarial than
traditional court.

© Ingram Publishing/Thinkstock

- Probation, either standard or intensive
- Community-based intermediate sanctions like fines, community service, day-reporting programs, and home confinement with or without electronic monitoring
- Split sentences, also known as shock probation, whereby the defendant serves the first part of his or her sentence in jail or prison and the remainder of the sentence on probation
- Bootcamps, wilderness camps, and ranches, designed primarily for adolescent and young adult offenders

Drugs and Corrections

Once convicted and sentenced, an individual is remanded to the care of the state or federal correctional system. Corrections can take place in an institution (jail, prison) or in the community (community corrections). Whether it takes place in the institution or community, corrections serves three interrelated functions: classification, management, and reintegration.

Classification

Initial Classification

The first order of business, once an individual enters the correctional system, is **classification** and the first classification decision that must be made concerns the individual's security or supervision level. Security level is for prison classification and supervision level is for community classification. For prison-bound offenders, the classification decision is whether the individual should be housed in a high, medium, or low security institution. For community-bound offenders, the classification decision is the level of supervision required (standard, intensive) and the general and **special conditions** of that supervision. **General conditions** of supervision apply to all supervisees (i.e., do not associate with known felons, maintain employment), whereas special conditions apply to supervisees with specific issues and problems (i.e., drug testing, mental health follow-up).

Initial classification decisions make extensive use of historical or static risk factors like age, criminal history, and prior institutional/community adjustment. In the case of prison-bound offenders, initial classification is designed to answer three basic questions:

- What level risk does the individual present in terms of violence toward staff and other inmates?
- What level risk does the individual present for suicide and self-injury?
- What level risk does the individual present for escape?

Initial classification decisions for community-bound offenders also center around three questions:

- What level risk does the individual present to the community in terms of future violence and recidivism?
- What level risk does the individual present for suicide and self-injury?
- What level risk does the individual present for absconding?

Much of the information used to initially classify prison inmates and probationers comes from the **presentence investigation (PSI) report**. The PSI report is written by a probation officer after a defendant is convicted but before he or she is sentenced. In conducting the presentence investigation, the officer will review existing arrest and police reports, contact past employers and school officials, and interview the individual and key family members. The probation officer then writes up the results and submits a report to the judge who will use the report in arriving at a sentence. Although the PSI is written for the judge, it is used by both prison officials and probation departments to initially classify prison inmates and probationers, respectively. The PSI report normally consists of the following sections:

- Detailed description of the offense conduct
- Criminal history
- Family and marital history
- Medical and mental health history
- Substance abuse history
- Occupational/educational history
- Financial status

The most important section of the PSI report is the probation officer's recommendations to the judge. Because judges frequently have minimal contact with a defendant, particularly one who has accepted a **plea bargain**, judges will sometimes rely heavily on the views and perceptions of the PSI writer.[56]

Reclassification

Initial classification is important but so is periodic reclassification. Although the stable risk factors used in initial classification, with the exception of age, do not change, there are at least three reasons why **reclassification** is essential. First, as the individual ages his or her risk goes down. Second, as the individual gets closer to release we may want to gradually reduce the custody or supervision level to assist the individual in making the transition to release from prison or termination from probation. Third, there are important dynamic risk or needs factors that, if addressed, will reduce the individual's future chances of recidivism. Several of the principal needs that should be addressed through reclassification include:[57]

- Antisocial cognition
- Antisocial personality processes
- Antisocial associates
- Educational status
- Occupational status
- Substance abuse

It is critically important when performing reclassification that one get a good idea of the relationship between drugs and crime in the person being reclassified. The drug–crime connection is known to fluctuate among variables, situations, and circumstances. It also tends to vary across individuals. The first question that needs to be answered with respect to substance abuse, therefore, is whether the individual has a significant drug use problem. Research indicates that approximately two-thirds of offender populations have a history of significant substance misuse.[58–59] Once the substance misuse question has been answered in the affirmative the next question is the actual relationship between drugs and crime in this particular individual. In some cases, drugs are intimately tied to the individual's involvement in crime; in other cases, drug use and crime are unrelated. A drug user who steals solely to support his or her heroin addiction would be an example of the former, whereas a drug dealer who sells cocaine but smokes marijuana might be an example of the latter. It is probably best to think of offenders' drug–crime connections as falling along a continuum, with drug use that is maximally **criminogenic** at the high end and drug use that is noncriminogenic at the low end.

Management

Drug-using offenders can be difficult to manage in prison or on probation, and present a number of unique challenges. Five of these challenges are discussed in this section: continued drug usage, medication-seeking behavior, irresponsibility, opportunism, and multiple services.

Continued Drug Usage

Many drug-using offenders continue using drugs in prison or while on probation. It may come as a surprise to many readers but drugs are available in prison. They are smuggled into the institution by staff or visitors. In some cases they enter the institution through the mail. Drugs are less plentiful and more expensive in prison than they are in the community but if an inmate wants drugs and can afford them he or she can normally get access to them. Another option available to prison inmates looking to achieve an altered state of consciousness is to make their own alcohol. Taking fruit they have stolen from the food service department and letting it rot or adding yeast, inmates make an intoxicating beverage commonly referred to as "**prison pruno**" or "hooch." In addition, many drug-using offenders continue using drugs while on probation. Because they are already in the community they have greater access to drugs than someone confined in prison. One of the best ways to manage continued drug use in prison or on probation is through random drug testing and breathalyzer assessment. To be cost effective, testing should be: (1) *random*, so that inmates/probationers do not know when they are going to be tested, (2) *monitored*, so that inmates/probationers cannot manipulate the test results, and (3) *selective*, so that only inmates/probationers with a significant drug history are targeted and the expense of drug testing can be kept to a minimum.[60]

Drug testing is generally considered one of the best deterrents to continued drug usage and positive test results have been found to predict future recidivism.[61–62] Research on the deterrent effect of drug testing on drug use and crime, however, has produced mixed results. An early study on the deterrent effect of drug testing found that it reduced drug use in probationers under supervision.[63] More recently, John Roman and Adele Harrell ascertained that drug testing was effective in reducing both drug use and criminality in drug court participants included in a program of graduated sanctions.[64] Pretrial misconduct, on the other hand, was not deterred by drug testing in a study by Goldkamp and Jones,[65] and studies on intensive supervision for regular offenders have identified an elevated rate of violations in probationers and parolees subjected to drug testing without benefit of drug treatment.[66–67] Olson, Lurigio, and Alberden observed gender differences in probationers with drug problems, such that female probationers responded more positivity to urinalysis sanctions and drug treatment than did male probationers.[68]

Several factors need to be considered when interpreting the results of research on drug testing in parole and probation. First, the increased monitoring associated with drug testing will ordinarily accentuate the number of violations. This does not, in and of itself, nullify the utility of **urinanalysis** testing for drugs or the deterrent effect of drug testing for the purpose of reducing serious offending. Second, drug testing appears to be more effective with postconviction offenders than with pretrial defendants and with female probationers than with male probationers. More research is required to determine why drug testing is not more effective when conducted at the pretrial stage and why females are more responsive to urinalysis testing than males. Third, drug testing is most efficacious when included in a program of graduated sanctions. Many drug-involved offenders will periodically test positive for drugs and some offenders will consistently test positive for drugs. The key to managing these individuals is not revoking their parole or probation the first time they slip or lapse but to provide them with a program of evidence-based treatment and graduated sanctions designed to prevent the lapse from turning into a full-blown relapse.

Medication-Seeking

Some incarcerated offenders will feign symptoms of mental illness in an attempt to gain access to psychotropic medication, some of which, if taken in high enough doses, can produce effects similar to the street drugs to which they have grown accustomed. There have been frequent reports on the misuse of **psychotropic medication** by inmates, the more popular psychotropic drugs of abuse being the benzodiazepine, clonazapam (Klonipin); the second generation antipsychotic, quetiapine (Seroquel); and an antiseizure agent sometimes used to treat mania, known as gabapentin (Neurotin).[69–71] It should be noted that having a drug problem does not preclude an offender from also having a serious mental health problem given the **comorbidity** that exists between mental health and substance misuse disorders.[72] The key to managing medication-seeking behavior is a thorough diagnostic work-up by a psychologist or psychiatrist and a recommendation against medication when there is no evidence that the individual suffers from significant mental health problems.

Irresponsibility

The irresponsibility associated with reactive criminal thinking may be particularly prominent in drug-involved offenders.[73] Such irresponsibility can lead to an excess number of both drug-related and nondrug-related disciplinary problems in prison and technical rule violations on probation. Basic skills training (problem solving, anger/stress management) can help reduce the irresponsibility that is an integral a part of drug-involved offending.[74]

Opportunism

Given a limited supply of drugs in prison and a fairly strong demand, inmates can make substantial money supplying drugs to that portion of the prison population interested in using drugs to get high. Gangs gain power and influence by becoming involved in various schemes, one of the more lucrative being the distribution of illegal substances. Rival gangs compete for control of the drug trade, not only on the streets but in prison as well. In prison, gangs operate under the assumption that he who controls the contraband, particularly the drugs, controls the prison and much of their time in prison is spent doing just this.

Multiple Services

Drug-involved offenders ordinarily suffer from multiple problems. Consequently, they require **multiple services**. It is imperative then that a drug program for offenders address more than just drugs. Other areas requiring attention in a comprehensive program of multiple services include:

- Peer influence
- Criminal thinking
- Occupational/educational achievement
- Residential status
- Survival skills
- Problem solving and cognitive restructuring

The Federal Bureau of Prisons (BOP) has devised a comprehensive drug program that provides multiple services to prison inmates. There are currently 62 BOP facilities that offer the 500-hour residential drug abuse treatment program (RDAP), a unit based program grounded in cognitive behavioral principles. Components of the program include:

- Cognitive skills
- Communication skills
- Criminal thinking
- Anger management
- Relapse prevention
- Aftercare (halfway house and supervised release)

Bernadette Pelissier and several colleagues conducted a multisite evaluation of the 500-hour RDAP using 1,842 male and 473 female treatment and control participants. The results of the evaluation revealed that RDAP graduates displayed lower levels of subsequent drug use (see **Figure 9-11**) and crime (see **Figure 9-12**) than controls in a 3-year follow-up, although only the male effect was statistically significant. Women, but not men, with prior mental health treatment had lower levels of subsequent drug use.[75]

Reintegration

There are several advantages to managing offenders in the community rather than in jail or prison. First, community corrections are several times cheaper than institutional corrections.[76] Second, keeping lower risk, less violent

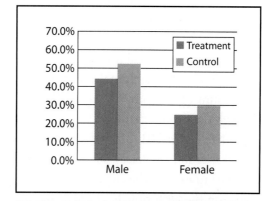

Figure 9-11
Percentage of male and female BOP drug program and control participants using drugs after 3 years.

Data From: Pelissier, B. M. M., Camp, S. D., Gaes, G. G., Saylor, W. G., & Rhodes, W. (2003). Gender differences in outcomes from prison-based residential treatment. *Journal of Substance Abuse Treatment, 24*, 149–160.

Figure 9-12
Percentage of male and female BOP drug program and control participants arrested during a 3-year follow-up.

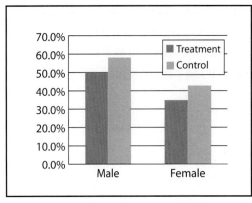

Data From: Pelissier, B. M. M., Camp, S. D., Gaes, G. G., Saylor, W. G., & Rhodes, W. (2003). Gender differences in outcomes from prison-based residential treatment. *Journal of Substance Abuse Treatment, 24,* 149–160.

individuals in the community saves precious jail and prison space for higher risk, more violent offenders.[77] Third, there are more programs available in the community than in jail or prison and research suggests that community-based programming is more effective than institution-based programming.[78] Fourth, incarceration can have a criminogenic effect in the sense that it makes many individuals' criminality worse.[79] Fifth, when offenders are managed in the community there is no need for them to reintegrate back into the community because they are already there.

Reentry

Reentry has become an important theme in correctional practice as correctional systems find themselves releasing the surfeit of prisoners who were originally incarcerated in the 1980s and 1990s and have now completed their sentences. We would do well to keep in mind that between the 1970s and late 2010, there was a sevenfold increase in the number of prisoners reentering society. A growing prison population gives rise to a growing need for reentry services. At present, 650,000 inmates are released from state and federal prison each year. Hence, nearly 1,800 former prisoners are released to the community each day.[80] The cost–benefit ratio for correctional programs that bear directly on reentry is 1:35, which means that for every dollar spent on prisoner reentry, $35 are saved in criminal justice and victimization costs.[81]

Ralph Fretz introduced a seamless **continuum-of-care** model designed to help released offenders successfully negotiate the precarious reentry process. There are three phases in the continuum-of-care model. First, there is the *step-down phase*, which begins about 6 months prior to release from prison. Second, there is the *structured reentry or transitional phase*, which ideally takes place in a halfway house as the individual makes his or her initial transition into the community. Third, there is the *integration or aftercare phase* beginning after release from the halfway house and ending 4 to 6 months later. **Community Education Centers (CEC),** where newly released inmates are provided with access to assessment, treatment, and occupational resources, play a particularly important role in the continuum-of-care model. Research indicates that prisoners who completed all three phases of the continuum-of-care program enjoyed 30% lower rates of recidivism than inmates released through traditional channels.[82]

In November 2011, New Jersey Governor Chris Christie, a former U.S. Attorney for the District of New Jersey, signed into law legislation that would create several pilot projects designed to expand the current drug court system into prisoner reentry. This legislation comes on the heels of federal legislation initiated by former President George W. Bush that created several federal programs designed to increase the chances of a successful reentry on the part of both drug-involved and nondrug-involved prisoners. Christie formed a task force to centralize the state's prisoner reentry program, identify barriers to inmate success upon release from prison, and find ways to increase drug treatment resources for newly released drug-involved offenders.[83] It will be interesting to see what effect this initiative has on recidivism in drug-involved individuals released from New Jersey state prisons.

Probation, Parole, and Supervised Release

Probation is a period of community supervision imposed by a judge on a convicted offender in lieu of incarceration. Parole is a period of community supervision following early release from prison for good behavior as granted by a parole board. **Supervised release** is a period of community supervision following release from prison on expiration of sentence minus whatever good-time credit the inmate may have earned in prison. The common denominator connecting these three dispositions is that the individual is followed in the community by a parole/probation officer who provides the individual with some measure of supervision. This supervision can range from minimal to intensive.

There is still much uncertainty whether more intensive forms of supervision are effective. Amy Solomon, Vera Kachnowski, and Avinash Bhati of the Urban Institute noted that postcustody supervision had minimal impact on subsequent offending. Two years after release, 62% of the individuals who had been released unconditionally (no supervision), 61% of the individuals who had been released on mandatory parole (supervision), and 54% who had released on discretionary parole (early release with supervision) had one or more arrests, with the mean number of rearrests being 2.5, 2.1, and 2.1, respectively.[84] A study by Doris Layton MacKenzie and colleagues demonstrated that although supervision often does not eliminate offending it does significantly reduce it. The mean annualized crime rate fell from 641.5 to 199.5 in offenders under supervision and the proportion of individuals involved in a wide variety of crime also dropped (see **Figure 9-13**).[85]

Supervision appears to work but perhaps not as well as many stakeholders would like. What needs to be kept in mind is that standard parole and probation normally provide minimal levels of supervision. With the advent of intensive supervised parole and probation (ISP) there was renewed optimism that supervision could be made more effective. An early study on ISP with drug-involved offenders, however, indicated that ISP supervisees had more technical violations and were rearrested at the same rate as offenders on regular parole.[86] More recently, Mario Paparozzi and Paul Gendreau compared 240 parolees enrolled in an intensive supervision program with 240 parolees undergoing traditional parole supervision and determined that the intensive supervision program reduced recidivism by 10–30% as long as the following conditions were met:[87]

- The greatest amount of supervision and treatment was provided to the highest risk individuals.
- The parole officers effectively balanced the law enforcement and social work functions of parole.
- The program received support from the organizational structure.

In addition to effectively balancing the law enforcement and social work functions, officers can be taught to effectively implement the risk-need-responsivity approach that is the backbone of evidence-based correctional practice.[88]

Figure 9-13
Percentage of
probationers involved
in crime prior to
arrest and while on
probation.

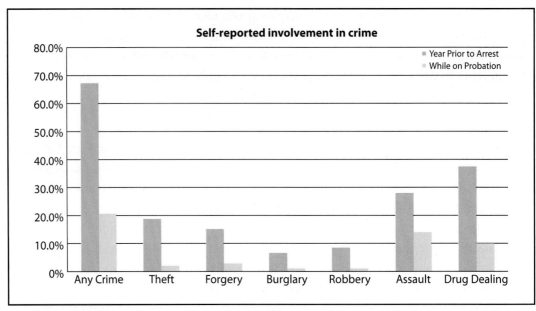

Data From: MacKenzie, D. L., Browning, K., Skroban, S. B., & Smith, D. A. (1999). The impact of probation on the criminal activities of offenders. *Journal of Research in Crime and Delinquency, 36,* 423–453.

Summary and Conclusions

- The three primary functions of law enforcement in working with drug-involved offenders are surveillance, intelligence, and apprehension. Surveillance is most effective when it is proactive and integrated. Intelligence begins at the microlevel (tactical) but should also be part of a larger or macrolevel approach. Nearly half of all arrests for drugs are for simple possession of marijuana.

- The two primary functions of the courts in working with drug-involved offenders are pretrial services and adjudication. Drug diversion and drug courts provide cost-effective alternatives to processing drug-involved offenders through the regular court system.

- The three primary functions of corrections in working with drug-involved offenders are classification, management, and reintegration. Classification for either prison or community supervision is important to successful correctional intervention. In addition, there are a number of unique management issues that drug-involved offenders present, from continued drug usage to the need for multiple services. Supervision, if properly implemented, can ease an individual's transition back into society.

Key Terms

Atavism   Throwback to an earlier stage in the evolution of humans.

Arrest   Process by which a law enforcement officer takes an alleged offender into custody.

Blood-Alcohol Concentration (BAC)   Amount of alcohol present in the blood; the legal limit in most states is .08.

Booking   Creating an official criminal justice record for an arrested individual by fingerprinting and taking pictures of the defendant.

Breathalyzer   Device that estimates the blood-alcohol concentration (BAC) of an individual from his or her breath.

Classicism   School of criminological thought that holds to the belief that individuals choose to engage in crime and can therefore be deterred in committing crime by the severity, certainty, and speed of punishment.

Classification   Method by which offender risks are balanced with security requirements to assign offenders to prison (high, medium, low) or community supervision (intensive, standard).

Comorbidity   Overlapping membership in two or more different diagnostic categories.

Community Education Center (CEC)   Center where released inmates can access resources useful in making the transition back into the community.

Confidential Informant   Individual who provides "inside information" to law enforcement.

Continuum-of-Care   Process designed to help an individual make a successful transition from prison to the community; normally composed of three phases: a step-down phase, a structured reentry phase, and an integration/aftercare phase.

Controlled Buy   A police officer purchases drugs from a dealer and uses this as evidence to build a case against the dealer.

Criminogenic   Causing crime.

Diversion   Diverting an individual out of the criminal justice system and redirecting them to an alternate system like the mental health or drug treatment systems.

Drug Court   Specialized court for nonviolent drug offenders marked by a cooperative and nonadversarial approach in which regular monitoring, a range of services, and integration between the treatment and criminal justice systems are emphasized.

DWI Court   Specialized court modeled after the Drug Court approach but for individuals accused of driving while intoxicated (DWI).

Entrapment   Enticement from law enforcement designed to encourage someone to commit a crime they would not have likely committed without inducement from law enforcement.

General Conditions   Standard requirements of probation or parole that all probationers and parolees must follow (e.g., alert probation/parole officer to any changes in job status or residence; no association with known felons).

Mandatory Minimum   Legislatively mandated minimum sentence to be served for a specific offense.

Multiple Services   Provision of different services to address the multiple problems of drug-involved offenders.

National Highway Traffic Safety Administration   Governmental agency concerned with research and policy on traffic safety.

Operational Intelligence   Mesolevel techniques used to gather information about regional drug activity.

Parole   Period of community supervision following early release from prison during which the individual must abide by certain conditions

Patrolling   To maintain order and control by passing through an area.

Plea Bargain   Agreement between the defense and prosecution in which defendant pleads guilty to an offense in exchange for a dismissal, downgraded charge, or reduced sentence.

Positivism   School of criminological thought that holds that crime is a function of factors outside the individual's personal control; also known as determinism.

Presentence Investigation (PSI)   An investigation conducted between a person's conviction for a crime and sentencing that typically covers the current offense, criminal history, family background, medical and mental health history, drug use history, and any relevant aggravating or mitigating circumstances.

Presentence Investigation (PSI) Report   A report submitted to the judge of the results of a presentence investigation that the judge will typically use to sentence the individual and prison and probation officials will use to classify the individual.

Pretrial Services   Information gathered after arrest and before trial to assist with bail and other important pretrial decisions.

Prison Pruno   Homemade alcohol manufactured by prison inmates; sometimes referred to as hooch.

Probation   Period of community supervision assigned in lieu of incarceration during which the individual must abide by certain conditions.

Psychotropic Medication   Drug designed to manage symptoms of mental illness.

Reclassification   Method used to integrate offender risks and needs for the purpose of determining programming needs and whether transfer to a higher or lower level of institutional or community supervision is required.

Reentry   Individual's reintegration back into society following a period of time in jail or prison.

Saturation Patrols   A large group of law enforcement officers are concentrated in a small geographical area with instructions to find individuals who are displaying behavioral signs of impaired driving (e.g., rough or erratic driving).

Selective Incapacitation   Practice of confining the most prolific criminal offenders for the longest periods of time.

Sentencing Reform Act of 1984   Section of the Comprehensive Crime Control Act of 1984 in which sentencing guidelines were changed for greater consistency, mandatory minimum sentences for drug offenses were implemented, and federal parole was abolished.

Sobriety Checkpoints   Roadblocks set up by law enforcement to evaluate if drivers have been drinking and driving.

Special Conditions   Special requirements of probation or parole that certain probationers and parolees must follow (e.g., regular drug testing, mental health counseling).

Strategic Intelligence   Macrolevel techniques used to gather information about national and international drug activity.

Supervised Release   Form of mandatory parole in which an individual has a set period of community supervision after he or she completes a prison sentence.

Surveillance   Law enforcement function designed to expose and control drug organizations.

Tactical Intelligence   Microlevel techniques used to gather information about local drug dealers.

Treatment Alternatives to Street Crime (TASC)   Diversion program for drug-involved offenders in which offenders sign a contract indicating that they agree to abide by the instructions of their case manager, submit to regular and random urinalyses, and participate regularly in drug treatment.

Undercover Operatives   Use of law enforcement officers trained in undercover operations to infiltrate a drug organization.

Urinanalysis   Drug test designed to identify the presence of illegal drugs in an individual's urine.

Wiretapping   Techniques that allow law enforcement to listen in on telephone and wireless phone conversations.

Critical Thinking

1. What are the most effective law enforcement models for apprehending drug offenders?
2. Are drug courts cost effective? Are there any limitations to drug courts?
3. Why should society be spending more money on community corrections programs and trying to limit the number of individuals in jail and prison?

Notes

1. Kalunta-Crompton, A. (1998). The prosecution and defence of black defendants in drug trials: Evidence of claim making. *British Journal of Criminology. 38*, 561–591.
2. Homel, R., Tomsen, S., & Thommeny, J. (1992). Public drinking and violence—not just an alcohol problem. *Journal of Drug Issues, 22*, 679–697.
3. Charest, M., Tremblay, P., Boivin, R., & D'Elia, M. (2010). Police video surveillance in public places: Learning technologies. *Canadian Journal of Criminology and Criminal Justice, 52*, 449–470.
4. Logue, D. (2008, February). The hidden badge: The undercover narcotics operation. *Law Enforcement Technology*, pp. 94–99.
5. Miller, J. M. (2011). Becoming an informant. *Justice Quarterly, 28*, 203–220.
6. Curriden, M. (1991). Making crime pay: What's the cost of using paid informants? *ABA Journal, 77*, 42–46.
7. Curriden (1991).
8. Miller (2011).
9. U.S. Courts. (2011). *Wiretap Report 2010*. Retrieved April 1, 2012, from http://www.uscourts.gov/statistics/WiretapReports/WiretapReport2010.aspx.
10. U.S. Legal. (2012). *Controlled buy law and legal definition*. Retrieved April 1, 2012, from http://definitions.uslegal.com/c/controlled-buy/.
11. *Illinois v. Caballes*, 543 U.S. 405 (2005; pp. 408–410).
12. National Highway Traffic Safety Administration. (2012, April). *Traffic safety factors. 2010 data: Alcohol-impaired driving* (DOT HS 811 606). Washington, DC: U.S. Department of Transportation.
13. Kloeden, C. N., McLean, A. J., Moore, V. M., & Ponte, G. (1997). *Travelling speed and the risk of crash involvement: Vol. 1. Findings*. Canberra, Australia: NHMRC Road Accident Research Unit, University of Adelaide.

14. Elder, R. W., Shults, R. A., Sleet, D. A., Nichols, J. L., Zaza, S., & Thompson, R. (2002). Effectiveness of sobriety checkpoints for reducing alcohol-involved crashes. *Traffic Injury Prevention, 3*, 266–274.

15. Greene, J. W. (2003). Battling DUI: A Comparative analysis of checkpoints and saturation patrols. *FBI Law Enforcement Bulletin, 72*, 1–6.

16. Ratcliffe, J. (2007). Integrated intelligence and crime analysis: *Enhanced information management for law enforcement leaders* (2nd ed.). Washington, DC: Police Foundation.

17. Ratcliffe (2007).

18. Ratcliffe (2007).

19. Ratcliffe (2007).

20. Kirby, S., Quinn, A., & Keay, S. (2010). Intelligence-led and traditional policing approaches to open drug markets—A comparison of offenders. *Drugs and Alcohol Today, 10*, 13–19.

21. Federal Bureau of Investigation. (2011). *Uniform crime reports, 2010.* Washington, DC: Author.

22. Grotenhermen, F. (2002). Review of therapeutic effects. In F. Grotenhermen & E. Russo (Eds.), *Cannabis and cannabinoids: Pharmacology, toxicology, and therapeutic potential* (pp. 123–142). New York: Haworth Press.

23. Torres, S., Elbert, M. J., Baer, J. D., & Booher, J. (1999). *Drug-involved adult offenders: Community supervision strategies and considerations.* Lexington, KY: American Probation and Parole Association.

24. Lemert, E. M. (1951). *Social pathology: A systematic approach to the theory of sociopathic behavior.* New York: McGraw-Hill.

25. Bureau of Justice Statistics. (2012). *The justice system: What is the sequence of events in the criminal justice system?* Retrieved September 26, 2012, from http://bjs.ojp.usdoj.gov/justsys.cfm.

26. DeLisi, M., & Conis, P. J. (2013). *American corrections: Theory, research, policy, and practice* (2nd ed.). Burlington, MA: Jones & Bartlett Learning.

27. Clark, J., & Henry, D. A. (2003). *Pretrial services programming at the start of the 21st Century.* Washington, DC: U.S. Department of Justice, Office of Justice Programs, Bureau of Justice Assistance.

28. Britt, C., Gottfredson, M., & Goldkamp, J. (1992). Drug testing and pre-trial misconduct: An experiment on the specific deterrent effects of drug monitoring defendants on pretrial release. *Journal of Research in Crime and Delinquency, 29*, 62–78.

29. Goldkamp, J., Gottfredson, M. R., & Weiland, D. (1990). Pretrial drug testing and defendant risk. *Journal of Criminal Law and Criminology, 81*, 585–652.

30. Goldkamp, J., & Jones, P. (1992). Pretrial drug-testing experiments in Milwaukee and Prince George's County: The context of implementation. *Journal of Research in Crime and Delinquency, 29*, 430–465.

31. DeLisi & Conis (2013).

32. Substance Abuse and Mental Health Services Administration. (1998). *Services Research Outcomes Study* (DHHS Publication No. 98-3177). Washington, DC: Author.

33. Gendreau, P., French, S. A., & Gionet, A. (2004). What works (what doesn't work): The principles of effective correctional treatment. *Journal of Community Corrections, 13*, pp. 4–6, 27–30.

34. Harvey, E., Shakeshaft, A., Hetherington, K., Sannibale, C., & Mattick, R. P. (2007). The efficacy of diversion and aftercare strategies for adult drug-involved offenders: A summary and methodological review of the outcome literature. *Drug and Alcohol Review, 26*, 379–387.

35. Anglin, M. D., Longshore, D., & Turner, S. (1999). Treatment Alternatives to Street Crime: An evaluation of five programs. *Criminal Justice and Behavior, 26*, 168–195.

36. National Association of Drug Court Professionals. (2011). *Facts about drug courts.* Retrieved April 2, 2012, from http://www.ndcrc.org/faq.

37. National Association of Drug Court Professionals. (1997). *Defining drug courts: The key components.* Washington, DC: Bureau of Justice Assistance, U.S. Department of Justice.

38. Aos, S., Miller, M., & Drake, E. (2006). *Evidence-based adult corrections programs: What works and what does not.* Olympia, WA: Washington State Institute for Public Policy.

39. Latimer, J., Morton-Bourgon, K., & Chretien, J. (2006). *A meta-analytic examination of drug treatment courts: Do they reduce recidivism?* New Brunswick, Canada: Canada Department of Justice, Research & Statistics Division.

40. Lowenkamp, C. T., Holsinger, A. M., & Latessa, E. J. (2005, Fall). Are Drug Courts effective? A meta-analytic review. *Journal of Community Corrections*, 5–28.

41. Shaffer, D. K. (2006). *Reconsidering Drug Court effectiveness: A meta-analytic review* [Doctoral Dissertation]. Las Vegas, NV: Dept. of Criminal Justice, University of Nevada.

42. Wilson, D. B., Mitchell, O., & MacKenzie, D. L. (2006). A systematic review of Drug Court effects on recidivism. *Journal of Experimental Criminology, 2,* 459–487.

43. Mitchell, O., Wilson, D. B., Eggers, A., & MacKenzie, D. L. (2012). Assessing the effectiveness of drug courts on recidivism: A meta-analytic review of traditional and non-traditional drug courts. *Journal of Criminal Justice, 40,* 60–71.

44. Rossman, S. B., Roman, J. K., Zweig, J. M., Rempel, M., & Lindquist, C. H. (2011). *The multi-site adult drug court evaluation: Executive summary.* Washington, DC: Urban Institute.

45. Bhati, A. S., Roman, J. K., & Chalfin, A. (2008). *To treat or not to treat: Evidence on the prospects of expanding treatment to drug-involved offenders.* Washington, DC: Urban Institute.

46. Walsh, N. (2011). *Addicted to courts: How a growing dependence on drug courts impacts people and communities.* Washington, DC: Justice Policy Institute.

47. Drug Policy Alliance. (2011). *Drug courts are not the answer: Toward a health-centered approach to drug use.* New York: Author.

48. Taylor, E., Zold-Kilbourn, P., Carey, S. M., Fuller, B. E., & Kissick, K. (2008). *Michigan DUI courts outcome evaluation: Final report.* Portland, OR: NPC Research.

49. Hiller, M. L., Saum, C. A., & Taylor, L. (2010). Outcome evaluation of a DUI court. *Criminal Justice Research Review, 11,* 70–76.

50. National Highway Traffic Safety Administration. (2011). *An evaluation of three Georgia DUI courts* (DOT HS 811 450). Washington, DC: U.S. Department of Transportation.

51. Mitchell et al. (2012).

52. King, R. S., & Mauer, M. (2002). *Distorted priorities: Drug offenders in state prisons.* Washington, DC: The Sentencing Project.

53. Mauer, M., & King, R. S. (2007). *A 25-year quagmire: The War on Drugs and its impact on American society.* Washington, DC: The Sentencing Project.

54. Walters, G. D. (2012). Criminal predatory behavior in the Federal Bureau of Prisons. In M. DeLisi & P. J. Conis (Eds.), *Violent offenders: Theory, research, and practice* (pp. 369–381). Burlington, MA: Jones & Bartlett Learning.

55. DeLisi & Conis (2013).

56. Bayens, G., & Smykla, J. O. (2013). *Probation, parole, and community-based corrections: Supervision, treatment, and evidence-based practices.* New York: McGraw-Hill.

57. Andrews, D. A., Bonta, J., & Wormith, J. S. (2006). The recent past and near future of risk and/or need assessment. *Crime and Delinquency, 52,* 7–27.

58. Karberg, J. C., & James, D. J. (2005). Substance dependence, abuse, and treatment of jail inmates, 2002. *Bureau of Justice Statistics Special Report* (NCJ 209588). Washington, DC: U.S. Department of Justice.

59. Mumola, C. J., & Karberg, J. C. (2006). Drug use and dependence, state and federal prisoners, 2004. *Bureau of Justice Statistics Special Report* (NCJ 213530). Washington, DC: U.S. Department of Justice.

60. Torres et al. (1999).

61. Wish, E., & Gropper, B. (1990). Drug testing by the criminal justice system: Methods, research and applications. In M. Tonry and J. Wilson (Eds.) *Drugs and Crime* (pp. 321–392). Chicago: University of Chicago Press.

62. Smith, D. A., & Polsenberg, C. (1992). Specifying the relationship between arrestee drug test results and recidivism. *Journal of Criminal Law and Criminology, 83,* 364–377.

63. Vito, G.F., Wilson, D.G., & Holmes, S.T. (1993). Drug testing in community corrections: Results from a four-year program. *The Prison Journal, 73,* 343–354.

64. Harrell, A., & Roman, J. (2001). Reducing drug use and crime among offenders: The impact of graduated sanctions. *Journal of Drug Issues, 31,* 207–232.

65. Goldkamp & Jones (1993).

66. Turner, S., & Petersilia, J. (1992). Focusing on high-risk parolees: An experiment to reduce commitment to the Texas Department of Corrections. *Journal of Research in Crime and Delinquency, 29,* 34–61.

67. Springer, D. W., McNeece, C. A., & Arnold, E. M. (2003). Monitoring offenders. In D. W. Springer, C. A. McNeece, & E. M. Arnold (Eds.), *Substance abuse treatment for criminal offenders: An evidence-based guide for practitioners* (pp. 157–173). Washington, DC: American Psychological Association.

68. Olson, D. E., Lurigio, A. J., & Alberden, M. (2003). Men are from Mars, women are from Venus, but what role does gender play in probation recidivism? *Justice Research and Policy, 5,* 33–54.

69. Pinta, E. R., & Taylor, R. E. (2007). Quetiapine addiction [Letter to the Editor]. *American Journal of Psychiatry, 164,* 174.

70. Reccoppa, L., Malcolm, R., & Ware, M. (2004). Gabapentin abuse in inmates with prior history of cocaine dependence. *American Journal of Addiction, 13,* 321–323.

71. Sec, I., Questel, F., Rey, C., & Pourriat, J. L. (2009). Misuse of psychotropic medications in a population of subjects held for custody in the city of Paris. *Therapie, 64,* 129–134.

72. Conway, K. P., Compton, W., Stinson, F.S., & Grant, B. F. (2006). Lifetime comorbidity of DSM-IV mood and anxiety disorders and specific drug use disorders: Results from the National Epidemiologic Survey on Alcohol and Related Conditions. *Journal of Clinical Psychiatry, 67,* 247–257.

73. Walters, G. D. (2012). Substance abuse and criminal thinking: Testing the countervailing, mediation, and specificity hypotheses. *Law and Human Behavior, 36,* 506–512.

74. Tripodi, S. J., & Bender, K. (2011). Substance abuse treatment for juvenile offenders: A review of quasi-experimental and experimental research. *Journal of Criminal Justice, 39,* 246–252.

75. Pelissier, B. M. M., Camp, S. D., Gaes, G. G., Saylor, W. G., & Rhodes, W. (2003). Gender differences in outcomes from prison-based residential treatment. *Journal of Substance Abuse Treatment, 24,* 149–160.

76. Pew Center on the States. (2009). *One in 31: The long reach of American corrections.* Washington, DC: Pew Charitable Trusts.

77. West, H. C., & Sabol, W. J. (2008). *Prisoners in 2007. Bureau of Justice Statistics Bulletin* (NCJ 224280). Washington, DC: U.S. Department of Justice.

78. Gendreau et al. (2004).

79. Bales, W. D., & Piquero, A. R. (2012). Assessing the impact of imprisonment on recidivism. *Journal of Experimental Criminology, 8,* 71–101.

80. Petersilia, J. (2004), What works in prisoner reentry? Reviewing and questioning the evidence. *Federal Probation, 68*(2), 4–8.

81. Welsh, B. C. (2004). Monetary costs and benefits of correctional treatment programs: Implications for offender reentry. *Federal Probation, 68*(2), 9–13.

82. Fretz, R. (2005). Step down programs: The missing link in successful inmate reentry. *Corrections Today, 67,* 102–107.

83. Hester, T. (2011, November 28). Gov. Christie announces initiative to help criminal offenders re-enter N.J. society. *Newsroom Jersey.* Retrieved April 3, 2012, from http://www.newjerseynewsroom.com/state/gov-christie-announces-initiative-to-help-criminal-offenders-re-enter-nj-society.

84. Solomon, A. L., Kachnowski, V., & Bhati, A. (2009). *Does parole work? Analyzing the impact of postprison supervision on rearrest outcomes.* Washington, DC: Urban Institute.

85. MacKenzie, D. L., Browning, K., Skroban, S. B., & Smith, D. A. (1999). The impact of probation on the criminal activities of offenders. *Journal of Research in Crime and Delinquency, 36,* 423–453.

86. Turner & Petersilia (1992).

87. Paparozzi, M., & Gendreau, P. (2005). An intensive supervision program that worked: Service delivery, professional orientation, and organizational supportiveness. *The Prison Journal, 85,* 445–466.

88. Bonta, J, Bourgon, G., Rugge, T., Scott, S.-T., Yessine, A. K., Gutierrez, L., et al. (2011). An experimental demonstration of training probation officers in evidence-based community supervision. *Criminal Justice and Behavior, 38,* 1127–1148.

CHAPTER 10

ASSESSING THE DRUG-INVOLVED OFFENDER

© Juanmonino/iStockphoto

Assessment of the drug-involved offender is most effective when guided by principles from Andrews, Bonta, and Hoge's Risk-Need-Responsivity (RNR) model, an outgrowth of the treatment classification system created by Ted Palmer, Lee Sechrest, and others during the 1960s and 1970s.[1] **Risk** refers to the static or historical risk factors that have been found to predict violence, recidivism, and institutional adjustment (see **Table 10-1**). **Needs** represents the dynamic or changeable risk factors that can be used to identify goals for treatment (see **Table 10-2**). **Responsivity** describes the demographic, learning style, and personal strength variables that help identify the most effective interventions for specific individuals (see **Table 10-3**). The RNR model consequently serves a vital function in the assessment of drug-involved offenders and is the foundation upon which this chapter is based. This chapter has three primary objectives, one for each component of the RNR model:

- Appreciate the role of risk factors in classifying and managing drug-involved offenders as exemplified by two second-generation and two third-generation risk measures for crime and two popular risk measures for drug abuse.
- Understand the function of needs factors in establishing goals for change in such areas as alcohol and drugs, antisocial personality processes, antisocial cognition, and antisocial peer associations.
- Apply the responsivity principle to various combinations of risk and needs factors in an effort to create an optimally effective intervention for drug-involved offenders.

Table 10-1 What, Why, and When of Risk Factors

RISK
WHAT
• Static (historical) risk factors that predict recidivism and violence
WHY
• Helpful in classifying and managing offenders
• Useful in identifying levels of service
WHEN
• At intake and periodically thereafter as the individual's status changes

Table 10-2 What, Why, and When of Needs Factors

NEEDS
WHAT
• Dynamic (changeable) risk factors that change in accordance with the person's chances of recidivism (criminogenic)
WHY
• Helpful in identifying programming needs
• Useful in assessing degree of change
WHEN
• Periodically over the course of the prison or probation sentence

Table 10-3 What, Why, and When of Responsivity Factors

RESPONSIVITY
WHAT
• Variables that influence an offender's responsiveness to a specific intervention (demographics, learning style, personal strengths, thinking, and preference)
WHY
• Tailoring an intervention to the client's demographic status, learning style, strengths, or thinking so it optimizes the intervention
WHEN
• At the beginning of an intervention and periodically after that

Risk

Risk is an estimate of the likelihood that a person will engage in a negative, dangerous, or destructive behavior. The negative behaviors we are primarily concerned with are institutional and community violence, recidivism, drug-related crime, disciplinary infractions, relapse, escape, absconding, and suicide. Measures of risk are used to predict and manage an individual's behavior and are of major significance in assigning offenders to institutions (high, medium, low), community supervision (standard, intensive), and specialized housing (suicide watch in the case of a suicidal inmate). When risk assessment and management fail, the results can be disastrous as reflected in the story described in News Spot 10-1.

NEWS SPOT 10-1

Title: Teenager's Sex Killing Should Have Been Prevented
Source: *Yorkshire (England) Post*
Author: None reported
Date: March 6, 2012

The brutal murder of a teenage girl at the hands of a convicted rapist could have been prevented but for a series of failings by key agencies in Yorkshire charged with protecting the public from highly dangerous offenders, a report finds today.

Polish-born Zuzanna Zommer had only been living in Leeds for six weeks when she was raped and left in a pool of blood at the family home in a frenzied attack by killer Michael Clark.

A serious case review said it had been "highly probable" that Clark would attack someone after his release from prison for the latest of a string of vicious assaults which saw him receiving sentences totalling 22 years between the ages of 20 and 40.

It found the murder of 14-year-old Zuzanna 11 months later in October 2007 was not foreseeable but could have been prevented had agencies involved worked more effectively or had there been measures to restrict the freedom of high-risk repeat offenders.

It said: "More should have been done to effectively manage the risk posed by the perpetrator and, had everything been done that should have been done, the outcome may have been different."

The report found Humberside Police. . .only told colleagues in Leeds that Clark planned to live in the city the day before his arrival, leaving no time to draw up a plan to manage the risks he posed.

There were further failings by West Yorkshire Police due to the "weaknesses" of a computer system which meant officers who questioned Clark over four unrelated incidents did not know he was a high-risk sex offender. His behaviour was not flagged up to specialist staff who were monitoring him and they later downgraded their checks despite his history of serious offending.

The prison and probation service also failed to share a report compiled a decade earlier on Clark which showed he was a psychopath. He befriended the Zommers after they moved in near him in Harehills, Leeds. They had no idea he was a violent sex offender.

The report makes 15 recommendations including calling on the Home Secretary to review controls on high-risk offenders.

Today Jane Held, chair of the Leeds Safeguarding Children Board, said: "This was a tragic and deeply upsetting case for the family and the local community and my deepest sympathies lie with Zuzanna's family."

"There were a number of things we could have done better. It is still extremely regrettable that we didn't always do things as well as we could and we accept that is not good enough. The agencies involved accept all the findings and have acted on all the recommendations."

Questions to Ponder

1. **How would you assess the murderer Clarke's risk to the community coming out of prison?**
2. **Risk management flows directly from risk assessment. What problems in risk assessment, communication, and risk management led to the murder of this 14-year-old girl?**
3. **In another article on this case, neighbors described Clarke as a "glue-sniffing weirdo." What role do you think drugs may have played in the crime?**

Clinical Versus Statistical Prediction

One of the first decisions evaluators must make in conducting risk assessments is how to collect and combine risk variables to make predictions. In his groundbreaking 1954 book, *Clinical versus Statistical Prediction*, Paul Meehl made a case for the superiority of statistical or mechanical prediction over clinical prediction. Meehl was interested, not in how data were gathered, but in how they were combined. For instance, a psychological test typically yields scores on several scales. These scores can be combined or interpreted clinically by a trained and experienced clinician, or they can be combined mechanically using cutting scores or computerized formulae. Meehl found that the mechanical method of data combination and interpretation was at least as accurate and in many cases more accurate than clinical judgment in predicting a range of behaviors.[2] Grove and Meehl reviewed 136 studies comparing **clinical prediction** and **statistical prediction** and determined that only 8 studies produced results substantially supporting clinical prediction.[3] Grove and colleagues performed a meta-analysis of these same 136 studies and discovered that, on average, **actuarial prediction** was 10% more accurate than clinical prediction. The statistical model proved superior to the clinical model in all six comparisons involving recidivism or delinquency prediction.[4]

Three Generations of Risk Assessment Measures

Several decades ago, the **first-generation risk assessment** method of relying on unstructured clinical judgment (e.g., an experienced clinician offers an appraisal of an offender's chances of success on parole) was replaced by **second-generation risk assessment** methods. Second-generation risk assessment methods code static risk factors like age, gender, and criminal history that are then entered into empirically derived decision rules, matrices, or cut scores that sort cases into categories of high and low risk. **Third-generation risk assessment** methods, the most recent innovation in risk assessment, combine the static risk factors from second-generation methods and dynamic risk factors in an attempt to assess both risk and needs (see **Figure 10-1**).

In a meta-analysis comparing second- and third-generation instruments, Campbell, French, and Gendreau discerned that second-generation instruments did a slightly better job of predicting institutional violence whereas third-generation instruments did a slightly better job of predicting community violence.[5] Given the fact that second-generation instruments emphasize static risk factors and static risk factors are among the strongest predictors of future criminal behavior it was not surprising that third-generation instruments did not significantly improve on the predictive efficacy of second-generation instruments. Third-generation instruments clearly have an advantage over second-generation measures because they are capable of predicting risk of recidivism on par with second-generation instruments yet are more sensitive to change and possess greater utility in managing risk and establishing goals for intervention.

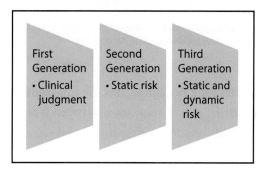

Figure 10-1
Three generations of risk assessment procedures.

Risk Instruments

In this section we examine two second-generation criminal risk measures (**Lifestyle Criminality Screening Form**, Salient Factor Score), two third-generation criminal risk measures (Historical, Clinical, Risk-20, Level of Service Inventory-Revised), and two drug abuse risk measures (**Addiction Severity Index**, Risk and Needs Triage).

Lifestyle Criminality Screening Form (LCSF)

The LCSF is a 14-item chart audit form completed using information found in an offender's central file or presentence investigation (PSI) report (see **Table 10-4**). Although the LCSF is divided into four sections (Irresponsibility, Self-Indulgence, Interpersonal Intrusiveness,

Table 10-4 Items on the Lifestyle Criminality Screening Form (LCSF)

Section I (Irresponsibility)
A. Failed to provide support for at least one child (Yes = 1)
B. Terminated education prior to graduating from high school (Yes = 1)
C. Longest job ever held (< 6 months = 2, 6–23 months =1, 24 or more months = 0)
D. Fired from/quit job (two or more times = 2, once = 1, no times = 0)
Section II (Self-Indulgence)
A. History of drug/alcohol abuse (Yes = 2)
B. Marital Background (two or more divorces = 2, 1 divorce = 1, illegitimate child = 1, married with no divorce/single with no children = 0)
C. Physical Appearance (4 separate tattoos/tattoos on neck or face = 2, 1–4 tattoos = 1, no tattoos = 0)
Section III (Interpersonal Intrusiveness)
A. Intrusive confining offense (Yes = 1)
B. Prior arrests for intrusive behavior (three or more = 2, one or two = 1, none = 0)
C. Use of a weapon during confining offense (Yes = 1)
D. Physical abuse of significant others/family members (Yes = 1)
Section IV (Social Rule Breaking)
A. Prior non-traffic arrests (5 or more = 2, 2–4 = 1, 0–1 = 0)
B. Age at time of first arrest (< 15 = 2, 15–18 = 1, > 18 = 0)
C. History of disruptive behavior in school (Yes = 1)

Data From: Walters, G. D., White, T. W., & Denney, D. (1991). The Lifestyle Criminality Screening Form: Preliminary data. *Criminal Justice and Behavior, 18*, 406–418.

Social Rule Breaking), it is the total score (range = 0–22) that is of primary concern in assessing risk. A total score between 0 and 6 indicates low risk, a total score between 7 and 9 signals moderate risk, and a total score of 10 or higher indicates high risk. The factor structure of the LCSF indicates the presence of a general or superordinate factor, two higher order factors (Violation and Impulse) and the four section scores (see **Figure 10-2**).

To be considered effective and useful an assessment instrument should possess both reliability and validity. **Reliability** means consistency of scores across time (test-retest reliability) or across raters (interrater reliability) and **validity** means that the test measures what it purports to measure (as represented by its correlation with certain external criteria). The interrater reliability of the LCSF is excellent and its predictive validity is moderate. Interestingly, the V and I factor scores appear to predict different behaviors: V does a better job of

Figure 10-2
Hierarchical organization of the Lifestyle Criminality Screening Form (LCSF).

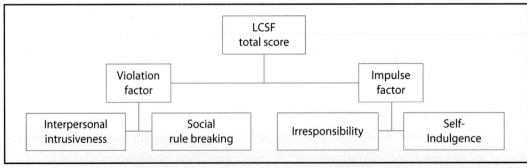

Walters, G. D. (2012a). *Crime in a psychological context: From career criminals to criminal careers.* Thousand Oaks, CA: Sage.

predicting institutional adjustment and recidivism, whereas I appears to do a better job of predicting social and occupational adjustment.[6–8]

Because the LCSF is a chart audit form there is no need for the offender to be present during the evaluation. Furthermore, raters need not hold advanced degrees in psychology to reliably score the LCSF and it takes less than an hour to train someone to competently score the LCSF. Because of its brevity the LCSF can be completed in less than 10 minutes, yet it is capable of predicting recidivism and prison adjustment on par with more time-intensive procedures like the Psychopathy Checklist.[9] The LCSF suffers from two principal limitations. First, it cannot be completed in the absence of file information or a PSI. Second, it is insensitive to change due to the fact that it is based exclusively on static (historical) risk factors.

Salient Factor Score (SFS)

Another second-generation risk measure is the **Salient Factor Score**. The SFS was developed by the federal parole commission to assist in making decisions about parole. It is a simple checklist consisting of six items, all of which reflect static risk: prior adjudications/convictions, prior commitments of 30 or more days, age at time of current offense, recent commitment free periods, probation/parole/confinement escape or violation, and history of heroin/opiate dependence. Whereas higher scores on the LCSF indicate higher risk for recidivism, higher scores on the SFS indicate lower risk for recidivism. Scores on the SFS can range from 0 to 10 with the following ranges being associated with poor (0–3), fair (4–5), good (6–7), and very good (8–10) predicted outcome.[10]

Published reliability data on the SFS are unavailable but correlations between the SFS and recidivism after 2 and 3 years in federal prisoners released on parole show evidence of moderately strong predictive validity and correlations (r) near the range associated with a high effect size.[11] It is unfortunate that the SFS has been studied only with federal prisoners because it would seem to have relevance to state prisoners as well. The strength of the SFS is that it is optimally weighted toward those static risk factors (criminal history, age, substance abuse history) that have demonstrated the strongest predictive relationships with recidivism. Like the LCSF, it is limited to situations where a central file or PSI is available, but unlike the LCSF, several of its items are subject to change in a positive direction (e.g., Recent Commitment Free Period).

Historical, Clinical, Risk-20 (HCR-20)

As a third-generation risk measure, the **Historical, Clinical, Risk-20** measure is composed of both static and dynamic risk factors. The HCR-20 is an empirically derived checklist scored using a procedure known as structured clinical judgment. Structured clinical judgment differs from the pure actuarial approach used with the LCSF and SFS in that it allows the clinician to deviate from a score or emphasize one item over another. The HCR-20 is made up of 20 items, each of which are scored on a three-point scale (0 = not present, 1 = may be present or partially present, 2 = present). Items are grouped into three subscales: Historical, Clinical, and Risk (see **Table 10-5**).[12]

Table 10-5 Items on the HCR-20

Historical Subscale
● H1 Previous Violence
● H2 Young Age at First Violent Incident
● H3 Relationship Instability
● H4 Employment Problems
● H5 Substance Use Problems
● H6 Major Mental Illness
● H7 Psychopathy (as measured by the Psychopathy Checklist-Revised)
● H8 Early Maladjustment
● H9 Personality Disorder
● H10 Prior Supervision Failure
Clinical Subscale
● C1 Lack of Insight
● C2 Negative Attitudes
● C3 Active Symptoms of Major Mental Illness
● C4 Impulsivity
● C5 Unresponsiveness to Treatment
Risk Subscale
● R1 Plans Lack Feasibility
● R2 Exposure to Destabilizers
● R3 Lack of Personal Support
● R4 Noncompliance with Remediation Effects
● R5 Stress

Data From: Webster, C. K., Douglas, D. E., Eaves, D., & Hart, D. (1997). *HCR-20 assessing risk for violence: Version II.* Burnaby, British Columbia, Canada: Mental Health, Law & Policy Institute, Simon Fraser University.

Interrater reliability estimates for the HCR-20 Total score and Historical subscale score are high. The Risk subscale, on the other hand, displays moderate interrater reliability and the interrater reliability of the Clinical subscale is modest.[13] In a meta-analysis of 16 studies using the HCR-20 to predict violence, the pooled effect size was just below the level associated with a large effect size.[14] The primary strengths of the HCR-20 are that it includes dynamic risk factors and so can be used to establish goals for intervention and assess change, yet it is capable of predicting violence and recidivism at a level comparable to the best second-generation instruments. A major weakness of the HCR-20 is that its developers recommend interpreting the results with structured clinical judgment rather than combining the results statistically despite research showing that interpretations based on a statistical model are clearly superior to ones based on clinical judgment.

Level of Service Inventory-Revised (LSI-R)

The **Level of Service Inventory-Revised** is an interview-based instrument developed by Donald Andrews and James Bonta designed to assess both static and dynamic risk. The measure's 54 items are organized into 10 broad topical areas:[15]

1. Criminal History
2. Education/Employment
3. Financial

4. Family/Marital
5. Accommodations
6. Leisure/Recreation
7. Companions
8. Alcohol/Drug Problems
9. Emotional/Personal
10. Attitudes/Orientation

Only the first domain (criminal history) is a static risk factor, the other nine domains are made up of acute and/or stable dynamic risk factors.

Chris Lowenkamp and colleagues had a large group of trained raters score a vignette with the LSI-R and discovered that raters achieved 85% or higher agreement on many of the individual items and in 9 of the 10 domains (financial being the lone exception).[16] Andrews, Bonta, and Wormith examined the results of several meta-analyses in which the LSI-R was compared to first- and second-generation risk measures. In predicting general and violent recidivism, the LSI-R achieved an average effect size that was several times higher than the first-generation effect size and slightly higher than the second-generation effect size.[17] Most correctional assessment procedures were originally designed for males and only a handful have been validated for use with females. The LSI-R is one of these procedures. A meta-analysis of studies using the LSI-R to predict female recidivism revealed a moderate effect size.[18]

Strengths of the LSI-R include the fact that it:

- can be used reliably by case managers and probation officers to evaluate prisoners, parolees, and probationers,
- predicts as well if not better than most second-generation procedures, and
- is useful in program planning because of the broad range of dynamic needs it assesses.

The LSI-R also has documented efficacy with drug-involved offenders. Christopher Kelly and Wayne Welsh, for instance, examined the predictive utility of the LSI-R in drug-involved offenders released from a 12-month in-prison drug program. After controlling for age, criminal history, instant offense, type of release, and time at risk, both the total LSI-R score and the Alcohol/Drug Problem subscale successfully predicted future recidivism at a modest to moderate level.[19] The primary weakness of the LSI-R is that it provides only superficial coverage of several important dynamic risk factors (e.g., antisocial cognition, antisocial peer associations, antisocial personality processes) and so needs to be supplemented by additional measures of these constructs.

Addiction Severity Index (ASI)

The ASI is a semistructured interview designed to address seven potential problem areas in substance-abusing individuals:[20]

- Medical Status
- Employment and Support
- Drug Use
- Alcohol Use

- Legal Status
- Family/Social Status
- Psychiatric Status

A trained rater gathers information on recent (past 30 days) and lifetime problems in each of these seven areas. Because risk in drug-involved offenders is measured in terms of both crime and drug use, the ASI has a great deal to offer those working with drug-involved offenders.

The interrater reliability of the ASI is good.[21–22] The validity of the ASI is also fairly well established. Lawrence Appleby and colleagues, for instance, witnessed strong correlations between the ASI-Alcohol scale and the Michigan Alcoholism Screening Test and between the ASI-Drug scale and the Drug Abuse Screening Test.[23] David Zanis, Thomas McLellan, and Mary Randall observed a robust relationship between the ASI and urinanalysis results indicating the presence of drugs.[24] The ASI is also capable of predicting general and violent recidivism in drug-involved offenders when age and criminal history are controlled.[25–26] The primary strength of the ASI is that it provides a reliable estimate of drug use that is clearly relevant to crime. Its primary weakness is that because it was not originally designed for use with correctional populations there is limited guidance on how to use it clinically with offenders.

Risk and Needs Triage (RANT)

Unlike the ASI, the **Risk and Needs Triage** was developed specifically for correctional populations. Items for the RANT were selected on the basis of a literature review and from a preliminary analysis of data provided by the community corrections sample used to construct the RANT. With only 19 items, the RANT can be administered in less than 15 minutes and the automated format allows probation personnel to administer the procedure after a brief period of training. A scoring algorithm yields 10 binary (yes/no) risk indices such as age of onset of substance use and delinquency and antisocial peer associations and 5 binary needs indices such as substance dependence and chronic substance-related medical problems. Based on the risk and needs computations, the individual is assigned to one of four quadrants: high risk/high need, low risk/high need, high risk/low need, and low risk/low need.[27]

The interrater reliability of the RANT is very good,[28–29] and preliminary validity studies are encouraging. In one such study, Marlowe observed a statistically significant predictive effect for the RANT (see **Figure 10-3**) and several nonstatistically significant trends with respect to matching risk/needs level with service level (e.g., higher risk/needs being assigned to more intensive service). The trend was greatest for high risk/high need offenders charged with property crimes. Rearrest (41% vs. 56%) and reconviction (24% vs. 44%) rates were lower for high-risk/high-need offenders assigned to drug court (high intensity) than for high-risk/high-need offenders assigned to traditional probation (low intensity).[30] The absence of a statistically significant effect makes these results suggestive and preliminary. The lack of statistical significance could have been the result of small cell sizes or the mixing of risks and needs. Further research on the RANT is clearly warranted given these promising preliminary findings.

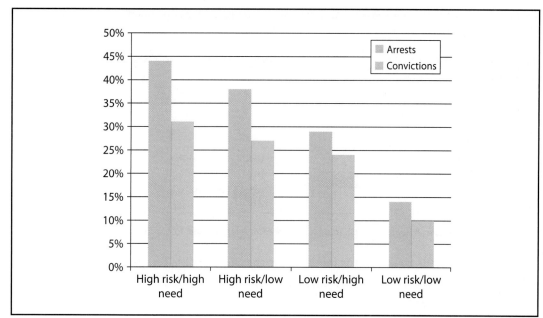

Figure 10-3
Percent arrests and convictions for different risk/needs levels of the RANT.

Data From: Marlowe, D. B., Festinger, D. S., Dugosh, K. L., Caron, A. Podkopacz, M. R., & Clements, N. T. (2011). Targeting dispositions for drug-involved offenders: A field trial of the Risk and Needs Triage (RANT). *Journal of Criminal Justice, 39,* 253–260.

Needs

Whereas risk measures are designed to identify custody/supervision (high, medium, low) and level of service (standard, intensive), needs measures are designed to identify specific areas requiring attention. Accordingly, needs measures typically offer a deeper and more detailed analysis of a problem behavior than risk measures. Some procedures attempt to assess both risks and needs (e.g., LSI-R, RANT), and although this approach has its advantages, particularly with respect to saving time and money and demonstrating that risks and needs are often two sides of the same coin, it may also dilute the risk assessment and provide only a superficial assessment of needs. I would therefore recommend that in most cases risk and needs assessment be carried out separately, using different procedures. Whereas the LSI-R is one of the best risk measures available to clinicians and probation officers, its ability to serve as a needs measure is limited. Therefore, although the nine LSI-R dynamic risk domains may be helpful in identifying areas in need of attention, a more thorough evaluation of each needs area may be required. Four of the nine dynamic risk/needs areas covered by the LSI-R are discussed in this section (see **Table 10-6**).

Alcohol and Drugs

The ASI and RANT can be used to assess alcohol- and drug-related risk and needs, although different sections of each instrument may be better equipped to handle one function or the other. For instance, the total ASI score and ASI Legal Status subscale along with the RANT risk items (current age, age of onset of substance abuse and delinquency, criminal history, and treatment history, in particular) would appear to be best suited for risk and general needs assessment. All of the ASI scales except legal status, all of the RANT needs items, and some of the RANT risk items (e.g., antisocial peers, employment/living stability) could be used to address specific needs. Because many substance abuse programs for drug-involved offenders must be sufficiently generic to be applicable to the greatest number of

Table 10-6 The Four Dynamic Risk Domains from the LSI-R that Serve as the Foundation for Primary Criminogenic Needs

LSI-R Dynamic Risk Domains	Primary Criminogenic Needs
• Education/Employment	
• Financial	
• Family/Marital	
• Accommodations	
• Leisure/Recreation	
• Alcohol/Drug Problems	Alcohol and Drugs
• Emotional/Personal	Antisocial Personality Processes
• Attitudes/Orientation	Antisocial (Criminal) Cognition
• Companions	Antisocial Peer Associations

Data From: Andrews, D. A., & Bonta, J. (1995). *The Level of Service Inventory-Revised*. Toronto, Canada: Multi-Health Systems.

clients, specific needs assessment is required for the best possible results. To this end, alcohol and drug needs can be broken down into four core issues:

- **Central versus Peripheral**
- Alcohol versus Illicit Drugs
- **Dependence versus Abuse**
- Drug-Related Problems

Central versus Peripheral

The first question that must be answered whenever one is conducting a needs assessment of the alcohol and drug domain is whether the person's drug use is central or peripheral to his or her criminal conduct. In other words, to what extent is the person's drug use **criminogenic**? The stronger the connection between a person's drug use and criminality the more central or criminogenic the drug use. Individuals whose drug use is peripheral to their criminality can sometimes be a disruptive influence in treatment, particularly if treatment takes place in a group setting. Not only can they detract from the group discussion but they can also serve as negative role models for less criminally inclined individuals. I am not suggesting that individuals with peripheral drug use be denied treatment, simply that they not be placed in the same group as those whose drug use is more central to their criminality.

Three bits of data can be useful in determining where along the central-peripheral continuum an individual's drug use falls. First, by comparing the age of onset of drug use and the age of onset of delinquency one can get an idea of the degree to which drug use is central (drug use started before delinquency) or peripheral (delinquency started before drug use) to crime. Second, the type of drug used can also be helpful in answering the central versus peripheral question. Some drugs (heroin, cocaine) tend to be more criminogenic than other drugs (marijuana, LSD). Third, examining usage patterns provides clues as to whether drugs normally support criminal involvement or crime normally supports drug involvement. The answers to these three questions can provide a wealth of information about the nature of the drug–crime relationship in a specific individual.

Alcohol versus Illicit Drugs

Being a legal substance, alcohol presents a different set of challenges than an illegal substance does. Hence, what works with alcohol may not work with illicit drugs and vice versa. Encouraging controlled drug usage is a viable harm reduction option with alcohol but not with illicit drugs. As a law enforcement agent and government employee, a probation officer cannot realistically or ethically encourage someone to control their use of cocaine or heroin, though they could certainly encourage them to control their use of alcohol or even refer them to a harm reduction program for alcohol. Given the ubiquity of alcohol, cue avoidance (avoiding drug-related cues) would be a more viable option in dealing with an illicit drug problem than with a drinking problem. Assessing the degree to which alcohol versus illicit drug is problematic for an individual could perhaps best be accomplished by comparing the alcohol and drug subscales of the ASI.

Dependence versus Abuse

Drug dependence suggests a more serious or engrained pattern of drug use than drug abuse. There is a general belief among many in the drug treatment field that abuse may be a precursor to dependence.[31] A recent study by a group of researchers from the University of Manitoba in Canada under the direction of Laurence Katz, however, produced results suggesting that drug abuse and drug dependence are distinct processes, with dependence displaying significantly greater **comorbidity** or crossover diagnoses than abuse. The crime–drug dependence relationship may, in fact, be stronger than the crime–drug abuse relationship as observed in comorbidity patterns involving **antisocial personality disorder** (ASPD). The drug dependence–ASPD correlation was four times higher than the drug abuse–ASPD correlation in the Katz et al. study and the alcohol dependence–ASPD correlation was nearly six times higher than the alcohol abuse–ASPD correlation.[32] The differential significance of substance dependence to criminality is further indicated by research showing that drug dependence is twice as common as drug abuse in criminal populations, a complete reversal of the abuse-dependence relationship in the general population (see **Figure 10-4**).

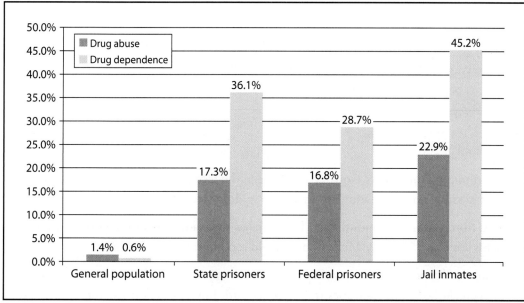

Figure 10-4
Prevalence of drug abuse and dependence in the general population, state prisoners, federal prisoners, and jail inmates.

Data From: Karberg, J. C., & James, D. J. (2005). Substance dependence, abuse, and treatment of jail inmates, 2002. Bureau of Justice Statistics Special Report (NCJ 209588). Washington, DC: U.S. Department of Justice, Mumola, C. J., & Karberg, J. C. (2006). Drug use and dependence, state and federal prisoners, 2004. Bureau of Justice Statistics Special Report (NCJ 213530). Washington, DC: U.S. Department of Justice, & U.S. Department of Health and Human Services. (2003). National Epidemiologic Survey on Alcohol and Related Conditions, 2002. Bethesda, MD: National Institutes of Health, National Institute on Alcohol Abuse and Alcoholism.

The RANT drug dependence scale would be a good place to start in assessing the drug dependence component of the alcohol and drug needs complex.

Drug-Related Problems

Substance abuse and dependence, particularly the latter, can lead to a wide range of additional problems, some of which are needs factors in their own right:

- Medical and mental health problems
- Financial problems/homelessness
- Social/relationship problems
- Occupational problems
- Time structuring problems

With respect to time structuring, drugs are highly effective in structuring a person's time. Consequently, after a person desists from drugs he or she will ordinarily have a lot of spare time on his or her hands. This time must be filled with productive activity or the individual risks returning to drugs out of boredom or for want of sufficient time structuring.

A needs assessment can be helpful, not only in setting goals for intervention, but also in determining whether a defendant should be processed through the criminal justice system or diverted to a drug or mental health program. Proposition 36 is a California program that diverts nonviolent offenders charged with drug possession into drug treatment. In treating substance abuse as a public health problem rather than as a criminal justice concern, Proposition 36 provides substance abuse treatment to individuals with elevated drug and alcohol needs. The program saved Californian taxpayers $1.4 billion in taxes over a 5-year period because the cost of treating nonviolent drug offenders in the community is several times less than the cost of incarcerating these same individuals in prison.[33] News Spot 10-2 describes how one person, actor Robert Downey Jr., personally benefitted from this program.

NEWS SPOT 10-2

Title: Downey Could Test New Drug Law—PROPOSITION 36: Measure Requires Treatment, Not Jail Time, for Many Users
Source: *Associated Press*
Author: Don Thompson
Date: May 13. 2001

Award-winning actor Robert Downey Jr. has been the face of young Hollywood drug addiction and possibly now the nation's most sweeping drug treatment experiment.

Released from prison nine months ago Downey has since added two more drugs arrests that ended his stint on TV's "Ally McBeal" and could send him back to prison.

But thanks to Proposition 36 a law California voters approved last November that might not happen. Although the law doesn't take effect until July 1 some prosecutors are already following it.

So if the 36-year-old Downey avoids prison he'll be like every other Californian with a nonviolent drug record and start with a clean slate under the new law.

That's because Proposition 36 takes away the threat of jail for drug offenders unless they are charged three more times with drug violations or repeatedly fail to cooperate in treatment programs.

Arizona started four years ago but California—the nation's most populous state—poses greater challenges and presents a larger proving ground for a plan that drug treatment advocates hope will spread elsewhere.

In Arizona about 6,000 offenders go through the system each year. Early projections indicate California will have to find room in already crowded community treatment programs for six times as many or 36,000 offenders. California's county probation departments also were far less prepared to oversee the coming flood of offenders.

The new law takes away the threat of jail or prison as an element of punishment for addicts said Alameda County District Attorney Tom Orloff president of the California District Attorneys Association.

But Robert Waters, Downey's attorney, said prison works for neither his client nor other addicts.

"What they need is treatment through either counseling or medication," Waters said. "Jail doesn't even address the problem."

Sixty percent of voters agreed with Waters so California will spend $660 million over 5½ years to funnel drug offenders to community treatment programs instead of prison and jail.

While estimates in some counties suggest fewer offenders will qualify for treatment than originally anticipated officials said more money is needed to give addicts long-term treatment and frequent drug tests to ensure they stay clean.

At the greatest premium are more expensive live-in drug treatment programs which county treatment coordinators said means some offenders who need residential programs will end up in outpatient counseling instead.

However they generally expect to expand existing community treatment programs to handle the influx ending fears that fly-by-night treatment programs might spring up across California to deal with the demand.

County probation departments and treatment providers are competing with each other for their share of the limited state allotment of $120 million a year but joining in support of a bill budgeting money for limited drug tests.

Questions to Ponder

1. How would you judge the success of the Proposition 36 program in the case of Robert Downey, Jr. more than a decade after he entered the program?
2. How can a state like California, which is already in deep financial trouble, afford to spend $120 million a year on drug treatment? Consider in your answer the

Robert Downey Jr. in court.

fact that it costs over $45,000 to keep an adult housed in a Californian prison for one year.

3. Are there other offender issues and problems that a program like Proposition 36 might be able to address?

Antisocial Personality Processes

Two higher order psychological constructs are commonly used to organize antisocial personality processes like low self-control, impulsivity, and stimulation-seeking into a single entity: **psychopathy** and antisocial personality disorder. Different measures are available for each construct.

Psychopathy

Psychopathy Checklist-Revised (PCL-R)

The **Psychopathy Checklist-Revised** is a 20-item clinical rating scale designed to assess the clinical construct of psychopathy. Each PCL-R item is scored on a three-point scale (0 = not present, 1 = possibly or partially present, 2 = definitely present). These items are then summed to form various scores. Clinicians usually examine the total PCL-R score first (range = 0–40) followed by a review of the four facet scores (interpersonal, affective, impulsive behavior, antisocial). Robert Hare, author of the PCL-R, recommends a cutting score of 30 on the total score for a definitive diagnosis of psychopathy. The facet scores can be helpful in identifying the aspects of the psychopathy construct that are most prominent in an individual's profile.[34]

The interrater reliability of the PCL-R in research studies is good.[35] However, when actual clinical cases are used to assess reliability, a procedure known as "field reliability," interrater agreement drops to a modest and barely acceptable level.[36–37] Moderate mean effect sizes were obtained in a meta-analysis of the PCL-R as a predictor of general and violent recidivism,[38] although the PCL-R was incapable of predicting recidivism above and beyond the effects of age and criminal history in another study.[39] Furthermore, when Walters and colleagues tested the incremental validity of the PCL-R facet scores they determined that the predictive strength of the PCL-R was due largely to the antisocial facet.[40]

Psychopathic Personality Inventory-Revised (PPI-R)

The **Psychopathic Personality Inventory-Revised** is a 154-item self-report measure designed to assess psychopathic personality disorder distinct from criminal behavior. The PPI-R assesses psychopathic traits covered by the PCL-R (egocentricity, superficial charm, lying, lack of remorse, emotional shallowness, risk taking, and manipulativeness) as well as psychopathic traits not covered by the PCL-R (inability to learn from punishment, lack of anxiety, fearlessness). The PPI-R yields a total score and eight subscale scores (Machiavellian Egocentricity, Social Potency, Coldheartedness, Carefree Nonplanfulness, Fearlessness, Blame Externalization, Impulsive Nonconformity, and Stress Immunity). Test-retest reliability is good when college students complete the PPI-R, although the reliability of the PPI-R has not been tested in offender samples.[41] One-, two-, and three-factor models have been proposed for the PPI-R but there is no consensus at this time as to which model is best.[42] The PPI-R has been found to correlate reasonably well with the PCL-R and other measures of psychopathy, though it has not been used to assess psychopathy in drug-involved offenders.[43]

Antisocial Personality Disorder

The Antisocial Personality Disorder (ASP) module of the **Structured Clinical Interview for DSM-IV Axis II Personality Disorders (SCID-II)**[44] and the Antisocial Features scale (ANT) of the Personality Assessment Inventory[45] can be used to assess antisocial personality disorder (ASPD). Questions remain, however, as to the ability of these measures and the previous psychopathy measures to predict recidivism independent of criminal history; as such, they are probably better used for needs assessment. Individuals high in psychopathy may be particularly difficult to treat because of their tendency to manipulate and charm therapeutic staff. With diagnostic criteria for ASPD gravitating toward the psychopathy construct,[46] information on either psychopathy or ASPD may be helpful in creating a treatment plan for this challenging but not untreatable[47] group of individuals.

Antisocial Cognition

Antisocial cognition or criminal thinking can be assessed in one of two ways: criminal thought process and criminal thought content. The **Psychological Inventory of Criminal Thinking Styles** (PICTS) is a measure of criminal thought process and the **Criminal Sentiments Scale-Modified** (CSS-M) is a measure of criminal thought content.

Psychological Inventory of Criminal Thinking Styles (PICTS)

The PICTS is an 80-item self-report measure made up of eight thinking style (TS) scales, two higher order factor scores (P and R), and a superordinate scale (GCT).[48] The higher-order scores, Proactive (P) and Reactive (R), measure planned and impulsive criminal thinking, respectively, and the General Criminal Thinking (GCT) score assesses an individual's overall level of criminal cognition. A recent **item response theory** (IRT) analysis indicates that the PICTS Sentimentality (Sn) thinking style scale does not load onto the general criminal thinking factor and so it is no longer used to calculate the GCT score.[49] **Figure 10-5** illustrates the hierarchical structure of the PICTS and the rules for computing the higher order and superordinate scores. Specifically, P is calculated by summing the raw scores for Mo, En, Po, and So, R is calculated by summing the raw scores for Co, Ci, and Ds, and GCT is calculated by summing the raw scores for P and R.

The test-retest reliability of the GCT, P, and R scores is good, whereas the test-retest reliability of the eight thinking style scales ranges from weak to good. The GCT is slightly more predictive of institutional adjustment and recidivism than the P and R scores, and all three possess moderate predictive validity. Results are more variable when the individual thinking style scores are analyzed. The GCT score is the most reliable and valid score or

Figure 10-5
Hierarchical organization of the PICTS; GCT = General Criminal Thinking, P = Proactive Criminal Thinking, R = Reactive Criminal Thinking, Mo = Mollification, En = Entitlement, Po = Power Orientation, So = Superoptimism, Co = Cutoff, Ci = Cognitive Indolence, Ds = Discontinuity.

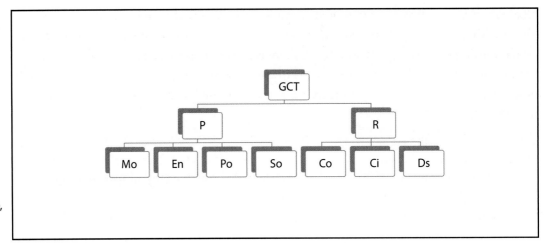

scale on the PICTS, largely because of its size (56 GCT items versus 32 P items, 24 R items, and 8 items for each TS scale). When using the PICTS to assess risk, emphasis should be placed on the GCT score. When using the PICTS to assess needs, all three levels of scores should be considered, starting with the GCT score, then moving to the P and R scores, and ending with the eight thinking style scales.

Incremental validity refers to the fact that a measure continues to predict an outcome even after controlling for other important and usually more easily obtainable measures. A useful predictor of criminal justice outcomes should therefore be capable of predicting recidivism and violence above and beyond the contributions of age and criminal history. As previously stated, the PCL-R failed to do so in two different samples.[51] Controlling for age and three different measures of criminal history (the LCSF-V score, prior convictions, and prior institutional infractions), the PICTS GCT score successfully predicted recidivism in two samples of released federal prisoners (see **Figure 10-6**).[52] The PICTS is

Figure 10-6
Effect size enhancement to age and criminal history with inclusion of a criminal thinking measure.

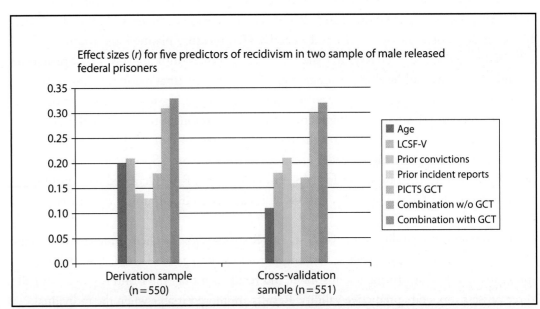

Data From: Walters, G. D. (2011). Taking the next step: Combining incrementally valid indicators to improve recidivism prediction. *Assessment, 18,* 227–233.

also effective for use with drug-involved offenders. Walters, as a case in point, determined that reactive criminal thinking not only correlated with a history of prior substance misuse but also mediated the relationship between prior substance abuse and subsequent recidivism.[53]

Criminal Sentiments Scale-Modified (CSS-M)

The PICTS is designed to measure criminal thought process (*how* an offender thinks). A complete evaluation of antisocial cognition requires that we also assess criminal thought content (*what* an offender thinks). The CSS-M is a 41-item self-report inventory that yields scores on three subscales:[54–55]

* Attitudes Toward the Law, Court, and Police (LCP)
* Tolerance for Law Violations (TLV)
* Identification with Criminal Others (ICO)

Whereas the TLV assesses Sykes and Matza's techniques of neutralization[56] and is therefore more reflective of criminal thought process, the LCP and ICO subscales are strong indicators of criminal thought content.

Test-retest reliability for the original CSS LCP and ICO subscales are moderate and modest, respectively,[57] and Simourd reports that the reliability of the total CSS-M and its three subscales is adequate.[58] There is evidence for the construct validity of the CSS-M[59] and it has been found to correlate with the behavioral (lifestyle, antisocial) but not personality (interpersonal, affective) components of psychopathy,[60] and predict violent recidivism in general offenders[61] and nonsexual but not sexual recidivism in sex offenders.[62] Research comparing and contrasting the PICTS and CSS-M may be particularly helpful in advancing antisocial cognition needs assessment with drug-involved offenders because as has been previously reported, drug users, even those without an official arrest record, display signs of criminally oriented thinking.

Antisocial Peer Associations

The **Self-Appraisal Questionnaire (SAQ)** is another self-report measure that might be helpful in the risk and needs assessment of drug-involved offenders. The SAQ's 67 items are spread across six scales:[63]

* Criminal Tendencies (CT)—antisocial attitudes, beliefs, and behaviors that reflect criminal thought content
* Antisocial Personality Problems (AP)—antisocial personality processes, patterns, and tendencies
* Conduct Problems (CP)—childhood and early adolescent behavioral problems
* Criminal History (CH)—one of the few self-report measures of criminal history available
* Alcohol/Drug Abuse (AD)—substance abuse difficulties
* Antisocial Associates (AS)—antisocial peer associations

One-week test-retest reliability estimates for the SAQ range from moderate to very high, with the total score achieving the highest reliability. The criterion validity of the SAQ is acceptable given its correlation with the PCL-R and LSI-R (see **Figure 10-7**).[64] Two-, 5-,

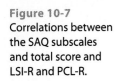

Figure 10-7
Correlations between the SAQ subscales and total score and LSI-R and PCL-R.

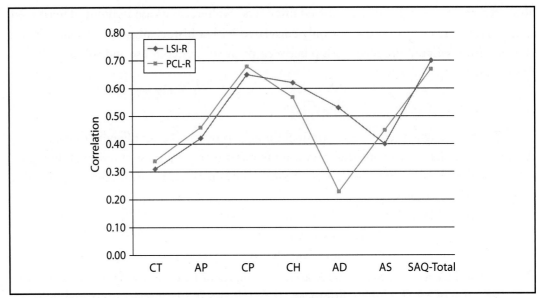

Data From: Loza, W., Dhaliwal, G., Kroner, D. G., & Loza-Fanous, A. (2000). Reliability, construct and concurrent validities of the Self-Appraisal Questionnaire (SAQ): A tool for assessing violent and non-violent recidivism. *Criminal Justice and Behavior, 27*, 356–374.

and 9-year follow-ups have shown that the SAQ is capable of predicting both violent and nonviolent recidivism.[65–67] The SAQ is not only capable of assessing the antisocial peer association needs factor but the other three needs factors discussed in this section as well (i.e., alcohol and drugs, antisocial personality processes, and antisocial cognition).

Responsivity

The responsivity principle asserts that the offender's ability to learn from an intervention or rehabilitation program is maximized by: (1) behavioral and cognitive-behavioral programs of intervention and (2) efforts to tailor the intervention to the participant's strengths, learning styles, and abilities. In accordance with this bifurcated view of responsivity, Andrews, Bonta, and Hoge divide responsivity into general and specific. General responsivity calls for the use of behavioral and cognitive-behavioral techniques when working with offenders. **Specific responsivity** entails "fine tuning" the behavioral and cognitive-behavioral intervention to take advantage of the individual's demographic status (age, gender), learning style, strengths, and personal proclivities.[68]

General Responsivity

The **general responsivity** principle asserts that interventions based on learning and social learning principles offer the greatest benefit to offender populations because they are applicable to the widest range of offender learning styles. Accordingly, behavioral and cognitive behavioral intervention techniques and strategies like role-playing, skills training, cognitive restructuring, and graduated reinforcement are more appropriate for use with offenders than nondirective relationship-oriented and psychodynamic insight-oriented techniques and strategies.[69]

Specific Responsivity

The effectiveness of a program that satisfies the general responsivity requirement of being behavioral or cognitive-behavioral in nature can be enhanced by taking specific responsivity into account. Specific responsivity involves tailoring the intervention to the demographic status, learning style, personal strengths and weaknesses, and thinking of the treated individual. Responsivity factors act as moderators of the treatment-outcome relationship. If Treatment A is found to reduce recidivism in males but not in females, then gender is said to moderate the Treatment A-recidivism relationship by way of specific responsivity. Four responsivity factors are discussed in this section:

- Gender
- Learning style and ability
- Self-esteem
- **Proactive versus reactive** criminal thinking

First, however, we examine a study that tried, unsuccessfully, to match substance abuse interventions to particular client characteristics, in what has become known as Project MATCH.

Project MATCH

Project MATCH was a multisite clinical trial (outpatient and aftercare) of alcoholism treatment designed to assess the effect of patient-treatment matching on outcome. Participants were randomly assigned to one of three conditions, each of which lasted 12 weeks: Twelve-Step Facilitation, Cognitive-Behavioral Coping Skills, and Motivational Enhancement Therapy. Upon completion of treatment, participants were evaluated every 3 months for a period of 1 year. Results indicated that participants in all three groups displayed decreased drinking, improved quality of life, and increased use of treatment services. However, there were no meaningful outcome differences between the groups nor was there any evidence of a significant interaction between any of the treatments and any of the person characteristics (e.g., gender, motivation, drinking severity) examined in this study. In short, the matching hypothesis failed to find support in this study.[70]

Project MATCH has been heavily criticized on both methodological and conceptual grounds. Stanton Peele has been one of the more vocal critics of this $30 million study. Peele lists several rather serious problems with the study. First, there was no control group to rule out the effects of natural recovery or unassisted change. Second, the brevity of the interventions (12 weeks) may have precluded any meaningful change in participants. Third, the focus on objective matching, in which individuals are matched with interventions based on various traits or symptoms, may not be as effective or useful as subjective matching, in which individuals are matched with interventions based on their values, preferences, and beliefs.[71] Research conducted in Europe, Peele notes, has consistently supported the efficacy of subjective matching.[72–74]

Gender

Both gender and a history of physical and/or sexual abuse can be considered potential responsivity factors. Many more females than males have been victimized by physical and sexual abuse and the gender gap is even wider when male and female offenders are compared.[75] Females, particularly females who have suffered sexual abuse, may be less responsive to certain forms of intervention (e.g., group therapy) than males or females who have not been abused. As such, they may require additional sessions to supplement the correctional intervention, even if it involves the use of noncriminogenic factors. Program content may need to be varied depending on gender, in that not only are female offenders more likely to have a history of physical and sexual victimization, but drug use, mental health problems, and relationship issues tend to be more prominent in female offenders than in male offenders.[76] A national survey of correctional administrators and supervisors, in fact, revealed that 80% believed a different set of management strategies were required in working with male and female offenders.[77]

Learning Style and Ability

Learning style is another putative responsivity factor capable of influencing an offender's responsiveness to a behavioral or cognitive-behavioral intervention. Some offenders are visual learners, others are auditory learners, and still others are hands-on learners. Cognitive-behavioral intervention will probably work best with auditory and visual learners, whereas hands-on learners will more often be responsive to a straight behavioral intervention. Meredith Thanner and Faye Taxman tested both the risk and responsivity principles in a study in which offenders were matched to different forms of substance abuse treatment. The results indicated that high-risk offenders benefitted significantly more from the intervention and that the intervention was most effective when the service was delivered in a manner consistent with the learning style of the treated offender.[78]

Self-Esteem

Although **self-esteem** is not a criminogenic need, it can serve as a responsivity factor. James Bonta speculates that offenders with low self-esteem may not participate in group interventions and may require more support from an experienced therapist than offenders with high self-esteem.[79] Exploring the relationship between self-esteem and recidivism, Dana Hubbard found that self-esteem failed to correlate with recidivism in the total sample, but interacted with race such that higher self-esteem correlated with recidivism in black participants and lower self-esteem correlated with recidivism in white participants.[80] Other research suggests that although self-esteem is uncorrelated with recidivism in male offenders, it tends to be negatively correlated with recidivism in female offenders.[81] Self-esteem, it would seem, could be used to modify an intervention to make it more relevant to subgroups of offenders.

Proactive versus Reactive Criminality

Subjective matching involves matching clients to interventions based on their attitudes, thoughts, and preferences. As such, criminal thinking, proactive and reactive criminal thinking in particular, could be considered a potential responsivity factor. Research indicates that reactive criminal thinking but not proactive criminal thinking responds to skill-based interventions like anger and stress management (see **Figure 10-8**).[82] In addition, reactive criminal thinking but not proactive criminal thinking correlates with prior substance misuse and may mediate the relationship between substance misuse and recidivism.[83] Additional research is required to identify intervention strategies effective in reducing proactive criminal thinking, although it is speculated that challenging the outcome and efficacy expectancies believed to support proactive criminality would be a good place to start.[84]

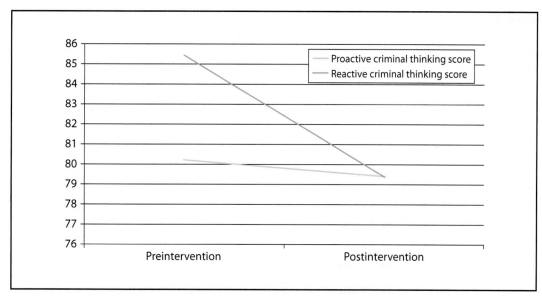

Figure 10-8
Pre- to postintervention changes in proactive and reactive criminal thinking in offenders participating in a 10-week anger management class.

Data From: Walters, G. D. (2009). Anger management training in incarcerated male offenders: Differential impact on proactive and reactive criminal thinking. *International Journal of Forensic Mental Health, 8,* 214–217.

It is interesting and noteworthy that criminal thinking, as measured by the PICTS, could potentially play an important role in all three functions of the RNR model. Not only is the PICTS GCT score a reasonably consistent predictor of recidivism, but it also has been found to predict recidivism above and beyond the contributions of such popular static risk factors as age and criminal history.[85] It therefore makes sense that it could play a role in risk assessment. The eight PICTS thinking style scales, on the other hand, seem better suited to needs assessment in that they represent different facets of criminal thinking that could serve as goals for intervention. Although the Proactive (P) and Reactive (R) Criminal Thinking scores would also appear to be relevant to needs assessment, their greatest role may be as responsivity factors.

Summary and Conclusions

- Risk factors for criminality and drug abuse are helpful in determining an individual's risk of violence and recidivism. These risk factors can either be static (unchangeable) or dynamic (changeable) and are included in popular risk assessment instruments. Two second-generation risk measures, two third-generation risk measures, and two substance abuse risk measures were examined.
- Needs factors are used to establish goals for change and intervention. Four general groupings of needs were reviewed in this chapter. Alcohol and drug needs were explored as were needs pertaining to antisocial personality processes, antisocial cognition in the form of criminal thought process and criminal thought content, and antisocial peer associations.
- Responsivity optimizes an intervention by identifying the format (behavioral or cognitive-behavioral) most likely to benefit an offender. This is referred to as general responsivity. The goal of specific responsivity is to match certain client characteristics or preferences to a specific form or version of behavioral or cognitive-behavioral intervention in an effort to achieve an optimal treatment effect.

Key Terms

Actuarial Prediction   Making use of static risk factors like age, gender, and criminal history and empirically derived decision rules, matrices, or cutting scores to sort cases into categories of high and low risk.

Addiction Severity Index (ASI)   Semistructured interview designed to assess seven areas relevant to substance abuse risk.

Antisocial Personality Disorder   Personality disorder characterized by blatant disregard for the rights of others and frequent violation of the rules of society.

Central versus Peripheral   Degree to which drug involvement is criminogenic (central) or noncriminogenic (peripheral).

Clinical Prediction   Use of professional judgment to predict a behavior.

Comorbidity   Overlapping membership in two or more different diagnostic categories.

Criminal Sentiments Scale-Modified (CSS-M)   A 41-item self-report inventory designed to measure criminal thought content (i.e., *what* an offender thinks).

Criminogenic   Capable of causing crime.

Dependence versus Abuse   Degree to which drug involvement is more (dependence) or less (abuse) severe.

First-Generation Risk Assessment   Risk assessment based exclusively on professional judgment.

General Responsivity   Improving the odds of an offender benefitting from an intervention by using behavioral or cognitive-behavioral techniques.

Historical, Clinical, Risk-20 (HCR-20)   Rating scale composed of 20 static and dynamic risk factors.

Item Response Theory (IRT)   A modern approach to test development and validation that focuses on how individual test items perform; also known as latent trait theory.

Learning Style   Manner in which a person approaches new learning situations, either visually, auditorily, or behaviorally (hands-on).

Level of Service Inventory-Revised (LSI-R)   A 54-item interview procedure that produces scores for one static risk domain and nine dynamic risk domains.

Lifestyle Criminality Screening Form (LCSF)   A 14-item chart audit form used to assess criminal risk composed exclusively of static risk factors.

Needs   Targets for intervention in the form of criminogenic variables known to correlate with recidivism.

Project MATCH   Multisite clinical trial in which certain client characteristics were matched to one of three interventions: Twelve-Step Facilitation, Cognitive-Behavioral Coping Skills, and Motivational Enhancement Therapy.

Psychological Inventory of Criminal Thinking Styles (PICTS)   An 80-item self-report inventory designed to measure criminal thought process (i.e., *how* an offender thinks).

Psychopathic Personality Inventory-Revised (PPI-R)   A 154-item self-report inventory designed to measure psychopathic personality disorder distinct from criminal behavior.

Psychopathy   Personality disorder marked by callousness, selfishness, irresponsibility, impulsiveness, lack of remorse, and a tendency to get involved in a variety of antisocial behaviors.

Psychopathy Checklist-Revised (PCL-R)   A 20-item rating scale designed to assess the clinical construct of psychopathy.

Proactive versus Reactive   Degree to which a person is planful (proactive) or impulsive (reactive) in his or her criminal thinking and behavior.

Reliability   The consistency of test scores over time, across ratings, or for different versions of a test.

Responsivity   Maximizing an offender's odds of benefitting from an intervention by using a behavioral or cognitive-behavioral approach and attempting to match the intervention to the individual's learning style and personal strengths.

Risk   Estimate of the danger presented by an individual for violence, recidivism, relapse, or suicide.

Risk and Needs Triage (RANT)   A 19-item automated assessment procedure designed to assess drug risks and needs in a criminal justice context.

Salient Factor Score   A six-item checklist used to assess criminal risk composed exclusively of static risk factors.

Second-Generation Risk Assessment   Risk assessment based exclusively on static (historical) risk factors.

Self-Appraisal Questionnaire (SAQ)   A 67-item self-report inventory used to assess criminal history, antisocial personality processes, early conduct problems, criminal thought content, alcohol and drug abuse, and antisocial peer associations.

Self-Esteem   A person's appraisal of his or her value to self and others.

Specific Responsivity   Improving the odds of an offender benefitting from an intervention by matching the intervention to the individual's learning style and personal strengths.

Statistical Prediction   Use of actuarial or mechanical formulae or cutting scores to predict a behavior.

Structured Clinical Interview for DSM-IV Axis II Personality Disorders (SCID-II)   Structured interview designed to assess the 10 personality disorders contained in the fourth edition of the *Diagnostic and Statistical Manual of Mental Disorders*, including Antisocial Personality Disorder.

Third-Generation Risk Assessment   Risk assessment based on a combination of static (historical) and dynamic (changeable) risk factors.

Validity   Degree to which a test measures what it purports to measure.

Critical Thinking

1. If third-generation risk procedures tend to perform at about the same general level as second-generation risk procedures in predicting recidivism or relapse, what is their value?

2. Three of the "Big Four" risk factors are actually needs factors. Drug abuse is not listed as one of these "Big Four" needs factors but can you make a case for drug abuse deserving at least as much attention as antisocial personality processes, antisocial cognition, and antisocial peer associations in assessing and classifying offenders?

3. Differentiate between general and specific responsivity. How can both be assessed in the same interview and with the same questions?

Notes

1. Andrews, D. A., Bonta, J., & Hoge, R. (1990). Classification for effective rehabilitation: Rediscovering psychology. *Criminal Justice and Behavior, 17*, 19–52.

2. Meehl, P. E. (1954). *Clinical versus. statistical prediction: A theoretical analysis and a review of the evidence.* Minneapolis: University of Minnesota Press.

3. Grove, W. M., & Meehl, P. E. (1996). Comparative efficacy of informal (subjective, impressionistic) and formal (mechanical, algorithmic) prediction procedures: The clinical-statistical controversy. *Psychology, Public Policy, and Law, 2*, 293–323.

4. Grove, W. M., Zald, D. H., Lebow, B. S., Snitz, B. E., & Nelson, C. (2000). Clinical versus mechanical prediction: A meta-analysis. *Psychological Assessment, 12*, 19–30.

5. Campbell, M. A., French, S., & Gendreau, P. (2009). The prediction of violence in adult offenders: A meta-analytic comparison of instruments and methods of assessment. *Criminal Justice and Behavior, 36*, 567–590.

6. Walters, G. D., White, T. W., & Denney, D. (1991). The Lifestyle Criminality Screening Form: Preliminary data. *Criminal Justice and Behavior, 18*, 406–418.

7. Walters, G. D. (1998). The Lifestyle Criminality Screening Form: Psychometric properties and practical utility. *Journal of Offender Rehabilitation, 27*, 9–23.

8. Walters, G. D. (2012a). *Crime in a psychological context: From career criminals to criminal careers.* Thousand Oaks, CA: Sage.

9. Walters, G. D. (2003a). Predicting criminal justice outcomes with the Psychopathy Checklist and Lifestyle Criminality Screening Form: A meta-analytic comparison. *Behavioral Sciences & the Law, 21*, 89–102.

10. Hoffman, P. B. (1983). Screening for risk: A revised salient factor score (SFS 81). *Journal of Criminal Justice, 11*, 539–547.

11. Hoffman, P. B. (1984). Twenty years of operational use of a risk prediction instrument: The United States Parole Commission's Salient Factor Score. *Journal of Criminal Justice, 22*, 477–494.

12. Webster, C. K., Douglas, D. E., Eaves, D., & Hart, D. (1997). *HCR-20 assessing risk for violence: Version II.* Burnaby, British Columbia, Canada: Mental Health, Law & Policy Institute, Simon Fraser University.

13. Warren, J. I., South, S. C., Burnette, M. L., Rogers, A., Friend, R., Bale, R., et al. (2005). Understanding the risk factors for violence and criminality in women: The concurrent validity of the PCL-R and HCR-20. *International Journal of Law and Psychiatry, 28*, 269–289.

14. Yang, M., Wong, S. C. P., & Coid, J. (2010). The efficacy of violence prediction: A meta-analytic comparison of nine risk assessment tools. *Psychological Bulletin, 136*, 740–767.

15. Andrews, D. A., & Bonta, J. (1995). *The Level of Service Inventory-Revised.* Toronto, Canada: Multi-Health Systems.

16. Lowenkamp, C. T., Holsinger, A. M., Brusman-Lovins, L., & Latessa, E. J. (2004). Assessing the inter-rater agreement of the Level of Service Inventory-Revised. *Federal Probation, 68*(3), 34–38.

17. Andrews, D. A., Bonta, J., & Wormith, J. S. (2006). The recent past and near future of risk and/or need assessment. *Crime & Delinquency, 52,* 7–27.

18. Smith, P., Cullen, F. T., & Latessa, E. J. (2009). Can 14,737 women be wrong? A meta-analysis of the LSI-R and recidivism for female offenders. *Criminology and Public Policy, 8,* 183–208.

19. Kelly, C. E., & Welsh, W. N. (2008). The predictive validity of the Level of Service Inventory-Revised for drug-involved offenders. *Criminal Justice and Behavior, 35,* 819–831.

20. McLellan, A. T., Luborsky, L., Woody, G. E., & O'Brien, C. P. (1980). An improved diagnostic evaluation instrument for substance abuse patients. The Addiction Severity Index. *Journal of Nervous and Mental Disorders, 168,* 26–33.

21. McLellan et al. (1980).

22. McLellan, A. T., Luborsky, L., Cacciola, J., Griffith, J., Evans, F., Barr, H. L., et al. (1985). New data from the Addiction Severity Index: Reliability and validity in three centers. *Journal of Nervous and Mental Disorders, 173,* 412–422.

23. Appleby, L., Dyson, V., Altman, E., & Luchins, D. J. (1997) Assessing substance use in multiproblem patients: Reliability and validity of the Addiction Severity Index in a mental hospital population. *Journal of Nervous and Mental Disease, 185,* 159–165.

24. Zanis, D. A., McLellan, A. T., & Randall, M. (1994). Can you trust patient self-reports of drug use during treatment? *Drug and Alcohol Dependence, 35,* 127–132.

25. Gresnigt, J. A. M., Breteler, M. H. M., Schippers, G. M., & Van den Hurk, A. A. (2000). Predicting violent crime among drug-using inmates: The Addiction Severity Index as a prediction instrument. *Legal and Criminological Psychology, 5,* 83–95.

26. Jaffe, A., Du, J., Huang, D., & Hser, Y.-I. (2012). Drug-abusing offenders with co-morbid mental disorders: Problem severity, treatment participation, and recidivism. *Journal of Substance Abuse Treatment, 43,* 244–250.

27. Marlowe, D. B. (2009). Evidence-based sentencing for drug offenders: An analysis of prognostic risks and criminogenic needs. *Chapman Journal of Criminal Justice, 1,* 167–201.

28. Festinger, D. S., Marlowe, D. B., Lee, P. A., Kirby, K. C., Bovasso, G., & McLellan, A. T. (2002). Status hearings in drug court: When more is less and less is more. *Drug and Alcohol Dependence, 68,* 151–157.

29. Marlowe, D. B., Festinger, D. S., Lee, P. A., Dugosh, K. L., & Benasutti, K. M. (2006). Matching judicial supervision to clients' risk status in drug court. *Crime and Delinquency, 52,* 52–76.

30. Marlowe, D. B., Festinger, D. S., Dugosh, K. L., Caron, A., Podkopacz, M. R., & Clements, N. T. (2011). Targeting dispositions for drug-involved offenders: A field trial of the Risk and Needs Triage (RANT). *Journal of Criminal Justice, 39,* 253–260.

31. Samet, J. H. (2007). Drug abuse and dependence. In L. Goldman and D. Ausiello (Eds.), *Cecil Medicine* (23rd ed., pp. 174–181). Philadelphia, PA: Saunders Elsevier.

32. Katz, L. Y., Cox, B. J., Clara, I. P., Oleski, J., & Sacevich, T. (2011). Substance abuse versus dependence and the structure of common mental disorders. *Comprehensive Psychiatry, 52,* 638–643.

33. Drug Policy Alliance. (2006). *Proposition 36: Improving lives, delivering results.* Los Angeles: Author.

34. Hare, R. D. (2003). *The Hare Psychopathy Checklist-Revised manual.* (2nd ed.). Toronto, Canada: Multi-Health Systems.

35. Hare (2003).

36. Murrie, D. C., Boccaccini, M. T., Turner, D. B., Meeks, M., Woods, C., & Tussey, C. (2009). Rater [dis]agreement on risk assessment measures in sexually violent predator proceedings: Evidence of adversarial allegiance in forensic evaluation? *Psychology, Public Policy, and Law, 15,* 19–53.

37. Edens, J. F., Boccaccini, M. T., & Johnson, D. W. (2010). Inter-rater reliability of the PCL-R total and factor scores among psychopathic sex offenders: Are personality features more prone to disagreement than behavioral features? *Behavioral Sciences & the Law, 28,* 106–119.

38. Gendreau, P., Goggin, C., & Smith, P. (2002). Is the PCL-R really the "unparalleled" measure of offender risk? A lesson in knowledge cumulation. *Criminal Justice and Behavior, 29,* 397–426.

39. Walters, G. D. (2012b). Psychopathy and crime: Testing the incremental validity of PCL-R-measured psychopathy as a predictor of general and violent recidivism. *Law and Human Behavior, 36,* 404–412.

40. Walters, G. D., Knight, R. A., Grann, M., & Dahle, K.-P. (2008). Incremental validity of the Psychopathy Checklist facet scores: Predicting release outcome in six samples. *Journal of Abnormal Psychology, 117*, 396–405.

41. Lilienfeld, S. O., & Widows, M. R. (2005). *Psychopathic Personality Inventory—Revised (PPI-R)*. Lutz, FL: Psychological Assessment Resources.

42. Anestis, J. C., Caron, K. M., & Carbonell, J. L. (2011). Examining the impact of gender on the factor structure of the Psychopathic Personality Inventory—Revised. *Assessment, 18*, 340–349.

43. Copestake, S., Gray, N. S., & Snowden, R. J. (2011). A comparison of a self-report measure of psychopathy with the Psychopathy Checklist-Revised in a UK sample of offenders. *Journal of Forensic Psychiatry & Psychology, 22*, 169–182.

44. First, M. B., Gibbon, M., Spitzer, R. L., Williams, J. B., & Benjamin, L. (1997). *Structured clinical interview for DSM-IV Axis II personality disorders (SCID-II)*. Washington, DC: American Psychiatric Press.

45. Morey, L. C. (2007). *The Personality Assessment Inventory (PAI): Professional manual* (2nd ed.). Lutz, FL: Psychological Assessment Resources.

46. Hesse, M. (2010). What should be done with antisocial personality disorder in the new edition of the diagnostic and statistical manual of mental disorders (DSM-V)? *BMC Medicine, 8*, 66.

47. Walters, G. D. (1995). The Psychological Inventory of Criminal Thinking Styles: Part I. Reliability and preliminary validity. *Criminal Justice and Behavior, 22*, 307–325.

48. Walters, G. D., Hagman, B. T., & Cohn, A. M. (2011). Towards a hierarchical model of criminal thinking: Evidence from item response theory and confirmatory factor analysis. *Psychological Assessment, 23*, 925–936.

49. Walters, G. D. (2012a).

50. Walters, G. D. (2012b).

51. Walters, G. D. (2011). Taking the next step: Combining incrementally valid indicators to improve recidivism prediction. *Assessment, 18*, 227–233.

52. Walters, G. D. (2012c). Substance abuse and criminal thinking: Testing the countervailing, mediation, and specificity hypotheses. *Law and Human Behavior, 36*, 506–512.

53. Gendreau, P., Grant, B. A., Leipciger, M., & Collins, C. (1979). Norms and recidivism rates for the MMPI and selected empirical scales on a Canadian delinquency sample. *Canadian Journal of Behavioral Science, 11*, 21–31.

54. Simourd, D. J. (1997). The Criminal Sentiments Scale-Modified and Pride in Delinquency Scale: Psychometric properties and construct validity of two measures of criminal attitudes. *Criminal Justice and Behavior, 24*, 52–70.

55. Sykes, G., & Matza, D. (1957). Techniques of neutralization: A theory of delinquency. *American Sociological Review, 22*, 664–670.

56. Simourd (1997).

57. Andrews, D. A., & Wormith, J. S. (1990). [A summary of normative, reliability, and validity statistics on the Criminal Sentiments Scale]. Unpublished data.

58. Simourd (1997).

59. Simourd, D. J., & Olver, M. E. (2002). The future of criminal attitudes research and practice. *Criminal Justice and Behavior, 29*, 427–446.

60. Simourd (1997).

61. Simourd, D. J., & Van De Ven, J. (1999). Assessment of criminal attitudes: Criterion-related validity of the Criminal Sentiments Scale-Modified and Pride in Delinquency Scale. *Criminal Justice and Behavior, 26*, 90–106.

62. Witte, T. D., Di Placido, C., Gu, D., & Wong, S. C. P. (2006). An investigation of the validity and reliability of the Criminal Sentiments Scale in a sample of treated sex offenders. *Sexual Abuse: A Journal of Research and Treatment, 18*, 249–258.

63. Loza, W. (1996). Self-Appraisal Questionnaire (SAQ): A tool for assessing violent and nonviolent recidivism. Unpublished manuscript.

64. Loza, W., Dhaliwal, G., Kroner, D. G., & Loza-Fanous, A. (2000). Reliability, construct and concurrent validities of the Self-Appraisal Questionnaire (SAQ): A tool for assessing violent and non-violent recidivism. *Criminal Justice and Behavior, 27*, 356–374.

65. Loza et al. (2000).

66. Loza, W., & Loza-Fanous, A. (2003). More evidence for the validity of the Self-Appraisal Questionnaire for predicting violent and nonviolent recidivism. *Criminal Justice and Behavior, 30*, 709–721.

67. Loza, W., MacTavish, A., & Loza-Fanous, A. (2007). A nine-year follow-up study on the predictive validity of the Self-Appraisal Questionnaire for predicting violent and nonviolent recidivism. *Journal of Interpersonal Violence, 22*, 1144–1155.

68. Andrews et al. (1990).

69. Andrews et al. (1990).

70. Project MATCH Research Group. (1997). Matching alcoholism treatments to client heterogeneity: Project MATCH posttreatment drinking outcomes. *Journal of Studies on Alcohol, 58*, 7–29.

71. Peele, S. (1998). Ten radical things NIAAA research shows about alcoholism. *The Addictions Newsletter, 5*(2), 6, 17–19.

72. Heather, N., Rollnick, S., & Winton, M. (1983). A comparison of objective and subjective measures of alcohol dependence as predictors of relapse following treatment. *British Journal of Clinical Psychology, 22*, 11–17.

73. Orford, J., & Keddie, A. (1986). Abstinence or controlled drinking: A test of the dependence and persuasion hypotheses. *British Journal of Addiction, 81*, 495–504.

74. Booth, P. G., Dale, B., Slade, P. D., & Dewey, M. E. (1992). A follow-up study of problem drinkers offered a goal choice option. *Journal of Studies on Alcohol, 53*, 594–600.

75. Harlow, C. W. (1999). Prior abuse reported by inmates and probationers. *Bureau of Justice Statistics: Selected findings*. Washington, DC: U.S. Department of Justice.

76. Palmer, E. J., Jinks, M., & Hatcher, R. M. (2010). Substance use, mental health, and relationships: A comparison of male and female offenders serving community sentences. *International Journal of Law and Psychiatry, 33*, 89–93.

77. Schram, P. J., Koons-Witt, B. A., & Morash, M. (2004). Management strategies when working with female prisoners. *Women & Criminal Justice, 15*, 25–50.

78. Thanner, M. H., & Taxman, F. S. (2003). Responsivity: The value of providing intensive services to high-risk offenders. *Journal of Substance Abuse Treatment, 24*, 137–147.

79. Bonta, J. (1995). The responsivity principle and offender rehabilitation. *Forum on Corrections Research, 7*, 34–37.

80. Hubbard, D. J. (2006). Should we be targeting self-esteem in treatment for offenders: Do gender and race matter in whether self-esteem matters? *Journal of Offender Rehabilitation, 44*, 39–57.

81. Epstein, J. A., Griffin, K., & Botvin, G. (2004). Efficacy, self-derogation, and alcohol use among inner-city adolescents: Gender matters." *Journal of Youth and Adolescence, 33*, 159–166.

82. Walters, G. D. (2009). Anger management training in incarcerated male offenders: Differential impact on proactive and reactive criminal thinking. *International Journal of Forensic Mental Health, 8*, 214–217.

83. Walters (2012c).

84. Walters (2012a).

85. Walters (2011).

CHAPTER 11

INTERVENING WITH THE DRUG-INVOLVED OFFENDER

© Alina555/iStockphoto

Of the five core goals of corrections (**retribution**, **incapacitation**, **deterrence**, **rehabilitation**, and **restoration**), rehabilitation may be the least well understood. As a means of facilitating change in drug-involved offenders, rehabilitation encompasses experiences, programs, and interventions designed to alter the thinking and behavior of lawbreakers and make it less likely that they will participate in criminal activity in the future. Rehabilitation, in fact, was the dominant theme in corrections for 20 years, starting in the mid-1950s and ending in the mid-1970s. There were several events, however, that helped shift the emphasis from rehabilitation to punishment. First, an unprecedented increase in the crime rate that began in the mid-1960s showed no signs of abating a decade later despite a sizable increase in prison programming. Second, a nationwide rise in prison violence and several major prison riots, such as the one at New York's Attica State Prison in 1971, raised serious questions about the value of rehabilitation. Finally, in 1974 Robert Martinson, responding to the results of a meta-analysis he had just conducted with two colleagues,[1] published his highly influential essay entitled "What Works? Questions and Answers about Prison Reform," in which he concluded that "with few and isolated exceptions, the rehabilitative efforts that have been reported so far have had no appreciable effect on recidivism."[2,p.25] These events led to a devaluation of the rehabilitation ideal and a corollary reduction in interest on the part of scholars, practitioners, and policy-makers in prison rehabilitation programs.

This chapter attempts to make sense of correctional programming by addressing the relevant issues in sections organized around the following three objectives:

- Determine whether intervention should be a goal of the correctional system by examining the principles of effective intervention and offender change.
- Discuss models of intervention that have been employed with drug-involved offenders, including the 12-step model, the **cognitive-behavioral model**, the **motivational interviewing model**, and the **relapse prevention model**.
- Review major issues in implementing programs with drug-involved offenders, such as the prevalence of unassisted change, the role of the therapeutic relationship in fostering change, group versus individual counseling, community versus institutional corrections, inpatient versus outpatient intervention, therapeutic communities, compulsory treatment, and aftercare.

Principles of Effective Intervention

Between 1954 and 1974 the guiding philosophy of correctional programming was that practically "**everything works**" in bringing about change in offenders. After Martinson's stinging 1974 critique, however, the philosophy changed to one of "**nothing works**." In the mid-1980s a new philosophy emerged, one that sought to figure out "what works." The "**what works**" philosophy is based on the four principles of effective or evidence-based intervention. Three of these principles (risk, need, responsivity) are extensions of the three principles of effective correctional assessment. A fourth principle (fidelity) has been added to the list of evidence-based principles for intervention. The overlap in principles for effective assessment and effective intervention underscores the interrelatedness of the two constructs and reveals why assessment is so important. It is important precisely because it helps maximize the impact and effectiveness of intervention in bringing about offender change.[3]

Each of the four principles of effective or evidence-based intervention is designed to answer a different question. The **risk principle**, for instance, is designed to answer the question of *who* should be the primary target of correctional intervention. The **needs principle** seeks answers to the question of *what* is the proper focus of correctional intervention. The **responsivity principle** is geared toward answering yet another question; in this case, *how* a correctional intervention should be administered to achieve maximum benefit. Finally, the **fidelity principle** tries to answer the question of *how well* the correctional intervention needs to be implemented in order to be effective.[4] We begin by examining the risk principle and the question of who should be the primary target of correctional intervention and programming.

Risk Principle

The risk principle asserts that correctional programs are most effective when higher risk offenders are targeted. In the past, risk has been defined in terms of crime and recidivism but in working with drug-involved offenders, risk should also be defined in terms of drug use and relapse. Results from several meta-analyses indicate that interventions targeting high-risk offenders usually achieve the best results. Andrews and Dowden analyzed 374 effect sizes from 225 general correctional outcome studies and uncovered consistent support for the risk principle, with particularly strong effects for juveniles and females (see **Figure 11-1**).[5] Chris Lowenkamp, Edward Latessa, and Alexander Holsinger performed a meta-analysis of residential and nonresidential community-based programs (diversion, halfway house, community corrections) and discovered that higher risk individuals received the greatest benefit from programming above and beyond the use of behavioral and cognitive-behavioral interventions. As illustrated in **Figure 11-2**, the effect sizes became positive only when analyses were restricted to studies composed of at least 66% high-risk participants.[6]

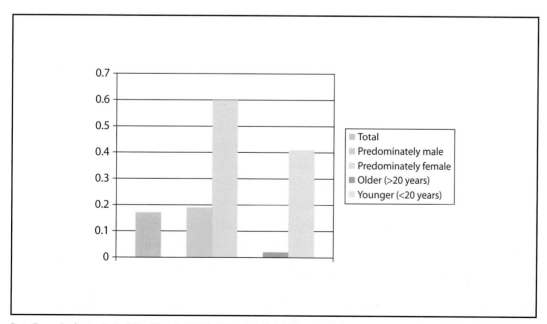

Figure 11-1
Degree of difference (η) between higher risk and lower risk effect sizes for the total sample of studies, studies composed predominately of male participants, studies composed predominately of female participants, studies composed of older participants, and studies composed of younger participants.

Data From: Andrews, D. A., & Dowden, C. (2006). Risk principle of case classification in correctional treatment : A meta-analytic investigation. *International Journal of Offender Therapy and Comparative Criminology, 50,* 88–100.

Figure 11-2
Effect size (*r*) as a function of the risk and responsivity (cognitive-behavioral or behavioral) principles in offenders participating in residential and nonresidential programs.

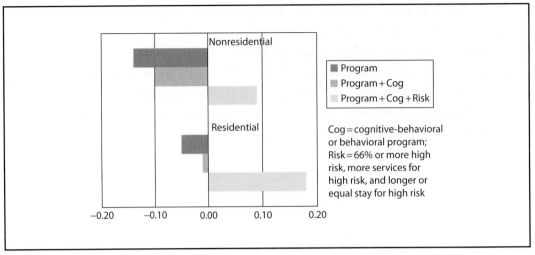

Data From: Lowenkamp, C. T., Latessa, E. J., & Holsinger, A. M. (2006). The risk principle in action: What have we learned from 13,676 offenders and 97 correctional programs? *Crime and Delinquency, 52,* 77–93.

The results of the Lowenkamp et al. meta-analysis revealed that low-risk offenders enrolled in treatment frequently experienced worse outcomes than low-risk offenders not enrolled in treatment. Nearly two-thirds of the effect sizes for low-risk offenders in the Lowenkamp et al. meta-analysis were negative, which is several times higher than the number of negative outcomes recorded for high-risk offenders (see **Figure 11-3**).[7] A study of recidivism in a group of electronically monitored offenders by Bonta, Wallace-Capretta, and Rooney also determined that more intensive services produced negative results for low risk offenders and positive results for high risk offenders (see **Figure 11-4**).[8] It is easy to understand why high-risk offenders might benefit from a more intensive program given their greater need for structure, supervision, control, and treatment, but why do low-risk offenders receiving treatment fare worse than untreated low-risk controls? There appear to be at least two reasons for the detrimental effect of more intensive treatment on lower risk offenders:[9–10]

- Receiving more supervision and scrutiny increases opportunities for noncompliance and a corresponding rise in technical violations for low-risk offenders.
- Most interventions are conducted in groups; therefore, by including high- and low-risk offenders in the same group one is increasing the odds of low-risk offenders being adversely affected by their association with high-risk offenders.

Several studies have examined the risk principle as applied specifically to drug-involved offenders. Kevin Knight, Dwayne Simpson, and Matthew Hiller conducted a 3-year follow-up of high- and low-risk drug-involved offenders previously enrolled in a prison-based **therapeutic community** and identified a significant treatment effect only for the high-risk group (see **Figure 11-5**).[11] Whereas Knight et al. estimated risk from the Salient Factor Score, Taxman, Thanner, and Weisburd estimated risk from indicators of both past criminality and prior drug use. Randomly assigning drug-involved probationers to either a seamless model of intensive drug treatment or a standard treatment protocol and using subsequent drug use and criminality as outcome measures, Taxman and colleagues recorded a small positive effect for the seamless treatment in high-risk probationers (*d* = .20 to .23) and a negative effect for the seamless protocol in moderate-risk probationers (*d* = −.18 to −.46).[12]

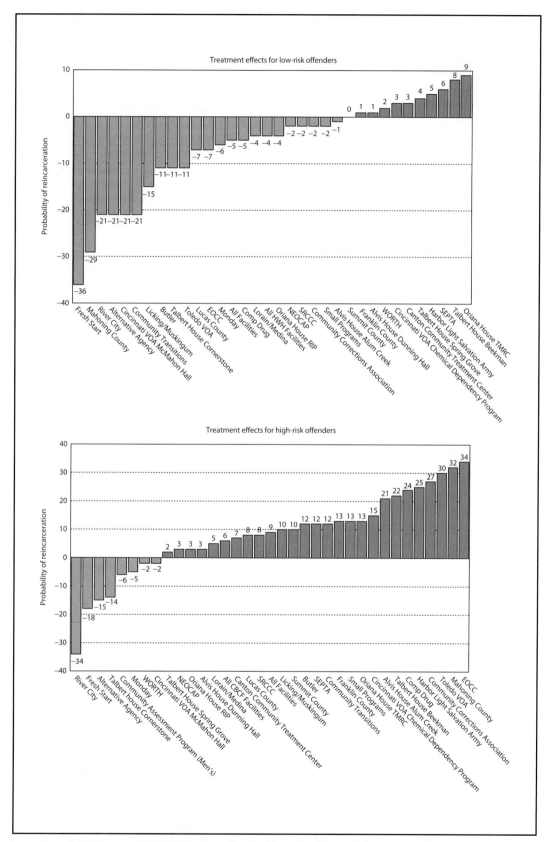

Figure 11-3
Individual effect sizes for each study included in the Lowenkamp and Latessa meta-analysis broken down into low-risk and high-risk offenders (blue = positive treatment effect; orange = negative treatment effect).

Lowenkamp, C. T., & Latessa, E. J. (2004). *Understanding the risk principle: How and why correctional interventions can harm low-risk offenders.* Washington, DC: U.S. Department of Justice, National Institute of Corrections, Topics in Community Corrections.

Figure 11-4
Percentage of recidivism in an intensive rehabilitation supervision program as a function of high versus low risk.

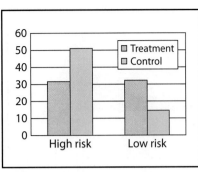

Data From: Bonta, J., Wallace-Capretta, S., & Rooney, J. (2000). A quasi-experimental evaluation of an intensive rehabilitation supervision program. *Criminal Justice and Behavior, 27*, 312–329.

Figure 11-5
Percentage of recidivism 3 years after treatment in high- and low-risk drug-involved offenders.

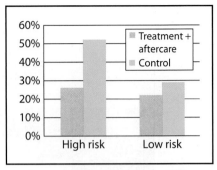

Data From: Knight, K., Simpson, D. D., & Hiller, M. L. (1999). Three-year reincarceration outcomes for in-prison therapeutic community treatment in Texas. *The Prison Journal, 79*, 337–351.

Needs Principle

The needs principle asserts that treatment will be maximally effective when it addresses **criminogenic** needs. Criminogenic needs are variables that correlate with recidivism and change in concert with a change in recidivism risk. A criminogenic need can also be considered a dynamic risk factor to the extent that it is capable of change and capable of predicting recidivism. Several examples of criminogenic needs include:

- Antisocial personality processes
- Antisocial attitudes and values
- Antisocial peer associations
- Family dysfunction
- Weak self-control, poor problem-solving skills
- Substance abuse and dependence
- Unemployment, lack of employment skills

Noncriminogenic needs are variables that do not correlate with recidivism and do not change in concert with changes in recidivism risk. Examples of noncriminogenic needs include:

- Self-esteem
- Anxiety
- Physical fitness
- Major mental illness

The results of several meta-analyses have shown that a concentrated focus on criminogenic needs is associated with more positive outcomes than a focus on noncriminogenic needs. In the original meta-analysis on this issue, Andrews and colleagues determined that programs holding to the principles of effective correctional programming (including a focus on criminogenic needs) were significantly more effective than programs not holding to these principles.[13] Andrews and Dowden confirmed these findings in a specific test of the needs principle, demonstrating that the needs effect surfaced in both high- and low-risk offenders (see **Figure 11-6**).[14] In a third meta-analysis, Dowden and Andrews observed a moderately strong positive effect for programs targeting criminogenic needs and various levels of negative effect for programs targeting noncriminogenic needs (see **Figure 11-7**).[15] Programs that target criminogenic needs can also have a positive impact on institutional adjustment. In a meta-analysis of studies testing the impact of programs on in-prison behavior, Sheila French and Paul Gendreau determined that programs addressing

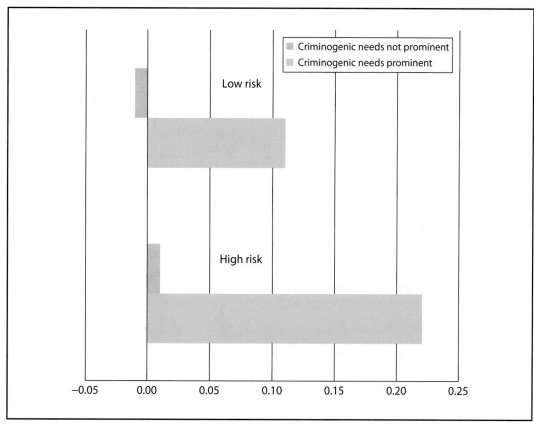

Figure 11-6
Effect size (*r*) as a function of need focus of program (prominent, not prominent) in low-risk and high-risk offenders.

Data From: Andrews, D. A., & Dowden, C. (2006). Risk principle of case classification in correctional treatment: A meta-analytic investigation. *International Journal of Offender Therapy and Comparative Criminology, 50*, 88–100.

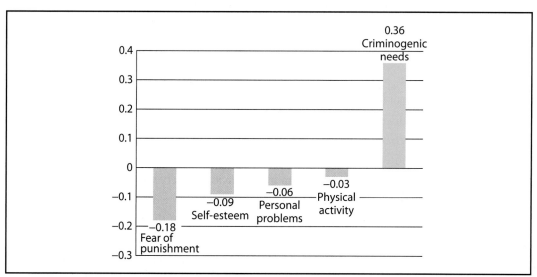

Figure 11-7
Effect sizes (*r*) for interventions targeting criminogenic and noncriminogenic needs in youthful offenders.

Data From: Dowden, C., & Andrews, D. A. (1999). What works in young offender treatment: A meta-analysis. *Forum on Corrections Research, 11(2)*, 21–24.

a larger number of criminogenic needs were more successful in reducing institutional misconduct than programs addressing only a few criminogenic needs (see **Figure 11-8**).[16]

In the previously mentioned Taxman et al. study, need, as represented by an elevated score on the Addiction Severity Index (ASI) drug use scale, moderated the relationship between participation in a seamless intensive drug program and subsequent drug use and criminality. Whereas high-need offenders who completed the seamless program exhibited lower levels of drug use and crime than controls, moderate-need program participants displayed higher levels of drug

Figure 11-8
Effect sizes (r) for programs targeting more or fewer criminogenic needs on institutional adjustment.

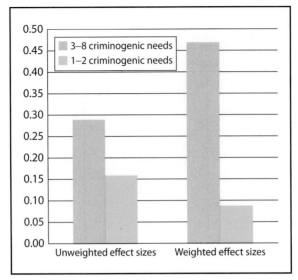

Data From: French, S. A., & Gendreau, P. (2006). Reducing prison misconducts: What works! *Criminal Justice and Behavior, 33*, 185–218.

use and crime than controls.[17] Mary McMurran notes that in England and Wales, one of the criteria for accreditation of an offender treatment program is that it targets one or more criminogenic needs. This requirement is waived for programs that target substance abuse because substance abuse is considered a major criminogenic need.[18] Nonetheless, for maximum efficiency an offender treatment program, whether designed for substance-involved offenders or offenders in general, should address as many criminogenic needs as possible.

Responsivity Principle

The responsivity principle holds that offenders will respond best to interventions that match their strengths, abilities, needs, and learning styles. There are two versions of responsivity covered by the responsivity principle: **general responsivity** and **specific responsivity**. General responsivity states that behavioral and cognitive-behavioral interventions provide the best match for the strengths, abilities, needs, and learning styles of most offenders and should produce results superior to those attained with nonbehavioral approaches. Specific responsivity holds that further improvements in outcome can be achieved by matching specific offender attributes to specific intervention strategies.

General Responsivity

The results of a 1994 meta-analysis by Don Andrews revealed that behavioral interventions for offenders produced an average effect size that was four times greater than the effect size produced by nonbehavioral interventions (see **Figure 11-9**).[19] Several meta-analyses conducted after the Andrews investigation indicated that cognitive-behavioral forms of intervention may be even more effective than straight behavioral interventions.[20–23] In the Landenberger and Lipsey meta-analysis, no differences were noted between the different versions of cognitive therapy commonly employed in corrections, including the four versions reviewed in

Figure 11-9
A comparison of effect sizes (r) for behavioral and nonbehavioral interventions with offenders.

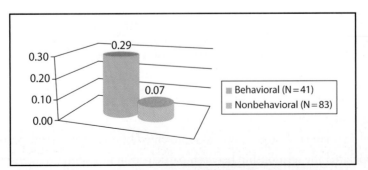

Data From: Andrews, D. A. (1994). An overview of treatment effectiveness: Research and clinical principles. Department of Psychology, Carleton University.

the next section of this chapter: Reasoning and Rehabilitation, Moral Reconation Therapy, Aggression Replacement Training, and Thinking for a Change.[24]

In a 1999 meta-analysis of drug programs for offenders, Pearson and Lipton uncovered mixed support

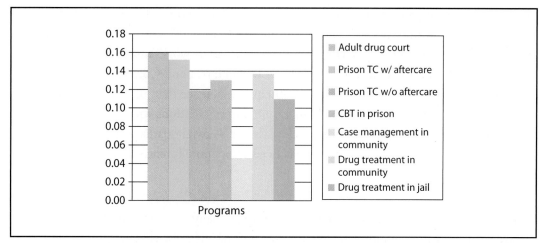

Figure 11-10
Effect sizes (*r*) obtained by different programs for drug-involved offenders.

Data From: Aos, S., Miller, M., & Drake, E. (2006). *Evidence-based adult corrections programs: What works and what does not.* Olympia, WA: Washington State Institute for Public Policy.

for cognitive-behavioral intervention for substance-abusing offenders. Except for therapeutic communities, which received fair-to-good support, nearly all of the other treatment modalities received poor ratings. In the Pearson and Lipton meta-analysis, cognitive-behavioral interventions achieved fair-to-poor results.[25] Two more recent meta-analyses, one by Aos, Miller, and Drake and the other by Landenberger and Lipsey, however, garnered support for the use of cognitive-behavioral interventions in samples of drug-involved offenders. In the Aos et al. study, prison-based cognitive-behavioral interventions achieved results comparable to community drug programs (see **Figure 11-10**),[26] despite the fact community interventions normally produce better results than prison-based programs.[27] In the Landenberger and Lipsey meta-analysis, the strongest effects were attained when high-risk offenders were targeted and anger management and interpersonal problem solving were included in the curriculum.[28]

Additional research is required to determine why cognitive-behavioral, and to a lesser extent, behavioral, interventions are so effective with adult and juvenile offenders. I would argue that there are at least three reasons for this. First, the cognitive and behavioral risk factors that maintain criminality are frequently targeted by traditional behavioral and cognitive-behavioral intervention programs. Second, the action-oriented nature of behavioral and cognitive-behavioral intervention (skills training, role playing) fits well with the "hands-on" learning styles of many offenders. Finally, the practice of reinforcing clients for positive change, so much a part of the behavioral and cognitive-behavioral traditions, would appear to be particularly effective with offenders, many of whom have never received much in the way of praise or positive feedback.

Specific Responsivity

In one of the few studies to examine specific responsivity, Dana Hubbard tested the effect of gender, intelligence, depression, self-esteem, and a history of sexual abuse on treatment response in a sample of community corrections clients and found little evidence of specific responsivity. Whereas females appeared to respond better to the cognitive-behavioral intervention than males, as evidenced by lower levels of subsequent recidivism, this may simply reflect the fact that females are arrested less often than males. Hence, this finding cannot be attributed to specific responsivity because there were no untreated male and female offenders to serve as controls.[29] A specific responsivity effect was recorded by Walters in a study where a skills-based program (i.e., anger management training) was found to be effective in reducing reactive but not proactive criminal thinking.[30] Robert Hare and others have argued that traditional treatment may make psychopathic offenders worse and so psychopathy may act as a specific responsivity factor.[31] A study by Rice, Harris, and Cormier, in fact, showed that treated psychopaths engaged in more subsequent violence than untreated psychopaths.[32] Randy Salekin has reviewed the literature on interventions with psychopathic individuals, however, and found that individuals classified as psychopaths may actually respond to treatment, although the intervention may need to be more intensive than usual.[33]

Fidelity Principle

The fidelity principle requires that program integrity be maintained over the course of an intervention. Poor program implementation can spoil an otherwise effective program. One of the reasons why Project Greenlight, a reentry program for inmates in New York State, failed despite its cognitive-behavioral format is that the program was poorly implemented. Not only did Project Greenlight fail to properly evaluate participant needs but it lacked a viable **aftercare** component.[34] Program fidelity requires that program participants be selected on the basis of need and that criminogenic needs be the focus of attention. Second, treatment staff should be adequately trained and supervised to make sure that they are implementing the program properly. Third, the program should have adequate administrative support.

Paul Gendreau and Don Andrews created the **Correctional Program Assessment Inventory (CPAI)** to assess the degree to which programs abide by the fidelity principle. The six sections of the CPAI each evaluate a different aspect of the fidelity principle:[35]

- Program Implementation—how is the program explained to participants, who is in charge, and how are roadblocks to effective implementation handled?
- Offender Preservice Assessment—how are program participants selected and risk-need-responsivity (RNR) principles assessed?
- Program Characteristics—how are the treatment techniques and strategies structured to address important criminogenic thoughts and behaviors?
- Staff Characteristics—what are the qualifications, training needs, and responsibilities of program staff?
- Evaluation—how is the attainment of program goals monitored and evaluated and is there a mechanism in place for periodic review of the entire program?
- Other Items—how strong is support from the community and administration, how stable is the funding, and are records completed and stored in a competent and ethical manner?

Matthews, Hubbard, and Latessa applied the CPAI to 86 programs and discovered that most were not abiding by the fidelity principle (see **Table 11-1**).[36] In the previously reviewed Landenberger and Lipsey meta-analysis, a significant relationship was observed between program fidelity and subsequent recidivism, with higher levels of fidelity predicting lower levels of future recidivism.[37] A meta-analysis by Lowenkamp, Latessa, and Smith also unearthed evidence of a fidelity–recidivism relationship. In this study, programs with higher estimated scores on the CPAI, indicating greater conformity to the fidelity principle, were more effective in suppressing recidivism, as reflected in a higher control–program difference in recidivism (see **Figure 11-11**).[38]

Table 11-1 Results from 86 Programs Using the Correctional Program Assessment Inventory (CPAI)

| | Programs in Each Catogary | | | | | | | | |
| | Very Satisfactory (70% to 100%) | | Satisfactory (60% to 69%) | | Needs Improvement (50% to 59%) | | Unsatisfactory (<50%) | | |
CPAI Area	%	n	%	n	%	n	%	n	M
Program implementation (11 items)	69.8	60	11.6	10	14	12	4.7	4	72.99
Client preservice assessment (11 items)	27.9	24	1.2	1	16.3	14	54.7	47	47.94
Progam characteristics (22 items)	7.0	6	12.8	11	25.6	22	54.7	47	43.91
Staff member characteristics (8 items)	34.9	30	17.4	15	25.6	22	22.1	19	60.12
Evaluation (8 items)	14.0	12	2.3	2	10.5	9	73.3	63	38.39
Other (6 items)	74.4	64	17.4	15	7.0	6	1.2	1	83.91
Overall (66 items)	10.6	9	27.1	23	28.2	24	34.1	29	54.87

Matthews, B., Hubbard, D. J., & Latessa, E. J. (2001). Making the next step: Using evaluability assessment to improve correctional programming. *The Prison Journal, 81,* 454–472. Reprinted by Permission of SAGE Publications.

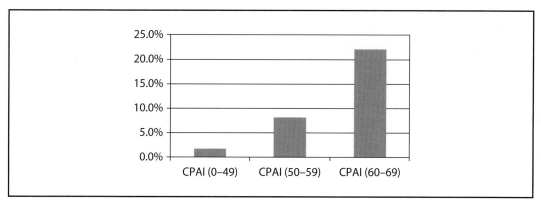

Figure 11-11
Differences in recidivism between program participants and controls for three different levels of program integrity as measured by the CPAI.

Data From: Lowenkamp, C. T., Latessa, E. J., & Holsinger, A. M. (2006). The risk principle in action: What have we learned from 13,676 offenders and 97 correctional programs? *Crime and Delinquency, 52,* 77–93.

Evidence-Based Treatment

The principles of effective correctional practice (risk, need, responsivity, and fidelity) provide an operational definition of what has become known in the medical and psychological fields as evidence-based treatment. To the extent that a correctional program focuses on higher risk individuals, targets criminogenic needs, is behavioral or cognitive-behavioral in nature, and is properly implemented, it is evidence based. Even if a program is effective, the taxpayer is well within his or her rights to ask whether the effect is worth the cost. There is no simple answer to this question, but Romani, Morgan, Gross, and McDonald have gathered some interesting data on this issue. Using results from the original Andrews et al. meta-analysis,[39] Romani and colleagues estimated the cost of traditional punishment, inappropriate services (not consistent with RNR principles), and appropriate services (consistent with RNR principles) to be $44, $69, and $60 per day, respectively. Factoring in the differential levels of recidivism associated with each program category, traditional punishment was found to cost $40.43 for a 1% reduction in recidivism, inappropriate services were found to cost $19.67 for a 1% reduction in recidivism, and appropriate services were found to cost $2.80 for a 1% reduction in recidivism.[40] These preliminary findings suggest that following RNR principles may reduce crime and save money.

Models of Intervention for Drug-Involved Offenders

Four different models of intervention commonly used with substance abusing offenders are covered in this section:

- 12-Step Model
- Cognitive-Behavioral Model
- Motivational Interviewing Model
- Relapse Prevention Model

Each model is evaluated using eight criteria for evidence-based correctional programming identified by Meghan Guevara and Enver Solomon. Even a cursory review of these criteria reveals that they overlap extensively with the principles of effective correctional practice. According to these criteria, an evidence-based correctional program should:[41]

- Assess risks and needs
- Enhance intrinsic motivation
- Target interventions for:
  - Risk, needs, and responsivity
  - Dosage level (40–70% high-risk offenders for 3–9 months)
- Offer skills training with direct practice (cognitive-behavioral)
- Supply positive reinforcement (behavioral)
- Build prosocial support systems in the community
- Measure and document offender change
- Provide participants with feedback on progress

Twelve-Step Model

The **12-step model** is probably the most commonly used approach with drug-involved offenders. It derives from **Alcoholics Anonymous (AA)** and has been applied to a wide range of substance-related and nonsubstance-related problems. Its popularity can be traced to its availability, simplicity, and the general absence of viable alternatives. A person can find a 12-step meeting in virtually any town in America with a church. In addition, the treatment philosophy and procedure are succinctly summarized in 12 simple steps. Finally, up until just recently, there have been few viable alternatives to the 12-step approach. Programs like AA and other substance-related 12-step programs are based on a self-help model in which the people who run the meetings are recovering alcoholics or addicts themselves and where external motivation ("higher power"), mentoring ("sponsor"), self-labeling, and powerlessness over alcohol and drugs are emphasized.

Judges, probation officers, and parole boards often send drug-involved offenders to 12-step meetings, unaware of the problems and confusion this can create. According to Mark Gornik, aspects of the 12-step philosophy and approach are potentially counterproductive when applied to offenders. Some of the potential pitfalls associated with the use of the 12-step model with corrections populations include:

- Limited structure and lack of formal recognized leadership
- Admission of powerlessness
- Religious emphasis

- Disclosure of shortcomings and handicaps in front of peers
- Failure to directly confront criminal thinking and behavior

Failure to directly confront criminal thinking is particularly problematic because aspects of the 12-step philosophy (e.g., powerlessness) can be used to justify past and future criminal behavior ("I am powerless over my urge to commit crime"). In conjunction with a program that focuses on criminal thinking, the 12-step model may be helpful in addressing certain substance-related issues but it is of limited value as a stand-alone procedure for drug-involved offenders.[42]

In my own experience, the 12-step insistence on abstinence is viewed as unacceptable by many adolescent and young adult offenders and its emphasis on powerlessness runs counter to one of the processes (i.e., self-efficacy) that has been found to support positive change in 12-step programs like AA.[43] In addition, 12-step models of intervention promote dependency, which is incompatible with the personality styles of offenders, which tend to be antisocial rather than dependent in nature. Finally, 12-step programs are not particularly receptive to research, thereby making it difficult to establish empirical efficacy. Evaluating the 12-step model against the eight criteria of evidence-based programming, there are twice as many areas of weakness as there are pockets of strength (see **Table 11-2**), suggesting that the 12-step model is not evidence based for use with correctional populations.

Cognitive-Behavioral Model

Cognitive-behavioral intervention or cognitive-behavior therapy (CBT), has received substantial empirical support and is the basis of the general responsivity principle discussed in the previous section. Research also supports the utility of CBT with drug-involved offenders, although the effect is less robust or perhaps more circumscribed. CBT is grounded in learning (classical conditioning, operant conditioning) and social learning (cognitive social) principles and follows one of two treatment methods: **cognitive skills training** and cognitive restructuring. Cognitive skills training involves learning cognitive or mental skills (e.g., problem solving, anger control, social skills), the acquisition of which tends to reduce

Table 11-2 Evidence-Based Status of the 12-Step Model

Evidence-Based Criteria the 12-Step Model Satisfies

(6) Build prosocial support systems in the community—*the 12-step community is composed of a fellowship of other users and the guidance of a sponsor.*

(8) Provide participants with feedback on progress—*12-step programs seek to provide participants with regular feedback on how their behavior is affecting those around them.*

Evidence-Based Criteria the 12-Step Model Does Not Satisfy

(1) Assess risks and needs—*without professional leadership there is no risk/needs assessment.*

(2) Enhance intrinsic motivation—*motivation in 12-step programs is almost exclusively external (i.e., higher power).*

(4) Offer skills training with direct practice—*skills training interventions are not normally used by 12-step programs.*

(7) Measure and document offender change—*12-step programs do not keep records and in some cases seem antagonistic to scientific research; consequently, measuring and documenting offender change is not typically part of the 12-step protocol.*

the individual's propensity for offending. **Cognitive restructuring** entails challenging and altering destructive or faulty beliefs (e.g., thinking styles, thinking errors), the elimination of which tends to reduce the individual's propensity for offending.[44] The four models described in this section—Reasoning and Rehabilitation, Moral Reconation Therapy, Aggression Replacement Training, and Thinking for a Change—employ one or both of these methods.

Reasoning and Rehabilitation

Reasoning and Rehabilitation (R&R) was the first formal cognitive-behavioral intervention created specifically for criminal offenders.[45] It is normally presented in 36 two-hour sessions and makes frequent use of role plays, group discussions, cognitive exercises, dilemma puzzles, and Socratic questioning. Because R&R targets cognitive and behavioral skill deficits identified by research as prevalent in offender populations, it focuses nearly exclusively on cognitive skills training. Listed here are some of the skills R&R attempts to teach offenders.

- Social and interpersonal skills
- Lateral thinking or creativity skills
- Critical reasoning skills
- Values clarification skills
- Assertiveness skills
- Negotiation skills
- Social perspective-taking skills

A meta-analysis of experimental studies by Joy Tong and David Farrington revealed that R&R participants achieved a mean reduction in recidivism of 14% compared to nontreated control participants. In addition, R&R has been found effective in the three countries where it has been studied: namely, Canada, where it was developed, the United States, and the United Kingdom. The Tong and Farrington meta-analysis further indicated that R&R was equally effective for institutional and community samples and for high as well as low risk participants.[46] These results suggest that R&R exerts a mild to moderate dampening effect on recidivism in adult and juvenile offenders who complete the program.

Moral Reconation Therapy

Moral Reconation Therapy (MRT) is a systematic step-by-step cognitive-behavioral intervention typically delivered in 12–16 sessions. Each session is normally 90 minutes in length. Overall, MRT attempts to:[47]

- Instruct participants in the identification and rectification of thinking errors
- Promote a healthy prosocial identity in participants
- Encourage participants to strive for higher levels of moral reasoning

Unlike R&R, which focuses almost exclusively on cognitive skill development, MRT employs heavy doses of cognitive restructuring and moral retraining to bring about cognitive and behavioral change in offenders.

Meta-analyses conducted on criminal justice clients enrolled in community- and prison-based programs indicate that recidivism is significantly reduced in graduates of MRT relative to control subjects, with slightly better outcomes for participants in community-based programs.[48–49] A 20-year follow-up by the developers of MRT revealed significantly lower rearrest (81.2% vs. 93.6%) and reconviction (60.8% vs. 81.8%) rates for graduates compared to controls.[50] Although these results are encouraging, much of the outcome research on MRT has been conducted by the developers of the program. Additional investigation by outside researchers is consequently required to rule out an **allegiance effect**.[51]

Aggression Replacement Training

Aggression Replacement Training (ART) is a cognitive-behavioral intervention designed for aggressive children and adolescents. The program is delivered in 30 sessions over a 10-week period, three sessions per week. The three weekly sessions are dedicated to one of the three principle program components of ART:[52]

- Social skills training
- Anger-control training
- Moral reasoning training

Like R&R, ART emphasizes cognitive skills training, and like MRT, it pays significant attention to the development of moral reasoning skills.

ART was originally designed for use with aggressive adolescents and demonstrates a clear ability to reduce aggression in youthful offenders.[53] It has also been used successfully with adult offenders. Ruth Hatcher and colleagues, for instance, compared violent male adult offenders enrolled in an ART probation program and a group of violent male control probationers matched with program participants on age, current offense, criminal history, and overall risk. In a 10-month follow-up, control subjects experienced a significantly higher rate of reconviction (50.9%) than ART participants (39.2%).[54] A meta-analysis by Landenberger and Lipsey also uncovered moderate support for the efficacy of ART, particularly the anger management component.[55]

Thinking for a Change

Thinking for a Change (T4C) is an integrated, cognitive-behavioral intervention for offenders developed by Barry Glick, Jack Bush, and Juliana Taymans, in cooperation with the National Institute of Corrections.[56] The curriculum consists of 25 lessons designed to teach the three core components of the program:

- Cognitive restructuring
- Social skills development
- Problem-solving skills training

Of the four models described in this section, T4C may do the best job of integrating the cognitive restructuring and cognitive skills methods into a single model.

Research has consistently shown that participation in T4C can lower recidivism. Golden, Gatchel, and Cahill, for instance, observed a 33% lower rate of recidivism in probationers graduating from a T4C program compared to a control group of nontreated probationers.[57] Chris Lowenkamp and colleagues discerned that community corrections clients exposed to, but not necessarily graduating from, a T4C intervention had an adjusted recidivism rate of 23% compared to 35% for controls.[58] The evidence-based status of CBT approaches like T4C is more firmly established than it is for the 12-step approach (see **Table 11-3**). **Table 11-4**, in addition, lists some of the more prominent differences between the cognitive-behavioral and 12-step models.

Table 11-3 Evidence-Based Status of the Cognitive-Behavioral Model

Evidence-Based Criteria the Cognitive-Behavioral Model Satisfies

(1) Assess risks and needs—*behavioral assessment is vital to CBT.*

(4) Offer skills training with direct practice—*nearly all interventions in CBT take a skills approach with plenty of opportunity for direct practice.*

(5) Supply positive reinforcement—*reinforcing success and positive behavior is an essential component of CBT.*

(6) Build prosocial support systems in the community—*aftercare is essential for effective CBT and is usually built into the program.*

(7) Measure and document offender change—*CBT programs are nearly all manualized and assessment of progress and achievement of treatment goals is practiced regularly.*

(8) Provide participants with feedback on progress—*participants are continually receiving feedback on how they are progressing.*

Evidence-Based Criteria the Cognitive-Behavioral Model Does Not Satisfy

(2) Enhance intrinsic motivation—*nothing in CBT directly ties into enhancing internal motivation for change.*

Table 11-4 Contrasting the 12-Step and Cognitive-Behavioral Models

FUNCTION	12-STEP	CBT
Source	Tradition	Innovation
Model	Disease	Social Learning
Emphasis	Powerlessness	Empowerment
Labeling	Person	Behavior or Lifestyle
Change	Hitting Bottom	Life Events
Objective	Abstinence	Harm Reduction

Although none of the four CBT programs described in this section were designed specifically for drug-involved offenders, many drug-involved offenders have successfully completed these programs. The Federal Bureau of Prisons (BOP) has been providing 500 hours of comprehensive drug treatment programming to drug-involved offenders for over 2 decades now. Each one of the 10-month residential programs operated by the BOP incorporates aspects of the four programs described in this section (i.e., cognitive skills training, cognitive restructuring, anger management training, criminal thinking) and offers participants aftercare services that continue treatment while the individual is in the halfway house or on supervised release. The results, as described in News Spot 11-1, are quite encouraging.

NEWS SPOT 11-1

Title: Federal Study Touts Effectiveness of Prison-Based Treatment
Source: *Alcoholism & Drug Abuse Weekly*
Author: none cited
Date: March 9, 1998

Prison inmates who complete residential drug abuse treatment programs while incarcerated are substantially less likely to be rearrested or become involved in further drug use after their release, according to a recent study conducted by researchers at the Federal Bureau of Prisons.

Federal inmates who completed a residential treatment program were 73 percent less likely to be rearrested in the first six months after release than were similar inmates who did not receive treatment. The respective rearrest rates were 3.3 percent for inmates completing treatment and 12.1 percent for those who did not receive treatment.

In addition, inmates who completed residential drug abuse treatment were 44 percent less likely to test positive for drug use in the first six months after release than were inmates who had not received treatment. Positive urinalysis rates were 20.5 percent for those who received treatment and 36.7 percent for those who did not receive treatment.

These findings are noteworthy because prior research has stated that the first six to 12 months following an offender's release are critical to successful reintegration into the community.

Daniel Dunne, a spokesman for the Bureau of Prisons, told ADAW that residential substance abuse treatment for inmates is not only making a difference in the lives of offenders, but it is also saving taxpayer money in terms of decreased health care and criminal-justice costs.

Dunne notes that 61 percent of all inmates in the federal prison system were incarcerated for an alcohol or drug-related offense (see ADAW, Jan. 19), and that about 30 percent of federal prisoners have a chronic substance abuse problem. The total number of federal inmates has increased from 41,000 in 1987 to 115,000 at present.

Dunne said that in the federal prison system, treatment is generally available for any inmate who wants it. Those who are identified as having a need for treatment but are resistant to entering treatment may be given incentives to enter a program, including higher pay for their prison jobs or more desirable placement in halfway-house programs.

The federal treatment study involved 1,866 inmates at more than 30 facilities. Inmates were treated in a comprehensive prison-based program affording them up to 500 hours of treatment while in prison; the program included participation in community transitional services when the inmate was transferred to a halfway house prior to release. The treatment focused on assuming individual responsibility and changing future behavior.

Alcoholism & Drug Abuse Weekly. "Federal study touts effectiveness of prison-based treatment." Copyright 1998, John Wiley & Sons, Inc. This material is printed with the permission of John Wiley & Sons, Inc.

Questions to Ponder

1. **In what ways could a program like the Federal BOP's residential drug program save taxpayers money?**
2. **What are the active ingredients in the BOP's residential drug program? In other words, what makes it work?**
3. **Why are the first 6 to 12 months so critical to offender reentry?**

Motivational Interviewing

Motivational interviewing (MI) is a procedure developed by William Miller, professor emeritus of psychology at the University of New Mexico. MI is not so much a stand-alone procedure as it is an adjunct or supplement to behavioral and cognitive-behavioral interventions. Miller has challenged traditional conceptualizations of motivation—such as the ones held by groups like AA—that view motivation as a stable trait. He argues instead that motivation evolves out of an unfolding helping relationship. Hence, a therapist, counselor, or probation officer can enhance an offender's motivation for change by developing a positive helping relationship with the offender.[59] MI was originally designed for substance abusing clients but its applicability to corrections and drug-involved offenders, in particular, seems self-evident.

Some of the motivation-enhancing recommendations made by proponents of MI include:[60]

- Avoid labels like addict and alcoholic
- Provide feedback and give advice
- Avoid dictating solutions, maximize personal choice
- Support self-efficacy and reinforce successive approximations to the end goal
- Express empathy and demonstrate understanding
- Roll with the resistance and avoid arguments
- Develop and explore discrepancies between goals and current behavior

Prochaska and DiClemente's **stages-of-change (SOC) model** fits nicely into the MI framework and the two are often used together. The five stages of the SOC model are precontemplation, contemplation, preparation, action, and maintenance, with relapse sometimes included as a sixth stage (see **Figure 11-12**). Someone in the **precontemplation** stage is not currently considering change, whereas someone in the **contemplation** stage is thinking about change but is ambivalent or "on the fence" about the prospect of making a change. Once an initial commitment to change has been made, the individual enters the **preparation** stage where arrangements are made to bring about change. This is followed by a period of **action** in which skills and information designed to bring about change are acquired and practiced. Once change occurs it must be reinforced and strengthened to remain viable; this is the goal of the **maintenance** stage. Relapse is often included as a stage in the SOC because lapse and relapse are frequently parts of the change process.[61] The clinical significance of the SOC is that because each stage expresses a different need, different intervention strategies are required for individuals at each stage (see **Table 11-5**). This is a prime example of specific responsivity.[62]

Figure 11-12
The stages-of-change (SOC) model.

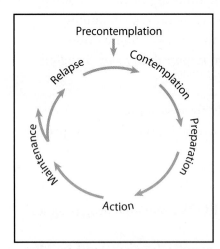

Walters, S. T., Clark, M. D., Gingerich, R., & Meltzer, M. L. (2007). Motivating offenders to change: A guide for probation and parole (NIC #022253). Washington, DC: National Institute of Corrections (page 14), although originally from Miller and Rollnick.

Table 11-5 Needs and Intervention Strategies for the First Five Stages of the SOC Model

---

PRECONTEMPLATION
- Need: information on the impact substance abuse is having on the person
- Intervention: establish rapport and provide information

CONTEMPLATION
- Need: explore feelings of ambivalence
- Intervention: free will, self-efficacy, and the consequences of not changing

PREPARATION
- Need: strengthen commitment to change
- Intervention: clarify goals and establish a change plan

ACTION
- Need: put change plan into action
- Intervention: provide skills training and establish a program of self-reinforcement

MAINTENANCE
- Need: avoid relapsing back into old negative patterns
- Intervention: practice coping strategies and develop a relapse prevention plan

---

Data From: Walters, S. T., Clark, M. D., Gingerich, R., & Meltzer, M. L. (2007). *Motivating offenders to change: A guide for probation and parole (NIC #022253)*. Washington, DC: National Institute of Corrections.

In a review of results from four separate meta-analyses, Brad Lundahl and Brian Burke determined that MI was significantly (10–20%) more effective than no treatment in reducing both substance abuse (alcohol, tobacco, marijuana, other illegal drugs) and risky behavior (unprotected sex, needle sharing).[63] Mary McMurran reviewed 10 studies in which MI was used with drug-involved offenders and concluded that MI can lead to retention of participants in programming and improved motivation for change, although its effect on subsequent drug use and recidivism is equivocal and perhaps only short lived. Despite questions about its long-range impact on behavior,[64] MI would appear to satisfy six of the eight criteria for evidence-based correctional programming (see **Table 11-6**). In addition, it satisfies the one criterion (enhance intrinsic motivation) on which CBT models are weak, implying that the two models may complement one another.

Table 11-6 Evidence-Based Status of the Motivational Interviewing Model

---

Evidence-Based Criteria the Motivational Interviewing Model Satisfies

(2) Enhance intrinsic motivation—*this is what MI is all about.*

(3) Target interventions for risks, needs, and responsivity—*the stages of change (SOC) model incorporates all three aspects of the RNR model.*

(4) Offer skills training with direct practice—*skills training is part of both the MI and SOC models.*

(5) Supply positive reinforcement—*reinforcing success and positive behavior is as vital to MI as it is to CBT.*

(7) Measure and document offender change—*measuring and documenting change is central to the SOC approach.*

(8) Provide participants with feedback on progress—*feedback is a tool commonly used by advocates of MI.*

Evidence-Based Criteria the Motivational Interviewing Model Does Not Satisfy

(6) Build prosocial support systems in the community—*there is little to no evidence that MI or SOC models spend much time on natural support systems.*

Relapse Prevention

Like motivational interviewing, relapse prevention (RP) was originally designed for substance abusers. Unlike motivational interviewing, RP is more likely to be employed as a stand-alone procedure. Developed by Alan Marlatt in response to the dichotomous view of relapse held by proponents of AA and the disease model, RP hypothesizes that high-risk situations can facilitate either an effective or ineffective coping response. Ineffective coping responses lead to relapse, by way of outcome expectancies, decreased self-efficacy, and the Abstinence Violation Effect (AVE). Effective coping responses, by contrast, do not generally lead to relapse (see **Figure 11-13**).[65]

Proponents of RP believe that it is important to differentiate between a lapse and a relapse. A lapse is a momentary slip, whereas a relapse is a return to a former pattern of drug abuse or crime. According to the tenets of RP, people can learn from a lapse and so it need not be viewed as a total failure, as it often is by proponents of the 12-step model. People who fail to differentiate between a lapse and a relapse tend to view the lapse as a sign of failure that can only be rectified by starting over again. This can lead to a state known as the Abstinence Violation Effect (AVE), which, in turn, can significantly increase a person's odds of full-blown relapse.[66] People who fail to differentiate between a lapse and a relapse and who interpret a lapse as evidence of failure make internal, stable, and global attributions for the lapse ("I'm a failure"). This is more likely to lead to full-blown relapse than when a lapse is attributed to external, unstable, and specific factors ("I drank after receiving some bad news").

Figure 11-13
Chain of events leading from a high-risk situation to an effective coping response and a decreased probability of relapse and to an ineffective coping response and an increased probability of relapse.

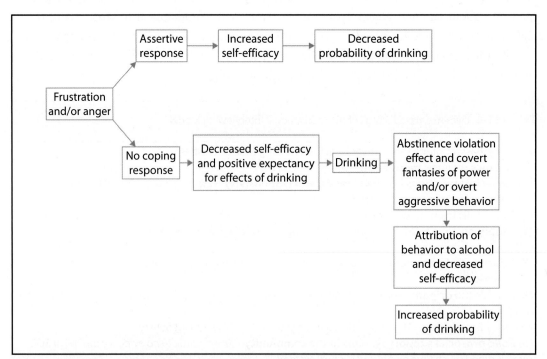

Marlatt, G. A., & Gordon, J. R. (Eds.). (1999). Relapse prevention: Maintenance strategies in the treatment of addictive behaviors. *Alcohol Research & Health. Vol. 23*, No. 2. New York: Guilford Press.

A meta-analysis of 26 RP treatment outcome studies (N = 9,504) by Irwin, Bowers, Dunn, and Wang revealed that RP was successful in reducing substance use and had a particularly powerful effect on psychosocial functioning. In this study, RP was equally efficacious across treatment modalities (individual vs. group) and settings (inpatient vs. outpatient). Irwin's analyses showed that RP was more effective in reducing alcohol and polysubstance use than it was in reducing tobacco and cocaine use.[67] More recently, Lissa Dutra and her colleagues conducted a meta-analysis on the effect of several different cognitive and behavioral techniques on subsequent drug use and determined that although RP reduced drug use, it failed to achieve the level of effect produced by contingency (reinforcement) management.[68]

A meta-analysis of research on the use of RP with offender populations was conducted by Craig Dowden, Daniel Antonowicz, and Donald Andrews. A total of 40 tests of RP revealed moderate mean reductions in recidivism (r = .15). Offense chain, relapse rehearsal, and training significant others in the model were associated with the greatest reductions in recidivism. Small moderating effects were noted for age, gender, and offense type in this meta-analysis (see **Figure 11-14**).[69] Comparing RP to the criteria for evidence-based practice it would appear that RP is more evidence based than the 12-step model but less evidence based than CBT (see **Table 11-7**).

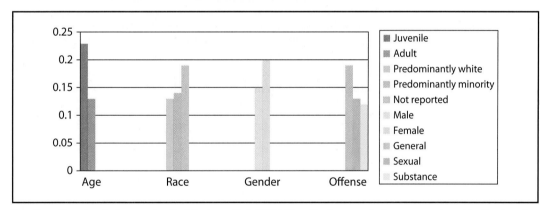

Figure 11-14
Effect sizes (r) for relapse prevention with offenders, broken down by age, race, gender, and offense.

Data From: Dowden, C., Antonowicz, D., & Andrews, D. A. (2003). The effectiveness of relapse prevention with offenders: A meta-analysis. *International Journal of Offender Therapy and Comparative Criminology, 47*, 516–528.

Table 11-7 Evidence-Based Status of the Relapse Prevention Model

Evidence-Based Criteria the Relapse Prevention Model Satisfies
(1) Assess risks and needs—*assessing both risks and needs is a central feature of RP.*
(3) Target interventions for risks, needs, and responsivity—*RP emphasizes interventions for risks and needs; responsivity less certain.*
(4) Offer skills training with direct practice—*relapse rehearsal is an example of a coping skills technique commonly used in RP.*
(5) Supply positive reinforcement—*positive reinforcement is as important to RP as it is to CBT and MI.*
Evidence-Based Criteria the Relapse Prevention Model Does Not Satisfy
(2) Enhance intrinsic motivation—*there is nothing in the RP model that addresses internal motivation for change.*
(6) Build prosocial support systems in the community—*there are no provisions in RP for the development of natural support systems in the community.*

Treatment Implementation

Proper treatment implementation is required in the name of program fidelity. Eight issues central to treatment implementation are discussed in this section, starting with unassisted change.

Unassisted Change

Most individuals desist from drugs and/or crime on their own, without professional help or assistance. This is variously referred to as unassisted change, spontaneous remission, natural recovery, and maturing out. In a review of the literature on desistance from drug abuse, Walters detected a high incidence of **unassisted change** over an average follow-up of 5 years. Using a broad definition of remission, 26.2% of participants had been abstinent or were experiencing significantly fewer problems with substance use for 6 months or longer. Using a narrow definition of remission, 18.2% of participants had been totally abstinent from the problem substance or substances for a period of at least 6 months. The Walters review uncovered few meaningful differences between spontaneous remitters and persons who either continued misusing substances or remitted through treatment on pre-remission measures of prior drug involvement.[70] Common reasons given by self-remitters for initiating and maintaining desistance from drugs can be found in **Tables 11-8** and **11-9**, respectively.

Table 11-8 Reasons Given for Initiating Desistance from Substance Abuse for Those Who Have Abused Alcohol/Other Drugs and for Those Who Have Abused Tobacco

	Alcohol/other drug (N = 755)		Tobacco (N = 205)		Chi square
	n	%	n	%	
Changes in values and goals	59	7.8	1	0.5	14.73[a]
Developed aversion to drugs	8	1.0	8	3.9	8.01
Drug-related problems					
Family	11	1.4	3	1.5	0.01
Financial	50	6.6	16	7.8	0.35
Legal	21	2.8	3	1.5	1.12
Medical	143	18.9	94	45.8	63.80[a]
Social	37	4.9	0	0.0	10.44[a]
Work	23	3.0	0	0.0	6.38
Extraordinary events	74	9.8	10	4.9	4.86
"Hitting bottom"	32	4.2	10	4.9	0.16
Increased responsibility	46	6.1	7	3.4	2.20
Pressure from friends/family	68	9.0	21	10.2	0.30
Religious experience	28	3.7	0	0.0	7.87
"Spiritual" awakening	20	2.6	0	0.0	5.59
Tired/disgusted	9	1.2	17	8.3	30.41[a]
Willpower/decision to stop	22	2.9	24	11.7	27.35[a]

[a] $p < .0031$ = Bonferroni correction: alpha level (.05) ÷ number of comparisons (16).
Walters, G. D. (2000). Spontaneous remission from alcohol, tobacco, and other drug abuse: Seeking quantitative answers to qualitative questions. *American Journal of Drug and Alcohol Abuse, 26,* 443–460.

Table 11-9 Reasons Given for Maintaining Desistance from Substance Abuse for Those Who Have Abused Alcohol/Other Drugs and for Those Who Have Abused Tobacco

	Alcohol/other drug (N = 817)		Tobacco (N = 89)		Chi square
	n	%	n	%	
Change in recreational/leisure activities	128	15.7	10	11.2	1.24
Change in lifestyle	56	6.8	0	0.0	6.49
Change residence/avoid drug areas	64	7.8	0	0.0	7.51
Exercise/physical fitness	95	11.6	10	11.2	0.01
Find new relationships/avoid old relations	198	24.2	0	0.0	27.65[a]
Loss of desire for drugs	11	1.3	0	0.0	1.23
Religion	54	6.6	7	7.9	0.20
Reminding self of negative consequences	50	6.1	0	0.0	5.74
Self-confidence	51	6.2	18	20.2	22.73[a]
Self-help groups (e.g., AA)	21	2.5	0	0.0	2.39
Support from family/friends	226	27.7	9	10.1	12.89[a]
Substitute activities/dependencies	34	4.2	26	29.2	81.33[a]
Transform identity/reject addict identity	173	21.2	0	0.0	23.04[a]
Willpower/resist urge to use	142	17.4	37	41.6	29.52[a]
Work or school	64	7.8	0	0.0	7.51

[a] $p < .0033$ = Bonferroni correction: alpha level (.05) ÷ number of comparisons (15).
Walters, G. D. (2000). Spontaneous remission from alcohol, tobacco, and other drug abuse: Seeking quantitative answers to qualitative questions. *American Journal of Drug and Alcohol Abuse, 26*, 443–460.

Unassisted change has also been reported for crime, although it has not been studied as extensively as unassisted change from drug and alcohol abuse. A 10-year follow-up of 65 individuals involved in the international drug trade revealed that 13 (20%) had completely desisted from crime in the absence of formal intervention. The motivations for unassisted change in these 13 self-remitters included:[71]

- return of previously held conventional hobbies and interests.
- extension of entrepreneurial skills learned in the drug trade to legal activities.
- development of noncriminal interpersonal relationships.

Decreased preoccupation with material success, appreciation of the futility of crime, and construction of a prosocial self-view were mentioned by 50 former habitual property offenders attempting to explain how they successfully exited a criminal lifestyle without formal intervention or assistance.[72] A group of 23 property offenders who had managed to avoid reconviction for 10 years reported that self-efficacy, remorse for past criminal behavior, and social bonding (marital and occupational attachments) were instrumental in their remaining crime free.[73]

Regardless of whether the person is desisting from drugs or crime, three factors appear to be instrumental in the decision to remain drug and crime free for an extended period of time. First, involvements—what people do and who they do it with—change. Those who successfully abandon a drug or criminal lifestyle often do so by avoiding people who abuse drugs and commit crime, refraining from drug use and crime themselves, and developing an entirely new system of associations and bonds with conventional people and activities. The second factor that frequently accompanies self-remission from drugs or crime is a change in commitments—what is important to the individual in terms of goals and values. Short-term hedonistic goals and values characterize drug and criminal behavior; change occurs when the individual starts considering long-term consequences and learns to balance pleasure with social, work, and intellectual values. The third factor involved in desistance from drugs and crime is a change in identification—how the individual sees him or herself relative to others and the larger environment. Labels like addict, alcoholic, and criminal keep people locked in a negative lifestyle. Avoiding labels and seeing oneself as a contributing member of conventional society is the type of self-image people who desist from drugs and crime often project.[74]

The Therapeutic Relationship

Researchers who study psychotherapy differentiate between change resulting from the treatment protocol or technique (specific factors) and change resulting from something other than the treatment protocol or technique (nonspecific factors). When it comes to promoting psychotherapeutic change, one of the most powerful nonspecific factors is the client–therapist relationship. Even behaviorists recognize the salience of the therapeutic relationship in promoting change through psychotherapy. Hence, a strong therapeutic relationship, regardless of the specific techniques used, will nearly always produce a better outcome than a weak therapeutic relationship.[75]

Joe, Simpson, Dansereau, and Rowan-Szal had counselors and clients rate the rapport they had with one another. Counselor ratings were eventually used in the analyses because clients' ratings were highly skewed toward the upper end of the scale. The results indicated that a higher level of rapport or counselor-client relationship predicted a lower level of subsequent drug use and criminality (see **Figure 11-15**). Counselors who reflected warmth,

Figure 11-15
Positive drug test (+), self-reported weekly drug use, and any self-reported illegal activity and arrests for two cohorts of outpatients enrolled in methadone maintenance divided by those with low versus high rapport with their drug counselor.

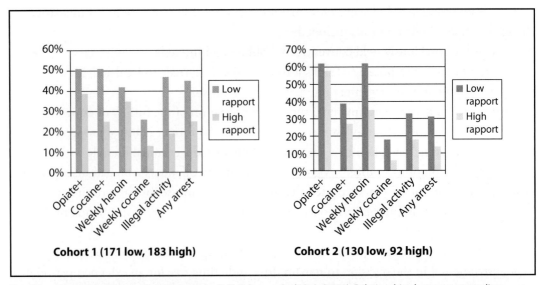

Data From: Joe, G. W., Simpson, D. D., Dansereau, D. F., & Rowan-Szal, G. A. (2001). Relationships between counseling rapport and drug abuse treatment outcomes. *Psychiatric Services, 52,* 1223–1229.

honesty, and understanding and who were easy to talk to had clients who were significantly less likely to engage in future drug use and crime.[76]

Group Versus Individual Counseling

Most criminal justice interventions are conducted in groups because they are cheaper and potentially more cost effective than individual counseling. There are situations, however, where individual counseling may be preferable to group counseling and the results of at least one study suggest that motivational interviewing works best when an individual rather than group format is followed.[77] At this point in time there are no hard and fast rules as to which is better, group or individual counseling, because there are no reliable studies contrasting the two methods. Selecting a group or individual format is therefore largely a matter of preference, although before making a decision one may want to take into account the individual strengths and weakness of each method. A partial list of these strengths and weaknesses can be found in **Table 11-10**.[78]

Community Versus Institutional Corrections

There are several reasons why it is preferable to place nonviolent drug-involved offenders in community or intermediate sanction programs rather than sending them to jail or prison. One reason is that is saves money. Another is that it reduces prison overcrowding. A third reason is that community placement avoids the criminogenic (crime-causing) effects of incarceration. Finally, placing a nonviolent drug offender in a community program obviates the need for reintegration because the individual is already in the community. There are two additional reasons why community placement is often preferred over prison for nonviolent drug offenders: (1) there are a greater number and diversity of treatment programs in the community than there are in prison;[79] (2) programs conducted in the community tend to produce better results than programs conducted in jail or prison (see **Figure 11-16**).[80] The value of working with offenders in the community is also recognized by those in the news media (see News Spot 11-2).

Table 11-10 Strengths and Weaknesses of the Group and Individual Formats in Working with Drug-Involved Offenders

Format	Advantages	Disadvantages
Group	1. Cost-effectiveness 2. Social support 3. Modeling of appropriate behavior 4. Role play/behavioral rehearsal 5. Providing an alternative perspective 6. Learning by teaching	1. Less privacy/confidentiality 2. Destructive group feedback 3. Modeling of inappropriate behavior 4. Forced to listen to others' problems
Individual	1. Privacy/confidentiality 2. Depth of analysis 3. Attention to personal issues 4. Flexible meeting times	1. Time and cost intensive 2. Relatively high drop-out rate 3. Dependency on therapist

Source: Walters, G. D. (2012). *Crime in a psychological context: From career criminals to criminal careers*. Thousand Oaks, CA: Sage.

Figure 11-16
Average effect sizes (*r*) for programs conducted in the community and programs conducted in prison.

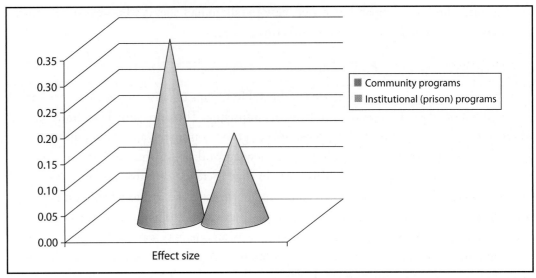

Data From: Gendreau, P., French, S. A., & Gionet, A. (2004, Spring). What works (what doesn't work): The principles of effective correctional treatment. *Journal of Community Corrections*, pp. 4–6, 27–30.

NEWS SPOT 11-2

Title: Stop Locking Up Nonviolent Drug Offenders
Source: *Chicago (IL) Sun-Times*
Author: Melody M. Heaps
Date: November 14, 2006

Drug-involved offenders continue to cycle through the state's prisons at an enormous cost to taxpayers and communities ["Jailing drug convicts costs us billions; Study urges options to 'revolving door,'" news story, Oct. 31]. Illinois taxpayers spend an estimated $240 million per year to house individuals convicted of nonviolent drug offenses, according to the Crime and Justice report released last month by Chicago Metropolis 2020.

The fundamental problem is that Illinois sends thousands of nonviolent, drug-involved offenders to prison when there are more effective and cost-efficient alternatives available.

For example, the Cook County State's Attorney Drug School reduces drug abuse-linked recidivism. Only 11 percent of the State's Attorney Drug School participants who receive substance abuse treatment care were re-arrested within a year, contrasted to 55 percent who failed to finish the program.

Moreover, supervised substance abuse treatment is far more cost effective than incarceration. Treatment costs range from $3,100 to $12,500 per year, in contrast to the average Illinois incarceration cost of $20,929 per adult inmate per year, excluding the prison building costs.

Unfortunately, the ability of effective programs like the State's Attorney Drug School, other intensive substance abuse treatment services and community-based support that provide housing and job training to reduce recidivism significantly is limited because they are habitually under-funded by local, state and federal governments.

Substance abuse treatment is a tested and proven strategy that can block an individual from entering a life of crime and prison. These "no entry" to prison policies—drug school, supervised substance abuse treatment, and community-based support—can undermine habitual drug-linked recidivism. If Illinois were to divert another 1,000 nonviolent offenders with substance abuse problems from prison to supervised treatment alternatives, the state would conservatively save almost $8.5 million. The solution seems simple.

Questions to Ponder

1. **What are some reasons why the community option is not used more often than it is with nonviolent drug offenders given that it is cheaper and more cost effective than incarceration?**
2. **How effective do you think education would be in helping the general public appreciate the benefits of community programming over incarceration?**
3. **In some situations defendants are given a mixed or blended sentence where they spend a small amount of time in jail or prison followed by a longer period of time on probation or intensive supervision. Under what conditions do you think this option would be most appropriate?**

One of the primary reasons why community corrections programs may be more effective than institutional programs is that they generally incorporate more evidence-based practices (EBPs) than institutional programs. Friedmann, Taxman, and Henderson surveyed the clinical directors of programs for drug-involved offenders and discovered that except for length of programming, community-based programs satisfied a greater portion of EBPs than prison-based programs (see **Figure 11-17**).[81] Other research indicates that community aftercare programs are superior to prison programs.[82] This suggests that another reason community-based programs tend to produce better results than prison-based programs is that the generalizability or transfer of learning between the community-based program and the community is greater than the generalizability or transfer of learning between the prison-based program and the community.

Inpatient Versus Outpatient

Community-based treatment is clearly superior to prison-based treatment but community-based intervention can take one of several forms. The most common differentiation is between inpatient or residential treatment and outpatient treatment. Accordingly, another important implementation decision is whether community-based treatment should be conducted on an inpatient or outpatient basis. Research has fairly convincingly demonstrated that inpatient and outpatient drug treatment produce comparable results. Analyzing data from the Drug Abuse Treatment Outcome Studies (DATOS), Robert Hubbard and colleagues observed minimal variation in the 1- and 5-year outcomes of individuals

Figure 11-17

Percentage of different evidence-based practices (EBPs) included in prison-based and community-based programs for drug-involved offenders.

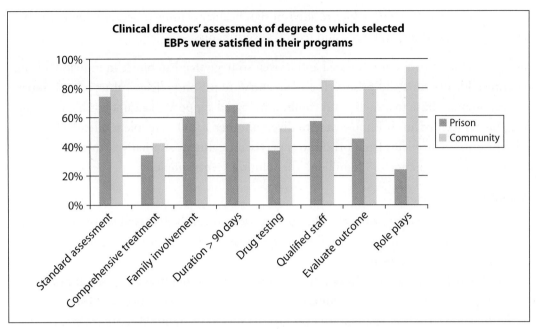

Source: Friedmann, P. D., Taxman, F. S., & Henderson, C. E. (2007). Evidence-based treatment practices for drug-involved adults in the criminal justice system. *Journal of Substance Abuse Treatment, 32,* 267–277.

completing inpatient and outpatient treatment. Length of treatment was the more important variable in this study, such that longer treatment was associated with more positive results.[83–84]

Norman Hoffmann and Norman Miller compared over 9,000 drug users subjected to inpatient treatment with 1,042 drug users subjected to intensive outpatient treatment. Three-quarters of the inpatients completed treatment compared to 70% of the outpatients. Abstinence rates after 1 year were 44–55% for inpatients and 52–63% for outpatients.[85] Anne Cornwall and Lowell Blood compared adolescent substance abusers who went through either an inpatient program or an intensive day treatment program. Completion rates and reductions in drug use and problem behaviors were comparable across the two groups.[86] William Burdon and colleagues studied male and female inmates who completed an in-prison therapeutic community and received either outpatient or residential aftercare. Regardless of the severity of the drug or alcohol problem, participants benefitted equally from outpatient and residential aftercare.[87]

Hser, Evans, Teruya, Huang, and Anglin analyzed short-term outcomes for drug-involved offenders referred to drug treatment through Proposition 36 and discovered that residential treatment was associated with higher levels of abstinence than outpatient treatment, although residential and outpatient treatment produced comparable results with respect to future offending. Length of treatment also correlated with better outcomes and because residential participants may have received more sessions than outpatient participants, these data need to be evaluated further before it is concluded that residential/inpatient drug treatment is superior to outpatient treatment for drug-involved offenders.[88] The preponderance of evidence suggests that inpatient and outpatient drug treatment produce comparable results. As such, intensive outpatient treatment would appear to be the optimal approach in most situations given that it costs less than residential treatment but is just as effective.

Therapeutic Communities

A therapeutic community (TC) is a group-based participative approach to intervention that normally, but not always, takes place in a residential setting. The two defining features of a TC are that participants (1) work together on a common problem (e.g., drug abuse), and (2) are actively involved in both supporting and challenging each other. In a TC, clients serve as both teachers and learners and the staff's job is to facilitate the participative approach. For example, staff members encourage clients to directly challenge a peer who is entertaining a negative thought or demonstrating a destructive behavior, a process commonly referred to as giving someone a "verbal haircut." In prison, TCs are often set apart from the general population as a separate housing area or unit, although it is important to note that residential placement does not in and of itself define a program as a TC. The Federal Bureau of Prisons' 10-month Residential Drug Abuse Program, for instance, is a residential program but it does not follow the TC model.

TCs can be found worldwide. In the United States, the TC movement can be traced back to **Synanon**. Through its charismatic leader, Charles "Chuck" Dederich (1913–1997), Synanon has had a powerful impact on the American approach to substance abuse. It started out in the late 1950s as an alternative living arrangement for people with various problems, including severe drug addiction, but soon became a model for treating substance abuse. It was endorsed by the humanist Abraham Maslow and was one of the principal components of the Asklepion Foundation's therapeutic community located within the walls of the United States Penitentiary at Marion, Illinois. Over time, however, Synanon became increasingly more cultlike, and there were accusations that former members who left the group received severe beatings and that outsiders who questioned the movement's practices and philosophy were threatened or even physically attacked. There are those who swear by Synanon and credit their recovery to the hardline tactics and confrontational approach adopted by Dederich and his followers, although Synanon itself is no longer a major therapeutic force in this country.[89]

TCs received strong support in a meta-analysis of correctional treatment programs for drug abuse. In this meta-analysis, Pearson and Lipton found that TCs achieved better results than any of the other programs or models evaluated, including boot camps, drug-focused group counseling, methadone maintenance, and cognitive-behavioral therapy.[90] It would appear, then, that TCs hold promise of promoting significant behavioral change in drug-involved offenders, provided staff are properly trained and actively involved in supervising participants, maximum structure and a sense of community are maintained, and a cognitive-behavioral curriculum is employed. It is important to keep in mind that offenders tend to be power oriented in their relationships, including their relationships with each other. As such, giving them too much control over a treatment program without strong staff supervision and oversight is simply asking for trouble.

Compulsory Treatment

Very few people would argue with the statement that people benefit more from a program they volunteer for than one they are forced into. When it comes to substance abuse treatment, however, the situation is not so cut-and-dried. First, it is naïve to think that people generally enter drug treatment voluntarily. Most people are coerced into treatment, if not by the criminal justice system, then by a spouse, an employer, or the family physician. Accordingly, **compulsory treatment** is the norm rather than the exception when it comes to substance abuse treatment and has been found, in some instances, to increase motivation for change.[91] Criminal justice coercion is therefore one method by which clinicians can gain leverage over an offender who resists treatment. In the end, compulsory treatment may actually benefit a portion of the drug-using criminal population.

An early study based on data from the Drug Abuse Reporting Program (DARP) revealed that people who entered TCs and drug-free outpatient counseling under legal pressure did as well as people who entered these programs voluntarily.[92] This preliminary research has been confirmed by more recent observational[93] and experimental[94] studies showing that offenders under legal pressure to complete methadone maintenance were just as likely to complete the program and be drug and crime free as offenders who were not under legal pressure to complete methadone maintenance. A study by Young, Fluellen, and Belenko also supports the efficacy of compulsory drug treatment for nonviolent offenders and notes that informing clients about the legal contingencies of participation and frequent contact between treatment and criminal justice (court, probation) staff contribute to the effectiveness of compulsory drug treatment.[95]

Wayne Hall and Jane Lucke reviewed the ethics of compulsory treatment and concluded that the most ethically defensible position is to use the fear of imprisonment or the fear of returning to prison as an incentive for enrolling in community treatment. They go on to state that allowing drug-involved offenders to choose between participating in drug treatment or returning to prison and having them select the specific treatment model provides offenders with the greatest freedom of choice.[96] Many of the programs discussed in this text, from drug diversion to drug courts to community aftercare programs for individuals receiving prison-based drug treatment, rely heavily on compulsory drug treatment and so the fact that it may be as effective as "voluntary" treatment is welcome news to those who are referring offenders to these programs.

Aftercare

Follow-up or booster sessions can be helpful in maintaining and strengthening the effects of a prison-based program. Stanley Sacks and others discerned that an aftercare program reinforced the effects of in-prison drug treatment for dually-diagnosed (drug and mental health problems) inmates.[97] James Inciardi, Steven Martin, and Clifford Butzin uncovered evidence that a prison-based TC achieved slightly improved results when a community aftercare component was added to the intervention (see **Figure 11-18**).[98] In a recent study on a group of female offenders, Christine Grella and Luz Rodriquez observed that community aftercare reduced levels of recidivism beyond the original effect of an in-prison treatment program.[99] These results suggest that for maximum efficiency, prison-based programs should be followed by a period of community aftercare designed to solidify and generalize the effects of the original intervention.

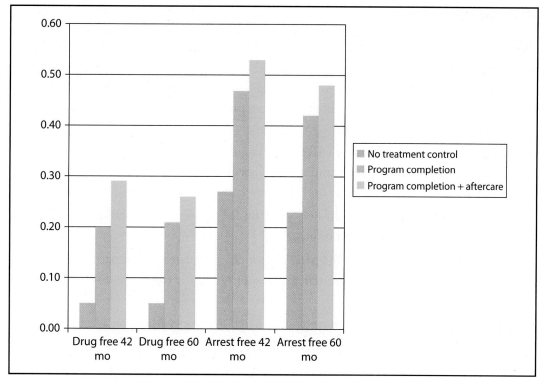

Figure 11-18
Proportion of participants who were drug and arrest free 42 and 60 months after completing a program, a program + aftercare, or a no treatment control condition.

Data From: Inciardi, J. A., Martin, S. S., & Butzin, C. A. (2004). Five-year outcomes of therapeutic community treatment of drug-involved offenders after release from prison. *Crime and Delinquency, 50,* 88–107.

Summary and Conclusions

- To be effective, an intervention should target higher risk offenders (in terms of both drug use and crime), address criminogenic needs (including substance abuse/dependency, antisocial personality processes, antisocial cognition, and antisocial peer associations); use a behavioral or cognitive-behavioral format; be maximally responsive to individual needs, abilities, and learning styles; and be properly implemented.

- Evidence-based criteria were applied to four models of intervention commonly employed with drug-involved offenders (12-step, cognitive-behavioral, motivational interviewing, and relapse prevention). Whereas the cognitive-behavioral, motivational interviewing, and relapse prevention models showed signs of being evidence based, the 12 step model failed to meet the majority of evidence-based criteria.

- Program implementation was also examined. Results indicated that unassisted change is a fairly common occurrence, the therapeutic relationship is vital to the change process, group and individual therapy have their strengths as well as their weaknesses, community-based programs produce better results than prison-based programs, inpatient and outpatient intervention are equally efficacious, therapeutic communities can play a role in drug treatment for offenders, coercion does not adversely affect treatment outcomes, and aftercare is vital to the ultimate success of prison-based programs.

Key Terms

Action   Fourth stage of the stages-of-change model; characterized by the learning of new skills designed to bring about change.

Aftercare   Follow-up or booster sessions taking place in the community in an effort to reinforce or generalize benefits obtained from a prison-based or inpatient/residential program.

Aggression Replacement Training (ART)   A cognitive-behavioral intervention that uses cognitive and moral skills training to reduce drug use and crime in drug-involved offenders.

Alcoholics Anonymous (AA)   Self-help program for people with alcohol problems based on the 12-step model of intervention.

Allegiance Effect   Tendency on the part of researchers affiliated with a particular school of psychotherapy to produce research results supporting the efficacy and superiority of their school of psychotherapy.

Cognitive-Behavioral Model   Treatment approach that views addiction as a learned process and seeks to instruct clients in cognitive skills and challenge destructive and irrational beliefs.

Cognitive Restructuring   Therapeutic method in which destructive and faulty beliefs are challenged as a means of reducing future drug use and crime.

Cognitive Skills Training   Therapeutic method in which basic cognitive skills are taught as a mean of reducing future drug use and crime.

Compulsory Treatment   Mandating intervention with the threat of incarceration or other severe sanction if the individual does not comply.

Contemplation   Second stage of the stages-of-change model; characterized by feelings of ambivalence about the prospect of change.

Correctional Program Assessment Inventory (CPAI)   Instrument, composed of six primary scales, designed to measure the degree to which a program follows the fidelity principle.

Criminogenic   Causing crime.

Deterrence   Theory of justice that attempts to discourage crime through the use of punishment that is swift, certain, and severe.

Everything Works   The view, popular during the 1960s and early 1970s, that nearly all programs are effective in reducing recidivism.

Fidelity Principle   Interventions are most effective when treatment staff are competently trained and supervised, the program is properly implemented, and the program receives adequate administrative support.

General Responsivity   Interventions for offenders are most effective when they use behavioral and cognitive-behavioral principles.

Incapacitation   Theory of justice that attempts to reduce offending by removing opportunities for crime through incarceration.

Maintenance   Fifth stage of the stages-of-change model; characterized by strategies designed to reinforce and strengthen changes made during the action stage.

Moral Reconation Therapy (MRT)   A cognitive-behavioral intervention that uses cognitive restructuring and moral retraining to reduce drug use and crime in drug-involved offenders.

Motivational Interviewing Model   Treatment approach that views addiction as a social-interactional process and seeks to improve a person's motivation for change.

Needs Principle   Interventions are most effective when they address criminogenic needs.

Nothing Works   The view, popular during the late 1970s and early 1980s, that programs are generally ineffective in reducing recidivism.

Precontemplation   First stage of the stages-of-change model; characterized by minimal interest in or motivation for change.

Preparation   Third stage of the stages-of-change model; characterized by a preliminary commitment to change.

Reasoning and Rehabilitation (R&R)   A cognitive-behavioral intervention that uses cognitive skills training to reduce drug use and crime in drug-involved offenders.

Rehabilitation   Theory of justice that attempts to restore or introduce the offender to a law-abiding state.

Relapse Prevention Model   Treatment approach that views addiction as a cognitive process and seeks to teach the individual skills designed to prevent relapse.

Responsivity Principle   Interventions are most effective when they use behavioral and cognitive-behavioral principles and are tailored to the individual abilities, needs, and learning styles of participants.

Restoration   Theory of justice that attempts to repair the damage caused by crime.

Retribution   Theory of justice that attempts to make offenders atone for their crimes through punishment.

Risk Principle   Interventions are most effective when they target higher risk individuals.

Specific Responsivity   Interventions are most effective when they are tailored to the individual abilities, needs, and learning styles of participants.

Stages-of-Change (SOC) Model   Theoretical model of psychotherapeutic change in which people are believed to progress through five stages of change (precontemplation, contemplation, preparation, action, and maintenance).

Synanon   Controversial organization that began by providing an alternate living arrangement for people with various problems, including drug addiction, and that eventually adopted a therapeutic community approach to intervention characterized by confrontation and hardline tactics.

Therapeutic Community (TC)   Group-based participant approach that normally takes place in a residential setting during which people with a common problem (e.g., drug abuse) both support and confront one another in an effort to resolve the problem.

Thinking for a Change (T4C)   A cognitive-behavioral intervention that uses cognitive restructuring and cognitive skills training to reduce drug use and crime in drug-involved offenders.

Twelve-Step Model   Treatment model that views addiction as a disease and uses a self-help format to reduce problem behavior.

Unassisted Change   Desistance from a drug or criminal pattern without formal or professional treatment; also referred to as spontaneous remission, natural recovery, and maturing out.

What Works   The view, popular since the mid-1980s, that certain programs are effective in reducing recidivism and that research is required to determine which programs work and which programs do not work.

Critical Thinking

1. What is meant by the term "evidence based" and how would you determine whether the 12-step, cognitive-behavioral, motivational interviewing, and relapse prevention models of intervention are evidence based?
2. When would you want to use an individual intervention format and under what conditions would a group intervention format be preferable?
3. Do you believe that coercive (mandatory) treatment is effective? If so, why does it work? If not, what would you do instead?
4. Why is aftercare vital to the success of programs conducted in jail and prison?

Notes

1. Lipton, D. S., Martinson, R., and Wilks, J. (1975). *The effectiveness of correctional treatment: A survey of treatment valuation studies.* New York: Praeger.
2. Martinson, R. (1974). What works? Questions and answers about prison reform, *The Public Interest, 35:* 22–54.
3. Andrews, D. A., Bonta, J., & Hoge, R. (1990). Classification for effective rehabilitation: Rediscovering psychology. *Criminal Justice and Behavior, 17,* 19–52.
4. Latessa, E. J., & Lowenkamp, C. (2006). What works in reducing recidivism. *University of St. Thomas Law Journal, 3,* 521–525.
5. Andrews, D. A., & Dowden, C. (2006). Risk principle of case classification in correctional treatment: A meta-analytic investigation. *International Journal of Offender Therapy and Comparative Criminology, 50,* 88–100.
6. Lowenkamp, C. T., Latessa, E. J., & Holsinger, A. M. (2006). The risk principle in action: What have we learned from 13,676 offenders and 97 correctional programs? *Crime and Delinquency, 52,* 77–93.
7. Lowenkamp et al. (2006).
8. Bonta, J., Wallace-Capretta, S., & Rooney, J. (2000). A quasi-experimental evaluation of an intensive rehabilitation supervision program. *Criminal Justice and Behavior, 27,* 312–329.
9. Andrews, D. A. (1980). Some experimental investigations of the principles of differential association through deliberate manipulations of the structure of social service systems. *American Sociological Review, 45,* 448–462.
10. Lowenkamp, C. T., & Latessa, E. J. (2004). Understanding the risk principle: How and why correctional interventions can harm low-risk offenders. *Topics in Community Corrections,* 3–8.

11. Knight, K., Simpson, D. D., & Hiller, M. L. (1999). Three-year reincarceration outcomes for in-prison therapeutic community treatment in Texas. *The Prison Journal, 79*, 337–351.

12. Taxman, F. S., Thanner, M., & Weisburd, D. (2006). Risk, need, and responsivity (RNR): It *all* depends. *Crime and Delinquency, 52*, 28–51.

13. Andrews et al. (1990).

14. Andrews, D. A., & Dowden, C. (2006). Risk principle of case classification in correctional treatment: A meta-analytic investigation. *International Journal of Offender Therapy and Comparative Criminology, 50*, 88–100.

15. Dowden, C., & Andrews, D. A. (1999). What works in young offender treatment: A meta-analysis. *Forum on Corrections Research, 11*(2), 21–24.

16. French, S. A., & Gendreau, P. (2006). Reducing prison misconducts: What works! *Criminal Justice and Behavior, 33*, 185–218.

17. Taxman et al. (2006).

18. McMurran, M. (2007). What works in substance misuse treatments for offenders? *Criminal Behaviour and Mental Health, 17*, 225–233.

19. Andrews, D. A. (1994). *An overview of treatment effectiveness: Research and clinical principles.* Ottawa, Ontario: Department of Psychology, Carleton University.

20. Landenberger, N. A., & Lipsey, M. W. (2006). The positive effects of cognitive–behavioral programs for offenders: A meta-analysis of factors associated with effective treatment. *Journal of Experimental Criminology, 1*, 451–476.

21. Lipsey, M. W., Chapman, G., & Landenberger, N. A. (2001). Cognitive-behavioral programs for offenders. *Annals of the American Academy of Political and Social Science, 578*, 144–157.

22. Pearson, F. S., Lipton, D. S., Cleland, C. M., & Yee, D. S. (2002). The effects of behavioral/cognitive-behavioral programs on recidivism. *Crime and Delinquency, 48*, 476–496.

23. Wilson, D. B., Bouffard, L. A., & MacKenzie, D. L. (2005). A quantitative review of structured, group-oriented, cognitive-behavioral programs for offenders. *Journal of Criminal Justice and Behavior, 32*, 172–204.

24. Landenberger & Lipsey (2006).

25. Pearson, F. S., & Lipton, D. S. (1999). A meta-analytic review of the effectiveness of corrections-based treatment for drug abuse. *The Prison Journal, 79*, 384–410.

26. Aos, S., Miller, M., & Drake, E. (2006). *Evidence-based adult corrections programs: What works and what does not.* Olympia, WA: Washington State Institute for Public Policy.

27. Gendreau, P., French, S. A., & Gionet, A. (2004, Spring). What works (what doesn't work): The principles of effective correctional treatment. *Journal of Community Corrections*, pp. 4–6, 27–30.

28. Landenberger & Lipsey (2006).

29. Hubbard, D. J. (2007). Getting the most out of correctional treatment: Testing the responsivity principle on male and female offenders. *Federal Probation, 71*(1), 2–8.

30. Walters, G. D. (2009). Anger management training in incarcerated male offenders: Differential impact on proactive and reactive criminal thinking. *International Journal of Forensic Mental Health, 8*, 214–217.

31. Hare, R. D. (1996). Psychopathy: A clinical construct whose time has come. *Criminal Justice and Behavior, 23*, 25–54.

32. Rice, M. E., Harris, G. T., & Cormier, C. (1992). Evaluation of a maximum security therapeutic community for psychopaths and other mentally disordered offenders. *Law and Human Behavior, 15*, 625–637.

33. Salekin, R. T. (2002). Psychopathy and therapeutic pessimism: Clinical lore or clinical reality? *Clinical Psychology Review, 22*, 79–112.

34. Wilson, J. A. (2007). *Habilation or harm: Project Greenlight and the potential consequences of correctional programming.* Washington, DC: U.S. Department of Justice, Office of Justice Programs, National Institute of Justice.

35. Gendreau, P., & Andrews, D. A. (1989). *The Correctional Program Assessment Inventory*. Fredericton, New Brunswick, Canada: University of New Brunswick.

36. Matthews, B., Hubbard, D. J., & Latessa, E. J. (2001). Making the next step: Using evaluability assessment to improve correctional programming. *The Prison Journal, 81,* 454–472.

37. Landenberger & Lipsey (2005).

38. Lowenkamp, C. T., Latessa, E. J., & Smith, P. (2006). Does correctional program quality really matter? The impact of adhering to the principles of effective intervention. *Criminology and Public Policy, 5,* 201–220.

39. Andrews et al. (1990).

40. Romani, C. J., Morgan, R. D., Gross, N. R., & McDonald, B. R. (2012). Treating criminal behavior: Is the bang worth the buck? *Psychology, Public Policy, and Law 18,* 144–165.

41. Guevara, M., & Solomon, E. (2009). *Implementing evidence-based policy and practice in community corrections* (2nd ed.). Washington, DC: U.S. Department of Justice, National Institute of Corrections.

42. Gornik, M. (2001). *Moving from correctional program to correctional strategy: Using proven practices to change criminal behavior*. Washington, DC: U.S. Department of Justice, National Institute of Corrections.

43. Kelly, J. F., Magill, M., & Stout, R. L. (2009). How do people recover from alcohol dependence? A systematic review of the research on mechanisms of behavior change in Alcoholics Anonymous. *Addiction Research and Theory, 17,* 236–259.

44. Gornik (2001).

45. Ross, R. R., & Fabiano, E. A. (1985). *Time to think: A cognitive model of delinquency prevention and offender rehabilitation*. Johnson City, TN: Institute of Social Sciences and Arts.

46. Tong, L. S. J., & Farrington, D. P. (2006). How effective is the "Reasoning and Rehabilitation" programme in reducing reoffending? A meta-analysis of evaluations in four countries. *Psychology, Crime & Law, 12,* 3–24.

47. Little, G. L., & Robinson, K. D. (1986). *How to escape your prison*. Memphis, TN: Eagle Wing Books.

48. Little, G. L. (2001). Meta-analysis of MRT recidivism research on post-incarceration adult felony offenders. *Cognitive-Behavioral Treatment Review, 10*(3/4), 4–6.

49. Little, G. L. (2005). Meta-analysis of Moral Reconation Therapy: Recidivism results from probation and parole implementations *Cognitive-Behavioral Treatment Review, 14*(1/2), 14–16.

50. Little, G. L., Robinson, K. D., Burnette, K. D., & Swan, E. S. (2010). Twenty-year recidivism results for MRT-treated offenders. *Journal of Community Corrections, 19*(3), 15–17.

51. Luborsky, L., Diguer, L., Seligman, D. A., Rosenthal, R., Krause, E. D., Johnson, S., et al. (1999). The researcher's own therapeutic allegiances—A "wild card" in comparisons of treatment efficacy. *Clinical Psychology: Science and Practice, 6,* 95–132.

52. Goldstein, A. P, Glick, B., & Reiner, S. (1987). *Aggression Replacement Training*. Champaign, IL: Research Press.

53. Goldstein, A. P., Nensén, R., Daleflod, B., & Kalt, M. (Eds.). (2004). *New perspectives on aggression replacement training—Practice, research and application*. West Sussex, England: Wiley.

54. Hatcher, R. M., Palmer, E. J., McGuire, J., Hounsome, J. C., Bilby, C. A. L., & Hollin, C. R. (2008). Aggression Replacement Training with adult male offenders within community settings: A reconviction analysis. *Journal of Forensic Psychiatry and Psychology, 19,* 517–532.

55. Landenberger & Lipsey (2005).

56. Bush, J., Glick, B., & Taymans, J. (1997). *Thinking for a change: Integrated cognitive behavior change program*. Washington DC: U.S. Department of Justice, National Institute of Corrections.

57. Golden, L., Gatchel, R. J., & Cahill, M. (2006). Evaluating the effectiveness of the National Institute of Corrections' "Thinking for a Change" program among probationers. *Journal of Offender Rehabilitation, 43*(2), 55–73.

58. Lowenkamp, C. T., Hubbard, D., Makarios, M. D., & Latessa, E. J. (2009). A quasi-experimental evaluation of Thinking for a Change: A "real-world" application. *Criminal Justice and Behavior, 36,* 137–146.

59. Miller, W. R. (1985). Motivation for treatment: A review with special emphasis on alcoholism. *Psychological Bulletin, 98,* 84–107.

60. Miller, W. R., & Rollnick, S. (2002). *Motivational interviewing: Preparing people for change* (2nd ed.). New York: Guilford.

61. Prochaska, J. O., & DiClemente, C. C. (1992). Stages of change in the modification of problem behaviors. In M. Hersen, R. M. Eisler, & P. M. Miller (Eds.), *Progress in behavior modification* (pp. 184–214). Sycamore, IL: Sycamore.

62. Walters, S. T., Clark, M. D., Gingerich, R., & Meltzer, M. L. (2007). *Motivating offenders to change: A guide for probation and parole* (NIC #022253). Washington, DC: National Institute of Corrections.

63. Lundahl, B., & Burke, B. L. (2009). The effectiveness and applicability of motivational interviewing: A practice-friendly review of four meta-analyses. *Journal of Clinical Psychology, 65,* 1232–1245.

64. McMurran, M. (2009). Motivational interviewing with offenders: A systematic review. *Legal and Criminological Psychology, 14,* 83–100.

65. Marlatt, G. A., & Gordon, J. R. (Eds.). (1985). *Relapse prevention: Maintenance strategies in the treatment of addictive behaviors.* New York: Guilford Press.

66. Marlatt & Gordon (1985).

67. Irwin, J. E., Bowers, C. A., Dunn, M. E., & Wang, M. C. (1999). Efficacy of relapse prevention: A meta-analytic review. *Journal of Consulting and Clinical Psychology, 76,* 563–570.

68. Dutra, L., Stathopoulou, G., Basden, S. L., Leyro, T. M., Powers, M. B., & Otto, M. W. (2008). A meta-analytic review of psychosocial interventions for substance use disorders. *American Journal of Psychiatry, 165,* 179–187.

69. Dowden, C., Antonowicz, D., & Andrews, D. A. (2003). The effectiveness of relapse prevention with offenders: A meta-analysis. *International Journal of Offender Therapy and Comparative Criminology, 47,* 516–528.

70. Walters, G. D. (2000). Spontaneous remission from alcohol, tobacco, and other drug abuse: Seeking quantitative answers to qualitative questions. *American Journal of Drug and Alcohol Abuse, 26,* 443–460.

71. Adler, P. A. (1993). *Wheeling and dealing: An ethnography of an upper-level drug dealing and smuggling community* (2nd ed.). New York: Columbia University Press.

72. Shover, N. (1996). *Great pretenders: Pursuits and careers of persistent thieves.* Oxford, England: Westview.

73. LeBel, T. P., Burnett, R., Maruna, S., & Bushway, S. (2008). The "chicken and egg" of subjective and social factors in desistance from crime. *European Journal of Criminology, 5,* 131–159.

74. Walters, G. D. (2012). *Crime in a psychological context: From career criminals to criminal careers.* Thousand Oaks, CA: Sage.

75. Strupp, H. H., & Hadley, S. W. (1979). Specific vs. nonspecific factors in psychotherapy: A controlled study of outcome. *Archives of General Psychiatry, 36,* 1125–1136.

76. Joe, G. W., Simpson, D. D., Dansereau, D. F., & Rowan-Szal, G. A. (2001). Relationships between counseling rapport and drug abuse treatment outcomes. *Psychiatric Services, 52,* 1223–1229.

77. Lundahl & Burke (2009).

78. Walters (2012).

79. Centers for Disease Control (CDC). (2001). *Substance abuse and treatment for drug users in the criminal justice system.* Washington, DC: Department of Health and Human Services.

80. Gendreau et al. (2004).

81. Friedmann, P. D., Taxman, F. S., & Henderson, C. E. (2007). Evidence-based treatment practices for drug-involved adults in the criminal justice system. *Journal of Substance Abuse Treatment, 32,* 267–277.

82. Prendergast, M. L., Wellisch, J., & Wong, M. M. (1996). Residential treatment for women parolees following prison-based drug treatment: Treatment experiences, needs, and service outcomes. *The Prison Journal, 76,* 253–274.

83. Hubbard, R. L., Craddock, S. G., Flynn, P. M., Anderson, J., & Etheridge, R. M. (1997). Overview of 1-year follow-up outcomes in the Drug Abuse Treatment Outcome Study (DATOS). *Psychology of Addictive Behaviors, 11,* 261–278.

84. Hubbard, R. L., Craddock, S. G., & Anderson, J. (2003). Overview of 5-year follow-up outcomes in the Drug Abuse Treatment Outcome Studies (DATOS). *Journal of Substance Abuse Treatment, 25*, 125–134.

85. Hoffmann, N. G., & Miller, N. S. (1993). Perspectives of effective treatment for alcohol and drug disorders. *Psychiatric Clinics of North America, 16*, 127–140.

86. Cornwall, A., & Blood, L. (1998). Inpatient versus day treatment for substance abusing adolescents. *Journal of Nervous & Mental Disease, 186*, 580–582.

87. Burdon, W. M., Dang, J., Prendergast, M. I., Messina, N. P., & Farabee, D. (2007). Differential effectiveness of residential versus outpatient aftercare for parolees from prison-based therapeutic community treatment programs. *Substance Abuse Treatment, Prevention, and Policy, 2*, 16.

88. Hser, Y.-I., Evans, E., Teruya, C., Huang, D., & Anglin, M. D. (2007). Predictors of short-term treatment outcomes among California's Proposition 36 participants. *Evaluation and Program Planning, 30*, 187–196.

89. Janzen, R. (2005). The rise and fall of Synanon. *Review of Arts, Literature, Philosophy and the Humanities*, No. 128. Retrieved May 5, 2012, from http://www.ralphmag.org/DF/synanon.html.

90. Pearson & Lipton (1999).

91. Miller, H. V., Miller, J. M., Tillyer, R., & Lopez, K. M. (2010). Recovery and punishment: Reconciling the conflicting objectives of coercive treatment in correctional settings. *Research in Social Problems and Public Policy, 17*, 241–261.

92. Hubbard, R., Marsden, M., Rachal, J., Harwood, H., Cavanaugh, E., & Ginzburg, H. (1989). *Drug abuse treatment: a national study of effectiveness*. Chapel Hill: University of North Carolina Press.

93. Brecht, M., Anglin, M. D., & Wang, J. (1993). Treatment effectiveness for legally coerced versus voluntary methadone maintenance clients. *American Journal of Drug and Alcohol Abuse, 19*, 89–106.

94. Gordon, M., Kinlock, T., Schwartz, R., & O'Grady, K. (2008). A randomized clinical trial of methadone maintenance for prisoners: Findings at 6 months post-release. *Addiction, 103*, 1333–1342.

95. Young, D., Fluellen, R., & Belenko, S. (2004). Criminal recidivism in three models of mandatory drug treatment. *Journal of Substance Abuse Treatment, 27*, 313–323.

96. Hall, W., & Lucke, J. (2010). Legally coerced treatment for drug using offenders: Ethical and policy issues. *Crime and Justice Bulletin*, No. 144.

97. Sacks, S., Sacks, J. Y., McKendrick, K., Banks, S., & Stommel, J. (2004). Modified TC for MICA offenders: Crime outcomes. *Behavioral Sciences and the Law, 22*, 477–501.

98. Inciardi, J. A., Martin, S. S., & Butzin, C. A. (2004). Five-year outcomes of therapeutic community treatment of drug-involved offenders after release from prison. *Crime and Delinquency, 50*, 88–107.

99. Grella, C. E., & Rodriguez, L. (2011). Motivation for treatment among women offenders in prison-based treatment and longitudinal outcomes among those who participate in community aftercare. *Journal of Psychoactive Drugs, 43*, 58–67.

PART IV

POLICY

© iStockphoto/Thinkstock

© VladKol/ShutterStock, Inc.

© iStockphoto/Thinkstock

CITY HALL

The fourth and final part of this book on drugs and crime is devoted to policy. Societies differ in how they conceptualize and manage drugs, crime, and the drug–crime connection. Understanding these differences in conceptualization can be helpful in explaining the origins of drug abuse and crime and are also invaluable in identifying cost-effective ways of reducing the impact of these behaviors on society. In the next three chapters the policy implications of the drug–crime nexus for prevention, harm reduction, and drug prohibition/legalization will be examined. The current chapter serves as a bridge between Parts III and IV to the extent that it focuses on issues of risk and intervention (Part III) as well as on the policy implications of prevention programs (Part IV).

PREVENTION

In this chapter, drug and crime prevention is explored in an effort to achieve the following three objectives:

- Differentiate between primary, secondary, and tertiary prevention.
- Understand the strengths and weaknesses of primary prevention as a means of slowing the development of drug use and crime.
- Prevent harmful patterns of drug use and criminal engagement by constructing and implementing an effective program of secondary prevention.

Three Categories of Prevention

The public health and preventive medicine literatures identify three categories of prevention: primary prevention, secondary prevention, and tertiary prevention.

Primary Prevention

Primary prevention seeks to reduce drug use and crime by assessing, identifying, and neutralizing drug and criminal influences within the general population. Programs employing a primary prevention format focus primarily on psychological well-being and crime prevention education. Whereas primary prevention can be effective when implemented as a situational crime prevention strategy (e.g., target hardening, property marking, environmental design, neighborhood watches), it is expensive and of questionable utility when used as a person-level drug or crime prevention strategy.[1] Primary prevention, by definition, has a populationwide scope and targets a general audience. To reach a general audience, a primary prevention program must, by necessity, be low impact.[2] Because of their low impact, such programs are unlikely to benefit high-risk/high-need individuals. Primary prevention consequently sacrifices depth for the widest possible dissemination.

In the past, primary prevention programs for drug use and crime have relied heavily on basic, and sometime faulty, information (drug or crime education) and fear techniques (the affective approach). Affective approaches are particularly ineffective in changing people's attitudes. There are several reasons for this. Before a fear message can alter behavior, several conditions must be satisfied, including

- understanding the message
- relating the message to one's behavior
- accepting the messenger as credible and the message as accurate
- having confidence in one's ability to change the behavior
- believing that changing the behavior will reduce the fear.[3]

If any one of these conditions is not met then the fear message will have little or no impact on behavior. Until primary prevention of drug use and crime has been more thoroughly studied we may want to take heed of research documenting the inability of simple drug education and affective approaches like **Drug Abuse Resistance Education (DARE)** to alter drug use behavior in children and adolescents.[4]

Secondary Prevention

Secondary prevention seeks to reduce drug use and crime by focusing on a small group of high-risk individuals. Because our prevention efforts are confined to a relatively small group of individuals we can save money while maximizing the intensity of the intervention, which, in turn, improves outcome. Tertiary prevention or treatment of adults and adolescents with an existing drug or crime problem is effective with high-risk individuals but is either ineffective or harmful with low-risk individuals. The risk principle may be as relevant to secondary prevention as it is to tertiary prevention but because high risk in the secondary prevention context refers to asymptomatic individuals who have not yet experienced a problem, risk needs to be measured with variables other than the criminal history measures used to assess risk in a tertiary prevention context.

One challenge facing those wishing to employ secondary prevention with drug use and crime is finding evidence-based drug or crime secondary prevention programs. One of the more popular secondary prevention programs for drugs (general drug education) and one of the more popular secondary prevention programs for crime (**Scared Straight**) have been found to be either totally ineffective (i.e., drug education)[5] or unintentionally harmful (i.e., Scared Straight)[6] when employed with high-risk youth. Those who oversee secondary prevention programs for adolescents must also be familiar with risk factors that predict drug use and crime because these risk factors are vital in identifying candidates for secondary prevention. Both of these issues are taken up in the final section of this chapter.

Tertiary Prevention

Tertiary Prevention seeks to alter the course of an existing pattern of drug use and/or criminality. Tertiary prevention programs for drugs give rise to drug treatment, whereas tertiary prevention programs for crime evolve from policies of incapacitation, punishment, and rehabilitation.[7] Like primary prevention, tertiary prevention can be expensive because it is much more intense although more narrow in scope than primary prevention. As such, tertiary prevention may be no more cost effective than primary prevention and less cost-effective than secondary prevention; for what it saves in scope, it spends on intensity. To the extent that the direct and indirect costs of chronic drug abuse and habitual criminal offending are high, we cannot simply ignore tertiary prevention.

Primary Prevention of Drug Use and Crime

Hammersley asserts that there are three realistic goals when it comes to preventing drug abuse, crime, and the drug–crime connection.[8]

- Slow the development of drug use
- Prevent harmful patterns of drug use
- Prevent criminal engagement through drug use

Hammersley's first (slow the development of drug use) and second (prevent harmful patterns of drug use) goals relate to both primary and secondary prevention and are discussed in this section. Hammersley's third goal (prevent criminal engagement through drug use) relates to issues of drug decriminalization and legalization.

Slowing the Development of Drug Use

An earlier onset of drug use and/or crime is associated with more serious drug and/or crime problems in late adolescence and early adulthood, although a causal connection has yet to be established.[9–10] One possible goal for drug prevention might therefore be to delay initial use of drugs and experimentation with crime. Programs like DARE are designed to do just this but have been found to be ineffective (see News Spot 12-1).[11] According to Hammersley, DARE is ineffective, not because of its emphasis on delaying drug initiation, but because:[12]

- Police officers do not necessarily make the best educators.
- The "no use" message is unrealistic and inconsistent with the "it's OK for parents to drink as long as they do so responsibly" message that accompanies it.
- The message is often delivered to children who have not yet been exposed to peer usage and who don't have much curiosity about drugs.

With respect to the last point, DARE has been found to increase drug usage in some studies, allegedly by stimulating curiosity about drugs.[13] Prevention programs that view substance use as a personal choice, honestly assess the dangers and benefits of drug use, offer realistic guidelines for patterns and ages of usage, and focus on competencies rather than just drugs are better options, says Hammersley.[14]

NEWS SPOT 12-1

Title: DARE Officials Admit Program's Weakness May Lie in its Long-Term Effects on Drug Prevention
Source: *The (Red Bank, NJ) Hub*
Author: Alison Granito
Date: November 23, 2001

DARE has become an educational institution and a household name, garnering the lion's share of government drug education dollars and maintaining a presence in the vast majority of America's classrooms.

Drug Abuse Resistance Education (DARE) is the most recognizable and widely used drug education program worldwide. DARE has been taught to 36 million schoolchildren in 52 countries, including 26 million students in the United States alone, according to information from the DARE Web site www.dare.com.

More than 80 percent of the nation's school districts in all 50 states use DARE as their primary form of drug education.

Along with its popularity as the anti-drug education program of choice for the vast majority of American school systems, DARE enjoys massive public and political support, including that of the President George W. Bush, who signed a proclamation proclaiming April 1, 2001, national DARE day, continuing a presidential tradition begun in 1988.

DARE officially describes its program as a police officer-led "anti-drug, anti-gang, anti-violence program for schoolchildren around the world." The primary mission of DARE is "to provide children with the information and skills they need to live drug- and violence-free lives," according to the DARE Web site.

Started primarily as an anti-drug program in 1983 by a partnership between the Los Angeles Police Department and the Los Angeles Unified School District, the DARE program began with 10 officers who were sent into that city's school system in an attempt to reduce drug use and violence that were plaguing the city's schools....

Many surveys of school districts, students and their parents throughout the country report the short-term positive effects of DARE.

However, the long-term success rate of the DARE program is less certain.

Some critics even dare to suggest that the program might have a boomerang effect, giving youngsters ideas they wouldn't have come up with themselves.

Many of those who are critical of DARE claim that every dollar spent on the program is a dollar that could be going to a more effective anti-drug education program, commonly arguing that despite, or perhaps because of, so much anecdotal evidence, immense popularity, and the receipt of nearly all of drug education dollars spent by the government, DARE has enjoyed a sacred cow status and has not been required to scientifically prove its success.

DARE's official Web site concedes that "the impact of DARE on long-term drug use prevention is not well supported."

However, DARE recognizes the fact that its program cannot stand alone, suggesting that "communities can strengthen the impact of the program by ensuring that DARE is a part of an ongoing, multi-dimensional approach to prevention that spans the elementary, middle and high school years."

Questions to Ponder

1. **Many present-day college students were exposed to DARE while in elementary school. Were you one of those students? If so, how valuable did you find the DARE experience?**
2. **What do you think can be done to make DARE evidence based?**
3. **DARE officials have brought lawsuits against several publications that have made statements that DARE does not work. Why do you think they went through the trouble of suing these publications?**

Delaying the onset of substance abuse may have little preventive effect if age of onset is simply a marker for other problem behaviors. In the previously reviewed McGue et al. study, age of onset of alcohol use only predicted future alcohol problems by virtue of its common association with preexisting differences in disinhibitory behavior and psychopathology.[15] This does not matter, however, for primary and secondary prevention because either everyone will be targeted (primary prevention) or we will target individuals who are high risk but have not yet begun drinking, using drugs, or engaging in crime (secondary prevention).

Preventing Harmful Patterns of Use

Moderate alcohol consumption would appear to be relatively harmless, provided the individual is not too young or does not engage in risky behaviors while drinking.[16] Research indicates that children who start smoking, drinking, and using illegal drugs significantly earlier than their peers tend to have more substance use problems in later life compared to children who wait until mid to late adolescence to start experimenting with substances.[17] Hammersley believes that society needs to work out the functional rules of what is acceptable drug use and avoid falling into the moralistic trap of believing that personal fulfillment can only be achieved through abstinence. This requires programs that are both more effective and less tied to zero tolerance than DARE. Hammersley believes that several such programs exist, two of which are described next.[18]

Life Skills Training

Life Skills Training (**LST**) is a widely researched school-based prevention program developed by Gilbert Botvin, professor of Public Health and Psychiatry at Cornell University's Weill Medical College. The elementary school curriculum consists of 24 45-minute sessions and the middle school curriculum consists of 30 45-minute sessions, both conducted over a period of 3 years. Three different sets of skills are taught to participants:[19]

- Resistance skills designed to correct common misconceptions about tobacco, alcohol, and illegal drugs and where older students help participants resist peer and media pressure to drink and use drugs
- Personal self-management skills designed to help students solve problems, set goals, and deal effectively with adversity
- General social skills designed to improve students' communication and assertiveness skills

Research clearly supports the efficacy of LST when students and schools receiving LST are compared to students and schools not receiving LST. Elementary students from schools randomly assigned to LST reported 64% less tobacco use and 25% less alcohol use than students from control schools (see **Figure 12-1**).[20] Compared to untreated control

Figure 12-1
Rate of tobacco and alcohol use reported by LST graduates and control participants.

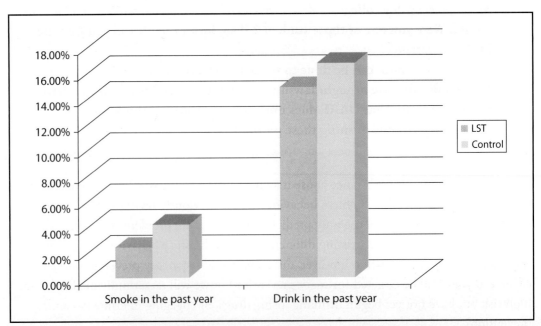

Data From: Botvin, G. J., Griffin, K. W., Paul, E., & Macaulay, A. P. (2003). Preventing tobacco and alcohol use among elementary school students through Life Skills Training. *Journal of Child and Adolescent Substance Abuse, 12*(4), 1–17.

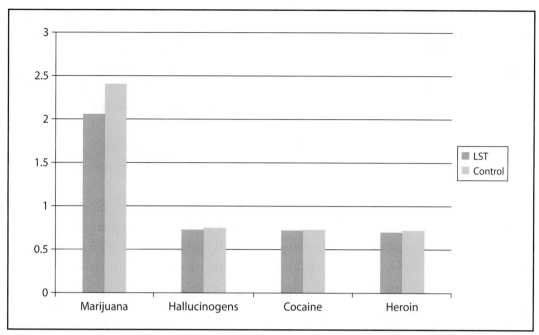

Figure 12-2
Adjusted mean scores for illicit drug use in LST graduates and control participants after 6.5 years.

Data From: Botvin, G. J., Griffin, K. W., Diaz, T., Schieier, L. M., Williams, C., & Epstein, J. A. (2000). Preventing illicit drug use in adolescents: Long-term follow-up data from a randomized control trial of a school population. *Addictive Behaviors, 25,* 769–774.

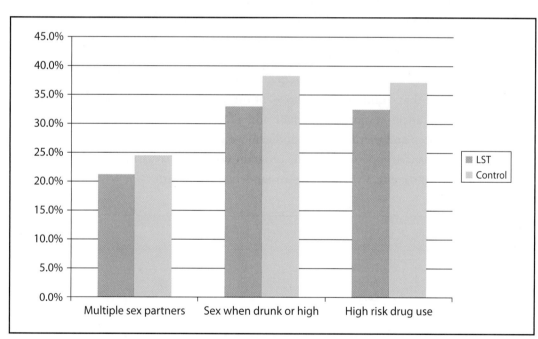

Figure 12-3
Percentage of LST graduates and control participants who engaged in HIV-risk behaviors while using drugs or alcohol.

Data: Griffin, K. W., Botvin, G. J., & Nichols, T. R. (2006). Effects of a school-based drug abuse prevention program for adolescents on HIV risk behavior in Young adulthood. *Prevention Science, 7,* 103–112.

participants, students who received LST in junior high school reported less illicit drug use 6 years later, when they were in 12th grade (see **Figure 12-2**).[21] A 3-month follow-up of sixth grade LST participants revealed a significant pre-post reduction in aggression and delinquency.[22] The positive results of LST extend beyond drug use and crime. Junior high school students receiving LST when they were in the seventh through ninth grades were less likely to engage in HIV-risk behaviors during early adulthood (multiple sex partners, sex when drunk or high, unprotected sex and other high-risk drug use behaviors) compared to students from schools that did not receive LST (see **Figure 12-3**).[23]

Project ALERT

Project ALERT is a school-based program developed over a 10-year period by researchers at the RAND Corporation. It is designed for middle school students (grades 6–8) and is delivered in 11 45-minute lessons during the first year and three booster sessions during the second year. The program focuses on four "gateway drugs"—tobacco, alcohol, marijuana, and inhalants—and has two primary goals:

- Prevent adolescent nonusers from experimenting with gateway drugs
- Prevent adolescents who have experimented with gateway drugs from using them regularly

With the aid of small-group activities, question-and-answer sessions, and role plays, Project ALERT seeks to motivate early adolescents to avoid drugs, while building norms against drug use. Program content includes learning to weigh the consequences of drug use, recognizing the benefits of not using drugs, and learning how to resist social pressure to use drugs. Frequently, slightly older students serve as positive role models for middle school participants.[24]

Research conducted on Project ALERT, like research conducted on LST, is generally supportive of the approach. In an early study on Project ALERT, Phyllis Ellickson, Robert Bell, and Kimberly McGuigan followed a sample of approximately 4,000 seventh- and eighth-grade students exposed to an 11-session version of Project ALERT. Although the program had an immediate effect on tobacco and marijuana use, the effect dissipated over time (see **Figures 12-4** and **12-5**). The authors recommended changes to the curriculum in the form of booster sessions.[25] In a subsequent study, Bonnie Ghosh-Dastidar and colleagues determined that eighth graders who went through an updated version of the program, consisting of an 11-session initial phase and a follow-up phase with booster sessions, reduced their tobacco and marijuana risk and achieved more modest reductions in alcohol risk after 18 months (see **Figure 12-6**). The program was found to assist individuals at all risk levels but was most effective with low- to moderate-risk youth.[26]

Figure 12-4
Percentage of Project ALERT (Adult only leader versus Teen leader) and control participants initiating marijuana use from grades 7 through 12.

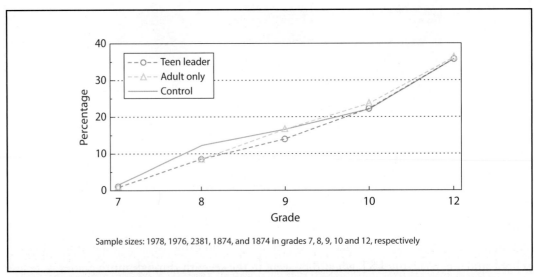

Sample sizes: 1978, 1976, 2381, 1874, and 1874 in grades 7, 8, 9, 10 and 12, respectively

Ellickson, P. L., Bell, R. M., & McGuigan, K. (1993). Preventing adolescent drug use: Long-term results of a Junior High program. *American Journal of Public Health, 83*, 856–861.

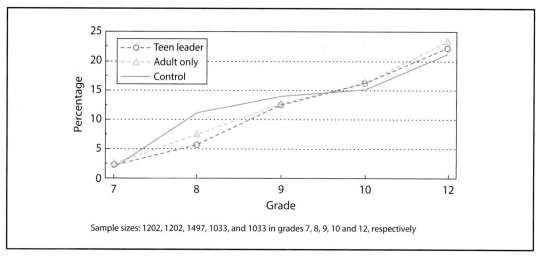

Figure 12-5
Percentage of Project ALERT (Adult only leader versus Teen leader) and control participants who used cigarettes weekly from grades 7 through 12.

Ellickson, P. L., Bell, R. M., & McGuigan, K. (1993). Preventing adolescent drug use: Long-term results of a Junior High program. *American Journal of Public Health, 83,* 856–861.

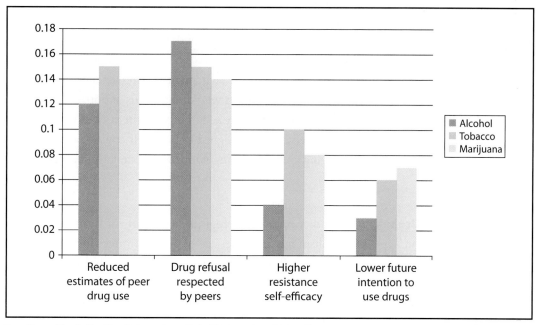

Figure 12-6
Effect sizes (beta weights from a regression equation) for alcohol, tobacco, and marijuana risk that differentiate between Project ALERT and control students.

Data From: Ghosh-Dastidar, B., Longshore, D. L., Ellickson, P. L., & McCaffrey, D. F. (2004). Modifying pro-drug risk factors in adolescents: Results from Project ALERT. *Health Education and Behavior, 31,* 318–334.

Secondary Prevention of Drug Use and Crime

Even evidence-based primary prevention programs like LST and Project ALERT have only a modest effect on future drug use and criminal behavior. This is probably due to the fact that primary prevention must, by necessity, be of low intensity/dosage because of its wide scope. Perhaps more powerful results could be attained with secondary prevention. Because secondary prevention programs target high-risk youth, the scope of the intervention is much narrower than the scope of a primary prevention program. Due to its more limited scope, the secondary prevention intervention can be made more intensive than the primary prevention intervention. Using 10 variables that appear prior to the onset of drug use and delinquency, an additive risk model is examined next. In an additive model, risk increases in concert with a rise in the number of active risk factors. The 10 risk factors to be discussed in this section are:

- dopamine dysregulation and Type 2 alcoholism
- three temperament styles
- three agents of socialization
- access and stress

Biological Risk Factors

Dopamine Dysregulation

The neurotransmitter dopamine has been linked to pleasure, motivation, and reward pursuit and so it may play a role in both drug use and crime. It remains to be seen whether the problem involves excessive amounts of dopamine in various regions of the central nervous system or a dearth of dopamine receptors in certain dopamine-rich areas of the brain, but it seems clear that people who engage in drug use and crime experience a rush of dopamine when engaging in these activities. In addition, the dopamine system is thought to be modulated by another neurotransmitter, serotonin. Weak or ineffective modulation of dopamine by serotonin has been shown to correlate with drug use and crime.[27] The behavioral markers of **dopamine dysregulation** include impulsivity, irresponsibility, and excitement-seeking tendencies. Secondary preventive measures that could be taken with youths who display signs of dopamine dysregulation include prescription drugs that potentiate the action of serontin, such as the selective serotonin reuptake inhibitors (SSRIs), interventions designed to build self-control, and efforts to keep the individual engaged in interesting and stimulating nondrug and noncriminal activities.

Type 2 Alcoholism

Cloninger's **Type 2 alcoholism** is another putative biological **risk factor** for future drug use and criminal behavior. Type 2 alcoholism has an earlier age of onset, stronger inheritance, and a more lucid connection to crime than Type 1 alcoholism.[28] Type 2 alcoholism tends to be passed down from father to son; hence, it is sometimes referred to as male-limited alcoholism. The Type 2 risk factor is theoretically restricted to males but could apply to some females as well. The marker in this case is a close paternal figure, such as a biological father, uncle, or grandfather, who demonstrates severe alcohol and/or drug abuse along with a pattern of chronic criminality. The risk goes up as the number of first- and second-degree male relatives with the pattern increases. Secondary prevention of this high-risk biological characteristic could entail furnishing at-risk youth with substitute paternal role models and mentoring through a program like Big Brothers Big Sisters. In fact, the Coalition for Evidence-Based Policy lists Big Brothers Big Sisters as an evidence-based intervention on the strength of a large-scale study showing that program involvement reduced alcohol and drug initiation and aggressive behavior, although it had no apparent effect on theft or property damage.[29]

Psychological Risk Factors

With roots in biology, a prominent role in development, and moderate correlations with drug use and crime, temperament would appear to be a good candidate for a risk factor in a program of secondary prevention. Three temperament dimensions, in particular, are highlighted in this section:

- Negative emotionality
- High activity level
- Novelty seeking

Negative Emotionality

Negative emotionality is strongly correlated with self-reported drug use and abuse[30] and also correlates with antisocial behavior.[31] In using negative emotionality as a risk factor in a program of secondary prevention, it is important that we first clarify the individual relationships linking specific negative emotions to drug use and crime. Research, for instance, indicates that angry negative emotionality is more closely linked to antisocial conduct than to drug use, whereas anxiety and depression are more closely tied to drug use than to antisocial conduct.[32–33] A temperament marked by low anxiety and depression (fearlessness) can also put a child at risk for future antisocial conduct. Given the role of negative emotionality in predisposing someone to drug use or delinquency it would seem to make sense that secondary prevention in cases where negative emotionality is a factor should involve some form of emotions management. In addition to learning how to control their anger and tolerate frustration, high-risk individuals should also be taught how to cope with anxiety and depression. ART (Aggression Replacement Training) does the former and LST the latter.

High Activity Level

A temperament style marked by high physical activity has been observed in children at risk for future drug use[34] and delinquency.[35] Abnormally high levels of physical activity have also been shown to correlate with impulsiveness,[36] lack of empathy,[37] antisocial responses on a moral dilemma task,[38] and a general pattern of disinhibition. A **high activity level** is not always observed in children who later develop problems with drugs or delinquency and not every child with a high activity level will develop a drug or crime problem, but a high activity level is a risk factor for future drug use and crime in a fair number of cases. Where hyperactivity puts a child at risk for future drug and criminal involvement, stimulant medication (Ritalin), substitution (having the child divert his or her energy into positive activities), and environmental manipulation (structuring the child's immediate environment) may serve a secondary prevention function.

Novelty Seeking

Novelty seeking has been found to predict early onset drug use[39] as well as aggression and delinquency.[40] The fact that novelty seeking correlates positively with externalizing disorders like drug abuse and delinquency suggests that high novelty seeking is a risk factor for externalizing behavior.[41] Furthermore, adolescents high in novelty seeking tend to be impulsive[42] and aggressive.[43] Substitution, modeling, and internalization are methods by which secondary prevention of high-risk novelty seeking in children can be achieved. By encouraging high-risk youth to enter into exciting prosocial activities (substitution), follow the example of someone who engages in socially appropriate stimulation seeking (modeling), and helping them develop self-discipline and inner-directedness (internalization) it may be possible to significantly reduce their future liability for drug abuse and crime.

Sociological Risk Factors

Risk factors extend beyond the biological and psychological characteristics of the individual. They can also encompass external variables like socialization. People acquire the beliefs, norms, values, and behaviors of a larger group or culture through socialization. Socialization can therefore increase or decrease opportunities for drug use and crime by bringing the individual into contact with definitions congruent with drug use and crime or definitions incongruent with drug use and crime, respectively. Three agents of socialization may be particularly noteworthy as risk factors in a program of secondary prevention:

- Parents
- Peers
- Media

Parenting

Parental socialization can be either direct or indirect. Parents socialize their children indirectly through love, encouragement, and respect (support dimension of parenting) and they socialize them directly through discipline, order, and restraint (control dimension of parenting). Jane Petrie, Frances Bunn, and Geraldine Byrne reviewed experimental studies on **parenting** programs and found that statistically significant reductions in self-reported substance use following parenting training were reported in 6 out of 14 studies on alcohol, 9 out of 13 studies on tobacco, and 5 out of 9 studies on illicit drugs. Overall, they uncovered moderate support for a secondary preventive effect for parenting programs on offspring substance use and abuse, with the most effective programs being those that integrated the control and support dimensions.[44] Machteld Hoeve and colleagues performed a meta-analysis of studies investigating the relationship between parenting and delinquency by breaking parenting down into its support and control dimensions. Authoritative parenting (inductive discipline, incorporating aspects of both high control and high support) correlated with reduced levels of offspring delinquency. Lack of paternal warmth and support, on the other hand, was a stronger correlate of delinquency than lack of maternal warmth and support, particularly in male children.[45]

Although the control and support dimensions of parenting are equally important in the development and prevention of drug use and crime, the goal of most parenting-centered secondary prevention programs is teaching parents to be more effective disciplinarians. Both drug abuse[46] and delinquency[47] have been prevented in high-risk youth whose parents have received training in how to improve their child management skills. Kumpfer and Alvarado report that the Center for Substance Abuse Prevention's 1998 expert review of family-focused approaches to secondary prevention certified three programs as evidence based.[48] Gerald Patterson's **Behavioral Parent Training (BPT)** model received some of the highest marks. BPT is a highly structured approach in which parents meet with trainers in small groups for a period of 6 to 15 sessions, during which parents are instructed in basic child management techniques (e.g., limit-setting, monitoring and supervision, family problem solving, positive parental involvement). The **Family Skills Training (FST)** approach supplements parental training with life and social skills training for the high-risk child and family practice sessions.[49] As a result, retention is one-third higher in FST than in BPT.[50] **Behavioral Family Therapy (BFT)** is a brief intervention that has produced the weakest effects of the three evidence-based parenting programs.[51]

Peer Associations

Research indicates that peers have both a direct and indirect effect on subsequent drug use and that **peer associations** may moderate the relationship between parenting and drug use.[52–53] Research has shown that some youth overestimate the degree to which their peers drink and use drugs; even though this trend is neither as robust or as consistent as has traditionally been assumed, it nonetheless exists.[54] Secondary prevention programs that seek to correct these erroneous perceptions have been shown to reduce self-reported drug experimentation and use.[55] In a review of studies on peers and delinquency, Gifford-Smith, Dodge, Dishion, and McCord concluded that peers are critical in initiating, exacerbating, and maintaining delinquent behavior. The peer effect persisted even after preexisting levels of delinquency were taken into account, thereby supporting Gifford-Smith et al.'s contention that the peer-delinquency relationship is the direct result of exposure to antisocial peers rather than a self-selection effect.[56]

Peers can serve as either risk or protective factors depending on whether the peers are prosocial or antisocial. In situations where peers serve as risk factors the best approach to secondary prevention may be to limit the child's contact with antisocial peers. In situations where peers serve as protective factors it may be possible to enlist their help, provided they:

- hold prosocial attitudes, values, and beliefs.
- genuinely want to serve as role models.
- are properly supervised by responsible adults.
- have credibility with the audience with whom they are working.

Project ALERT makes effective use of this approach by having responsible high school students teach sections of the curriculum. Black, Tobler, and Sciacca concluded that prosocial peers can serve a vital secondary prevention function through a process known as "peer helping."[57]

Media Influences

Drugs have often been portrayed in a positive light by the media, especially in movies and popular music, and this has been shown to promote the use of alcohol, tobacco, and illegal drugs in juveniles.[58] Facets of the media may also promote violence as indicated by the results of a review of five meta-analyses, in which the authors concluded that violent images from movies, television, and computer games may lead to a short-term increase in aggressive and fearful behavior on the part of younger male children.[59] However, the media can also play a role in primary and secondary prevention, as Michael Slater and colleagues discovered when they examined the effect of a media campaign referred to as "Above the Influence." Unlike the previous campaign, "My Anti-Drug," which focused on the risks of marijuana use, the "Above the Influence" campaign tapped into adolescents' goals, aspirations, and desire for

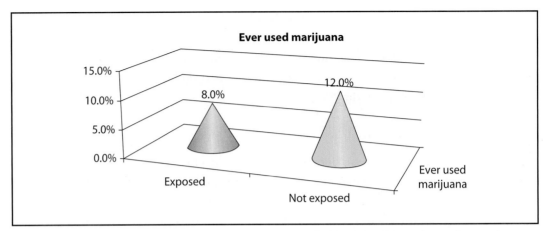

Data From: Slater, M. D., Kelly, K. J., Lawrence, F. R., Stanley, L. R., & Comello, M. L. G. (2011). Assessing media campaigns linking marijuana non-use with autonomy and aspirations: "Be Under Your Own Influence" and ONDCP's "Above the Influence". *Prevention Science, 12*, 12–22.

autonomy, shifting the message from "is this hurting you" to "is this what you really want." Whereas the "My Anti-Drug" campaign promoted increased levels of drug use because most drug users are sensations seekers and not risk aversive, the "Above the Influence" campaign appeared to cut marijuana use by a third (see **Figure 12-7**).[60]

Acute Dynamic Risk Factors

A final group of risk factors that should be considered when assessing risk for future drug and crime problems is acute dynamic risk factors. Two primary acute dynamic risk factors, **access** and stress, are reviewed here.

Access

Objects (e.g., drug paraphernalia, burglary tools) and resources (drug-using associates, criminal knowledge) can make drugs more available and create criminal opportunities. Routine activities theory holds that certain routine activities of everyday life increase opportunities for drug use and crime.[61] Wayne Osgood and colleagues studied routine activities in a large sample of high school students and discerned that three of four unstructured socializing activities (going to parties, riding for fun, evenings out) correlated with criminal behavior and that the fourth activity (visiting with friends) correlated with the use of alcohol, marijuana, and other drugs.[62] Limiting access to alcohol and firearms are ways of reducing drug availability and criminal opportunities, respectively.

Limiting Access to Alcohol

Two ways to limit access to alcohol are to increase taxes on alcoholic beverages and to raise the drinking age. Alexander Wagenaar, Matthew Salois, and Kelli Komro conducted a meta-analysis of studies exploring the effect of tax increases on alcohol consumption and found that raising the price of alcohol through increased taxation led to a significant reduction in alcohol consumption (see **Figure 12-8**), heavy drinking, and several alcohol-related problems like fatal accidents.[63] Whereas some individuals will respond to price increases by switching to a cheaper brand of liquor,[64] there is no getting around the fact that raising the price of alcohol does, in

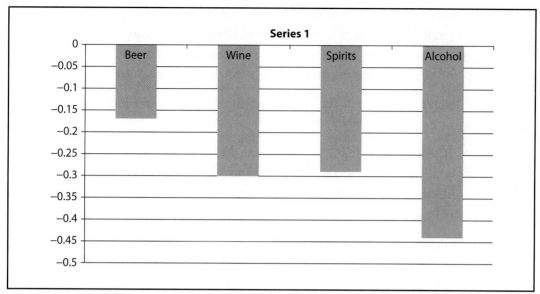

Figure 12-8
Effect sizes (*r*) obtained in a meta-analysis of the relationship between alcohol taxation/price and beer, wine, spirits, and total alcohol consumption.

Data From: Wagenaar, A. C., Salois, M. J., & Komro, K. A. (2009). Effects of beverage alcohol price and tax levels on drinking: A meta-analysis of 1003 estimates from 112 studies. *Addiction, 104,* 179–190.

fact, reduce access, consumption, and alcohol-related problems. Wagenaar has also studied the effect of raising the drinking age on alcohol-related problems. By making it more difficult for 18- to 20-year-olds to access alcohol, society benefits from significant reductions in alcohol-related automobile accidents and other problems.[65–66] It is estimated that raising the drinking age from 18 to 21 saves as many as 1,000 young lives each year (see also News Spot 12-2).[67]

NEWS SPOT 12-2

Title: Teen Drinking Less Common in Road Death: State Credits Boost in Legal Age for Rise in Drivers' Sobriety
Source: *The Milwaukee (WI) Journal*
Author: Lawrence Sussman
Date: April 4, 1990

Fewer teenage drivers are dying in alcohol-related accidents on Wisconsin highways, and officials say the decline is due in large part to the state's higher drinking age.

A state study shows that the number of teenage drivers found to be drunk when they died in traffic accidents was cut nearly in half during the first full year that the drinking age was 21, compared with figures available for the last full year the drinking age was 19.

Drivers ages 16 to 20 traditionally have had the highest rate of fatal accidents for those who were found to be drinking beforehand. But figures compiled by the State Departments of Transportation and Health and Social Services show a significant decrease in the death rates of these drivers between 1986 and 1989.

The study also indicates, however, that drinking among high school students has not subsided.

The study evaluated the impact of the higher drinking age in Wisconsin. The law was phased in over a two-year period beginning in September 1986, when the minimum drinking age was 19, and ending in September 1988, when it became 21. The Transportation and Health and Social Services Departments conducted the study for the Legislature and presented it earlier this year.

In 1983, the legal drinking age in Wisconsin was 18. A law raising the minimum drinking age from 18 to 19 took effect July 1, 1984.

According to the report, from July 1, 1985, to June 30, 1986, 78 drivers ages 16 through 20 died in traffic accidents. Of those, 65 were tested and 35 drivers, or nearly 54%, were found to have had a blood-alcohol content of 0.10% or greater, which is considered evidence of intoxication in Wisconsin.

In contrast, from Sept. 1, 1988, through Aug. 31, 1989, the first full year that the drinking age was 21, only 34% of drivers ages 16 through 20 who were killed in traffic accidents and tested were found to have been intoxicated, according to the study. A total of 78 died, and 55 were tested. Only 19 drivers were found to have been intoxicated, a 45% reduction.

Among drivers 21 and older who died in accidents, 48% of those tested were found to have been intoxicated at the time of fatal accidents in 1985 and 1986 and 43% in 1988 and 1989, the report said.

In comparison, in 1983, when the drinking age was 18, 88 drivers ages 16 to 20 were killed in traffic accidents. Tests were done on 72 of the victims and of those, 50 drivers or 69% were found to have been intoxicated.

Republished with permission of *Milwaukee Journal Sentinel*; permission conveyed through Copyright Clearance Center, Inc.

Questions to Ponder

1. **What are the pros and cons of raising the legal drinking age?**
2. **Why do you suppose younger people have a higher rate of both automobile accidents and alcohol-related fatalities?**
3. **In addition to raising the legal drinking age, what other policy changes could potentially help reduce alcohol-related problems?**

Controlling **outlet density** is another way to limit access to alcohol and reduce various alcohol-related problems. After reviewing the literature on alcohol availability and its effect on alcohol consumption and alcohol-related problems, Paul Gruenewald offered the following conclusions:[68]

- Greater outlet (place where alcohol is sold) densities (number of outlets in an area) are associated with greater amounts of alcohol usage.
- Greater densities of bars and taverns are associated with more drunk driving incidents and alcohol-related accidents.
- Greater densities of bars and taverns are associated with an increase in the incidence of assault and related violence.

This would seem to suggest that alcohol consumption and alcohol-related problems could be reduced by limiting the number of outlets that sell and serve alcohol.

Limiting Access to Firearms

It is often stated that guns do not kill people, people kill people. While accepting the basic logic of this argument, David Cook and Jens Ludwig contend that the statement should be amended to read, "Guns don't kill people; they just make it real easy."[69,p590] Cook, himself, performed a study in which he discovered that gun robberies were three times more likely to lead to the victim's death than nongun robberies.[70] Controlling guns is therefore one way society could potentially limit access to criminal opportunities. In discussing the controversial topic of gun control, it is important to understand that **gun control** policies are based on two premises:

- Premise 1: The more guns in the community, the greater the violence.
- Premise 2: Controlling guns will reduce violent crime.

Support for the first premise (i.e., the more guns in the community, the greater the violence) is strong. Albert Reiss and Jeffrey Roth noted that regardless of whether the unit of analysis was neighborhoods, cities, states, or nations, the conclusion was the same: jurisdictions with more guns suffered higher rates of violence.[71] Alfred Blumstein and Joel Wallman have also studied this issue and found that the single most important factor in the post-1993 drop in the U.S. violent crime rate was the plunge in recruitment of young black males with handguns to replace other black males who had been incarcerated for distributing crack cocaine—the direct result of reduced demand for crack cocaine.[72]

Whereas the first premise is strongly supported, there is virtually no support for the second premise (i.e., controlling guns will reduce violence). The results of an evaluation by the Task Force on Community Preventive Services revealed that policies banning certain firearms or ammunition, prohibiting felons from purchasing firearms, requiring a waiting period prior to acquiring a firearm, and compelling urban communities to install metal detectors in schools all proved inconclusive in preventing future violence.[73] **Gun buyback** programs, where individuals receive cash in exchange for turning in firearms to the police department, also appear to be ineffective.[74] Sherman and Rogan speculate that gun buyback programs fail because:[75]

- guns frequently come from outside the jurisdiction to which they are returned
- many of the guns had previously been locked up
- offenders use the funds to purchase newer and more lethal firearms

Stress

Stress can be defined as a reaction or orienting response to a change in the internal or external environment. There are two dimensions along which stressors are believed to vary:
- origin of the change (internal-external)
- direction of the orienting response (approach-avoidance)

Arbitrarily dichotomizing and crossing the dimensions produces a system of four stressor pseudo-categories:[76]

- Internal-approach stressors
- External-approach stressors

- Internal-avoidance stressors
- External-avoidance stressors

All four stressor categories are theoretically capable of increasing opportunities for drug use and/or crime, but it is the external-avoidance category that has received the most attention from researchers. Examples of stressors from each category capable of increasing risk for drug use and crime are listed in **Table 12-1**.

The stress created by risk can be managed by removing the stressor, adding buffers, or teaching the individual **stress management** techniques.

Removing the Stressor

Removing mild to moderate stressors in a child's life is not typically the best approach to use in secondary prevention of stress. In fact, shielding a child from failure and disappointment can lead to internalizing disorders like depression, which then put the child at increased risk for future substance abuse and other adjustment difficulties because the child has never learned to cope effectively with disappointment.[77] For stressors that are more severe, like physical abuse or bullying, a more direct approach may be required, up to and including removal of the child from the home or a change in classroom. The value of limiting a child's exposure to severe stressors can be traced to the fact that physical abuse predicts subsequent delinquency and future interpersonal violence,[78] whereas bullying can lead to serious emotional difficulties in the bullied child and an increased probability of the child becoming a bully him or herself.[79]

Adding Buffers

Buffering stress with family support, new friendships, or school programs can serve a vital secondary prevention function.[80] Social support is a common **buffer** that reduces the odds that an individual who grows up in a socially isolated neighborhood will abuse alcohol or drugs.[81] Promotional and protective factors that buffer against drug use and delinquency include:[82]

- Low parental stress
- Strong parental supervision and consistent parental discipline
- Minimal parental use of physical punishment
- Involvement of the child in family activities
- Residence in a good neighborhood

Table 12-1 Examples of Drug- and Crime-Related Stressors in Each of Four Stressor Categories

Stressor Category	Drug Example	Crime Example
Internal-Approach	Positive outcome expectancies for alcohol	Reminiscing about a gratifying prior offense
External-Approach	Environmental cues associated with past drug use	An open cash register or an unattended jewelry case
Internal-Avoidance	Chronic boredom	Fear of becoming a "working stiff" like one's father
External-Avoidance	Physical or sexual abuse	Peer rejection or bullying

Stress Management

Teaching children to cope with stress by providing them with stress management training and arming them with basic social/coping skills is another way to assist children at risk for future drug use and delinquency as a consequence of elevated environmental stress.[83] Some of the social and coping skills useful in preventing future substance abuse and delinquency are as follows:[84]

- Communication
- Assertiveness
- Empathy and perspective taking
- Resistance (to negative social influences)
- Problem solving
- Anger management
- Stress management and coping

Resilience

Children exposed to high levels of stress do not necessarily suffer long-term negative consequences. The fact that some children experience good outcomes despite exposure to severe stress, marked adversity, or other threats to normal development is known as resilience. In other words, they are resilient to the effects of stress.[85] **Resilience** has been attributed to both person and situation variables. Several person variables have been found to promote resilience in children exposed to high levels of life stress and adversity, to include:

- Above average intelligence[86]
- Mild-mannered temperament[87]
- Ego strength[88]
- Good social skills[89]
- Perseverence[90]

The results of one study showed that personal resources were often insufficient to protect children living in multiproblem families from the debilitating effect of stress and that situational supports were often required to protect these children from developing long-term problems.[91] Situational supports can play a particularly important role in secondary prevention by providing:

- Early exposure to controllable stressors[92]
- Positive parenting[93]
- High-quality preschool education[94]
- Social support[95]

Risk Prediction and Management

An effective program of secondary prevention rests on an effective program of **risk assessment**, which involves both **risk prediction** and **risk management**.[96] Risk prediction involves assessing a child's overall level of risk and identifying specific areas of concern. The 10 risk factors described in this chapter reflect personal characteristics (dopamine dysregulation, Type 2 alcoholism, negative emotionality, high activity level, novelty seeking), immediate environmental issues (parenting, peer associations, stress), and wider environmental

Table 12-2 Specific Secondary Prevention Interventions for Each of 10 Risk Factors

Risk Factor	Specific Interventions
Dopamine Dysregulation	Serotonin-enhancing medications (e.g., SSRIs) Self-Control Training
Type 2 Alcoholism	Restricting contact with antisocial male relatives Mentoring programs like *Big Brothers Big Sisters*
Negative Emotionality	Emotions Management Anger Management Training
High Activity Level	Stimulant medication (e.g., Ritalin) Substitution Environmental manipulation
Novelty Seeking	Substitution Modeling Internalization
Parenting	Parenting Skills Training to help parents improve both control and support
Peer Associations	Avoiding antisocial peers Approaching prosocial peers
Media Influence	Parental monitoring of TV viewing/computer games Evidence-based media campaigns
Access	Access-limiting changes in policy Access-limiting changes in environment
Stress	Removing stressors Adding buffers Teaching stress-management techniques

issues (**media influences** and access). When summed, these 10 risk factors provide an overall assessment of risk (i.e., total number of areas of risk) and, when examined individually, they identify specific pockets of concern (i.e., areas of highest risk). Because each of these risk factors can be observed in an individual who has not yet begun using drugs or committing crime, this system is ideal for secondary prevention, which, as the reader will recall, is designed to prevent the onset of drug and crime problems in high-risk individuals. Drug and criminal history, including an early age of onset of drug use or crime, are strong predictors of risk. However, identifying individuals who have already begun using drugs or engaging in crime comes under the heading of tertiary prevention and requires a program of treatment rather than prevention. Even individuals in the early stages of a drug or delinquency pattern are more properly classified as candidates for tertiary prevention than as candidates for secondary prevention.

Like risk prediction, risk management possesses both general and specific features. The general features of risk management in the secondary prevention of drug abuse and crime are an expansion of evidence-based primary prevention programs like LST and Project ALERT. Emotions management, improved problem solving, increased self-esteem, and resistance skills training all play major roles in evidence-based primary prevention programs. Secondary prevention programs should be teaching these same skills to high-risk children and adolescents; because of the smaller number of participants, secondary prevention

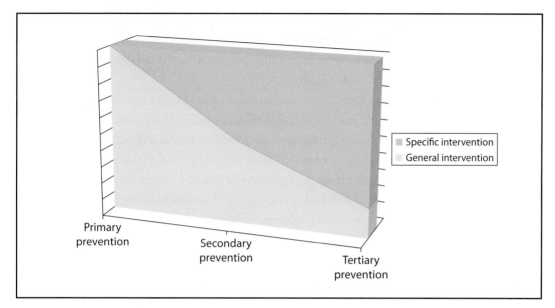

Figure 12-9
Relative emphasis placed on general and specific intervention by primary, secondary, and tertiary prevention programs.

programs have the luxury of increasing the intensity or dosage level of the intervention above what is normally found in primary prevention programs. Risk management for secondary prevention of drug abuse and crime can also target specific areas of concern. A list of specific interventions for each of the ten risk factors discussed in this chapter can be found in **Table 12-2**. The continuum that runs from primary to tertiary prevention responds differentially to general and specific interventions, with primary prevention relying exclusively on general intervention and tertiary prevention relying more on specific than general intervention (see **Figure 12-9**). In closing this section, it is important to keep in mind that prevention programs cannot prevent all or even most cases of drug abuse and crime, but the degree to which they can delay the onset of drug use and crime and prevent the emergence of more serious patterns of drug use and crime points to the practical utility of secondary prevention programs.

Summary and Conclusions

- Primary prevention is designed to reduce the overall occurrence of a problem in the general population. As such, an intervention based on primary prevention targets the entire population. Secondary prevention is designed to prevent and delay the onset of a problem in high-risk individuals. Accordingly, an intervention based on secondary prevention targets certain high-risk groups. Tertiary prevention is designed to ameliorate an already existing pattern of drug use or crime and so an intervention based on tertiary prevention targets those individuals in the early or middle stages of drug or criminal involvement.

- Given the fact that they adopt a wide scope, primary prevention programs are expensive. It is accordingly important to document whether these programs are evidence based. Popular primary prevention drug education programs like DARE have not been shown to be effective in reducing future drug use and a popular secondary prevention program for crime, Scared Straight, may actually increase future criminality.

Evidence-based primary prevention programs like LST and Project ALERT have achieved modest reductions in future drug use and general antisocial behavior and with an increase in intensity may have value in preventing or delaying drug use and delinquency in high-risk individuals.

- A program of secondary prevention was introduced based on 10 primary risk factors (dopamine dysregulation, Type 2 alcoholism, negative emotionality, high activity level, novelty seeking, parenting, peer associations, media influences, access, and stress). These 10 risk factors can be used to determine an individual's overall level of risk as well as identify specific areas or pockets of risk. By taking into account the individual's overall level of risk and specific areas of concern, a program of risk management can be constructed and implemented with individuals at risk for future drug and criminal involvement.

Key Terms

Access   Putative risk factor for future drug abuse and crime as manifested in objects and resources that increase opportunities for drug use and/or crime.

Behavioral Family Therapy (BFT)   Brief family-oriented program designed to change interactive patterns within the family and support parents in managing their children.

Behavioral Parent Training (BPT)   Highly structured program for disruptive children in which the parents of these children are instructed in basic child management strategies and techniques.

Buffer   Situation or resource that protects an individual against the debilitating effects of stress.

Dopamine Dysregulation   Putative risk factor for future drug abuse and crime in the form of poor modulation of the neurotransmitter dopamine as manifest in behavioral impulsivity and low self-control.

Drug Abuse Resistance Education (DARE)   Primary prevention program administered in schools where police officers present basic drug information to primary school students; research does not support this program as evidence based.

External-Approach Stressor   External stimulus that directs the individual toward it.

External-Avoidance Stressor   External stimulus that directs the individual away from it.

Family Skills Training (FST)   Program designed to improve parenting skills in the parents of disruptive children, while at the same time providing the child with life and social skills training.

Gun Buyback   Program that provides individuals with cash for firearms turned in at the local police station.

Gun Control   Policy designed to regulate the sale and ownership of rifles and handguns as a means of reducing gun-related violence.

High Activity Level   Putative risk factor for future drug abuse and crime as manifest in a temperament marked by excessive motor activity and easy distractibility.

Internal-Approach Stressor   Internal stimulus that directs the individual toward it.

Internal-Avoidance Stressor   Internal stimulus that directs the individual away from it.

Life Skills Training (LST)   Primary prevention program for elementary and middle school children designed to teach student participants drug resistance skills, personal self-management skills, and general social skills; research supports this program as evidence based.

Media Influences   Putative risk factor for future drug abuse and crime as manifest in excessive exposure to media violence and limited exposure to prosocial media messages.

Negative Emotionality   Putative risk factor for future drug abuse and crime as manifest in a temperament dominated by negative affect (anger, depression, and anxiety).

Novelty Seeking   Putative risk factor for future drug abuse and crime as manifest in a temperament characterized by thrill-seeking and the desire for new experiences.

Outlet Density   The number of establishments selling or serving alcohol per unit area.

Parenting   Putative risk factor for future drug abuse and crime as manifest in poor child management skills and a lack of supportive interactions with the child.

Peer Associations   Putative risk factor for future drug abuse and crime as manifest in an excess of antisocial peer associations and a dearth of prosocial peer associations.

Primary Prevention   Seeking to reduce a problem like drug abuse or crime by promoting general well-being and affording population-wide protection (immunization) against the problem.

Project ALERT   Primary prevention program for middle school children that makes use of small group exercises, question-and-answer sessions, and role plays to discourage children from experimenting with drugs; research supports this program as evidence based.

Resilience   Internal and external resources that allow a child to overcome severe stress, marked adversity, or other negative developmental experiences.

Risk Factor   Variable capable of predicting a future behavior of interest, such as drug use or crime.

Risk Assessment   System of risk evaluation designed to predict and manage individuals considered to be at risk for future drug or crime problems.

Risk Management   Use of risk factors to reduce an individual's chances of future problems with drugs or crime.

Risk Prediction   Use of risk factors to predict future problems with drugs and crime as a means of establishing supervision level or treatment need.

Scared Straight   Secondary prevention program designed for high-risk youth who may have gotten in trouble for a relatively minor offense, where inmate volunteers graphically depict the realities of prison life in an effort to frighten participants away from crime; research indicates that this program is not evidence based.

Secondary Prevention   Seeking to reduce a problem like drug abuse or crime by intervening with high-risk individuals who do not yet exhibit the problem (asymptomatic) but who are at increased risk for developing the problem in the future.

Stress   Putative risk factor for future drug abuse and crime as manifest in an orienting response that increases the incentive for drug use and/or crime.

Stress Management   Techniques designed to help an individual learn to cope more effectively with stress.

Tertiary Prevention   Seeking to reduce a problem like drug abuse or crime by providing treatment (amelioration) to individuals who have already developed the problem.

Type 2 Alcoholism   Putative risk factor for future drug abuse and crime as manifest in an excess of first- and second-degree male relatives with serious alcohol/drug problems and extensive criminal histories.

Critical Thinking

1. What are the advantages and disadvantages of primary, secondary, and tertiary prevention?
2. Why does drug awareness resistance (DARE) not appear to work as well as programs like Life Skills Training (LST) and Project Alert?
3. How would you go about assessing risk in a 8-year-old child who has no history of substance use or delinquency using the ten risk factors described in this chapter?

Notes

1. Clarke, R. V. (1983). Situational crime prevention: Its theoretical basis and practical scope. *Crime and Justice, 4,* 225–256.
2. World Health Organization. (2000). *Primary prevention of substance abuse: A workbook for project operators.* Geneva: Department of Mental Health and Substance Dependence, World Health Organization.
3. Hammersley, R. (2008). *Drugs and crime.* Cambridge, England: Polity Press.
4. Soole, D., Mazerolle, L., & Rombouts, S. (2008). School based drug prevention: A review of what works. *Australia and New Zealand Journal of Criminology, 41,* 259–286.
5. Brown, J. H. (2001). Youth, drugs and resilience education. *Journal of Drug Education, 31,* 83–122.
6. Petrosino, A., Turpin-Petrosino, C., & Buehler, J. (2003). "Scared Straight" and other juvenile awareness programs for preventing juvenile delinquency (Updated C2 Review). *The Campbell Collaboration Reviews of Intervention and Policy Evaluations.* Philadelphia, PA: Campbell Collaboration.
7. Andresen, M. A., & Jenion, G. W. (2008). Crime prevention and the science of where people are. *Criminal Justice Policy Review, 19,* 164–180.
8. Hammersley (2008).
9. Zhang, L., Wieczorke, W. F., & Welte, J. W. (1997). The impact of age of onset of substance use on delinquency. *Journal of Research in Crime and Delinquency, 34,* 253–268.
10. Gordon, M. S., Kinlock, T. W., & Battjes, R. J. (2004). Correlates of early substance use and crime among adolescents entering outpatient substance abuse treatment. *American Journal of Drug and Alcohol Abuse, 30,* 39–59.
11. Ennett, S. T., Tobler, N. S., Ringwalt, C. L., & Flewelling, R. L. (1994). How effective is Drug Abuse Resistance Education? A meta-analysis of Project DARE outcome evaluations. *American Journal of Public Health, 84,* 1394–1401.
12. Hammersley (2008).
13. Ennett et al. (1994).
14. Hammersley (2008).

15. McGue, M., Iacono, W. G., Legrand, L. N., Malone, S., & Elkins, I. (2001). Origins and consequences of age at first drink. I. Associations with substance-use disorders, disinhibitory behavior and psychopathology, and p3 amplitude. *Alcoholism: Clinical and Experimental Research, 25,* 1156–1165.

16. Roche, A. M., Evans, K. R., & Stanton, W. R. (1997). Harm reduction: Roads less traveled to the Holy Grail. *Addiction, 92,* 1207–1212.

17. Hingson, R. W., Heeren, T., & Winter, M. R. (2006). Age at drinking onset and alcohol dependence: Age at onset, duration, and severity. *Archives of Pediatrics and Adolescent Medicine, 160,* 739–746.

18. Hammersley (2008).

19. Botvin, G. J. (1990). Substance abuse prevention: Theory, practice, and effectiveness. *Crime and Justice, 13,* 461–519.

20. Botvin, G. J., Griffin, K. W., Paul, E., & Macaulay, A. P. (2003). Preventing tobacco and alcohol use among elementary school students through Life Skills Training. *Journal of Child and Adolescent Substance Abuse, 12*(4), 1–17.

21. Botvin, G. J., Griffin, K. W., Diaz, T., Schieier, L. M., Williams, C., & Epstein, J. A. (2000). Preventing illicit drug use in adolescents: Long-term follow-up data from a randomized control trial of a school population. *Addictive Behaviors, 25,* 769–774.

22. Botvin, G. J., Griffin, K. W., & Diaz-Nichols, T. (2006). Preventing youth violence and delinquency through a universal school-based prevention approach. *Prevention Science, 7,* 403–408.

23. Griffin, K. W., Botvin, G. J., & Nichols, T. R. (2006). Effects of a school-based drug abuse prevention program for adolescents on HIV risk behavior in young adulthood. *Prevention Science, 7,* 103–112.

24. Ellickson, P. L., & Bell, R. M. (1990). Drug prevention in junior high: A multi-site longitudinal test. *Science, 247,* 1299–1305.

25. Ellickson, P. L., Bell, R. M., & McGuigan, K. (1993). Preventing adolescent drug use: Long-term results of a Junior High program. *American Journal of Public Health, 83,* 856–861.

26. Ghosh-Dastidar, B., Longshore, D. L., Ellickson, P. L., & McCaffrey, D. F. (2004). Modifying pro-drug risk factors in adolescents: Results from Project ALERT. *Health Education and Behavior, 31,* 318–334.

27. Soderstrom, H., Blennow, K., Sjodin, A.-K., & Forsman, A. (2003). New evidence for an association between the CSF HVA:5-HIAA ratio and psychopathic traits. *Journal of Neurology, Neurosurgery, and Psychiatry, 74,* 918–921.

28. Cloninger, C. R. (1987). Neurogenetic adaptive mechanisms in alcoholism. *Science, 236,* 410–416.

29. Grossman, J. B., & Tierney, J. P. (1998). Does mentoring work? An impact study of the Big Brothers Big Sisters program. *Evaluation Review, 22,* 403–426.

30. James, L. M., & Taylor, J. (2007). Impulsivity and negative emotionality associated with substance use problems and Cluster B personality in college students. *Addictive Behaviors, 32,* 714–727.

31. Pulkkinen, L., Lyrra, A.-L., & Kokko, K. (2009). Life success of males on nonoffender, adolescence-limited, persistent, and adult onset antisocial pathways: Follow-up from age 8 to 42. *Aggressive Behavior, 35,* 117–135.

32. Eisenberg, N., Valiente, C., Spinrad, T. L., Cumberland, A., Liew, J., Zhou, Q., Losoya, S. H,. et al. (2009). Longitudinal relations of children's effortful control, impulsivity, and negative emotionality to their externalizing, internalizing, and co-occurring behavior problems. *Developmental Psychology, 45,* 988–1008.

33. Zvolensky, M. J., Buckner, J. D., Norton, P. J., & Smits, J. A. J. (2011). Anxiety, substance use, and their co-occurrence: Advances in clinical science. *Journal of Cognitive Psychotherapy: An International Quarterly, 25*(1), 3–6.

34. Windle, M. (2000). Parental, sibling, and peer influences on adolescent substance use and alcohol problems. *Applied Developmental Science, 4,* 98–110.

35. Windle, M., & Mason, W. A. (2004). General and specific predictors of behavioral and emotional problems among adolescents. *Journal of Emotional and Behavioral Disorders, 12,* 49–61.

36. Shoda, Y., Mischel, W., & Peake, P. K. (1990). Predicting adolescent cognitive and self-regulatory competencies from preschool delay of gratification: Identifying diagnostic conditions. *Developmental Psychology, 26*, 978–986.

37. Rothbart, M. K., Ahadi, S. A., & Hershey, K. L. (1994). Temperament and social behavior in childhood. *Merrill-Palmer Quarterly, 40*, 21–39.

38. Kochanska, G., Murray, K., & Cox, K. C. (1997). Inhibitory control as a contributor to conscience in childhood: From toddler to early school age. *Child Development, 68*, 263–277.

39. Masse, L. C., & Tremblay, R. E. (1997). Behavior of boys in kindergarten and onset of substance abuse during adolescence. *Archives of General Psychiatry, 54*, 62–68.

40. Kim, S. J., Lee, S. J., Yune, S. K., Sung, Y. H., Bae, S. C., Chung, A., et al. (2006). The relationship between the biogenetic temperament and character and psychopathology in adolescents. *Psychopathology, 39*(2), 80–86.

41. Copeland, W., Landry, K., Stranger, C., & Hudziak, J. J. (2004). Multi-informant assessment of temperament in children with externalizing behavior problems. *Journal of Clinical Child and Adolescent Psychology, 33*, 547–556.

42. Nagoshi, C. T., Walter, D., Muntaner, C., & Haertzen, C. A. (1992). Validation of the Tridimensional Personality Questionnaire in a sample of male drug users. *Personality and Individual Differences, 13*, 401–409.

43. Ruchkin, V. V., Eisemann, M., Hägglöf, B., & Cloninger, C. R. (1998). Interrelations between temperament, character, and parental rearing in male delinquent adolescents in northern Russia. *Comprehensive Psychiatry, 39*, 225–230.

44. Petrie, J., Bunn, F., & Byrne, G. (2007). Parenting programmes for preventing tobacco, alcohol or drugs misuse in children <18: A systematic review. *Health Education Research, 22*, 177–191.

45. Hoeve, M., Dubas, S., Eichelsheim, V. I., van der Laan, P. H., Smeenk, W., & Gerris, J. R. M. (2009). The relationship between parenting and delinquency: A meta-analysis. *Journal of Abnormal Child Psychology, 37*, 749–775.

46. Dishion, T. J., & Andrews, D. W. (1995). Preventing escalation in problem behaviors with high-risk young adolescents: Immediate and 1-year outcomes. *Journal of Consulting and Clinical Psychology, 63*, 538–548.

47. Lundahl, B. W., Nimer, J., & Parsons, B. (1996). Preventing child abuse: A meta-analysis of parent training programs. *Research on Social Work Practice, 16*, 251–262.

48. Kumpfer, K. L., & Alvarado, R. (2003). Family-strengthening approaches for the prevention of youth problem behaviors. *American Psychologist, 58*, 457–465.

49. Patterson, G. R. (1976). *Living with children: New methods for parents and teachers.* Champaign, IL: Research Press.

50. Forehand, R. L., & McMahon, R. J. (1981). *Helping the noncompliant child: A clinician's guide to parent training.* New York: Guilford Press.

51. Alexander, J. F., Robbins, M. S., & Sexton, T. L. (2000). Family-based interventions with older, at-risk youth: From promise to proof to practice. *Journal of Primary Prevention, 21*, 185–206.

52. Bahr, S. J., Hoffmann, J. P., & Yang, X. (2005). Parental and peer influence on the risk of adolescent drug use. *Journal of Primary Prevention, 26*, 529–551.

53. Henry, K. L. (2008). Low prosocial attachment, involvement with drug-using peers, and adolescent drug use: A longitudinal examination of mediational mechanisms. *Psychology of Addictive Behaviors, 22*, 302–308.

54. Pape, H. (2012). Young people's overestimation of peer substance use: An exaggerated phenomenon? *Addiction, 107*, 878–884.

55. Donaldson, S. I., Graham, J. W., & Hansen, W. B. (1994). Testing the generalizability of intervening mechanism theories: Understanding the effects of adolescent drug use prevention interventions. *Journal of Behavioral Medicine, 17*, 195–216.

56. Gifford-Smith, M., Dodge, K. A., Dishion, T. J., & McCord, J. (2005). Peer influence in children and adolescents: Crossing the bridges from developmental to intervention science. *Journal of Abnormal Child Psychology, 33*, 255–265.

57. Black, D. R., Tobler, N. S., & Sciacca, J. P. (1998). Peer helping/involvement: An efficacious way to meet the challenge of reducing alcohol, tobacco, and other drug use among youth? *Journal of School Health, 68*, 87–93.

58. Villani, S. (2001). Impact of media on children and adolescents: A 10-year review of the research. *Journal of the American Academy of Child and Adolescent Psychiatry, 40*, 392–400.

59. Browne, K. D., & Hamilton-Giachritsis, C. (2005). The influence of violent media on children and adolescents: A public-health approach. *Lancet, 365*, 702–710.

60. Slater, M. D., Kelly, K. J., Lawrence, F. R., Stanley, L. R., & Comello, M. L. G. (2011). Assessing media campaigns linking marijuana non-use with autonomy and aspirations: "Be Under Your Own Influence" and ONDCP's "Above the Influence". *Prevention Science, 12*, 12–22.

61. Cohen, L. E., & Felson, M. (1979). Social change and crime rate trends: A routine activity approach. *American Sociological Review, 44*, 588–608.

62. Osgood, D. W., Wilson, J. K., O'Malley, P. M., Bachman, J. G., & Johnston, L. D. (1996). Routine activities and individual deviant behavior. *American Sociological Review, 61*, 635–655.

63. Wagenaar, A. C., Salois, M. J., & Komro, K. A. (2009). Effects of beverage alcohol price and tax levels on drinking: A meta-analysis of 1003 estimates from 112 studies. *Addiction, 104*, 179–190.

64. Gruenewald, P. J., Ponicki, W. R., Holder, H. D., & Romelsjö, A. (2006). Alcohol prices, beverage quality, and the demand for alcohol: Quality substitutions and price elasticities. *Alcoholism: Clinical and Experimental Research, 30*, 96–105.

65. Wagenaar, A. C. (1993). Minimum drinking age and alcohol availability to youth: Issues and research needs. In M. E. Hilton & G. Bloss (Eds.), *Economics and the prevention of alcohol-related problems* [NIAAA Research Monograph No. 25, NIH Publication No. 93-3513] (pp. 175–200). Rockville, MD: Department of Health and Human Services.

66. Wagenaar, A. C., & Wolfson, M. (1995). Deterring sales and provision of alcohol to minors: A study of enforcement in 295 counties in four states. *Public Health Reports, 110*, 419–427.

67. Wechsler, H., & Nelson, T. F. (2010). Will increasing alcohol availability by lowering the minimum legal drinking age decrease drinking and related consequences among youths? *American Journal of Public Health, 100*, 986–992.

68. Gruenewald, P. J. (2011). Regulating availability: How access to alcohol affects drinking and problems in youth and adults. *Alcohol Research and Health, 34*, 248–256.

69. Cook, P. J., & Ludwig, J. (2004). Principles for effective gun policy. *Fordham Law Review, 73*, 589–613.

70. Cook, P. J. (1987). Robbery violence. *Criminal Law and Criminology, 78*, 371–372.

71. Reiss, A. J., & Roth, J. A. (Eds.). (1993). *Understanding and preventing violence.* Washington, DC: National Academy Press.

72. Blumstein, A., & Wallman, J. (2006). The crime drop and beyond. *Annual Review of Law and Social Science, 2*, 125–146.

73. Hahn, R. A., Bilukha, O. O., Crosby, A., Fullilove, M. T., Liberman, A., Moscicki, E. K., et al. (2003). *First reports evaluating the effectiveness of strategies for preventing violence: Firearms laws.* Findings from the Task Force on Community Preventive Services. Atlanta, GA: Centers for Disease Control and Prevention.

74. Callahan, C. M., Rivara, F. P., & Koepsell, T. D. (1994). Money for guns: Evaluation of the Seattle Gun Buy-Back program. *Public Health Reports, 109*, 472–477.

75. Sherman, L. W., & Rogan, D. (1995). Effects of gun seizures on gun violence: "Hot spots" patrol in Kansas City. *Justice Quarterly, 12*, 673–694.

76. Walters, G. D. (2012). *Crime in a psychological context: From career criminals to criminal careers.* Thousand Oaks, CA: Sage.

77. Seligman, M. E. P. (1990). Why is there so much depression today? The wasting of the individual and the waning of the commons. In R. E. Ingram (Ed.), *Contemporary psychological approaches to depression: Theory, research, and treatment* (pp. 1–9). New York: Plenum.

78. Widom, C. S. (1995). Victims of childhood sexual abuse—Later criminal consequences. *National Institute of Justice: Research in Brief.* Washington, DC: U.S. Department of Justice.

79. Griffin, R. S., & Gross, A. M. (2004). Childhood bullying: Current empirical findings and future directions for research. *Aggression and Violent Behavior, 9,* 379–400.

80. Cicognani, E., Albanesi, C., & Zani, B. (2008). The impact of residential context on adolescents' subjective well being. *Journal of Community and Applied Social Psychology, 18,* 558–575.

81. Stockdale, S. E., Wells, K. B., Tang, L., Belin, R. R., Zhang, L., & Sherbourne, C. D. (2007). The importance of social context: Neighborhood stressors, stress-buffering mechanisms, and alcohol, drug, and mental health disorders. *Social Science and Medicine, 65,* 1867–1881.

82. Loeber, R., Burke, J., & Pardini, D. A. (2009). Perspectives on oppositional defiant disorder, conduct disorder, and psychopathic features. *Journal of Child Psychology and Psychiatry, 50,* 133–142.

83. Kraag, G., Zeegers, M. P., Kok, G., Hosman, C., & Abu-Saad, H. H. (2006). School programs targeting stress management in children and adolescents: A meta-analysis. *Journal of School Psychology, 44,* 449–472.

84. Northeast Center for the Application of Prevention Technologies. (1999). *School-based prevention: Critical components.* Newton, MA: Health and Human Development Programs at Education Development Center, Inc.

85. Masten, A. S. (2001). Ordinary magic: Resilience processes in development. *American Psychologist, 56,* 227–238.

86. Fergusson, D. M., & Lynskey, M. T. (1996). Adolescent resiliency to family adversity. *Journal of Child Psychology and Psychiatry, 37,* 281–292.

87. Martinez-Torteya, C., Bogat, G. A., von Eye, A., & Levendosky, A. A. (2009). Resilience among children exposed to domestic violence: The role of risk and protective factors. *Child Development, 80,* 562–577.

88. Cicchetti, D., & Rogosch, F. A. (2007). Personality, adrenal steroid hormones, and resilience in maltreated children: A multilevel perspective. *Development and Psychopathology, 19,* 787–809.

89. Greenberg, M. T. (2006). Promoting resilience in children and youth. *Annals of the New York Academy of Sciences, 1094,* 139–150.

90. Floyd, C. (1996). Achieving despite the odds: A study of resilience among a group of African America high school seniors. *Journal of Negro Education, 65,* 181–189.

91. Jaffee, S. R., Caspi, A., Moffitt, T. E., Polo-Thomas, M., & Taylor, A. (2007). Individual, family, and neighborhood factors distinguish resilient from non-resilient maltreated children: A cumulative stressors model. *Child Abuse and Neglect, 31,* 231–253.

92. Garmezy, N. (1993). Children in poverty: Resiliency despite risk. *Psychiatry, 56,* 127–136.

93. Werner, E. E., & Smith, R. S. (1992). *Overcoming the odds: High risk children from birth to adulthood.* Ithaca, NY: Cornell University Press.

94. Hall, J., Sylva, K., Melhuish, E., Sammons, P., Siraj-Blatchford, I., & Taggart, B. (2009). The role of preschool quality in providing resilience in the cognitive development of young children. *Oxford Review of Education, 35,* 331–352.

95. Ungar, M. (2010). Families as navigators and negotiators: Facilitating culturally and contextually specific expressions of resilience. *Family Process, 49,* 421–435.

96. Heilbrun, K. (2009). *Evaluation for risk of violence in adults.* New York: Oxford University Press.

HARM REDUCTION

Harm reduction is a set of strategies designed to reduce the negative consequences of drug use for the individual and for society. Rather than insisting on **abstinence** as the only possible goal for recovery, harm reduction allows for controlled usage, alternate drugs, different routes of administration, or less harmful practices than the individual's normal routine. Compared to traditional prevention and intervention programs, where the focus is on preventing usage, the goal of harm reduction is to prevent or reduce the harm associated with usage. The clinical significance of harm reduction is that many clients will refuse to enter treatment if one of the conditions of treatment is total abstinence from all drug use, legal and illegal, starting at day one. Harm reduction programs attract people who never would have entered treatment had they been told they had to immediately stop using drugs and never use again. However, many of the individuals who go through harm reduction programs eventually become abstinent or near abstinent.[1] The principal policy implication of harm reduction is that it provides an avenue by which treatment professionals and public health workers gain access to and potentially influence normally difficult-to-reach clientele (e.g., **intravenous** drug users, sex workers).[2]

Some might argue that given the public health emphasis of harm reduction, a book on drugs and crime could do without a chapter on harm reduction. I disagree. Although the primary harm that harm reduction is designed to ease is physical, there are other negative consequences addressed by harm reduction techniques. Crime and violence are among these negative consequences. More importantly, a major goal of harm reduction is influencing difficult-to-reach clients. Many of these difficult-to-reach clients engage in crime, either as a way of supporting their drug habit (e.g., heroin) or because drugs lower their inhibitions and interfere with their judgment (e.g., alcohol). There are five objectives pursued in this chapter, each of which is capable of clarifying drug–crime relationships through harm reduction:

- Acknowledge the reality and feasibility of controlled drug usage
- Understand the strengths and weaknesses of drug replacement programs
- Recognize the health benefits of **needle** exchange programs
- Describe the function of drug consumption facilities
- Consider the role of decriminalization in a comprehensive program of harm reduction

Principles of Harm Reduction

Before examining the five major areas of harm reduction it may be helpful to first review the eight principles of harm reduction as put forth by the Harm Reduction Coalition:[3]

- Acknowledge that drug use is part of many people's lives and that the emphasis should be on reducing the harm associated with usage rather than on total abstinence
- Appreciate the complexity of drug use and the fact that it responds to a myriad of mitigating and aggravating conditions
- Advocate for nonjudgmental and noncoercive forms of intervention for drug-related problems
- Affirm drug users as the primary agents of change in reducing the harm created by their use of substances
- Accentuate quality of life and well-being over total abstinence as the primary goals of intervention and policy

- Assure users and former users that they will have an active voice in the development of programs and policies relating to drug use and abuse
- Account for race, social class, trauma, and social inequality in the development of a drug problem
- Analyze the effect of licit and illicit drug abuse on the user, community, and society

Controlled Drug Use

Controlled Drinking

The **controlled drug use** controversy began in the early 1960s when British psychiatrist D. L. Davies reported that 7 out of 93 individuals participating in a long-term follow-up of patients treated for "alcohol addiction" at Maudsley Hospital had been able to drink in a nonproblematic fashion following discharge for periods spanning 7 to 11 years. Davies characterized each of these patients as "alcoholics" who had experienced "loss of control" drinking prior to enrolling in the abstinence-oriented treatment program at Maudsley. None of the seven controlled drinking patients had ever been "drunk" during the follow-up and all demonstrated stable employment and good family relationships. On the basis of these results, Davies concluded that "some alcohol addicts do return to normal drinking."[4,p102] This conclusion ran counter to the total abstinence philosophy espoused by **Alcoholics Anonymous (AA)**, the dominant treatment philosophy at the time.

In 1973, Mark and Linda Sobell added a new dimension to the controlled drinking controversy by suggesting that it was possible to teach problem drinkers to control their drinking. This was even more threatening to the disease model's philosophy of total abstinence than the Davies study because it suggested that goals other than abstinence could guide substance-abuse treatment. Sobell and Sobell randomly assigned 40 alcohol dependent volunteer clients from an inpatient alcohol treatment unit at Patton State Hospital in California to either a traditional abstinence program or a controlled drinking regimen. Half were assigned to the abstinence program and half were assigned to the controlled drinking program. One- and 2-year follow-ups of both groups revealed that the controlled drinking clients experienced twice as many good functioning days as the abstinence clients (see **Figure 13-1**).[5–6]

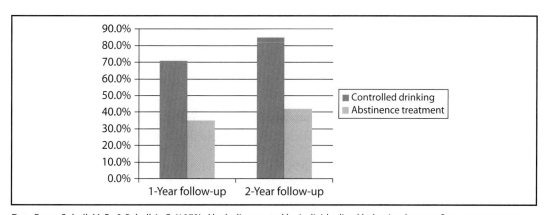

Figure 13-1
Percentage of "good functioning" days in 1- and 2-year follow-ups of participants receiving controlled drinking and traditional abstinence treatment.

Data From: Sobell, M. B., & Sobell, L. C. (1973). Alcoholics treated by individualized behavior therapy: One year treatment outcome. *Behaviour Research and Therapy, 11,* 599–618 & Sobell, M. B., & Sobell, L. C. (1976). Second year treatment outcome of alcoholics treated by individualized behavior therapy: Results. *Behaviour Research and Therapy, 14,* 195–215.

Many in the traditional alcoholism treatment community took exception to the Sobells' results and conclusions. Mary Pendery, Irving Maltzman, and Jolyon West went so far as to accuse the Sobells of professional misconduct and fraud.[7] The irony is that the experimental design the Sobells used in their original study—random assignment of cases to experimental and control groups—was superior to Pendery, Maltzman, and West's reanalysis. At the core of the Pendery et al. critique were retrospective accounts by members of the controlled drinking group of what had allegedly transpired 9 years earlier. The Pendery group, as well as several media sources, highlighted the fact that four members of the controlled drinking group had died in the 9 years since the original study. What they failed to report, because they interviewed only participants from the controlled drinking group, was that 6 out of 20 members of the abstinence group had also died in the preceding 9 years. An independent blue ribbon panel fully exonerated the Sobells after conducting an independent investigation of the Pendery group's charges.[8]

Controlled drinking is more consistent with a behavioral skills approach to intervention than the disease or 12-step model. Self-help programs like Moderation Management[9] and **SMART Recovery**[10] were subsequently introduced as alternatives to the ubiquitous abstinence-oriented Alcoholics Anonymous (AA) self-help program. In March 2000, Audrey Kishline, founder of **Moderation Management** (MM), a nonabstinence self-help program, killed two people in a head-on collision. Her blood alcohol level at the time was .26, more than three times the legal limit. Several AA advocates used this tragic event to point out the hazards of nonabstinence programs (see News Spot 13-1). What these advocates forgot to mention was that 2 months before the accident, Kisline had quit MM after posting a message on the MM listserv advising that she had decided to change her goal to total abstinence and would be attending AA on a regular basis. Hence, Kishline was attending AA rather than MM at the time of the accident.[11]

NEWS SPOT 13-1

Title: Vehicular Manslaughter Charges Against Author of Moderation Management
Source: *National Council on Alcoholism & Drug Dependence*
Author: Stacia Murphy, former President of NCADD
Date: June 20, 2000

It was with great sadness that the National Council on Alcoholism and Drug Dependence, Inc. (NCADD) today learned that Audrey Kishline, author of Moderation Management and founder of a movement with the same name, has been charged by the state of Washington with two counts of vehicular manslaughter. According to the Seattle Times, Ms. Kishline had a blood alcohol content of 0.26—more than three times the legal limit—when the pickup truck she was driving in the wrong direction on an interstate highway crashed into a second vehicle, killing a man and his daughter on March 25. NCADD offers its belated condolences to the family of Richard and LaSchell Davis.

The Seattle Times also has reported that Ms. Kishline's trial, scheduled to have begun today, has been postponed pending completion of intensive treatment for alcoholism. Her lawyer has been quoted as saying that Ms. Kishline realizes that "moderation management is nothing but alcoholics covering up their problem."

This dreadful tragedy might have been avoided if Ms. Kishline had come to this realization earlier. Unfortunately, the disease of alcoholism, which is characterized by denial, prevented this from occurring. While this does not excuse Ms. Kishline's actions, it provides a harsh lesson for all of society, particularly those individuals who collude with the media to continually question abstinence-based treatment for problems related to alcohol and other drugs.

What makes Ms. Kishline's present situation even more distressing is the fact that her denial, amplified by the media, undoubtedly contributed to the progression of alcoholism and other alcohol-related problems for thousands more unidentified Americans and their families. In March 1995, representatives of this organization debated Ms. Kishline several times on national television and in newspapers all over the country. How many of these television programs and newspapers will give as much prominence to the consequences of "moderation management" five years later? As is often repeated in training courses for alcoholism counselors, "if it's a problem in March, it's going to be a disaster by December."

The National Council on Alcoholism and Drug Dependence hopes Ms. Kishline will finally achieve sobriety and recognize how high a price denial of her illness has exacted. But more significantly, we should all remember the names of Richard and LaSchell Davis the next time a problem drinker claims to be able to "drink a little" without harm. As a society we must finally accept that abstinence offers the safest and most predictable course for the treatment of alcohol and other drug-related problems and we must do everything we can to break through the denial of those who are actively addicted.

Reprinted with permission from the National Council on Alcoholism and Drug Dependence, Inc. (NCADD) www.ncadd.org

About NCADD: The National Council on Alcoholism and Drug Dependence, Inc. (NCADD) and its Affiliate Network is a voluntary health organization dedicated to fighting the Nation's #1 health problem – alcoholism, drug addiction and the devastating consequences of alcohol and other drugs on individuals, families and communities.

Questions to Ponder

1. **Is it legitimate to pin the success or failure of a particular program, strategy, or movement on the outcome of a single case, no matter how dramatic?**
2. **Can you see a connection between the type of thinking manifest in this article and the fact that the Alcoholics Anonymous/12-Step model continues to fall well behind the behavioral approach in terms of its evidence base?**
3. **The "circling the wagons" mentality of Drug Abuse Resistance Education (DARE) is understandable in the sense that there is a great deal of money at stake; but why do so many AA/12-Step advocates seem to adhere to the same mentality, despite the fact AA is free to all?**

Behavioral self-control training as a harm reduction measure for alcohol use problems normally consists of six elements:

- **Blood alcohol concentration (BAC)** discrimination training
- Rate control (increasing the amount of time between drinks, prolonging the duration of a single drink, or switching to a lower proof beverage)
- Functional analysis (identifying high-risk situations)
- Self-monitoring

- Goal setting
- Contingency management and self-reinforcement

With the exception of BAC discrimination training, the other five elements can be effectively taught to clients.[12] Research tends to support the efficacy of controlled drinking programs as evidenced by the results of a meta-analysis of 17 randomized control studies comparing individuals randomly assigned to behavioral self-control training or an abstinence/no treatment control group. The results of this meta-analysis revealed reduced levels of alcohol consumption and alcohol-related problems in behavioral self-control participants compared to control subjects. Controlled drinking programs have been characterized as inappropriate for seriously addicted individuals, but as the results in **Table 13-1** indicate, the effect sizes for studies composed of alcohol dependent and less severe problem drinking participants were nearly identical.[13]

There are no hard-and-fast rules when it comes to determining who is and who is not appropriate for controlled drinking. The results of the Walters meta-analysis indicated that more and less severe alcohol problems appear to respond equally well to controlled drinking protocols.[14] In considering whether to go with a traditional abstinence program or a controlled drinking regimen, the first thing a clinician should do is find out what the client prefers and work from there. Dictating to the client which program he or she should attend does not generally lead to positive results and will greatly detract from the developing client–therapist relationship. Other factors that should probably be considered in recommending either an abstinence or controlled drinking protocol to a client are age and prior attempts. Younger individuals may be more responsive to controlled drinking and drug use programs than older individuals and individuals who have attempted and repeatedly failed to achieve controlled drinking outcomes are poorer risks than individuals who have never attempted to control their drinking.[15] Offenders may be particularly receptive to controlled drinking programs given their desire to be in control and their tendency to reject authoritative mandates.

Table 13-1 Effect Sizes (d) Obtained in a Meta-Analysis of 17 Controlled Drinking Studies

Inclusion Criteria	n	d	SE	95% CI
All studies	17	.33	.08	.17 to .49
No-contact control group	4	.94	.16	.63 to 1.25
Abstinent control group	6	.28	.16	−.03 to .59
Other control group	11	.20	.10	.01 to .39
Alcohol-dependent subjects	7	.32	.14	.05 to .59
Problem-drinking subjects	10	.34	.11	.12 to .56
Alcohol-consumption outcome	11	.22	.09	.04 to .40
Problem-drinking outcome	7	.29	.14	.02 to .56
Follow-up < 1 year	11	.45	.10	.25 to .65
Follow-up ≥ 1 year	11	.21	.10	.01 to .41

Note. n = number of effect sizes aggregated; *d* = mean effect-size estimate; *SE* = standard error of the mean effect-size estimate; 95% CI = 95% confidence interval for the aggregate mean effect-size estimate.

Reprinted from Walters, G. D. (2000). Behavioral self-control training for problem drinkers: A meta-analysis of randomized control studies. *Behavior Therapy, 31*, 135–149, with permission from Elsevier.

Controlled Use of Illicit Drugs

Controlled use of marijuana, cocaine, and heroin has been reported in the literature. Medical marijuana has not presented a significant problem for those prescribed the drug for glaucoma, debilitating muscle spasms, or the nausea caused by cancer treatment. In addition, there is no evidence that medical marijuana interferes with drug treatment for other substances.[16] Murphy, Reinarman, and Waldorf followed a network of social cocaine users and discovered that only 1 of the 21 members lapsed into habitual cocaine consumption during an 11-year follow-up.[17] Of servicemen who underwent detoxification for heroin addiction prior to leaving the Vietnam combat theatre, only 12% relapsed into heroin dependence upon their return to the United States, despite the fact that half the sample used heroin after their return.[18] Norman Zinberg identified a small enclave of controlled heroin users who kept their usage secret from everyone except each other and their dealers.[19] Hence, it would appear that the controlled use of illegal substances is possible, though probably not practical given that those who work in the criminal justice system are charged with upholding the law, regardless of whether or not they agree with it.

Controlled Criminal Involvement

At first glance, controlled criminal involvement would seem an absurd concept. Upon further reflection, however, there may be some value in a notion like controlled criminal involvement. Most people would agree that shoplifting is not as serious as armed robbery, scalping tickets at a sporting event is not as bad as burglarizing someone's home, and cheating on taxes is not the same as embezzling millions of dollars from a public company. Harm reduction does not mean making drug use or crime more palatable but rather reducing the harm associated with these behaviors. There is another consideration that must be taken into account whenever one broaches the topic of controlled criminal involvement. Less harmful criminal activity should not trigger or serve as a stimulus to more harmful criminal activity. Unfortunately, in some cases, particularly when habitual criminals are involved, such triggering may occur. This is one reason why offender classification is so important in offender management. Higher risk individuals require maximum community supervision because with them, a small criminal act can lead to a major criminal event. Lower risk individuals, on the other hand, can engage in a variety of minor offenses (e.g., driving over the speed limit, having a few drinks or smoking marijuana, associating with a known felon) and this will often have little bearing on their future propensity to engage in serious criminality. Low-risk individuals can be handled with minimal supervision and actually do worse when their supervision level is raised.[20] Minimal supervision of low-risk offenders could therefore be considered a form of controlled criminal involvement.

Drug Replacement

Methadone and Heroin Maintenance

Beginning with the introduction of **methadone maintenance** in the 1960s, drug replacement programs have been implemented in an effort to improve the clinical outcomes of drug-using individuals and reduce drug-related medical problems, criminality, and public nuisance.

Methadone is a synthetic opiate that achieves its effect by occupying opiate receptor sites in the brain. Although methadone relieves the craving for heroin and reduces symptoms of heroin withdrawal, it does not cause euphoria at standard and stable dosing levels, and need only be administered once a day because it is excreted more slowly than heroin. In fact, at higher doses it can block the euphoric effects of heroin and morphine. Treatment with methadone allows individuals to work and maintain a relatively normal social routine.[21]

Methadone Maintenance Treatment (MMT) is effective provided the client and clinic staff abide by the treatment protocol. One aspect of the protocol that is often overlooked or ignored by staff is the recommendation that MMT be part of a larger program of resocialization and vocational training. MMT was originally designed as a stepping stone to sobriety, although in many cases a person will remain on methadone indefinitely.[22] Despite less than perfect application of the standard MMT treatment protocol across the United States, multiple studies have documented the many benefits of MMT, including:[23]

- Decreased and, in some cases, complete cessation of injected drug use
- Lowered risk of overdose and decreased transmission of HIV and hepatitis C
- Reduced mortality of up to 30%
- Diminished violent and nonviolent criminality
- Improved family relationships
- Greater employment stability
- Better pregnancy outcomes

The results of a comparative meta-analysis of MMT studies published between 1966 and 1999 revealed that high doses of methadone ($\geq$ 50 mg/day) were more effective than low doses of methadone (< 50 mg/day) in reducing illicit opiate usage. The authors of this meta-analysis, Farré, Mas, Torrens, Moreno, and Cami, also discovered that high doses of methadone were more effective than low doses of a semisynthetic opiate sometimes used to treat opiate addiction, buprenorphine (< 8 mg/day), and that high doses of methadone were as effective as high doses of buprenorphine ($\geq$ 8 mg/day) in retaining participants and reducing illicit opiate usage. Although **levo-acetylmethadol** (LAAM), another synthetic opiate with chemical properties similar to methadone, was as effective as high-dose methadone in reducing illicit opiate usage, patients treated with LAAM were significantly less likely to remain in treatment than those treated with high-dose methadone.[24]

Lisa Marsch had previously conducted a meta-analysis on MMT in which she examined the effect of MMT on crime. From the results of her 24-study meta-analysis, Marsch concluded that MMT produced a large effect size in studies examining drug-related crime ($r = .70$), a moderate effect size in studies examining drug- and property-related crime ($r = .23$), and a small-to-moderate effect size in studies examining both drug- and nondrug-related crime ($r = .17$).[25] Among the MMT patients included in a study by Ball and Rossi, there was a 70.8% decline in crime-days within the first 4 months of MMT. This decline was followed by continuing, but less dramatic, reductions in mean crime-days among those in treatment for 1 to 3 years (see **Figure 13-2**). Those in treatment for 6 or more years experienced the lowest number of crime-days per year (i.e., 14.5).[26]

MMT is the most common form of drug replacement therapy for heroin addiction. Another option, however, would be to provide maintenance doses of heroin alone or in combination with MMT to opiate addicts. The British have been treating opiate addiction with

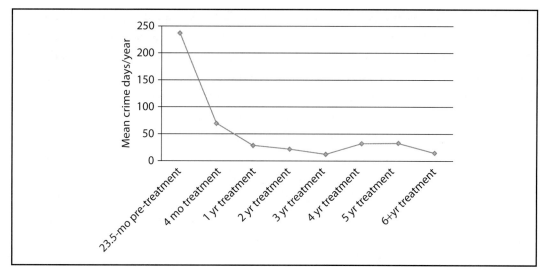

Figure 13-2
Mean crime-days per
year as a function
of length of time
in Methadone
Maintenance
Treatment.

Data From: Ball, J. C., & Ross, A. (1991). *The effectiveness of methadone maintenance treatment: Patients, programs, services, and outcomes.* New York: Springer-Verlag.

legally prescribed heroin since the 1920s and the Swiss and Dutch are currently experiment-ing with harm reduction techniques that involve administering maintenance doses of heroin to heroin addicts.[27] The results of two Swiss studies determined that supervised medical pre-scription of heroin was associated with good treatment retention, reduced illicit drug usage, reduced criminal activity, improved health outcomes, and better social/legal adjustment (see **Table 13-2**).[28–29] Peter Blanken and colleagues studied two randomized clinical trials in the Netherlands in which patients on a trial of MMT plus medically prescribed heroin were com-pared to patients on MMT alone. The results indicated significantly better physical, mental, and social functioning on the part of individuals in the methadone plus heroin group (51.8%) compared to MMT alone (28.7%).[30] Heroin-assisted substitution treatment, with or without MMT, may be a viable option for individuals who do not respond to MMT alone.

Table 13-2 Social and Legal Adjustment of 237 Opioid-Dependent Patients Receiving Heroin-Assisted Substitution Treatment over an 18-Month Period

	Admission	6 months	12 months	18 months	p*
Unstable housing situation	102 (43%)[†]	74 (31%)	57 (24%)	49 (21%)	< 0.0001
Homeless	42 (18%)	19 (8%)	3 (1%)	3 (1%)	< 0.0001
Unemployed	173 (73%)	113 (48%)	104 (44%)	106 (45%)	< 0.0001
Receiving disability pension	51 (22%)	53 (22%)	60 (25%)	65 (27%)	0.001
Receiving welfare payments	149 (63%)	143 (60%)	145 (61%)	129 (54%)	0.035
No debts	61 (26%)[‡]	61 (26%)[§]	64 (27%)[ǁ]	77 (33%)[¶]	0.026
Illegal income	164 (69%)	40 (17%)	32 (14%)	25 (11%)	< 0.0001
No visit to illegal drug scene last month	33 (14%)[**]	107 (46%)	120 (52%)[††]	137 (59%)[‡‡]	< 0.0001

Data are number of patients (% of patients with valid data at admission). *Based on last observation carried forward. Number of data missing: [†] 1; [‡] 4, [§] 4, [ǁ] 6, [¶] 2, [**] 4, [††] 1, [‡‡] 1

Reprinted from Rehm, J., Gschwend, P., Steffen, T., Guzwiller, F., Dobler-Mikola, A., & Uchtenhagen, A. (2001). Feasibility, safety, and efficacy of injectable heroin prescription for refractory opioid addicts: A follow-up study. Reprinted from *The Lancet, 358,* 1417–1420, with permission from Elsevier.

A **natural experiment** of sorts was set into motion after 91 Canadian heroin addicts moved to the United Kingdom (UK) between 1958 and 1969 to take advantage of a newly announced medical prescription program. Interestingly enough, over half these individuals returned to Canada within a few years even though the UK prescription program was still in effect. One of the reasons cited by several of these individuals for returning to Canada was that they missed aspects of the drug lifestyle that were available only in situations where heroin could not be legally obtained (e.g., clandestine meetings, hiding from the police).[31] What this means is that illegal drug use is often supported by behaviors (rituals), activities (crime), and environmental cues (location where drugs are used) that supersede the chemical substance in maintaining the drug use pattern. As such, these behaviors, activities, and cues need to be addressed as part of a comprehensive program of drug treatment and resocialization.

Cocaine and Amphetamine Substitution

There is no chemical substitute for cocaine comparable to methadone. Harm reduction of the drug replacement type can nonetheless be implemented with cocaine by stressing substitute or alternate paths of drug administration. It is well known that injecting and smoking (freebasing, crack) cocaine can lead to more compulsive usage patterns and greater physical and social problems than snorting cocaine. One reason why injecting and smoking cocaine leads to a more compulsive pattern of usage than snorting cocaine is that these routes of administration generate a more rapid, intense, and short-lived effect than snorting.[32] A program of harm reduction for cocaine might include encouraging someone who injects or smokes cocaine to start snorting it because snorting the drug is associated with fewer long-term problems than injecting or smoking it. In fact, successful controlled users of cocaine in the Murphy, Reinarman, and Waldorf study actively avoided injecting and smoking cocaine and disparagingly referred to those who smoked or injected cocaine as "junkies."[33]

Amphetamine replacement therapy has been growing in popularity, particularly in Great Britain. Harm reduction of the drug replacement type for amphetamines entails replacing the intravenous use of methamphetamine with orally administered amphetamine pills. Such an approach implements harm reduction principles by reducing the harm associated with injectable drugs, in much the same manner as snorting cocaine is a less harmful route of administration than smoking or injecting cocaine. In a perfect world, an individual should not feel the need to use amphetamines, but given the fact that the world in which we live is less than perfect and some people will use drugs no matter what the cost, a procedure that reduces the harm associated with drug use should be considered at least on par with one that achieves abstinence in only a small portion of cases. Stimulant replacement therapy would appear to hold promise but there are currently no empirical data to either support or refute the practice of replacing more harmful routes of administration with less harmful routes of drug administration.[34]

Tobacco Substitution

Legal drugs are also subject to harm reduction through drug replacement or substitution therapy. Switching to a lower proof beverage is a common way this can be achieved with alcohol. Most of the research on legal drug substitution, however, has been conducted on tobacco. **Smokeless tobacco** (snuff or chewing tobacco) and **e-cigarettes** (electronic devices that sometimes look and feel like real cigarettes and that produce a vapor composed of water, propylene glycol, and nicotine that is allegedly less harmful than tobacco smoke) are two of the more popular tobacco substitutes. In an extensive review of alternatives to tobacco smoking, Brad Rodu discovered that:[35]

- Smokeless tobacco presented significantly fewer health hazards to users than regular cigarettes.
- Smokeless tobacco was responsible for declining rates of smoking and smoking-related diseases in Sweden and Norway.
- E-cigarette users are not exposed to the same level of toxins and carcinogenic agents as those who smoke tobacco.
- Use of e-cigarettes sufficiently simulates the cigarette handling rituals and cues associated with regular smoking, producing a suppressing effect on craving and withdrawal beyond the simple reduction in nicotine delivery.

Needle Exchange Programs

It is estimated that in the United States 15–20% of intravenous drug users are infected with human immunodeficiency virus (HIV) and over 70% are infected with hepatitis C. A report from the National Institutes of Health estimates that one in five new cases of hepatitis C is transmitted through dirty needles.[36] **Needle exchange programs (NEPs)** attempt to reduce the incidence of disease transmission by providing users with replacement syringes and by discouraging the practice of sharing needles. Like controlled usage and drug replacement programs, NEPs are based on a philosophy of harm reduction. Some jurisdictions require an equal exchange of old and new syringes or needles; other jurisdiction do not have such requirements. In addition, most NEPs offer ancillary services and items:[37]

- HIV and hepatitis C testing
- Alcohol swabs
- Bleach water and normal saline that can be used to rinse eyedroppers

© Steve Liss/TIME & LIFE Images/Getty Images

Needle exchange programs have been found to reduce disease and litter without increasing drug use or crime.

- Containers for needles
- Voluntary counseling

Katy Turner and her colleagues examined the effectiveness of opiate substitution treatment (OST) and NEPs on the rate of hepatitis C virus transmission among injecting drug users in six United Kingdom sites. Surveys were conducted with nearly 3,000 injecting drug users between 2000 and 2009. The results indicated that full harm reduction (enrollment in OST and high NEP coverage) reduced the odds of hepatitis C infection by nearly 80%.[38] OST[39] and needle and **syringe** exchange programs[40] have also been found to reduce the transmission of HIV in long-term intravenous heroin users.

Kate Ksobiech conducted a meta-analysis of 47 studies on NEPs published between 1988 and 2001 and discovered that participation in these programs led to significant reductions in needle sharing, lending, and borrowing ($r = -0.16$ to -0.19).[41] In a review of reviews, Norah Palmateer and colleagues found strong evidence that NEPs significantly decreased high-risk injecting behaviors, modest but sufficient evidence that NEPs reduced the rate of HIV infections, and insufficient evidence that NEPs reduced the rate of hepatitis C infections.[42] Obviously, more research is required to determine whether NEPs have a significant effect on hepatitis C transmission in light of the fact that Turner and colleagues found that NEPs reduced hepatitis C by 80% when combined with opiate substitution therapy.[43]

NEPs are more common in Europe than they are in the United States. The United States initially had a ban on using federal funds for NEPs. This ban was lifted in 2009 but then reinstated in December 2011. A concern expressed by many U.S. politicians and citizens is that NEPs promote injecting behavior and drug usage, much like condom distribution in schools is believed to promote premarital sex. Empirical data, however, do not support these concerns. A study conducted in Spain found that NEPs were followed by a sharp decline in injecting drug use[44] and a study conducted in the United States found that NEPs had no bearing on adolescents' attitudes toward drug use.[45] Many European countries take a pragmatic approach to drug injection and have been using NEPs for years. The U.S. government has been much less supportive of NEPs, although both the Centers for Disease Control and the National Institutes of Health advocate for the use of NEPs as a public health initiative in promoting the safety not only of the drug user but also of his or her sexual partners, children, and neighbors.

A second concern expressed by critics of NEPs is that they promote crime and disrespect for the law. Melissa Marx and colleagues examined this issue by comparing neighborhoods in Baltimore, Maryland that had NEPs with neighborhoods in Baltimore that did not have NEPs. Comparing arrest rates 6 months before and 14 months after implementation of the NEPs, Marx and colleagues uncovered no support for the view that crime rose in NEP neighborhoods relative to non-NEP neighborhoods (see **Figure 13-3**). In fact, there was no change in arrests for resisting the police or for property crimes between the two time periods in the NEP neighborhoods, compared to a small to moderate increase in these offenses in non-NEP neighborhoods.[46]

Drug Consumption Facilities

Drug Consumption Facilities (DCFs), also known as supervised injection facilities and safe or safer injection sites, are legally sanctioned and medically supervised facilities, typically a room, where individuals go to inject or use drugs in a hygienic and stress-free environment. The framework for nurses and other professionals working in DCFs is summarized in **Figure 13-4**. As should

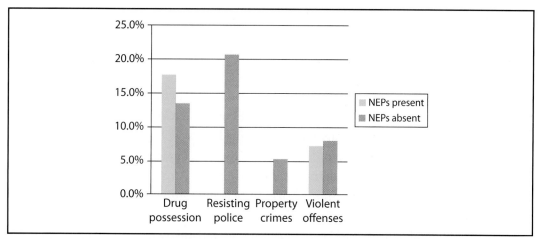

Figure 13-3
Percentage increase in arrests before and after implementation of Needle Exchange Programs (NEPs) in Baltimore, Maryland.

Data From: Marx, M. A., Crape, B., Brookmeyer, R. S., Junge, B., Latkin, C.,…Strathdee, S. A. (2000). Trends in crime and the introduction of a needle exchange program. *American Journal of Public Health, 90*, 1933–1936.

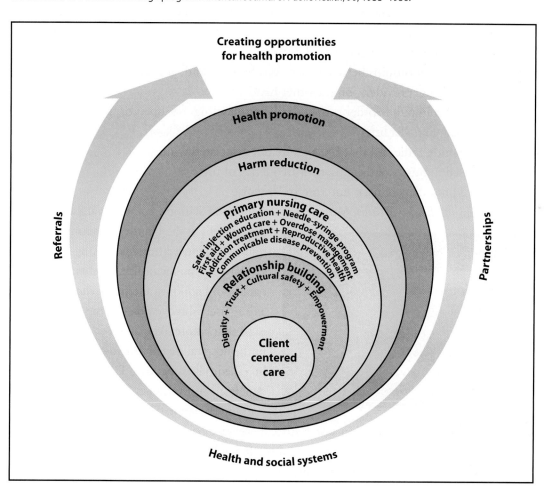

Figure 13-4
Insite Nursing Framework.

Lightfoot, B., Panessa, C., Hayden, S., Thumath, M., Goldstone, I., & Pauly, B. (2009). Gaining INSITE: Harm Reduction in Nursing Practice. *Canadian Nurse, 105*(4), 16–22.

be clear from the figure, the model adopted in these programs borrows heavily from the public health tradition. In 2012, there were 65 DCFs operating worldwide in the following countries:

- Australia
- Canada
- Germany

- Holland
- Luxembourg
- Norway
- Spain
- Switzerland

There are currently no DCFs in the United States or in the United Kingdom and the only two DCFs in North America are located in Canada[47–48].

One frequently voiced criticism of DCFs is that they discourage intravenous drug users from entering treatment and in so doing, facilitate drug use. A recent study conducted at the Vancouver DCF, however, determined that participation in the DCF was associated with increased rather than decreased use of treatment and was followed by a declining rather than rising rate of drug use.[49] A report from Switzerland, which makes fairly extensive use of DCFs, revealed that DCF programs were associated with:[50]

- a reduction in risk behaviors linked to the transmission of infectious diseases like HIV and hepatitis C
- a reduction in the number of fatal overdoses
- improved relationships between users, on the one hand, and social service workers and healthcare providers, on the other hand
- a reduction in public order problems like public drug use, open drug scenes, and drug paraphernalia litter

This same study indicated that DCFs were not associated with:

- increased numbers of drug users or frequency of use
- reduced numbers of users entering treatment

Writing in the *British Medical Journal*, Nat Wright and Charlotte Tompkins argue that creating DCFs in the United Kingdom would result in a reduced number of drug deaths and several other public health benefits. They cite data from Frankfort, Germany showing that a drug user who overdoses in the community is 10 times more likely to spend at least 1 day in the hospital than a drug user who overdoses in a medically supervised DCF. They also cite data from an Australian DCF indicating that staff intervened in 329 overdose incidents in a 1-year period with at least four lives saved. Also, there was no increase in the number of cases of hepatitis B or C in the area of the center and those individuals who frequented the center were more likely to enter drug treatment. Finally, community residents and local businesses reported fewer incidents of public injection, a reduction in drug paraphernalia litter, and no increase in thefts or robberies after the center opened.[51]

Figure 13-5
Baskets filled with supplies and drug paraphernalia to be used by clients of the InSite safe injection clinic in Vancouver, B.C.

© Darryl Dyck/AP Photos

An expert advisory committee appointed by the Canadian government reviewed all available data on the relationship between the Vancouver DCF and crime and determined that public disorder offenses (e.g., public drug use) dropped significantly and that drug-related crime did not increase after the DCF opened its doors on September 22, 2003. What is more, local police began referring drug users to the center instead of arresting them, thereby reducing police workload and freeing space in the local jail for serious criminals.[52]

Not everyone, however, was happy with the committee's findings (see News Spot 13-2). Crime continues to be a major issue for DCF opponents, although there is no documented proof that crime increases with the introduction of a DCF. In addition to the previously reviewed Australian and Vancouver studies, a review of DCF openings in Switzerland and the Netherlands failed to show evidence of a corresponding increase in drug-related crime.[53]

NEWS SPOT 13.2

Title: Federal Government Should Follow the Evidence and Stop Trying to Close Insite, Co-authors of New CMAJ Article Say
Source: *CNW Group*
Author: None indicated
Date: August 30, 2010

CNW Telbec—Drs. Kathleen Dooling and Michael Rachlis, the two co-authors of a new review of the evidence and events surrounding Insite—Vancouver's supervised drug consumption public health facility—say the federal government "should drop its last-ditch Supreme Court appeal that would allow the government to permanently close this public health facility. They should stand back so public health and law enforcement professionals can do the work that their local community wants them to do."

Their article, published Monday in the *Canadian Medical Association Journal*, reviews the scientific research, public policies, and community actions related to the establishment and operation of Vancouver's supervised drug consumption site.

They conclude that "the evidence shows that this public health facility reduces harms of drug addiction while creating positive relationships between users and caregivers which result in more of them entering treatment and rehabilitation programs. Insite also helps to reduce the adverse impact of addiction on the immediate community in various ways, such as decreasing litter like used needles."

"On a less positive note" the authors said their review "also shows that, unfortunately, since 2006, the Government of Canada, and the Prime Minister of Canada in particular, have consistently misrepresented scientific evidence on Insite to justify their opposition. The government even ignored its own Expert Advisory Panel's conclusions."

The authors express general concern about the federal government's attitude towards evidence-based policy making, also exemplified in the recent canceling of the long-form census. They said that recent revelation in *Macleans* magazine indicating that the federal government ordered the RCMP last year not to participate with scientific experts in a public statement supporting Insite "has demolished any remaining credibility for federal addictions policy."

Reprinted from: http://www.newswire.ca/en/story/673759/federal-government-should-follow-the-evidence-and-stop-trying-to-close-insite-co-authors-of-new-cmaj-article-say

Questions to Ponder
1. **What concerns might the Canadian government have about the Vancouver DCF?**
2. **Are these concerns justified?**
3. **Why are there no DCFs in the United States?**

Decriminalization

Some scholars and public health experts believe that drug laws may be more harmful or criminogenic than the drugs themselves.[54] Under such circumstances, harm reduction involves changing the law or decriminalizing the behavior. Two examples are reviewed in this section: decriminalization of drug possession, particularly marijuana, and decriminalization of a crime-related activity (i.e., prostitution).

Decriminalization of Marijuana and Other Drugs

The results of a 2011 Gallup Poll indicated that approximately half of all Americans are currently in favor of making personal use of marijuana legal. This was the first time in the 40-year history of this poll question that more people were in favor of legalizing marijuana than were opposed to it (see **Figure 13-6**).[55] Since 1973, 14 states—Alaska, California, Colorado, Maine, Massachusetts, Minnesota, Mississippi, Nebraska, Nevada, New York, North Carolina, Ohio, Oregon, and Washington—have decriminalized or legalized marijuana. What this means is that marijuana users in these states no longer receive jail or prison time (or even arrest, in most cases) for small amounts of marijuana. Joy, Watson, and Benson note that marijuana decriminalization has led to a substantial reduction in the cost of arrest and prosecution for marijuana possession. States that decriminalized marijuana experienced no increase in marijuana, alcohol, or other drug usage, whereas states with the most severe penalties for marijuana possession experienced the greatest increases in marijuana usage.[56]

In the 1970s the Netherlands began what has become known as the "**Dutch experiment**" by legalizing marijuana. The results of this natural experiment brought marijuana's role as a gateway drug into question and showed that marijuana was much less criminogenic than most other drugs, including alcohol. Studies conducted in the Netherlands and several other European countries with liberal policies toward marijuana indicate

Figure 13-6
Results from the October 6-9, 2011 Gallup poll on public support for marijuana legalization.

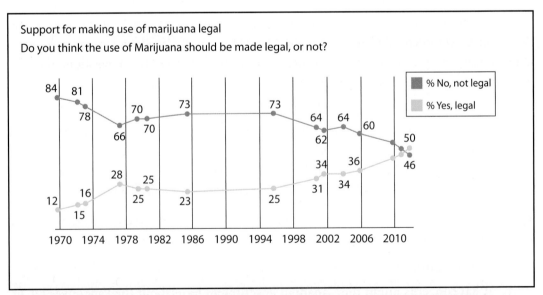

Support for making use of marijuana legal

Do you think the use of Marijuana should be made legal, or not?

% No, not legal
% Yes, legal

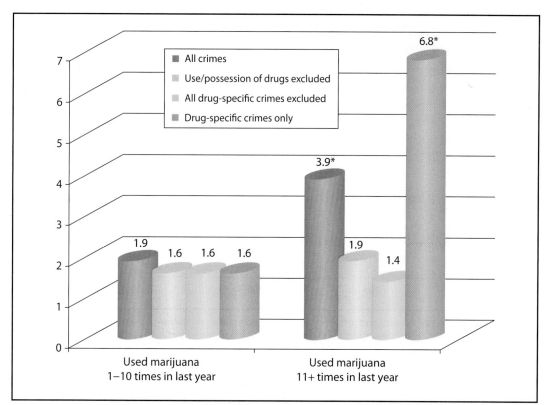

Figure 13-7
Level of cannabis use at age 20 as a predictor of crime involvement at ages 20 to 27 in the form of odds ratios.

Data From: Pedersen, W., & Skardhamar, T. (2009). Cannabis and crime: Findings from a longitudinal study. *Addiction, 105*, 109–118.
*statistically significant effect

that removing criminal sanctions against cannabis possession did not increase the amount of marijuana or other illicit drugs being used and actually seemed to reduce crime slightly.[57] Ever since the La Guardia Commission published its report on marijuana use in New York City in the mid-1940s, research has consistently failed to show evidence of a relationship between marijuana use and crime.[58–59] Willy Pedersen and Torbjørn Skardhamar explored this issue in a longitudinal panel study of individuals interviewed at age 20 and followed for 8 years. The results indicated that when arrests for drug use and possession were dropped from the analysis, there was no relationship between marijuana use at age 20 and criminality between the ages of 20 and 27 (see **Figure 13-7**).[60]

Faced with a rising number of overdose deaths, a growing HIV population, and a mounting problem with drug-related crime, the Portuguese government decriminalized the use and possession of marijuana, LSD, cocaine, heroin, and other illegal drugs in 2001. Under the new law, individuals caught with drugs were given a citation instead of being arrested, were instructed to report to a special addictions board rather than to court, and received treatment in place of punishment. After 5 years, the "**Portuguese experiment**" was judged a resounding success by Libertarian Glenn Greenwald[61] and an utter failure by Manuel Pinto Coelho, an abstinence-oriented treatment provider and head of the Association for a Drug Free Portugal.[62] The truth, it would seem, lies somewhere in between. Greenwald and Pinto Coelho apparently let their personal biases color their interpretation of the data, leaving it to Caitlin Hughes and Alex Stevens to sort through the facts.

Figure 13-8
Changes in the number of total, private, street, and managed sex workers before (2003) and after (2006, 2007) decriminalization of prostitution in New Zealand.

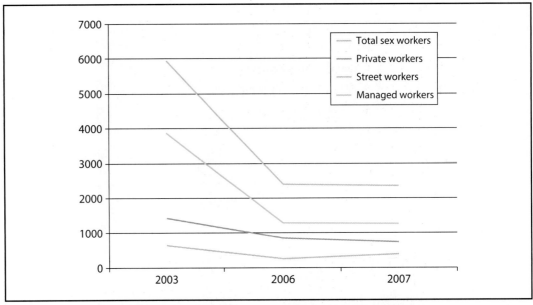

Data From: Prostitution Law Review Committee (PLRC). (2008). Report of the Prostitution Law Review Committee on the operation of the Prostitution Reform Act of 2003. Wellington, New Zealand: Ministry of Justice.

Although Portugal experienced a rise in adult drug use shortly after decriminalization, it did not rise as dramatically as Pinto Coelho has argued and was accompanied by a reduction in adolescent drug usage. Furthermore, although Portugal has a lower rate of drug use than most other European countries, it does not have the lowest rate of cannabis use in Europe, as Greenwald asserts.[63] Decriminalization, like other programs of harm reduction, is no panacea but there are two conclusions that can be drawn from the Portuguese experiment. First, it was not the unmitigated disaster that critics claimed it would be. Second, it allowed one of the poorest countries in Europe to divert funds from law enforcement to treatment, and as has been demonstrated, properly implemented treatment is more effective than incarceration in changing the lives of individuals who abuse drugs and commit nonviolent crime.

Decriminalization of Prostitution

Prostitution is another crime-related behavior that could potentially be handled through decriminalization. A number of countries (e.g., Australia, Canada, Germany, Mexico) and one U.S. state (Nevada) have legalized prostitution, but it was not until New Zealand decriminalized prostitution that researchers had an opportunity to take a close look at the effect of decriminalization on the sex trade. Researchers uncovered no evidence of an increase in the number of sex workers following implementation of **New Zealand's Prostitution Reform Act** of 2003 (see **Figure 13-8**) and discovered that organized crime seemed to be less involved in prostitution once decriminalization took effect.[64–65] Harm reduction through decriminalization achieves its effect via increased regulation, improved health and welfare, and decreased contact with criminals both in and out of jail and prison.

Harm Reduction and the U.S. Treatment Industry

In a review of research on harm reduction techniques and strategies for alcohol, tobacco, and illicit drugs, Alison Ritter and Jacqui Cameron unearthed support for the utility of

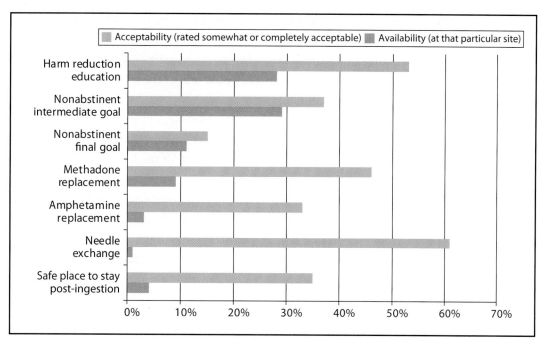

Figure 13-9
Degree to which treatment programs find various harm reduction procedures acceptable and the extent to which they are available in the rated site.

Data From: Rosenberg, H., & Phillips, K. T. (2003). Acceptability and availability of harm-reduction interventions for drug abuse in American substance abuse treatment agencies. *Psychology of Addictive Behaviors, 17,* 203–210.

harm reduction techniques with illicit drugs but less support for their utility in managing alcohol and tobacco consumption.[66] Despite the documented efficacy of harm reduction procedures in managing drug abuse, they are rarely used by traditional treatment providers. Harold Rosenberg and Kristina Phillips mailed surveys to 500 randomly selected U.S. substance abuse agencies inquiring about the acceptability and availability of various harm reduction programs. They received 222 responses from the 435 eligible agencies (51% response rate). A number of harm reduction procedures were rated as somewhat or completely acceptable by 50% or more of the respondents but very few of these programs were available to clients (see **Figure 13-9**). The primary reasons given for program unavailability were limited resources and conflicts with the guiding philosophy of the agency, which in nearly all cases was the disease model.[67] Funding issues can be overcome with data showing that harm reduction is cost effective, data that are already beginning to accumulate.[68–70] Overcoming the disease model, which is still the guiding philosophy of most American drug treatment programs, however, will require a major shift in attitude given the popularity of the disease model and its 12-step treatment offshoot.

Summary and Conclusions

- Five areas or aspects of harm reduction were covered in this chapter (controlled drug usage, drug replacement programs, needle exchange programs, drug consumption facilities, and decriminalization). Very few programs teach individuals to control their drinking or drug use any longer, although the evidence for controlled usage is strong and the philosophy of controlled usage survives in Marlatt and Witkiewitz's harm reduction approach[71] and in such self-help programs as moderation management and SMART recovery.

- **Drug replacement** programs, particularly those in which heroin addicts are maintained on methadone, have produced decreased drug use and crime and improved life outcomes in the areas of employment and relationships. In fact, drug replacement therapy, at least with heroin addicts, is one of the most **cost-effective** harm reduction programs available.
- Needle exchange programs (NEPs) have been found to significantly reduce high-risk injecting behaviors and appear to have a dampening effect on the transmission of HIV, although their utility in reducing the transmission of the hepatitis C virus is less certain and in need of more research.
- Drug Consumption Facilities (DCFs) are a relatively new addition to the harm reduction arsenal of techniques, although they have been found to reduce mortality and encourage treatment participation. Like NEPs, they do not lead to an increase in crime. In fact, police in Vancouver have started bringing intravenous drug users to the local DCF rather than arresting then, thus reserving scarce jail space for more serious offenders.
- **Decriminalization** of drug use is another harm reduction technique with a great deal of potential. In states where marijuana has been decriminalized there has been no increase in either drug use or crime. In a country (Portugal) that has decriminalized nearly all drugs, a slight increase in adult drug usage was associated with a slight drop in adolescent drug use and none of the problems its critics anticipated.

Key Terms

Abstinence   Belief held by many clients, substance abuse counselors, and policy-makers that only total cessation of drug use will bring about lasting happiness and personal fulfillment.

Alcoholics Anonymous (AA)   Self-help program based on a philosophy of powerlessness, surrender, and total abstinence.

Behavioral Self-Control Training   Formal program designed to teach alcoholics and problem drinkers how to drink in a controlled manner through BAC discrimination training, rate control, functional analysis, self-monitoring, goal-setting, and contingency management.

Blood-Alcohol Concentration (BAC)   Amount of alcohol present in the blood.

Buprenorphine   Semisynthetic opiate used in the treatment of opiate addiction.

Controlled Drug Use   Harm reduction strategy based on the belief that a person with a problem with alcohol or drugs can learn to drink or use drugs in a controlled manner.

Cost-Effective   The degree of benefit that can be achieved with a program in proportion to its overall cost; more cost-effective programs have greater benefit per unit cost than less cost-effective programs.

Decriminalization   Policy in which a behavior that was previously illegal is handled in a way other than through the criminal justice system.

Drug Consumption Facility (DCF) A medically supervised facility, often just a room, where drug users go to ingest drugs in a hygienic and stress-free environment.

Drug Replacement Harm reduction strategy in which a less harmful or more controllable drug or substance is substituted for a more harmful or less controllable drug or substance.

Dutch Experiment Marijuana has been legal in the Netherlands since the 1970s and this provided an opportunity for a natural experiment on the effects of legalization on drug use behavior and crime.

E-Cigarettes Electronic devices that produce a vapor of water, propylene glycol, and nicotine that is believed to be less harmful than tobacco smoke.

Harm Reduction Set of strategies designed to reduce the negative consequences of drug use for the person and for society.

Intravenous Administration of a substance, such as a drug or vitamin, directly into the vein.

Levo-Acethylmethadol Synthetic opiate with chemical properties similar to methadone used in the treatment of opiate addiction.

Methadone Synthetic opiate commonly used in drug replacement therapy for opiate addiction.

Methadone Maintenance Administration of a daily maintenance dose of methadone to opiate addicts designed to reduce the craving for heroin, improve the individual's social adjustment, and reduce or eliminate drug-related crime.

Moderation Management Self-help program developed around controlled drinking and harm reduction principles that holds to the belief that some problem drinkers can learn to control their drinking.

Natural Experiment An observational study where treatments have not been randomly assigned but the policy change or intervention is so dramatic that it provides potentially useful information on the phenomenon of interest.

Needle Device consisting of a simple plunger in a cylindrical tube used to inject drugs; also known as a syringe.

Needle Exchange Programs (NEP) Harm reduction strategy designed to reduce the incidence of disease transmission by providing users with replacement syringes and discouraging the practice of sharing needles.

New Zealand Prostitution Reform Act In 2003 the New Zealand government decriminalized prostitution; this provides a natural experiment on the effect of decriminalization on the number of sex workers and patterns of organized crime.

Portuguese Experiment Portugal decriminalized most drugs in 2001 and this provides a natural experiment of the effects of decriminalization on drug use behavior and crime.

Prostitution Act of offering sexual favors or services for money.

SMART Recovery   Self-help program that makes use of motivational interviewing, cognitive-behavioral principles, and methods derived from evidence-based therapeutic techniques.

Smokeless Tobacco   Tobacco consumed in a manner other than smoking (e.g., snuff, chewing tobacco).

Syringe   Device consisting of a simple plunger in a cylindrical tube used to inject drugs; also referred to as a needle.

Critical Thinking

1. If you were working as a probation officer, how would you handle the issue of controlled drug usage with your clients, keeping in mind that you are an agent of the (local, state, or federal) government?

2. Methadone maintenance has been criticized for enabling drug users and maintaining people on opiate drugs indefinitely. How do you respond to this characterization of modern methadone maintenance?

3. Why does the United States government seem to be so adamantly opposed to needle exchange programs? Are its concerns justified?

4. How would you go about setting up a drug consumption facility (DCF) in your local community? What local groups would you want to include in the planning and implementation of the DCF?

Notes

1. Witkiewitz, K., & Marlatt, G. A. (2006). Overview of harm reduction treatments for alcohol problems. *International Journal of Drug Policy, 17*, 285–294.

2. Walthers, J., Weingardt, K. R., Witkiewitz, K., & Marlatt, G. A. (2012). Harm reduction and public policy. In G. A. Marlatt, M. E. Lamimer, & K. Witkiewitz (Eds.), *Harm reduction: Pragmatic strategies for managing high risk behavior* (pp. 339–380). New York: Guilford.

3. Harm Reduction Coalition. (2012). *Principles of harm reduction.* Retrieved May 30, 2012, from http://harmreduction.org/about-us/principles-of-harm-reduction/.

4. Davies, D. L. (1962). Normal drinking in recovered alcohol addicts. *Quarterly Journal of Studies on Alcohol, 23*, 94–104.

5. Sobell, M. B., & Sobell, L. C. (1973). Alcoholics treated by individualized behavior therapy: One year treatment outcome. *Behaviour Research and Therapy, 11*, 599–618.

6. Sobell, M. B., & Sobell, L. C. (1976). Second year treatment outcome of alcoholics treated by individualized behavior therapy: Results. *Behaviour Research and Therapy. 14*, 195–215.

7. Pendery, M. L., Maltzman, I. M., & West, L. J. (1982). Controlled drinking by alcoholics? New findings and a reevaluation of a major affirmative study. *Science, 217*, 169–175.

8. Dickens, B. M., Doob, A. N., Warwick, O. H., & Winegard, W. C. (1982). *Report of the Committee of Inquiry into allegations concerning Drs. Linda and Mark Sobell*, Toronto, Canada: Addiction Research Foundation.

9. Kishline, A. (1994). *Moderate drinking: The Moderation Management guide for people who want to reduce their drinking.* New York: Crown.

10. Steinberger, H. (2004). *SMART Recovery handbook.* Mentor, OH: Alcohol & Drug Abuse Self-Help Network.

11. Peele, S. (2000). Comment on Audrey Kishline's accident and statement. Retrieved May 30, 2012, from http://www.positiveatheism.org/rw/kishpeel.htm.

12. Werch, C. E. (1990). Perception of intoxication and blood-alcohol concentration of drinkers in social settings. *International Journal of the Addictions, 25*, 253–262.

13. Walters, G. D. (2000). Behavioral self-control training for problem drinkers: A meta-analysis of randomized control studies. *Behavior Therapy, 31*, 135–149.

14. Walters (2000).

15. Klaw, E., Luft, S., & Humphreys, K. (2003). Characteristics and motives of problem drinkers seeking help from Moderation Management self-help groups. *Cognitive and Behavioral Practice, 10*, 384–389.

16. Schwartz, R. (2010). Medical marijuana users in substance abuse treatment. *Harm Reduction Journal, 7*, 3.

17. Murphy S. B., Reinarman, C., & Waldorf, D. (1989). An 11-year follow-up of a network of cocaine users. *British Journal of Addiction, 84*, 427–436.

18. Robins, L. N., Helzer, J. E., & Davis, D. H. (1975). Narcotic use in southeast Asia and afterward. *Archives of General Psychiatry, 32*, 955–961.

19. Zinberg, N. E. (1984). *Drug, set, and setting: The basis for controlled intoxicant use.* New Haven, CN: Yale University Press.

20. Paparozzi, M., & Gendreau, P. (2005). An intensive supervision program that worked: Service delivery, professional orientation, and organizational supportiveness. *The Prison Journal, 85*, 445–466.

21. Centers for Disease Control and Prevention (CDC). (2002). *Methadone maintenance treatment [IDU HIV Prevention].* Atlanta, GA: U.S. Department of Health and Human Services.

22. Wechsberg, W. M., Kasten, J. J., Berkman, N. D., & Roussel, A. E. (2007). *Methadone maintenance treatment in the U.S.: A practical question and answer guide.* New York: Springer.

23. CDC (2002).

24. Farré, M., Mas, A., Torrens, M., Moreno, V., & Cami, J. (2002). Retention rate and illicit opioid use during methadone maintenance interventions: A meta-analysis. *Drug and Alcohol Dependence, 65*, 283–290.

25. Marsch, L. A. (1998). The efficacy of methadone maintenance interventions in reducing illicit opiate use, HIV risk behavior and criminality: A meta-analysis. *Addiction, 93*, 515–532.

26. Ball, J. C., & Ross, A. (1991). *The effectiveness of methadone maintenance treatment: Patients, programs, services, and outcomes.* New York: Springer-Verlag.

27. Nordt, C., & Stohler, R. (2006). Incidence of heroin use in Zurich, Switzerland: A treatment case register analysis. *Lancet, 367*, 1830–1834.

28. Perneger, T. V., Giner, F., del Rio, M., & Mino, A. (1998). Randomised trial of heroin maintenance programme for addicts who fail in conventional drug treatments. *British Medical Journal, 317*, 13–18.

29. Rehm, J., Gschwend, P., Steffen, T., Guzwiller, F., Dobler-Mikola, A., & Uchtenhagen, A. (2001). Feasibility, safety, and efficacy of injectable heroin prescription for refractory opioid addicts: A follow-up study. *Lancet, 358*, 1417–1420.

30. Blanken, P., Hendriks, V. M., Koeter, M. W., van Ree, J. M., & van den Brink, W. (2005). Matching of treatment-resistant heroin-dependent patients to medical prescription of heroin or oral methadone treatment: Results from two randomized controlled trials. *Addiction, 100*, 89–95.

31. Spear, H. B., & Glatt, M. M. (1971). The influence of Canadian addicts on heroin addiction in the United Kingdom. *British Journal of Addiction, 66*, 141–149.

32. National Institute on Drug Abuse (NIDA). (2010). DrugFacts: Cocaine. Retrieved May 30, 2012, from http://www.drugabuse.gov/publications/drugfacts/cocaine.

33. Murphy et al. (1989).

34. Shearer, J., Sherman, J., Wodak, A., & Van Beek, I. (2002). Substitution therapy for amphetamine users. *Drug and Alcohol Review, 21*, 179–185.

35. Rodu, B. (2011). The scientific foundation for tobacco harm reduction, 2006–2011. *Harm Reduction Journal, 8*,19.

36. National Institutes of Health (2002, November). National Institutes of Health consensus development conference statement: Management of hepatitis C. *Hepatology, 36*(5 Suppl 1), S3–S20.

37. Centers for Disease Control and Prevention. (2010). Syringe exchange programs—United States, 2008. *Morbidity and Mortality Weekly Report, 59*, 1488–1491.

38. Turner, K. M. E., Hutchinson, S., Vickerman, P., Hoope, V., Craine, N., Palmateer, N., et al. (2011). The impact of needle and syringe provision and opiate substitution therapy on the incidence of hepatitis C virus in injecting drug users: Pooling of UK evidence. *Addiction, 106*, 1978–1988.

39. Gowing, L., Farrell, M., Bornemann, R., Sullivan, L. E., & Ali, R. (2008). Substitution treatment of injecting opioid users for prevention of HIV infection. *Cochrane Database Systematic Review, 2*, CD004145.

40. Hurley, S. F., Jolley, D. J., & Kaldor, J. M. (1997). Effectiveness of needle-exchange programmes for prevention of HIV infection. *Lancet, 349*, 1797–1800.

41. Ksobiech, K. (2003). Meta-analysis of needle sharing, lending, and borrowing behaviors of needle exchange program attenders. *AIDS Education and Prevention, 15*, 257–268.

42. Palmateer, N., Kimber, J., Hickman, M., Hutchinson, S., Rhodes, T., & Goldberg, D. (2010). Evidence for the effectiveness of sterile injecting equipment provision in preventing hepatitis C and human immunodeficiency virus transmission among injecting drug users: A review of reviews, *Addiction, 105*, 844–859.

43. Turner et al. (2011).

44. Bravo, M. J., Royuela, L., Barrio, G., de la Fuente, L., Suarez, M., & Bruga, M. T. (2007). More free syringes, fewer drug injectors in the case of Spain. *Social Science and Medicine, 65*, 1773–1778.

45. Marx, M. A., Brahmbhatt, H., Beilenson, P., Brookmeyer, R. S., Strathdee, S. A., Alexander, C., et al. (2001). Impact of needle exchange programs on adolescent perceptions about illicit drug use. *AIDS and Behavior, 5*, 379–386.

46. Marx, M. A., Crape, B., Brookmeyer, R. S., Junge, B., Latkin, C., Vlahov, D., et al. (2000). Trends in crime and the introduction of a needle exchange program. *American Journal of Public Health, 90*, 1933–1936.

47. Lightfoot, B., Panessa, C., Hayden, S., Thumath, M., Goldstone, I., & Pauly, B. (2009). Gaining INSITE: Harm reduction in nursing practice. *Canadian Nurse, 105*(4), 16–22.

48. Wood, A., Zettel, P., & Stewart, W. (2003). The Dr. Peter Centre: Harm reduction nursing. *Canadian Nurse, 99*(5), 20–24.

49. DeBeck, K., Buxton, J., Kerr, T., Qi, J., Montaner, J., & Wood, E. (2011). Public crack cocaine smoking and willingness to use a supervised inhalation facility: Implications for street disorder. *Substance Abuse Treatment, Prevention, and Policy, 6*, 4.

50. Zobel, F., & Dubois-Arber, F. (2004). *Short appraisal of the role and usefulness of drug consumption facilities (DCF) in the reduction of drug-related problems in Switzerland.* Appraisal produced at the request of the Swiss Federal Office of Public Health. Lausanne: University Institute of Social and Preventive Medicine.

51. Wright, N. M. J., & Tompkins, C. N. E. (2004). Supervised injecting centres. *British Medical Journal, 328*, 100–102.

52. Expert Advisory Committee. (2008). Vancouver's INSITE service and other supervised injection sites: What has been learned from research? *Final report of the Expert Advisory Committee on Supervised Injection Site Research.* Ottawa, ON: Health Canada.

53. Hedrich, D., Kerr, T., & Dubois-Arber, F. (2010). Drug consumption facilities in Europe and beyond. In T. Rhodes & D. Hedrich (Eds.), *Harm reduction: Evidence, impacts, and challenges* (pp. 305–331). Lisbon: EMCDAA.

54. Birdwell, J., Chapman, J., & Singleton, N. (2011). *Taking drugs seriously: A Demos and UK Drug Policy Commission report on legal highs.* London: Demos.

55. Newport, F. (2011, October). *Record-high 50% of Americans favor legalizing marijuana use: Liberals and those 18 to 29 most in favor; Americans 65 and older most opposed.* Princeton, NJ: Gallop.

56. Joy, J. E., Watson, S. J., & Benson, J. A. (Eds.). (1999). *Marijuana and medicine: Assessing the science base*. Washington, DC: Institute of Medicine, National Academy Press.

57. MacCoun, R. J., & Reuter, P. (2001). *Drug War heresies: An agnostic look at the legalization debate*. Cambridge, England: Cambridge University Press.

58. Mayor's Committee on Marihuana. (1944). *The marihuana problem in the city of New York: The La Guardia Committee Report*. New York: New York Academy of Medicine.

59. Dembo, R., Washburn, M., Wish, E., Schmeidler, J., Getreu, A., Berry, E., et al. (1987). Further examination of the association between heavy marijuana use and crime among youth entering a juvenile detention centre. *Journal of Psychoactive Drugs, 19*, 361–373.

60. Pedersen, W., & Skardhamar, T. (2009). Cannabis and crime: Findings from a longitudinal study. *Addiction, 105*, 109–118.

61. Greenwald, G. (2009). *Drug decriminalization in Portugal: Lessons for creating fair and successful drug policies*. Washington, DC: CATO Institute.

62. Pinto Coelho, M. (2010). *The "resounding success" of Portuguese drug policy: The power of an attractive fallacy*. Lisbon: Association for a Drug Free Portugal.

63. Hughes, C. E., & Stevens, A. (2012). A resounding success or disastrous failure: Reexamining the interpretation of evidence on the Portuguese decriminalization of illicit drugs. *Drug and Alcohol Review, 31*, 101–113.

64. Abel, G., Fitzgerald, L., & Bruton, C. (2009). The impact of decriminalization on the number of sex workers in New Zealand. *Journal of Social Policy, 38*, 515–531.

65. Prostitution Law Review Committee (PLRC). (2008). *Report of the Prostitution Law Review Committee on the operation of the Prostitution Reform Act of 2003*. Wellington, New Zealand: Ministry of Justice.

66. Ritter, A., & Cameron, J. (2006). A review of the efficacy and effectiveness of harm reduction strategies for alcohol, tobacco and illicit drugs. *Drug and Alcohol Review, 25*, 611–624.

67. Rosenberg, H., & Phillips, K. T. (2003). Acceptability and availability of harm-reduction interventions for drug abuse in American substance abuse treatment agencies. *Psychology of Addictive Behaviors, 17*, 203–210.

68. Alistar, S. S., Owen, D. K., & Brandeau, M. L. (2011). Effectiveness and cost effectiveness of expanding harm reduction and antiretroviral therapy in a mixed HIV epidemic: A modeling analysis for Ukraine. *PLoS Medicine, 8*(3), e1000423.

69. Belani, H. K., & Muennig, P. A. (2008). Cost-effectiveness of needle and syringe exchange for the prevention of HIV in New York City. *Journal of HIV/AIDS and Social Services, 7*, 229–240.

70. Vickerman, P., Kumaranayake, L., Balakireva, O., Guinness, L., Artyukh, O., Semikop, T., et al. (2006). The cost-effectiveness of expanding harm reduction activities for injecting drug users in Odessa, Ukraine. *Sexually Transmitted Disease, 33*, S89–S102.

71. Marlatt, G. A., & Witkiewitz, K. (2002). Harm reduction approaches to alcohol use: Health promotion, prevention, and treatment. *Addictive Behavior, 27*, 867–886.

DRUGS, CRIME, AND SOCIETY

Figure 14-1
International drug
trafficking routes.

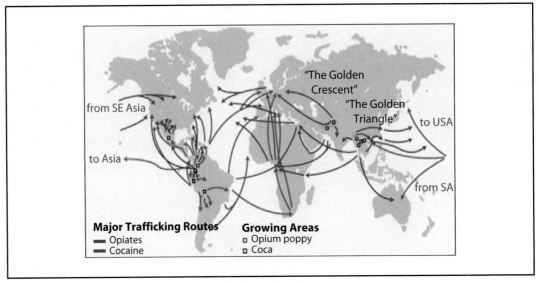

CIA, 2000.

The drug trade, like the economy, is global. Very few of the drugs used in the United States are grown or produced here. Instead, they are grown in one country, processed in another, and transported through one or more other countries. These international trade routes all have hubs, whether in Central America, West Africa, or Central Asia (see **Figure 14-1**).[1] The hubs provide protection for the drug cartels because direct routes between the source and destination are often tracked by the authorities, whereas flights going through hub countries frequently are not. Because hub countries are nearly always poor, they provide an opportunity for bribery of local police and government officials. In addition, hubs are used to store large amounts of illegal drugs and allow the drug cartels to transport drugs when they want and in the quantity they need. To enforce a program of drug **prohibition** authorities must find ways to identify and neutralize these hubs and the trade routes through which drugs travel.

NEWS SPOT 14-1

Title: US Concerned About Kenyan Drugs Trade, Plans DEA Office—Local Officials Said to be Complicit in Trafficking of Heroin and Other Drugs Through Kenya
Source: *Global Post: Africa*
Author: Tristan McConnell
Date: April 7, 2011

Kenya is a hub for the international drugs trade, according to a new United States State Department report.

"The trafficking of narcotics in and through Kenya is a major and growing problem that has permeated all strata of the society," according to the latest report on the global drugs trade by the State Department that has been presented to the U.S. Congress.

The report warns that hard drugs are being trafficked in Kenya. Heroin, in particular, is reaching East Africa from the poppy fields of central Asia and then being smuggled on to the United States, according to the report. The report reveals that "the U.S. Drug Enforcement Administration is in the process of opening a country office in Nairobi."

The beefing up of capacity shows the extent of U.S. concern about the drugs trade through East Africa and the corrosive effect it has in Kenya itself.

"Drug trafficking is linked to the prevailing culture of impunity, and presents serious ramifications to the nation's health, security, and stability," states the 2011 International Narcotics Control Strategy Report.

"Kenya is a significant transit country for a host of illegal narcotics, including heroin and cocaine," says the report.

According to a recently published report by the International Narcotics Control Board, an estimated 35 tons of heroin is smuggled into Africa every year, "mainly through the major airports of Addis Ababa and Nairobi." The Vienna-based group says that 25 tons of this is for consumption by Africa's 1.2 million addicts.

"Narcotics trafficking is a grave reflection of the culture of impunity which pervades Kenya," said U.S. Ambassador to Kenya Michael Ranneberger in a speech in November.

He went on to accuse five Kenyans, including politicians, of involvement in the drugs trade.

"Based on reliable and corroborative reports, we have taken steps to ensure that four senior government officials and one prominent businessman will be permanently prevented from entering the US for business or tourism," said Ranneberger.

The names, which have not been revealed publicly, have been forwarded to the Kenya Anti-Corruption Commission.

© 2011 GlobalPost.

Questions to Ponder

1. **What effect does the fact that Kenya serves as a major hub for drugs have on the citizens of Kenya?**
2. **How do hubs like Kenya enhance the efficiency of the international drug trade?**
3. **Name three other countries that serve as hubs for the international drug trade?**

The purpose of this chapter is to track the drug trade from its origins in foreign coca and poppy fields and foreign and domestic marijuana fields and laboratories, to its destination, the streets of America's cities, suburbs, and towns, and what happens in between. This discussion on the international drug trade and America's response to it is organized into three major objectives:

- Understand the nature of drug trafficking networks from their largely international origins to their local destinations
- Appreciate the nature and ultimate success of America's "War on Drugs"
- Explore policy alternatives to America's "War on Drugs" as a means of dealing with the drug problem

Drug Trafficking Networks

Three issues are discussed in this section: where drugs come from, drug distribution hierarchies, and the international drug trade.

Where Do Drugs Come From?

Marijuana

Approximately half the marijuana consumed in the United States is produced domestically. Marijuana cultivation is particularly prominent in the states of California, Tennessee, Kentucky, Hawaii, and Washington. In 2006, domestic marijuana cultivation was worth $35.8 billion, more than corn and wheat combined, making it the largest cash crop in the United States. The other half of the marijuana consumed in the United States comes from Mexico, Canada, Colombia, and several small countries in Latin America.[2]

LSD

The hallucinogen LSD is produced by a limited number of chemists, perhaps as few as a dozen, in clandestine laboratories located primarily in northern California. The **Drug Enforcement Administration** (DEA) acknowledges that they have not been able to shut down a major LSD synthesizing lab since 1987.[3]

Methamphetamine

Approximately 80% of the methamphetamine consumed in the United States is produced in large laboratories run by the Mexican drug cartels. These labs are located near the U.S.-Mexican border in both countries. The remaining 20% of methamphetamine used by American citizens is manufactured in small, often makeshift, labs scattered throughout the United States and Canada.[4]

Cocaine

Nearly all of the cocaine consumed in the United States (approximately 95%) is produced in Colombia, South America from plants grown in Colombia, Peru, and Bolivia. The drug is then transported to the United States either directly or through hubs in Mexico, Panama, and the Dominican Republic.[5]

Heroin

Although Afghanistan (the **Golden Crescent**) is the major source of heroin for the world, the majority of heroin consumed in the United States comes from Mexico, in a form known as black tar, and Colombia. The **Golden Triangle** (Burma, Thailand, Laos, and Vietnam) is another major source, producing a form of heroin known as china white. Although America receives most of its heroin from Mexico and Colombia, a significant portion reaches the United States from Afghanistan and Asia through hubs located in West Africa, India, and Europe.[6]

Drug Distribution Hierarchies

Bruce Johnson, Eloise Dunlap, and Sylvie Tourigny analyzed a crack cocaine drug trafficking network in New York City. Their analyses revealed a loose five-level hierarchy, each with different roles. The five levels are:[7]

- Growers and manufacturers
- Traffickers
- Dealers
- Sellers
- Low-level distributors

Growers and Manufacturers

Farmers grow cannabis for marijuana, coca for cocaine, and opium for heroin. The raw drug is processed, manufactured, and/or prepared for consumption by a group of individuals loosely connected to a drug lord or kingpin. Drugs like methamphetamine and LSD are manufactured by a chemist, who is the origin of these drugs. The drug lord, kingpin, or origin then makes the drug available to wholesale distributors who disperse the drug through lower level suppliers.

Traffickers

Drug **traffickers** and wholesale distributors are responsible for transporting a drug from one location to another, often over long distances and across international borders. The importer role is assumed by a pilot, boat captain, or "mule" who smuggles small to large amounts of the drug into a country over land, sea, or air. The wholesale distributor, on the other hand, transports and redistributes multikilogram amounts of the drug.

Dealers

Dealers are middle managers in the drug trade, involved either in the adulteration and sale of the product (weight dealers), adulteration and sale of significant quantities of dosage units of the drug, or security and distribution. **Regional distributors**, also known as weight dealers, cut the product with another substance and package the drug in unit dosage bags. **Retail store owners** either supply or manage a crack house, shooting gallery, or drug store. Assistant managers and security chiefs supervise the distribution of unit dosage bags of the drug, collect money, or manage security.

Sellers

Further down the hierarchy are the sellers. A seller's job is to sell drugs to individual customers. The **seller** will purchase a small number of unit dosage bags of the drug and sell these unit dosage bags to customers at retail prices. Sellers may work in a set location like a crack house or shooting gallery or they may have a territory and act more like a salesman. Individuals functioning at this level of the hierarchy handle both drugs and money.

Figure 14-2
Elements of a drug
distributing hierarchy.

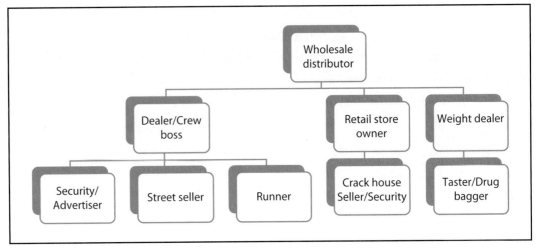

Data From: Johnson, B. D., Dunlap, E., & Tourigny, S. C. (2000). Crack distribution and abuse in New York. In M. Natarajan &
M. Hough (Eds.), Illegal drug markets: From research to policy (*Crime Prevention Studies*, Vol. 11, pp. 19–57). Monsey, NY:
Criminal Justice Press.

Low-Level Distributors

At the bottom of the hierarchy are the **low-level distributors** who serve as runners, look-outs, baggers, holders, guards, or tasters. Their job is to advertise the product, package the product, or protect the seller from the police, competitors, or other criminals looking to rob the seller. Individuals at this level may handle drugs or money but not both. **Figure 14-2** provides a schematic diagram of the hierarchy from the **wholesale distributor** down to the lowest levels of the hierarchy.

Additional Research on Drug Distributing Hierarchies

Analyzing wiretap and other records collected on a drug trafficking operation in New York City, Mangai Natarajan discovered that the network adopted a corporate structure with hierarchical organization and clear division of labor. Field workers had minimal contact with others in the organization so that if they were caught they had no useful information to share with law enforcement officials. The results of the analysis further revealed that individuals higher up in the hierarchy relied extensively on telephone contact to make deals and dispense orders, thus providing an additional layer of protection between them and the individuals who were actually selling the drugs and who were most likely to get caught by the police.[8]

Using investigative data gathered by state, federal, and local law enforcement agencies, John Eck and Jeffrey Gersh tested the fit of two different models of crime organization to drug dealing in the Baltimore-Washington area. The two models they tested were the **conspiracy/bureaucratic model**, which holds to a well-defined hierarchy of distributional relationships, and the **enterprise or cottage industry model**, which holds to a loosely connected group of fluid distributional relationships. The results indicated that drug dealing in the Baltimore-Washington area was more consistent with the enterprise model than with the conspiracy/bureaucratic model.[9] This is the exact opposite of what Jacobs and Gouldin found when they examined the hierarchy of relationships in organized crime **Cosa Nostra** families.[10]

One big difference between those at the top of the drug distribution hierarchy and those at the bottom is that those at the bottom make a lot less money and are more likely to be drug users themselves than those at the higher echelons of the drug trade. Many drug users, in fact, support their habit by selling drugs or serving as tasters, runners, or lookouts. Dan Werb and a group of colleagues interviewed a large group of drug users who reported dealing drugs between November 2005 and March 2009. Out of 381 users who were dealing drugs at baseline, 194 (51%) stopped dealing. Desistance from drug dealing was positively associated with age and spending less than $50 a day on drugs and negatively associated with buying drugs from the same source and injecting crystal methamphetamine.[11] This not only illustrates the fluid nature of drug distribution operations but also underscores the fact that desistance from crime (drug dealing) is important in maintaining desistance from drugs. Previous research, in fact, denotes that continued involvement in crime can retard the natural maturing out of drug use process that is frequently observed in older drug users.[12]

Different Drug Trafficking Patterns

Trafficking of the three major illicit drugs (marijuana, cocaine, and heroin) differs in several key respects. Unlike the users of cocaine and heroin, a substantial number of marijuana users grow their own product. Indoor growing is becoming increasing more popular in the United States but outdoor growing is still the primary mode of production. Marijuana is consequently more conducive to small-scale trafficking than either cocaine or heroin.[13] Cocaine is grown almost exclusively in South America, with nearly all production occurring in Colombia and major **drug distribution networks** running through Mexico and West Africa.[14] Heroin is frequently the preferred drug of sale for many in the drug trade. There are two reasons for this. First, heroin has a much greater yield than cocaine and therefore provides greater profit per unit of risk compared to cocaine. A kilogram of heroin is worth 8–10 times that of a kilogram of cocaine.[15] Second, heroin customers are more loyal than cocaine customers in the sense that the average heroin career is several times longer than the average cocaine career. This makes the heroin trade more stable and reliable than the cocaine trade.[16]

The International Drug Trade

Drug trafficking is a truly global enterprise, but some countries play a more important role than other countries in the international drug trade. The role of three of the most important regions in the international drug trade (South America, Mexico, and Afghanistan) is covered in this section, followed by a brief discussion of the CIA's role in the international drug trade and national and international factors that support the drug trade.

South America

For years, Colombia was under the control of two warring factions, the Medellin **drug cartel** and the Cali drug cartel. The Medellin cartel was centered in the Colombian city of Medellin. Under the leadership of Pablo Escobar, the Medellin cartel waged a war with the Colombian government that left hundreds of government officials, lawyers, judges, police officers, and innocent bystanders dead. In 1994, Escobar was hunted down and killed by Colombian police. Centered in the town of Cali, Colombia, the Cali cartel conducted their business more subtly than did the Medellin cartel and began reinvesting their profits in

Figure 14-3
Coca cultivation in Bolivia, Colombia, and Peru between 1995 and 2009.

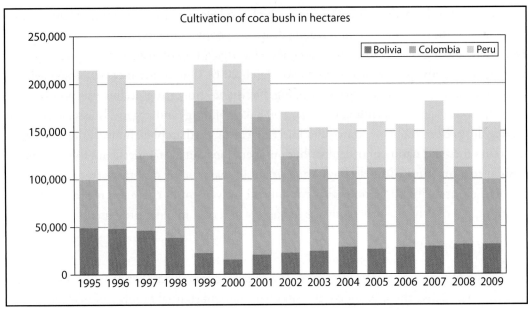

Data From: United Nations Office on Drugs and Crime (UNODC). (2011). *World drug report 2011*. New York: Author.

sophisticated equipment, political protection, and legal businesses. The Cali cartel was also suspected of providing the Colombian government and U.S. DEA with information on the whereabouts of Pablo Escobar. The leaders of the Cali cartel were eventually arrested and imprisoned but made deals with the government to serve their 10- to 15-year sentences in Colombia instead of the United States.

Most of the cocaine sold worldwide is grown in three countries, Colombia, Bolivia, and Peru. After the 9/11 terrorist attacks, President George W. Bush began tying the narcotics trade to international terrorism and accelerated **eradication** programs in Colombia. Eradication programs involve spraying coca and opium poppy fields with a herbicide that kills the plants. The overall effect on cocaine production, however, was minimal because coca cultivation increased in Bolivia and Peru to compensate for the modest loss of coca production in Colombia (see **Figure 14-3**). As in a game of chess, every move made to limit the production and distribution of illegal drugs in Colombia was countered by the opposition. Presently, those in charge of the drug trade in Colombia have realized that larger organizations are vulnerable to attack and so have formed smaller, more loosely knit operations in which responsibilities are compartmentalized and less tied to a central organization or hierarchy.[17]

Mexico

Mexico produces a good portion of the heroin, methamphetamine, and marijuana consumed in the United States. Through the combined efforts of the DEA and Colombian government, cocaine and heroin production have dropped modestly in Colombia in recent years. Some of the demand for heroin and cocaine has therefore shifted to Mexico. Mexican heroin production has increased in the last several years and the country has become a major transportation hub for cocaine coming from South America. There are currently seven major drug-trafficking organizations operating in Mexico, each located in a different region of the country: La Familia Michoacán, the Gulf cartel, Los Zetas, the Beltrán-Leyva organization, the Sinaloa cartel, the Tijuana cartel, and the Juarez cartel.

Drug trafficking generates annual revenues of $35–$45 billion for the Mexican cartels, money they are unwilling to surrender without a fight. The lucrative drug trade has fueled violence among the cartels and between the cartels and the Mexican government. Drug-related violence escalated dramatically after President Felipe Calderón assumed office in December 2006 and pledged that he would do everything within his power to wipe out the cartels. Compared to previous administrations, Calderón has aggressively attacked the drug cartels in the belief that they pose a serious threat to national security. The results are such that the U.S. government has advised American tourists to avoid Mexico at the present time.[18]

Afghanistan

Afghanistan is the world's largest producer of opium and its most prolific supplier of heroin. Located in an area known as the "Golden Crescent," Afghanistan is well positioned geographically, politically, and environmentally to be a key player in the international heroin trade. During the Taliban period (1993–2001), the supply of opium fell dramatically as a result of the Taliban's efforts to eradicate the opium trade in Afghanistan. After the Taliban was overthrown in early 2002, poppy production returned to and exceeded pre-Taliban levels. Today, Afghanistan supplies over 85% of the world's heroin (see **Figure 14-4**), most of which goes to Western Europe and Russia. It is no coincidence that Russia harbors more heroin addicts than any other country in the world.[19]

Drug Trafficking and the CIA

The United States government, or, more precisely, elements of the U.S. government, has been accused of being involved in the international drug trade. Since its inception in 1947, the Central Intelligence Agency (CIA) has been suspected of dealing with various drug lords in an effort to influence world affairs, but its direct involvement in drug trafficking was no longer a matter of speculation once the infamous Iran-Contra Affair became public. A deal was apparently struck between Oliver North and others in the Reagan White House to sell weapons to Iran, with Israel serving as the middle man, in exchange for the release of six

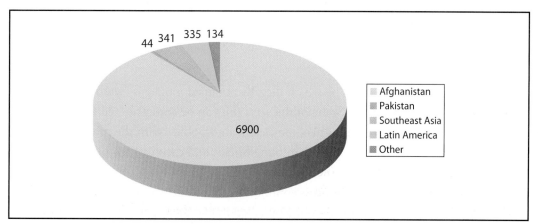

Figure 14-4
Opium production worldwide in metric tons.

Data From: United Nations Office on Drugs and Crime (UNODC). (2011). *World drug report 2011.* New York: Author.

American hostages. Some of the profits from the arms sales would then go to the Contra rebels in Nicaragua who were financing their cause, in part, by smuggling cocaine into the United States, apparently with the help of the CIA.[20]

Factors that Support the Drug Trade

In his book, *Drugs in American Society*, Erich Goode highlights eight factors that appear to support the drug trade, each of which is described next.[21]

Prohibition

The drug trade is supported, first and foremost, by prohibition. No drug **dealer** wants to see drugs legalized, for this would mean that he or she would be out of a job. Making a commodity illegal creates a black market. Greater prohibition means greater profit, and with both comes greater incentive to enter into the prohibited activity.

Organized Crime

Prohibition encourages the entrance of organized crime into the prohibited activity. The entrance of organized crime into the prohibited activity makes the activity more successful because organized crime can call upon existing relationships and connections to increase the operational efficiency of the prohibited activity. This was observed during Prohibition with the rise of the American Cosa Nostra and in modern times with the rise of the Russian mob.[22]

Weak National and Local Governments

A weak central or local government is an open invitation for organized crime and other criminal groups to enter into a prohibited activity like drug trafficking. Countries such as Colombia, Mexico, and Afghanistan have traditionally been plagued by weak central governments and the associated problems of graft, corruption, and ineffective criminal justice response to crime. After the collapse of the Soviet Union, weakened central control and mass patterns of migration and immigration opened up new markets for drugs and new drug trade routes, particularly between Afghanistan and Russia.[23]

Economic Privatization

Deregulation and a variety of free trade agreements like the North American Free Trade Agreement (NAFTA) have been good for international business and trade. Unfortunately, they have also facilitated drug trafficking by opening up new trade and trafficking routes and making it easier for criminals to launder drug money.[24]

Money Laundering

Money laundering is the process by which illegally obtained money is "washed" for the purpose of concealing its origin. Some of the ways this can be accomplished is by:[25-26]

- purchasing large-ticket items like homes and automobiles with the money
- bringing the money to a casino, gambling briefly, and then cashing out
- breaking a large amount of money down into smaller units and purchasing bearer bonds or money orders (a process commonly referred to as smurfing)
- acquiring a financial institution in a jurisdiction like the Cayman Islands with weak antilaundering laws and laundering the cash through the institution

Globalization

The global economy has facilitated the international drug trade. Expanded travel, particularly air travel, has opened up new trade routes and new opportunities for drug distribution.[27] **Globalization** also facilitates the international drug trade by reducing the cost of illegal drugs.[28]

Technology

Technology facilitates the drug trade by allowing drug traffickers the opportunity to purchase the knowledge, equipment, and access necessary to effectively transport drugs; this includes Global Positioning System (GPS) devices, planes, boats, tunnels, and even submarines (see News Spot 14-2). In many jurisdictions, drug dealers are better armed than the police and in some jurisdictions they are better armed than the military.[29]

NEWS SPOT 14-2

Title: U.S. Probes for Drug Tunnel to Mexico
Source: *Associated Press*
Authors: Elliot Spagat
Date: April 14, 2004

CALEXICO, Calif. (AP)—The federal government began drilling holes Tuesday in this border town, searching for a tunnel it believes may be used to smuggle drugs from Mexico. But after seven hours of work, officials said they had come up empty.

With technology developed by geophysicists, the Department of Homeland Security identified the possible tunnel—two feet wide and about 15 feet below ground—two weeks ago.

On Tuesday, a giant drill plugged ten holes in a dirt road used by the Border Patrol. The crew reported a change in soil at about 14 feet and struck water at about 18 feet. They brought along a camera on a six-foot pole to scope underground.

But Lauren Mack, a spokeswoman for Homeland Security, said the crew by late Tuesday had found nothing amiss and tentatively concluded there was no drugtunnel in the area.

The offensive marked a shift in the government's efforts to locate the clandestine tunnels. Previously, agents have relied on human intelligence and sheer luck, such as when a Border Patrol agent on patrol in Calexico, about 120 miles east of San Diego, struck a sink hole in November.

Officials were mum on what kind of technology they used, saying they want to avoid tipping off smugglers. Calexico Police Chief Mario Sanchez said officials told him they used a sonic recording device.

U.S. and Mexican officials have discovered at least 10 cross-border tunnels since the Sept. 11, 2001, terror attacks prompted heightened security along the border.

U.S. officials said increased border enforcement may be forcing drug smugglers to be more creative. Each tunnel is estimated to cost between $800,000 and $1 million to build, said Misha Piastro, a spokesman for the Drug Enforcement Administration.

In Calexico, an arid town of about 30,000 people that abuts the large industrial Mexican city of Mexicali, city workers discovered an incomplete tunnel in September that zigzagged about 250 yards into a residential area.

Mexican authorities arrested four people where the tunnel allegedly originated in Mexicali. The suspected ringleader said he planned to rent the ventilated tunnel to a large drugsmuggling ring, according to investigators.

Questions to Ponder

1. **Drug traffickers have been known to use airplanes, speed boats, and submarines to smuggle drugs into the country and to hide drugs in clothing, food, and children's toys. There appears to be no limit to the ingenuity of the drug cartels when it comes to smuggling drugs into the United States. How else might a drug trafficker smuggle drugs across international borders?**
2. **What can U.S. Customs and Border Patrol officials do to combat the creativity and technology employed by drug smugglers?**
3. **If drug traffickers are capable of smuggling drugs into the country with relative ease, what is stopping terrorists from smuggling weapons of mass destruction across these same borders?**

Poverty

The poor may view the drug trade as a way of getting rich or in some situations, a means of survival. Survival for oneself and for one's family may literally apply to poor farmers in Colombia who grow the coca and poppy plants used to make cocaine and heroin, respectively. It is usually not a matter of physical survival in the United States, yet poor minority youth may start selling drugs in hopes of capturing the American dream of material wealth when other avenues of advancement seem closed off to them.[30]

America's "War on Drugs"

America has not always been obsessed with drugs or had a "War on Drugs." When then, did the war begin? Many people mistakenly believe that America's "War on Drugs" began in the late 1980s with the George Herbert Bush administration. Actually, America's current "War on Drugs" can be traced back to the Nixon administration and its roots extend all the way back to the 1914 Harrison Narcotics Tax Act. This section begins with a brief history of the "War on Drugs" and ends with a review of the war's current status.

History of America's "War on Drugs"

This summary of the history of America's "**War on Drugs**" is based on a number of sources, the three most prominent being Judge James Gray's book *Why Our Drug Laws Have Failed*,[31] James Inciardi's book *The War on Drugs*,[32] and a timeline of America's "War on Drugs" constructed by staff from National Public Radio and PBS's *Frontline* series.[33]

Harrison Act

The **Harrison Narcotics Tax Act** was passed on December 17, 1914 and went into effect on April 1, 1915. On the face of it, the Harrison Act was not a prohibition act but a simple attempt to license and/or tax **manufacturers**, importers, pharmacists, and physicians involved in manufacturing and prescribing opiate-based drugs like morphine.

> Nothing contained in this section shall apply … to the dispensing or distribution of any of the aforesaid drugs to a patient by a physician, dentist, or veterinary surgeon registered under this Act in the course of his professional practice only.[34]

There was a catch phrase in the law, however. The statement "in the course of his professional practice only" was interpreted by law enforcement to mean that doctors could not legally prescribe maintenance doses of opiates to "addicts" because addiction was not a disease and addicts were not patients. The medical profession soon learned that to prescribe opiates was to risk one's medical career. A number of physicians lost their medical licenses for being in violation of the reinterpreted Harrison act and a few were even jailed.[35]

Prohibition

Prohibition is the next major event leading up to the modern American "War on Drugs." Spurred by the temperance movement that grew in popularity over the course of the 19th century and then in political power during the first 2 decades of the 20th century, Congress passed the **Eighteenth Amendment** to the Constitution on December 16, 1917. The amendment, which outlawed the manufacture, sale, and transportation of liquor or intoxicating beverages within the borders of the United States, was fully ratified by the required 36 states by January 16, 1919. The Eighteenth Amendment was signed into law on January 16, 1920 and was enforced by the **Volstead Act** of October 1919.[36]

The Eighteenth Amendment was repealed on December 5, 1933 by the **Twenty-First Amendment**. The "noble experiment," as it was called, was driven, it would seem, more by politics than by concern for drug-using citizens.[37] The positive effects of Prohibition were that drinking declined slightly during the early stages of Prohibition and the death rate from liver cirrhosis was cut in half from its peak in 1907.[38] The negative effects included a rise in violent crime (see Figure 14-5),[39] expansion of organized crime, increased potency and decreased quality control of the alcohol that was consumed, and no real meaningful reduction in alcohol consumption over time (see Figure 14-6).[40–41]

Federal Bureau of Narcotics

The **Federal Bureau of Narcotics** (FBN) was founded in 1930. Under its director, Harry J. Anslinger, the FBN actively and fervently pursued the eradication of marijuana, cocaine, and opiates from the American landscape. It lobbied, often successfully, for harsh penalties, for both the distribution and use of drugs. The FBN attempted to strengthen the Harrison Act of 1914 and severely restrict the medical use of opiates and cocaine. It was also instrumental in pushing through the Marijuana Tax Act of 1937, which criminalized the use and sale of marijuana. Anslinger personally lobbied to get the Opium Poppy Control Act of 1942 passed in Congress and assigned agents to overseas offices in areas intimately involved in the manufacturing and distribution of opiate drugs (France, Turkey, Lebanon, Thailand).

Figure 14-5
Murder rate before, during, and after prohibition.

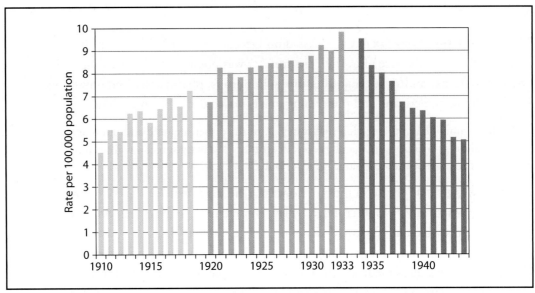

U.S. Bureau of the Census. (1975). *Historical statistics of the United States, colonial times to 1970.* Washington, DC: Government Printing Office.

Figure 14-6
Per capita consumption of alcoholic beverages in the United States (gallons of pure alcohol) before and during Prohibition.

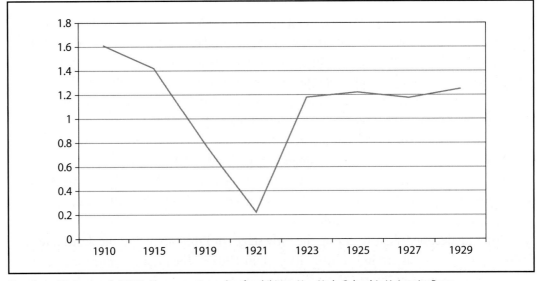

Data From: Warburton, C. (1932). *The economic results of prohibition.* New York: Columbia University Press.

The 1960s

The late 1960s was a period of social unrest and political upheaval. The women's movement was gaining momentum, racial conflict was at its peak, the generation gap had become a chasm, and the Vietnam War was raging. Drugs like marijuana and LSD became symbols of rebellion and nonconformity and those in charge viewed them as a threat. It was in this atmosphere that President Richard Nixon initiated the modern "War on Drugs" in America.

Nixon Administration

The opening salvo of the modern American "War on Drugs" was fired on June 17, 1971 when Richard Nixon officially declared a war on drugs. In his speech, Nixon characterized drugs as "public enemy number one." Two years later he created the Drug Enforcement

Administration. The image of Vietnam veterans returning home hooked on heroin is said to have played a major role in Nixon's decision. There are two versions of the GI heroin epidemic theory. First, the Nixon administration launched the "War on Drugs" to prevent a domestic crime wave by heroin-addicted military veterans. Second, the Nixon administration was concerned that heroin addiction among servicemen returning from Vietnam would undermine public support for the war.[42]

Carter Administration

In his 1976 campaign for President, Jimmy Carter ran on a platform of marijuana decriminalizaton and spoke about eliminating criminal penalties for possession of up to one ounce of marijuana. In a speech before Congress in 1977 Carter stated, "penalties against possession of a drug should not be more damaging to an individual than the use of the drug itself." There was very little change in actual government policy, however, and so it is probably most accurate to say that during Carter's watch, there was a modest deescalation in the "War on Drugs." Rapid reescalation would soon follow, however, with the election of Ronald Reagan.[43]

Reagan Administration

Even Ronald Reagan's most ardent supporters admit that the Reagan administration did virtually nothing to improve the drug situation in the United States and did a great deal to make it worse. The Reagan administration is not the only culpable party, however; Democrats in Congress went along with many of the missteps of the Reagan administration and must share in the blame. There were four areas, in particular, where the Reagan administration and Congress may have made things worse:[44]

1. Eroding the Posse Comitatus Act of 1868 that bans federal troops from domestic law enforcement duties.
2. Introducing the naïve "Just Say No" campaign and the exclusionary zero-tolerance policy.
3. Passing the 1986 crime bill, which created mandatory minimum sentences, eliminated parole, and led to a marked increase in sentence length for drug offenders.
4. Passing the 1988 Anti-Drug Abuse Act, which included a provision for a federal death penalty for "drug kingpins."

The First Bush Administration

The first Bush administration continued many of the policies of the Reagan administration and added a few new wrinkles of its own. First, the administration put pressure on the states to do more of the legwork in the "War on Drugs." States were threatened with loss or reduction in their federal highway funds if they did not abide by the federally recommended policy of revoking the driver's licenses of citizens convicted of drug crimes. Second, the goal of the "War on Drugs" was clearly defined as the immediate cessation of even casual drug use. There was a drop in middle-class cocaine use during Bush's presidency but drug use in the lower social classes increased. Third, the Bush administration emphasized **interdiction** to the detriment of **treatment** and research. Fourth, Bush appointed William

Bennett to be the first "drug czar" of the newly formed **Office of National Drug Control Policy** (ONDCP).

Clinton Administration

Compared to the two previous administrations, the Clinton administration was more aware of the problems associated with the "War on Drugs," yet did nothing to stop it. When Clinton's first Surgeon General, Dr. Jocelyn Elders, suggested that alternatives to drug prohibition should be "studied," she was promptly fired. Clinton sought to handle the "Drug War" with benign neglect but several policies inadvertently made things worse. First, NAFTA made it easier to smuggle drugs from Mexico into the United States. Second, Clinton deemphasized interdiction but then redirected the money to foreign governments (e.g., Colombia) in an attempt to combat drugs where they were produced, escalating the eradication programs in place at the time he took office and increasing the spraying of the coca and opium poppy fields in Colombia.

The Second Bush Administration

George W. Bush continued many of the policies of the previous three administrations, although he placed greater emphasis on treatment than previous Republican presidents. Reentry programs, increased funding for community and institutional corrections, and faith-based counseling were among the programs initiated or expanded during the second Bush administration.

The Obama Administration

The Obama administration has not deviated much from previous administrations in its handling of the "War on Drugs" other than to stop calling it a war. Like Clinton, Obama seems to be trying to distance himself from the drug prohibition issue without doing much to bring about change. Obama's drug czar, Gil Kerlikowske, indicated openness to rethinking the government's response to drugs and recommended an end to the nearly 40-year "War on Drugs." Yet, actual policy remains one of prohibition rather than of change and so the "War on Drugs" continues.[45]

Progress of the "War on Drugs"

Most scholars believe that America is either losing or has already lost the "War on Drugs." An international commission composed of high-ranking dignitaries, intellectuals, and former heads of state, the Global Commission on Drug Policy, in fact recently concluded that the worldwide war on drugs has failed miserably and should be replaced by an alternative approach.[46] Perhaps the best way to evaluate the progress and current status of America's "War on Drugs" is to take a look at the costs and benefits of this war, much as the commission did for the worldwide drug war, but with special reference to the situation in America.

Perceived Costs of the "War on Drugs"

A pie chart of the costs of illegal drugs, constructed by the Lewin group for the Office of National Drug Control Policy, is reproduced in **Figure 14-7**.[47] The entire expense of two

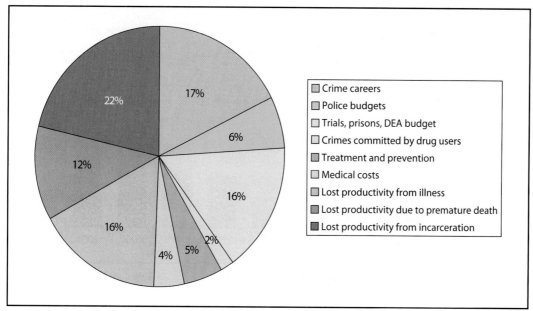

Figure 14-7
The costs of illegal drugs.

Crime careers
Police budgets
Trials, prisons, DEA budget
Crimes committed by drug users
Treatment and prevention
Medical costs
Lost productivity from illness
Lost productivity due to premature death
Lost productivity from incarceration

Data from the Lewin Group, 1998. Courtesy of the DEA.org.

categories from **Figure 14-7** can be considered the direct result of drug prohibition: Trials, prisons, and DEA (16%) and lost productivity from incarceration (21.3%). About three-quarters of the medical costs (diseases contracted from sharing infected needles) can be attributed to drug prohibition and failure to implement harm reduction policies: medical ($4 \times .75 = 3\%$). In addition, at least half the expense of three categories listed in **Figure 14-7** is a likely consequence of drug prohibition: police budgets ($6.4 \times .5 = 3.2\%$), crime careers ($17.4 \times .5 = 8.7\%$), and crimes committed by drug users ($1.7 \times .5 = 0.8\%$). Summing the percentages yields a figure of 53%, which represents a conservative estimate of the portion of the total cost of illegal drugs in the United States that is a direct result of drug prohibition. This translates into $95.9 billion in 2002, the last year a full analysis of the total cost of illegal drugs in the United States was conducted (total cost = $180.9 billion).

The perceived costs of the "War on Drugs" are both direct and indirect. Direct costs would be the cost of law enforcement and prisons to house drug offenders. A significant increase in the American prison population has taken place over the last 25 years. Passage of the 1986 crime bill, which provided for abolition of federal parole, mandatory minimum sentences for drug-related crimes, and increased prison time for drug offenders, ushered in a period of unprecedented prison growth. Starting in the late 1980s the prison population began to grow and it has continued to grow up until the present time. Increases in the total number of federal prisoners and the proportion of federal prisoners serving time for drug offenses between 1970 and 2004 is illustrated in **Figure 14-8**.[48] Indirect costs of drug prohibition include loss of revenue from taxes on illegal drugs and the corruption of police and public officials that occurs whenever large amounts of illegal money are available.

Perceived Benefits of the "War on Drugs"

Most of the perceived benefits of the "War on Drugs" hinge on the belief that prohibition significantly reduces usage and with it, some of the negative consequences of usage.

Figure 14-8
Number of inmates serving time in Federal Bureau of Prisons facilities for drug and nondrug offenses, 1970–2004.

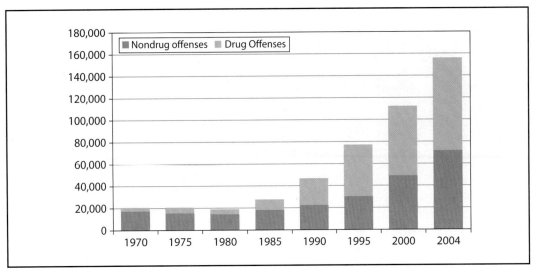

Data From: Bureau of Justice Statistics. (2005). *Sourcebook of criminal justice statistics, 2003*. Washington, DC: U.S. Department of Justice Table 6.57.

After **American Prohibition** went into effect in 1920, the drinking rate fell (see **Figure 14-6**). It is important to note, however, that drinking had been declining even before Prohibition went into effect and that it shot back up to pre-Prohibition levels several years into Prohibition. In the years following Prohibition's repeal, drinking rose slightly. **Decriminalization** of all drugs in Portugal led to a moderate increase in lifetime drug use but little change in what researchers consider better estimates of population drug use: recent use (last 12 months) and current use (last 30 days). In fact, recent use and current use both went down in the 15- to 24-year-old age group (see **Figure 14-9**).[49] Although Sweden, a country with a zero-tolerance drug policy, has a lower rate of drug use than most European countries, its rate of nonmarijuana drug use is comparable to the Netherlands, a country that has legalized marijuana, and Portugal, a country that has decriminalized all drugs; furthermore, all three countries have a much lower rate of drug use than the United States (see **Figure 14-10**).[50]

Whether longitudinal (Prohibition in the United States, decriminalization in Portugal) or cross-sectional (current comparisons between the United States and nonprohibition countries) data are brought to bear on the issue, there is little evidence that prohibition significantly reduces drug use in the overall population. Some policy-makers nonetheless insist that prohibition can have a beneficial effect on public health and crime. There was a dramatic drop in mortality from alcoholism and cirrhosis during the first several years of Prohibition.[51] However, this drop began during World War I (1914–1918) and carried over into the early years of Prohibition (1920–1933). In fact, the death rate from alcoholism had bottomed out by the time Prohibition went into effect and soon returned to pre-World War I levels. An increase in the consumption of more potent and poisonous alcoholic beverages like wood alcohol may have more than compensated for any reduction in drinking that occurred during Prohibition. Interestingly enough, alcohol-related mortality rates also dropped in Denmark, Ireland, and Great Britain during World War I and continued to drop through the decade of the 1920s even though none of these countries followed a policy of alcohol prohibition.[52]

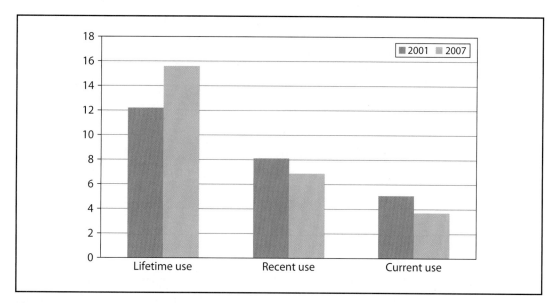

Figure 14-9
Prevalence of lifetime, recent, and current use of any illicit drugs by Portuguese citizens between the ages of 15 and 24, 2001 versus 2007.

Hughes, C. E., & Stevens, A. (2012). A resounding success or disastrous failure: Re-examining the interpretation of evidence on the Portuguese decriminalization of illicit drugs. *Drug and Alcohol Review, 31,* 101–113.

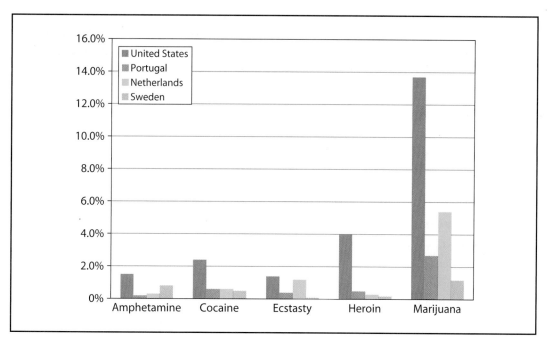

Figure 14-10
Annual prevalence of amphetamine, cocaine, ecstasy, heroin, and marijuana use in the United States, Portugal, Netherlands, and Sweden for general population individuals aged 15 to 64.

Data From: United Nations Office on Drugs and Crime (UNODC). (2011). *World drug report 2011.* New York: Author.

Whereas the evidence that prohibition promotes public health is weak, the notion that prohibition reduces crime is even weaker. In fact, most studies indicate that crime tends to rise in response to prohibition and drug law enforcement. This was certainly true of American Prohibition in the 1920s and early 1930s. During Prohibition, arrests for drunkenness and disorderly conduct rose 41%, arrests for drunk driving jumped 81%, thefts and burglaries increased by 9%, homicides and assault climbed 13%, the federal prison population grew

Figure 14-11
Costs (orange) and
benefits (blue) of
America's "War on
Drugs."

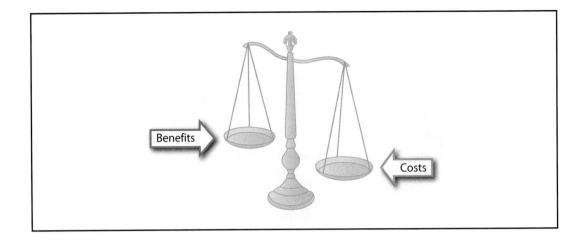

by 366%, and organized crime gained a powerful foothold.[53] In a review of studies on drug prohibition and crime, Dan Werb and colleagues discovered that 14 out of 15 studies (93%) revealed an adverse effect of drug law enforcement on drug market violence and 10 out of 11 longitudinal studies (91%) recorded a significant correlation between drug law enforcement and drug market violence.[54]

In weighing the costs and benefits of America's "War on Drugs" it would seem that the costs clearly outweigh the benefits (see **Figure 14-11**). This is consistent with the general belief among a wide cross-section of scholars, intellectuals, and policy-makers that the "War on Drugs" has been less than fully successful. Some have even questioned whether the war was ever designed to be won. In the final section of this chapter we consider several alternatives to America's "War on Drugs."

Alternatives to the "War on Drugs"

In searching for alternatives to America's "War on Drugs" we need to review basic economic principles. Like any commodity, illegal drugs respond to the laws of supply and demand. Whereas the **law of supply** proposes an inverse relationship between supply and price (as the supply goes down, the price goes up), the **law of demand** proposes a direct relationship between demand and price (as the demand goes up so too does the price). Dealing with the drug problem means restricting supply, reducing demand, or both. Consequently, there are two sets of strategies for dealing with the drug problem: supply-side strategies and demand-side strategies.

Supply-Side Strategies

Supply-side economic policies are based on three drug control strategies:

- Interdiction
- Eradication
- Incarceration

Interdiction

Interdiction means using law enforcement to keep the drugs out of the country. Even advocates of interdiction admit that the majority of drugs make it through to their intended destinations. Estimates are that only 8–15% of heroin shipments and 30% of cocaine shipments bound for the United States are intercepted before reaching their destination.[55] What that means is that 85–92% of heroin shipments and 70% of cocaine shipments make it into the country. Marijuana is bulkier than either cocaine or heroin, and as a result, is more difficult to smuggle and transport. Accordingly, the number of marijuana seizures is often greater than the number of cocaine or heroin seizures. The result has been a large increase in domestic marijuana production and a sizeable increase in the number of people cultivating indoors.[56] Even when large shipments of heroin and cocaine are seized, this simply increases the price of the drugs and the incentive for people to get involved in the transportation and selling of these drugs. The unit cost of cocaine is nearly twice as high in nations with strong prohibition policies as it is in nations with weak prohibition policies and the unit cost of heroin is three to four times higher in nations with strong as opposed to weak prohibition policies (see **Figure 14-12**).[57]

Eradication

Crop eradication programs in Colombia, Peru, and Bolivia have been moderately successful in destroying coca and poppy plants in the region. In 2001, crop eradication programs resulted in a 22% reduction in coca cultivation and a 67% reduction in opium poppy cultivation, with the greatest reductions occurring in Colombia. Even so, the region was able to produce 640 metric tons of cocaine and 3.8 metric tons of heroin in 2004. In addition, crop eradication programs pose certain ecological (crop damage from spray drift and rain forest destruction from **growers** moving further into the jungle to escape the spray planes) and political (farmers aligning with armed rebels against the government) risks.[58] Eradication programs in Afghanistan have also been successful, though their success has shifted the opium trade to Taliban-held areas not covered by eradication programs, and have thereby made these areas more financially stable than the rest of the country.[59]

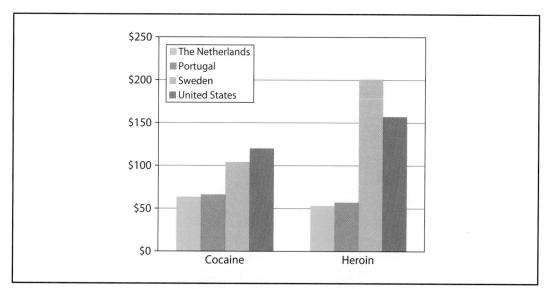

Figure 14-12
Unit cost (1 gram) of cocaine and heroin in U.S. dollars across four different nations.

Data From: United Nations Office on Drugs and Crime (UNODC). (2011). *World drug report 2011.* New York: Author.

Incarceration

The third prong of supply-side economic policies is incarceration. By locking up those who transport, deal, sell, and consume drugs we are reducing the supply of individuals who deliver drugs to others and we are theoretically preventing some individuals from using drugs. There are two problems with this strategy. First, as soon as a drug dealer is locked up, someone is there to take his or her place given how much money can be made selling drugs. Second, jailing and imprisoning drug users does not necessarily prevent them from using drugs because drugs can be found in jail and prison. What it will do, is make them more criminal and less able to fit back into society. The United States has the highest rate of **incarceration** of all the nations in the entire world (see **Figure 14-13**) but this has done little to stem the tide of drug use.[60] In a paper presented to the U.S. Commission on Civil Rights, Marc Mauer identified four reasons for the high U.S. incarceration rate, two of which relate directly to drug prohibition (2 and 4) and one of which relates indirectly to drug prohibition (3):[61]

1. More violent crime compared to other industrialized nations.
2. Harsher penalties, especially for property and drug crimes.
3. A shift in the 1980s toward determinate and mandatory sentencing, changes in early release policies (parole), decreased judicial discretion, and increased utilization of imprisonment as a sanction.
4. Policy changes relating directly to the "War on Drugs" whereby drug dealers and drug users have been incarcerated in state and federal prison in record numbers.

Demand-Side Strategies

Demand-side economic policies are also based on three drug control strategies:

- Education
- Treatment
- Deglamorization

Figure 14-13
Prisoners per 100,000 population in the United States and several other countries.

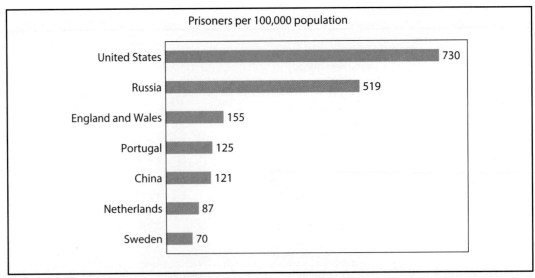

Data From: International Centre for Prison Studies. (2012). Entire world—Prison population rates per 100,000 of the national population. Retrieved on May 27, 2012 from http://www.prisonstudies.org/info/worldbrief/wpb_stats.php?area=all&category=wb_poprate.

Education

Experimentation with alcohol and tobacco is normative and experimenting with marijuana, although not normative, is fairly common among American adolescents.[62] Trying drugs is not, in and of itself, pathological or predictive of a future drug problem. What is predictive of a future drug problem is early initiation of drug use (< 16 years of age). If experimentation with substances, particularly illegal substances, can be delayed until mid- to late-adolescence then there is a much better chance that the individual will be able to avoid serious problems with drugs in the future.[63] **Skill-based education** is important because it is one of the best ways to reach adolescents.[64] If properly implemented, it can be successful as part of a larger program of primary or secondary prevention. Scare tactics and horror stories, however, should be avoided because they do not deter drug use nor do they delay the onset of drug experimentation. Furthermore, they run the risk of discrediting the source of the information to where adolescents begin ignoring even credible warnings about the dangers of drugs.[65]

Treatment

If properly conceptualized, organized, and implemented, treatment can reduce drug abuse as well as crime. Proper conceptualization means that the intervention is behavioral or cognitive-behavioral in nature (general responsivity). Proper organization means that it focuses on moderate- to high-risk individuals (risk principle) and targets criminogenic needs (needs principle). Proper implementation means that the intervention is conducted in a manner consistent with the intentions of the program developers and that treatment staff are afforded adequate training and supervision (fidelity principle). To the extent that harm reduction techniques encourage people to enter treatment, they are also an important feature of proper treatment conceptualization, organization, and implementation.[66–69]

American officials often use Sweden, with its zero-tolerance policy toward drug use, as a model of what can be accomplished with prohibition (namely, low drug use and low crime). The problem with using Sweden as a benchmark for U.S. drug policy is that there are a number of cultural, demographic, geographic, and sociopolitical differences between the two nations that make a direct comparative analysis difficult. Moreover, when Peter Reuter compared the amount of money (in Euros) that the United States and Sweden spent on drug enforcement and drug treatment in 2002, he discovered that Sweden spent twice as much on law enforcement and five times as much on drug treatment as the United States (see **Figure 14-14**). Proportionally, Sweden devoted twice as much of its drug budget to treatment as did the United States (see **Figure 14-15**).[70]

Deglamorization

In his book, *Why Our Drug Laws Have Failed*, Judge Gray emphasizes **deglamorization** as a means of reducing the demand for drugs.[71] Taking the glamour out of drugs starts by determining why drug use is viewed as glamorous in the first place. It is glamorous because

Figure 14-14
Amount of money (in Euros) spent per problem drug user in 2002 by the United States and Sweden for drug enforcement and drug treatment.

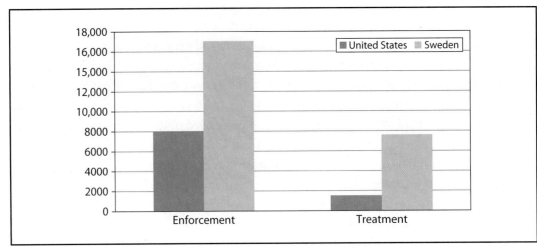

Data From: Reuter, P. (2006). What drug policies cost: Estimating government drug policy expenditures. *Addiction, 101,* 315–322.

Figure 14-15
Proportion of money (in Euros) spent per problem drug user in 2002 on drug enforcement versus drug treatment in Sweden and the United States.

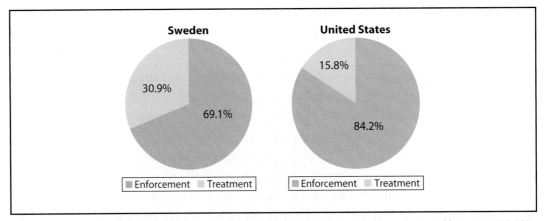

Data From: Reuter, P. (2006). What drug policies cost: Estimating government drug policy expenditures. *Addiction, 101,* 315–322.

friends do it, famous people do it, and it is forbidden (illegal). Taking the glamour out of drugs consequently requires:

- Good primary and secondary prevention programs that highlight the genuine problems with drugs, correct misperceptions about how often illegal drugs are used, and employ positive peer role models.
- Greater media responsibility in how alcohol and drugs are depicted and honest reporting about the dangers of both.
- Serious study on the ramifications of decriminalizing and legalizing drugs.

Deglamorization may have taken place in a study previously described where several Canadian heroin addicts who had emigrated to England to take advantage of a heroin prescription program returned to Canada within a few years because they missed the illegal drug lifestyle.[72]

Supply versus Demand

The vast majority of money in America's "War on Drugs" goes to supply-side strategies (interdiction, eradication, incarceration). By restricting supply, the price goes up, as does the incentive to become involved in the drug trade because it is so lucrative. Every time a shipment is seized, every time a coca field is sprayed, every time a drug dealer is incarcerated, it increases the profit for those shipments that make it through, those fields that are not sprayed, and those drug dealers who are not incarcerated. There seems to be no winning when the emphasis is on supply-side economics. Demand-side economics, on the other hand, appear to hold a great deal more promise. Reducing demand through education, treatment, and deglamorization will drive the price of illegal drugs down, thereby making the production, trafficking, and sale of drugs less lucrative and the risk of selling drugs not worth the anticipated benefits in many people's minds.

Perspectives on Drug Control

There are three major perspectives on drug control:

- Prohibition—imposition of criminal penalties for the sale, possession, and use of drugs
- Decriminalization—replacing criminal sanctions with fines or treatment for drug users, while maintaining criminal penalties for selling and trafficking drugs
- Legalization—repeal of laws against selling, possessing, and using drugs

Although a few countries abide by a single perspective (e.g., prohibition in some Muslim countries), most countries adopt a mixed approach to drug control. In the United States, for instance, alcohol and tobacco are legal, marijuana has been decriminalized in several states, and cocaine and heroin are prohibited except when prescribed by a physician.

Arguments for Prohibition (and against Decriminalization/Legalization)

- Prohibition reduces drug use
  - In an Australian study, 29% of those who had never used cannabis listed the illegality of marijuana as one of the reasons for not using the drug, and 19% of a group of former cannabis users cited illegality as a reason for their decision to stop using marijuana. The authors of this study, Don Weatherburn and Craig Jones, conclude that although prohibition may discourage drug use in some individuals, most people are deterred from using marijuana for reasons other than its illegality.[73] It should be noted that this study asked only about marijuana; it would seem likely that even fewer people avoid using harder drugs like cocaine and heroin simply because they are illegal.
  - Research conducted on American Prohibition[74] and postdecriminalization Portugal[75] suggests that any increase in drug use following the lifting of prohibition is modest at best.
- Prohibition protects health and lowers healthcare costs.
  - There is some evidence that health improved during the early stages of American Prohibition but that as more people began using harmful alcohol substitutes (e.g., wood alcohol) the health benefits quickly dissipated.[76]
- Prohibition protects society from drug-related crime and violence.
  - Research reviewed in this chapter clearly demonstrates that prohibition is associated with higher rather than lower rates of drug-related crime and violence.
- Prohibition is the morally correct thing to do.

■ This may or may not be true, but is trying to protect people from themselves a legitimate function of government? Even Ronald Reagan didn't think so.[77]

Arguments against Prohibition (and for Decriminalization/Legalization)

- Decriminalization/**legalization** may increase drug use temporarily but there are other benefits that potentially outweigh the small rise in drug use associated with increased availability through legalization/decriminalization.
  - ■ Greater quality control reduces health-related problems.
  - ■ Drug-related crime and violence are reduced.
  - ■ Revenue from taxes increases.
- Prohibition creates a strong supply vacuum via incarceration; a vacuum that is rapidly filled by new recruits who figure the reward is worth the risk.
- Prohibition draws children into the drug trade because dealers reason that the authorities will not punish a child as severely as they would an adult.
- Prohibition corrupts police and public officials because of all the money that is available to drug kingpins, traffickers, dealers, and sellers.

The Successive Approximations Approach

A complement to the mixed perspective on drug control is the **successive approximations** approach to drug decriminalization/legalization proposed by Ethan Nadelmann. The successive approximations approach begins by rank ordering currently illegal drugs by level of perceived hazard or dangerousness and then legalizing or decriminalizing the drug with the lowest perceived hazard. After a period of evaluation and adjustment the next least hazardous drug is decriminalized or legalized and the results evaluated and the procedures adjusted. The process continues to the point of diminishing returns whereby no further perceived benefit is anticipated.[78] Decriminalization would seem a safer bet than legalization, at least initially, because we have little recent experience with jurisdictions that have legalized drugs (except, of course, for marijuana legalization in the Netherlands). Legalization of at least some drugs, however, may be advisable after successful decriminalization in order to remove the incentive for drug trafficking and dealing.

Summary and Conclusions

- Drug trafficking networks range from local to international. These networks, though hierarchically organized, are fluid, particularly at the lower levels, where individuals move into and out of the network on a fairly regular basis. Individuals functioning at the higher levels of a drug trafficking hierarchy attempt to insulate themselves from arrest by limiting their contact with those at the lower levels of the hierarchy who are at the greatest risk of coming into contact with the police.
- America's current "War on Drugs" officially began during the Nixon administration but has its roots in the Harrison Narcotics Tax Act of 1914. A review of existing evidence suggests that the "War on Drugs" has been ineffective in reducing both drug

use and drug-related problems. In fact, some problems, such as drug-related crime, appear to have been aggravated by the "War on Drugs."

- In an attempt to find an alternative to the "War on Drugs," supply-side economic strategies (interdiction, eradication, incarceration) and demand-side economic strategies (education, treatment, deglamorization) were compared and contrasted. Three perspectives on crime control (prohibition, decriminalization, legalization) were also examined. Results indicated that demand-side strategies may be more useful than supply-side strategies in controlling drug use and abuse.

Key Terms

American Prohibition   With passage of the Eighteenth Amendment, outlawed the manufacture, distribution, and sale of alcoholic beverages.

Conspiracy/Bureaucratic Model   Postulates that drug distribution networks constitute well-defined hierarchies of distributional relationships.

Cosa Nostra   Italian-American criminal society also known as the American Mafia.

Dealer   Middle manager in the drug trade who works for a wholesale distributor and supervises a group of sellers; also referred to as a crew boss.

Decriminalization   Replacing criminal sanctions with fines or treatment for drug users, while maintaining the illegality of drug sales and trafficking.

Deglamorization   Demand-side strategy designed to reduce the demand for drugs by reducing the glamour associated with drug use.

Drug Cartel   Criminal organization whose primary purpose is the transportation and distribution of illegal drugs.

Drug Distribution Network   Loose organization of individuals involved in the manufacturing, transportation, and/or distribution of illegal drugs.

Drug Enforcement Administration   Federal law enforcement agency responsible for making drug cases inside the United States and keeping drugs from entering the country.

Drug Mule   Low-level drug trafficker who smuggles drugs on his or her person (by wearing or swallowing the drug), luggage, or automobile.

Drug Trade Hub   Country or jurisdiction through which drugs travel and where drugs are often stored.

Eighteenth Amendment   Amendment to the U.S. Constitution outlawing the manufacture, distribution, and sale of alcoholic beverages.

Enterprise/Cottage Industry Model   Postulates that drug distribution networks constitute a loosely connected group of fluid distributional relationships.

Eradication   Supply-side strategy designed to reduce supply by destroying plants and closing down laboratories from which drugs are grown and manufactured.

Federal Bureau of Narcotics   U.S. federal law enforcement agency founded in 1930 and tasked with controlling illegal drugs.

Globalization   International integration of worldwide resources.

Golden Crescent   Area in central Asia known for heroin production; Afghanistan and Pakistan in particular.

Golden Triangle   Area in Southeast Asia known for heroin production; includes Burma, Thailand, Laos, and Vietnam.

Grower   Individual who raises the marijuana, coca, or opium poppy plants used to make illegal drugs.

Harrison Narcotics Tax Act   1914 act originally designed for licensing and taxation purposes but progressively used by law enforcement to keep physicians from prescribing drugs like morphine and cocaine.

Incarceration   Supply-side strategy designed to reduce supply by incarcerating drug dealers and users.

Interdiction   Supply-side strategy designed to reduce supply by attempting to keep drugs from entering the country.

Law of Demand   Proposes a direct relationship between the demand for a commodity and its price; as the demand for drugs goes up, so too does the price of drugs.

Law of Supply   Proposes an inverse relationship between the supply of a commodity and its price; as the supply of drugs goes down, the price of drugs goes up.

Legalization   Repeal of laws prohibiting the distribution, transportation, and use of drugs.

Low-Level Distributor   Worker at the lowest level of the drug distribution hierarchy who serves as a runner, lookout, bagger, holder, guard, or taster.

Manufacturer   Individual who either manufactures the marijuana, coca, or opium poppy plant into a usable drug or chemically creates a drug like LSD or amphetamine.

Money Laundering   Process by which money obtained illegally is "washed" for the purpose of concealing its origin.

Office of National Drug Control Policy   Executive branch office designed to establish policy, priorities, and objectives for the purpose of eradicating illegal drug use and abuse.

Prohibition   Imposition of criminal penalties for the sale, possession, and use of drugs.

Regional Distributor   Individual responsible for cutting the drugs with other substances and packaging the drug in unit dosage bags; also referred to as a weight dealer.

Retail Store Owner   Supplies or manages a crack house, shooting gallery, or drug store.

Seller   Individual who actually sells drugs to customers either in a set location (crack house) or territory (salesman).

Skill-Based Education   Demand-side strategy designed to reduce the demand for drugs by providing accurate information through evidence-based primary and second prevention programs.

Successive Approximations   Program for decriminalizing and legalizing drugs by selecting the least dangerous illegal drug for decriminalization/legalization and continuing the process using feedback from previous attempts until a point of diminishing returns is reached.

Trafficker   Individual responsible for transporting a drug from one location to another.

Treatment   Demand-side strategy designed to reduce the demand for drugs by alleviating drug problems through evidence-based treatment.

Twenty-First Amendment   Repealed the Eighteenth Amendment and Prohibition.

Volstead Act   Legislation that gave law enforcement the power to enforce Prohibition and laid out penalties for violations of Prohibition.

"War on Drugs"   Formal program of drug prohibition, that began in the United States during the Nixon administration and has been supported by every administration since.

Wholesale Distributor   Transports and redistributes multikilogram amounts of a drug.

Critical Thinking

1. If you were police commissioner how would you go about setting up your drug task force?
2. Do you think there is a chance that the United States will ever win the "War on Drugs?" Why or why not?
3. Compare and contrast supply-side economic strategies with demand-side economic strategies for dealing with illegal drugs. Which do you think has the better chance of succeeding?

Notes

1. Central Intelligence Agency. (2000). *Major narco trafficking routes and crop areas*. Retrieved October 20, 2012, from http://www.pbs.org/wgbh/pages/frontline/shows/drugs/business/map.html.
2. Gettman, J. (2006). Marijuana production in the United States. *Bulletin of Cannabis Reform*, Issue 2. Retrieved October 2, 2012, from http://www.drugscience.org/Archive/bcr2/bcr2_index.html.
3. Drug Enforcement Administration. (2003). *LSD in the United States*. Retrieved May 25, 2012, from http://www.egodeath.com/lsdus.htm.
4. Drug Enforcement Administration. (2007, March 22). *Drug threats and enforcement challenges* [DEA Congressional Testimony].
5. United Nations Office on Drugs and Crime (UNODC). (2011). *World drug report 2011*. New York: Author.
6. Drug Enforcement Administration. (2004). *Drug trafficking in the United States*.
7. Johnson, B. D., Dunlap, E., & Tourigny, S. C. (2000). Crack distribution and abuse in New York. In M. Natarajan & M. Hough (Eds.), *Illegal drug markets: From research to policy* (Crime Prevention Studies, Vol. 11, pp. 19–57). Monsey, NY: Criminal Justice Press.
8. Natarajan, M. (2000). Understanding the structure of a drug trafficking organization: A conversational analysis. In M. Natarajan & M. Hough (Eds.), *Illegal drug markets: From research to policy* (Crime Prevention Studies, Vol. 11. pp. 273–298). Monsey, NY: Criminal Justice Press.
9. Eck, J., & Gersh, J. S. (2000). Drug trafficking as a cottage industry. In M. Natarajan & M. Hough (Eds.), *Illegal drug markets: From research to policy* (Crime Prevention Studies, Vol. 11, pp. 241–271). Monsey, NY: Criminal Justice Press.
10. Jacobs, J. B., & Gouldin, L. P. (1999). Cosa Nostra: The final chapter? In M. Tonry (Ed.), *Crime and justice: A review of research* (Vol. 25, pp. 129–189). Chicago, IL: University of Chicago Press.

11. Werb, D., Bourchard, M., Kerra, T., Shoveller, J., Qia, J., Montaner, J., et al. (2011). Drug dealing cessation among a cohort of drug users in Vancouver, Canada. *Drug and Alcohol Dependence, 118,* 459–463.

12. Anglin, M. D., & Speckart, G. (1986). Narcotics use, property crime, and dealing: Structural dynamics across the addiction career. *Journal of Quantitative Criminology, 2,* 355–375.

13. Gettman (2006).

14. DEA (2004).

15. Drug Enforcement Administration. (2005, November 9). *The illicit drug transit zone in central America* [DEA Congressional Testimony]. Retrieved on October 20, 2012 from http://commdocs.house.gov/committees/intlrel/hfa24517.000/hfa24517_0f.htm.

16. Bourgois, P., & Schonberg, J. (2009). *Righteous dopefiend.* Berkeley, CA: University of California Press.

17. Abadinsky, H. (2010). *Organized crime* (9th ed.). Belmont, CA: Thomson/Wadsworth Learning.

18. Grillo, I. (2011). *El narco: Inside Mexico's criminal insurgency.* New York: St. Martin's Press.

19. UNODC (2011).

20. Webb, G. (1998). *Dark alliance: The CIA, the Contras, and the crack cocaine explosion.* New York: Seven Stories Press.

21. Goode, E. (2012). *Drugs in American society* (8th ed.). New York: McGraw-Hill.

22. Abadinsky (2010).

23. Paoli, L. (2002). The price of freedom: Illegal drug markets and polices in post-Soviet Russia. *Annals of the American Academy of Political and Social Science, 582,* 167–180.

24. Federation of American Scientists (FAS). (2012). *International crime threat assessment: Drug trafficking.* Retrieved May 25, 2012, from http://www.fas.org/irp/threat/pub45270chap2.html#3.

25. Ehlers, S. (1998). *Drug trafficking and money laundering.* Washington, DC: Foreign Policy in Focus. Retrieved May 25, 2012, from http://www.fpif.org/reports/drug_trafficking_and_money_laundering.

26. FAS (2012).

27. Karofi, U. A., & Mwanza, J. (2006). Globalisation and crime. *Bangladesh e-Journal of Sociology, 3*(1).

28. Costa Storti, C., & De Grauwe, P. (2009). The cocaine and heroin markets in the era of globalisation and drug reduction policies. *International Journal of Drug Policy, 20,* 488–496.

29. Grillo (2011).

30. Berg, C., & Gerhardus, B. (2003). *Drugs and poverty: The contribution of development-oriented drug control to poverty reduction.* Eschborn, Germany: Drugs and Development Programme, Poverty Reduction Project.

31. Gray, J. (2001). *Why our drug laws have failed: A judicial indictment of war on drugs.* Philadelphia, PA: Temple University Press.

32. Inciardi, J. A. (2007). *The War on Drugs IV: Continuing saga of the mysteries and miseries of intoxication, addiction, crime, and public policy* (4th ed.). Boston: Allyn & Bacon.

33. National Public Radio. (2007, April 2). *Timeline: America's War on Drugs.* Retrieved May 25, 2012, from http://www.npr.org/templates/story/story.php?storyId=9252490.

34. Harrison Act, P. L. 223, Sec 2(a), 63rd Cong., December 17, 1914.

35. Musto, D. F. (2008). *Drugs in America: A documentary history.* New York: NYU Press.

36. Musto (2008).

37. Behr, E. (1996). *Prohibition: Thirteen years that changed America.* New York: Arcade.

38. Musto (2008).

39. U.S. Bureau of the Census. (1975). *Historical statistics of the United States, colonial times to 1970.* Washington, DC: Government Printing Office.

40. Thornton, M. (1991). Alcohol prohibition was a failure. *Cato Institute Policy Analysis* (No. 157). Washington, DC: Cato Institute.

41. Warburton, C. (1932). *The economic results of prohibition.* New York: Columbia University Press.

42. Hickman, J. (2011, March 26). Nixon's war on drugs decision. Retrieved May 26, 2012, from http://likethedew.com/2011/03/26/nixon%E2%80%99s-war-on-drugs-decision-2/.

43. Musto, D. F., & Korsmeyer, P. (2002). *The quest for drug control: Politics and federal policy in a period of increasing substance abuse*. New Haven, CT: Yale University Press.

44. Merritt, J. (2004, June 18). Reagan's drug war legacy. *AlterNet*. Retrieved May 26, 2012, from http://www.alternet.org/drugs/18990/.

45. Frazier, M. (2012, April 15). Obama's disingenuous war on drugs. *The Daily Beast*. Retrieved May 26, 2012, from http://www.thedailybeast.com/articles/2012/04/15/obama-s-disingenuous-war-on-drugs.html.

46. Global Commission on Drug Policy. (2011, June). *War on drugs: Report of the Global Commission on Drug Policy*. Geneva: Author.

47. Office of National Drug Control Policy. (2001). *The economic costs of drug abuse in the United States, 1992–1998* (Publication No. NCJ-190636). Washington, DC: Executive Office of the President

48. Bureau of Justice Statistics. (2005). *Sourcebook of criminal justice statistics, 2003*. Washington, DC: U.S. Department of Justice.

49. Hughes, C. E., & Stevens, A. (2012). A resounding success or disastrous failure: Reexamining the interpretation of evidence on the Portuguese decriminalization of illicit drugs. *Drug and Alcohol Review, 31*, 101–113.

50. UNODC (2011).

51. Musto (2008).

52. Thornton (1991).

53. Thornton (1991).

54. Werb, D., Rowell, G., Guyatt, G., Kerra, T., Montaner, J., & Wood, E. (2011). Effect of drug law enforcement on drug market violence: A systematic review. *International Journal of Drug Policy, 22*, 87–94.

55. United Nations. (1997). *World drug report*. New York: Oxford University Press.

56. DEA (2007).

57. UNODC (2011).

58. Veillette, C., & Navarrete-Frías, C. (2005, November 18). *Report to Congress: Drug crop eradication and alternative development in the Andes* (Order Code RL33163). Washington, DC: Congressional Research Service, Library of Congress.

59. United Nations Office of Drugs and Crime (UNODC). (2012). *Afghanistan opium survey 2011*. New York: Author.

60. International Centre for Prison Studies. (2012). Entire world—Prison population rates per 100,000 of the national population. Retrieved May 27, 2012, from http://www.prisonstudies.org/info/worldbrief/wpb_stats.php?area=all&category=wb_poprate.

61. Mauer, M. (2003). *Comparative international rates of incarceration: An examination of causes and trends*. Washington, DC: The Sentencing Project.

62. Johnston, L. D., O'Malley, P. M., Bachman, J. G., & Schulenberg, J. E. (2011). *Monitoring the future: 1975–2010* (Vols. 1–2). Ann Arbor, MI: Institute for Social Research, University of Michigan.

63. Griffin, K. W., Bang, H., & Botvin, G. J. (2010). Age of alcohol and marijuana use onset predicts weekly substance use and related psychosocial problems during young adulthood. *Journal of Substance Use, 15*, 174–183.

64. Donaldson, S. I., Graham, J. W., & Hansen, W. B. (1994). Testing the generalizability of intervening mechanism theories: Understanding the effects of adolescent drug use prevention interventions. *Journal of Behavioral Medicine, 17*, 195–216.

65. Brown, S., & Locker, E. (2009). Defensive responses to an emotive anti-alcohol message. *Psychology & Health, 24*, 517–528.

66. DeBeck, K., Buxton, J., Kerr, T., Qi, J., Montaner, J., & Wood, E. (2011). Public crack cocaine smoking and willingness to use a supervised inhalation facility: Implications for street disorder. *Substance Abuse Treatment, Prevention, and Policy, 6*, 4.

67. Perneger, T. V., Giner, F., del Rio, M., & Mino, A. (1998). Randomised trial of heroin maintenance programme for addicts who fail in conventional drug treatments. *British Medical Journal, 317,* 13–18.

68. Witkiewitz, K., & Marlatt, G. A. (2006). Overview of harm reduction treatments for alcohol problems. *International Journal of Drug Policy, 17,* 285–294.

69. Wright, N. M. J., & Tompkins, C. N. E. (2004). Supervised injecting centres. *British Medical Journal, 328,* 100–102.

70. Reuter, P. (2006). What drug policies cost: Estimating government drug policy expenditures. *Addiction, 101,* 315–322.

71. Gray (2001).

72. Spear, H. B., & Glatt, M. M. (1971). The influence of Canadian addicts on heroin addiction in the United Kingdom. *British Journal of Addiction, 66,* 141–149.

73. Weatherburn, D., & Jones, C. (2001, August). Does prohibition deter cannabis use? *Bureau of Crime Statistics and Research.* Retrieved May 27, 2012, from http://www.cannabislegal.de/studien/nsw/b58.htm.

74. Thornton (1991).

75. Hughes & Stevens (2012).

76. Miron, J. A., & Zwiebel, J. (1991). Alcohol consumption during prohibition. *American Economic Review, 81,* 242–247.

77. Klausner, M. (1975, July). Inside Ronald Reagan: A Reason interview. Retrieved May 28, 2012, from http://reason.com/archives/1975/07/01/inside-ronald-reagan/singlepage.

78. Nadelmann, E. A. (1991). The case for legalization. In J. A. Inciardi (Ed.), *The drug legalization debate* (Vol. 7, pp. 17–44). Thousand Oaks, CA: Sage.

CHAPTER 15

THE FUTURE OF DRUG–CRIME RELATIONSHIPS

© Monkey Business Images/ShutterStock, Inc.

In an attempt to tie up loose ends from previous chapters, this final chapter on drugs, crime, and their relationships offers general comments and conclusions organized around the four parts into which this book was originally divided: theory, research, practice, and policy. The objectives of this final chapter are as follows:

- Review the characteristics of an effective theory of drug–crime relationships
- Understand the nature and empirical status of drug–crime relationships
- Provide general clinical guidelines for working with drug-involved offenders
- Examine the unintended consequences of drug prohibition

Characteristics of an Ideal Theory of Drug–Crime Relationships

As the reader may recall, there were four criteria against which the six drug theories, the six crime theories, and the two bidirectional theories were evaluated: comprehensiveness, parsimony, precision, and fruitfulness. A summary of how each of the 14 theories measured up on these four criteria is provided in **Table 15-1**. It should be clear from a cursory review of this table that none of the 14 theories constitutes an ideal theory or even an excellent theory of drug–crime relationships, though each has certain strengths that to some extent compensate for the weaknesses. Our search for an ideal theory of drug–crime relationships begins with efforts to expand the four criteria of a useful theory.

Comprehensiveness

A theory should cover a sufficient breadth of information in the area of interest to be considered comprehensive. The three theories rated as highly comprehensive in **Table 15-1** are the age-graded theory of crime, the biosocial theory of crime, and Thornberry's interactional theory. What these theories have in common is antipathy toward single variable explanations of complex behaviors like drug use, crime, and the drug–crime connection.

Table 15-1 Summary of Current Status of the Six Drug (Light Blue), Six Crime (Dark Blue), and Two Bidirectional (Purple) Theories

Theory	Comprehensiveness	Parsimony	Precision	Fruitfulness
Disease Model	L	H	L	L
Unified Biosocial	L	M	M	M
Cross-Cultural	M	H	L	L
Self-Medication	L	H	L	M
Gateway Theory	M	L	M	H
Social Learning	M	M	L	H
Psychopathy	L	L	H	M
Low Self-Control	M	H	L	H
Dev. Taxonomy	M	M	L	H
Age-Graded	H	L	M	M
Biosocial Theory	H	M	L	L
Social Learning	M	M	L	M
Interactional Theory	H	M	M	L
Overlapping Lifestyles	M	M	H	L

Unfortunately, single-variable theories have dominated both the drug abuse and criminology fields. The notion that genetics alone account for drug abuse or that crime is primarily a function of social structure are the kinds of noncomprehensive theories we want to avoid in our efforts to construct an ideal theory of drug–crime relationships.

Reciprocity or bidirectionality of relationships is a notion capable of improving the **comprehensiveness** of a theory by providing a network of reciprocating effects within which multiple variables interact. Six of the 14 theories evaluated in this book emphasize reciprocal relationships (age-graded theory of crime, biosocial theory of crime, the social learning theory of drug abuse, the social learning theory of crime, Thornberry's interactional theory, and overlapping lifestyles theory). Not unexpectedly, each of these theories received ratings of moderate to high comprehensiveness. An ideal theory of drug–crime relationships should accordingly avoid single variable explanations and emphasize bidirectional and reciprocal relationships, effects, and influences.

Parsimony

A useful theory should also be parsimonious, meaning that it should keep assumptions, postulates, and concepts to a minimum. The disease model of addiction, the cross-cultural theory of drug abuse, the self-medication hypothesis of drug abuse, and the low self-control theory of crime all received high marks on parsimony. Each of these theories keeps assumptions, postulates, and concepts to a minimum, but one way this is achieved is by focusing on single variables. This is how the disease model of addiction achieves maximum **parsimony** and is largely responsible for the high marks Gottfredson and Hirchi''s self-control theory of crime and the self-medication hypothesis of drug abuse received for parsimony. Parsimony and comprehensiveness are often at cross-purposes. How, then, can a proper balance be struck between parsimony and comprehensiveness?

I would argue that the best way to achieve balance between parsimony and comprehensiveness is to redefine parsimony as more a matter of **practicality** than of the number of postulates in a theory. A practical theory is, in effect, a parsimonious theory. Although it is important to keep postulates and concepts to a manageable number, a handful of postulates and concepts is often insufficient to adequately explain a phenomenon as complex as drug abuse or crime. By focusing on practicality or applicability to clinical situations (assessment, classification, supervision, intervention) we can see that an ideal theory of drug–crime relationships is one that is uncomplicated and practical enough to be meaningfully applied by criminal justice professionals and clinicians across a range of situations.

Precision

A useful theory is also a precise theory. **Precision** means that important variables are operationally and behaviorally defined. Only 2 of 14 theories reviewed in **Table 15-1** received high ratings on the precision criterion, whereas over half the theories were rated as low in precision. The two theories rated highest on precision were Hare's psychopathy model and the overlapping lifestyles model. What these two theories have in common is strong methodology in terms of validated measures that have been developed to assess constructs central to each theory. The Hare Psychopathy Checklist-Revised (PCL-R) provides an operational definition of psychopathy in Hare's model and the Lifestyle Criminality Screening Form and Psychological Inventory of Criminal Thinking Styles (PICTS) provide operational definitions of criminal lifestyle behavior and thinking, respectively, in the overlapping lifestyles model.

In deriving a maximally precise ideal theory of drug–crime relationships we need to pay close attention to instrumentation. One of the most frequently voiced criticisms of Gottfredson and Hirschi's self-control theory of crime is a lack of precision as to what constitutes low self-control. The measure most often used in research on low self-control, Grasmick et al.'s self-report low self-control scale,[1] is actually a weak representation of the behavioral measures that Gottfredson and Hirschi believe provide the most accurate estimate of low self-control. Unfortunately, they have neither developed nor identified a practical measure that meets their specifications. An ideal theory of drug–crime relationships consequently requires strong **instrumentation** in the form of a well-developed measure that possesses sufficient psychometric reliability and validity.

Fruitfulness

A useful theory stimulates interest and research. This is commonly referred to as **fruitfulness**. Four of the 14 theories were rated high on fruitfulness: the gateway theory of drug abuse, the social learning theory of drug abuse, the self-control theory of crime, and Moffitt's developmental taxonomy. Each of these theories has attracted the attention of researchers, clinicians, policymakers, or all three. The gateway theory of drug abuse is a driving force behind drug prohibition policies in the United States and other countries. Social learning theory is the foundation of some of the most effective clinical interventions for substance abuse.[2] Self-control theory is currently the most heavily researched theory in the field of criminology.[3] Moffitt's developmental taxonomy has drawn interest from researchers, clinicians, and policymakers alike.[4]

Just because a theory is fruitful, however, does not mean that it is valid. Much of the research conducted on gateway theory by researchers not affiliated with the theory has generated minimal support for core tenets, postulates, and assumptions.[5] In addition, aspects of Moffitt's theory, such as the assumption of categorical latent structure, have not been supported in several recent taxometric investigations.[6–7] On the other hand, some of the theories that received low ratings on fruitfulness in **Table 15-1** (biosocial theory of crime, interactional theory, overlapping lifestyles model) are new and have not yet been sufficiently tested by outside researchers. An ideal theory of drug–crime relationships is therefore not only fruitful but also evidence based, which means that the majority of research conducted on the theory supports the theory's underlying tenets.

Theoretical Overview

An ideal theory of drug–crime relationships is just that, an ideal that will never be fully realized. Such a concept is nonetheless useful because it can serve as a goal for theory development. An ideal theory of drug–crime relationships is one that is comprehensive and emphasizes reciprocal relationships between variables, keeps to a manageable number of postulates and is sufficiently uncomplicated to be applied to real-life situations, uses behaviorally and operationally defined terms and measures, and is both fruitful and evidence based. Future theoretical development in the field of drug–crime relationships depends on our ability to realize or at least approach these four ideals in our conceptualization of drugs, crime, and their relationships.

Research Foundations of Drug–Crime Relationships

As has been stated throughout this book, beginning with the preface, there is no single drug–crime relationship, but rather, multiple drug–crime relationships. At least eight such relationships have been identified in this book, each of which is reviewed here under the following subheadings: direct relationships and indirect relationships.

Direct Relationships

Direct relationships between drugs and crime can either be unidirectional or bidirectional.

Unidirectional Effects

There are two possible **unidirectional effects**: drugs cause crime or crime causes drugs (see **Figure 15-1**, panel a). An example of drugs causing crime would be a heroin addict who shoplifts in order to get money to buy drugs. When examining drugs-causing-crime

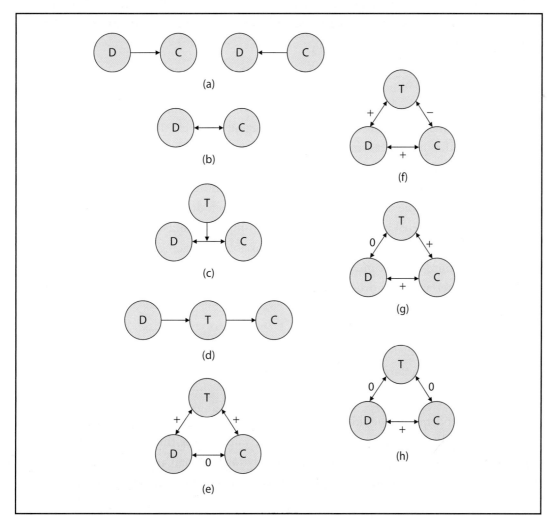

Figure 15.1
Eight different drug–crime effects:
(a) unidirectional effect,
(b) bidirectional effect,
(c) moderating effect,
(d) mediating effect,
(e) epiphenomenal effect,
(f) countervailing effect,
(g) exclusive effect,
(h) null effect.
D = Drugs
C = Crimes
T = Third Variable
+ = positive relationship
− = negative or inverse relationship
0 = no relationship

effects it is important to note that not all drugs are equally criminogenic (i.e., heroin and alcohol are more criminogenic than LSD and marijuana) and that certain drug–crime relationships are more likely to surface than other drug–crime combinations (i.e., alcohol correlates better with violent crime than with property crime and heroin correlates better with property crime than with violent crime). One example of crime causing drugs would be someone who receives a windfall of money from a successful bank robbery that he or she then uses to purchase cocaine; another example would be someone who plans to commit a burglary and then uses a drug to calm him or herself down prior to committing the crime. When examining crime-causing-drugs effects it is important to note that not all crimes are equally effective in promoting drug use and that the actual or anticipated payoff for a crime will influence the degree to which drug use follows crime.

Bidirectional Effects

A **bidirectional** or reciprocal **effect** is where drugs and crime influence one another in a pattern of mutually interacting forces (see **Figure 15-1**, panel b). In other words, opposing unidirectional effects (drugs-cause-crime, crime-causes-drugs) are merged into a single effect. Using a three-panel longitudinal design, Brook, Whiteman, and Finch determined that early childhood aggression predicted adolescent drug use and delinquency, whereas early adolescent drug use predicted later drug use and delinquency.[8] Hence, in this study, drug use and delinquency were found to be both a cause and effect of one another, a hallmark sign of a bidirectional relationship.

Indirect Relationships

Indirect relationships involve a third variable. Hence, it is no longer a simple matter of drugs causing crime, crime causing drugs, or crime and drugs causing each other. There is a third variable that moderates, mediates, or explains the drug–crime relationship or that correlates differentially with drugs and crime. Epiphenomenal interpretations of drug–crime correlations are examples of third variable explanations of the drug–crime nexus. There are many more third variable or indirect relationships between drugs and crime, however, than the classic epiphenomenal pattern. Indirect relationships can take the form of a third variable interfacing with drugs *and* crime or a third variable interfacing with drugs *or* crime. In the former, the third variable interfaces with the drug–crime relationship; in the latter, the third variable interfaces with drugs and crime separately.

Third Variable Interfacing with Drugs and Crime

There are three effects that stem from third variables interfacing with drugs *and* crime: **moderator effects**, **mediator effects**, and **epiphenomenal effects**.

Moderator Effects

In the case of moderation, the third variable interacts with the drug–crime relationship (see **Figure 15-1**, panel c). Hence, one level or range of values of the third variable (moderator) gives rise to a significantly different drug–crime relationship than another level or range of values. The moderator variable can either be continuous or categorical. Moderation by a categorical variable is easier to visualize than moderation by a continuous variable and therefore serves as the example in this section. In a study conducted by Forsythe and Adams, sex was found to moderate the relationship between drugs and crime. Although a relationship was observed between drug and crime in both males and females, the drug–crime relationship was significantly stronger in females than in males; hence, sex was a moderator variable in this study.[9]

Mediator Effects

Mediation involves interposing a variable between two other variables, in this case, drugs and crime (see **Figure 15-1**, panel d), to either partially or fully explain the drug–crime relationship. Full mediation means that once the mediating variable is entered into the equation the relationship between drugs and crime disappears. In partial mediation, even after a significant mediating effect is observed, there is still a significant direct relationship between drugs and crime. Walters recorded a significant partial mediating effect when an operational measure of criminal thinking (PICTS Reactive Criminal Thinking score) was interposed between a history of substance abuse and subsequent criminal recidivism.[10] It is important to keep in mind that mediational analysis requires proper temporal ordering between variables (i.e., the predictor should precede the mediator and the mediator should precede the outcome).

Epiphenomenal Effects

When a third variable fully accounts for the drug–crime relationship (see **Figure 15-1**, panel e) the relationship between drugs and crime is said to be an epiphenomenon. If the effect is epiphenomenal, then once the third variable is controlled the correlation between drugs and crime becomes nonsignificant. Full mediation is a special case of epiphenomenalism in a longitudinal design, although epiphenomenal effects can also be observed in cross-sectional designs. Hence, all full mediation effects are epiphenomenal effects but not all epiphenomenal effects are full mediation because to have full mediation one must have proper temporal order. Wendy Slutske and colleagues determined that 76% of the phenotypic association between alcohol abuse and conduct disorder in men and 71% of the phenotypic association between alcohol abuse and conduct disorder in women was the result of common genetic risk factors, suggesting minimal relationship between alcohol abuse and conduct disorder once common genetic factors were controlled.[11]

Third Variable Interfacing with Drugs *or* Crime

Three third variable interfacing with drugs *or* crime effects have also been observed in drug–crime research: countervailing effects, exclusive effects, and null effects.

Countervailing Effects

A countervailing relationship is said to occur when a third variable correlates in opposite directions with two correlating variables, in this case, drugs and crime (see **Figure 15-1**, panel f). Measured intelligence, for instance, appears to form a countervailing relationship with drugs and crime. There is growing evidence of a modest to moderate positive correlation between intelligence and drug use.[12] This contrasts sharply with the moderate negative or inverse relationship that has been repeatedly observed between intelligence and criminality.[13] A **countervailing effect** identifies areas of divergence for drugs and crime because for at least that one third variable, drugs and crime form opposing relationships.

Exclusive Effects

An **exclusive effect** is similar to a countervailing effect except that instead of correlating in opposite directions with drugs and crime, a third variable correlates (positively or negatively) with one variable and does not correlate at all with the other variable. **Figure 15-1** (panel g) displays one of several possible exclusive effects, in this case, a positive relationship between the third variable and crime and no relationship between the third variable and drugs. Ambient temperature, as a case in point, is a variable that forms an exclusive relationship with aggressive criminality in the sense that it correlates modestly with violent crime but does not appear to correlate with drug use, drug abuse, or nonviolent criminality.[14]

Null Effects

A **null effect** (see **Figure 15-1**, panel h) denotes the absence of a relationship between the third variable and two correlated variables, which in the current set of examples would be drugs and crime. The value of null effects is that they help define the limits or boundaries of drug–crime relationships. Social class, under certain circumstances, forms a null relationship with drugs and crime.[15–16]

Overview of Research Relationships

The six indirect effects reviewed in this section are not the only possible effects connecting drugs and crime to various third variables. A number of possible combinations involving two or even three of these effects further increases the complexity of drug–crime relationships. It is possible, for instance, that a third variable could serve as a moderating variable and also enter into a countervailing or exclusive relationship with drugs and crime. Combinations that have already been studied, but not with respect to drugs and crime, are dual effect relationships referred to as mediated moderation and moderated mediation.[17] It is also possible for direct and indirect relationships to intermingle, interact, and coexist. Understanding that drug–crime relationships are contextualized by drug, crime, drug–crime, third variable, and developmental factors will go a long way toward helping us understand the complexity of these relationships.

Practical Issues in Working with Drug-Involved Offenders

As a way of teaching students how to apply information from this book to real-life situations and case material I will often have them write a paper on someone famous who has had public problems with both drugs and the law. A wide variety of celebrities have been written about by my students, but Charlie Sheen (see **News Spot 15-1**), Paris Hilton, Robert Downey Jr., Lindsay Lohan, Courtney Love, and rapper Earl Simmons (DMX) seem to be particularly popular. Using public information gathered from the Internet, students create a clinical profile of their chosen celebrity. Because the Internet contains both accurate and inaccurate information, this exercise provides students with the opportunity to

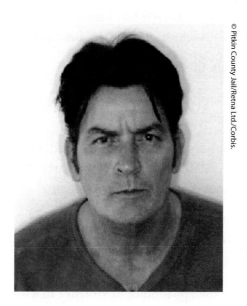

Figure 15.2
Actor Charlie Sheen.

check their sources, cross-validate information against different sources, and critically evaluate information. Students then write a report divided into three sections:

- History and Background
- Evaluation
- Recommendations

NEWS SPOT 15-1

Title: Actor Charlie Sheen is arrested in Colorado
Source: *Pittsburgh Post-Gazette*
Author: The Associated Press
Date: December 26, 2009

ASPEN, Colo.—Actor Charlie Sheen was arrested yesterday in this Colorado resort town and released from jail on bond hours later on charges related to domestic violence, police said.

The star of CBS's "Two and a Half Men" was taken into custody on suspicion of second-degree assault and menacing, both felonies, along with criminal mischief, a misdemeanor, Aspen police spokeswoman Stephanie Dasaro said.

Police arrested the 44-year-old actor after responding to a 911 call regarding a report of domestic violence at 8:34 a.m. at a historic house up for sale for $7.5 million. The alleged victim in the case, whose name was withheld, did not have to be taken to the hospital, police said.

Ms. Dasaro says Mr. Sheen posted $8,500 bond after speaking with a county judge and was advised on the conditions of his release. No date for his court appearance has been set.

Aspen, a ski resort town, is about 200 miles west of Denver.

Mr. Sheen's publicist Stan Rosenfield released a statement saying, "It would benefit everyone not to jump to any conclusion."

Mr. Sheen is the son of actor Martin Sheen. He is married to Brooke Mueller Sheen, who gave birth to the couple's first children, twin boys, in March. They married in May 2008 following Charlie Sheen's bitter divorce from Denise Richards.

Charlie Sheen's screen credits include "Platoon," "Wall Street" and the "Hot Shots!" movies. He nearly died of a drug overdose in 1998 but received court-ordered rehabilitation.

Questions to Ponder

1. **How do you explain the appearance of violence in a 44-year-old man with no apparent history of violence?**
2. **Do you think the fact that Charlie Sheen is a famous actor made his legal situation better or worse?**
3. **What form of intervention, if any, would you recommend in this case?**

History and Background

Drugs

In a paragraph or two describe the types of drugs the celebrity has allegedly used in the past. Whenever possible, indicate the frequency (how often), duration (how long), and intensity (how much) of drug use. Also ask students to indicate whether the usage suggests a pattern of abuse or dependence, although this is often difficult to gauge from public information.

Crime

List the crimes for which the celebrity has allegedly been arrested, including information on outcome (conviction, disposition, sentence), if available. It should also be noted whether the celebrity has ever been incarcerated, where, and for how long.

Drug–Crime Connection

Indicate the degree to which drug use is connected to the celebrity's alleged criminal activities. In other words, are drugs central or peripheral to the individual's criminal behavior?

Evaluation

Risk

Risk should be evaluated for both crime (recidivism) and drug use (relapse). Using standard risk assessment nomenclature (high, moderate, low), the celebrity's recidivism risk should be evaluated from an analysis of such well-known predictors as age, gender, criminal history, and time since last criminal offense. Using the same three-level system (high, moderate, low) the celebrity's relapse risk should also be evaluated, perhaps using both static (age, drug history) and dynamic (stress, opportunity) risk factors.

Need

Besides drug abuse/dependence, what other criminogenic **needs** does the celebrity display? The three most important criminogenic needs (i.e., antisocial personality processes, antisocial cognition, antisocial peer associations) should be evaluated in every case and additional criminogenic needs (e.g., housing, finances, leisure/recreation, educational/occupational assistance) can be evaluated if they appear to apply in the case under investigation.

Responsivity

Are there abilities, strengths, weaknesses, and learning styles that need to be taken into account when matching the celebrity to a particular treatment program or supervision level?

Recommendations

Custody/Supervision Level

Is institutional placement (jail, prison, or hospital) warranted in this case or can the celebrity be handled in a community corrections program? If placement in a correctional institution is deemed necessary, what would be the appropriate security level (maximum, medium, minimum)? If community placement is appropriate, what level of supervision is required (intensive, standard, none)?

Programming

In a paragraph or two, the student should discuss the celebrity's programming needs and identify the program characteristics that should be emphasized in treating the celebrity's alleged problems with drugs and crime. Program type (drug, anger management, social skills training), setting (inpatient, outpatient), and duration (length of treatment in months) should also be specified.

Unintended Consequences of Drug Prohibition Policies

There are several unintended consequences of drug prohibition policies that go beyond the costs of drug prohibition and America's "War on Drugs." Five of these unintended consequences are discussed here.

Strengthens Drug–Crime Relationships

Research conducted before and after American Prohibition suggests that crime increased during Prohibition but then fell once Prohibition was lifted. A portion, although clearly not the totality, of the effect of prohibition on crime is due to the fact that legalizing alcohol or decriminalizing drugs reduces the number of people arrested for the manufacture and sale of alcohol or the trafficking and use of drugs. Data provided by U.S. Census Bureau reveals that the murder rate went up during Prohibition and then dropped after it was repealed.[18] Although the nature of these murders cannot be determined from the Census results, it could very well be that competition between different criminal groups for control of the alcohol trade was primarily responsible for this increase in the murder rate. Property crimes are also likely to rise in situations where drugs are illegal because prohibition makes drugs more expensive and the legitimate resources of many users are insufficient to cover the price of illegal drugs.[19]

This would be a good time to reintroduce an interesting finding from my own analysis of the National Longitudinal Study of Adolescent Health (Add Health) data. For the purpose of review, the correlation between marijuana use and crime increased over the first three waves of the Add Health study and then leveled off between the third and fourth waves, whereas the correlation between drunkenness and crime progressively decreased after the second wave of the Add Health study.[20] All or most of the participants during the first two waves of the Add Health study were under the legal drinking age, whereas most if not all of the Add Health participants were beyond the legal drinking age during the study's third and fourth waves. Marijuana was illegal for all waves and so the relationship between drugs and crime never changed. However, as the number of legal drinkers rose, the correlation between drunkenness and crime decreased. This is further evidence that drug prohibition strengthens the drug–crime correlation.

Limits Law Enforcement's Ability to Respond to Serious Crime

At one time there was a rough correspondence between the damage done by a crime and the amount of time the offender spent on probation or in prison. This correlation has been all but wiped out by the "War on Drugs." At the present time there is the distinct possibility that a person could spend less time in prison for raping, robbing, or killing someone than they would for possessing a modest amount of cocaine or heroin. The chances of someone convicted of a drug crime going to federal prison rather than being placed on probation (92.9%) are nearly as high as the chances of someone convicted of a violent offense going to federal prison rather than being placed on probation (94.2%). In this same study, the average federal sentence for a drug offense was only 19% shorter than the average federal sentence for a violent offense (see **Figure 15-3**).[21] Because drug offenders outnumber violent offenders 11 to 1 in the federal system, even a 50% reduction in the number of low-level drug offenders sentenced to federal prison would free up prison space for violent offenders who, on average, serve less than 9 years in prison.

Corrections is not the only component of the criminal justice system likely to benefit from an end to the "War on Drugs." The courts and police would also benefit. State and federal courts have been inundated with drug cases and although drug courts and drug diversion have helped reduce the burden, more drug offenders are processed through the regular courts than anywhere else.[22] The police could also benefit from an end to the "War on Drugs." Currently, many police departments are spending so much time chasing, catching, and processing low-level drug sellers and users that they do not have sufficient time and resources to pursue cases against more violent criminals. Many jurisdictions, for instance, do not have the resources to process rape kits and so the kits remain unopened

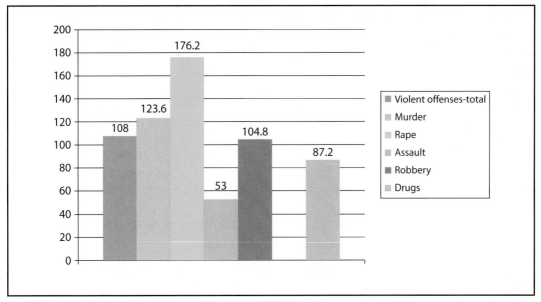

Figure 15.3
Average sentence (in months) for violent and drug offenders confined in federal prison.

Data From: Motivans, M. (2009). *Federal justice statistics, 2006—Statistical tables (NCJ 225711)*. Washington, DC: Bureau of Justice Statistics.

and the perpetrators go unpunished (see News Spot 15-2). Ending the "War on Drugs" would in all likelihood free police departments to spend the necessary resources analyzing rape kits and bringing a greater number of serious criminals to justice.

NEWS SPOT 15-2

Title: Buried Amid Rape Kit Backlog: Justice for Victims
Source: *Associated Press*
Author: Corey Williams
Date: March 18, 2012

DETROIT (AP)—For nearly two decades, Carol Bart's untested rapekit collected dust in a police evidence room. Her attacker, who kidnapped her from outside her Dallas apartment and repeatedly raped her at knifepoint, had spent time in prison by coincidence, but not for sexually assaulting Bart.

Bart, now a 52-year-old mother of four, fears that among the thousands of backlogged, untested kits pulled from a Detroit police evidence room are stories of women similarly violated only to be forgotten by a justice system that seemingly has placed its priorities and resources elsewhere.

"Women go to the hospital and their bodies are a crime scene and treated as such," said Bart, who still lives in Texas. "For these kits then to just to sit in a laboratory or in police vaults or wherever they sit, denies victims of sexual assault any opportunity for justice. I just wonder how many more there are?"

Bart and other rape victims spoke recently to The Associated Press in hope that other women about to go through the same painful process in Detroit learn from their experiences and know they are not alone. Detroit has begun testing some of its rapekits.

The women—who agreed to use their names for this story—know testing years-old rapekits holds no guarantee the attacker will be found and brought to justice. They also know the tangled legal process can reopen wounds that took years to heal and send horrific memories of the assault flooding back.

According to some estimates, between 180,000 and 400,000 rapekits remain untested nationwide, despite DNA technology that can swiftly link rapists to crimes. …

Bart was attacked in 1984, and DNA swabbed during a hospital exam was stored in a rapekit. When the kit finally was tested 24 years later, DNA was added to the FBI's Combined DNA Index System and produced a hit on Joseph Houston Jr.

"Four months after he kidnapped and raped me, he attempted to do the same with another young lady and a security guard chased him off," Bart said.

Houston was sentenced in 1985 for kidnapping and served 19 of 50 years. His DNA was taken while in prison, even as Bart's rapekit sat forgotten. He eventually was released but now is serving a 20-year sentence in Texas for indecency with a child.

"He could not be prosecuted for his crime against me. The statute of limitations was only five years at the time of my assault," Bart said. "DNA evidence is tested quickly following a murder, but is not always when a woman has been raped by a stranger."

About 55 percent of victims never report being raped, according to Scott Berkowitz, president of the Washington D.C.-based nonprofit Rape, Abuse and Incest National Network.

"When they see stories like this, that's even more discouragement for them," he said. …

Questions to Ponder

1. **Why do you suppose so many rape kits have not been opened?**
2. **How do DNA test results stack up against other sources of criminal evidence (fingerprints, voice analysis, eyewitness testimony)?**
3. **What are some ways police departments can reduce the backlog of unopened rape kits?**

Weakens the Person-Community Bond

Another unintended consequence of America's "War on Drugs" is a weakening of the person–community bond. Whenever a crime is committed, the person–society bond weakens. To the extent that the community represents society, crime also weakens the person–community bond. The whole idea behind restorative justice is to repair the harm done by a criminal offense and reestablish the person–community bond. The "War on Drugs" makes it difficult to reestablish the person–community bond because the majority of individuals convicted of drug offenses, even relatively minor ones, are being sent to prison (92.9% in the federal system) rather than being managed in the community. It is more difficult to establish a bond or connection to the community from a prison cell than it is from one's home in the community. The informal social control afforded by the community has been weakened by modernization and is weakened further by mass incarceration.

A process known as **coercive mobility** helps explain what happens when low-level drug offenders are removed from the community and placed in jail or prison. As described by Dina Rose and Todd Clear, coercive mobility involves a disruption in social relationships in communities and neighborhoods where mass incarceration is practiced. Family and community functions are disturbed and the individual's sense of community is upset. Given current emphasis on locking up drug dealers and drug users, a good portion of this mass incarceration is a direct result of the "War on Drugs." The second part of the coercive mobility process is that once the individual completes his or her sentence the prison system dumps the individual back into the community or neighborhood, usually worse off than when they left.[23] Now, the community must cope with an influx of angry, alienated, and mostly unemployed individuals who lack the skills necessary to successfully transition back into the community.

Threatens National Security

A fourth unintended consequence of the "War on Drugs" is that it makes the world less safe. The drug trade has ties to organized crime, armed rebel groups, and international terrorism. Organized criminal groups like the Italian Mafia, Russian mob, and Chinese triads are all heavily involved in the drug trade. In fact, American Prohibition was a major shot in the arm for organized crime. Armed rebel groups like the FARC in Colombia and the Taliban in Afghanistan provide protection to drug growers, traffickers, and dealers. There is a virtual civil war currently being fought between the Mexican government and Mexican drug cartels. Although drug traffickers and terrorists have different goals, terrorists have been known to finance their operations with proceeds from the drug trade and to periodically work with drug traffickers to achieve their aims.[24]

Mexico, Colombia, and Afghanistan have been destabilized by the drug trade and dozens more countries have been marginalized by the violence and corruption that goes hand-in-hand with international drug trafficking. The situation is particularly tense in Mexico where the government is literally at war with the drug cartels. To be fair, the Mexican government is in a difficult position. Nearly all the drugs grown, produced, and processed in Mexico are destined for the United States. Hence, the Mexican government must rely on the American government to provide U.S. citizens with the most effective interventions available (demand-side economic strategies), something that has been slow in coming. With tourism and drugs as its two big money makers, Mexico needs American dollars, both legal and illegal. The Mexican government has been handed a war that is not its own and which it has no chance of winning.

It Is Not Evidence Based

Drug policy should be **evidence based** in the sense that it is responsive to empirical research results. Unfortunately, the "War on Drugs" and the policy of prohibition from which it springs are based more on tradition than on evidence. "We do what we do because that is what we have done for the last 100 years" is a motto that seems to drive America's

"War on Drugs." Yet, if what we do makes things worse we need to reevaluate our priorities. As former President Jimmy Carter once stated, drug policies should not be more damaging than the drugs they are designed to control. Some writers have characterized America's "War on Drugs" as an elaborate hoax, something akin to the "smoke and mirrors" magicians use to fool their audiences.[25] This characterization may be unfair in that many of those who have supported drug prohibition in the past have done so with the best of intentions. The fact remains, however, that our intentions must be informed by the facts.

In November 2012 two western states, Colorado and Washington, legalized marijuana for recreational use. The voters of Colorado and Washington have provided us with the unique opportunity to empirically test whether legalized marijuana leads to increased drug usage or crime. The Dutch experiment revealed that legalized marijuana neither encouraged drug use nor increased crime; now we have the opportunity to test the generalizability of these findings to two U.S. states. Adopting an evidence-based approach to drug policy can serve as a model for dealing with other aspects of the drug-crime nexus. Borrowing ideas and principles from biology, psychology, sociology and criminal justice it should be possible to construct a rational model of drug-crime research, treatment, and policy. If the past has taught us anything it is that we cannot be content with unproven theories and practices. Change, as evidenced by recommendations recently made by the Global Commission on Drug Policy,[26] may be on the horizon but this change must be built on an empirical foundation.

Summary and Conclusions

- The characteristics of an ideal theory of drug–crime relationships include comprehensiveness and a focus on reciprocal relationships, parsimony and practicality, precision and instrumentation, and fruitfulness and evidence based. Although no single theory will possess the maximum of each of these characteristics, the degree to which a theory approaches these ideals is a measure of its usefulness or utility.

- Research indicates that there are eight basic drug–crime effects: two direct effects (unidirectional and bidirectional), three indirect effects with drugs and crime (moderation, mediation, epiphenomenal), and three indirect effects with drugs or crime (countervailing, exclusive, null). Understanding drug–crime relationships means understanding these eight basic effects and how they interact with one another.

- Practical application of the material in this book requires a solid understanding of theory and research and the ability to organize this information into clinically relevant categories. A three-section, eight-subsection format is recommended: Background and History (Drugs, Crime, Drug-Crime Connection), Evaluation (Risk, Needs, **Responsivity**), and Recommendations (Custody/Supervision Level, Programming).

- A policy of drug prohibition such as America's "War on Drugs" has several negative unintended consequences. Five such consequences were discussed in this chapter: strengthening drug-crime relationships, limiting law enforcement's ability to respond to serious crime, weakening the person-community bond, threatening national security, and failing to be evidence based. Change, it is argued, will require an educated and undaunted public that is no longer distracted by the "bright lights" of the "War on Drugs."

Key Terms

Bidirectional Effect Causal relationship that goes in both directions; drugs and crime are both a cause and effect of one another.

Coercive Mobility Two-part process in which the social cohesion of a neighborhood is disrupted by mass incarceration of a good portion of its (usually male) residents and then disrupted once again when these individuals are released from prison and returned to the neighborhood unchanged or worse off than when they left.

Comprehensiveness One of the four characteristics of a useful theory; degree to which the theory covers a sufficient breadth of information in the area of interest.

Countervailing Effect A third variable has the opposite relationship with two correlated variables.

Epiphenomenal Effect A third variable that fully explains the relationship between two other variables (e.g., drugs and crime) such that there is no longer a significant correlation between the two variables once the third variable is controlled.

Evidence Based Theory, practice, or policy that is based on research evidence.

Exclusive Effect A third variable has a significant relationship with one but not the other of two correlated variables.

Fruitfulness One of the four characteristics of a useful theory; degree to which the theory stimulates interest and research.

Instrumentation Extent to which a theory makes use of reliable and valid measures.

Mediator Effect A third variable temporally inserts itself between two other variables (e.g., drugs and crime) such that it explains a portion of or the entire relationship between these two variables.

Moderator Effect A third variable alters the relationship between two other variables (e.g., drugs and crime) such that the drug–crime relationship is significantly different at different levels or values of the third variable.

Needs Targets for intervention in the form of criminogenic variables known to correlate with recidivism.

Null Effect A third variable does not correlate with either of two correlated variables.

Parsimony One of the four characteristics of a useful theory; degree to which the theory sufficiently explains the phenomenon with the fewest number of assumptions, postulates, and concepts.

Practicality The degree to which a theory is applicable to real-life clinical situations in terms of assessment, classification, supervision, and treatment.

Precision One of the four characteristics of a useful theory; degree to which the theory defines its constructs with behavioral and operationally defined terms.

Reciprocity   Mutual interchange or bidirectional influence.

Responsivity   Maximizing an offender's odds of benefitting from an intervention by attempting to match the intervention to the individual's learning style and personal strengths and weaknesses.

Risk   Estimate of the danger presented by an individual for violence, recidivism, or relapse.

Unidirectional Effect   Causal relationship that goes in one direction; drugs cause crime or crime causes drugs.

Critical Thinking

1. None of the 14 theories profiled in this book provides a complete explanation of drug–crime relationships, but which theory, in your opinion, comes closest to the ideal established by the four criteria of comprehensiveness, parsimony, precision, and fruitfulness? Justify your selection.

2. Epiphenomenal explanations are just one way to explain drug-crime connections. In this chapter we learned that there are at least six different third variable explanations of drug-crime relationships. What are these six explanations? Provide an example of each.

3. Select a celebrity who has experienced public problems with drugs/alcohol and the law and construct a three-section report (History and Background, Evaluation, Recommendations) based on public information found on the Internet.

4. Some American politicians use Sweden as an example of what could be accomplished with drug prohibition in the United States. How appropriate is Sweden as a point of comparison to the United States and is it any better than European countries like the Netherlands and Portugal where drugs have been legalized and/or decriminalized?

Notes

1. Grasmick, H. G., Tittle, C. R., Bursick, R. J., & Arneklev, B. J. (1993). Testing the core implications of Gottfredson and Hirschi's general theory of crime. *Journal of Research in Crime and Delinquency, 30,* 5–29.

2. Landenberger, N. A., & Lipsey, M. W. (2006). The positive effects of cognitive–behavioral programs for offenders: A meta-analysis of factors associated with effective treatment. *Journal of Experimental Criminology, 1,* 451–476.

3. Pratt, T. C., & Cullen, F. T. (2000). The empirical status of Gottfredson and Hirschi's general theory of crime: A meta-analysis. *Criminology, 38,* 931–964.

4. Van Dulmen, M., Goncy, E., Vest, A., & Flannery, D. (2009). Group-based trajectory modeling of externalizing behavior problems from childhood through adulthood: Exploring discrepancies in the empirical findings. In J. Savage (Ed.). *The development of persistent criminality* (pp. 288–314). New York: Oxford University Press.

5. Tarter, R. E., Vanyukov, M., Kirisci, L., Reynolds, M., & Clark, D. B. (2006). Predictors of marijuana use in adolescents before and after licit drug use: Examination of the gateway hypothesis. *American Journal of Psychiatry, 163,* 2134–2140.

6. Walters, G. D. (2011). The latent structure of life-course-persistent antisocial behavior: Is Moffitt's developmental taxonomy a true taxonomy? *Journal of Consulting and Clinical Psychology, 79,* 96–105.

7. Walters, G. D., & Ruscio, J. (in press). Trajectories of youthful antisocial behavior: Categories or continua? *Journal of Abnormal Child Psychology*.

8. Brook, J. S., Whiteman, M. M., & Finch, S. (1992). Childhood aggression, adolescent delinquency, and drug use: A longitudinal study. *Journal of Genetic Psychology, 153*, 369–383.

9. Forsythe, L., & Adams, K. (2009). Mental health, abuse, drug use and crime: Does gender matter? *Trends and Issues in Crime and Criminal Justice* (No. 384). Canberra, Australia: Australian Institute of Criminology.

10. Walters, G. D. (2012). Substance abuse and criminal thinking: Testing the countervailing, mediation, and specificity hypotheses. *Law and Human Behavior, 36*, 506–512.

11. Slutske, W. S., Heath, A. C., Dinwiddie, S. H., Madden, P. A. F., Bucholtz, K. K., Dunne, M. P., et al. (1998). Common genetic risk factors for conduct disorder and alcohol dependence. *Journal of Abnormal Psychology, 107*, 363–374.

12. Kanazawa, S., & Hellberg, J. E. E. U. (2010). Intelligence and substance use. *Review of General Psychology, 14*, 382–396.

13. Wilson, J. Q., & Herrnstein, R. (1985). *Crime and human nature.* New York: Simon and Schuster.

14. Anderson, C. A. (1987). Temperament and aggression: Effects on quarterly, yearly, and city rates of violent and nonviolent crime. *Journal of Personality and Social Psychology, 52*, 1161–1173.

15. Room, R. (2004, February 25–27). Thinking about how social inequalities relate to alcohol and drug use and problems. *Presented at the 1st International Summer School on Inequalities and Addictions.* National Centre for Education and Training in Addictions, Adelaide, South Australia. Retrieved from http://www.robinroom.net/inequal.htm.

16. Tittle, C., Villemez, W. J., & Smith, D. (1978). The myth of social class and criminality: An empirical assessment of the evidence. *American Sociological Review, 43*, 643–656.

17. Miller, D., Judd, C. M., & Yzerbyt, V. Y. (2005). When moderation is mediated and mediation is moderated. *Journal of Personality and Social Psychology, 89,* 852–863.

18. U.S. Bureau of the Census. (1975). *Historical statistics of the United States, colonial times to 1970.* Washington, DC: Government Printing Office.

19. Riley, K. J. (1997). *Crack, powder cocaine, and heroin: Drug purchase and use patterns in six U.S. cities* (Research Report). Washington, DC: National Institute of Justice.

20. Udry, J. R. (2003). *The National Longitudinal Study of Adolescent Health (Add Health).* Chapel Hill, NC: Carolina Population Center, University of North Carolina.

21. Motivans, M. (2009). *Federal justice statistics, 2006—Statistical tables* (NCJ 225711). Washington, DC: Bureau of Justice Statistics.

22. King, R. S., & Mauer, M. (2002). *Distorted priorities: Drug offenders in state prisons.* Washington, DC: The Sentencing Project.

23. Rose, D. R., & Clear, T. (1998). Incarceration, social capital, and crime: Implications for social disorganization theory. *Criminology, 36*, 441–479.

24. Isralowitz, R. (2002). Drugs and terrorism: The need for immediate policy change. *Journal of Social Work Practice in the Addictions, 2*(2), 97–99.

25. Baum, D. (1996). *Smoke and mirrors: The war on drugs and the politics of failure.* New York: Little Brown.

26. Global Commission on Drug Policy. (2011, June). *War on drugs: Report of the Global Commission on Drug Policy.* Geneva: Author.

Tables and figures are indicated by an italic *t* or *f* following the page number.